The SQL Server 2000 Book

Anthony Sequeira
Brian Alderman

PARAGLYPH
PRESS

President

Keith Weiskamp

Editor-at-Large

Jeff Duntemann

Vice President, Sales, Marketing, and Distribution

Steve Sayre

Vice President, International Sales and Marketing

Cynthia Caldwell

Editorial Director

Sharon Linsenbach

Production Manager

Kim Eoff

The SQL Server 2000 Book

Limits of Liability and Disclaimer of Warranty

The author and publisher of this book have used their best efforts in preparing the book and the programs contained in it. These efforts include the development, research, and testing of the theories and programs to determine their effectiveness. The author and publisher make no warranty of any kind, expressed or implied, with regard to these programs or the documentation contained in this book.

The author and publisher shall not be liable in the event of incidental or consequential damages in connection with, or arising out of, the furnishing, performance, or use of the programs, associated instructions, and/or claims of productivity gains.

Trademarks

Trademarked names appear throughout this book. Rather than list the names and entities that own the trademarks or insert a trademark symbol with each mention of the trademarked name, the publisher states that it is using the names for editorial purposes only and to the benefit of the trademark owner, with no intention of infringing upon that trademark.

Paraglyph Press, Inc.
2246 E. Myrtle Avenue
Phoenix, Arizona 85202
Phone: 602-749-8787
www.paraglyphpress.com

ISBN 1-932111-67-0

Printed in the United States of America
10 9 8 7 6 5 4 3 2 1

The Paraglyph Mission

This book you've purchased is a collaborative creation involving the work of many hands, from authors to editors to designers and to technical reviewers. At Paraglyph Press, we like to think that everything we create, develop, and publish is the result of one form creating another. And as this cycle continues on, we believe that your suggestions, ideas, feedback, and comments on how you've used our books is an important part of the process for us and our authors.

We've created Paraglyph Press with the sole mission of producing and publishing books that make a difference. The last thing we all need is yet another tech book on the same tired, old topic. So we ask our authors and all of the many creative hands who touch our publications to do a little extra, dig a little deeper, think a little harder, and create a better book. The founders of Paraglyph are dedicated to finding the best authors, developing the best books, and helping you find the solutions you need.

As you use this book, please take a moment to drop us a line at **feedback@paraglyphpress.com** and let us know how we are doing - and how we can keep producing and publishing the kinds of books that you can't live without.

Sincerely,

Keith Weiskamp & Jeff Duntemann
Paraglyph Press Founders

Paraglyph Press
2246 East Myrtle Ave.
Phoenix, AZ 85020

email:
feedback@paraglyphpress.com
Web: **www.paraglyphpress.com**
Phone: 602-749-8787
Fax: 602-861-1941

I dedicate this book to my lovely wife, Joette Sequeira. She is truly my best friend and I love her very much. Everyone that has ever met her knows exactly how lucky I am. Too bad we can't seem to bring that luck to Vegas with us!
—Anthony Sequeira

❧

To my family and friends who supported me during this enjoyable experience.
—Brian Alderman

❧

About the Authors

Anthony Sequeira (Fountain Hills, AZ) has been a professional speaker and writer in the IT industry for the last eight years. He holds every major Microsoft certification including MCT, MCSE+I, MCSE 2000, MCDBA, and MCSD. Anthony's books include Windows 2000 Server and Active Directory titles. He currently speaks about SQL Server 2000 technologies and Cisco networking for KnowledgeNet.com.

Brian Alderman (Scottsdale, AZ) is a Senior Technical Instructor with KnowledgeNet, a Phoenix-based provider of proven "next generation" e-learning solutions for Information Technology professionals. In this role, Brian delivers live instruction over the Web to KnowledgeNet students seeking certification in Microsoft technology. As a subject-matter expert, he also assists KnowledgeNet in the design and development of class courseware. He holds numerous major Microsoft certifications including MCT, MCSE+I, MCSE 2000, and MCDBA. Brian also authored *Windows 2000 Professional On Site*.

Acknowledgments

First and foremost, thanks to Brian Alderman for his many contributions to this book. Brian not only knows SQL Server 2000 better than anybody, but he is also a great friend. Thanks, as always, to Charlotte Carpentier for securing this project for me, and Jessica Choi for helping to get it started. Thanks also to Karen Swartz, Project Editor for The *SQL Server 2000* Book. If not for her tireless efforts, this book might never have seen the light of the bookstore. Thanks also to copyeditor Mary Swistara, technical editor Buck Woody, Production Coordinator Kim Eoff, and Editorial Director Sharon Linsenbach.

Finally, thanks to all of my family and friends for their understanding while I was working on this and other books. It is so difficult to stay in touch as it is, and when you are working around the clock, it seems an impossible task. Please know that in between all of the SQL Server 2000 thoughts, practically all I think of is you.
—*Anthony Sequeira*

Contents at a Glance

Table of Contents

Part II
Planning and Installing SQL Server 2000

Part III
Administering and Optimizing SQL Server 2000

Part IV
Using SQL Server 2000

Introduction

Thanks for buying The *SQL Server 2000 Book*. We have worked very hard to make sure that this book provides you with critical information you need to succeed with SQL Server 2000 in an enterprise environment.

You should consider mastering SQL Server 2000 for the following reasons:

• There is a very strong demand for Microsoft Certified Database Administrators in the IT industry today.

• SQL Server 2000 continues to make great strides in cornering the market share for enterprise capable relational database servers.

• SQL Server 2000 is a key product in the important .NET strategy from Microsoft.

• The new features of SQL Server 2000 make it even more powerful and easy to use than previous versions.

Is This Book for You?

The SQL Server 2000 Book was written with the intermediate or advanced user in mind. Among the topics covered are:

• Properly planning for and deploying SQL Server 2000 in your environment.

• Creating and maintaining new user databases.

• Monitoring and optimizing SQL Server 2000.

• Automating administrative tasks, including backups and restores of SQL Server 2000.

• Configuring replication properly in distributed data environments.

• Configuring SQL Server 2000 for key .NET integration including XML support.

How to Use This Book

You should use this book when you are actually on site and responsible for the installation, configuration, or maintenance of a SQL Server 2000 system. Although some users will read this book cover to cover, others will first attack those chapters relevant to individual tasks they are performing in the field. For example, if you are responsible for configuring SQL Server 2000 to integrate with another XML system, you might start with Chapter 16, "Configuring XML and Internet Support." The book is divided into four parts: "SQL Server 2000 in Your Organization," Planning and Installing SQL Server 2000," "Administrating and Optimizing SQL Server 2000," and "Using SQL Server 2000." Use these part divisions to help you easily locate the material most relevant to your needs.

Each chapter of this book contains powerful reference information you will find yourself returning to again and again. Key tables listing features and utilities will be invaluable references.

Another powerful feature of this book are the decision trees. The decision trees will help you quickly and efficiently make key decisions regarding administrative tasks.

Part I

SQL Server 2000 in Your Organization

Configuration Deployment
Planning
Troubleshooting

Chapter 1

What Is SQL Server 2000?

Chapter 1 of *The SQL Server 2000 Book* provides you with a solid understanding of exactly what SQL Server 2000 is and why it is such an important product. Not only does this chapter define SQL Server 2000 for you, it also details the exact feature set this product provides. In addition, to assist you in selecting the edition that best suits your needs, this chapter provides similar information about the many editions of SQL Server 2000 that are available. Finally, the chapter also provides you with a look at some competing applications in the industry and at the feature sets these products include, for purposes of comparison.

A Relational Database Management System

SQL Server 2000 is Microsoft's premier relational database management system. A relational database management system (RDBMS) stores data in the form of multiple related tables. A relational database designer creates the tables that store the data and defines the relationships that exist among these tables. One of the beauties of a relational database management system is that the system makes no assumptions about the design of the tables it stores. It ensures that data is retrieved efficiently, in whatever fashion the system's users require.

A key to the efficiency of the RDBMS is the fact that the data can be spread across many tables. This is in direct contrast to a flat-file database system in which the data is stored in a single table. One of the inefficiencies with a flat-file database system is the amount of wasted space that accumulates in the file. Also, as more and more data is added and the file gets increasingly larger, queries of the file become much more time-consuming.

Figure 1.1 presents an example of the table structure in a sample database stored on SQL Server 2000. This sample database—Northwind—ships with SQL Server 2000 and will serve for many of the examples provided in this book. You should feel free to use this database as you experiment with SQL Server 2000 in a non-production environment.

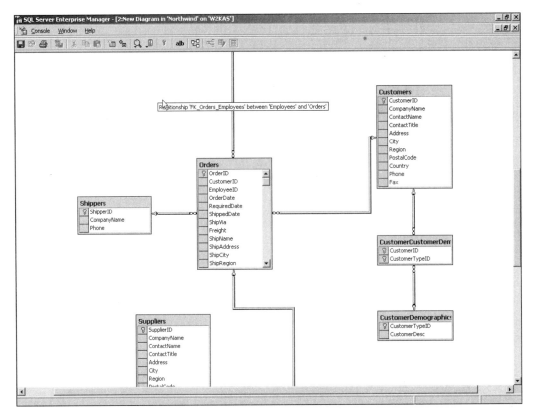

Figure 1.1
A sample table structure in a relational database management system.

Tip: During experimentation with the Northwind database, you may find that it becomes unusable or has transformed so dramatically that it is no longer useful for your learning purposes. Microsoft anticipated this and provides a simple method for restoring the Northwind database to its original form. To accomplish this restoration, follow these steps: 1. Launch a command prompt session, 2. Switch to the Mssql\Install directory, 3. Use the osql utility to run the **Instnwnd.sql** *script with the following syntax:* **osql /Usa /Psapassword /Sservername /iinstnwnd.sql /oinstnwnd.rpt**, *and 4. Check the oinstnwnd.rpt file for any errors that may have occurred during the rebuilding of Northwind.*

A Key Element in the Microsoft .NET Strategy

Microsoft is excited that high bandwidth is becoming more readily available at a steadily decreasing cost. Combine this with the fact that computer processing power tends to double every 18 months while the cost of this processing power tends to decrease by about 50 percent, and you have the recipe for truly distributed computing. As far as the Microsoft application development strategy is concerned, under .NET, you can have processing occur wherever it is most optimal in the design.

Microsoft points to some recently popular applications as near-perfect examples of the .NET strategy in action—Napster and any of the new Windows instant messaging applications. These apps feature a rich client that communicates with a directory service somewhere in the Wide Area Network (WAN) cloud. It is certainly tough to argue against the success of these applications.

In order to be successful with the .NET initiative, Microsoft's strategy is to focus on three areas:

- Creating all components of the application as Web services, specifically Web services that support a common language—Extensible Markup Language (XML)

- Ensuring these Web services can be aggregated and integrated readily

- Succeeding in the creation of a simple and compelling user experience

Microsoft addresses these three areas using five main components:

- *Developer tools*—Visual Studio.NET—which includes Visual Basic.NET— is intended to make the creation of Web services as easy as possible.

- *Servers*—The first class of servers—Windows 2000, SQL Server 2000, and Exchange 2000—provides the core foundation for the .NET strategy. They do this primarily through their support of XML, a key language in the Web service environment. A second class of servers, including BizTalk Server 2000 and Commerce Server, seeks to ensure the Web services can be easily integrated and aggregated.

- *Building Block Services*—Microsoft is constructing a set of .NET Building Block Services intended to create a simple and compelling user experience. These services will reside in the WAN cloud and enable users to move from one Web service to another with ease and flexibility. For example, .NET Building Block Services would ensure that a user will be authenticated seamlessly across Web services so that there only needs to be a single logon to the distributed application.

- *Devices*—Microsoft wants to make certain that the .NET strategy reaches the entire family of devices that are available in today's computing environment. This includes PCs, handhelds, phones, tablet PCs, and more.

- *User experiences*—Microsoft also desires to deliver a rich end-user experience by providing simple integrated Web service environments through such products as MSN, bCentral, Office XP, and Visual Studio.NET.

As a central server in the .NET strategy, SQL Server 2000 is one of the most important products for the future success of Microsoft. This explains the intense development efforts and the resulting robust feature set provided by SQL Server 2000.

SQL Server 2000's Key Features

While the following list of features is by no means comprehensive, it does describe the most important aspects of the relational database management system. The features described here are also (not coincidentally) the feature set that Microsoft is most excited about. In many cases, you will find a reference directing you to a chapter, or chapters, in this book that can help you learn more about a specific topic.

Integration with Other Core .NET Servers

SQL Server 2000 is designed to integrate with all of the core .NET servers and performs best when running on one of the Windows 2000 Server family of operating systems, or later versions of these OSs. The Windows 2000 Server family includes Windows 2000 Server, Windows 2000 Advanced Server, and Windows 2000 Datacenter Server. SQL 2000 also integrates with all other 32-bit or higher Windows operating systems (with the exception of Windows 95), but to a lesser degree.

When running on Windows 2000 Server systems, SQL Server 2000 leverages Active Directory, Memory Management, Failover Clustering, MS Distributed Transaction Coordinator, Symmetric Multiprocessors, Asynchronous and Scatter-gather I/O, Event Logging, and System Monitor. For an example of this integration with Windows 2000 Event Logging, see Figure 1.2. This book examines SQL Server 2000's integration with the Windows 2000 Server family to some degree in almost every chapter.

Microsoft BizTalk Server 2000 runs on top of a SQL Server 2000 installation. BizTalk Server 2000 simplifies the construction of e-commerce Web services. XML acts as the language for sophisticated purchase order and electronic invoice transactions from a Web interface. For enhancing the end user e-commerce experience, SQL Server 2000 integrates with Commerce Server 2000, thus providing personalization and simple electronic ordering services.

XML Support

SQL Server 2000 features robust XML support. XML is quickly gaining ground as the standard for the exchange of data on Web-based systems. Accordingly, this new technology serves as the glue that helps to hold the Microsoft .NET strategy together.

XML support in SQL Server 2000 includes the use of XPath and URL queries, helping to shield developers from the complexities of relational database programming. In addition to supporting elaborate XML query possibilities, SQL Server 2000 also serves as a highly effective storage medium for XML data. S2K provides XML Views of relational data and also provides the ability to map XML data into relational data structures. Finally, SQL Server 2000 provides XML Updategrams and Bulk Load as methods for adding XML data documents to databases quickly and efficiently. This book covers SQL Server 2000's XML support in great detail in Chapter 16, "Configuring XML and Internet Support."

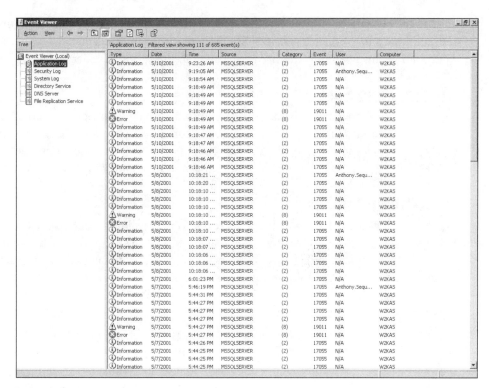

Figure 1.2
SQL Server 2000 logging events in the Event Log of Windows 2000 Server.

Web-Enabled Analysis

Analysis Services now boasts two exciting new features that make it simple for database users to study data via the Web-linked cubes and Hyper Text Transfer Protocol (HTTP) access to cubes. Linked cubes are data structures used for analysis that can be stored on another remote SQL Server 2000 system and still used locally by data consumers. S2K also permits access to remote cubes via HTTP or Secure Hypertext Transfer Protocol (HTTPS).

Web Access to Data

SQL Server 2000 now offers several different options for accessing data stored on the server via the Web. The user simply constructs queries in Uniform Resource Locators (URLs) so that the data is returned in standard rowsets or an XML document. This book covers these exciting new capabilities in Chapter 16, "Configuring XML and Internet Support."

Multiple Instances

Another dramatic enhancement to SQL Server 2000 permits multiple, independent installations on the same server. Among numerous benefits, this permits application service providers (ASPs) to host multiple business applications on a single server, which ensures the business applications' independence when it comes to a security configuration and from a performance perspective. This book covers multiple SQL Server instances in Chapter 4, "Installation Planning" and Chapter 5, "Installing SQL Server 2000."

Disk Imaging Support

SQL Server 2000 now makes it easier than ever to distribute an image of a perfect SQL Server installation. This is critical for administrators responsible for setting up many SQL systems in a short period of time. This technology also guarantees consistent, efficient configurations. This book examines this new technology in Chapters 4 and 5.

Clickstream Analysis

SQL Server 2000's integration with Commerce Server 2000 allows e-commerce operators to easily collect, cleanse, and analyze the data created as Web site users click through the site's pages. This information helps operators gain an understanding of their "virtual" customers and dramatically aids in future site design and marketing efforts.

Security

S2K features a dramatically enhanced security subsystem, thanks, in great part, to its tight integration with the Windows 2000 Server family of operating systems. For example, SQL Server 2000 now features support for the Kerberos authentication system, a key component of Windows 2000 Active Directory. This and other security features guarantee that the relational database management system will maintain its C2-level security certification. Figure 1.3 provides an illustration of some of S2K's security objects.

This book covers the security features of S2K in detail in Chapter 8, "Securing SQL Server 2000."

Full-Text Search

The full-text search capability in SQL Server 2000 allows queries to be executed against data stored in formatted documents or HTML files. The ability to query unstructured textual data permits more and more "raw data" storage in the relational database system, enabling more efficient searching and retrieval of this data.

High Availability

Microsoft SQL Server 2000 provides "five 9s" reliability with new and enhanced availability features. (Five 9s refers to the server being available 99.999% of the time.) Previously, only products from Oracle or IBM could offer this level of availability. SQL Server 2000's availability is a result of online backups, log shipping, and failover clustering.

The online backup feature allows SQL Server databases to be backed up while the database is in use. Differential backups and server-less snapshots assist in backing up databases as well. These backup types, illustrated in Figure 1.4, enhance availability by

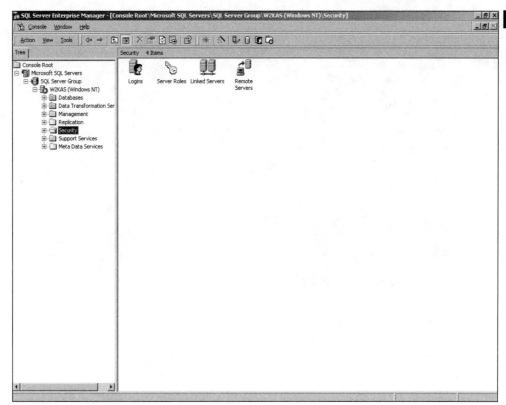

Figure 1.3
Security objects in SQL Server 2000.

promoting quick recoverability of the server and its databases. They also reduce the impact on resources during backups. This book examines SQL Server 2000 backups in great detail in Chapter 10, "Automating Administrative Tasks."

Log shipping automates the movement of transaction logs to remote servers in the interest of keeping these servers synchronized with the main production SQL Server. These "warm" standby servers are an excellent resource in the event of a problem with the main server. These systems can also provide excellent scalability. Log shipping is covered in detail in Chapter 11, "Configuring Failover Support."

SQL Server 2000 also supports failover and failback clustering. This means additional servers automatically provide services in the event of a system failure. The additional systems help load balance as well. This book describes these features in Chapter 11.

Scalability

Thanks mainly to the Windows 2000 Datacenter Server operating system, SQL Server 2000 provides new levels of scalability. This includes tremendous support for hardware, specifically 64GB of RAM and 32 CPUs. In addition to this excellent hardware support,

Figure 1.4
Backup types in SQL Server 2000.

other scalability enhancements abound, including parallel index creation, distributed portioned views, standby servers, and robust server clusters.

Distributed Partitioned Views

Distributed partitioned views provide an excellent way to distribute the processing load across multiple SQL Servers. Data is horizontally portioned across multiple servers. The servers all respond to queries, and neither users nor applications realize the data is not centrally located.

Indexed Views

Views created in SQL Server 2000 can now contain a clustered index. This index provides enhanced performance when these views are used and even improves query performance when these views are not explicitly referenced in a query. The SQL Server query optimizer is actually smart enough to use the indexed view (if appropriate), even if this view is not mentioned in the **FROM** clause of a query.

Virtual Interface System Area Network (VI SAN)

A new and exciting technology used by many e-commerce and enterprise business applications is System Area Networks (SANs). SQL Server 2000 supports Virtual VI SAN technology, which means that SQL Server can communicate directly with these SAN devices for the transfer of data at much higher throughput.

Replication

SQL Server 2000 provides a robust, built-in replication system. This system permits data to be distributed easily and efficiently throughout the enterprise and beyond. Three main types of replication appear in S2K–snapshot, transactional, and merge replication. This book covers replication thoroughly in Chapter 15, "Using Replication."

Simplified Database Administration

SQL Server 2000 provides more tools than in previous editions to self-administer the relational database management system. It uses dynamic algorithms to optimize database storage, memory usage, disk system usage, and more. Also, almost all of the administration tools boast enhancements, making their use simpler or more efficient. This book covers these new administration tools throughout.

Improved Developer Productivity

Programmability enhancements are plentiful in SQL Server 2000. Most notable are the enhancements found in SQL Server 2000 Query Analyzer. This tool provides a scripting medium for developers and now features a Transact-SQL (T-SQL) debugger, templates, and object browser. In addition, plenty of new language features aid application development, including cascading referential integrity constraints, **INSTEAD OF** and **AFTER** triggers, and indexes on computed columns.

Data Transformation Services (DTS)

Moving data in or out of SQL Server 2000 can be done very easily thanks to DTS. DTS, illustrated in Figure 1.5, not only transports data to or from just about any data source, it can also manipulate the data as it does so. You create DTS packages that can include any number of transformation steps as data is moved from one system to another. You can then save these packages (with security, of course) and even schedule them for periodic or sporadic executions. This book covers DTS in detail in Chapter 14.

Extended Applications

SQL Server 2000's support for the Windows CE 2.11 operating system means database applications can extend to a much wider variety of devices, including Handheld and Pocket PCs, as well as embedded systems. SQL Server 2000 Windows CE Edition excels at transferring data in low bandwidth and/or wireless environments to synchronize data between portable devices and network servers. For example, a remote user could easily use the HTTP protocol and the Internet to transfer data from a remote location back to a central SQL Server 2000 system. This also has tremendous implications in SQL Server replication environments. Chapter 15 covers replication in SQL Server 2000 in great detail.

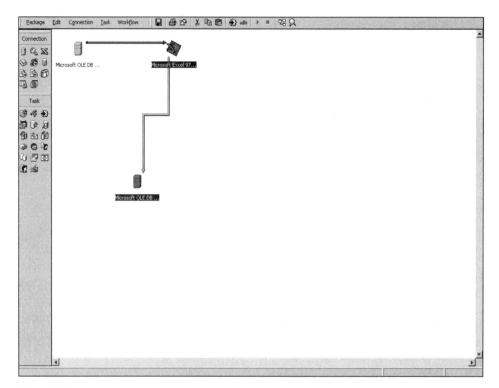

Figure 1.5
DTS in SQL Server 2000.

English Query

Thanks to English Query functionality in SQL Server 2000, users with absolutely no knowledge of SQL can pose queries to the server using plain English language. This offers simple access to data stored in databases within SQL Server 2000 and also enhances Web integration, because Web site users have come to expect simple search capabilities for data.

Data Mining and Analysis (OLAP) Services

Data mining assists advanced users of databases in analyzing data stored in OLAP data sources. Microsoft Decision Tree Algorithms and Microsoft Clustering Algorithms both provide assistance with uncovering patterns and trends that make data analysis exceedingly valuable.

SQL Server's Competition

SQL Server 2000 is not the only relational database management system that offers the various features described earlier. In fact, many competing products paved the way for the success of SQL Server 2000. This section examines several of these competing products and lists the features *they* offer. Be sure to note the consistency in themes here that help define the industry today. Also realize that all of these products run on the Windows 2000 Server platform; in fact, DB2 Universal Database version 7 is the first non-Microsoft RDBMS to be certified as built for Windows 2000 Server.

Oracle9i

The Oracle database is considered by most today as the industry standard. This is fitting perhaps, because this RDBMS was the first to support the SQL language. The latest version of this relational database management system from Oracle Corporation stresses Internet integration more than any other feature it offers (notice the "i" in the title?).

Oracle9i features:

- *Scalability*—Oracle Real Application Clusters provide support for staggering numbers of users and vendor independence for server hardware
- *Availability*—new features in Oracle9i assist the system in achieving five 9 uptime
- *System management and security*
- *Data warehousing*
- *Java support*
- *XML support*

Sybase Adaptive Server Enterprise 12

Sybase is another longtime player in the relational database management software game. Its latest high-end product features the following:

- *Availability*—two node cluster capabilities
- *Integration*—features the Enterprise Information Portal for easy integration of data from disparate data stores
- *Java support*
- *XML support*
- *Web Transaction Management*—featuring distributed transaction support using industry standard XA interfaces

DB2 Universal Database version 7

IBM has also included an RDBMS in its product lineup. DB2 Universal Database version 7 features:

- *Developer support*—tight integration with Microsoft Visual Studio and IBM VisualAge
- *Integration*—simplified access to OLE DB data sources
- *In memory text search capabilities*

- *Data warehousing*

- *Java support*

- *XML support*

SQL Server 2000 Editions

SQL Server 2000 currently ships in seven different editions. It is critical to select the correct edition of the application in order to ensure you possess the feature set you need in production. In fact, only four of these editions are appropriate for production servers. The remaining three editions are for more specialized usage, as you will see in this section.

Enterprise Edition

If you need all of the possible features offered by SQL Server 2000, you need the Enterprise Edition. This edition supports the largest of production environments; it is the most scalable version of SQL Server 2000 currently available.

SQL Server 2000 Enterprise Edition installs on the following operating systems:

- Windows 2000 Datacenter Server

- Windows 2000 Advanced Server

- Windows 2000 Server

- Windows NT 4 Server, Enterprise Edition

- Windows NT 4 Server

Standard Edition

Smaller workgroups might find the SQL Server 2000 Standard Edition appropriate for their installation. It does not provide the scalability that the Enterprise Edition features, nor does it support the full feature set of SQL Server 2000.

Features not supported in this version include:

- Failover clustering

- Failover support

- Parallel **CREATE INDEX**

- Parallel DBCC

- Log shipping

- Enhanced read-ahead and scan

- Indexed views

- Federated Database Server

- SAN Support

- Graphical utilities support for language settings

In addition to the lack of the above features, the Standard Edition does not support the full set of SQL Server 2000 Analysis Services features found in the Enterprise Edition. The features missing from Analysis Services in the Standard Edition are as follows:

- User-defined OLAP partitions

- Linked OLAP cubes

- Real-time OLAP

- Partition Wizard

- Relational OLAP dimension support

- HTTP Internet support

- Calculated cells

- Writeback to dimensions

- Very large dimension support

- Distributed portioned cubes

SQL Server 2000 Standard Edition installs on the following operating systems:

- Windows 2000 Datacenter Server

- Windows 2000 Advanced Server

- Windows 2000 Server

- Windows NT 4 Server, Enterprise Edition

- Windows NT 4 Server

Personal Edition

For standalone application usage, or for mobile users running notebooks or other less powerful portable devices, Microsoft provides the SQL Server 2000 Personal Edition. This feature does not provide the performance found in either the Enterprise Edition or the Standard Edition. In fact, there is a workload governor that actually forces this limited performance.

The Personal Edition lacks the same features that are lacking in the Standard Edition. It also lacks:

- Transactional replication support

- Full-text search (if installed on Windows 98 or Windows ME)

SQL Server 2000 Personal Edition installs on the following operating systems:

- Windows 2000 Datacenter Server

- Windows 2000 Advanced Server

- Windows 2000 Server

- Windows 2000 Professional

- Windows NT 4 Server, Enterprise Edition

- Windows NT 4 Server

- Windows NT 4 Workstation

- Windows Millennium Edition

- Windows 98

Developer Edition

If you are a developer interested in creating SQL Server 2000 applications, you might be interested in the Developer Edition. This special edition is licensed only for use in development and testing and cannot be used in a production environment. The Developer Edition supports all of the features of SQL Server 2000, with one exception—it does not support graphical utilities' support for language settings.

SQL Server 2000 Developer Edition installs on the following operating systems:

- Windows 2000 Datacenter Server

- Windows 2000 Advanced Server

- Windows 2000 Server

- Windows 2000 Professional

- Windows NT 4 Server, Enterprise Edition

- Windows NT 4 Server

- Windows NT 4 Workstation

Evaluation Edition

Microsoft makes it very easy to learn, test, and evaluate SQL Server 2000 by providing a complimentary copy of the Enterprise Edition–the Evaluation Edition. This version stops running 120 days after installation. The Evaluation Edition supports all of the features of SQL Server 2000, with one exception—it does not support graphical utilities' support for language settings.

SQL Server 2000 Enterprise Evaluation Edition installs on the following operating systems:

- Windows 2000 Datacenter Server

- Windows 2000 Advanced Server

- Windows 2000 Server

- Windows 2000 Professional

- Windows NT 4 Server, Enterprise Edition

- Windows NT 4 Server

- Windows NT 4 Workstation

Windows CE Edition

Windows CE Edition of SQL Server 2000 provides robust data storage services on Windows CE devices. SQL Server 2000 Windows CE Edition is especially effective when the CE devices are connected to the network and accessing larger SQL Server 2000 systems using Remote Data Access (RDA) components. Windows CE Edition also performs well in wireless networks. It accomplishes this through the use of data compression and messaging to reduce the size of data transmissions. SQL Server 2000 Windows CE Edition installs on Windows CE.

Desktop Engine

The Desktop Engine Edition of SQL Server 2000 is a redistributable version of the SQL Server 2000 relational database engine. Developers that need robust data storage capabilities in an application can license this special version of SQL Server 2000. Naturally, this version requires no end-user administration and ships with no graphical utilities or tools.

The Desktop Engine Edition lacks the same features that are lacking in the Personal Edition. In addition, the Desktop Edition does not have full-text search capabilities; nor does it have graphical administration and developer tools and wizards. Finally, Desktop Edition does not support Analysis Services.

SQL Server 2000 Desktop Engine addition installs on the following operating systems:

- Windows 2000 Datacenter Server

- Windows 2000 Advanced Server

- Windows 2000 Server

- Windows 2000 Professional

- Windows NT 4 Server, Enterprise Edition

- Windows NT 4 Server

- Windows NT 4 Workstation

- Windows Millennium Edition

- Windows 98

Decision Tree 1.1 is designed to help you choose the SQL Server 2000 Edition that is best for your needs. Spend some time with this job aid to be sure you save yourself money and time in the long run.

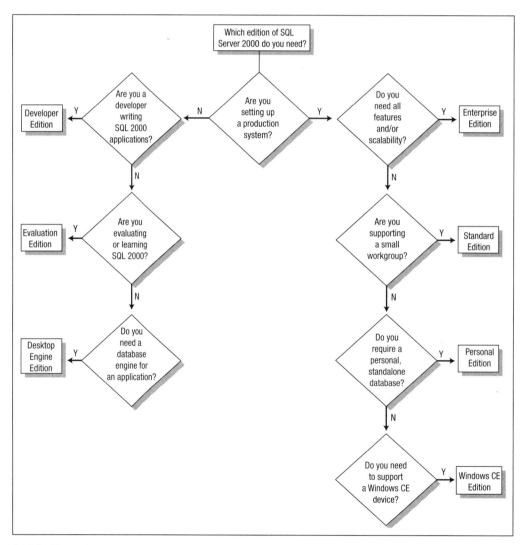

Decision Tree 1.1
Which edition of SQL Server 2000 do you need?

Summary

It is important for you to understand just what Microsoft SQL Server 2000 is and how this important product fits into Microsoft's overall project strategy. Remember, SQL Server 2000 is a key element in the important .NET strategy that should define the future of the software giant. SQL Server 2000 features a robust set of key features that parallel those of major competing products. You should become familiar with these features.

SQL Server 2000 ships in many different editions. Use the decision tree in this chapter to help you select an edition that is appropriate for your installation. Selecting the wrong edition can be a costly and time-consuming error.

The next chapter of this book deals with the architecture and components that make up SQL Server 2000. An understanding of the SQL Server 2000 architecture provides an excellent framework for the rest of your career as a SQL Server administrator, and knowledge of the components that makeup SQL Server ensure that you select the appropriate tool for a particular need or situation.

Chapter 2

SQL Server 2000 Architectures and Components

SQL Server 2000 is a relational database management system built completely upon databases. The system consists of user databases—created by database administrators for storing and retrieving data used by database clients—and system databases that store the information needed for SQL Server 2000, enabling it to actually function. This chapter examines these user databases and system databases, and explores additional aspects of the SQL Server 2000 architecture. It also examines the actual components that make up SQL Server 2000 Enterprise Edition–these are the tools that you will learn to master as you move through this book. Like the previous overview chapter, this chapter frequently points to specific chapters in the book for more specific information regarding certain topics.

SQL 2000 Architectures

The architecture of SQL 2000 is amazingly diverse and complex. To facilitate your understanding of it, this section breaks down this architecture into five main categories. While this is not a complete coverage of the architecture, it stresses the topics that are most important to an administrator. Let's begin with a look at the basic architecture of databases.

Database Architecture

The database is the core building block of SQL Server 2000. It consists of *logical components*—such as tables, views, and stored procedures—and also *physical components,* which consist primarily of the files that make up the database and that are stored on a disk subsystem.

Logical Database Components

Logical database components consist of the following objects:

- *Tables*—If the database is the core building block of SQL Server, then the table is the building block of the database. This structure stores data in columns (known as attributes) and rows (known as records). By its very nature, a relational database consists of more than one of these tables, most of which are related to each other in some way. Typically, these tables represent entities modeled from the business environment and needing storage and retrieval. For example, a university might require a database to store information about its courses and faculty. Tables that might be created in this database would typically contain information about Courses, Instructors, Assistants, and Curriculum.

- *Data types*—Data types specify the form of data that can be stored in columns of a table. For example, SQL Server 2000 provides such data types as money, integer, and character; money for storing currency values, integer for storing numbers, and character for storing text. In addition to the many system-supplied data types in SQL Server, you can create your own user-defined data types for specific data storage situations.

- *Views*—Views, as their name implies, present data to users from one or more underlying tables. Why not simply have the users access tables directly? Most of the time, views are employed to improve performance or enhance security. Thanks to views, many underlying columns can be completely hidden, for example.

- *Stored procedures*—Stored procedures are groups of Transact-SQL statements compiled into a single execution plan. These groups of statements perform tasks that applications might need to process frequently. Stored procedures ensure these transactions get processed correctly and efficiently. Stored procedures can exist in nontransactional environments as well, however. SQL Server 2000 provides many prewritten stored procedures for performing a variety of administrative tasks. These stored procedures are known as system stored procedures and begin with **sp_** in their name. For example, **sp_renamedb** assists administrators in efficiently renaming databases.

- *Functions*—Functions assist developers by manipulating data with a single group of prewritten code. It should come as no surprise that SQL Server 2000 provides functions (system functions) and also permits the creation of user-defined functions. Transact-SQL supports three types of functions–rowset, aggregate, and scalar functions.

  - *Rowset functions*—These return an object that can be used in place of a table reference in a Transact-SQL statement. For example, **OPENDATASOURCE** connects to a remote table in a Transact-SQL statement.

  - *Aggregate functions*—These analyze a collection of values and return a single, summarizing value. For example, **AVG** returns the average of a series of values.

  - *Scalar functions*—These examine a single value and return a single value. For example, **CHAR** converts an integer ASCII code value to a character value.

- *Indexes*—Just as in a book, an index assists in the quick and efficient retrieval of data from tables in the database. SQL Server 2000 supports two types of indexes on tables–clustered and nonclustered.

  - *Clustered indexes*—These sort and store the data rows in a table based on a key value. Because the rows are actually stored in order, data retrieval can be extremely efficient. Also because of this special sorted storage order, only one clustered index is permitted per table.

- *Nonclustered indexes*—These do not store data in any special order. Instead, pointers are used to quickly retrieve specific information. SQL Server 2000 supports multiple clustered indexes per table. S2K features the Index Tuning Wizard to assist administrators and developers in constructing the most effective collection of indexes for a particular table.

- *Constraints*—Constraints help maintain the integrity of data stored in a database. You assign constraints to tables to ensure that only valid data can be inserted within select columns. For example, the statement **CONSTRAINT chk_employid CHECK (employ_id BETWEEN 0 and 2000)** in a **CREATE TABLE** statement mandates that the **employ_id** is a value between 0 and 2000.

- *Rules*—Rules perform essentially the same functions as constraints. They are provided in SQL Server 2000 for backward compatibility with previous versions of SQL that did not offer constraints. You should choose constraints over rules whenever possible, mainly because constraints are a SQL-92 standard, whereas rules are not.

- *Defaults*—Defaults are data values that are assigned automatically to a row if a user does not provide a value. For example, you can assign the value "USA" as the default to a **Country** column if most of the values will be from the U.S., and data entry staff might tend to omit typing this value.

- *Triggers*—Triggers are a special class of stored procedure. These stored procedures are designed to execute automatically when an **UPDATE, INSERT,** or **DELETE** statement is issued against a table or view. Based on your needs, you can place one or more of these trigger objects on a table or view. Triggers help to ensure the integrity of data stored in a database and also can enforce business rules required by the enterprise needing the database.

For a glimpse of these database objects as they appear in SQL Server 2000, see Figure 2.1. Note that databases also contain additional components that relate specifically to security. These objects include logins, users, and roles. This book covers the use of these components in full in Chapter 8, "Securing SQL Server 2000."

Physical Database Components

The physical database architecture of SQL Server 2000 is extremely important for the performance and stability of SQL Server databases. Understanding this physical architecture is critical for any SQL administrator.

Each SQL Server 2000 database stores data using two or more operating system files. These files consist of the following:

- *Primary data files*—Every database has a primary data file. By default, the file has an .mdf extension, which follows the naming convention Microsoft recommends that you

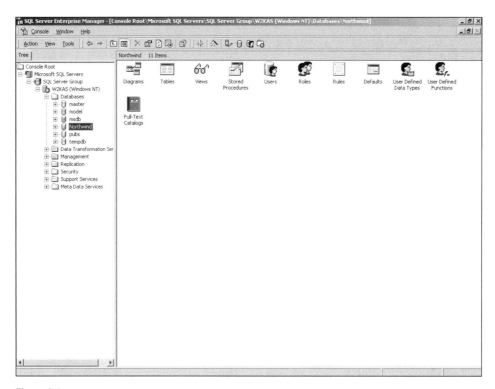

Figure 2.1
Logical database components in SQL Server 2000.

use. One of the jobs of the primary data file (in addition to storing data) is to point to all other operating system files that make up the database.

- *Secondary data files*—Secondary data files are optional and store additional data for databases. Databases can be made up of any number of additional secondary data files. This depends on the file system strategy that the administrator uses. This book examines these strategies and the use of secondary data files in Chapter 7, "Creating Databases." The default extension for these files is .ndf, and again, you should use this default.

- *Log files*—Log files store the transaction log for a database. The transaction log allows the database to be restored to any particular point in time, and is, therefore, extremely important. There must be at least one log file for the database, but more can be used, depending on the strategy employed. The default extension for these files is .ldf; again, Microsoft recommends this not be changed. For a glimpse of these data and log files as they exist on the file system, see Figure 2.2.

Administrators have the ability to group these files that make up a database into structures called *filegroups*. Filegroups provide additional administration options for data storage in SQL Server 2000. For example, a SQL Server administrator creates filegroups

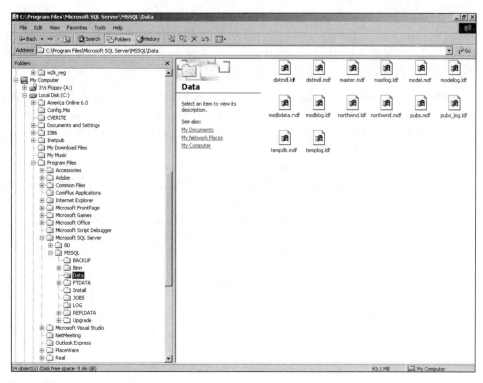

Figure 2.2
Data files for SQL Server 2000 databases.

for each disk drive, and then assigns specific tables or indexes to specific filegroups. This is an advanced system administration technique discussed in more detail in Chapter 7.

System Databases

SQL Server 2000 is made up of four system databases—**master**, **tempdb**, **msdb**, and **model**. Naturally, SQL Server 2000 also provides user databases. These databases are created by database administrators and developers and provide a storage location for SQL server data. As was mentioned in Chapter 1, Microsoft provides the Northwind user database as a sample database for experimentation and practice. It is important to realize that a single instance of SQL Server 2000 has the ability to host many user databases. In addition to this, a server can host many instances of SQL Server 2000. This makes the relational database management system (RDBMS) extremely scalable and flexible for administrators.

Obviously, the four system databases of S2K are critical to the operation of the server. Each of these system databases performs a specific function, as follows:

- *master*—This database records all system-level information for the SQL Server; this includes all login accounts and system configuration settings. It is also responsible for tracking information regarding all user databases on the system. For obvious reasons, it is imperative to have a backup of the master database readily available at all times. Chapter 9, "Backing Up and Restoring SQL Server 2000," details backing up **master** databases and other important information. See Figure 2.3 for a look at the **master** system database and the tables it contains.

- *tempdb*—This database stores all temporary data that SQL Server 2000 creates during normal database operations. This could include entire temporary tables or temporary stored procedures. To ensure a clean **tempdb**, temporary information created as a result of a user connection is immediately dropped when the user disconnects from the server. Also, SQL Server 2000 recreates the **tempdb** database from scratch each time the system restarts. By default, **tempdb** grows in size as needed during production and also resets its size each time the database engine starts. It is possible to minimize the resource impact these resizes create using the **ALTER DATABASE** statement or Enterprise Manager to increase the size of **tempdb**. This book covers these techniques in Chapter 8, "Securing SQL Server 2000."

- *msdb*—This database stores information regarding scheduled alerts and jobs. **Msdb** also stores information about operators who receive notifications regarding these jobs. This system database is critical for automating administrative tasks in SQL Server 2000. The SQL Server Agent service maintains this automation and is driven by this system database. This book looks at automating administrative tasks more fully in Chapter 10.

- *model*—This database serves as a template for the creation of new user databases on the system. If there are certain parameters you will need consistently across all subsequent databases created on the system, modify the **model** database accordingly.

Relational Database Engine Architecture

The relational database engine is one of SQL Server 2000's real strengths. Examining exactly how this architecture functions is not only a fascinating study; it can also ensure that an administrator truly understands SQL Server 2000 processes.

Tabular Data Stream (TDS)

Clients of the SQL Server 2000 system send SQL statements to the server using a proprietary application-level protocol called Tabular Data Stream (TDS). The Microsoft OLE DB Provider for SQL Server, the SQL Server Open Database Connectivity (ODBC) driver, or the DB-Library dynamic link library (DLL) builds these TDS packets and passes them to a SQL Server client Net-Library. The client Net-Library encapsulates these packets into network protocol packets. At the SQL Server, a server Net-Library receives the network protocol packets and extracts the TDS packets. The server Net-Library then passes these TDS packets to the relational database engine for processing.

This process reverses when results need to be passed back to a client from the relational database engine. The exact format of TDS packets returned is variable, however. This format depends on whether **FOR XML** is specified in the Transact-SQL statement trans-

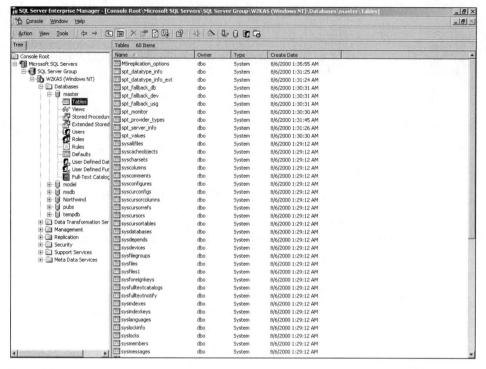

Figure 2.3
The system tables of the **master** system database.

mitted to the database engine. The **FOR XML** clause causes results to be returned as Extensible Markup Language (XML) data instead of standard rowsets. This book details the use of the **FOR XML** clause in Chapter 16, "Configuring XML and Internet Support."

If **FOR XML** is specified, the database engine streams an XML document back to the client. The XML document is formatted in the TDS packets as if it were a single, long Unicode value, with each packet approximately 4KB in size. If **FOR XML** is not specified, the database engine sends a relational result set back to the client. The TDS packets contain the rows of the result set, with each row comprised of one or more columns, as specified in the select list of the **SELECT** statement.

An advanced SQL Server administration technique permits you to configure the size of TDS packets. The size of the TDS packets defaults to 4KB on most clients, which is optimal in almost all scenarios.

Relational Database Engine

SQL Server 2000's relational database engine consists of two main parts—the relational engine and the storage engine. These components are separate from each other and use the OLE DB API in order to communicate. The relational engine accepts statements and compiles them into an optimized execution plan. As the relational engine steps through this plan, it calls upon the storage engine for data retrieval. This is not to trivialize the role of the storage engine, as its duties also include:

- Managing the files on which the database is stored and managing the use of space in the files.

- Managing the data buffers and all I/O to the physical files.

- Managing transactions and using locking to control concurrent user access to rows in the database.

- Logging and recovery.

- Implementing utility functions such as the **BACKUP, RESTORE,** and **DBCC** statements and bulk copy.

This separation of duties in the relational database engine began in version 7 of SQL Server and dramatically enhances performance for the server.

Administration Architecture

SQL Server 2000 provides a robust administration architecture that permits new levels of automation and management simplicity. This is made possible by a wide variety of technologies. The following sections present the main components of the administration architectures of SQL Server 2000, including the SQL Distributed Management Framework, Transact-SQL, graphical tools, and automated administration components. I also discuss the backup and restore architecture and the data import and export architectures in SQL Server 2000.

SQL Distributed Management Framework (SQL-DMF)

The SQL Distributed Management Framework (SQL-DMF) provides an integrated system of services, components, and objects for managing SQL Server 2000. This framework provides astonishing flexibility when it comes to managing SQL Server 2000. Some organizations can standardize on graphical tools provided by Microsoft; others can create their own tools using Web interfaces.

Figure 2.4 displays the objects that make up the SQL-DMF. This book covers many of these components in detail later in this chapter and in other chapters.

As you can see from the figure, there are three main application types that administrators use to harness the power of SQL-DMF:

- *SQL Server Enterprise Manager*—The main graphical user interface for server management and configuration. This GUI is actually a Microsoft Management Console snap-in.

- *Distributed Component Object Model (DCOM) applications* and *Active Server Pages*— Allow creation of custom Web interfaces for specialized management of SQL Server systems.

2

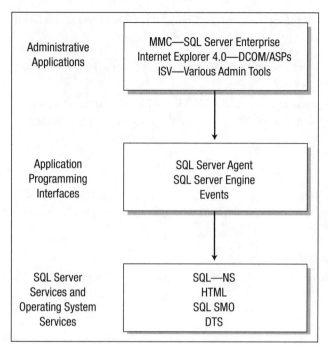

Figure 2.4
The components of SQL-DMF.

• *Applications and Independent Software Vendors (ISV) tools*—Allow non-Microsoft software vendors to easily develop administrative applications for the various SQL Server 2000 editions.

Notice also that several application programming interfaces are available to provide easy access to key administrative operating system and SQL Server services. The most important one for discussion here is SQL Distributed Management Objects (SQL-DMO).

SQL-DMO provides object interfaces for SQL Server 2000 and its components. You use the main object, SQLServer, in conjunction with other objects such as Database and Table. These SQL-DMO objects provide properties and methods and are easily manipulated using Visual Basic or C++ and other key .NET components.

Once you install SQL-DMO support in Visual Basic (see the VB documentation regarding Add-Ins for Visual Basic), creating a SQL Server object and connecting to a server are simple. The following code snippet demonstrates this:

```
Dim ServerObject As New SQLOLE.SQLServer
ServerObject.Connect "ServerName", "sa", "password"
```

Once a connection is made to the server, manipulating the objects within SQL Server 2000 is also simple. Examine the examples here:

- This code snippet modifies the SelectIntoBulkCopy database option for the Northwind database:

```
ServerObject.Databases("Northwind").DBOption.SelectIntoBulkCopy = TRUE
```

- This code snippet demonstrates using SQL-DMO to add a new column named NewColumn to a table called SampleTable in a database named SampleDatabase:

```
Dim NewColobject as New SQLOLE.Column
NewColobject.Name = "OrderCategory"
NewColobject.Datatype = "char"
NewColobject.Length = 2
ServerObject.Databases("SampleDatabase").Tables("SampleTable").Columns.Add
NewColobject
```

DDL, DML, DCL, and Stored Procedures

Chapter 3 of this book provides a detailed look at Transact-SQL, the main, high-level language of SQL Server 2000. There, you will learn about four T-SQL categories that will be invaluable to you as an S2K administrator:

- *Data Definition Language (DDL)*—You use Data Definition Language T-SQL statements to create and manage all of the objects central to SQL databases. For each object class, there are usually **CREATE, ALTER,** and **DROP** statements, such as **CREATE TABLE, ALTER TABLE,** and **DROP TABLE.** These are perfect examples of DDL statements.

- *Data Manipulation Language (DML)*—Data Manipulation Language statements select, insert, update, and delete data in the objects defined using DDL. Examples include **INSERT, UPDATE,** and **DELETE** statements, of course.

- *Data Control Language (DCL)*—Data Control Language statements provide security for objects in SQL Server. Examples include **GRANT, REVOKE,** and **DENY.** This book covers these statements not only in Chapter 3, but also in Chapter 8, which deals with security.

- *Stored procedures*—As discussed earlier in this chapter, stored procedures are groups of statements that perform tasks that many applications might need to frequently process. If you have administrative needs not met by DDL, DML, or DCL, one of the system stored procedures—or a stored procedure that you create—just might be the solution you are looking for.

Graphical Tools

SQL Server 2000 abounds with graphical tools, utilities, and wizards that guide administrators through complex server and database management tasks. These tools are discussed in the "SQL Server 2000 Components" section of this chapter.

It is important to realize that many of these tools can function within the Microsoft Management Console interface, now native to Windows 2000. The MMC provides a "blank slate" for administrators to plug-in graphical management tools. If you would like the Event Viewer graphical interface in the same console with the SQL Enterprise Manager, you could easily accomplish this by following the steps below:

1. Select Start|Programs|Accessories|Windows Explorer.

2. Navigate to the directory that stores the Enterprise Manager MMC used by SQL Server 2000. In a default installation, this directory is C:\Program Files\Microsoft SQL Server\80\Tools\Bin. The file name is SQL Server Enterprise Manager.MSC.

3. Right-click this file and choose Author from the shortcut menu (see Figure 2.5).

4. The Enterprise Manager launches in Author mode so you can modify the MMC interface. Choose the Console menu and select Add/Remove Snap-In.

5. In the Add/Remove Snap-In dialog, choose the Add button. Select Event Viewer and click the Add button.

6. Choose the Finish button from the Select Computer dialog to choose Event Viewer for the Local computer.

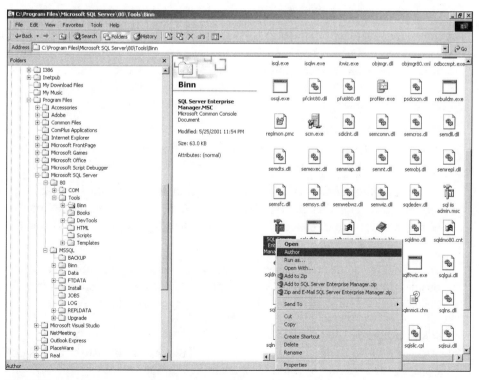

Figure 2.5
Opening the SQL Server Enterprise Manager console in Author mode.

7. Choose the Close button in the Add Standalone Snap-In dialog box.

8. Choose OK in the Add/Remove Snap-In dialog box to close it.

9. Notice the Enterprise Manager MMC now features the graphical Event Viewer controls as well. Choose the Console menu, Save As option to save your new Enterprise Manager/Event Viewer MMC using an appropriate name and location.

Automated Administration

SQL Server 2000 makes automating the administration of the server and its databases very simple (covered in Chapter 10 of this book). A classic example of automating administrative tasks is having the server periodically back up its own database information. This backup certainly needs to be performed regularly, and having the server handle it automatically frees you up for more sophisticated management tasks.

The architectural features that make this automation possible are:

- *SQL Server Agent*—The key to automation in SQL Server 2000 is the SQL Server Agent. The SQL Server Agent handles the execution of jobs you create and alerts operators you define on the system. The agent runs as a service in Windows 2000/NT or as an executable on Windows 98, or ME systems.

- *Jobs*—You create jobs that define the administrative task you would like to automate. Jobs can consist of multiple steps and can also execute Transact-SQL statements, Windows commands, executables, and even ActiveX compliant scripts. After carefully creating these jobs, you can then schedule them to occur at appropriate intervals. See Figure 2.6 for an example of creating a new job in SQL Server 2000.

- *Events and alerts*—SQL Server 2000 reports significant events to the Event Log system of Windows 2000. Using alerts, you can schedule jobs to be executed when certain events occur on the system.

- *Operators*—You define operators in SQL Server 2000 to be notified of specific occurrences surrounding the jobs you create. For example, if you need certain individuals to be paged or emailed when a certain critical job fails, you configure this through the use of operators.

- *Triggers*—Remember, triggers are a special class of stored procedure and enforce business logic in the database. Triggers integrate nicely with automation in SQL Server 2000. A specific event can fire an alert that in turn fires a trigger.

Backup/Restore

SQL Server 2000 provides a robust backup and restore architecture. This is critical for operations that cannot tolerate any data loss or operational disruption. Backups stored offsite help reduce or eliminate the consequences of catastrophic events such

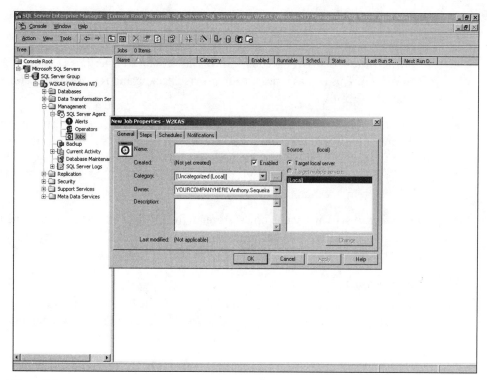

Figure 2.6
Creating a new job in SQL Server 2000.

as fires or floods. Also, backups make it easier to recover from security breaches. Chapter 9, "Backing Up and Restoring SQL Server 2000," covers backing up and restoring in great detail.

The backup and restore architecture of SQL Server 2000 provides the following components and features:

• *A variety of backup types*—Full database backups, transaction log backups, differential backups, and file or filegroups backups can all be used to ensure you have the correct backup and restore strategy in place.

• *Control with the **BACKUP** and **RESTORE** statements and graphical tools*—Administrators have a variety of methods for carrying out backups and restores. The **BACKUP** and **RESTORE** Transact-SQL statements allow the creation of stored procedures and/or jobs, and Enterprise Manager features simple Graphical User Interfaces and wizards for maintaining backups and restores.

• *History tables in the **msdb** database*—The **msdb** system database automatically records the history of database backups, including the type of backup performed. When it comes time for database restoration, SQL Server 2000 provides advice regarding which backups need to be restored and in what order.

- *Backups during database utilization*—The backup and restore architecture of S2K permits the administrator to backup databases while they are in use.

- *Fast transfer rates*—SQL Server 2000 features faster data transfer rates than any previous version. This makes it possible to provide backup and restore support for very large databases (VLDB).

- *Database creation on **RESTORE***—The **RESTORE** Transact-SQL statement has the ability to create databases upon execution of the statement. This eliminates the need to create the database with separate statements should the database not exist when the restore is performed. This is obviously critical when restoring a database to a different SQL Server system, for example.

- *Additional features*—The backup and restore architecture of S2K also supports better recovery from interrupted backups or restores, and, on top of that, supports verification of backups prior to restores.

Data Import/Export

SQL Server 2000 also provides a robust architecture for the transfer of data to and from the RDBMS. These architectural components, covered more completely in Chapters 14 and 15, include:

- Data Transformation Services

- Replication

- Bulk copying

Data Warehousing and OLAP Architecture

SQL Server 2000 provides a sophisticated architecture for the creation of data warehouses and data marts. These structures provide for intense data activities and reporting, including trend analysis. Such a system is known as an Online Analytical Processing (OLAP) system. This is in contrast to an Online Transaction Processing (OLTP) system designed to process transactions as quickly as possible. Earlier versions of SQL Server possessed the architecture for OLTP environments only. It was not until version 7 and higher that Microsoft offered OLAP in SQL Server.

The OLAP functionality in SQL Server 2000 results from the inclusion of OLAP Services and the PivotTable Service. OLAP Services and PivotTable Service provide the capability to design, create, and manage cubes from data warehouses and provide client access to OLAP data. The OLAP server manages the data, and PivotTable Service works with the server to provide client access to the data.

Application Development Architecture

SQL Server 2000 also provides a powerful architecture for developers to easily create applications that use the RDBMS. Application developers use one of two programming language technologies to access databases from applications—a database language (Transact-SQL or XPath) or an Application Programming Interface (API).

T-SQL follows conventions created specifically for Relational Database Management Systems, as it complies with the Entry Level of the SQL-92 standard.

SQL Server 2000 supports a subset of the XPath language. XPath's specialty is the selection of nodes from XML documents. XPath is a language defined by the World Wide Web Consortium (W3C). Chapter 16, "Configuring XML and Internet Support" covers XPath queries in detail.

SQL Server supports a number of APIs:

- ActiveX Data Objects (ADO)
- OLE DB
- Open Database Connectivity (ODBC)
- Remote Data Objects (RDO)
- Data Access Objects (DAO)
- Embedded SQL for C (ESQL)
- DB-Library

SQL Server 2000 also supports queries submitted via Internet URLs. These URLs may consist of XPath, T-SQL, or template based queries. This Internet application support is critical for Microsoft's .NET initiative.

Not all of these APIs include support for all of the features SQL Server 2000 provides. Also, particular programming languages support only some of these APIs. Table 2.1 presents comparisons of these key features.

Table 2.1 Application Programming Interfaces supported in SQL Server 2000.

API	SQL Server Feature Support	Native Language Support
ADO	Most	Microsoft Visual Basic, Microsoft Visual C++, Microsoft Visual J++
OLE DB	All	Visual C++
ODBC	All	Visual C++, Visual Basic, Visual J++
RDO	Most	Visual Basic, Visual J++
DAO	Few	Visual Basic, Visual C++
ESQL	Few	Visual C++, COBOL
DB-Library	Few	Visual C++

SQL Server 2000 Components

SQL Server 2000 initially intimidates many newcomers because of the large number of components that make up the relational database management system. This section details all of these components for you and should provide a valuable reference as you master all aspects of SQL Server 2000.

Server Components

One of the advantages of running SQL Server 2000 on top of the Windows NT/2000 platform is that key components of S2K run as services on these operating systems. If you are running one of the other 32-bit Windows platforms, S2K must run these key components as executables. When these server components run as services, they benefit from preferential treatment by the operating system, including additional memory and resources, compared to other applications.

Here are the server components that help make up SQL Server 2000:

- *SQL Server service*—Every instance of SQL Server 2000 running on a system must have an instance of the SQL Server service. This all-important service actually implements the relational database engine of SQL Server described earlier in this chapter. When viewed in the various Windows system interfaces, this service displays as MSSQLServer. The service relies upon the executable sqlservr.exe and can be found in the respective \MSSQL\binn\ directory. As you might guess, almost all other components of SQL Server 2000 rely upon this important service, including the SQL Server Agent service.

- *Analysis Services service*—Analysis Services provides the Online Analytical Processing environment of SQL Server 2000. All instances of SQL Server 2000 share a single instance of Analysis Services running on the system. This service has a very appropriate display name of MSSQLServerOLAPService.

- *SQL Server Agent service*—Every instance of SQL Server 2000 running on a system enjoys its own SQL Server service instance. The primary responsibility of the SQL Server Agent service is to run scheduled jobs created by administrators. This service also detects specific conditions for which administrators have defined an action and also runs replication tasks. The display name for this service is SQLServerAgent.

- *Microsoft Search service*—This service is shared by all instances of SQL Server running on the system. The Microsoft Search service is responsible for implementing the full-text search engine present in S2K. The display name for this service is Microsoft Search. This service is only installed on a system when it is selected using a custom installation, or is added later by an administrator.

- *Microsoft Distributed Transaction Coordinator (MS DTC) service*—All instances of SQL Server share the MS DTC service. This service manages distributed transactions exchanged between multiple instances of SQL Server 2000. Thanks to MS

DTC, client applications may present several different sources of data in one transaction—MS DTC manages them all. The display name of this service is Distributed Transaction Coordinator.

Client-based Administration Tools

SQL Server 2000 provides many client-based administration tools for managing the system. In addition to a large and powerful group of graphical tools, SQL Server 2000 features a good number of command-prompt utilities for managing the system.

Command-Prompt Tools

You often find yourself using a command-prompt tool to make a configuration change or submit a query to the server because command-prompt tools are often the quickest way to perform these actions. Certainly these command-prompt tools require less resource usage on the server, and therefore, are often preferred. These command prompt tools include:

- *bcp*—The Bulk Copy Program utility efficiently transfers large amounts of data between SQL Server 2000 and text files in a variety of formats. Although bcp employs a lengthy and complex syntax, it is often used with large text files because of its excellent performance.

- *console*—The console command-prompt utility displays backup and restore messages when backing up to or restoring from tape dump devices. This utility assists backup administrators by permitting them to easily monitor the status of large backup or restore tasks.

- *distrib*—The Replication Distribution Agent utility configures and begins the Distribution Agent, which moves the snapshot (for snapshot replication and transactional replication) held in the distribution database tables (for transactional replication) to the destination tables at the Subscribers.

- *dtsrun*—The dtsrun utility executes a package created using Data Transformation Services. The ability to run these packages from a command prompt environment is a nice convenience for administrators. There are many options for using dtsrun, as you can see from Figure 2.7.

- *dtswiz*—The dtswiz utility starts the DTS Import/Export Wizard, using command-prompt options provided by an administrator. With this utility, you create DTS packages that import, export, or transform data between data sources. Again, this command-prompt utility provides convenience for administrators who are looking for an alternative to the graphical wizard equivalent: DTS Import/Export Wizard.

- *isql*—The isql utility allows you to enter Transact-SQL statements, system procedures, and script files from the command-prompt environment. This utility uses the DB-Library API to communicate with S2K.

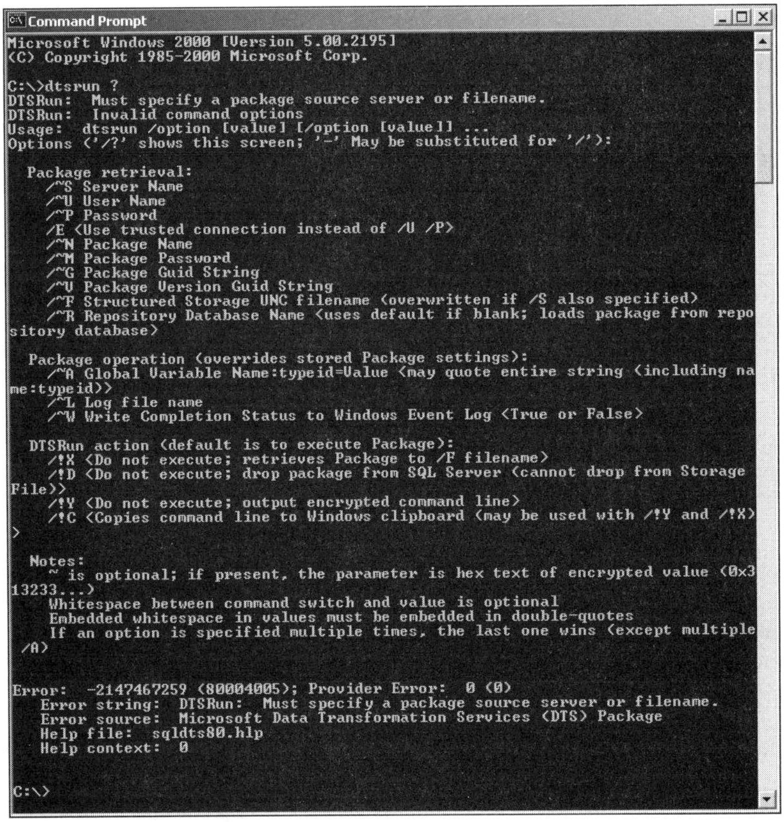

Figure 2.7
dtsrun command-prompt options.

- *isqlw*—The isqlw utility is a convenient way to launch the graphical SQL Query Analyzer from a command-prompt environment. This utility also allows you to set up shortcuts or create batch files to launch preconfigured SQL Query Analyzer sessions.

- *itwiz*—The itwiz utility allows you to execute the Index Tuning Wizard from a command-prompt environment.

- *logread*—The Replication Log Reader Agent utility configures and begins the Log Reader Agent, which monitors the transaction log of each database configured for replication and copies the transactions marked for replication from the transaction log into the distribution database.

- *makepipe*—You use the makepipe utility to test the integrity of the network Named Pipe services. Often you use this utility in conjunction with another command-prompt utility called readpipe.

- *odbccmpt*—This utility enables or disables the compatibility option for an ODBC application executable file.

- *odbcping*—This utility tests the integrity of an ODBC data source and the ability of the client to connect to a server.

- *osql*—This utility allows you to enter Transact-SQL statements, system procedures, and script files. The osql utility uses ODBC to communicate with the server.

- *queueread*—The Replication Queue Reader Agent utility configures and begins the Queue Reader Agent, which reads messages stored in a SQL Server queue or a Microsoft Message Queue and then applies those messages to the Publisher. Queue Reader Agent is used with snapshot and transactional publications that allow queued updating.

- *readpipe*—This utility tests the integrity of the network Named Pipe services in conjunction with makepipe.

- *rebuildm*—The Rebuild master (rebuildm) utility changes the collation settings for an instance of Microsoft SQL Server 2000, or fixes a corrupted **master** database.

- *replmerg*—The Replication Merge Agent utility configures and begins the Merge Agent, which applies the initial snapshot held in the database tables to the Subscribers. It also merges incremental data changes that occurred at the Publisher after the initial snapshot was created and reconciles conflicts either according to the rules you configure or using a custom resolver you create.

- *scm*—The Service Control Manager utility creates, modifies, starts, stops, or pauses any of the SQL Server 2000 services that run under Windows 2000/NT. Under Windows 9X or ME, the scm utility starts, stops, or pauses the equivalent SQL Server applications.

- *snapshot*—The Replication Snapshot Agent utility configures and begins the Snapshot Agent, which prepares snapshot files containing schema and data of published tables and database objects, stores the files in the snapshot folder, and records synchronization jobs in the distribution database.

- *sqlagent*—This utility starts SQL Server Agent from the command prompt. Only run sqlagent from the command prompt when you are diagnosing SQL Server Agent, or when you are directed to by your primary support provider.

- *sqldiag*—This utility gathers and stores diagnostic information and the contents of the query history trace (if running). The output file includes error logs, output from **sp_configure** and additional version information. If the query history trace was running when the utility was invoked, the trace file will contain the last 100 SQL events and exceptions. The sqldiag utility is intended to expedite and simplify information gathering by Microsoft Product Support Services.

- *sqlftwiz*—This utility executes the Full-Text Indexing Wizard.

- *sqlmaint*—This utility performs a specified set of maintenance operations on one or more databases. Use sqlmaint to run DBCC checks, backup a database and its transaction log, update statistics, and rebuild indexes. All database maintenance activities generate a report that can be sent to a designated text file, HTML file, or email account.

- *sqlservr*—This utility starts, stops, pauses, and continues an instance of Microsoft SQL Server 2000 from a command prompt.

- *vswitch*—This utility switches the active instance of SQL Server between SQL Server 2000, SQL Server 6.5, and SQL Server 6.

Almost all of these tools install automatically when you install SQL Server 2000. They are found by default in the locations described in Table 2.2.

Graphical Tools

In addition to many command-prompt utilities for administration, SQL Server 2000 ships with a full complement of graphical utilities for managing the server. These GUI tools include:

- *SQL Server Enterprise Manager*—This is the main administration tool for SQL Server 2000. It is a Microsoft Management Console snap-in; therefore you can combine this tool with many others in the MMC interface. This tool permits almost every server and database configuration possible in a graphical or even wizard based environment.

- *SQL Query Analyzer*—You use the Query Analyzer to administer the SQL Server system and its databases using Transact-SQL scripts. The Query Analyzer is also perfect for testing such scripts and for creating and testing batches and stored procedures.

- *SQL Profiler*—You use SQL Profiler to monitor and capture specific events in SQL Server 2000. Profiler allows security auditing, as well as advanced query analysis. Many times, the Profiler allows you to enhance the performance of queries by catching "hidden" inefficiencies.

- *SQL Server Service Manager*—This utility, shown in Figure 2.8, starts, stops, and pauses the SQL Server services. It also configures the automatic startup options for these services.

- *Client Network Utility*—This utility manages the client Net-Libraries used to connect to SQL Server 2000.

- *Server Network Utility*—This utility manages the server Net-Libraries.

Table 2.2   Default installation locations for the command-prompt utilities.

Directory	Tools
\Program Files\Microsoft SQL Server\MSSQL\Binn	bcp, console, isql, sqlagent, sqldiag, sqlmaint, sqlservr, vswitch
\Program Files\Microsoft SQL Server\80\Tools\Binn	bcp, dtsrun, dtswiz, isql, isqlw, itwiz, odbccmpt, osql, rebuildm, sqlftwiz
\Program Files\Microsoft SQL Server\80\Com	distrib, logread, replmerg, snapshot
\Program Files\Common Files\Microsoft Shared\Service Manager	scm
\Program Files\Common Files\Microsoft Shared\<your dir name>	regxmlss

2

Figure 2.8
SQL Server Service Manager.

Client Communication Components

Remember, clients take advantage of a large number of Application Programming Interfaces to make connections with SQL Server 2000 and manipulate data. For example, Internet applications access SQL Server 2000 using a URL, the ADO API, or the OLE DB API. Once the connection is made, the Internet application executes XPath queries or Transact-SQL statements against the server.

In addition to these new .NET compliant client communication methods, SQL Server 2000 also supports more "traditional" methods of client communication. The client must possess a Net-Library that matches a Net-Library hosted by the server. You can protect these communications across the Net-Libraries using encryption, thanks to the industry standard Secure Sockets Layer (SSL).

Because of the number of diverse Local Area and Wide Area Network technologies used today, SQL Server 2000 supports a diverse selection of Net-Libraries. Clients and the server can run multiple Net-Libraries as needed. Table 2.3 presents the current Net-Libraries supported by SQL Server 2000.

Table 2.3   SQL Server 2000 Net-Libraries.

Net-Library	Summary
Shared Memory	This default Net-Library permits a client connection to the server on the same computer. It uses a segment of local memory for this connection.
Named Pipes	Default protocol that uses Named Pipes for the client connection.
TCP/IP Sockets	Default Net-Library that uses TCP/IP for the client connection.
NWLink IPX/SPX	Used in legacy Novell environments where there is no TCP/IP support.
VIA GigaNet SAN	Supports the new high-speed SAN technology on GigaNet's clan server farm network.
Multiprotocol	Provided mainly for backward compatibility, this Net Library permits server-to-server communication over any available network protocol.
AppleTalk ADSP	Allows client communication using the AppleTalk protocol.
Banyan VINES	Used to permit Banyan VINES support. This only allows SQL Server 7 level functionality, however.

Books Online

SQL Server 2000 provides remarkably in-depth documentation on almost all aspects of the relational database management system, thanks to an application known as Books Online. Books Online is a collection of HTML documents organized in a powerful application interface. This interface permits administrators or students to read content by chapter or search for specific information using either a powerful index or an even more powerful search capability.

You can install Books Online on any 32-bit Windows platform, and you do not need to install any other components of SQL Server 2000. This means you can ensure Books Online is always available on any system you have access to, a very handy feature if you work with SQL Server 2000 very often. This is also a good reason to hold on to any Evaluation Edition of SQL Server 2000 you may acquire–it can function as your install mechanism for Books Online.

To install just Books Online on a Windows system, follow these steps:

Note: These instructions use the SQL Server 2000 Evaluation Edition CD-ROM to install Books Online on a Windows 98 system.

1. Insert the SQL Server 2000 CD-ROM in your CD-ROM drive.

2. If the SQL Server 2000 introductory screen does not automatically appear, use Windows Explorer to navigate to the root of the CD-ROM and double-click autorun.exe. The introductory screen is shown in Figure 2.9.

3. Choose SQL Server 2000 Components from the Welcome screen.

4. Choose Install Database Server from the Install Components screen.

5. Click OK in the warning dialog. This warning concerns the installation of client components only.

6. Choose Next at the Setup Welcome screen.

7. Choose Next to select Local Computer from the Computer Name screen.

8. Choose Next at the Installation Selection screen to create a new instance of SQL Server 2000 or to install Client Tools.

9. Complete the user information and choose Next.

10. Agree to the License Agreement by clicking Yes.

11. From the Installation Definition screen, select Client Tools Only and click Next.

12. In the Select Components screen, clear all components except Books Online and click Next.

13. Click Next again to begin the installation of Books Online.

14. In the Setup Complete screen, click Finish to complete the installation.

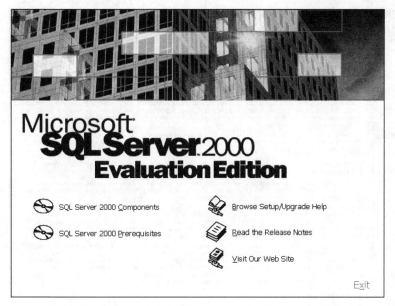

Figure 2.9
The SQL Server 2000 introductory screen.

You launch Books Online from the Start menu. The Microsoft SQL Server program group contains a shortcut aptly named Books Online. In order to use the powerful search capabilities of Books Online, follow these instructions:

1. Launch Books Online by selecting Start|Programs|Microsoft SQL Server|Books Online. Notice that Books Online launches with the Index tab selected by default in the left pane.

2. Choose the Search tab in the left pane.

3. In the Type In The Word(s) To Search For field, type the following (illustrated in Figure 2.10):

```
"relational database engine" memory
```

4. Choose the List Topics button. Notice that Books Online lists HTML documents that contain the phrase "relational database engine" and that also include the word "memory."

5. To view a document, double-click the document title in the Select Topic list. The document appears in the right pane.

6. To add this document to a list of your favorite Books Online topics, choose the Favorites tab and use the Add button at the bottom of the Favorites tab to add the document to your favorites list.

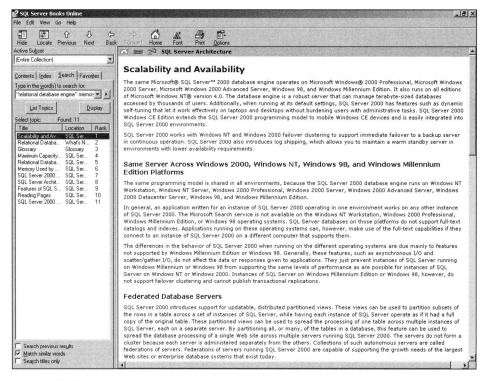

Figure 2.10
Using the Search capability of SQL Server 2000 Books Online.

Summary

It is very important for you to understand the various architectures that make up SQL Server 2000. Understanding these architectures builds a foundation for your full comprehension of all SQL Server 2000 topics to follow. You also need to understand the many varied components that comprise SQL Server 2000. These include both client and server components. Most importantly, remember the Microsoft SQL Server Service and the SQL Agent Service. Without these services, there is no SQL Server 2000. Finally, remember the critical client components of Enterprise Manager and Query Analyzer. The rest of this book relies heavily upon these tools.

The next chapter presents an overview of the Transact-SQL language. SQL Server 2000 uses this language to make all configuration changes to the product, and this language is also used to interact with data stored on the server. It is obviously critical, therefore, that you have a solid understanding of Transact-SQL.

Chapter 3

Transact-SQL

To be most effective in managing SQL Server 2000, you should master the Transact-SQL(T-SQL) language. Most people believe Transact-SQL is simply a language for manipulating the data in SQL databases, but in reality, it is much more powerful than that. Transact-SQL also provides commands that manage and maintain the server. While graphical user interfaces abound for these purposes, it is often much more efficient for administrators to use Transact-SQL. In fact, some server and database configurations can still only be made using T-SQL. Interestingly enough, it is Transact-SQL that actually makes all configuration changes in SQL Server 2000. When you use any of the graphical tools to manage server instances or databases, Transact-SQL statements are being formed for you and sent to the server.

In addition to teaching you the most important aspects of the Transact-SQL language, this chapter also serves as a reference for you as you move throughout this book. You should find yourself returning to this chapter frequently as you configure SQL Server 2000 in other chapters. Using the T-SQL scripting techniques shown here can literally save you countless hours in server administration time. You can also use this chapter to help decipher scripts that you may "inherit" from other SQL Server 2000 administrators or designers.

Note: Many of the exercises in this chapter assume you have an installation of SQL Server 2000 accessible. If you do not, you may want to return to this chapter after you learn how to install SQL Server in Chapters 4 and 5.

The Transact-SQL Language

Transact-SQL extends the standard Structured Query Language defined by the International Organization for Standardization (ISO) and the American National Standards Institute (ANSI). This section should serve as a reference to this important language for you. It covers the most important and most frequently used components of the language. SQL Server 2000 Books Online provides a complete reference for any components not covered here.

The first component you will learn about involves statements. Transact-SQL statements are the crux of the language. As you learned in Chapter 2, Transact-SQL statements can be divided into three main groups–Data Definition Language, Data Manipulation Language, and Data Control Language.

Data Definition Language Statements

DDL statements create and manage the objects of SQL Server databases. These language components center on the **CREATE**, **ALTER**, and **DROP** statements. As a database administrator, here are the statements you need to be most familiar with:

- **CREATE DATABASE**

- **CREATE PROCEDURE**

- **CREATE STATISTICS**

- **ALTER DATABASE**

- **DROP DATABASE**

- **DROP PROCEDURE**

- **DROP STATISTICS**

These statements are discussed in detail in the next sections.

CREATE DATABASE

This statement creates a database and the physical files that make up the database. The syntax of this statement is as follows:

```
CREATE DATABASE database_name
[ ON
 [ < filespec > [ ,...n ] ]
 [ , < filegroup > [ ,...n ] ]
]
[ LOG ON { < filespec > [ ,...n ] } ]
[ COLLATE collation_name ]
[ FOR LOAD | FOR ATTACH ]
< filespec > ::=
[ PRIMARY ]
( [ NAME = logical_file_name , ]
    FILENAME = 'os_file_name'
    [ , SIZE = size ]
    [ , MAXSIZE = { max_size | UNLIMITED } ]
    [ , FILEGROWTH = growth_increment ] ) [ ,...n ]
< filegroup > ::=
FILEGROUP filegroup_name < filespec > [ ,...n ]
```

Although this syntax looks intimidating, almost all of it is optional, allowing the administrator to specify advanced database management techniques. Here is an explanation of key arguments used in the syntax:

- **ON**—specifies the files and their location that make up the database.

- **n**—indicates that you can specify multiple files to make up the database.

- **LOG ON**—specifies the files and their location that make up the transaction log.

- **COLLATE**—allows you to define the collation for the database. Collation is a set of rules that determines how data is compared, ordered, and presented.

- **FOR LOAD**—allows you to create the database with the "dbo use only" database option enabled, while the status of the database is set to loading.

- **FOR ATTACH**—permits you to specify that the database be created from an existing set of database files.

- **PRIMARY**—allows you to specify the primary file for the database.

- **FILEGROUP**—allows you to specify a filegroup; filegroups allow files to be grouped together for advanced administrative purposes.

To further help you understand the **CREATE DATABASE** statement, take a look at the following example, which creates a database named sampleDB. This statement creates the database primary file and the transaction log file with default parameters because there are no user specifications in the statement:

```
CREATE DATABASE sampleDB
```

Here is another example of the use of this statement. This time more parameters are specified:

```
CREATE DATABASE EntSales
ON
(NAME = EntSales_dat,
   FILENAME = 'c:\data\entsaledat.mdf',
   SIZE = 10,
   MAXSIZE = 50,
   FILEGROWTH = 5)
LOG ON
(NAME = 'EntSales_log',
   FILENAME = 'd:\data\entsalelog.ldf',
   SIZE = 5,
   MAXSIZE = 25,
   FILEGROWTH = 5)
```

This example creates a database named EntSales. The statement creates the primary data file on the C: drive and creates the transaction log file on the D: drive. The primary data file is 10MB in size and can grow to 50MB, using 5MB increases. The transaction log file is 5MB in size, can grow to 25MB, and grows in 5MB increments.

CREATE PROCEDURE

This statement creates a stored procedure. The syntax is as follows:

```
CREATE PROC [ EDURE ] procedure_name [ ; number ]
    [ { @parameter data_type }
        [ VARYING ] [ = default ] [ OUTPUT ]
    ] [ ,...n ]

[ WITH
    { RECOMPILE | ENCRYPTION | RECOMPILE , ENCRYPTION } ]

[ FOR REPLICATION ]

AS sql_statement [ ...n ]
```

Below is an explanation of some of the elements of the syntax:

- **; number**—allows you to specify an optional integer you can use later to group procedures of the same name so they can be dropped together with a single **DROP PROCEDURE** statement.

- **@parameter**—allows you to specify a parameter in the stored procedure. You may define up to 2,100 parameters in a stored procedure.

- **VARYING**—applies only to cursor parameters and specifies the result set supported as an output parameter.

- **default**—specifies a default value for the parameter.

- **OUTPUT**—indicates that the parameter is a return parameter.

- **n**—indicates that you can specify multiple parameters in the stored procedure.

- **{RECOMPILE|ENCRYPTION|RECOMPILE, ENCRYPTION}**—**RECOMPILE** forces SQL Server to not cache an execution plan for the procedure and recompile the stored procedure at run time. **ENCRYPTION** causes SQL Server to encrypt the **syscomments** table entry containing the text of the **CREATE PROCEDURE** statement.

- **FOR REPLICATION**—specifies that the stored procedure is created for replication and cannot be executed on the Subscriber.

Here is an example of the **CREATE PROCEDURE** statement:

```
CREATE PROCEDURE author_info
    @lastname varchar(30) = 'D%',
    @firstname varchar(18) = '%'
AS
SELECT au_lname, au_fname, title, pub_name
FROM authors a INNER JOIN titleauthor ta
    ON a.au_id = ta.au_id INNER JOIN titles t
    ON t.title_id = ta.title_id INNER JOIN publishers p
    ON t.pub_id = p.pub_id
WHERE au_fname LIKE @firstname
    AND au_lname LIKE @lastname
```

This stored procedure named **author_info** returns only the specified authors (first and last names supplied), their titles, and their publishers from a four-table join. **author_info** uses the pattern match the parameter is passed or the stored procedure uses the preset defaults. For example, the statement

```
EXECUTE author_info 'Hunter', 'Sheryl'
```

returns the title and publisher information for the author Sheryl Hunter.

CREATE STATISTICS

This statement creates statistical information for columns of a table or view. A database administrator can then use this information to optimize the RDBMS. The syntax is as follows:

```
CREATE STATISTICS statistics_name
ON { table | view } ( column [ ,...n ] )
    [ WITH
        [ [ FULLSCAN
            | SAMPLE number { PERCENT | ROWS } ] [ , ] ]
        [ NORECOMPUTE ]
    ]
```

Brief explanations for elements in the above syntax are as follows:

- *n*—is a placeholder indicating multiple columns can be specified.

- **FULLSCAN**—specifies that all rows in the table specified should be read to gather the statistics.

- **SAMPLE *number* {PERCENT|ROWS }**—specifies that a percentage (or a specified number of rows) of the data should be read using random sampling to gather the statistics. This option cannot be used with the **FULLSCAN** option.

- **NORECOMPUTE**—specifies that automatic recomputation of the statistics should be disabled.

The following example creates a sample statistics group. These statistics calculate random sampling statistics on five percent of the **CompanyName** and **ContactName** columns of the **Customers** table:

```
CREATE STATISTICS sample
   ON Customers (CompanyName, ContactName)
   WITH SAMPLE 5 PERCENT
```

Chapter 13 of this book helps you optimize your SQL Server 2000 database. In that chapter, you will learn how these statistics can help in that regard.

ALTER DATABASE

You use the **ALTER DATABASE** statement when you need to make changes to a database configuration. This includes adding or removing files or filegroups and changing the size of any of these objects. Here is the syntax:

```
ALTER DATABASE database
{ ADD FILE < filespec > [ ,...n ] [ TO FILEGROUP filegroup_name ]
| ADD LOG FILE < filespec > [ ,...n ]
| REMOVE FILE logical_file_name
| ADD FILEGROUP filegroup_name
| REMOVE FILEGROUP filegroup_name
| MODIFY FILE < filespec >
| MODIFY NAME = new_dbname
| MODIFY FILEGROUP filegroup_name {filegroup_property | NAME =
new_filegroup_name }
| SET < optionspec > [ ,...n ] [ WITH < termination > ]
| COLLATE < collation_name >
}
```

This syntax is self-explanatory, except for the **WITH <termination>** syntax. This clause specifies when to roll back incomplete transactions when the database is transitioned from one state to another.

The following example changes the size of a data file in the sampleDB database to 20MB:

```
ALTER DATABASE sampleDB
MODIFY FILE
   (NAME = sampledat2,
   SIZE = 20MB)
```

Statements of this nature become critical when you are creating and managing databases following the guidelines set forth in Chapter 7 of this book.

ALTER PROCEDURE

Use the **ALTER PROCEDURE** statement to make changes to a stored procedure that you have created. The syntax for this statement is as follows:

```
ALTER PROC [ EDURE ] procedure_name [ ; number ]
    [ { @parameter data_type }
        [ VARYING ] [ = default ] [ OUTPUT ]
    ] [ ,...n ]
[ WITH
    { RECOMPILE | ENCRYPTION
        | RECOMPILE , ENCRYPTION
    }
]
[ FOR REPLICATION ]
AS
    sql_statement [ ...n ]
```

A brief explanation of some of the elements in the above syntax follows:

- *;number*—allows you to specify an optional integer you can use later to group procedures of the same name so they can be dropped together with a single **DROP PROCE-
  DURE** statement.

- *@parameter*—allows you to specify a parameter in the stored procedure. You may
  define up to 2,100 parameters in a stored procedure.

- **VARYING** —applies only to cursor parameters and specifies the result set supported as
  an output parameter.

- *default*—specifies a default value for the parameter.

- **OUTPUT**—indicates that the parameter is a return parameter.

- *n*—indicates that you can specify multiple parameters in the stored procedure.

- {**RECOMPILE|ENCRYPTION|RECOMPILE, ENCRYPTION**}—**RECOMPILE** forces
  SQL Server to not cache an execution plan for the procedure and recompile the stored
  procedure at run time. **ENCRYPTION** causes SQL Server to encrypt the **syscomments**
  table entry containing the text of the **CREATE PROCEDURE** statement.

- **FOR REPLICATION**—specifies that the stored procedure is created for replication and
  cannot be executed on the Subscriber.

Here is an example that modifies the procedure **author_info** created earlier in this
chapter using the **CREATE PROCEDURE** statement:

```
ALTER PROCEDURE author_info
    @lastname varchar(30) = 'A%',
    @firstname varchar(18) = '%'
AS
SELECT au_lname, au_fname, title, ytd_sales, pub_name
```

```
FROM authors a INNER JOIN titleauthor ta
   ON a.au_id = ta.au_id INNER JOIN titles t
   ON t.title_id = ta.title_id INNER JOIN publishers p
   ON t.pub_id = p.pub_id
WHERE au_fname LIKE @firstname
   AND au_lname LIKE @lastname
```

The procedure now defaults to providing information on authors whose last names begin with the letter A, and it also now provides the year-to-date sales information for each title. Although you may not often need to alter stored procedures you have created, it is critical that you have the ability to do so as a SQL Server 2000 administrator.

DROP DATABASE

The **DROP DATABASE** statement removes one or more databases from SQL Server 2000; this includes deleting the database and the disk files used by the database. The syntax for this statement is as follows:

```
DROP DATABASE database_name [ ,...n ]
```

In this statement *n* indicates that you can specify multiple databases to be dropped in a single statement.

Here is an example of the **DROP DATABASE** statement:

```
DROP DATABASE sampleDB, pubs
```

This example removes the **sampleDB** and the **pubs** database from SQL Server 2000. Remember, this statement also deletes the associated database files.

DROP PROCEDURE

You will use the **DROP PROCEDURE** statement to remove stored procedures from SQL Server 2000. The syntax is as follows:

```
DROP PROCEDURE { procedure } [ ,...n ]
```

In this statement *n* indicates that you can specify multiple stored procedures to be dropped in a single statement.

Here is an example of the **DROP PROCEDURE** statement:

```
DROP PROCEDURE author_info
```

This example removes the **author_info** stored procedure from SQL Server 2000.

DROP STATISTICS

The **DROP STATISTICS** statement removes statistics created on a table or view using the **CREATE STATISTICS** statement, as in:

```
DROP STATISTICS table.statistics_name | view.statistics_name [ ,...n ]
```

In this statement *n* indicates that you can specify multiple statistics groupings to be dropped in a single statement.

Here is an example of the **DROP STATISTICS** statement:

```
DROP STATISTICS Customers.sample
```

This example removes the statistics called **sample** from the **Customers** table in the appropriate SQL Server 2000 database.

Data Manipulation Language Statements

Data Manipulation Language Transact-SQL statements manipulate data in SQL Server 2000 databases. This section presents the following statements, which are the most popular examples for database administrators:

- **SELECT**

- **INSERT**

- **UPDATE**

- **DELETE**

SELECT

The **SELECT** statement is one of the most frequently used and most complex statements in SQL Server 2000. It retrieves information from SQL databases using a wide variety of criteria. The basic syntax for this statement is as follows:

```
SELECT select_list
[ INTO new_table ]
FROM table_source
[ WHERE search_condition ]
[ GROUP BY group_by_expression ]
[ HAVING search_condition ]
[ ORDER BY order_expression [ ASC | DESC ] ]
```

A brief explanation of some of the elements in the above syntax is as follows:

- **select_list**—specifies the columns included in the result set; * is often used to retrieve all columns from a table or tables.

- **INTO**—a powerful clause that actually creates a new table based on the result set from the **SELECT** statement.

- **FROM**—specifies the table or tables used in the **SELECT** statement.

- **WHERE**—allows you to specify search conditions to restrict the number of rows returned by the **SELECT** statement.

- **GROUP BY**—specifies how the result set should be organized and summarized.

- **HAVING** —used with the **GROUP BY** clause and permits you to specify a search condition for a group or an aggregate.

- **ORDER BY**—specifies how the result set should be ordered.

To help you better understand Transact-SQL **SELECT** statements, take a look at the following example:

```
SELECT au_fname, au_lname, phone AS Telephone
FROM authors
WHERE state = 'CA'
ORDER BY au_lname ASC
```

This example returns first names, last names, and phone numbers from the **authors** table. It displays the phone column as **Telephone**. The result set includes only authors from California and sorts this result set by author's last name in ascending order.

Here's another example:

```
SELECT type, AVG(price)
FROM titles
GROUP BY type
ORDER BY AVG(price)
```

This **SELECT** statement finds the average price of each type of book in the pubs database and orders the results by average price.

INSERT

The **INSERT** statement adds a new row to a table or a view. The basic syntax for the **INSERT** statement is as follows:

```
INSERT [ INTO]
table_name
( column_list )
VALUES ( { DEFAULT | NULL | expression } [ ,...n] )
```

Here is an example of the **INSERT** statement in use:

```
INSERT TestTable VALUES (1, 'Sequeira')
```

This example inserts the values of **1** and **Sequeira** into the next available row in the **TestTable** table. Here is another example:

```
INSERT Jobs (address, priority) VALUES ('100 Main',1)
```

This example inserts the values of **100 Main** and **1** in the **address** and **priority** columns of the **Jobs** table.

UPDATE

You use the **UPDATE** Transact-SQL statement to modify data in a table or view. The basic syntax of the statement is as follows:

```
UPDATE
table_name
SET{ column_name}
FROM { < table_source > }
WHERE { < search_condition > }
```

Here is an example of how it is used:

```
UPDATE customers
SET areacode = '508'
WHERE areacode = '602'
```

This example updates the **customers** table by changing all area code values of **508** to a value of **602.**

DELETE

The **DELETE** statement removes rows from tables. Obviously, this statement needs to be used with caution. The basic syntax for the statement is as follows:

```
DELETE
    [ FROM ]
        { table_name }
    [ WHERE ]
        { < search_condition > }
```

Here is an example of a **DELETE** statement in use:

```
DELETE FROM authors
WHERE au_lname = 'Jones'
```

This example deletes any rows from the **authors** table where the last name is equal to Jones. Notice this may be more than one row.

Data Control Language Statements

You use Data Control Language Transact-SQL statements to control security in a SQL Server 2000 environment. You accomplish this primarily by creating statements that control the permission on SQL Server objects. The most common Transact-SQL statements for accomplishing these tasks are:

- **GRANT**

- **REVOKE**

- **DENY**

GRANT

The **GRANT** statement allows you to permit specific users to access database objects and data or execute specific Transact-SQL statements. You might use the **GRANT** statement to permit a group of users to execute **SELECT** statements against a particular table, for example. The basic syntax of the command is as follows:

```
GRANT
{ ALL [ PRIVILEGES ] }
ON table_name
TO security_account
```

The following example permits the Managers role to execute **SELECT** statements against the **Invoices** table:

```
GRANT SELECT
ON Invoices
TO Managers
```

REVOKE

The **REVOKE** statement permits you to remove a previously granted or denied permission from a user or group of users in the database. The basic syntax for this statement is as follows:

```
REVOKE
{ ALL [ PRIVILEGES ] }
ON table_name
TO security_account
```

This example revokes the permissions granted on the **Invoices** table by the earlier **GRANT** statement example:

```
REVOKE SELECT
ON Invoices
TO Managers
```

DENY

The **DENY** statement is most likely the most powerful of all of the Data Control Language statements. This statement permits you to deny access to specific database resources and statements to a user or groups of users. This **DENY** statement effectively overrules all other permissions settings a user might possess. The basic syntax of the command is as follows:

```
DENY
{ ALL [ PRIVILEGES ] }
ON table_name
TO security_account
```

For example, this statement prohibits the Fools role from running **SELECT** statements against the **Invoices** table:

```
DENY SELECT
ON Invoices
TO Fools
```

Identifiers

As you have seen from the Transact-SQL statement examples in this chapter, most database objects are identified with a name. This name is known as an identifier in SQL Server 2000. You typically create the identifier for an object when you create the object, and then you reference this identifier whenever you need to refer to the object later. For example, you use the following code to create a database with the identifier of **Sales**:

```
CREATE DATABASE Sales
```

Later, you can reference this database very simply by referring to the identifier of **Sales**.

There are two types of identifiers—*regular identifiers* and *delimited identifiers*. You should use regular identifiers whenever possible as they conform to the SQL Server 2000 rules for identifiers and are simpler. Delimited identifiers do not conform to the rules for identifiers and, therefore, must be delimited using either double quotation marks or square brackets. For example, here the identifier for the database must be delimited because it contains a space:

```
CREATE DATABASE [East Sales]
```

Because you should get in the habit of using regular identifiers, you need to understand the rules for the format of regular identifiers. These rules are dependent on the database compatibility level, which you set using the **sp_dbcmptlevel** stored procedure or by using

Enterprise Manager. Here are the rules for a compatibility level of 80, which is the default compatibility level for a new database (unless you change it):

- The first character of the identifier must be a letter, an underscore, an @ symbol, or a # symbol.

- Subsequent characters can be letters, decimal numbers, @ symbols, dollar signs, # symbols, or underscores.

- The identifier cannot be a Transact-SQL reserved word—for example, "select".

- The identifier cannot contain embedded spaces or other special characters.

Variables

Transact-SQL variables are objects that hold data values in batches or scripts. Variables are necessary ingredients for many Transact-SQL scripts and can function as a counter or can save data values that are to be returned by stored procedures.

You first declare a variable in the body of a Transact-SQL batch or procedure using the **DECLARE** statement. Variable identifiers start with an @ symbol. Once the variable is declared, you then assign the variable a value using the **SET** statement. Here is an example that shows how to declare a variable named **@CustNum** in a Transact-SQL batch, assign this variable a value, and then use this variable in a **SELECT** statement:

```
DECLARE @CustNum
SET @CustNumVar = 1001
SELECT * FROM Customers
WHERE CustomerNumb = @CustNumVar + 1000
```

Variables provide you with much flexibility in your Transact-SQL scripts. You can use these as a counter— either to count or to control the number of times a loop is performed. You can also use variables to hold a data value to be tested by a control-of-flow statement or to save a data value to be returned by a stored procedure return code.

Functions

Functions assist database administrators and designers, as they provide simple, pre-written methods for manipulating data and SQL Server objects. There are built-in functions in SQL Server that you cannot modify, and then there are user-defined functions you actually create. The following sections detail each for you.

Built-In Functions

Built-in functions consist of *rowset*, *aggregate*, and *scalar* functions. Each is useful for a particular situation in SQL Server 2000 administration and design.

You use rowset functions like table references in a Transact-SQL statement. These functions actually return an object used in place of a table reference in a T-SQL statement. The most common rowset functions you will use in SQL Server 2000 are shown in Table 3.1.

Aggregate functions process a group of data values and return a single value that summarizes the analyzed values. A common example is the **AVG** function that provides the average value for a group of data values. Table 3.2 lists the built-in aggregate functions of SQL Server 2000.

3

Table 3.1   Common rowset functions.

Rowset Function	Usage
CONTAINSTABLE	Used in full-text queries to return rows for those columns containing text matches
FREETEXTTABLE	Also used in full-text queries to return rows for those columns containing text matches based on meaning
OPENDATASOURCE	Provides ad hoc connection information as part of a four-part object name without using a linked server name
OPENQUERY	Executes a specified pass-through query on a given linked server
OPENROWSET	Includes all connection information necessary to access remote data from an OLE DB data source
OPENXML	Provides a rowset view over an XML document

Table 3.2   Aggregate functions.

Aggregate Function	Usage
AVG	Returns the average of the values in a group
BINARY_CHECKSUM	Returns the binary checksum value computed over a row of a table or over a list of expressions
CHECKSUM	Returns the checksum value computed over a row of a table or over a list of expressions
CHECKSUM_AGG	Returns the checksum of the values in a group
COUNT	Returns the number of items in a group
COUNT_BIG	Returns the number of items in a group — **COUNT_BIG** always returns a **bigint** data type value
GROUPING	Causes an additional column to be output with a value of 1 when the row is added by either the **CUBE** or the **ROLLUP** operator
MAX	Returns the maximum value in the expression
MIN	Returns the minimum value in the expression
SUM	Returns the sum of all the values
STDEV	Returns the statistical standard deviation of all values in the given expression
STDEVP	Returns the statistical standard deviation for the population for all values in the given expression
VAR	Returns the statistical variance of all values in the given expression
VARP	Returns the statistical variance for the population for all values in the given expression

Scalar functions operate on a single value and then return a single value. There are many types of scalar functions built into SQL Server 2000 including date and time, mathematical, string, and text and image functions. Table 3.3 details the most popular scalar functions for you.

Table 3.3   Scalar functions.

Scalar Function	Usage
@@DATEFIRST	Returns the current value of the **SET DATEFIRST** parameter, which indicates the specified first day of each week
@@LANGID	Returns the local language identifier (ID) of the language currently in use
@@LOCKTIMEOUT	Returns the current lock time-out setting, in milliseconds, for the current session
@@MAX_CONNECTIONS	Returns the maximum number of simultaneous user connections allowed on the SQL Server
@@OPTIONS	Returns information about current SET options
@@REMSERVER	Returns the name of the remote SQL Server database server as it appears in the login record
@@SERVERNAME	Returns the name of the local server running SQL Server
@@SPID	Returns the server process identifier (ID) of the current user process
@@VERSION	Returns the date, version, and processor type for the current installation of SQL Server
@@CURSOR_ROWS	Returns the number of qualifying rows currently in the last cursor opened on the connection
@@FETCH_STATUS	Returns the status of the last cursor **FETCH** statement issued against any cursor currently opened by the connection
DATEADD	Returns a new **datetime** value based on adding an interval to the specified date
DATEDIFF	Returns the number of date and time boundaries crossed between two specified dates
DATENAME	Returns a character string representing the specified **datepart** of the specified date
DATEPART	Returns an integer representing the specified **datepart** of the specified date
DAY	Returns an integer representing the day **datepart** of the specified date
GETDATE	Returns the current system date and time in the SQL Server standard internal format for **datetime** values
GETUTCDATE	Returns the **datetime** value representing the current UTC time
MONTH	Returns an integer that represents the month part of a specified date
YEAR	Returns an integer that represents the year part of a specified date
ABS	Returns the absolute, positive value of the given numeric expression
RAND	Returns a random float value from 0 through 1
ROUND	Returns a numeric expression, rounded to the specified length or precision
SIGN	Returns the positive (+1), zero (0), or negative (-1) sign of the given expression
DB_ID	Returns the database identification (ID) number

(continued)

Table 3.3   Scalar functions *(continued)*.

Scalar Function	Usage
OBJECT_ID	Returns the database object identification number
@@PROCID	Returns the stored procedure identifier (ID) of the current procedure
USER_ID	Returns a user's database identification number
USER	Allows a system-supplied value for the current user's database username to be inserted into a table when no default value is specified
ASCII	Returns the ASCII code value of the leftmost character of a character expression
CHAR	Converts an integer ASCII code to a character
LEFT	Returns the part of a character string starting at a specified number of characters from the left
LOWER	Returns a character expression after converting uppercase character data to lowercase
LTRIM	Returns a character expression after removing leading blanks
RIGHT	Returns the part of a character string starting a specified number of ***integer_expression*** characters from the right
RTRIM	Returns a character string after truncating all trailing blanks
STR	Returns character data converted from numeric data
SUBSTRING	Returns part of a character, binary, text, or image expression
UPPER	Returns a character expression with lowercase character data converted to uppercase
@@ERROR	Returns the error number for the last Transact-SQL statement executed
@@IDENTITY	Returns the last-inserted identity value
@@ROWCOUNT	Returns the number of rows affected by the last statement
@@TRANCOUNT	Returns the number of active transactions for the current connection
@@CONNECTIONS	Returns the number of connections or attempted connections, since SQL Server was last started
@@CPU_BUSY	Returns the time in milliseconds that the CPU has spent working since SQL Server was last started
@@TOTAL_ERRORS	Returns the number of disk read/write errors encountered by SQL Server since last started
PATINDEX	Returns the starting position of the first occurrence of a pattern in a specified expression

User-Defined Functions

In order to create your own functions as a database administrator or database designer, you will use the **CREATE FUNCTION** statement. Modifying or removing user-defined functions is a simple matter of using **ALTER FUNCTION** or **DROP FUNCTION** statements. You may create functions that return either a scalar value or a table.

Data Types

Data types define the type of data that a SQL Server object can contain. For example, when defining a column in a SQL Server table, you specify the data type for the column. Table 3.4 defines the data types built into SQL Server, yet you can also define your own data types. The data types you define are based on the system-supplied data types of SQL Server 2000. In order to define your own data types, use the **sp_addtype** stored procedure.

Table 3.4   SQL Server data types.

Data Type	Values
bigint	Integer data from -2^{63} through 2^{63} -1
binary	Fixed-length binary data with a maximum length of 8,000 bytes
bit	Integer data with either a 1 or 0 value
char	Fixed-length non-Unicode character data with a maximum length of 8,000 characters
cursor	A reference to a cursor
datetime	Date and time data from January 1, 1753 through December 31, 9999
decimal	Fixed precision and scale numeric data from -10^{38} +1 through 10^{38} −1
float	Floating precision number data from -1.79E+308 through 1.79E+308
image	Variable-length binary data with a maximum length of 2^{31} - 1 bytes
int	Integer data from -2^{31} through 2^{31} - 1
money	Monetary data values from -2^{63} through 2^{63} - 1
nchar	Fixed-length Unicode data with a maximum length of 4,000 characters
ntext	Variable-length Unicode data with a maximum length of 2^{30} - 1 characters
nvarchar	Variable-length Unicode data with a maximum length of 4,000 characters
real	Floating precision number data from -3.40E + 38 through 3.40E + 38
smalldatetime	Date and time data from January 1, 1900 through June 6, 2079, with an accuracy of one minute
smallint	Integer data from 2^{15} through 2^{15} - 1
smallmoney	Monetary data values from -214,748.3648 through +214,748.3647
text	Variable-length non-Unicode data with a maximum length of 2^{31} - 1 characters
timestamp	A database-wide unique number that gets updated every time a row gets updated
tinyint	Integer data from 0 through 255
varbinary	Variable-length binary data with a maximum length of 8,000 bytes
varchar	Variable-length non-Unicode data with a maximum of 8,000 characters
uniqueidentifier	A globally unique identifier

Expressions

Expressions permit you to use a combination of operators that SQL Server evaluates to produce a single data value. SQL Server provides seven categories of operators you may use in expressions, including the most popular—arithmetic. For example, the following code snippet uses an arithmetic operator to display a salesperson's last name along with 25 percent of yearly sales:

```
SELECT LastName, YTDSales * .25
```

Table 3.5 provides the other operator types and examples found in SQL Server 2000.

Control-of-Flow Language Elements

Control-of-flow T-SQL elements control the flow of execution of statements. This is important when you are constructing long and complex Transact-SQL scripts. Perhaps you require the script to pause for some period of time as another process completes, or perhaps you need the script to take different actions depending upon a particular value. The possible control-of-flow language elements are described in Table 3.6.

Table 3.5   Operator types in SQL Server 2000.

Operator Type	Examples
Comparison	<, >, =, <=, >=, <>, !=, !<, !>
Logical	ALL, AND, ANY, BETWEEN, EXISTS, IN, LIKE, NOT, OR, SOME
Arithmetic	+, -, *, %, /
Unary	+, -
Bitwise	&, I, ^
String concatenation	+
Assignment	=

Table 3.6   Control-of-flow elements.

Keyword	Description
BEGIN...END	Defines a group of statements for execution
BREAK	Exits the innermost **WHILE** loop
CONTINUE	Restarts a **WHILE** loop
GOTO	Causes execution of a T-SQL batch to jump to a label
IF...ELSE	Provides a condition on the execution of a statement
RETURN	Terminates a query, stored procedure, or batch
WAITFOR	Suspends execution
WHILE	Repeats a statement as long as a specified condition remains true

Comments

Comments permit you to make remarks in Transact-SQL scripts or batches that are not processed. These remarks assist you or another administrator in interpreting the script and ensuring you use it properly. Well-designed comments in code can assist dramatically in your efficiency as an administrator.

There are two methods for placing comments in code in SQL Server 2000. You may use double hyphens, or you may use forward slash-asterisk pairs. Examples of each type follow:

```
SELECT *  --This is a sample comment
FROM Customers
--Here is another sample comment

UPDATE customers
SET areacode = '508'
WHERE areacode = '602'
/* Here is another example of a comment using the
forward slash-asterisk pair method! */
```

Notice that the forward slash-asterisk pair method is excellent for multiple lines of comments. In fact, Microsoft recommends you use this method in Transact-SQL scripts, because the double hyphen method often causes errors if the comment wraps to another line. Notice with the double hyphen method that you do not have to end the comment with a double hyphen, however. This can save time for very short comments.

Executing Transact-SQL Statements

There are multiple methods for executing Transact-SQL statements in SQL Server 2000. This section of the chapter explores these various methods, and the "Transact-SQL Tools" section provides guidance for using Transact-SQL tools.

Single Statements

The simplest, most basic method for executing Transact-SQL statements is to execute a single statement. The SQL Server query optimizer ensures this statement executes in the most efficient manner possible. You can execute this single Transact-SQL statement by submitting the statement to SQL Server 2000 using any number of client tools. The tool can be one you designed yourself or one of the many client tools provided by Microsoft with SQL Server 2000, such as osql, for example.

Batches

A batch is a group of one or more Transact-SQL statements sent to SQL Server for execution by an application. SQL Server 2000 compiles the statements in the batch into an execution plan and then executes this plan one step at a time.

There are certain rules you must follow with batches in SQL Server 2000; these rules are as follows:

- **CREATE DEFAULT**, **CREATE PROCEDURE**, **CREATE RULE**, **CREATE TRIGGER**, and **CREATE VIEW** statements cannot be combined with other T-SQL statements in a batch. These statements must begin the batch.

- You cannot alter a table by modifying columns and then reference these new columns in the batch.

- If an **EXECUTE** statement is the first statement in the batch, the **EXECUTE** keyword is not required.

Most Transact-SQL tools use the **GO** command to signal the end of a batch. **GO** is not actually a T-SQL command but is used by these tools to signify the last statement in the batch. The following is an example of the use of the **GO** command. This example switches to the pubs database, creates a view, and then queries this view. Because the **CREATE VIEW** statement must stand alone in a batch, **GO** commands surround it here to isolate it from other statements. The example is as follows:

```
USE pubs
GO
CREATE VIEW auth_info
AS
SELECT *
FROM authors
GO
SELECT * FROM auth_info
GO
```

You specify batches to SQL Server by using one of the following methods:

- Send several statements together from an application

- Use stored procedures or triggers that contain multiple statements

- Use the **EXECUTE** statement

- Use the **sp_executesql** system stored procedure

Stored Procedures and Triggers

Use the **CREATE PROCEDURE** or **CREATE TRIGGER** statement to create SQL Server 2000 stored procedure and trigger objects. As you learned in the previous section, these objects can contain multiple T-SQL statements that execute on the server together as a batch, which results in optimal performance and assists in administration and server usage.

Scripts

You may store multiple Transact-SQL statements together in a text file. The default extension for this file is .SQL for SQL Server 2000. Once you create and save the .SQL file, you can use it as input for many of the Transact-SQL tools explored in the next section. Here is an example of a Transact-SQL script file that creates a sample database and then reports information about the new database using the **sp_helpdb** system stored procedure:

```
/*
** SAMPLEDB.SQL
** This sample T-SQL script file
** creates a database and then runs sp_helpdb.
**
*/
CREATE DATABASE sampledb
ON
  PRIMARY (NAME=sampledb_data,
  FILENAME='c:\data\sampledb_sql.mdf',
  SIZE=2MB,
  FILEGROWTH=2MB)
LOG ON
  (NAME=sampledb_sql_log,
  FILENAME='c:\data\sampledb_sql.ldf',
  SIZE=1MB,
  MAXSIZE=10MB,
  FILEGROWTH=1MB)
GO
/* Notice the use of the GO command
** due to the CREATE DATABASE statement.
*/
EXEC sp_helpdb sample_sql
```

Transact-SQL Tools

Because Transact-SQL is the language of SQL Server 2000, there are plenty of tools for submitting your statements to the server. There is also an awesome tool named Query Analyzer that not only submits your statements to the server but also helps test, optimize, and debug your statements. This section explores these tools and ensures that you master their usage.

Query Analyzer

The SQL Server 2000 Query Analyzer is the most important tool provided by the server product when it comes to Transact-SQL. You will use this tool more than any other when it comes to your Transact-SQL statements. Query Analyzer allows you to test and debug your statements and scripts. You can also submit them to the server for processing using this tool, and you can even examine detailed information about your scripts to ensure they are fully optimized. In order to use this graphical user interface tool, you must launch it and establish a connection with SQL Server 2000. Follow the steps presented here to do so:

1. Select Start|Programs|Microsoft SQL Server|Query Analyzer.

2. In the Connect To SQL Server window, click OK to connect to your default instance of SQL Server 2000 using Windows Authentication (You may also use SQL Server authentication if necessary.).

3. SQL Query Analyzer launches with an empty Query window displayed (see Figure 3.1).

The Object Browser is a new and exciting feature of SQL Query Analyzer. This enhancement assists you as you compose Transact-SQL statements in the query window. You simply drag and drop objects from the browser into the query window to reference these objects in code. You may test the functionality of the Object Browser by performing several queries against the **INFORMATION_SCHEMA** views of SQL Server 2000. SQL Server provides the **INFORMATION_SCHEMA** views to assist you as an administrator by

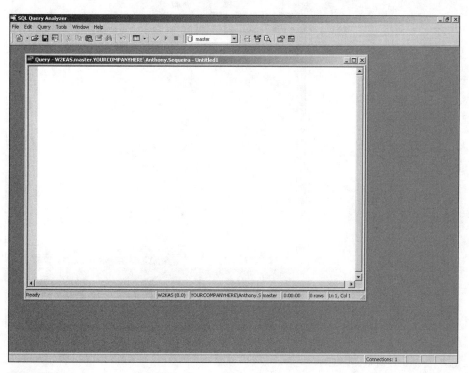

Figure 3.1
SQL Query Analyzer.

providing database objects that contain key information about the server. The steps for testing the Object Browser are as follows:

1. Launch Query Analyzer and connect to the default instance of SQL Server.

2. Select the Tools menu and choose Object Browser|Show/hide. Notice the Object Browser window appears (see Figure 3.2). You can also use the F8 key to prompt this window to appear.

3. In the Object Browser window, double-click the master database to expand this object.

4. Double-click the Views container to expand that object. Notice the **INFORMATION_ SCHEMA** views included in SQL Server 2000 by default.

5. If necessary, drag the right border of the Object Browser window to the right so you can view the full object names in the window.

6. Select **INFORMATION_SCHEMA.SCHEMATA** from the available views, drag this object to the Query window, and drop it there.

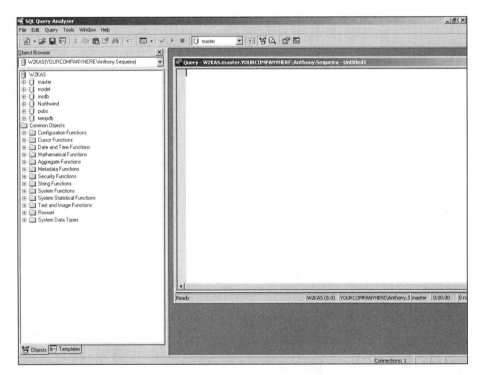

Figure 3.2
The Object Browser in SQL Query Analyzer.

7. Click in front of this object in the Query window to place the cursor and add the following Transact-SQL before the view:

```
SELECT * FROM
```

Be sure to include a space between **FROM** and the view identifier.

8. Parse the statement to be sure it is constructed properly by clicking the Parse button on the toolbar. This button has a blue checkmark icon on it. Results of the parse appear in the Results tab at the bottom of the Query window.

9. Use the Execute button on the toolbar to execute the query. Notice the query displays the system and user databases that exist on the SQL Server and key information about these databases (see Figure 3.3).

10. Use the Clear Window button on the toolbar to clear the Query window.

11. Select the **INFORMATION_SCHEMA.TABLES** object from the Object Browser window and drag and drop it into the Query window.

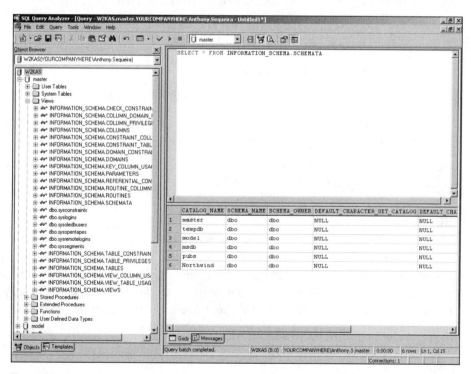

Figure 3.3
The results of a query execution in Query Analyzer.

12. With the object still selected, press Shift + F1 on the keyboard. Notice SQL Server 2000 Books Online launches with the **INFORMATION_SCHEMA.TABLES** help topic highlighted.

13. Use the Taskbar to switch back to Query Analyzer.

14. Click in front of this object in the Query window to place the cursor and add the following Transact-SQL before the view:

```
SELECT * FROM
```

Be sure to include a space between **FROM** and the view identifier.

15. Use the Execute button on the toolbar to execute the query.

16. Notice this query displays key table information for all of the tables in the current database.

17. Select the Database drop down menu in the toolbar and choose the Northwind database.

You have now changed the active database to the Northwind database. This is the equivalent of the **USE** Northwind T-SQL statement.

18. Run the query again using the shortcut key of F5.

19. Close Query Analyzer using the Close button.

20. In the SQL Query Analyzer window, choose Yes to save the query.

21. In the Save Query window, browse to the folder of your choice and save the query as sample.sql by renaming the default file and clicking Save.

There are many other features to explore in the SQL Server Query Analyzer. This On Site book explores these many features throughout.

isqlw

The isqlw utility allows you others ways in which to launch the Query Analyzer tool. Thanks to the command-line isqlw utility, you have the ability to launch Query Analyzer in a pre-configured state or launch Query Analyzer without the graphical user interface at all. In order to run Query Analyzer without an interface, you must provide valid logon information and input and output files for your query and the query results respectively.

The syntax for the isqlw utility is as follows:

```
isqlw
    [-?] |
    [
        [-S server_name[\instance_name]]
        [-d database]
```

```
      [-E] [-U user] [-P password]
      [{-i input_file} {-o output_file} [-F {U|A|O}]]
      [-f file_list]
      [-C configuration_file]
      [-D scripts_directory]
      [-T template_directory]
  ]
```

Here is an explanation of the switches used with isqlw:

- **-?**—displays the syntax for using isqlw.

- **-S**—specifies the instance of SQL Server 2000 to connect to.

- **-d**—specifies the database to connect to.

- **-E**—forces a trusted connection instead of requiring a username and password.

- **-U**—specifies a username to connect with.

- **-P**—specifies a password for the username.

- **-i**—identifies the input file.

- **-o**—identifies the output file.

- **-F**—specifies the format of the input and output files; values include **Unicode**, **ANSI**, and **OEM**.

- **-f**—permits you to load multiple files into Query Analyzer.

- **-C**—uses the settings specifies in a configuration file.

- **-D**— overwrites the default saved script directory specified in the registry or the configuration file specified with **-C**.

- **-T**— overwrites the default template directory specified in the registry or the configuration file specified with **-C**.

To help you further understand how this works, the following example connects to the pubs database on the server SQLServer2K. The sa account is used (no password), and the command executes SQL statements from **input_file** and stores the results of the execution in **output_file**. The example is as follows:

```
isqlw -S SQLServer2K -d pubs -U sa -P -i input_file -o output_file
```

To continue, the following example launches the graphical user interface version of Query Analyzer with two files loaded. It uses Windows authentication to make a connection to the default instance of SQL Server 2000. The example is as follows:

```
isqlw -d pubs -E -f "c:\sample.sql" "c:\sample2.sql"
```

isql

isql is a command-line utility for submitting Transact-SQL statements to SQL Server for processing. The isql utility uses DB-Library to communicate with SQL Server 2000. SQL Server returns results to isql formatted for display on the screen. The syntax of isql is as follows:

```
isql
    [-?] |
    [-L] |
    [
        {
            {-U login_id [-P password]}
            | -E
        }
        [-S server_name] [-H wksta_name] [-d db_name]
        [-l time_out] [-t time_out] [-h headers]
        [-s col_separator] [-w column_width] [-a packet_size]
        [-e] [-x max_text_size]
        [-c cmd_end] [-q "query"] [-Q "query"]
        [-n] [-m error_level] [-r {0 | 1}]
        [-i input_file] [-o output_file] [-p]
        [-b] [-O]
    ]
```

Here is an explanation for the switches used by isql:

- **-?**—displays the syntax for using isql.

- **-L**— lists the locally configured servers and the names of the servers broadcasting on the network.

- **-U**—is the user login ID.

- **-P**—is the user password.

- **-E**—forces a trusted connection instead of requiring a username and password.

- **-S**—specifies the default instance of SQL Server to connect to.

- **-H**—is a workstation name.

- **-d**—issues a **USE *db_name*** statement when isql is started.

- **-I**—specifies the number of seconds before an isql login times out.

- **-t**—specifies the number of seconds before a command times out.

- **-h**—specifies the number of rows to print between column headings.

- **-s**—specifies the column-separator character, which is a blank space by default.

- **-w**—allows the user to set the screen width for output.

- **-a**—allows you to request a different-sized packet.

- **-e**— echoes input.

- **-x**—specifies, in bytes, the maximum length of text data to return.

- **-c**—specifies the command terminator.

- **-q**—executes a query when isql starts but does not exit isql when the query completes.

- **-Q**—executes a query and immediately exits isql when the query completes.

- **-n**—removes numbering and the prompt symbol (>) from input lines.

- **-m**—customizes the display of error messages.

- **-r**—{0 | 1} redirects message output to the screen (stderr).

- **-i**—identifies the file that contains a batch of SQL statements or stored procedures.

- **-o**—identifies the file that receives output from isql.

- **-p**—prints performance statistics.

- **-b**—specifies that isql exits and returns a **DOS ERRORLEVEL** value when an error occurs.

- **-O**—specifies that isql reverts to the behavior of earlier versions.

The following example logs on to the default instance of SQL Server 2000 using the anthony username and a password of "password". The server processes the sample.qry file and returns the results to the file results.res. The example is as follows:

```
isql /U anthony /P password /i sample.qry /o results.res
```

osql

The osql utility is yet another command-prompt utility that allows you to pass Transact-SQL statements to the server for processing. This utility uses ODBC to connect to the server, however. The syntax of this command is as follows:

```
osql
    [-?] |
    [-L] |
    [
        {
                {-U login_id [-P password]}
                | -E
        }
        [-S server_name[\instance_name]] [-H wksta_name] [-d db_name]
```

```
        [-l time_out] [-t time_out] [-h headers]
        [-s col_separator] [-w column_width] [-a packet_size]
        [-e] [-I] [-D data_source_name]
        [-c cmd_end] [-q "query"] [-Q "query"]
        [-n] [-m error_level] [-r {0 | 1}]
        [-i input_file] [-o output_file] [-p]
        [-b] [-u] [-R] [-O]
    ]
```

Here is an explanation for the switches used by osql:

- **-?**—displays the syntax summary of osql switches.

- **-L** —lists the locally configured servers and the names of the servers broadcasting on the network.

- **-U**—is the user login ID.

- **-P**—is the user password.

- **-E**—forces a trusted connection instead of requiring a username and password.

- **-S**—specifies the default instance of SQL Server to connect to.

- **-H**—is a workstation name.

- **-d**—issues a **USE** *db_name* statement when osql is started.

- **-l**—specifies the number of seconds before an osql login times out.

- **-t**—specifies the number of seconds before a command times out.

- **-h**—specifies the number of rows to print between column headings.

- **-s**—specifies the column-separator character, which is a blank space by default.

- **-w**—allows the user to set the screen width for output.

- **-a**—allows you to request a different-sized packet.

- **-e**—echoes input.

- **-I**—sets the **QUOTED_IDENTIFIER** connection option on.

- **-D**—connects to an ODBC data source that is defined using the ODBC driver for Microsoft SQL Server.

- **-c**—specifies the command terminator.

- **-q**—executes a query when osql starts, but does not exit osql when the query completes.

- **-Q**—executes a query and immediately exits osql.

- **-n**—removes numbering and the prompt symbol (>) from input lines.

- **-m**—customizes the display of error messages.

- **-r**—redirects message output to the screen (stderr).

- **-i**—identifies the file that contains a batch of SQL statements or stored procedures.

- **-o**—identifies the file that receives output from osql.

- **-p**—prints performance statistics.

- **-b**—specifies that osql exits and returns a **DOS ERRORLEVEL** value when an error occurs.

- **-u**—specifies that *output_file* is stored in Unicode format, regardless of the format of the *input_file*.

- **-R**—specifies that the SQL Server ODBC driver use client settings when converting currency, date, and time data to character data.

- **-O**—specifies that certain osql features be deactivated to match the behavior of earlier versions of isql.

Both isql and osql may run interactively. Follow these steps for an example of running osql interactively from a command prompt:

1. Select Start|Programs|Accessories|Command Prompt.

2. At the prompt, type the following:

```
osql -E
```

This command logs you into the default instance of SQL Server using Windows authentication. Notice the prompt changes to a 1> and is ready to accept your first line of Transact-SQL code (see Figure 3.4).

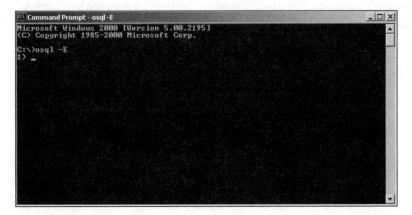

Figure 3.4
Using osql interactively.

3. Type the following line of code:

```
SELECT @@VERSION
```

Press Enter to move to the next line.

4. On the next line, type the following command and press Enter:

```
GO
```

Notice this command sends the query to the SQL Server for processing. S2K returns the results, formatted for the screen.

5. To exit this interactive osql session, type the following command and press Enter:

```
exit
```

Summary

Transact-SQL is the language of SQL Server 2000. In order to truly master SQL Server, you should understand this language and be able to use it to your advantage. Even if you rely upon the graphical user interfaces of the client tools to make configuration changes, Transact-SQL is making all of the modifications behind the scenes. Remember, using Transact-SQL is often much more efficient than any other method for manipulating your server or the data it stores. This chapter should serve as a reference as you move through the rest of this book. Depending on your comfort level with Transact-SQL, you may need to return here frequently as you examine code examples used throughout the remaining chapters.

Now that you have a solid introduction to SQL Server 2000, it is time to begin a discussion of installing the product in a production environment. Chapter 4 begins this journey with an examination of issues you face as you plan an installation of SQL Server 2000.

Part II

Planning and Installing SQL Server 2000

Configuration Deployment

Planning

Troubleshooting

Chapter 4

Installation Planning

You should not even consider plunging into the installation of SQL Server 2000 without doing a substantial amount of installation planning. This chapter will help you with this important task. You must not only select the appropriate operating system to use in conjunction with SQL Server 2000, but you must also choose the appropriate hardware, and pre-plan for the selection of important configuration options during the actual setup. Poorly planned installations may result in the loss of valuable time, data, money, or all three of these.

Selecting the Appropriate Operating System

Installation planning begins with the selection of the appropriate operating system that powers SQL Server 2000. Thanks to the many different versions of Microsoft Windows, you actually have many operating systems to choose from, so the selection may not be as easy as it sounds. In order to make this decision, you must first look back to Chapter 1 of this book and complete Decision Tree 1.1 that guides you through your selection of a SQL Server 2000 Edition. Once you have determined the edition of SQL Server 2000 that fits your needs, you should then examine Table 4.1. This table details the Windows operating systems that support the various SQL 2000 Editions and even provides the recommended platform given a particular edition. Decision Tree 4.1 assists further with your choice of operating system to ensure you acquire the recommended platform.

Planning Your Hardware

The success of your SQL Server 2000 installation and the success of your server in a production environment rely heavily upon your successful hardware planning. A server with too little or incompatible hardware resources is doomed to fail, and a server with an overabundance of hardware resources can deplete budgets unnecessarily.

This section examines hardware planning for SQL Server 2000 in great detail—all the detail you require, in fact, to make effective hardware purchasing decisions for your SQL Server 2000 implementation.

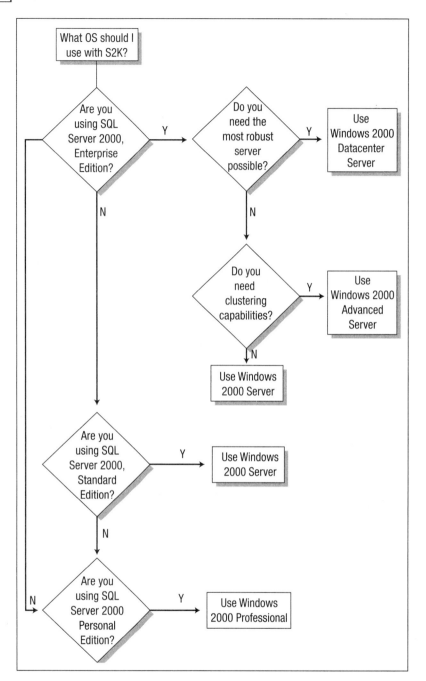

Decision Tree 4.1
Choosing an operating system for your SQL Server 2000 implementation.

Table 4.1   SQL Server 2000 editions and operating system choices.

Operating System	Enterprise	Standard	Personal	Evaluation Edition	Desktop Engine	Developer	Windows CE
Windows 2000 Datacenter	R	S	S	R	S	S	NS
Windows 2000 Advanced Server	R	S	S	R	S	S	NS
Windows 2000 Server	R	R	S	R	S	S	NS
Windows 2000 Professional	NS	NS	R	S	S	S	NS
Windows NT 4 Server, Enterprise	S	S	S	S	S	S	NS
Windows NT 4 Server	S	S	S	S	S	S	NS
Windows NT 4 Workstation	NS	NS	S	S	S	S	NS
Windows, Millennium Edition	NS	NS	S	NS	S	NS	NS
Windows 98	NS	NS	S	NS	S	NS	NS
Windows CE	NS	NS	NS	NS	NS	NS	S

NS=Not supported   R=Recommended   S=Supported

Hardware Requirements

To begin with, you should know a little something about the hardware requirements for SQL Server 2000 in a variety of configurations. You will not only find hardware minimums detailed but also have the opportunity to take a closer look at production hardware requirements in this section. First, let's look at the minimum hardware you must provide to run SQL Server 2000.

Minimum Hardware Requirements

You might be surprised to see this section at all in this book, since minimum hardware requirements are hardly ever appropriate for production environments. Don't forget—these minimum hardware requirements often serve valuable purposes for testing and experimentation in the lab environment. They also provide a nice baseline to build from when planning hardware expenditures.

Although this section breaks down minimum hardware requirements based on SQL Server 2000 editions running on recommended operating system platforms, it is important to realize there are minimum hardware requirements that all editions of SQL Server 2000 share (with the exception of the Windows CE edition). These minimums are listed in Table 4.2.

Table 4.2   Minimum hardware requirements for all editions of SQL Server 2000.

Resource	Minimum Hardware Requirement
Computer	IBM or compatible
Processor	Pentium 133MHz or higher
Display	800x600 for graphical tools usage
Pointing Device	Microsoft Mouse or compatible

In addition to the above hardware minimums, remember that if you plan on installing SQL Server 2000 from CD-ROM, you need a CD-ROM drive. And if you require network connectivity, you must also have a network interface card (NIC).

SQL Server 2000 Enterprise Edition running on Windows 2000 Datacenter Server features the most robust SQL Server 2000 configuration possible. It is no surprise, then, that the minimum hardware requirements for this configuration are quite extensive. Table 4.3 presents these minimums for you.

Another powerful Windows 2000/SQL Server 2000 combination is S2K Enterprise Edition running on Windows 2000 Advanced Server. This provides robust support for hardware and built-in clustering capabilities, thanks to Advanced Server. Table 4.4 details the minimum hardware requirements for this configuration.

If you are not in need of clustering capabilities, Windows 2000 Server provides another excellent platform for SQL Server 2000 Enterprise Edition. Table 4.5 presents the minimum hardware requirements for this configuration.

For standalone application usage, Microsoft provides SQL Server 2000 Personal Edition. Personal Edition runs best on Windows 2000 Professional. Table 4.6 presents the minimum hardware requirements for this configuration.

Table 4.3   Minimum hardware requirements for Windows 2000 Datacenter/SQL Server 2000 Enterprise Edition.

Resource	Minimum Hardware Requirement
Processor	Pentium chip 400MHz or higher
Memory	256MB
Free Disk Space	1GB

Table 4.4   Minimum hardware requirements for Windows 2000 Advanced Server/SQL Server 2000 Enterprise Edition.

Resource	Minimum Hardware Requirement
Processor	Pentium chip 133MHz or higher
Memory	128MB
Free Disk Space	1GB

Table 4.5   Minimum hardware requirements for Windows 2000 Server/SQL Server 2000 Enterprise Edition.

Resource	Minimum Hardware Requirement
Processor	Pentium chip 133MHz or higher
Memory	128MB
Free Disk Space	1GB

4

Table 4.6   Minimum hardware requirements for Windows 2000 Professional/SQL Server 2000 Personal Edition.

Resource	Minimum Hardware Requirement
Processor	Pentium chip 133MHz or higher
Memory	64MB
Free Disk Space	1GB

Depending on the Operating System you use with SQL Server 2000, you should also make sure that your hardware matches the hardware found in the appropriate Hardware Compatibility List (HCL). Again, realize these lists are operating system-dependent and they contain hardware tested to function properly with the Windows operating systems. You should rely on Microsoft's Web site for your HCL lookups, because the copies found there are the most recently updated (see Figure 4.1). Hardware Compatibility Lists constantly grow as more and more hardware is found to function with Windows. Unfortunately, finding these HCLs for the various operating systems can be a bit like finding a needle in a haystack. Use Table 4.7 for assistance.

Production Hardware Requirements

It is very important to realize that minimum hardware requirements typically will not work in production environments. In production, you need to constantly monitor resource usage on the server to ensure adequate response times to SQL Server 2000 clients. You must select the appropriate Windows 2000 version for your SQL Server 2000 installation to ensure you have enough resources supported in the operating system. Table 4.8 provides a look at recommended and maximum hardware configuration supported across the various editions of Windows 2000.

Table 4.7   Hardware Compatibility List Web locations.

Operating System	HCL Location
Windows 2000 Datacenter	**www.microsoft.com/windows2000/datacenter/hcl**
Windows 2000	**www.microsoft.com/hcl**
Windows NT 4	**www.microsoft.com/hcl**
Windows ME	**www.microsoft.com/hcl**
Windows 98	**www.microsoft.com/hcl**

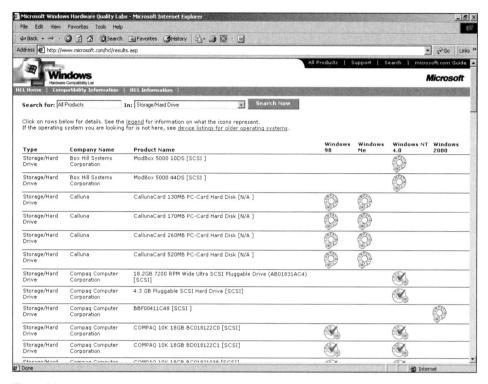

Figure 4.1
The Web-based Windows Hardware Compatibility List in action.

Table 4.8   Recommended and maximum hardware configurations for Windows 2000 versions.

Operating System	Resource	Recommended	Maximum Supported
Windows 2000 Datacenter	Processor	800MHz Pentium	32 Pentium processors
	Memory	1GB	64GB
	Free Disk Space	30GB	Exabytes
Windows 2000 Advanced Server	Processor	800MHz Pentium	8 Pentium processors
	Memory	1GB	8GB
	Free Disk Space	30GB	Exabytes
Windows 2000 Server	Processor	450MHz Pentium	4 Pentium processors
	Memory	512MB	4GB
	Free Disk Space	10GB	Exabytes
Windows 2000 Professional	Processor	333MHz	2 Pentium processors
	Memory	128MB	4GB
	Free Disk Space	6GB	Terabytes

Optimizing Hardware

There are numerous ways to optimize your server hardware for use with SQL Server 2000. This section examines these methods using the main categories of server hardware.

Processor

SQL Server 2000 is very processor-intensive. The simplest way to improve the performance of processing for S2K systems is to add additional processors. As you learned in the previous section, all versions of Windows 2000 provide support for symmetric multiprocessing (SMP).

SMP is a computer architecture that provides fast performance by making multiple CPUs available to complete individual processes simultaneously (multiprocessing). Unlike asymmetrical processing, any idle processor can be assigned any task, and additional CPUs can be added to improve performance and handle increased loads. SMP uses a single operating system and shares common memory and disk input/output resources.

In a perfect world, adding an additional processor to a SQL Server 2000 system scales the system out by 100 percent. For example, if your SQL Server is currently able to process 20 transactions in a second and you add a second symmetrically multiprocessing processor, you could now achieve 40 transactions per second. In the real world, this perfect 100 percent scalability is virtually impossible to achieve. A solid baseline to work against is a 60 percent increase in scalability due to the addition of a processor. You can use Performance Monitor to ensure the level of scalability you are achieving (see Chapter 12).

If your SQL Server 2000 system is to be used for decision support activities, as opposed to transactional processing, you can still benefit from the addition of processors to the system. This was not always the case in previous versions of SQL Server. Now, thanks to new parallel query processing capabilities, the addition of multiple processors is almost always beneficial.

Disks

Choose the disk systems you purchase for use with SQL Server 2000 carefully. Disk system bottlenecks are often a performance problem for many implementations. Be sure to avoid disk controllers that contain write-caching functionality. These controllers typically cause issues with database recoverability. If you purchase one, be sure it is designed to function with SQL Server 2000.

Typically, when purchasing storage space for your SQL Server system, you want to purchase smaller, fast drives as opposed to slower, large drives. Multiple drives are also needed for your RAID solutions and permit you to separate database files and logs.

You should implement some version of Redundant Array of Inexpensive Disks (RAID) in almost every SQL Server installation. You use RAID to improve performance, reliability, storage, and/or capacity. You should consider hardware RAID implementations (although more expensive) over software RAID implementations (those implemented by Windows 2000). Hardware RAID almost always outperforms software RAID.

You must choose what level of RAID your system should use. Table 4.9 details the various RAID levels and their respective advantages.

File System

When installing Windows 2000 in preparation for SQL Server 2000, you have a choice between three file systems to use on the server. Windows 2000 (and SQL Server 2000) supports FAT, FAT32, and the NTFS file system. Table 4.10 highlights these file systems and their differences.

If you are not dual-booting your Windows 2000 system (and you should not be), you should choose NTFS. NTFS provides performance enhancements and the highest levels of security possible for data files.

Warning! *You cannot place SQL Server 2000 database files or log files on compressed file systems.*

Memory

As long as the operating system you choose for SQL Server 2000 can support it, you can always add memory to improve server performance. Unlike previous versions of SQL Server, S2K dynamically manages the additional RAM that you provide. One of the main advantages with additional memory is SQL Server's ability to store more data in cache

Table 4.9   RAID levels and their advantages.

RAID Level	Description	Advantages
RAID 0	Disk striping	Improved read/write performance
RAID 1	Disk mirroring	Improved (sequential) read performance; fault-tolerance
RAID 5	Striping with parity	Improved (random) read/write performance; fault-tolerance
RAID 10	Mirroring with striping	Improved read/write performance; fault-tolerance

Table 4.10   File systems supported by Windows 2000.

File System	Maximum File Size	Maximum Volume Size	Advantage
FAT	2GB	4GB	Compatibility
FAT32	4GB	2TB	Compatibility; compression support
NTFS	Size of volume	2TB	Security

memory, thus making the data available to clients much more quickly. If there is inadequate memory on the server, SQL Server 2000 must constantly read data from the relatively slow disk subsystem.

SQL Server 2000 Enterprise Edition uses the Windows 2000 Address Windowing Extensions (AWE) Application Programming Interface (API) to support very large amounts of physical memory. This permits SQL Server 2000 Enterprise Edition to access 8GB of RAM on Windows 2000 Advanced Server and 64GB of RAM on Windows 2000 Datacenter Server.

4

AWE is a set of extensions to the memory management functions of the Microsoft Win32 API that allows applications to address more memory than the 4GB that is available through standard 32-bit addressing. AWE lets applications acquire physical memory as nonpaged memory, and then dynamically maps views of the nonpaged memory to the 32-bit address space. Although the 32-bit address space is limited to 4GB, the nonpaged memory can be much larger. This enables SQL Server 2000 to address more memory than can be supported in a 32-bit address space.

You must specifically enable the use of AWE memory on an instance of SQL Server 2000 Enterprise Edition. To do this you use the **sp_configure** option **AWE Enabled**. When **AWE Enabled** is set to 0, AWE memory is not used, and the instance defaults to using dynamic memory in standard 32-bit virtual address spaces. When **AWE Enabled** is set to 1, SQL Server 2000 uses AWE memory.

When SQL Server 2000 uses AWE memory, the instance does not dynamically manage the size of the address space, and the instance holds all memory acquired at startup until it is shut down. Therefore, you must carefully manage memory in this configuration. If SQL Server 2000 acquires most of the available physical memory as nonpaged memory, other applications or system processes may not be able to get the memory they need to run. You should use the **Max Server Memory** configuration setting to control how much memory is used by each instance of SQL Server that uses AWE memory.

Network

Because clients typically access SQL Server 2000 from the network, your network's resources are also critical, and proper planning on your part can dramatically improve performance. You should concern yourself with the performance capabilities in your choice of network interface card (NIC), the bandwidth possible in your server's network connection, and the amount of utilization on your network.

Installation Considerations

During the installation of SQL Server 2000, you are faced with many decisions that can have a dramatic impact on your SQL implementation. This section describes these choices in detail and provides all the information you need to respond effectively.

Licensing

You have two basic choices when it comes to licensing SQL Server 2000—use a Processor License option, or use a Server/Per-Seat Client Access License (CAL) option. These options work as follows:

- *Processor License*—Using this option, you purchase a Processor License for each processor on the system running SQL Server 2000. This option provides an unlimited number of users access to the server. These users may be located inside the Local Area Network (LAN), inside the Wide Area Network (WAN), or anywhere outside the corporate firewalls. Under this licensing option, you do not need to purchase additional Server Licenses, Client Access Licenses, or Internet Connector Licenses.

- *Server/Per-Seat Client Access License*—This licensing option requires a separate Server License for each SQL Server system and a Client Access License for each client. This licensing method is optimal if you do not have many clients that need access to the SQL Server.

There is an exception to the licensing options described above. You may install SQL Server 2000 on a system and have it function as a purely passive server in an active/passive failover cluster configuration. In an active/passive failover cluster, the active server supports all clients, while the passive node remains idle as a dedicated backup. In this configuration, the passive system does not require a Processor or Server license.

Security Context for Services

In a Windows 2000 installation, each of the services that make up SQL Server 2000 run in the context of user accounts within the operating system. The exact user account to be provided for this task is your decision to make as the SQL Server administrator (see Figure 4.2). This section helps you determine which user account you should use and the implications of your choice.

Default Account

By default, SQL Server 2000 Setup chooses the domain user account of the logged on user that is performing the installation as the account to assign to the services. As this is typically your administrative user account, this is not usually the account you should use. Creating a dedicated domain user account and using this account for the SQL services is preferable.

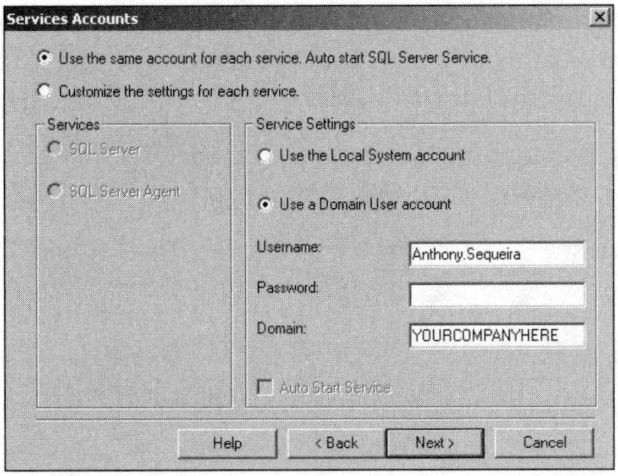

Figure 4.2
Selecting an account for the SQL services.

Local System

You can also use a local system account for the services. This is not often chosen, since this choice renders the services incapable of communicating with other, remote SQL Servers using trusted Windows connections.

Domain Account

A dedicated domain user account presents many advantages. Using such an account permits the following:

- SQL Server has the ability to access files on other computers in the domain.

- SQL Server can be configured for multiserver jobs—these are jobs that run across multiple SQL Servers. *The SQL Server 2000 Book* covers these jobs in Chapter 10.

- SQL Server can use a MAPI-compliant email server to send mail.

- SQL Server can communicate with other Microsoft servers.

Creating a domain user account dedicated to the services of SQL Server is simple. First, you must ensure the Password Never Expires option is set. This account also requires certain special access rights on the network, but it need not be a member of the Administrators group. The special rights the dedicated account needs include:

- The ability to log on as a service

- The ability to access and change the SQL Server folder

- The ability to access and change database files

- Read and write access to certain keys in the Windows registry

The SQL Server 2000 Setup program grants these rights automatically to the account for you. Additional rights may be necessary for this account, depending on certain administrative configurations, which are covered later in this book.

Follow these steps for creating a dedicated domain user account on a Windows 2000 domain controller:

1. Select Start|Programs|Administrative Tools and then choose Active Directory Users And Computers.

2. Expand your domain object so that the Users node is visible.

3. Right-click the Users container and choose New|User, from the shortcut menu. See Figure 4.3.

4. In the First Name text box, type SQLService.

5. In the User Logon Name text box, type SQLService, and then choose Next.

6. Type a password in the Password text box and confirm this password in the Confirm Password text box.

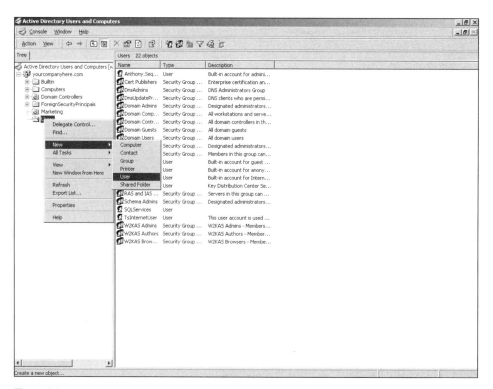

Figure 4.3
Creating a dedicated domain user account for the SQL services.

7. Select the Password Never Expires check box, and then click Next.

8. Click the Finish button.

Note: If you are running SQL Server 2000 on Windows 98 or Windows ME, the services run as executables, which do not run in the security context of a user account.

Autostart Services

By default, SQL Server 2000 Setup configures the SQL Server service and the Microsoft Search service to start automatically when Windows 2000 or Windows NT starts. As you learn in Chapter 5, you can configure these services to start manually or even configure the services that start manually by default to start automatically when the server starts.

Using Named and Multiple Instances

SQL Server 2000 offers a dramatic new installation feature—the ability to install multiple copies of SQL Server to run simultaneously on a system. Microsoft refers to these multiple installations of SQL Server 2000 as *instances*.

Remember, a single installation of SQL Server 2000 has the ability to host multiple databases. Therefore, be sure you do not install multiple instances of SQL Server 2000 unnecessarily. Multiple instances of SQL Server 2000 means additional administration for you and an increased demand for resources on the server. Installing multiple instances of SQL Server 2000 should be considered only in such circumstances as the following:

- You are testing SQL Server 2000, and multiple instances on a single system is more convenient.

- You are creating a single server to be shared by two or more customers, each of whom requires his own installation of SQL Server to ensure complete autonomous administrative control and security settings.

- Multiple Desktop Engine editions need to co-exist on a system because multiple applications using the edition have been installed.

During the installation of SQL Server 2000, the installation wizard asks if you are installing a default or named instance of S2K. The following sections describe these options for you.

Default Instance

The initial installation of SQL Server 2000 on a system defaults to the option for you to install a default instance of SQL Server 2000. When you choose this option, SQL Server 2000 is identified by the computer name of the host system; therefore, there can only be a single default instance per SQL Server system. If you are installing S2K on a system running a previous version of SQL Server, SQL 6.5 or 7 must function as the default instance. Also, keep in mind that previous SQL client software applications only have the ability to connect to default instances.

Named Instance

When you specify a named instance for your installation of SQL Server 2000, you will later reference the installation using the following syntax:

```
<computername>\<instancename>
```

When you are choosing an instance name, be sure to keep it relatively short. A name of under 10 characters in length ensures readability in most of the graphical user interface administration tools. Also, make certain you follow these naming rules:

- Instance names are not case sensitive.

- The name cannot be "Default" or "MSSQLServer."

- Instance names must follow the rules for regular identifiers specified in Chapter 3 of this book.

- Instance names must be 16 characters or shorter.

- The first character in the instance name must be a letter (Unicode Standard 2.0), an ampersand (&), an underscore (_), or a number sign (#).

- Subsequent characters can be letters (Unicode Standard 2.0), decimal numbers, the dollar sign ($), a number sign (#), or an underscore (_).

- Embedded spaces or special characters are not allowed in instance names.

- Instance names cannot contain the backslash (\), a comma (,), a colon (:), or the at sign (@).

You can have up to 16 named instances running on a system concurrently.

Multiple Instances

Remember, multiple instances of SQL Server 2000 occur when you have the default instance and one or more named instances installed on a system simultaneously. Multiple instances each have their own set of services and components, and they also share certain components and services with other instances.

Regardless of whether or not your instances of SQL Server are all 2000 versions or a mix of 2000, 7, and 6.5, there are components that are shared between these instances. These shared components are:

- Client management tools and utilities (SQL Server 6.5 and 7 client tools and utilities are upgraded to 2000 versions)

- Books Online (earlier versions are upgraded)

- Microsoft Search service

- Distributed Transaction Coordinator

Although SQL Server shares the above components between instances, several critical components remain unique to an instance. This is the reason resource demands can increase dramatically for the server. The following components are unique to each instance of SQL Server:

- System databases

- User databases

- SQL Server and SQL Agent services

As you know from Chapter 2, the default instance name for the SQL Server and SQL Agent Service is MSSQLServer and SQLServerAgent respectively. For named instances, the service names follow this syntax:

```
MSSQL$instancename
SQLAgent$instancename
```

Your default instance of SQL Server uses the standard network addresses. For example, named pipes uses \\.\pipe\sql\query, and TCP/IP sockets connect to port 1433. For your named instances, only the Named Pipes, TCP/IP, and NWLink IPX/SPX protocols are supported. Named Pipes defaults to a network address of \\Computername\Pipe\MSSQL$instancename\Sql\Query. The port addresses used by TCP/IP and NWLink IPX/SPX are chosen dynamically (by default) the first time the instance is started.

Multiple instances create another change to client connectivity configurations. A new *listener service* runs on UDP port 1434 but does not have a service name on the machine. This new listener service reveals the multiple instances of SQL Server 2000 and reveals both their network address information and other key information details needed by clients. The listener service is a component of every SQL Server instance—when SQL Server 2000 starts, the service looks to see whether any other instance is listening on UDP port 1434. If no other instance is on that port, the listener service on the newly started SQL Server instance starts listening and becomes the listener service for the machine.

When a client tries to connect to a machine, the client pings the machine to ask for information about all instances. After the client computer receives this information, it chooses a NetLib that is enabled on both the client computer and on the desired instance of SQL Server and makes a connection to the address listed for that NetLib.

Selecting a Security Mechanism

During installation of SQL Server 2000, you must make a very important decision regarding how login security will function for the server. You have two basic choices here—you can have users authenticate against either the Windows NT or Windows 2000 operating system, and then be granted access to the SQL Server automatically, or you can rely on a security database in SQL Server 2000 to provide authentication access.

Windows Authentication Mode

If you have installed SQL Server 2000 on a system participating in a Windows NT or Windows 2000 domain, you should seriously consider using Windows Authentication Mode to control how users access the SQL Server 2000 system. This mode provides convenience for the user and reduces the administrative overhead for you. In this mode, SQL Server 2000 simply relies upon the security mechanisms of the Windows operating system. If a user has been validated against NT Directory Services or Active Directory and you have specified that his account may access the server, once he logs on to either Windows NT Directory Services (NTDS) or Active Directory (AD), he can transparently access SQL Server 2000 without an additional logon.

Windows Authentication Mode means that a user requiring access to SQL Server 2000 must have a valid Windows 2000 or Windows NT account. The user also must log on to one of these operating systems in order to gain access to the server. Obviously, if you have users that are not participating in the security model of these operating systems, you will need another security method for your server. This method is called Mixed Mode.

Mixed Mode

Mixed Mode permits the same transparent logon authentication that Windows Authentication Mode provides, but it also permits SQL Server 2000 to control logon authentication using a security database hosted on the server. This accommodates those SQL Server 2000 users who do not authenticate against Windows NT or Windows 2000.

There is slightly more administrative work to be done when you are running in Mixed Mode. In this mode, you not only need to map the user accounts of Windows NT or 2000 that you would like to access SQL Server 2000, but you also must create SQL Server login accounts for those users not authenticated against Windows. Naturally, SQL Server 2000 provides both graphical methods, as well as Transact-SQL methods for quickly creating these accounts.

Collations and Sort Rules

How SQL Server 2000 stores character strings is controlled by the collation you choose during installation. A collation specifies the bit patterns that represent each character and the rules by which SQL Server sorts and compares these characters. Unlike previous versions of SQL Server, SQL Server 2000 supports objects that have different collations being stored in a single database. You may specify separate SQL Server 2000 collations down to the level of columns.

By default, the SQL Server 2000 Setup program selects your default collation for the server instance based on the Windows locale settings found in Windows 2000. This is often exactly what you require—so the default settings work well. You may need to make a change to this selection, however, if the primary language supported by SQL Server 2000 is different from the Windows locale information in W2K. You may also have to change the collation the setup program selects if your SQL Server instance participates in replication with other SQL Server systems running a different collation.

Follow these steps to determine the collation in use in your version of Windows 2000:

1. Select Start|Settings|Control Panel.

2. Double-click the Regional Options icon.

3. In the Your Locale (Location) drop-down list, determine your Windows locale (See Figure 4.4).

4. Click OK to close the Regional Options dialog box.

SQL Server 2000 not only supports the Windows collations but also provides support for its own SQL Server collations. SQL Server 2000 offers its own collations in order to provide support for previous versions of SQL Server. Earlier versions of SQL Server actually specified code page number, character sort order, and Unicode collations as separate values. Therefore, you can choose SQL Server 2000 collations instead of Windows collations to work with these earlier versions. If you are installing SQL Server 2000 on a system that contains a previous version installation, the SQL Server 2000 Setup program uses a SQL collation that matches the collation, sort order, and code page for the existing SQL Server installation (See Figure 4.5).

Selecting Network Libraries

As you learned in Chapter 2 of this book, SQL Server 2000 uses network libraries to send network packets between clients and SQL Servers. These network libraries support a variety of underlying network protocols including TCP/IP, IPX/SPX, and AppleTalk.

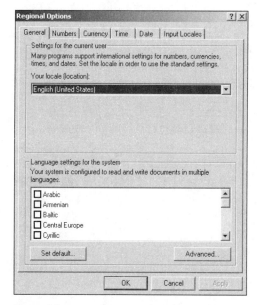

Figure 4.4
Determining your Windows locale.

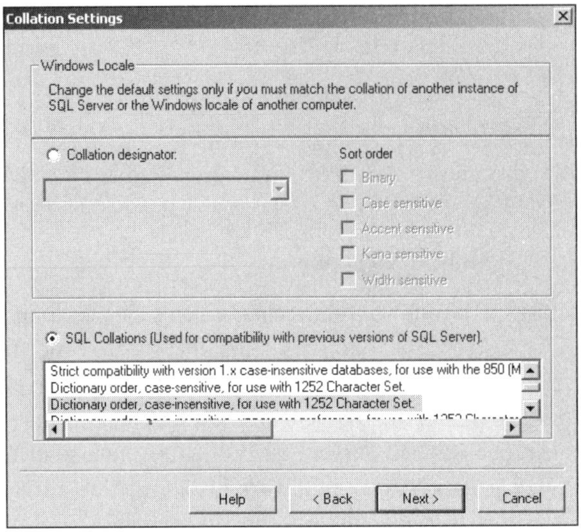

Figure 4.5
Choosing a SQL Server collation for SQL Server 2000.

By default, SQL Server 2000 Setup installs and configures SQL Server to use TCP/IP and named pipes. If you know you need additional network libraries installed and configured, you can do so at installation using Custom Setup. Should you need to configure additional network libraries following installation, you may do so using the Server Network Utility from the Microsoft SQL Server program group. You can configure additional network library support on a client using the Client Network Utility from the same program group.

New to SQL Server 2000 is the ability to use Secure Socket Layer (SSL) encryption over the network library to secure SQL client to server communications. This setting is made easily using the Server Network Utility following installation. This book discusses SSL encryption in more detail in Chapter 8.

Summary

Proper installation planning is critical for the successful installation and subsequent utilization of SQL Server 2000. Incorrect option selections during installation may result in the need for reinstallations at a later time, which can cause a substantial loss of time and money.

Remember, proper installation planning begins with the selection of the appropriate operating system on which SQL Server 2000 runs. Use the Decision Tree and the Table 4.1 in this chapter to help you make the best selection. You also need to ensure you have purchased the proper hardware for your operating system selection.

The next chapter of this book walks you through the actual installation of SQL Server 2000, whether from the original installation CD-ROM, or an unattended and/or remote installation that does not require your presence.

4

Chapter 5

Installing SQL Server 2000

This chapter covers everything you need to know about installing SQL Server 2000. It provides you with step-by-step information to guide you through the main methods for performing installations. This chapter also describes both post-installation tasks you should perform to ensure a successful installation and tips for troubleshooting your SQL Server 2000 installations. Troubleshooting tips are obviously of critical importance should problems arise during this important process.

Methods of Installation

There are several methods for actually installing SQL Server 2000. This section discusses the three main methods—standard, unattended, and remote installations. Be sure to use Decision Tree 5.1 to assist you in determining which installation method is right for you. You should approach this section armed with the knowledge you gained from Chapter 4 of this book, in which you learned to plan for a successful installation.

Note: This section focuses on the installation of SQL Server 2000 Enterprise Edition on Windows 2000 Server or greater, platforms which make up the overwhelming majority of production installations. These platforms also closely follow other installation platforms, so you should be able to use the information in this section as a guide under any circumstances.

Standard Installations

A standard installation—the most common method—involves actually visiting the computer system on which SQL Server 2000 is to be installed and using the installation CD-ROM to complete the setup. To carry out the standard installation, follow these steps:

1. Make sure that you are logged onto your Windows 2000/NT system with a user account that has sufficient permissions to perform the installation. The best account for this is an account with administrative privileges, of course.

2. Insert the SQL Server 2000 installation CD-ROM. An autorun application in the root of the CD-ROM presents a Setup dialog box. If you need to install Internet Explorer 5 or service packs for Windows NT 4 (both required for installation), choose SQL Server

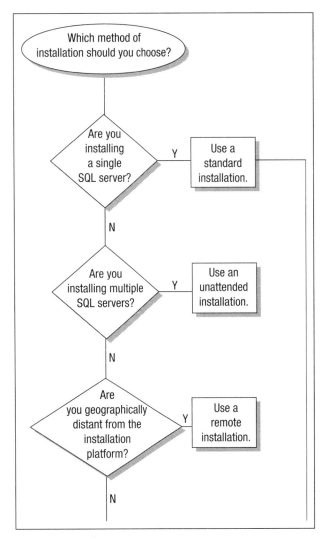

Decision Tree 5.1
Choosing an installation method.

2000 Prerequisites. If you have the prerequisites installed, choose SQL Server 2000 Components to begin the installation. Making this selection presents the SQL Server 2000 Install Components dialog box.

Note: You can also launch the installation by double-clicking the Setupsql.exe file in the \X86\Setup folder on the CD-ROM.

3. To begin the SQL Server 2000 Setup Wizard, choose Install Database Server from the SQL Server 2000 Install Components dialog box. This causes the Welcome page of the wizard to appear.

4. Choose Next in the SQL Server 2000 Setup Wizard's Welcome page. The Computer Name page appears.

5. Select Local Computer in the Computer Name page (see Figure 5.1). Once Local Computer is selected, choose Next in the Computer Name page. The Installation Selection page of the wizard appears.

5

Note: The options regarding Virtual Servers are covered in Chapter 11 of this book. Performing remote installations is covered later in this section.

6. On the Installation Selection page, choose Create A New Instance Of SQL Server, Or Install Client Tools (see Figure 5.2). You can also use this page to modify an existing installation or to assist in performing an unattended installation (these options are covered later in this section). Choose Next and the User Information page appears.

7. Complete the Name and Company information and choose Next. The Software License Agreement page appears. Choose Yes. The Installation Definition page appears.

8. On the Installation Definition page, you can choose to install the Client Tools Only, the Server and Client Tools, or the Connectivity Only option (see Figure 5.3). Here you are interested in installing the Server and Client Tools. Make this selection and choose Next. The Instance Name page appears.

9. If this is the first time you are installing SQL Server 2000 on a system, leave the Default checkbox selected. If you are installing a named instance of SQL Server 2000 on the system, provide an Instance Name in the appropriate field. Choose Next when finished. The Setup Type page appears.

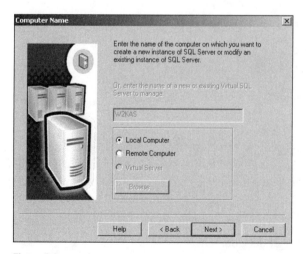

Figure 5.1
The Computer Name page of the SQL Server Setup Wizard.

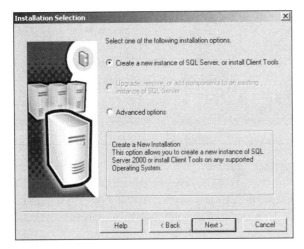

Figure 5.2
The Installation Selection page of the SQL Server Setup Wizard.

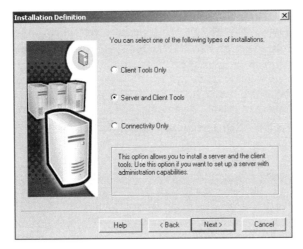

Figure 5.3
The Installation Definition page of the SQL Server Setup Wizard.

10. The Setup Type page permits you to choose between a Typical, Minimum, or Custom installation (see Figure 5.4). The Typical option sets up SQL Server 2000 with the default installation options. The Minimum option installs the minimum configuration necessary to run SQL Server. The Custom installation allows additional configurations to be made during setup. These include:

- The installation of additional development tools

- The installation of code samples

- The selection of specific components to install

- Modification of the default collation settings

- The selection of additional network libraries

- Modification of the default named pipe

- Modification of the default TCP/IP sockets port number

- Definition of a proxy server address

11. The Setup Type page also allows you to modify the default installation locations of the SQL Server 2000 program files and data files. You should consider storing the data files in a separate location from the program files. In fact, these data files should reside on a separate drive system (see Chapter 7 for more information). Select the Typical setup option and choose Next. The Services Account page appears.

12. As recommended in Chapter 4, you should use a dedicated domain user account for both of the services. Select Use The Same Account For Each Service. Autostart SQL Server Service. Also, select Use A Domain User Account. Provide the username, password, and domain name for the user account and choose Next. The Authentication Mode page appears.

13. Choose the appropriate authentication mode using Chapter 4 as a guide. Choose Next when finished. The Choose Licensing Mode page appears.

14. Use Chapter 4 as a guide to select the appropriate options in the Choose Licensing Mode page. Select Continue when finished. The Start Copying Files page appears. Choose Next to begin the file copy phase of installation. After the completion of this phase, the Setup Complete page appears.

15. Choose Finish from the Setup Complete page.

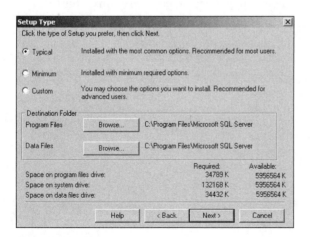

Figure 5.4
The Setup Type page of the SQL Server Setup Wizard.

The above steps perform the standard installation. You are now ready to verify this information and perform critical post-installation tasks, which are discussed in the remainder of this chapter.

Unattended Installations

A powerful alternative to the standard installation detailed above is the unattended installation option. This frees you from completing all of the options in the Setup Wizard during the installation. You can pre-select these options once, and then perform the installation rapidly across many different machines. This can save a dramatic amount of time when you need to install SQL Server 2000 on many systems.

To perform an unattended installation of SQL Server 2000, you execute a batch file that uses a setup initialization file (ISS). The syntax for this batch file follows:

```
Start /Wait D:\X86\Setup\Setupsql.exe k=SMS -s -m -SMS -f1 "d:\Sqlins.iss"
```

This ISS file contains all of the details SQL Server 2000 requires for setup. Table 5.1 details these files and their purpose.

Table 5.1   Pre-written unattended installation files for SQL Server 2000.

IIS File Name	Batch File Name	Purpose
Sqlins.iss	Sqlins.bat	Performs an unattended typical installation of SQL Server 2000
Sqlcli.iss	Sqlcli.bat	Installation of the client tools only
Sqlcst.iss	Sqlcst.bat	Custom installation including all components

Here is the Sqlins.iss file. Notice how simple it would be to customize this file:

```
[InstallShield Silent]
Version=v5.00.000
File=Response File

[File Transfer]
OverwriteReadOnly=NoToAll

[DlgOrder]
Dlg0=SdWelcome-0
Count=14
Dlg1=DlgMachine-0
Dlg2=DlgInstallMode-0
Dlg3=SdRegisterUser-0
```

```
Dlg4=SdLicense-0
Dlg5=DlgClientServer-0
Dlg6=DlgInstanceName-0
Dlg7=SetupTypeSQL-0
Dlg8=DlgServices-0
Dlg9=DlgSQLSecurity-0
Dlg10=DlgCollation-0
Dlg11=DlgServerNetwork-0
Dlg12=SdStartCopy-0
Dlg13=SdFinish-0

[SdWelcome-0]
Result=1

[DlgMachine-0]
Type=1
Result=1

[DlgInstallMode-0]
Type=1
Result=1

[SdRegisterUser-0]
szName=MSEmployee
Result=1

[SdLicense-0]
Result=1

[DlgCDKey-0]
Result=1
CDKey=XXXXX-XXXXX-XXXXX-XXXXX-XXXXX

[DlgClientServer-0]
Type=2
Result=1

[DlgInstanceName-0]
InstanceName=MSSQLSERVER
Result=1

[SetupTypeSQL-0]
szDir=%PROGRAMFILES%\Microsoft SQL Server
Result=301
szDataDir=%PROGRAMFILES%\Microsoft SQL Server
```

5

```
[DlgServices-0]
Local-Domain=3855
AutoStart=15
Result=1

[DlgSQLSecurity-0]
LoginMode=-1
Result=1

[DlgCollation-0]
collation_name=' '
Result=1

[DlgServerNetwork-0]
NetworkLibs=255
TCPPort=1433
TCPPrxy=Default
NMPPipeName=\\.\pipe\sql\query
Result=1

[SdStartCopy-0]
Result=1

[License]
LicenseMode=PERSERVER
LicenseLimit=5

[SdFinish-0]
Result=1
bOpt1=0
bOpt2=0
```

In addition to using one of the ISS files provided by Microsoft, you can easily create your own using the Setup Wizard. To do so, follow these steps:

1. Make sure you are logged on to the system and have the appropriate permissions.

2. Insert the SQL Server 2000 CD-ROM.

3. Choose SQL Server 2000 Components, and then select Install Database Server.

4. Choose Next in the Welcome page.

5. Choose Next in the Computer Name page.

6. Choose Advanced Options in the Installation Selection page.

7. Notice that the Record Unattended .ISS File is selected in the Advanced Options page (see Figure 5.5).

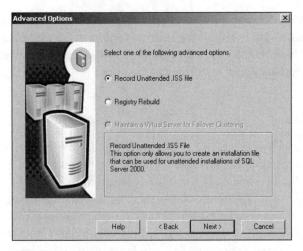

Figure 5.5
The Advanced Options page of the SQL Server Setup Wizard.

8. Choose Next.

9. Complete the remainder of the Setup Wizard screens with the appropriate information for your future unattended installations.

The above process creates your own custom ISS file in the winnt directory. The name of this file is Setup.iss. Use this file in conjunction with the syntax described earlier to perform unattended installations.

Note: SQL Server 2000 actually creates a Setup.iss file in the winnt directory following your initial installation. You may edit this file and use it for subsequent unattended installations of SQL Server. The above steps are useful, however, for creating an ISS file at any time without actually installing SQL Server 2000.

If you would like to perform disk-imaging installations of SQL Server 2000, this is easier than ever with SQL Server 2000, because SQL Server 2000 now supports the seamless renaming of the host operating system. When you change the name of the system running SQL Server 2000, the new name is automatically recognized during SQL Server startup. You no longer must rerun Setup to reset the computer name in SQL Server. However, in order to correct the **sysservers** system table, you should manually run the following procedures:

```
sp_dropserver <old_name>
go
sp_addserver <new_name>
go
```

You can also install SQL Server 2000 in an automated fashion using Microsoft's Systems Management Server (SMS) version 1.2 or later, which permits automatic deployments on multiple servers running Windows NT/2000. The SQL Server CD-ROM contains a Package Definition Format (PDF) file (Smssql.pdf) that automates creating a SQL Server package for use in SMS.

Remote Installations

Thanks to the Computer Name page of the SQL Server 2000 Setup Wizard, you can easily perform installations to a remote system. Choose the Remote Computer option in this wizard page to begin the installation. Obviously, the setup program must be able to establish a connection with this remote system, and you must be logged in using an account that has adequate permissions to access this remote system. You must also specify an account that has permissions to perform the installation on the remote system. Finally, to perform a remote installation you must specify a target path for the installation files and a source path for the setup files. You provide this information on the Remote Setup Information page of the Setup Wizard.

You should not be surprised that SQL Server 2000 Setup creates a Setup.iss file during this process. Setup then copies this file and the setup files to the remote computer and performs an unattended installation for you.

Post-Installation Tasks

Your installation of SQL Server 2000 should not end when the Setup Wizard completes. There are plenty of post-installation tasks a successful SQL administrator should perform. This section guides you through these post-installation tasks.

Reviewing Results

You should spend some time reviewing the results of installation not only to make sure that the installation completed successfully, but also to guarantee that you can adequately administer and troubleshoot the server following the install. The SQL Server Setup Wizard makes changes to the folder structure on your disk system, not only adding folders, but modifying permissions as well. The wizard also makes changes to the Windows registry. The sections that follow detail all of these changes for you.

File and Folder Modifications

SQL Server 2000 Setup adds the following folders to your system; these folders are shared by all instances of SQL Server running on the system (see Figure 5.6):

- \ *Program Files\Microsoft SQL Server\ 80\ Com*—contains DLLs for COM objects

- \ *Program Files\ Microsoft SQL Server\ 80\ Com\ Binn\ Resources\ 1033*—contains resource files (RLLs) used by the DLLs in this COM directory

- \ *Program Files\ Microsoft SQL Server\ 80\ Tools\ Binn*—contains Windows NT client executable files

- \ *Program Files\ Microsoft SQL Server\ 80\ Tools\ Binn\ Resources\ 1033*—contains resource files used by the DLLs in the Tools\ Binn directory

- \ *Program Files\ Microsoft SQL Server\ 80\ Tools\ Books*—contains SQL Server Books Online files, including online Help files

- \ *Program Files\ Microsoft SQL Server\ 80\ Tools\ DevTools*—contains header files, library files, and sample programs for use by developers

- \ *Program Files\ Microsoft SQL Server\ 80\ Tools\ Html*—contains Microsoft Management Console (MMC) and SQL Server HTML files

- \ *Program Files\ Microsoft SQL Server\ 80\ Tools\ Templates*—contains boilerplate files with SQL scripts to help you create objects in the database

SQL Server 2000 Setup also adds folders unique to each instance of SQL:

- \ *Program Files\ Microsoft SQL Server\ Mssql\ Backup*—provides a default location for backup files

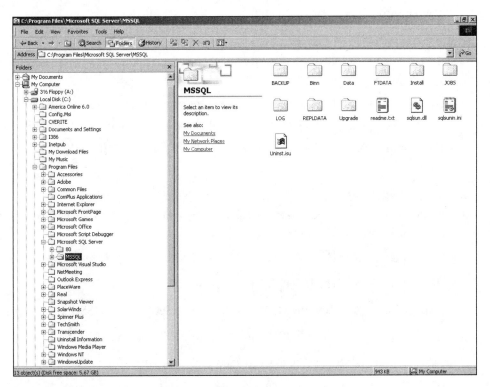

Figure 5.6
Common folders installed by SQL Server 2000.

- \ *Program Files\ Microsoft SQL Server\ Mssql\ Binn*—contains Windows NT Server executable files and DLL files for extended stored procedures

- \ *Program Files\ Microsoft SQL Server\ Mssql\ Binn\ Resources\ 1033*—contains resource files used by the DLLs in this Binn directory

- \ *Program Files\ Microsoft SQL Server\ Mssql\ Data*—contains system and sample database files

- \ *Program Files\ Microsoft SQL Server\ Mssql\ Ftdata*—contains full-text catalog files

- \ *Program Files\ Microsoft SQL Server\ Mssql\ Install*—contains scripts run during Setup and resulting output files

- \ *Program Files\ Microsoft SQL Server\ Mssql\ Jobs*—provides a storage location for temporary job output files

- \ *Program Files\ Microsoft SQL Server\ Mssql\ Log*—contains error log files

- \ *Program Files\ Microsoft SQL Server\ Mssql\ Repldata*—provides a working directory for replication tasks

- \ *Program Files\ Microsoft SQL Server\ Mssql\ Upgrade*—contains files used for version upgrades from SQL Server version 6.5 to SQL Server 2000

NTFS File Permission Changes

SQL Server Setup modifies select permissions on certain folders in a Windows NT/2000 environment. SQL Server makes the following changes:

- The Mssql or Mssql$InstanceName directory structure is set so that only the SQL Server service account(s) and the local administrator's group have read or write access.

- The Program and Data Files folders are set to Full Control for the SQL Server service account(s).

Registry Key Additions

SQL Server Setup adds several keys to the Registry and sets appropriate permissions on these keys. These keys are shared by all instances:

- HKEY_LOCAL_MACHINE\SOFTWARE\Microsoft\Microsoft SQL Server\80

- HKEY_LOCAL_MACHINE\SOFTWARE\Microsoft\MSDTC

- HKEY_LOCAL_MACHINE\SYSTEM\CurrentControlSet\Services\MSSQLServerADHelper

- HKEY_LOCAL_MACHINE\SOFTWARE\Microsoft\MSSQLServer\Client

Registry keys are added specific to the default instance. These keys are:

- HKEY_LOCAL_MACHINE\SOFTWARE\Microsoft\MSSQLServer

- HKEY_LOCAL_MACHINE\SYSTEM\CurrentControlSet\Services\MSSQLServer

Registry keys are also added for each named instance. These keys are:

- HKEY_LOCAL_MACHINE\SOFTWARE\Microsoft\Microsoft SQL Server\InstanceName

- HKEY_LOCAL_MACHINE\SYSTEM\CurrentControlSet\Services\MSSQL$InstanceName

Stopping, Starting, and Pausing Services

By default, SQL Server 2000 starts each instance of the SQL Server service automatically when the operating system starts. It also configures the SQL Server Agent service to be started manually by you, the administrator. You had the opportunity to change these default options during the SQL Server Setup, but if you would like to change the way these services start after installation, there are several simple methods for doing so:

- Use the SQL Server Manager to change the default starting configurations. SQL Service Manager can be found by using Start|Programs|Microsoft SQL Server to Service Manager.

- Use the Enterprise Manager to reconfigure the autostart options for the services. You can do this by right-clicking your server and choosing Properties. On the General tab of the Server Properties window are options for autostarting the services (see Figure 5.7).

- Use the Computer Management snap-in located in Administrative Tools. In this console, you can choose the Services And Applications node followed by the Services node and then reconfigure the default start-up option for any of the SQL services.

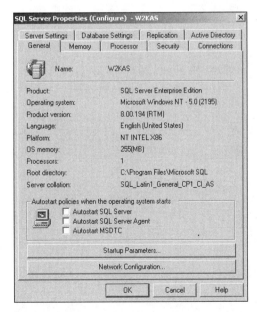

Figure 5.7
Changing autostart options in Enterprise Manager.

There are also several different methods for starting, stopping, and pausing the SQL services. Obviously, it is important to start the services in order for SQL Server 2000 to function properly, but stopping the services allows you to perform major configuration tasks and disconnects all users. Pausing the services is often useful as it does not disconnect current users, but it permits no additional connections to the server. In order to make these changes, you can use one of several methods:

- Use the SQL Service Manager (see Figure 5.8). Once you initially launch this utility using the Start menu, it can be found in the system tray of the Taskbar for easier access. Right-clicking this icon in the system tray produces a shortcut menu that allows for quicker starting, stopping, and pausing of services. In order to quickly launch the Service Manager in its "full-blown" configuration, simply double-click the icon in the system tray.

- When you use SQL Query Analyzer and SQL Profiler, you also have the ability to start the services.

- SQL Server Enterprise Manager permits you to stop, pause, or start the SQL Server service by right-clicking a server instance in the console.

- The Services node of the Computer Management snap-in also allows you to start, stop, or pause any of the SQL Services running on your system.

- The **NET** command used at the command prompt can also start, stop, and pause the services. The syntax of this command is simple:

```
NET START MSSQLServer
```

This particular example starts the SQL Server service.

Figure 5.8
The SQL Service Manager.

Connecting to the Server

An excellent way to test your installation following setup is to use one of the many client tools to make a connection to the server. This section presents two simple ways to do this using two of the tools provided by SQL Server 2000. One of these tools is a command prompt tool, and the other is a graphical user interface tool.

Perhaps the simplest way to test the installation is to use the Osql utility. To do so, follow these steps:

1. Select Start|Programs|Accessories|Command Prompt.

2. In the Command Prompt window, type the following and press Enter:

```
osql -E
```

This command uses Osql to connect to the default instance of SQL Server 2000 running on the computer. The **-E** argument logs on to the server using the security credentials of the currently logged on user account. If you receive an error message regarding security, be sure you are logged on using an account that has administrative privileges. Notice after pressing Enter that you are now in interactive Osql mode—the cursor changes to a 1> prompt waiting for your first line of Transact-SQL code. Enter the following sample query, pressing Enter at the end of each line (see Figure 5.9):

```
USE master
SELECT * FROM sysdatabases
GO
```

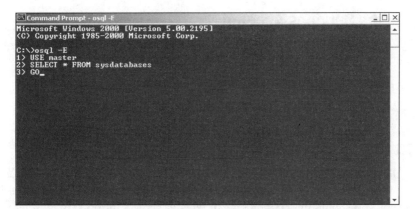

Figure 5.9
Using OSQL to test connectivity.

This query displays all the records from the **sysdatabases** system table in the master database. This is one way to view information about all of the databases stored on SQL Server. If this query returns information, you have successfully tested connectivity to the server.

Another way to test connectivity to the server is to use Query Analyzer. This graphical utility is your main tool for running and testing Transact-SQL queries. This book explored Query Analyzer with you in Chapter 3. Here, I use it to perform a simple test of connectivity:

1. Select Start|Programs|Microsoft SQL Server|Query Analyzer.

2. SQL Query Analyzer starts with the Connect to SQL Server dialog box open.

3. If you have configured your server to use Windows authentication, and you are currently using an account that has rights to the server (an administrative account, for example), simply click OK to connect using Windows authentication. If you are using Mixed Mode security, choose SQL Server authentication and provide a username and password.

4. Once you connect to the server, Query Analyzer presents you with a blank query pane to compose a new query. Type the following query:

```
SELECT * FROM INFORMATION_SCHEMA.SCHEMATA
```

5. When you have finished typing the query, execute the query by pressing the F5 key on the keyboard. Notice this is another method for examining all of the databases stored on SQL Server 2000.

Modifying the Services Account

If you need to modify the account assigned to the SQL Server services following installation, there are several methods for doing so. You can do either of the following:

- Use the Services node of the Computer Management console.

- Use the Security tab of the Server Properties dialog box in Enterprise Manager.

Configuring SQL Server Enterprise Manager

Enterprise Manager is the main graphical user interface for managing SQL Server. You use this tool throughout this book to manage and configure the server. In order to fully utilize this tool, you should understand how to register servers in this tool in order to access them.

Registering Additional Servers

In order to register a server in Enterprise Manager, you must be able to connect to the server. Your default SQL Server 2000 installation is registered in Enterprise Manager automatically when you first launch Enterprise Manager following the installation. To register additional servers, you must specify the following:

- The server name

- The named instance name if named instances are being used

- The authentication mode

- A server group, if you are using server groups in Enterprise manager to group multiple servers in the interface

The simplest method for registering a server in Enterprise Manager is to use the Register SQL Server Wizard. Follow these steps to do so:

1. With Enterprise Manager open, right-click the default SQL Server Group. From the shortcut menu, select New SQL Server Registration. Notice this launches the Register SQL Server Wizard.

2. Notice you can bypass the wizard for future registrations by choosing the From Now On, I Want To Perform This Task Without Using A Wizard checkbox. Choose Next from the wizard.

3. On the Select A Server page, type in the name of the server you would like to register and use the Add button to add this server to the list of added servers. Choose Next.

4. On the Select An Authentication Mode page, choose Windows or SQL Server authentication and choose Next.

5. On the Select SQL Server Group page, choose the group you want this new registered server to fall under, and choose Next.

6. Choose the Finish button to complete the wizard and register the server.

Registration information for servers is stored in the Windows Registry and is kept private by default. You can share registration information, however, to make it available to other administrators or yourself when using other Enterprise Manager installations. You can also share all registration information on a central server, to make multiple Enterprise Manager server registrations even more convenient. In order to change these settings, follow these steps:

1. From within Enterprise Manager, choose the Tools menu, then select Options.

2. On the General tab, notice the Read/Store user independent check box. Clearing this option allows your registration information to be shared.

3. Notice the Read From Remote option. Use this setting with the Server name box to store shared information on a central server.

Troubleshooting Installations

Hopefully, your installation has gone smoothly. But unfortunately, even if you have planned very carefully using Chapter 4 of this book and actually carried out the install using this chapter as a guide, things can still go wrong. This section teaches you how to troubleshoot installations with which you are having difficulties.

Microsoft designed SQL Server 2000 to catch many problems during installation on its own and either proactively correct these problems or prompt you to correct them. For example, the setup program catches several running programs that might cause problems for the installation. Setup also detects insufficient disk space and prompts you to restart the system if it detects that certain files it must access are locked. But even with all these measures, you might encounter problems that require additional troubleshooting.

Troubleshooting Logs

A key to successfully troubleshooting installations is to use the many logs that Microsoft provides in a Windows NT or Windows 2000 environment. Several of these logs specific to SQL Server 2000 are also available for installs on other Windows platforms. Table 5.2 describes these logs.

Naturally, SQL Server 2000 creates the SQL Server Setup Log during the installation of SQL. Notice the incredible detail this log provides, and what a valuable resource this log is for troubleshooting installation failures or oddities. Here is a portion of the sample log file from a typical (and completely successful) installation of Enterprise Evaluation Edition on Windows 2000 Advanced Server. You may use it for comparison purposes against your own SQL Server Setup Log. Here is the initial portion of the Setup Log:

Table 5.2   Troubleshooting logs.

Log	Description	Location
SQL Server Setup Log	Records all SQL Server Setup actions	c:\winnt\sqlstp.log
SQL Server Setup Completion Log	Records completion or failure of setup	c:\winnt\setup.log
SQL Server Search Service Log	Records actions during installation of Search service	c:\winnt\temp\SearchSetup.log
SQL Server Error Log	Records the process of starting SQL Server	c:\Program Files\Microsoft SQL Server\MSSQL\Log\ERRORLOG
SQL Server Agent Error Log	Records errors with SQL Server Agent service	c:\Program Files\Microsoft SQL Server\MSSQL\Log\SQLAGENT.OUT
Windows 2000 Application Log	Records information about application-related events	Start menu

```
16:46:54 Begin Setup
16:46:54 8.00.194
16:46:54 Mode = Normal
16:46:54 ModeType = NORMAL
16:46:54 GetDefinitionEx returned: 0, Extended: 0xf00000
16:46:54 ValueFTS returned: 1
16:46:54 ValuePID returned: 0
16:46:54 ValueLic returned: 0
16:46:54 System: Windows NT Enterprise Server
16:46:54 SQL Server ProductType: Enterprise Evaluation Edition [0x3]
16:46:54 IsNTCluster returned: 0
16:46:54 Begin Action: SetupInitialize
16:46:54 End Action SetupInitialize
16:46:54 Begin Action:  SetupInstall
16:46:54 Reading Software\Microsoft\Windows\CurrentVersion\CommonFilesDir ...
16:46:54 CommonFilesDir=C:\Program Files\Common Files
16:46:54 Windows Directory=C:\WINNT\
16:46:54 Program Files=C:\Program Files\
16:46:54 TEMPDIR=C:\WINNT\TEMP\
16:46:54 Begin Action:  SetupInstall
16:46:54 Begin Action:  CheckFixedRequirements
16:46:54 Platform ID: 0xf00000
16:46:54 Version: 5.0.2195
16:46:54 File Version - C:\WINNT\System32\shdocvw.dll: 5.0.3103.1000
16:46:54 End Action:  CheckFixedRequirements
16:46:54 Begin Action:  ShowDialogs
16:46:54 Initial Dialog Mask: 0x8300037, Disable Back=0x1
16:46:55 Begin Action ShowDialogsHlpr: 0x1
16:46:55 Begin Action:  DialogShowSdWelcome
16:46:57 End Action  DialogShowSdWelcome
16:46:57 Dialog 0x1 returned: 1
16:46:57 End Action ShowDialogsHlpr
16:46:57 ShowDialogsGetDialog returned: nCurrent=0x2,index=1
16:46:57 Begin Action ShowDialogsHlpr: 0x2
16:46:57 Begin Action:  DialogShowSdMachineName
16:46:58 ShowDlgMachine returned: 1
16:46:58 Name = W2KAS, Type = 0x1
16:46:59 Begin Action:  CheckRequirements
16:46:59 Processor Architecture: x86 (Pentium)
16:46:59 Service Pack:  256
16:46:59 ComputerName: W2KAS
16:46:59 User Name: Anthony.Sequeira
16:46:59 IsAllAccessAllowed returned: 1
16:46:59 OS Language: 0x409
16:46:59 End Action CheckRequirements
```

The SQL Server Setup Completion Log is very simple compared to the SQL Server Setup Log. This basic log file records the completion or failure of setup, and records any relevant information to this completion or failure. Here is a sample log:

```
[Status]
Completed=2
RebootRequired=0
```

The SQL Server Search Service Log performs a similar function to the SQL Server Setup Log. It does an excellent job of recording actions during the installation of the Microsoft Search service. Here is a portion of this log:

```
4/28/2001 7:31:39 INFO: Main, *******************************************
4/28/2001 7:31:39 INFO: Main, ***   Setup is beginning
4/28/2001 7:31:39 INFO: Main, *******************************************
4/28/2001 7:31:39 INFO: ParseCommandLine,
Command="C:\SQLSource\x86\FullText\MSSearch\Search\SearchStp.exe" /s /
a:SQLServer
4/28/2001 7:31:39 INFO: InstallInfo, Logging install info...
4/28/2001 7:31:39 INFO: InstallInfo, Setup Version=9.107.5512
4/28/2001 7:31:39 INFO: InstallInfo, Search is not installed.
4/28/2001 7:31:39 INFO: InstallInfo, IsNT4 (or higher)=1
4/28/2001 7:31:39 INFO: InstallInfo, IsNT5 (or higher)=1
4/28/2001 7:31:39 INFO: InstallInfo, IsIndexServer1x=0
4/28/2001 7:31:39 INFO: InstallInfo, IsQuiet=0
4/28/2001 7:31:39 INFO: InstallInfo, IsSilent=1
4/28/2001 7:31:39 INFO: InstallInfo, IsPostReboot=0
4/28/2001 7:31:39 INFO: InstallInfo, InstallPath=C:\Program Files\Common
Files\System\MSSearch
4/28/2001 7:31:39 INFO: InstallInfo, SystemPath=C:\WINNT\System32
4/28/2001 7:31:39 INFO: InstallInfo,
MediaPath=C:\SQLSource\x86\FullText\MSSearch\Search
4/28/2001 7:31:39 INFO: InstallInfo, RepairMode=0
4/28/2001 7:31:39 INFO: InstallInfo, InstallAction=Install
4/28/2001 7:31:39 INFO: CSearchSetupEngine::PreInstallSearch, Performing pre-
Install actions...
4/28/2001 7:31:39 INFO: CSearchSetupEngine::ChangeSearchClusterState, First
time search install, don't worry about clustering.
4/28/2001 7:31:39 INFO: CSetupEngine::StopServices, Stopping services...
4/28/2001 7:31:39 INFO: ManageServices, Stopping all services
4/28/2001 7:31:39 INFO: CSearchSetupEngine::InstallSearch, Performing Install
actions...
4/28/2001 7:31:39 INFO: CSetupEngine::CopyFiles, Incrementing shared file
RefCounts
4/28/2001 7:31:39 INFO: CSetupEngine::CopyFiles, Copying files...
4/28/2001 7:31:40 INFO: InstallFile, Successfully installed and verified file :
C:\Program Files\Common Files\System\MSSearch\Bin\acatctr.h.
```

```
4/28/2001 7:31:40 INFO: InstallFile, Successfully installed and verified file :
C:\Program Files\Common Files\System\MSSearch\Bin\acatctr.ini.
4/28/2001 7:31:40 INFO: InstallFile, Successfully installed and verified file :
C:\Program Files\Common Files\System\MSSearch\Bin\catutil.exe.
4/28/2001 7:31:40 INFO: InstallFile, Successfully installed and verified file :
C:\Program Files\Common Files\System\MSSearch\Bin\dsscntrs.h.
4/28/2001 7:31:40 INFO: InstallFile, Successfully installed and verified file :
C:\Program Files\Common Files\System\MSSearch\Bin\dsscntrs.ini.
4/28/2001 7:31:40 INFO: InstallFile, Successfully installed and verified file :
```

SQL Server 2000 creates the SQL Server Error Log each time the SQL Server service starts. This is an excellent resource to check for installation problems that might be keeping your implementation from running properly. Keep in mind that each time the SQL Server service starts, a new log is created. By default, SQL Server archives six of your previous logs and numbers these logs 1 through 6, although you can use the **sp_cycle_errorlog** stored procedure to close the current error log file and cycle the error log extension numbers just like a server restart. Your new error log contains version and copyright information and a line indicating that the new log has been created. You can also configure the number of logs SQL Server archives by following these steps:

1. Select Start|Programs|Microsoft SQL Server|Enterprise Manager.

2. Expand Microsoft SQL Servers, SQL Server Group, and your server.

3. Expand the Management node.

4. Right-click the SQL Server Error Logs node and choose Configure.

5. Select the Limiting The Number Of The Error Log Files Before They Are Recycled checkbox and then use the Maximum Number Of The Error Log Files field to configure a number of files from 1 through 99.

Here is a sample SQL Server Error Log:

```
2001-06-08 15:21:51.36 server    Microsoft SQL Server  2000 - 8.00.194 (Intel
X86)
        Aug  6 2000 00:57:48
        Copyright (c) 1988-2000 Microsoft Corporation
        Enterprise Edition on Windows NT 5.0 (Build 2195: Service Pack 1)
2001-06-08 15:21:51.40 server    Copyright (C) 1988-2000 Microsoft Corporation.
2001-06-08 15:21:51.40 server    All rights reserved.
2001-06-08 15:21:51.40 server    Server Process ID is 672.
2001-06-08 15:21:51.40 server    Logging SQL Server messages in file 'C:\Program
Files\Microsoft SQL Server\MSSQL\log\ERRORLOG'.
2001-06-08 15:21:51.62 server    SQL Server is starting at priority class
'normal'(1 CPU detected).
2001-06-08 15:21:51.98 server    SQL Server configured for thread mode
processing.
2001-06-08 15:21:52.02 server    Using dynamic lock allocation. [2500] Lock
Blocks, [5000] Lock Owner Blocks.
```

```
2001-06-08 15:21:52.05 server     Attempting to initialize Distributed
Transaction Coordinator.
2001-06-08 15:21:52.80 server     Failed to obtain
TransactionDispenserInterface: Result Code = 0x8004d01b
2001-06-08 15:21:52.97 spid3      Starting up database 'master'.
2001-06-08 15:21:54.26 server     Using 'SSNETLIB.DLL' version '8.0.194'.
2001-06-08 15:21:54.26 spid5      Starting up database 'model'.
2001-06-08 15:21:54.37 spid3      Server name is 'W2KAS'.
2001-06-08 15:21:54.43 spid8      Starting up database 'msdb'.
2001-06-08 15:21:54.43 spid9      Starting up database 'pubs'.
2001-06-08 15:21:54.48 spid10     Starting up database 'Northwind'.
2001-06-08 15:21:55.05 server     SQL server listening on TCP, Shared Memory,
Named Pipes.
2001-06-08 15:21:55.05 server     SQL server listening on 169.254.101.152:1433,
10.64.70.21:1433, 127.0.0.1:1433.
2001-06-08 15:21:55.05 server     SQL Server is ready for client connections
2001-06-08 15:21:56.33 spid5      Clearing tempdb database.
2001-06-08 15:22:02.45 spid5      Starting up database 'tempdb'.
2001-06-08 15:22:03.71 spid3      Recovery complete.
2001-06-08 15:22:20.22 spid51     Using 'xpstar.dll' version '2000.80.194' to
execute extended stored procedure 'sp_MSgetversion'.
2001-06-08 15:25:17.76 spid3      SQL Server is terminating due to 'stop'
request from Service Control Manager.
```

Microsoft creates a new SQL Server Agent Error Log each time the SQL Server Agent service starts. This log cycles and archives following the same rules as the SQL Server Error Log. Here is a sample Server Agent Log:

```
2001-06-18 22:08:42 - ? [100] Microsoft SQLServerAgent version 8.00.194 (x86
unicode retail build) : Process ID 1256
2001-06-18 22:08:42 - ? [101] SQL Server W2KAS version 8.00.194 (0 connection
limit)
2001-06-18 22:08:42 - ? [102] SQL Server ODBC driver version 3.80.194
2001-06-18 22:08:42 - ? [103] NetLib being used by driver is DBMSSHRN.DLL;
Local host server is (local)
2001-06-18 22:08:42 - ? [310] 1 processor(s) and 256 MB RAM detected
2001-06-18 22:08:42 - ? [339] Local computer is W2KAS running Windows NT 5.0
(2195) Service Pack 1
2001-06-18 22:08:42 - ? [129] SQLSERVERAGENT starting under Windows NT service
control
2001-06-18 22:08:42 - + [260] Unable to start mail session (reason: No mail
profile defined)
2001-06-18 22:08:42 - + [396] An idle CPU condition has not been defined -
OnIdle job schedules will have no effect
2001-06-18 22:08:49 - ? [131] SQLSERVERAGENT service stopping due to a stop
request from a user, process, or the OS...
2001-06-18 22:08:51 - ? [098] SQLServerAgent terminated (normally)
```

The Windows 2000 Application Log also proves very useful for installation troubleshooting. See Chapter 12 of this book for more information about the use of this log.

Starting SQL Server from the Command Line

You have the ability to start SQL Server 2000 from the command-line environment. This provides you with a large variety of switches you may use for troubleshooting and includes ways to start the server that have no graphical user interface equivalent.

In order to start SQL Server 2000 from the command prompt, make sure you navigate to the appropriate **BINN** directory for the instance you want to start (if you are using multiple SQL Server instances, of course). Once you are in the correct location, use the following syntax:

```
sqlservr [-sinstance_name] [-c] [-dmaster_path] [-f]
    [-eerror_log_path] [-lmaster_log_path] [-m]
    [-n] [-Ttrace#] [-v] [-x] [-g number] [-O] [-y number]
```

Here is an explanation of this syntax:

- **-s**—specifies the name of the instance to connect to.

- **-c**—indicates that an instance of SQL Server is started independently of the Windows NT Service Control Manager. This option shortens the amount of time it takes for SQL Server to start, but you cannot stop SQL Server by using SQL Server Service Manager or the **NET STOP** command. Also, logging off the Windows NT or Windows 2000 system stops the SQL Server.

- **-d**—indicates the fully qualified path for the master database file.

- **-f**—starts the server in minimally configured mode.

- **-e**—indicates the fully qualified path for the error log file.

- **-l**—indicates the fully qualified path for the master database transaction log file.

- **-m**—indicates to start an instance of SQL Server in single-user mode.

- **-n**—indicates that you do not want to use the Windows NT application log to log SQL Server events.

- **-T**—indicates that an instance of SQL Server should be started with a specified trace flag in effect. Trace flags are used to start servers with nonstandard behavior. SQL Server 2000 supports the following trace flags:

  - *260*—Prints versioning information about extended stored procedure dynamic-link libraries (DLLs).

  - *1204*—Returns the type of locks participating in a deadlock and the current command affected.

- *2528*—Disables parallel checking of objects by **DBCC CHECKDB**, **DBCC CHECKFILEGROUP**, and **DBCC CHECKTABLE**.

- *3205*—Disables hardware compression for tape drives.

- **-v**—indicates the server version number.

- **-x**—disables the maintenance of CPU statistics.

- **-g**—specifies an integer number of megabytes of memory to reserve for other applications running within SQL Server 2000.

- **-O**—specifies that **Distributed COM (DCOM)** is not required, thereby disabling heterogeneous queries.

- **-y**—if SQL Server 2000 encounters an error message specified in this option, it writes the symptom stack trace to the error log. You can specify multiple errors by using multiple **–y** arguments.

Troubleshooting Network Connections

Network connectivity is often an area of trouble for new installations. If you have local clients that can connect to your SQL Server 2000 installation but network clients that cannot, be sure to check the following:

- The network library you are using on the client must match a network library your SQL Server 2000 installation supports.

- The default client network library you chose must be appropriate for your network environment.

- You must have network connectivity between the client and the server. Utilize networking tools as necessary; for example, if you are in a TCP/IP network, use the PING utility to ensure network connectivity.

Troubleshooting Standard Installations

Should you receive an error during the standard installation using the Setup Wizard, follow this basic troubleshooting methodology:

1. If the underlying operating system reports an error, SQL Server 2000 translates most of these errors for you. If you do not understand the error you receive, check **http://support.microsoft.com** on the Internet for a more detailed explanation.

2. Check Sqlstp.log in the \Windows or \WINNT directory to see if the last few events in the log relate to the generation of the error message.

3. If you are performing a custom installation and the MSSearch service is failing to install properly, check the Mssearch.log in the \Temp directory. This log may contain additional information about the reason for the failure.

5

4. At this point, you should attempt to bypass the error message and continue setup. Often times, setup completes normally, as the error message was just a warning about a particular system configuration.

5. If you attempt to continue, the Setup program does in fact fail, and you cannot diagnose and fix the problem yourself, make a copy of Sqlstp.log and Setup.log from the \Windows or \WINNT directory. If you attempted to install Full-text Search, you should also make a copy of the Mssearch.log from the \Temp directory. These files are very valuable for tracking down the problem when working with a support technician.

There are several well-known and documented issues with setup that you need to be aware of. Here are those issues:

- SQL Server Setup may encounter problems installing MS DTC on computers with multiple network cards or SPX installed. If SQL Server Setup stops responding, check the Sqlstp.log in the \Windows or \WINNT directory to see if the problem is occurring at the installation of MS DTC. If this is the problem, uninstall one of the network cards or SPX, and then retry SQL Server Setup.

- If you try to install Microsoft Transaction Server (MTS) from the Windows NT 4.0 Option Pack after installing SQL Server2000, you might encounter an error message indicating that MTS could not be installed. You should check for the proper installation of MTS, because most likely it was installed properly, even though the error message states it could not be. This error message should not appear, and most of the time you can ignore it.

- If you click Back in the Select Components dialog box to change the type of installation during the installation of SQL Server 2000, nothing happens. This problem occurs only after you select Client Tools Only on the Installation Definition dialog box. This is a known problem with the setup program that Microsoft plans to fix in future versions. In order to select a different option, cancel the current setup process and run setup again.

- SQL Server 2000 setup may fail with the following error message—"The dynamic link library SQLUNIRL.dll could not be found in the specified path." This typically indicates you have a problem with your Microsoft Data Access Components (MDAC) installation. You may need to reinstall MDAC using the following steps:

1. Select Start|Run.

2. In the Run dialog box, type "regedt32", and then click OK.

3. Navigate to HKEY_LOCAL_MACHINE\SOFTWARE\Microsoft\Windows \CurrentVersion\Setup.

4. Click ExceptionComponents.

5. On the Edit menu, click Delete.

6. On the Registry menu, click Exit.

7. Restart your computer.

8. Finally, either reinstall SQL Server 2000 or run SQLREDIS.EXE.

- You may find that after you install SQL Server 2000 and you open the SQL Server Properties dialog box in Enterprise Manager, the path for Default Data Directory and Default Log Directory are blank on the Database Settings tab. This occurs because the Registry keys for the defaults are not present during setup. With the paths blank, a **CREATE DATABASE** statement uses the \Mssql\Data directory as the default location for the data and log files.

- You may receive the following error message when installing SQL Server 2000 Desktop Engine Edition on Windows 95 OSR2—"Cannot find file path (or one of its components). Check to ensure the path and filename are correct and that all required libraries are available." This error is by design, because SQL Server 2000 Desktop Engine Edition does not run on Windows 95. You should consider using Microsoft Data Engine (MSDE) **1** on 95 systems.

- The SQL Server 2000 Desktop Engine Edition features merge modules (.msm files) that you may embed into a Windows Installer—based setup application for the creation of an MSI file. When you try to modify the program or uninstall it later, the uninstallation may fail with the following error message—"The wizard was interrupted before <application name> could be successfully installed." Microsoft has solved this problem with a refresh CD. The refresh CD contains a new and full version of SQL Server 2000 Desktop Engine Edition and may be ordered from **support.microsoft.com**.

- The installation of the Desktop Engine Edition of SQL Server 2000 may fail on a system if any edition of SQL Server 2000 with Service Pack 1 is installed. The Desktop Engine Edition setup log includes the following error messages-"LoadLibrary failed for [path]\Binn\SEMNT.DLL.GetLastError() returned: 126" and "Microsoft SQL Server Desktop Engine—Installation operating failed." These errors occur when the Windows Installer does not copy certain essential files to the necessary directories because newer versions of these files already exist, even though these files are in a different location. To fix this problem, you should obtain the latest Service Pack for SQL Server 2000 at **support.microsoft.com**. You can also work around the problem by following these steps:

1. Prior to running the Desktop Engine Edition, you rename the following files as indicated:

   - \Program Files\Microsoft SQL Server\80\Tools\Binn\Resources\1033\Semnt.rll to Semnt.rld

   - \Program Files\Microsoft SQL Server\80\Tools\Binn\Resources\1033\Sqlsvc.rll to Sqlsvc.rld

- \Program Files\Microsoft SQL Server\80\Tools\Binn\Semnt.dll to Semnt.dld

- \Program Files\Microsoft SQL Server\80\Tools\Binn\Sqlsvc.dll to Sqlsvc.dld

- \Program Files\Microsoft SQL Server\80\Tools\Binn\Sqlresld.dll to Sqlresld.dld

2. Run the Desktop Engine Edition installation.

3. Rename the following files back to their original names as follows:

- \Program Files\Microsoft SQL Server\80\Tools\Binn\Resources\1033\Semnt.rld to Semnt.rll

- \Program Files\Microsoft SQL Server\80\Tools\Binn\Resources\1033\Sqlsvc.rld to Sqlsvc.rll

- \Program Files\Microsoft SQL Server\80\Tools\Binn\Semnt.dld to Semnt.dll

- \Program Files\Microsoft SQL Server\80\Tools\Binn\Sqlsvc.dld to Sqlsvc.dll

- \Program Files\Microsoft SQL Server\80\Tools\Binn\Sqlresld.dld to Sqlresld.dll

Note: You can also have a verbose setup log be written when installing the Desktop Engine Edition of SQL Server 2000. You do this by using the following command line switch:

```
/l*v [filename]
```

- Books Online contains an important error regarding the Desktop Engine Edition and Windows Installer. The "Merging the Desktop Engine into Windows Installer" topic incorrectly states that you can use the **SAPASSWORD** and **USEDDEFAULTSAPWD** parameters when you install the SQL Server 2000 Desktop Engine Edition by using Windows Installer Merge modules. By design,these parameters cannot be used.

- Running a setup program that uses the SQL Server 2000 Data Engine merge modules may produce the following error—"Setup requires Internet Explorer version 5.0.2314.0 or above." You may also receive the following error when you are installing on Windows 95,Windows 98, or Windows ME—"An internal error occurred during install (failed to load package id). Contact Microsoft Technical Support." Both of these errors have been resolved with a fix from Microsoft. This fix is available from **support.microsoft.com**.

- SQL Server 2000 Setup may stop responding after copying the files successfully. When this occurs, the hourglass displays without changing and there is no status change or message. This typically occurs because related services are running on the system. These related services are typically using ODBC or other shared components that prevent SQL Server Setup from using system resources. In order to work around this problem, follow these steps:

1. Make sure to notify all users that may be using ODBC-related services on the system.

2. Stop all services that may be using ODBC. These services include all Internet Information Services (Certificate Authority, Content Index, FTP Publishing Service, Gopher, IIS Admin Service, World Wide Web Publishing, Microsoft NNTP Service, Microsoft SMTP Service, Microsoft Message Queue Service, MSDTC), Microsoft Exchange Server, DBWeb, ARCserve backup, OnocuLAN virus protection, McAfee antivirus services, UniCenter system monitoring.

3. Setup should resume and complete normally. If you stopped setup, rerun it.

4. You may need to stop additional services in order for SQL Server Setup to complete normally.

- You may get the following error message when attempting to install SQL Server 2000—"Read Only File Detected. A read only file, c:\winnt\system32\mfc42u.dll, was found while attempting to copy files to the destination location. To overwrite the file, click the Yes button, otherwise click the No button." Another message that is displayed is "Setup. The specified file cannot be opened as write. Ensure the file is not in use and restart setup. File: C:\WINNT\System32\mfc42u.dll." Setup may complete if you ignore these error messages. There will be no shortcuts added to the Start menu, however. Installing SQL Server 2000 on a Windows NT 4 Server after the installation of Microsoft Visual Studio 6 causes this problem. In order to work around this problem, rename the file mfc42u.dll to mfc42u.original prior to attempting a reinstallation.

- If your Windows NT Server name is using mixed cases, you may have connection problems following installation. Specifically, connection attempts over the shared memory network library fail on a server where **GetComputerName** returns a lower- or mixed-case server name. When this connection attempt fails, SQL Server 2000 attempts to connect using an alternate protocol. A fix exists for this issue from **support.microsoft.com**.

- There is no option available to remove optional SQL Server 2000 components you may have installed. Using the Uninstall option in SQL Server 2000 Setup removes all of the components. This is by design and may change in future versions of SQL Server.

In addition to the above known problems, there are also common configuration problems that cause difficulties during installations. Examine Table 5.3 to be sure you are familiar with these possibilities.

Rerunning a failed installation, adding additional components to SQL Server 2000, or installing on a system that contains previous SQL Server versions can be tricky. You need to take certain steps before you attempt this:

- Be sure to shut down all SQL Services. This includes MSSQLServer, SQLServerAgent, MSSearch, and the MSDTC services.

Table 5.3   Common configuration problems and their solutions.

Problem	Solution
The SQL Server service does not start.	Often, this is a result of the user account assigned to the service. If this domain user account cannot be validated against a domain controller or it does not have the proper permissions, the service cannot start.
"Error 1069: The service did not start due to a logon failure."	The password for the user account assigned to the SQL Server service has expired.
The SQL Server Agent service does not start.	Often, this is a result of the user account assigned to the service. If this domain user account cannot be validated against a domain controller or it does not have the proper permissions, the service cannot start.
A SQL Server management tool cannot connect to the server.	This is often because the SQL Server service has not started.
"A connection could not be established to [servername]."	Check to see if the client and network libraries do not match, or you do not have the appropriate permissions.

- Close the SQL Server Service Manager icon in the system tray of the taskbar by right-clicking the icon and choosing Exit.

- Remove the read-only attribute for all ODBC* files on the system.

Note: You cannot remove Named Pipes from a Windows NT platform if you are trying to remove SQL Server 2000 from an NT system. Windows NT requires Named Pipes for other tasks.

Troubleshooting Remote Installations

There is one main issue Microsoft reports regarding installing SQL Server 2000 remotely: When performing remote installations of SQL Server 2000, the Upgrade, Remove, Or Add Components To An Existing Instance Of SQL Server option is not available. This is because a remote installation of SQL Server 2000 supports only a new instance, or client tool installations.

Troubleshooting Unattended Installations

Unattended installations of SQL Server 2000 may fail and return an error code. Use Table 5.4 to interpret these error codes.

There is also a known issue you should be aware of with unattended setups of SQL Server 2000: If you select the Per Processor licensing mode during a SQL Server installation, the licensing mode might be incorrectly saved to the Setup.iss file as Per Seat. As such, SQL Server Setup does not properly recognize the Per Processor licensing mode when you run an unattended installation. This problem has a fix located at **support.microsoft.com**. Reference article number Q273769.

Table 5.4 Unattended installation error codes.

Error Code	Description
0	Success
-1	General error
-2	Invalid mode
-3	Required data not found in the Setup.iss file
-4	Not enough memory available
-5	File does not exist
-6	Cannot write to the response file
-7	Cannot write to the log file
-8	Invalid path to the InstallShield Silent response file
-9	Not a valid list type (string or number)
-10	Data type is invalid
-11	Unknown error during setup
-12	Dialog boxes are out of order in the setup initialization file (Setup.iss)
-51	Cannot create the specified folder
-52	Cannot access the specified file or folder
-53	Invalid option selected

Rebuilding the Registry

If your installation proves to be troubled due to corruption, you might try to rebuild the SQL Server entries with the Registry Rebuild option in the Advanced Options Setup page of the Setup Wizard. This option allows you to rebuild the Registry automatically after a corrupt installation. This process fixes only the Registry; it does not fix data errors or modify the master database. To rebuild the master database, you should use the REBUILDM.EXE utility located in the Program Files\Microsoft SQL Server\80\Tools\Binn directory.

Troubleshooting Information Online

If, after all of the troubleshooting information in this chapter, you find you still need help, there are several excellent online resources you can turn to. These resources include:

- *SQL Troubleshooters* (**support.microsoft.com/support/sql/tshooter.asp**)—these interactive troubleshooters are there to help you with more than just setup issues. They actually interview you and assist in pinpointing problems.

- *MSDN* (**msdn.microsoft.com**)—The Microsoft Developers Network offers a massive "public" library free of charge. This library contains volumes and volumes of SQL information.

- *TechNet* (**www.microsoft.com/technet**)—Similar to MSDN, the TechNet site features a free library with excellent resources.

- *Microsoft Support* (**support.microsoft.com**)—This site allows you to type in specific error codes or messages you receive and find workarounds or fixes.

- *SQL Server Magazine* (**www.sqlmag.com**)—This is the online version of the popular SQL Server Magazine. This site also features robust search capabilities for problems and excellent forums.

- *SQL Server Home Page* (**www.microsoft.com/sql**)—This home page from Microsoft for SQL Server 2000 offers excellent information in addition to promoting the product.

- *Newsgroups*—There are many excellent SQL Server-related newsgroups. These can be found from the SQL Server Home Page.

Removing SQL Server

For a number of reasons, you might be interested in removing SQL Server 2000 from a system. Perhaps you were only testing server features or evaluating the product. You can remove instances of SQL Server 2000 using the following methods:

- Run SQL Server 2000 Setup and select the Uninstall option

- Run the Add/Remove Programs application in Control Panel (see Figure 5.10)

You must remove each named instance of SQL Server 2000 separately, and you cannot remove individual components of SQL Server 2000. In order to remove components, you must remove the entire instance of SQL Server 2000.

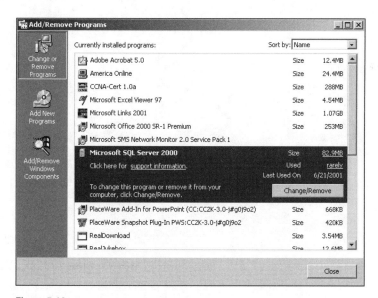

Figure 5.10
Removing SQL Server 2000 using Control Panel.

Before removing SQL Server 2000, you should end all applications, including the following:

- Windows NT Event Viewer

- Registry editor

- All SQL Server applications

- All applications dependent on SQL Server

Summary

Whether you are installing SQL Server 2000 remotely, performing an unattended installation, or physically sitting at the server with the installation media, there are many factors you need to consider for a successful installation. This chapter presented those factors and provided a step-by-step guide you should follow to ensure installation success. The importance of this chapter and Chapter 4 cannot be stressed enough. As you might imagine, without a successful installation of SQL Server 2000, the content presented in the remainder of this book is completely useless.

One very important installation topic remains to be addressed: upgrading an existing SQL Server installation to the 2000 version. Chapter 6 covers this important topic. If you are running *any* previous version of SQL Server, be sure you read the next chapter closely.

Upgrading to SQL Server 2000

Many of you reading this book are running previous versions of SQL Server in your networks. You may want to upgrade to SQL Server 2000, as opposed to replacing this previous version. Upgrading, if performed properly using this chapter as a guide, provides the simplest method of moving from a previous version to SQL Server 2000 with all data present and available in the new version.

You may have heard horror stories about upgrading to SQL Server 2000. Have no fear; just be sure to follow the advice provided here.

Planning for an Upgrade

Before you launch into the upgrade of a previous version of SQL Server, you need to plan for this dramatic step. This section discusses planning for upgrades from SQL Server 6.5 or 7.

Note: You cannot upgrade directly from SQL Server 6.0 to SQL Server 2000. You must upgrade to SQL Server 7, then SQL Server 2000, or convert the SQL Server 6.0 data to SQL Server 6.5, then perform the upgrade. Most prefer to upgrade first to SQL Server 7.

Running Multiple Versions of SQL Server

In addition to running multiple instances of SQL Server 2000, you may also run multiple versions of SQL Server on a single server. In fact, you can actually run SQL Server 6.5, 7, and 2000 all on the same system.

One method that allows you to accomplish this is version switching. Version switching permits SQL Server 7 or SQL Server 2000 to install as the default instance on a system already running SQL Server 6.5. In this configuration, you use the VSWITCH.EXE utility to switch between SQL Server 6.5 and SQL Server 7 or SQL Server 2000. Note that version switching does not permit you to run the different versions of SQL Server simultaneously, nor does it permit you to switch between SQL Server 7 and SQL Server 2000. You can run VSWITCH from the Start menu, or you can locate it in \Program Files\Microsoft SQL Server\Mssql\Binn.

Named instances offer another method for running multiple versions of SQL Server on a single system. Chapter 4 covers named instances in detail. If your system is running SQL Server 6.5 or SQL Server 7, you may install SQL Server 2000 as a named instance. Unlike version switching, this method permits multiple versions of SQL Server to run simultaneously.

NOTE: *When you install SQL Server 2000 as a named instance on a system running SQL Server 7, the SQL Server 7 client tools are upgraded to SQL Server 2000 versions.*

Selecting an Appropriate Upgrade Method

You have many options when it comes to upgrading your systems to SQL Server 2000. Be sure to read this section and refer to it as you are making key upgrade decisions. Notice there are many factors to consider when upgrading.

Upgrading SQL Server 6.5

To perform an upgrade of SQL Server 6.5 to SQL Server 2000 requires the use of the SQL Server Upgrade Wizard. Keep these facts in mind when considering this upgrade process:

- SQL Server 6.5 must be running Service Pack 5 to ensure a successful upgrade.

- SQL Server 6.5 must be offline, and therefore unavailable, to users of the network during the upgrade.

- You may be selective with the user databases that are upgraded, choosing to only upgrade select databases. All system databases are upgraded, of course.

- The Upgrade Wizard transfers replication settings, SQL Executive settings, and most other server configurations during the upgrade.

- Performing the upgrade process in this fashion features built-in recovery methods—the Upgrade Wizard restarts and resumes the upgrade in the event of major failures.

- The Upgrade Wizard does not remove SQL Server 6.5. The Wizard leaves this installation intact, as a fallback solution in case there are major problems with the upgraded version of SQL Server 2000.

- If hard disk space is at a premium during the upgrade, you may use a tape drive for additional storage space, although this is not recommended because it can negatively impact performance and reliability during the upgrade process.

- You may use the Upgrade Wizard to upgrade a SQL Server 6.5 system to another system that will run SQL Server 2000. This is an excellent method for both upgrading and moving your server as part of a single administrative process. This also permits you to have two version of SQL Server running simultaneously in your network.

- The Upgrade Wizard can only upgrade SQL Server 6.5 to the role of a SQL Server 2000 default instance. You cannot use the upgrade process to create named instances of SQL Server 2000.

Another available option is to migrate your SQL Server 6.5 data instead of performing the server upgrade. You have many ways of doing this, thanks to SQL Server 2000. You can use Data Transformation Services (DTS) or Bulk Copy Program (BCP), or you can perform a query between linked servers. Chapter 14 of this book examines these options for you.

To help you determine the upgrade method that is right for you, use Decision Tree 6.1.

6

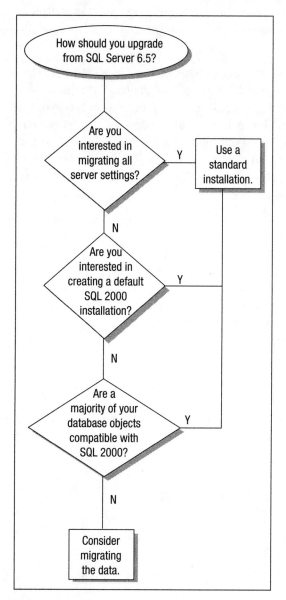

Decision Tree 6.1
Upgrading from SQL Server 6.5.

Upgrading SQL Server 7

Just as you have several options when it comes to upgrading SQL Server 6.5, you have several options when it comes to upgrading SQL Server 7. You can use the SQL Server 2000 Setup program to perform a version upgrade. However, this does not allow you to fall back to the previous version of SQL Server, as this process upgrades and overwrites all of the SQL Server 7 components. This upgrade method retains most of the SQL Server 7 settings, including replication, SQL Server Agent, and most server configuration settings. During this version upgrade process, SQL Server 7 must be offline, and therefore unavailable, to users of the databases.

You an also upgrade SQL Server 7 by using the Copy Database Wizard (See Figure 6.1) to perform an online database upgrade of the user databases of your choice. With this method, you can retain SQL Server 7 after the upgrade process, providing an excellent fallback solution in the event there are major problems with the upgrade. Also, when you upgrade databases in this manner, all user logon information and user-specific objects are migrated as well. And, this method gives you the option of leaving SQL Server 7 available and online while the upgrade takes place. Thus, users are able to interact with the server and access other data stores on the server.

If you decide to perform the upgrade using the Copy Database Wizard, you still have choices to consider. You can install SQL Server 2000 as a named instance on the SQL Server 7 system and then use the wizard. This obviously provides the speediest performance for the wizard. Yet, you can also use the Copy Database Wizard from one system to another. You can also use Data Transformation Services technology to schedule and automate this type of upgrade. For guidance in how to do this, see Chapter 14.

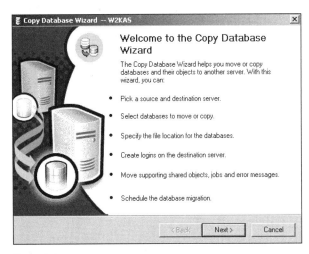

Figure 6.1
The Copy Database Wizard of SQL Server 2000.

Note: The Copy Database Wizard method of upgrading cannot be used with databases participating in replication.

To help you determine the upgrade method that is right for you, use Decision Tree 6.2.

Replication Issues with Upgrading

6

As you might gather from the previous note, the upgrading of servers participating in replication requires some special considerations and planning. If your servers for upgrade are participating in replication, you must upgrade the Distributor(s) first, the Publisher(s) second, and finally, the Subscribers(s). Proceeding in this order lets you continue to replicate data even though you have a substantial upgrade project in process.

Note: If you are using transactional replication, you can upgrade the Subscribers before the Publisher. If you are using immediate updating with snapshot replication or transactional replication, there are additional upgrade recommendations in this section.

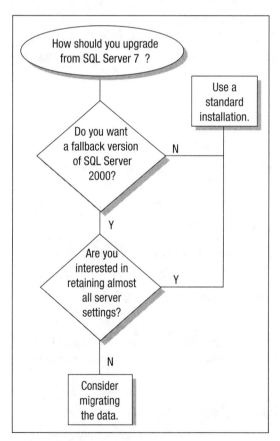

Decision Tree 6.2
Upgrading from SQL Server 7.

Be sure to review these other replication issues regarding SQL Server 2000 upgrades prior to performing them:

- For upgrading to SQL Server 2000 from SQL 7 systems participating in replication, you should set the database compatibility level to 70 or later. If you have servers running in the 65 compatibility level or earlier, you should temporarily change them to 70 or later during the upgrade process. If the Publisher or Subscriber is running in the 65 compatibility level or earlier during an upgrade to SQL Server 2000, error 15048 is raised. This error states that the operation is supported only on SQL Server version 7 or SQL Server 2000. (Database compatibility levels are covered in detail in Chapter 7.)

- If you are upgrading replication on a failover cluster, you must *uncluster* the previous installation before upgrading. Unclustering requires that you delete all publications, remove replication, then reconfigure replication after upgrading to SQL Server 2000.

- If you are using immediate updating with snapshot replication or transactional replication, you should be aware of changes to these replication types in SQL Server 2000. In SQL Server 2000, rows in immediate updating articles use a **unique identifier** column to identify versions. In SQL Server 7.0, a **timestamp** column was used. In addition, the triggers generated for immediate updating have been changed to accommodate queued updating. Therefore, if you are using immediate updating you should:

  1. Upgrade both the Publisher and Subscriber before replicating data.

  2. Drop the publication and all subscriptions to the publication.

  3. Use an **ALTER TABLE DROP COLUMN** Transact-SQL statement to drop the **timestamp** column from the tables on the Publisher and from the tables on the Subscriber that allow Subscriber updates.

  4. Re-create the publication and subscriptions.

- If errors occur while upgrading replication servers, they might be related to the database being offline or unavailable. You should also be wary of script failures.

- You should stop all data modifications at the replication server while it is being upgraded.

- When upgrading from SQL Server 6.5, you must run the Log Reader Agent and Distribution Agent before upgrading to make sure there are no replicated commands pending delivery to Subscribers.

Additional Hardware and Software Requirements

In Chapter 4 of this book, you learned the hardware and software requirements for installing SQL Server 2000. You must modify these requirements slightly for upgrades from previous versions of SQL Server. In fact, the exact modifications you must make will differ depending on which previous version of SQL Server you are upgrading, and exactly how you are performing the upgrade.

SQL Server 6.5 Upgrades

Upgrades from SQL Server 6.5 to SQL Server 2000 require both specific software and specific hardware requirements. Be sure to meet the following requirements when performing this task:

- If you are upgrading SQL Server 6.5 running on a Windows NT 4 system and you are going to install SQL Server 2000 on that same system, you must be running Service Pack 5 or higher for Windows NT 4. You also must be running Internet Explorer 5.0 or higher.

- As mentioned earlier, you also must be running Service Pack 5 for SQL Server 6.5. If you are not installing SQL Server 2000 on the same system as SQL Server 6.5, only Service Pack 3 must be applied to SQL Server 6.5.

- For the upgrade to succeed, SQL Server 6.5 and SQL Server 2000 must be set to use named pipes, and both must be set to use the default pipe \\.\pipe\sql\query.

- Additional free hard disk space is required to perform an upgrade. Space that is approximately 1.5 times the size of the SQL Server 6.5 user databases must be available. The SQL Server Upgrade Wizard can help you estimate this amount.

SQL Server 7 Upgrades

Upgrades from SQL Server 7 to SQL Server 2000 also require both specific software and specific hardware requirements. Be sure to meet the following requirements when performing this task:

- Version upgrades for SQL Server 7 running on Windows NT 4 require Service Pack 5 or higher for Windows NT 4 and Internet Explorer 5 or higher.

- SQL Server 7 requires no service pack levels prior to the upgrade.

- Version upgrades require the use of named pipes. Both SQL Server 7 and SQL Server 2000 must be set to use the default pipe \\.\pipe\sql\query.

- Online database upgrades using the Copy Database Wizard do not require the use of named pipes. In this configuration, any available Net-Library may be used.

- Version upgrades of SQL Server 7 to SQL Server 2000 require no additional hard disk space.

- Online database upgrades require additional hard disk space if a database copy is used, as opposed to a database move.

Preparing for the Upgrade

In addition to the considerations mentioned above, there are some final steps you should take prior to performing version upgrades of the previous SQL Server versions. This section describes these steps.

SQL Server 6.5 Upgrades

If you are performing a version upgrade of SQL Server 6.5, be sure to perform these steps prior to the upgrade:

- Set the tempdb system database size to 10MB or more. (25MB for the database size is recommended.)

- Verify that the master database has at least 3MB of free space more.

- Verify that the master database contains logon information for all users.

- Disable any startup stored procedures.

SQL Server 6.5 and SQL Server 7 Upgrades

Additional steps for performing a version upgrade for either SQL Server 6.5 or SQL Server 7 include:

- Stop all user activity in all databases and obtain exclusive use of all SQL Server files.

- Back up all system and user databases.

- Run the appropriate DBCC commands to ensure database consistency. (See Chapter 12 for more information on these commands.)

- Disable all jobs.

- Close all applications.

- Stop replication.

- Ensure the replication log is empty.

- Ensure enough free disk space is available.

- Upgrade all databases with cross-database dependencies at the same time.

Upgrading from SQL Server 6.5

This section guides you through the actual process of upgrading from SQL Server 6.5 to SQL Server 2000. Keep in mind that this upgrade is more difficult than upgrading from SQL Server 7 to SQL Server 2000, and there are many more compatibility issues to consider.

Performing the Upgrade

Performing a version upgrade of SQL Server 6.5 to SQL Server 2000 begins by running the SQL Server Upgrade Wizard from a computer on which you have installed SQL Server 2000 running as a default instance. In addition to finding this wizard on the Start menu as depicted in the steps below, you can also find it in the Upgrade folder of your SQL Server 2000 installation. The executable is named UPGRADE.EXE. You also need to connect to this SQL Server 2000 instance using SQL Server authentication. You may need to set the server for this authentication mode for purposes of the installation.

Follow these steps for launching the SQL Server Upgrade Wizard and performing the upgrade process from SQL Server 6.5:

1. Select Start|Programs|Microsoft SQL Server-Switch to SQL Server Upgrade Wizard. Selecting this shortcut launches the SQL Server Upgrade Wizard and the Welcome page of the wizard appears. (See Figure 6.2.) Choose Next to advance to the Data and Object Transfer page of the wizard.

2. The Data And Object Transfer page allows you to select the upgrade method to use. (See Figure 6.3.) You can perform a direct upgrade on the same computer using named pipes or a tape drive if one is installed. You can also choose to perform additional verification options. If you do, the wizard compares a list of all of the SQL Server 6.5 objects prior to the upgrade to a list of objects following the upgrade. Any discrepancies are reported by the wizard, and this verification is above and beyond verifications provided by the logs described in the previous chapter. You can also specify that the Upgrade Wizard perform an exhaustive byte-by-byte comparison of data in each column to make sure that no data has changed or been corrupted during the upgrade. Note that selecting this option dramatically increases the time required for the upgrade. Once you have selected the appropriate options for your upgrade, choose Next to advance to the Logon page of the wizard.

3. The Logon page permits you to specify the name of the SQL Server 6.5 system that you want to upgrade. (See Figure 6.4.) The Wizard refers to this system as the export server. Note that the SQL Server 2000 system you are upgrading to must be the SQL Server 2000 system running the Upgrade Wizard and this system is referred to as the import server. You must also specify the password for the SQL Server administrator account (sa) for both the import and the export servers. This page of the Wizard also permits you to specify optional startup arguments for the import and export servers. These optional startup arguments may include trace flags as discussed in the last chapter. When you have completed this page, choose Next.

4. The Upgrade Wizard now presents a warning dialog box to remind you that both of the SQL Server installations need to be restarted using the authentication information and startup parameters you provided. Choose Next.

Figure 6.2
The SQL Server Upgrade Wizard.

5. The Code Page Selection page appears. SQL Server examined the code page used by SQL Server 6.5 during the restart of this version. Because you most likely want to use the same code page, most of the time you can select the code page presented by the wizard here. Choose Next once you have made your selection.

6. The Upgrade Databases To SQL Server 2000 page appears. Here you select the specific user databases you are interested in upgrading. You should upgrade as many data-bases at the same time as possible. Choose Next once you have made your selections.

7. The Database Creation page appears. Here you can modify the data file and log file specifications the Upgrade Wizard uses to create the databases. This is an excellent opportunity to move these data and log files, or modify their size. When you have made these selections, choose Next.

8. The System Configuration page appears. Here you select system objects to transfer, including server configuration information, replication settings, and SQL Executive settings. Here you also select the **ANSI_NULLS** and **QUOTED_IDENTIFIER** settings. **ANSI_NULLS** settings specify the SQL-92 compliant behavior of the Equals (=) and Not Equal To (<>) comparison operators when used with null values, whereas **QUOTED_IDENTIFIER** settings prompt SQL Server to follow the SQL-92 rules regarding quotation mark delimiting identifiers and literal strings. Identifiers delimited by double quotation marks can be either Transact-SQL reserved keywords or can contain characters not usually allowed by the Transact-SQL syntax rules for identifiers. Choose Next when you are finished with these selections.

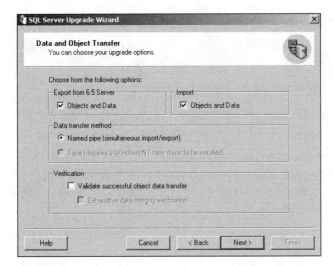

Figure 6.3
The Data And Object Transfer page.

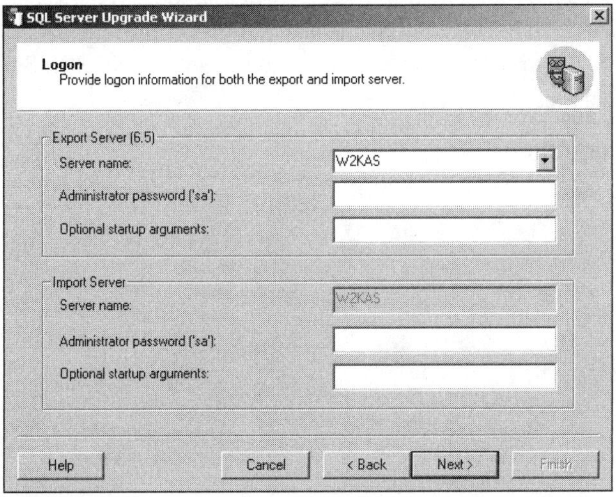

Figure 6.4
The Logon page.

9. The Completing The SQL Server Upgrade Wizard appears. This page provides a summary of your Upgrade Wizard selections and lists any warning messages that apply to your upgrade. When you are ready to actually start the upgrade process, choose Finish.

10. As the upgrade transpires, the wizard displays each step in the SQL Server Upgrade Script Interpreter dialog box. Details of any errors are displayed here as well.

Backward Compatibility Factors

For the most part, SQL Server 2000 is compatible with SQL Server 6.5. Issues can arise, however, in the following areas:

- *Configuration options*—Some server configuration options have changed.

- *Tasks*—SQL Server 2000 uses jobs instead of tasks, and provides new system tables and system stored procedures for automating administrative procedures.

- *Replication and Triggers*—Replication types that allow data modifications at the Subscriber use triggers to track changes to published tables. If you use triggers in your SQL Server application to modify published tables, you should use the **sp_configure** server option to ensure nested triggers are enabled.

- *Segments and Devices*—SQL Server 2000 use files and filegroups instead of segments and devices for storing indexes and tables. This should not cause problems for your SQL Server applications, unless they are specifically looking for the earlier segments and devices.

- *System Tables*—If your SQL Server application needs to access system tables, it is recommended that you use system stored procedures or information schema views. Also be aware that some SQL Server 6.5 system tables no longer exist in SQL Server 2000. Tables that no longer exist are:

  - **master.dbo.spt_datatype_info**
  - **sysbackupdetail**
  - **sysbackuphistory**
  - **syshistory**
  - **syskeys**
  - **syslocks**
  - **sysprocedures**
  - **sysrestoredetail**
  - **sysrestorehistory**
  - **syssegments**
  - **systasks**
  - **sysusages**

- *Backup and Restore*—SQL Server 2000 uses **BACKUP** and **RESTORE** statements in place of **DUMP** and **LOAD**. Although **DUMP** and **LOAD** can still be used with SQL Server 2000, you should avoid them as there are some limitations and caveats with their usage.

- *System Stored Procedures*—Be aware that some SQL Server 6.5 system stored procedures are no longer supported under SQL Server 2000.

Post-Upgrade Tasks

There are tasks that you typically need to perform following the upgrade process, such as removing SQL Server 6.5 from the system and troubleshooting upgrade problems. This section describes those tasks.

Troubleshooting the SQL Server 6.5 Upgrade

The most common problem with the SQL Server 6.5 upgrade is the Upgrade Wizard failing to create certain database objects in SQL Server 2000. The most common reasons for this problem are as follows:

- Text regarding the missing objects is not present in the **syscomments** table.

- Objects were renamed using the **sp_rename** stored procedure. SQL Server does not update the **syscomments** table when this stored procedure is used.

- Stored procedures were embedded in other stored procedures. Unfortunately, **syscomments** does not contain entries for these stored procedures.

- Tables and views have **NULL** column names. These objects cannot be scripted by the Upgrade Wizard.

- Tables were created on behalf of a user who does not have **CREATE** permissions.

- A stored procedure modifies a system table or references a system table that does not exist in SQL Server 2000.

Problems also occur with the upgrade if you have a server name that does not match the server name returned by the **@@SERVERNAME** function. If this happens, you should use the **sp_dropserver** and **sp_addserver** system stored procedures to change the server name returned by **@@SERVERNAME**.

Removing SQL Server 6.5

When you have thoroughly tested your new SQL Server 2000 implementation, and you are satisfied that the upgrade was a complete success, you can remove SQL Server 6.5, if you so desire. Thankfully, removing SQL Server 6.5 is a simple matter. Use the Start menu to navigate to the SQL Server 6.5 group. In this group, select Remove SQL Server 6.5.

Upgrading from SQL Server 7

Performing a version upgrade of SQL Server 7 to SQL Server 2000 is a much simpler task than performing the version upgrade of 6.5 to 2000, because the two platforms are much more similar. This section walks you through this version upgrade process and provides key post-upgrade tasks that you should perform.

Performing the Upgrade

Performing a version upgrade of SQL Server 7 to SQL Server 2000 is amazingly simple: simply run the SQL Server 2000 Setup program from the installation CD-ROM on the system running SQL Server 7. The setup program detects the 7 version of SQL Server running on the system and provides you with the option of upgrading, removing, or adding components to this existing installation. Obviously, choose the option to Upgrade Your Existing Installation From The Existing Installation dialog box when it appears.

The only other configuration information you must provide is the security settings used to connect to the SQL Server 7 installation. After you provide this information, and the setup program verifies that it can truly connect using this information, the upgrade commences. System databases, the registry, MDAC 2.6, and all of the client tools are included in the upgrade automatically.

Post-Upgrade Tasks

There are a number of tasks you should perform following this version upgrade process. In addition to troubleshooting the upgrade using the information provided in this section, you should also:

• Review the SQL Server error logs described in Chapter 5 of this book.

• Repopulate all full-text catalogs if you were using full-text search capabilities in SQL Server 7.

• Update database statistics.

• Register servers in Enterprise Manager, as SQL Server 7 systems are not registered automatically with the Enterprise Manager of SQL Server 2000.

You also need to manually upgrade the Meta Data Services Information Models used by DTS, as the SQL Server Setup program does not do this for you. To upgrade the information models, you need the SQL Server 2000 installation files in order to access the appropriate *.rdm files. You also need INSREPIM.EXE, the model installation program that creates or updates the Meta Data Services tables and installs information models. This program installs on your system during the SQL Server 2000 installation. Finally, you need a batch file to install the models. This file must reside in the directory that contains the INSREPIM.EXE file. After creating the batch file, simply run it from a command prompt.

Use the following batch file to perform this manual upgrade of these services. Simply replace **<path>**, **<servername>**, **<sa>**, and **<password>** in the batch file with information specific to your installation:

```
REM  Usage:  InsRepIM.exe
REM  Syntax:  /f[Model File] /r[Repository connect string] /u[User] /
p[Password]
REM
insrepim.exe /f<path>\uml.rdm /rserver=<servername>;database=msdb /u<sa> /
p<password>
insrepim.exe /f<path>\umx.rdm /rserver=<servername>;database=msdb /u<sa> /
p<password>
insrepim.exe /f<path>\gen.rdm /rserver=<servername>;database=msdb /u<sa> /
p<password>
insrepim.exe /f<path>\dtm.rdm /rserver=<servername>;database=msdb /u<sa> /
p<password>
insrepim.exe /f<path>\dbm.rdm /rserver=<servername>;database=msdb /u<sa> /
p<password>
insrepim.exe /f<path>\tfm.rdm /rserver=<servername>;database=msdb /u<sa> /
p<password>
insrepim.exe /f<path>\dts.rdm /rserver=<servername>;database=msdb /u<sa> /
p<password>
insrepim.exe /f<path>\sql.rdm /rserver=<servername>;database=msdb /u<sa> /
p<password>
insrepim.exe /f<path>\db2.rdm /rserver=<servername>;database=msdb /u<sa> /
p<password>
insrepim.exe /f<path>\ocl.rdm /rserver=<servername>;database=msdb /u<sa> /
p<password>
insrepim.exe /f<path>\ifx.rdm /rserver=<servername>;database=msdb /u<sa> /
p<password>
insrepim.exe /f<path>\olp.rdm /rserver=<servername>;database=msdb /u<sa> /
p<password>
insrepim.exe /f<path>\mds.rdm /rserver=<servername>;database=msdb /u<sa> /
p<password>
insrepim.exe /f<path>\sim.rdm /rserver=<servername>;database=msdb /u<sa> /
p<password>
```

You must also manually upgrade the repository database used by Meta Data Services. In order to accomplish this, pass the **REPOS_CONN_UPGRADE** flag when you open the repository database using the new repository engine 3.0 that SQL Server 2000 installs on your system. This **REPOS_CONN_UPGRADE** flag upgrades the repository database tables to the most recent version.

Troubleshooting SQL Server 7 Upgrades

If you try to install SQL Server 7 on a computer that already has a default instance of SQL Server 2000, SQL Server 7 Setup displays the following warning message—"Setup has detected a previous 6.x version of SQL Server but cannot obtain the sort order and character set from the 6.x SQL Server service. If you continue with setup it will install a sort order and character set which may be different from the previous 6.x version. Should you choose to convert your existing data at a later time to the newer version, successful conversion cannot be guaranteed. Do you wish to continue?" Unfortunately, continuing causes Setup to fail. SQL Server 7 Setup mistakenly treats SQL Server 2000 as if it were SQL Server 6.5, because SQL Server 7 cannot properly recognize the newer version of SQL Server 2000. You can work around this problem by performing the Registry rebuild through SQL Server 2000 setup.

Also, be sure you provide sufficient space for database growth during the upgrade process. Failure to do so may corrupt the **sysdepends** table in the model database or may cause the upgrade process to stop responding without providing you with any informational message during the upgrade.

Removing SQL Server 7

When you are ready to remove the SQL Server 7 instance from your upgraded system, simply use the Start menu to navigate to the SQL Server 7 group. Once there, select Uninstall SQL Server 7.

Performing an Online Database Upgrade from SQL Server 7

Remember, another powerful option for upgrading your SQL Server 7 installation is to not really upgrade it at all! Instead, you use the Copy Database Wizard to upgrade user databases that you select. This section describes this process for you, and also details post-upgrade tasks you should follow.

Performing the Online Database Upgrade

In order to perform an online database upgrade, follow these steps on your SQL Server 2000 system:

1. Select Start|Programs|Microsoft SQL Server|Enterprise Manager.

2. In Enterprise Manager, expand your server and select the Databases mode.

3. Select the Tools menu option and choose Wizards.

4. In the Select Wizard dialog box, expand the Management option and select Copy Database Wizard and click OK.

5. Choose Next in the Welcome to the Database Wizard page.

6. In the Select A Source Server page of the wizard, select a server to copy databases from. (See Figure 6.5.) You can use the ellipses [...] button to browse for the server on your network. Provide the security credentials to make the connection to this server and choose Next.

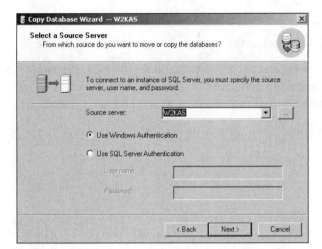

Figure 6.5
Selecting a source server.

7. In the Select A Destination Server page, select a destination for the databases you choose to copy. Once again, you may browse for the server using the ellipses button. Also, specify the security credentials to make a connection to the server you select. Click Next when you finish with these selections.

8. In the Select A Database To Move Or Copy page, select the appropriate databases to move or copy. You can select multiple databases for these tasks. Be sure that a database with the same name does not exist on the destination server or the process will fail. Also notice that you can only move user databases. Click Next when you finish.

9. Use the Database File Locations page to change the default locations for data or log files. Notice this page also informs you of available hard disk space on the destination drive. Choose Next when finished.

10. Use the Select Related Objects page to exclude specific login accounts for the move or copy. Choose Next when finished.

11. Use the Schedule The DTS Package page to schedule this online database upgrade process. You can perform the upgrade immediately, or you can schedule it to occur at some later point in time. Configure the appropriate settings and choose Next.

12. In the Completing The Copy Database Wizard page, review the options you have selected and choose Finish.

13. If you scheduled the move or copy to take place immediately, the Log Detail dialog box displays as the process completes. This dialog displays information about each step of the process. This dialog also displays most errors should they occur.

Post-Upgrade Tasks

You should perform the following actions following an online database upgrade:

- Remove the data and log files from the source system if you no longer require them there, as is typically the case if you performed database moves. The wizard does not remove these files from the source system in either a copy or a move operation.

- Repopulate all full-text catalogs if you were using full-text search capabilities in SQL Server 7.

- Update database statistics.

Summary

Use this chapter if you need to upgrade a previous version SQL Server to SQL Server 2000. Remember, there are specific concerns you should be aware of depending on which version of SQL Server you are currently running, and exactly how you wish to perform the upgrade.

Now that SQL Server 2000 is installed, it is time to cover other database administrator responsibilities. The next chapter of this book discusses creating databases on SQL Server 2000, a logical starting point following proper installation.

Chapter 7

Creating and Maintaining Databases

SQL Server is only as functional as the administrator who creates and manages the databases. By constructing an effective design plan, you save yourself hours of needless effort moving and resizing your databases to continue to meet the databases' original intended purpose. Therefore, it is important to your success to adequately plan for the size of the database before you begin to create the database.

In this chapter, I focus on the components of a database, optimum placements of database files, how SQL Server stores and manipulates data and transactions, setting database options, continued maintenance of the database files, and actually creating the database.

What Is a SQL Server Database?

A database is a collection of tables that contain data and SQL Server objects such as views, stored procedures, triggers, and indexes. All of these objects work together to organize similar types of information.

A *table* is a grouping of rows (horizontal) and columns (vertical). Rows are commonly referred to as records or *tuples* and columns may be referred to as *attributes*. Each column is designed to store a specific type of information such as birth dates, employee ID numbers, dollar amounts, or serial numbers.

Tables feature several types of controls known as constraints, rules, triggers, defaults, and customized user data types. These data types guarantee the validity of the data. Tables may have indexes placed on them as well. Indexes are similar to those found in books—they allow quick location and retrieval of information. You can add declarative referential integrity (DRI) constraints to the tables to make sure that data in different tables remains consistent. A database can also store procedures that use Transact-SQL statements to perform specialized operations to the database.

Microsoft SQL Server physically stores your database using a set of primary, secondary, and transaction log operating-system files. These files store all data and objects in the database, including the tables, stored procedures, triggers, and views. (See Figure 7.1.) Table 7.1 describes these files.

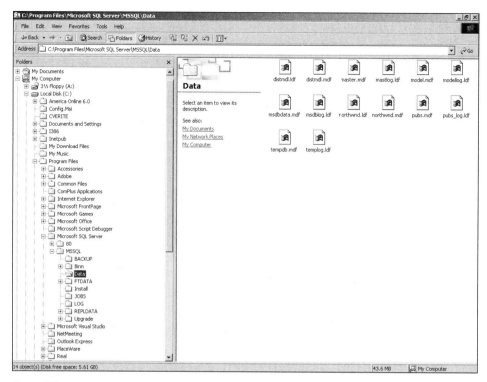

Figure 7.1
Physical database files of SQL Server 2000.

Table 7.1   The database files of SQL Server 2000.

File type	Description	Note
Primary (*.mdf)	Stores startup information and data	Mandatory for every database
Transaction log (*.ldf)	Stores log information for recovery operations	One or more in each database
Secondary (*.ndf)	Stores data that you want separate from the primary file	Optional number depending on your storage requirements

These files have both operating system file names and logical file names. Logical names are used in your Transact-SQL statements. The default location for all data files and transactions logs is C:\Program Files\Microsoft SQL Server\MSSQL\Data.

You might create a simple equipment inventory database named equipdb. You create this database with one primary file that contains all data and objects. This database also consists of a log file that contains transaction log information. You might also create a complex customer database named customerdb. This database might consist of one primary file and five secondary files along with four transactions log files. This permits you to store the data across these multiple files and not only to store it on different physical drives, but to manage the data separately as well.

Database Architectures

Understanding how SQL Server 2000 data is stored and the architectures used within your database is critical for you as a database administrator. This information helps you to plan your databases properly and can aid you dramatically when troubleshooting problems in your data storage endeavors.

Database Storage

When you create a new database, SQL Server 2000 copies the model system database and uses this system database as a template for the creation of your new database. Keep this in mind as you are creating new databases. Any features you would like new databases to have upon their initial creation, you can implement by modifying the model database. For example, increasing the size of the model database means that new databases begin with this initial size setting by default.

Obviously, as information is stored in your database, SQL Server 2000 must allocate space within the database files on disk to physically store the data. Data is physically stored on disk systems within the data files in 8KB (kilobyte) blocks of contiguous space called pages. Rows of data in a table within the database cannot span pages, which means the maximum amount of data that can be stored in a single row is 8060 bytes. This calculation does subtract some space for overhead involved in the process.

Tables and indexes, the main storage components of databases, are stored in structures called *extents*. An extent is eight contiguous pages—thus 64KB of space. If a particular table is so small that there is additional space in the extent, this additional space can be shared by other objects. Up to eight objects can share an extent. In this configuration, the extent is known as a *mixed extent*. If your extent contains a single object, it is known as a *uniform extent*.

When you create a new database—and therefore a new table or index—SQL Server 2000 uses free pages in mixed extents to store the new object. When the new object fills eight pages, SQL Server 2000 begins allocating uniform extents to the storage process for the object. SQL Server 2000 uses a Secondary Global Allocation Map (SGAM) to locate the mixed extents required in this data storage process. A Global Allocation Map (GAM) is used in order to identify uniform extents for data storage. An Index Allocation Map (IAM) is used to track all of the pages assigned to a particular object. Finally, Page Free Space (PFS) pages are used to quickly identify pages of free space when you create new objects in SQL Server. SQL Server 2000 uses these various maps and pages quite effectively to ensure efficient data storage whenever needed.

Without the use of indexes, SQL Server 2000 stores data on any available page allocated to your table using the process described above. This resultant group of data pages representing your data is referred to as a *heap*. If you need to locate specific data records, SQL Server 2000 must call upon the IAM and search all of the pages in the heap for the data. This is very inefficient, especially if there is a large amount of data in the table.

Indexes speed the retrieval of data stored by SQL Server 2000. SQL Server supports clustered indexes and non-clustered indexes. Clustered indexes actually force the physical ordering of data within the data files based on a key value. As additional data is stored in the database, existing data is moved as necessary to maintain this ordering. Obviously, this process dramatically speeds up the retrieval of data. Non-clustered indexes do not physically reorder the data as it is stored in the data files. Instead, these structures speed up the retrieval of data by creating an index of pointers to data-specific data rows.

SQL Server Transactions

Remember, every database must have at least one transaction log file associated with it. This transaction log holds the information necessary to recover the database in the event of a system failure. As its name implies, the transaction log maintains a record of transactions in SQL Server.

A transaction is a set of one or more Transact-SQL statements that SQL Server 2000 treats as a single unit of work and recovery. These logical units of work must provide four characteristics to qualify as a SQL transaction. You can remember these characteristics with the mnemonic ACID. The characteristics are atomicity, consistency, isolation, and durability. Table 7.2 describes these characteristics of transactions.

SQL Server 2000 performs either implicit transactions or explicit transactions. Which it uses is largely up to you as the database administrator or developer. SQL Server performs implicit transactions by default when it processes any of the following Transact-SQL statements:

• **ALTER TABLE**
• **CREATE**
• **DELETE**
• **DROP**
• **FETCH**
• **GRANT**
• **INSERT**
• **OPEN**
• **REVOKE**
• **SELECT**

- **TRUNCATE TABLE**

- **UPDATE**

These statements do not need to be followed with a **COMMIT TRANSACTION** statement, because, by default, SQL Server 2000 runs in autocommit mode. You can configure the server to run in implicit transaction mode, however. In this mode, even the above commands must be followed with **COMMIT TRANSACTION** to be processed as a transaction by the server. Use the **SET IMPLICIT_TRANSACTIONS ON** statement in your code to set the server in implicit transaction mode.

You can also specify explicit transactions in SQL Server 2000. With an explicit transaction, you explicitly define both the start and end of the transaction. In DB-Library applications and Transact-SQL scripts, you use the **BEGIN TRANSACTION**, **COMMIT TRANSACTION**, **COMMIT WORK**, **ROLLBACK TRANSACTION**, or **ROLLBACK WORK** Transact-SQL statements to define your explicit transactions. Table 7.3 describes these statements.

You can also use explicit transactions in OLE DB. To start a transaction; call the **ITransactionLocal:: StartTransaction** method. Call either the **ITransaction::Commit** or **ITransaction::Abort** method with *fRetaining* set to **FALSE** to end the transaction without automatically starting another transaction.

Table 7.2   Characteristics of transactions in SQL Server 2000.

Characteristic	Description
Atomicity	Either all of the transaction's data modifications are performed, or none of them are performed
Consistency	Upon completion, all of the data from the transaction must be in a consistent state
Isolation	Modifications made by concurrent transactions must be isolated from the modifications made by any other concurrent transactions
Durability	After a transaction has completed, its effects are permanently in place in the system

Table 7.3   Explicit transaction statements.

Statement	Description
BEGIN TRANSACTION	Marks the starting point of an explicit transaction
COMMIT TRANSACTION	Marks the end of a successful implicit or user-defined transaction
COMMIT WORK	Ends a transaction successfully if no errors were encountered
ROLLBACK TRANSACTION	Rolls back an explicit or implicit transaction to the beginning of the transaction, or to a savepoint inside a transaction
ROLLBACK WORK	Erases a transaction in which errors were encountered

In ActiveX Data Objects (ADO), you use the **BeginTrans** method on a Connection object to start an explicit transaction. To end the transaction, you call the Connection object's **CommitTrans** or **RollbackTrans** methods.

The Open Database Connectivity Application Programming Interface (ODBC API) does not support explicit transactions, only autocommit and implicit transactions.

You should note that explicit transaction mode lasts only for the duration of the transaction. When the transaction ends, the connection to SQL Server 2000 returns to the transaction mode it was in before the explicit transaction was started, either implicit or autocommit mode.

The SQL Server Transaction Log

Every SQL Server database must have at least one transaction log—even if you plan on configuring the database to not rely on the log system for recoverability. By default SQL Server 2000 records every transaction in this log to maintain database consistency and to aid in recovery should problems occur. SQL Server transaction logs are known as write-ahead logs. Transactions are logged as SQL Server 2000 processes the transactions, which means the logging occurs prior to the data being written to the database.

Note: The fact that transactions are logged prior to data being written to the database is one reason that write-caching disk controllers can cause such a problem for SQL Server 2000.

Here is the exact series of steps that occur with SQL Server 2000 transaction logging:

1. A data modification is sent to SQL Server 2000.

2. SQL Server loads the appropriate data pages into a buffer cache in memory.

3. SQL Server logs the data modifications to the transaction log as they are processed.

4. Periodically, a checkpoint process writes completed transactions to the database on the physical disk system.

Should there be a system failure during processing, SQL Server 2000 boasts an automatic recovery process, thanks to the write-ahead transaction log. All committed transactions are automatically rolled forward, and any incomplete transactions are automatically rolled back.

As you have already learned, the checkpoint process is critical to transaction logging. This process manages the number of pages stored in the buffer cache by ensuring these pages are periodically written to disk. This helps to minimize the time required for recovery should there be a server failure. Checkpoints occur in the overall transaction log process whenever any of the four following conditions occur:

- A **CHECKPOINT** Transact-SQL statement is issued.

- The **ALTER DATABASE** statement occurs.

- SQL Server 2000 stops normally.

- SQL Server 2000 issues an automatic checkpoint; the server does this periodically based on the number of records in the active portion of the transaction log.

Database Recovery Models

A new feature of SQL Server 2000 allows you to specify the exact recovery model any of your user databases follow in the RDBMS system. Each of these models affects not only the size of your transaction log, but also the methods by which you can recover the database in the event of failure. Having this flexibility on a per database basis increases the manageability of your database storage. You may configure each database for one of three recovery models: Full Recovery, Bulk-Logged, or Simple.

The Full Recovery model causes the heaviest possible use of the transaction log, because all database operations are fully logged to ensure recoverability to any point in time for the database. Included in transaction logging are large-scale data operations such as **BULK INSERT** statements, use of the bcp utility, and **SELECT INTO** statements. Use of this model increases your administrative workload because you must frequently back up transaction logs to guarantee proper truncation of the log, freeing up space for additional transaction logging. Backing up the transaction is covered in complete detail in Chapter 9 of this book.

The Bulk-Logged recovery model makes certain that transaction logging takes place for all data activity within a database with the exception of the large-scale data operations mentioned above. This negatively impacts the point-in-time recoverability of the database, but it does reduce your administrative workload because you must perform less frequent backups of the transaction log.

Finally, the Simple recovery model for a database logs all data activity, including large-scale operations. However, this model causes the transaction log to be truncated at each checkpoint. Thus, this transaction log cannot be used to restore the database to a certain point in time, nor even to the point of failure. With this method in place, the database can only be restored to the point of the last database backup. Obviously, this method eliminates the administrative work of transaction log backups, yet it is not often used in production because the recoverability factors are so minimal.

WARNING! Even using the Simple recovery model, you can still experience a transaction log that fills to capacity. Long-running transactions or transactions marked for replication that have not actually replicated can still exhaust the log.

Viewing the Architectural Properties of a Database

As you have noticed from the previous sections, there are many components that make up the architecture of your SQL Server databases. Follow these steps to view these architectural properties of a SQL Server 2000 database:

1. Select Start|Programs|Microsoft SQL Server|Enterprise Manager.

2. Expand the Microsoft SQL Servers, the SQL Server Group, and your server's node in the left pane.

3. Expand the databases container and right-click the pubs sample user database.

4. Choose Properties from the shortcut menu. Notice the pubs Properties window appears (see Figure 7.2).

5. Review the information the General tab contains and then select the Data Files tab (see Figure 7.3). Notice how this tab displays the physical data files (and their location) that actually store the data for this database.

6. Select the Transaction Log tab (see Figure 7.4). Notice how this tab displays information regarding this database's transaction log file and its location.

7. Finally, select the Options tab and note the ability to easily select the recovery model used by this database (see Figure 7.5).

Follow this series of steps to use Enterprise Manager to view the architectural elements of any of your SQL Server databases. Later, this chapter details steps you may take to change these configurations and even optimize them for the best possible performance.

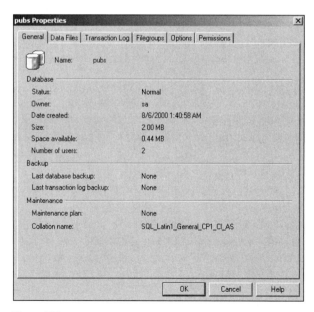

Figure 7.2
The pubs database Properties window in Enterprise Manager.

Figure 7.3
The Data Files tab.

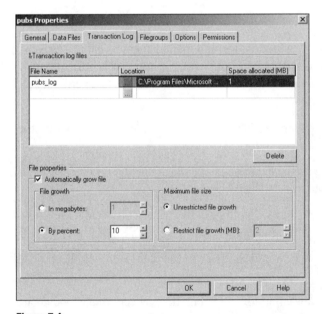

Figure 7.4
The Transaction Log tab.

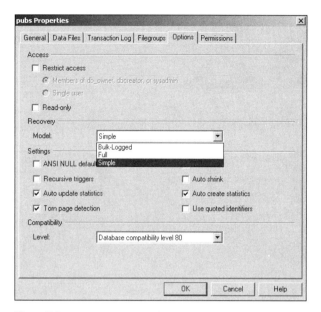

Figure 7.5
The Options tab.

Database Planning

An important step in the successful creation and management of databases is to properly plan for the amount of disk space such databases require. It is quite possible to accurately estimate such storage needs. Simply follow the guidelines and methods presented in this section.

You should consider the following key factors when you are planning for your new database:

- SQL Server 2000 uses the model database as a template for the new database's creation, including the initial size of this database.

- Consider the amount of data you are to store in the tables of this database (this section assists you in making this determination).

- Consider the number and type of indexes used in the database, including the fill factor used.

- Consider the size of the transaction log, including the recovery model you choose, and the number of backups you perform on this log—as a general rule, consider setting up a log that is 10 to 25 percent of the database size.

- Consider the size of system tables in the database.

Obviously, a key factor in planning for your new database is estimating the amount of data you are going to store in its tables. This factor has the greatest effect on the overall database size. Follow these steps for estimating the number of 8KB pages you need to store a particular table in the database:

1. Calculate the number of bytes in a row of the table. You accomplish this by totaling the byte lengths of each column. For variable length columns, use an average column width.

2. Calculate the number of rows stored in each data page by dividing 8060 by the number of bytes in a row. Round the result down.

3. Divide the number of rows you approximate for the table by the number of rows per page. This result equals an approximation of the number of pages your table requires.

Creating and Configuring Databases

This section covers everything you need to know when on site for creating and configuring new user databases. This is obviously critical information for a proper SQL Server 2000 implementation, and various methods and techniques are provided. This helps you select a method appropriate for a given situation.

Creating Databases

There are several methods for creating a database in SQL Server 2000. You can use a Transact-SQL statement, or you can use the appropriate dialog boxes in Enterprise Manager, or you can use a wizard. This section covers all of these methods.

First, however, it is important to realize just what occurs when you use one of these methods to actually create a new database. Remember, creating a database also creates the data file(s) and the transaction log(s) used to physically store the data. Creating a database records information in the master system database—specifically, the **sysdatabases** and **sysaltfiles** tables are given new entries. Also, as mentioned above, the model database is copied, including any settings and system tables included in this database.

Transact-SQL

Recall from Chapter 3 the Transact-SQL syntax for creating a database:

```
CREATE DATABASE database_name
[ ON
    [ < filespec > [ ,...n ] ]
    [ , < filegroup > [ ,...n ] ]
]
[ LOG ON { < filespec > [ ,...n ] } ]
[ COLLATE collation_name ]
[ FOR LOAD | FOR ATTACH ]
< filespec > ::=
```

```
[ PRIMARY ]
( [ NAME = logical_file_name , ]
    FILENAME = 'os_file_name'
    [ , SIZE = size ]
    [ , MAXSIZE = { max_size | UNLIMITED } ]
    [ , FILEGROWTH = growth_increment ] ) [ ,...n ]
< filegroup > ::=
FILEGROUP filegroup_name < filespec > [ ,...n ]
```

Remember, although this syntax looks intimidating, almost all of it is optional. Here is an example of the most minimal approach to creating such a database creation script:

```
CREATE DATABASE TestDB
```

Amazingly, this is all the syntax required for creating a database named TestDB.

Using such a minimal approach to your code leaves almost all of the configuration options to default settings, however. Here is a list of these default settings; notice how many of them rely upon the model database. Also notice these defaults are for the TestDB as created with the syntax above:

- *Logical primary data filename*—TestDB_Data

- *Physical primary data filename*—TestDB_Data.mdf

- *Physical primary data file location*—c:\Program Files\Microsoft SQL Server\Mssql\Data

- *Physical size of the primary data file*—the size of the model database data file

- *Physical primary data file growth properties*—autogrowth enabled, growth increment 10 percent, no maximum size

- *Logical transaction log filename*—TestDB_Log

- *Physical transaction log filename*—TestDB_Log.ldf

- *Physical transaction log file location*—c:\Program Files\Microsoft SQL Server\Mssql\Data

- *Physical size of the transaction log file*—the size of the model transaction log file

- *Physical transaction log file growth properties*—autogrowth enabled, growth increment 10 percent, no maximum size

This example creates a database with the logical name of Contacts:

```
USE master
GO
CREATE DATABASE Contacts
ON
( NAME = Contacts_dat,
```

```
    FILENAME = 'd:\sqldata\contacts.mdf',
    SIZE = 10,
    MAXSIZE = 50,
    FILEGROWTH = 5 )
LOG ON
( NAME = 'Contacts_log',
    FILENAME = 'e:\sqllogs\contacts.ldf',
    SIZE = 5MB,
    MAXSIZE = 25MB,
    FILEGROWTH = 5MB )
GO
```

Notice this statement creates the primary data file on the D: drive in the sqldata folder. This file's logical name is Contacts_dat and the physical file name is contacts.mdf. This file is 10MB in size. The maximum size the file may become is 50MB, and the file grows in 5MB increments.

The transaction log's logical name is Contacts_log and the physical name is contacts.ldf. This log is stored on the E: drive in a folder named sqllogs. The log is 5MB in size, and can grow to a maximum size of 25MB. This file grows in 5MB increments.

Note: *This example demonstrates a very important performance enhancement technique for SQL Server 2000. Storing the data file and the transaction log file on different physical hard drives improves performance thanks to the reduction in drive contention when writing to the transaction log and to the data file.*

This example creates a database with a logical name of Inventory. This database consists of both a primary and a secondary data file:

```
CREATE DATABASE Inventory
ON
( NAME = inventory_dat1,
    FILENAME = 'D:\data\inventory_dat1.mdf',
    SIZE = 50
    MAXSIZE = 300
    FILEGROWTH = 10 ),
( NAME = inventory_dat2,
    FILENAME = 'E:\data\inventory_dat2.ndf',
    SIZE = 200
    MAXSIZE = 500
    FILEGROWTH = 25 )
LOG ON
( NAME = inventory_log,
    FILENAME = 'F:\logs\inventory_log.ldf',
    SIZE = 100
    MAXSIZE = 400
    FILEGROWTH = 20% )
```

Notice in the previous example that three physical hard disks are used. The D: drive stores the primary data file, the E: drive stores the secondary data file, and the F: drive stores the transaction log.

Remember, you can use any SQL Server client tool you prefer to submit the above Transact-SQL statements for processing on the server. These tools include SQL Server Query Analyzer, isql, or osql.

SQL Enterprise Manager

Here you have the steps for creating a database using SQL Enterprise Manager. Although this method provides almost all of the options you have when using Transact-SQL to create the database, you are shielded from coding thanks to the graphical user interface provided by Enterprise Manager. The steps are:

1. Select Start|Programs|Microsoft SQL Server|Enterprise Manager.

2. Expand the nodes in the left pane to view your SQL Server instance and expand this instance.

3. Right-click the Databases container and choose New Database. The Database Properties window appears with the General tab selected.

4. Type the logical name for your database in the Name text box. When finished, select the Data Files tab.

5. Use this tab to rename the primary data file, or change its size and growth properties. You may also use this tab to create secondary data files by adding their entries to the appropriate rows of the data files display. When you are finished setting the data files properties, select the Transaction Log tab.

6. Use this tab to change any of the default parameters for the transaction log for your new database. Notice you can easily add multiple transaction logs for the database by adding appropriate rows in the transaction log files area of this tab.

7. When you are finished specifying the transaction log properties, click OK to create the new database with your specifications. Notice your new database appears in the console tree in the left pane under the databases node.

8. Right-click your new database and choose Properties to review or change any of your settings.

The Create Database Wizard

Yet another graphical user interface option for creating a new database in SQL Server 2000 is to use the Create Database Wizard. Although this wizard provides the least number of configuration options compared to other methods, it is certainly the simplest way to create your new database:

1. Select Start|Programs|Microsoft SQL Server|Enterprise Manager.

2. Expand the nodes in the left pane to view your SQL Server instance and expand this instance.

3. Select the Tools menu and choose Wizards.

4. In the Select Wizard window, expand the Database node (see Figure 7.6).

5. Choose Create Database Wizard and click OK.

6. Choose Next from the Welcome page of the Create Database Wizard.

7. In the Name The Database... page, type a name for your new database and specify the locations for the data file and transaction log locations, see Figure 7.7. When you have finished, click Next.

8. In the Name The Database Files page of the Wizard, create the database file names and initial sizes in the Database Files area (see Figure 7.8). When you are finished, click Next.

9. In the Define The Database File Growth page of the Wizard, specify the file growth properties you need for the data files (see Figure 7.9). When you are finished, click Next.

10. In the Name The Transaction Log Files page, specify the names and initial sizes for your transaction log files (see Figure 7.10). When you are finished, click Next.

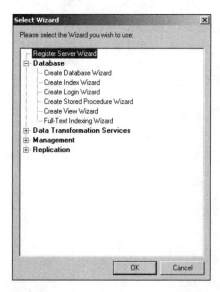

Figure 7.6
The Select Wizard window of Enterprise Manager.

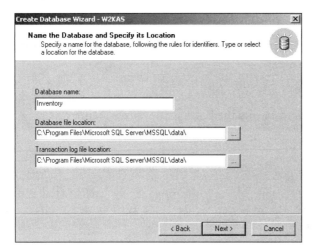

Figure 7.7
Naming your database and specifying a location for the data and log files.

11. In the Define The Transaction Log File Growth page, select the file growth options for your transaction log file (see Figure 7.11). When you are finished, click Next.

12. Review your configuration decisions in the Completing The Create Database Wizard page, and choose Finish when you are ready to create the database.

13. Click OK in the dialog box informing you that your database was created successfully.

14. Click No when you are presented with a dialog box asking you if you would like to create a maintenance plan for your database. (This wizard is covered later in Chapter 10.)

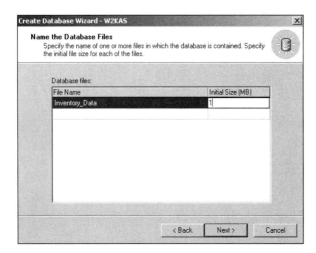

Figure 7.8
Naming your database files and specifying their sizes.

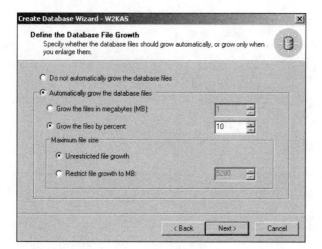

Figure 7.9
Selecting file growth properties for your data files.

15. Notice your new database appears in the console tree in the left pane under the databases node.

16. Right-click your new database and choose Properties to review or change any of your settings.

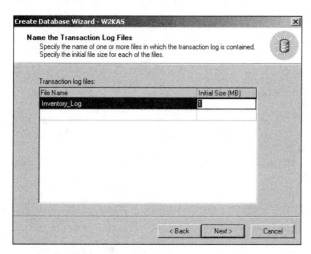

Figure 7.10
Naming the transaction log files and setting their initial sizes.

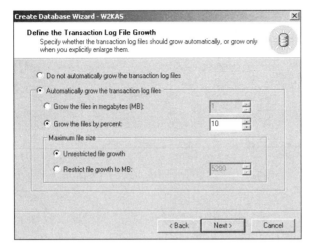

Figure 7.11
Setting the file growth properties for the transaction logs.

Setting Database Options

There are many database options you can set for your user databases in SQL Server 2000. The default settings for these many configuration options are inherited from the model database during the database creation process. In most production environments, you will never modify many of these options, yet there will be certain options you manipulate often. Obviously, in this book, it is important that you are provided with complete information regarding all of these possible options.

Database Options

There are five categories of database options:

• Auto options

• Cursor options

• Recovery options

• SQL options

• State options

Auto Options

You use auto options to control certain automatic behaviors regarding your SQL Server 2000 database. These options consist of the following:

• **AUTO_CLOSE**—When you set the **AUTO_CLOSE** option to **ON**, your database closes and shuts down cleanly when the last user of the database exits and all processes in the database complete. This frees any resources that were committed to the database operations. By default, this option is set to **ON** for all databases when you use SQL Server 2000 Desktop Engine Edition, and **OFF** for all other editions. When set to **OFF**, your database remains open even if no users are currently using the database. Setting this option to **ON** is excellent for desktop versions of SQL Server 2000 because database resources are reduced, and the database files can easily be manipulated, such as copy operations and even email. This setting should be set to **OFF** for most other production versions of SQL Server 2000, because the overhead of opening and closing the database would be too severe as client applications consistently connect and drop off.

7

- **AUTO_CREATE_STATISTICS**—When you set this database option to **ON**, statistics are automatically generated for indexes in the database. The creation of these statistics improves SQL Server performance, particularly when users query the database. If you choose to set this database option to **OFF**, you may still manually create statistics for the database. This database option is **ON** by default.

- **AUTO_UPDATE_STATISTICS**—When you set this database option to **ON**, existing database statistics automatically update when the statistics become out-of-date due to data changes. **AUTO_UPDATE_STATISTICS** is set **ON** by default.

- **AUTO_SHRINK**—Setting this option to **ON** causes SQL Server 2000 to periodically shrink the database files and transaction log files. This obviously helps to conserve hard disk space on the server. By default, this option is set to **ON** for all databases when using SQL Server Desktop Edition. This option is set to **OFF** by default for all other editions. This option causes files to be shrunk when more than 25 percent of the file contains unused space. SQL Server 2000 shrinks the file to a size where 25 percent of the file is unused space, or to the size of the file when it was created, whichever is greater.

Cursor Options

You use cursor options to control cursor behavior and scope within your SQL Server 2000 database. These options consist of the following:

- **CURSOR_CLOSE_ON_COMMIT**—Setting this database option to **ON** causes any open cursors to close automatically when a transaction is committed. By default, this setting is **OFF** and cursors remain open across transaction boundaries, closing only when the connection is closed or when they are explicitly closed. Setting this option to **ON** guarantees that your database will maintain SQL-92 compliance, but is otherwise not recommended.

- **CURSOR_DEFAULT**—Setting this database option to **CURSOR_DEFAULT LOCAL** sets the scope of the cursor to local for batches, stored procedures, or triggers in which the cursor was created. If you set **CURSOR_DEFAULT GLOBAL**, the scope of cursors are global to the connection. **CURSOR_DEFAULT GLOBAL** is the default setting.

Recovery Options

You use recovery options to control the recovery model used for your database. These options consist of the following:

- **RECOVERY**—You may specify **FULL, SIMPLE,** or **BULK_LOGGED,** using this option to control the recovery model used by your database. (See the discussion regarding recovery models earlier in this chapter for explanations of each mode.) **SIMPLE** is the default setting for SQL Server Desktop Edition and the Data Engine Edition; **FULL** is the default for all other editions.

- **TORN_PAGE_DETECTION**—This database recovery option allows SQL Server 2000 to detect incomplete I/O operations caused by power failures or other system outages. When you set this database option to **ON**, SQL Server 2000 reserves a bit for each 512-byte sector in an 8-kilobyte (KB) database page when the page is written to disk. If a bit is in the wrong state when the page is later read by SQL Server, the page was written incorrectly and SQL Server 2000 considers this a torn page. Torn pages are usually detected during recovery because any page that was written incorrectly is likely to be read by recovery. If the torn page is detected during recovery, the database is marked suspect. If you encounter a suspect database, your database backup should be restored and any transaction log backups applied, because your database is physically inconsistent. By default, **TORN_PAGE_DETECTION** is **ON**.

SQL Options

You use SQL options to control American National Standards Institute (ANSI) compliance for your database. These options consist of the following:

- **ANSI_NULL_DEFAULT**—This database option allows you to control the database default nullability. When **NULL** or **NOT NULL** is not specified explicitly, a user-defined data type or a column definition uses the default setting for nullability. SQL Server 2000 defaults to **NOT NULL**. For ANSI compatibility, setting the database option **ANSI_NULL_DEFAULT** to **ON** changes the database default to **NULL**. By default, ODBC and OLE DB clients issue a connection-level **SET** statement setting **ANSI_NULL_DEFAULT** to **ON** for the session when connecting to SQL Server.

- **ANSI_NULLS**—Setting this database option to **ON** causes all comparisons to a null value to evaluate to **NULL**. When you set this option to **OFF**, comparisons of non-Unicode values to a null value evaluate to **TRUE** if both values are **NULL**. By default, the **ANSI_NULLS** database option is **OFF**. By default, ODBC and OLE DB clients issue a connection-level **SET** statement setting **ANSI_NULLS** to **ON** for the session when connecting to SQL Server.

- **ANSI_PADDING**—Setting this database option to **ON** causes trailing blanks in character values inserted into **varchar** columns and trailing zeros in binary values inserted into **varbinary**. When you set this database option to **OFF**, the trailing blanks and zeros are trimmed. This setting affects only the definition of new columns. It is recommended that **ANSI_PADDING** always be set to **ON**; this is required when creating or manipulating indexes on computed columns or indexed views.

- **ANSI_WARNINGS**—Setting this database option to **ON** causes errors or warnings to be issued when conditions such as "divide by zero" occur or null values appear in aggregate functions. When you set this option to **OFF**, no warnings are raised when null values appear in aggregate functions, and null values are returned when conditions such as "divide by zero" occur. By default, **ANSI_WARNINGS** is **OFF**. **SET ANSI_WARNINGS** must be set to **ON** when you create or manipulate indexes on computed columns or indexed views. By default, ODBC and OLE DB clients issue a connection-level **SET** statement setting **ANSI_WARNINGS** to **ON**.

- **ARITHABORT**—Setting this database option to **ON** ensures that an overflow or divide-by-zero error causes the query or batch to terminate. If the error occurs in a transaction, the transaction is rolled back. When you set this option to **OFF**, a warning message displays if one of these errors occurs, but the query, batch, or transaction continues to process as if no error occurred. **SET ARITHABORT** must be set to **ON** when you create or manipulate indexes on computed columns or indexed views.

- **NUMERIC_ROUNDABORT**—Setting this database option to **ON** causes an error to be generated when loss of precision occurs in an expression. Setting this option to **OFF** guarantees that losses of precision do not generate error messages and the result is rounded to the precision of the column or variable storing the result. **SET NUMERIC_ROUNDABORT** must be set to **OFF** when you create or manipulate indexes on computed columns or indexed views.

- **CONCAT_NULL_YIELDS_NULL** —Setting this database option to **ON** guarantees that if one of the operands in a concatenation operation is **NULL**, the result of the operation is **NULL**. If you set this option to **OFF**, concatenating a null value with a character string yields the character string as the result; the null value is treated as an empty character string. By default, **CONCAT_NULL_YIELDS_NULL** is **OFF**. **SET CONCAT_NULL_YIELDS_NULL** must be set to **ON** when you create or manipulate indexes on computed columns or indexed views. By default, ODBC and OLE DB clients issue a connection-level **SET** statement setting **CONCAT_NULL_YIELDS_NULL** to **ON**.

- **QUOTED_IDENTIFIER**—Setting this database option to **ON** allows you to use double quotation marks to delimit identifiers. You can delimit literals with single quotation marks. Remember, quoted identifiers do not have to follow the Transact-SQL rules for identifiers. When this database option is set to **OFF**, identifiers cannot be in quotation marks and must follow all Transact-SQL rules for identifiers. Literals can be delimited by either single or double quotation marks. This database option is set to **OFF** by default.

- **RECURSIVE_TRIGGERS**—Setting this database option to **ON** allows your triggers to fire recursively. When this database option is set to **OFF**, triggers cannot be fired recursively. The default setting is **OFF**.

State Options

You use state options to control whether the database is online or offline, who can connect to the database, and whether the database is in read-only mode. These options consist of the following:

- **OFFLINE**—When you specify the **OFFLINE** option, the database is closed and shut down cleanly and marked offline. The database cannot be modified when the database is offline. When **ONLINE** is specified, the database is open and available for use. Obviously, **ONLINE** is the default setting.

- **READ_ONLY**—When you set the **READ_ONLY** database option, the database is in read-only mode. Users can retrieve data from the database but cannot modify data. If you place your database in this mode automatic recovery is skipped at system startup, shrinking the database is not possible, and no locking takes place in read-only databases. Read-only mode can result in faster query performance. If you set the database option to **READ_WRITE**, users can retrieve and modify data. **READ_WRITE** is the default setting.

- **SINGLE_USER**—Setting your database to **SINGLE_USER** allows one user at a time to connect to the database. Current user connections are broken and new connection attempts are refused. The database remains in **SINGLE_USER** mode even if the user who set the option logs off. At that point, a different user (but only one) can connect to the database. To allow multiple connections, you must set the database to **RESTRICTED_USER** or **MULTI_USER** mode. **RESTRICTED_USER** allows only members of the **db_owner** fixed database role and **dbcreator** and **sysadmin** fixed server roles to connect to the database, but it does not limit their number. Setting the database to **MULTI_USER** mode allows all users with the appropriate permissions to connect to the database. Obviously, **MULTI_USER** is the default setting.

Database Compatibility Levels

In order to accommodate applications developed for earlier versions of SQL Server, or to feature support for certain SQL-92 behaviors, you can set the compatibility level for the database. You can set the database compatibility level either by using the **sp_dbcmptlevel** stored procedure or by using the Options tab of the database Properties window. The syntax for this command follows:

```
sp_dbcmptlevel [ [ @dbname = ] name ]
    [ , [ @new_cmptlevel = ] version ]
```

You use the parameters in this statements as follows: **[@dbname =]** *name* allows you to specify the name of the database whose compatibility level you need to change and **[@new_cmptlevel =]** *version* allows you to specify the version of SQL Server with which the database is to be made compatible.

There are several valid values for database compatibility levels—these are 60, 65, 70, or 80. What follows is a summary of these database compatibility levels and the behaviors they effect.

Compatibility Level of 60 or 65

The following behaviors result from a database compatibility level of 60 or 65:

- The result sets of **SELECT** statements with a **GROUP BY** clause and no **ORDER BY** clause are sorted by the **GROUP BY** columns.

- Columns prefixed with table aliases are accepted in the **SET** clause of an **UPDATE** statement.

- Bit columns created without an explicit **NULL** or **NOT NULL** option in **CREATE TABLE** or **ALTER TABLE** are created as **NOT NULL**.

- The **ALTER COLUMN** clause cannot be used on **ALTER TABLE**.

- A trigger created for a table replaces any existing triggers of the same type.

- When a batch or procedure contains invalid object names, a warning is returned when the batch is parsed or compiled, and an error message is returned when the batch is executed.

- Queries of the following form are properly executed by ignoring table **Sales** and inserting the **SELECT** statement results into table **Invoices**:

```
INSERT Invoices
SELECT select_list INTO Sales
```

- The empty string literal (' ') is interpreted as a single blank.

- The **DATALENGTH, LEFT, LTRIM, REPLICATE, RIGHT, RTRIM, SPACE, SUBSTRING**, and **UPDATETEXT** all exhibit certain behaviors slightly different from the SQL Server 2000 versions of these commands. For complete details, see **sp_dbcmptlevel** in Books Online.

- The **CHARINDEX** and **PATINDEX** functions return **NULL** only if both the pattern and the expression are **NULL**.

- References to text or image columns in inserted and deleted tables appear as **NULL**.

- **UPDATETEXT** initializes text columns to **NULL**.

- The "concatenation of null yields null" setting of **sp_dboption** is off by default. This causes an empty string to be returned if any operands in a concatenation operation are **NULL**.

- In an **INSERT** statement, a **SELECT** returning a scalar value is allowed in the **VALUES** clause.

- A **ROLLBACK** statement in a stored procedure referenced in an **INSERT** table **EXEC** procedure statement causes the **INSERT** to be rolled back, but the batch continues.

- Retrieving text or image columns from the inserted or deleted tables inside a trigger returns **NULL** values.

- **AUTHORIZATION, CASCADE, CROSS, DISTRIBUTED, ESCAPE, FULL, INNER, JOIN, LEFT, OUTER, PRIVILEGES, RESTRICT, RIGHT, SCHEMA**, and **WORK** are all reserved keywords.

Compatibility Level of 70 or 80

The following behaviors result from a database compatibility level of 70 or 80:

- A **GROUP BY** clause does no sorting on its own. An **ORDER BY** clause must be explicitly specified for SQL Server to sort any result set.

- Table aliases are not accepted in the **SET** clause of an **UPDATE** statement.

- The nullability of bit columns without explicit nullability is determined by either the session setting of **SET ANSI_NULL_DFLT_ON** or **SET ANSI_NULL_DFLT_OFF**; or the database setting of **SET ANSI NULL DEFAULT**.

- The **ALTER COLUMN** clause can be used on **ALTER TABLE**.

- Triggers of the same type are appended. Trigger names must be unique.

- No warning is returned when a batch containing invalid object names is parsed or compiled, and an error message is returned when the batch is executed.

- SQL Server returns a syntax error when the following query is executed:

```
INSERT Invoices
SELECT select_list INTO Sales
```

- The empty string literal (' ') is interpreted as an empty string.

- The **CHARINDEX** and **PATINDEX** functions return **NULL** when any input parameters are **NULL**.

- References to text or image columns in the inserted and deleted tables are not allowed.

- **UPDATETEXT** initializes text columns to an empty string. **WRITETEXT** initializes text columns to **NULL**.

- The "concatenation of null yields null" setting of **sp_dboption** is on by default, which returns a **NULL** if any operands in a concatenation operation are null.

- The **INSERT** statement cannot have a **SELECT** statement in the **VALUES** clause as one of the values to be inserted.

- A **ROLLBACK** statement in a stored procedure referenced by an **INSERT...EXEC** statement causes the entire transaction to be rolled back, and the batch stops executing.

- Retrieving text or image columns from inserted or deleted tables inside a trigger is not allowed and causes an error.

- For database compatibility level 70, **BACKUP, CONTAINS, CONTAINSTABLE, DENY, FREETEXT, FREETEXTTABLE, PERCENT, RESTORE, ROWGUIDCOL**, and **TOP** are all reserved keywords.

- For database compatibility level 80, **COLLATE, FUNCTION**, and **OPENXML** are reserved keywords.

You can set the compatibility level of a database using Enterprise Manager as you learn in the next section, or you can use the **sp_dbcmptlevel** stored procedure. The syntax of this command follows:

```
sp_dbcmptlevel [ [ @dbname = ] name ]
    [ , [ @new_cmptlevel = ] version ]
```

For example, the following statement sets the compatibility level for the **Invoices** database to 65:

```
EXEC sp_dbcmptlevel 'Invoices', 65
```

Database Collation

Remember from our discussion of installing SQL Server 2000 that each user database hosted by the RDBMS can feature a different collation. When you create a database, you can use the **COLLATE** clause of the **CREATE DATABASE** statement to specify the default collation of the database. You can also specify a collation when you create a database using SQL Server Enterprise Manager. If you do not specify a collation, the database is assigned the default collation of the model database. This collation is the same as the default collation you selected when you installed SQL Server 2000. You can change the collation used by a database using the **ALTER DATABASE** statement as you see in the next section of this chapter.

Modifying Database Options

You can use SQL Server Enterprise Manager to set the most common database options. To do this, follow these steps:

1. Select Start|Programs|Microsoft SQL Server|Enterprise Manager.

2. Expand your server in the left pane and expand the database container.

3. Right-click the database you need to modify options for and choose Properties.

4. In the database properties window, select the Options tab (see Figure 7.12).

5. When you have finished configuring the appropriate options, choose OK.

In SQL Server 2000, you can also use the **ALTER DATABASE** Transact-SQL command to set any database option. The complete syntax of this command when used for setting database options follows:

```
ALTER DATABASE database
        { SINGLE_USER | RESTRICTED_USER | MULTI_USER }
        | { OFFLINE | ONLINE }
        | { READ_ONLY | READ_WRITE }
        ROLLBACK AFTER integer [ SECONDS ]
        | ROLLBACK IMMEDIATE
        | NO_WAIT
        CURSOR_CLOSE_ON_COMMIT { ON | OFF }
        | CURSOR_DEFAULT { LOCAL | GLOBAL }
        AUTO_CLOSE { ON | OFF }
        | AUTO_CREATE_STATISTICS { ON | OFF }
        | AUTO_SHRINK { ON | OFF }
        | AUTO_UPDATE_STATISTICS { ON | OFF }
        ANSI_NULL_DEFAULT { ON | OFF }
        | ANSI_NULLS { ON | OFF }
        | ANSI_PADDING { ON | OFF }
        | ANSI_WARNINGS { ON | OFF }
        | ARITHABORT { ON | OFF }
        | CONCAT_NULL_YIELDS_NULL { ON | OFF }
        | NUMERIC_ROUNDABORT { ON | OFF }
        | QUOTED_IDENTIFIER { ON | OFF }
        | RECURSIVE_TRIGGERS { ON | OFF }
        RECOVERY { FULL | BULK_LOGGED | SIMPLE }
        | TORN_PAGE_DETECTION { ON | OFF }
```

Here is an example of using the **ALTER DATABASE** command to set the **AUTO_SHRINK** database option to **OFF** for the Sales database:

Figure 7.12
The Options tab of the database properties window.

```
ALTER DATABASE Sales
SET AUTO_SHRINK OFF
```

You can also use the **sp_dboption** stored procedure for changing common database options. You should note, however, that this command is present in SQL Server 2000 mainly for backward compatibility purposes. As such, it cannot manipulate all of the database options found in SQL Server 2000. Here is the procedure:

```
sp_dboption [ [ @dbname = ] 'database' ]
    [ , [ @optname = ] 'option_name' ]
    [ , [ @optvalue = ] 'value' ]
```

In this syntax, **[@dbname =] 'database'** is the name of the database you want to set an option for, **[@optname =] 'option_name'** is the name of the option you would like to set, and **[@optvalue =] 'value'** allows you to specify the new setting for the database option.

This example sets the Customers database to Read Only:

```
EXEC sp_dboption 'Customers', 'read only', 'TRUE'
```

Viewing Database Options Settings

There are different methods for viewing the options set on your SQL Server 2000 database. One option is to use Enterprise Manager. You can follow the steps in the previous section to view the most common database settings using the Options tab of the database Properties window.

You can also use the **DATABASEPROPERTYEX** system function in a Transact-SQL query in order to check for a specific database option setting. The syntax for this function follows:

```
DATABASEPROPERTYEX( database , property )
```

Obviously, "database" in the above syntax allows you to specify the database you need to view the option setting for. Table 7.4 details the possibilities for the property value in the system function and the possible return values.

Table 7.4 DATABASEPROPERTYEX system function values.

Value	Possible return values
Collation	**Collation name**
IsAnsiNullDefault	1 = TRUE 0 = FALSE NULL = Invalid input
IsAnsiNullsEnabled	1 = TRUE 0 = FALSE NULL = Invalid input
IsAnsiPaddingEnabled	1 = TRUE 0 = FALSE NULL = Invalid input
IsAnsiWarningsEnabled	1 = TRUE 0 = FALSE NULL = Invalid input
IsArithmeticAbortEnabled	1 = TRUE 0 = FALSE NULL = Invalid input
IsAutoClose	1 = TRUE 0 = FALSE NULL = Invalid input
IsAutoCreateStatistics	1 = TRUE 0 = FALSE NULL = Invalid input
IsAutoShrink	1 = TRUE 0 = FALSE NULL = Invalid input
IsAutoUpdateStatistics	1 = TRUE 0 = FALSE NULL = Invalid input
IsCloseCursorsOn CommitEnabled	1 = TRUE 0 = FALSE NULL = Invalid input

(continued)

Table 7.4   DATABASEPROPERTYEX system function values *(continued)*.

Value	Possible return values
IsFulltextEnabled	1 = TRUE 0 = FALSE NULL = Invalid input
IsInStandBy	1 = TRUE 0 = FALSE NULL = Invalid input
IsLocalCursorsDefault	1 = TRUE 0 = FALSE NULL = Invalid input
IsMergePublished	1 = TRUE 0 = FALSE NULL = Invalid input
IsNullConcat	1 = TRUE 0 = FALSE NULL = Invalid input
IsNumericRoundAbortEnabled	1 = TRUE 0 = FALSE NULL = Invalid input
IsQuotedIdentifiersEnabled	1 = TRUE 0 = FALSE NULL = Invalid input
IsRecursiveTriggersEnabled	1 = TRUE 0 = FALSE NULL = Invalid input
IsSubscribed	1 = TRUE 0 = FALSE NULL = Invalid input
IsTornPageDetectionEnabled	1 = TRUE 0 = FALSE NULL = Invalid input
Recovery	FULL BULK_LOGGED SIMPLE
SQLSortOrder	0 = Database is using Windows collation >0 = SQL Server sort order ID
Status	ONLINE OFFLINE RESTORING RECOVERING SUSPECT

(continued)

Table 7.4   DATABASEPROPERTYEX system function values *(continued)*.

Value	Possible return values
Updateability	**READ_ONLY** **READ_WRITE**
UserAccess	**SINGLE_USER** **RESTRICTED_USER** **MULTI_USER**
Version	**Version number = Database is open** **NULL = Database is closed**

Here is an example that checks the default collation setting for the Customers database:

```
SELECT DATABASEPROPERTYEX('Customers', 'Collation')
```

Maintaining Databases

After you create your user databases, you are not done as a database administrator by any means. In fact, there are many database maintenance tasks that you will eventually be responsible for. This section explores many of these maintenance tasks; other chapters deal with the rest, such as backup and restore.

Note: *Anytime you perform the dramatic database maintenance activities specified in this section, you should back up the master database. This is necessary because the master database is responsible for storing all of the information about these user databases. Chapter 9 of this book covers backup and restore activities in detail.*

Scripting a Database

Enterprise Manager of SQL Server 2000 provides a simple interface for generating Transact-SQL scripts automatically for objects you have created or that otherwise exist in SQL Server 2000. These scripts allow you to easily re-create the objects anytime later—even on a different server entirely. Not only can you generate scripts to re-create databases, but to re-create any other object as well. These scripts can be separate for each object—or the scripts can create all the objects in one large script.

In order to accomplish this task in Enterprise Manager, simply follow these steps:

1. Select Start|Programs|Microsoft SQL Server|Enterprise Manager.

2. In the left pane, expand your server and expand the databases node.

3. Right-click the database you would like to generate a Transact-SQL script for and choose All Tasks from the shortcut menu. Now choose Generate Transact-SQL script. The Generate SQL Scripts window appears (see Figure 7.13).

4. Select the Show All button, and then select the Script All Objects check box to select all objects in the database for scripting.

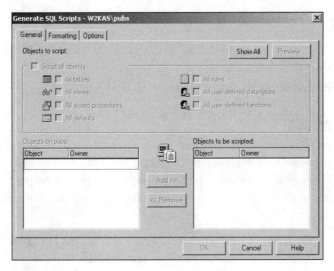

Figure 7.13
The Generate SQL Scripts window in Enterprise Manager.

5. Click the Options tab.

6. In the Security Scripting Options area, select the Script Database checkbox.

7. Return to the General tab.

8. Choose the Preview button and review this script in the Generate SQL Script Preview window (see Figure 7.14).

9. Click the Close button in the Generate SQL Script Preview window.

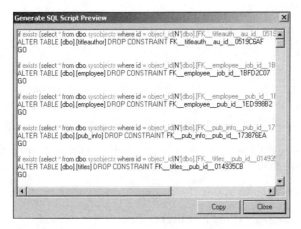

Figure 7.14
Previewing the Transact-SQL Script.

10. Choose OK in the Generate SQL Scripts window.

11. In the Save As window, name the script and select a location to save the script to and choose Save.

12. Click OK in the Scripting dialog box when the script has finished.

Renaming a Database

You may find it necessary to rename a database that you have created in SQL Server 2000. The great news is that there are simple Transact-SQL methods for you to accomplish this task. Before you actually perform the database rename using any of the methods described in this section, make sure that no one is using the database and that the database is set to single-user mode.

One method for changing the name of your database is to use the **ALTER DATABASE** command. This example syntax changes the name of the Test database to the Sample database:

```
ALTER DATABASE Test
MODIFY NAME = Sample
```

Another method is to use the **sp_renamedb** stored procedure. The complete syntax for this command follows:

```
sp_renamedb [ @dbname = ] 'old_name' ,
    [ @newname = ] 'new_name'
```

For example, this Transact-SQL statement changes the name of the Engineering database to EngResearch:

```
EXEC sp_renamedb 'Engineering', 'EngResearch'
```

Deleting a Database

Should you no longer require a database on your SQL Server 2000 system, you may delete the database and its underlying data and log files using one of the methods shown here. When you delete a database, you also delete all of the objects and data in the database as well.

There are restrictions that you should be aware of prior to deleting a database from SQL Server 2000, however. Be aware that you cannot delete a database if:

• The database is in the process of being restored

• The database is open for reading or writing by a user

• The database is publishing any of its tables as part of SQL Server replication

• The database is a system database

You should also keep in mind that after you delete a database, login IDs that relied upon the deleted database for a default database will no longer have a default database. For more information about login IDs and default database settings, see Chapter 8.

Perhaps the simplest method for deleting a database is to use Enterprise Manager. Simply follow these steps:

1. Select Start|Programs|Microsoft SQL Server|Enterprise Manager.

2. In the left pane, expand your server and expand the databases node.

3. Right-click the database that you would like to delete and choose Delete from the shortcut menu.

4. In the Delete Database dialog box, determine whether or not you would like to delete the backup and restore history information for the database and choose Yes when finished (see Figure 7.15).

You can also use the **DROP DATABASE** Transact-SQL statement to delete a database and the underlying data and log files. The syntax for this statement is extremely simple:

```
DROP DATABASE database_name [ ,...n ]
```

The *n* indicates that you can specify multiple databases to be dropped in a single statement.

Here is an example of the **DROP DATABASE** statement:

```
DROP DATABASE sampleDB, pubs
```

This example drops both the sampleDB and the pubs databases and their underlying data and log files.

Copying or Moving a Database

You may also find a time when you need to copy or move a database from one SQL Server system to another. One automated method for doing so is to use the Copy Database Wizard. This wizard can walk you through both a copy as well as a move. For detailed step-by-step instructions for using this wizard, see Chapter 6.

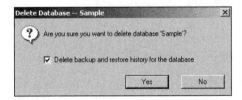

Figure 7.15
The Delete Database dialog box of Enterprise Manager.

In addition to using the Copy Database Wizard, you can also use Data Transformation Services (DTS) to perform both move and copy operations for databases (see Figure 7.16). This book covers DTS in full in Chapter 14.

Finally, you have Transact-SQL methods available to you for moving a database in SQL Server 2000. These methods center on the Detach and Attach stored procedures.

You use the **sp_detach_db** to remove a database from SQL Server 2000. This procedure does nothing with the data files and log files for the database, however. It is up to you to move the data and log files to a new location appropriate for your needs. You then use the **sp_attach_db** stored procedure to attach the database to a different SQL Server and reference the moved data and log files.

The syntax for the **sp_detach_db** stored procedure follows:

```
sp_detach_db [ @dbname = ] 'dbname'
    [ , [ @skipchecks = ] 'skipchecks' ]
```

In this syntax, **[@dbname =]** '**dbname**' is the name of the database to be detached. If **[@skipchecks =]** '**skipchecks**' is true, **UPDATE STATISTICS** is skipped. If false, **UP-DATE STATISTICS** is run. This option is useful for databases that are to be moved to read-only media.

The syntax for the **sp_attach_db** stored procedure follows:

```
sp_attach_db [ @dbname = ] 'dbname'
    , [ @filename1 = ] 'filename_n' [ ,...16 ]
```

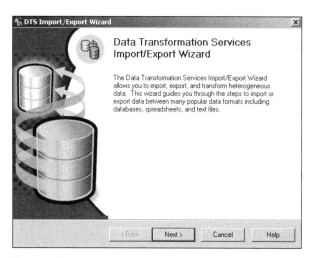

Figure 7.16
The DTS Import/Export Wizard.

In this syntax, **[@dbname =]** 'dbname' is the name of the database to be attached to the server. The name must be unique. **[@filename1 =]** 'filename_n' is the physical name, including path, of a database file. You can specify up to 16 file names. The parameter names start at **@filename1** and increment to **@filename16**. The file name list must include at least the primary file, which contains the system tables that point to other files in the database. The list must also include any files that were moved after the database was detached.

Here is an example of using these stored procedures to move a database named Customers from one SQL Server to another:

1. Run the following Transact-SQL statement against the SQL Server system currently hosting the Customers database:

```
EXEC sp_detach_db Customers, true
```

2. Move the underlying data and log files to the appropriate storage location on the new server. In this example this location is c:\data. You can use the **sp_helpdb** stored procedure in order to see a list of all of the files associated with a particular database, or you can use Enterprise Manager.

3. Run the following Transact-SQL statement against the destination SQL Server system:

```
EXEC sp_attach_db @dbname = 'Customers',
@filename1 = 'c:\data\cust_dat.mdf',
@filename2 = 'c:\data\cust_log.ldf'
```

Managing Database Size

Another common database maintenance task you should be prepared for is maintaining appropriate sizes for your databases. Although default configurations cause databases to grow automatically, certain environments may dictate that you change this default behavior and manually configure database sizes and adjust these sizes accordingly. This section explores all aspects of this topic.

Automatic Filegrowth

Provided that you have plenty of potential storage space and you have no time to physically monitor the sizes of your data and log files, automatic filegrowth in SQL Server 2000 can be a real benefit to you as an administrator. It is also critical in Desktop Engine Edition or Personal Edition installations where no database administrator may be present at all.

In order to provide for the best database performance possible, you should use autogrowth as a database administrator sparingly. This is because autogrowth causes performance degradation due to sudden resource usage increases on the server. Resources are also consumed in this configuration because SQL Server 2000 must constantly monitor the size of database files and logs, checking for the need to expand these files. Also, frequent automatic filegrowth can cause disk fragmentation.

If you are going to use automatic filegrowth, consider increasing the growth increment in large amounts, and consider setting a maximum size for the data or log file so that these files cannot consume entire volumes of disk space. You should also configure alerts to notify you when automatic filegrowth occurs. Chapter 10 of this book covers alerts in detail.

You can access the Properties of a database in Enterprise Manager to change the autogrowth settings using a graphical user interface, or you can rely on the **ALTER DATABASE** statement. The following example modifies the customers_data file of the Customers database, setting the autogrowth increment to 20 percent and configuring a maximum file size of 200MBs:

```
ALTER DATABASE Customers
MODIFY FILE (NAME = 'customers_data', FILEGROWTH = 20%, MAXSIZE = 200MB)
```

Automatic File Shrinkage

The ability for SQL Server 2000 to automatically shrink data or log files if there is an over abundance of free space is a luxury that should be reserved for Desktop Engine Editions or Personal Editions. In a higher load production environment, you should manually shrink files if necessary using the **DBCC SHRINKFILE** statement or Enterprise Manager. Remember, this autoshrink option is disabled by default in SQL Server 2000. Use the **ALTER DATABASE** command or Enterprise Manager to change this default setting if you must.

Changing Data File Size Manually

Monitoring the amount of free space in your data files (see Chapter 12) allows you to know exactly when it is necessary to manually resize a data file. You can use the Properties of a database in Enterprise Manager, or you can rely on Transact-SQL to make the change. The following example demonstrates the use of the **ALTER DATABASE** statement to change the size of the invoices_dat file in the Invoices database to 25MB:

```
ALTER DATABASE Invoices
MODIFY FILE (NAME = 'invoices_dat', SIZE = 25 MB)
```

To manually shrink a database file you must use the **DBCC SHRINKFILE** command, but to shrink an entire database including all of its data files and log files you use the **DBCC SHRINKDATABASE** command. The complete syntax for the **DBCC SHRINKFILE** command follows:

```
DBCC SHRINKFILE
   ( { file_name | file_id }
     { [ , target_size ]
         | [ , { EMPTYFILE | NOTRUNCATE | TRUNCATEONLY } ]
     }
  )
```

Target_size in this syntax specifies the target size in megabytes for the data file. **EMPTYFILE** migrates all data from the specified file to other files in the same filegroup. **NOTRUNCATE** causes the freed file space to be retained in the files. **TRUNCATEONLY** causes any unused space in the files to be released to the operating system and shrinks the file to the last allocated extent.

The following example reduces the size of the sample_dat file of the Sample database to 10MB:

```
USE Sample
DBCC SHRINKFILE ('sample_dat', 10)
```

DBCC SHRINKDATABASE shrinks an entire database. The command shrinks it to a specified percent of the current size—shrinking all data and log files in the process. The complete syntax of the command follows:

```
DBCC SHRINKDATABASE
   ( database_name [ , target_percent ]
       [ , { NOTRUNCATE | TRUNCATEONLY } ]
   )
```

In this syntax, **target_percent** is the desired percentage of free space left in the database file. **NOTRUNCATE** causes the freed file space to be retained in the database files, and **TRUNCATEONLY** causes any unused space in the data files to be released to the operating system and shrinks the file to the last allocated extent.

The following example decreases the size of the files in the Purchases user database to allow 10 percent free space.

```
DBCC SHRINKDATABASE (Purchases, 10)
```

Controlling Transaction Log File Size

You should carefully monitor the size of your transaction log file. Remember, a transaction log that completely fills eliminates the ability to add or modify data in a database. This means that when you are using the Full or Bulk-Logged Recovery models, you must consistently perform transaction log backups to truncate the data stored in the log, thus freeing space. Chapter 9 covers this process in detail.

Just as with data files, allowing your transaction log files to grow automatically is not preferred to manually adjusting the size of these files when necessary. If you need to increase the size, use the **ALTER DATABASE** command or Enterprise Manager just as if you were modifying data files. In order to manually shrink transaction log files, use Enterprise Manager or **DBCC SHRINKFILE**. You can also use **DBCC SHRINKDATABASE**.

Adding Data or Log Files

Remember that you can always add additional data files and transaction log files to a database. You can use the Properties window for a database in Enterprise Manager to do this, or you can use the **ALTER DATABASE** Transact-SQL statement. This example adds a file to the Invoices user database:

```
ALTER DATABASE Invoices
ADD FILE
(NAME = 'invoices_data2',
FILENAME = 'e:\data\invoices_dat2.ndf',
SIZE = 5,
MAXSIZE = 25,
FILEGROWTH = 5)
```

Filegroups and other Database Optimizations

There are many options for increasing the performance of databases in SQL Server 2000 that you should consider upon database creation. This section covers filegroups, the transaction log, and tembdb, all of which offer powerful opportunities for improving performance.

Filegroups

Most of your production SQL Server installations should feature the use of multiple disk drives. This increases the availability, performance, and fault-tolerance of your installations. Remember from Chapter 4 that Windows 2000 and SQL Server 2000 support a number of different RAID levels for improved performance and fault-tolerance.

In order to take full advantage of these RAID solutions, you should consider the use of SQL Server filegroups. There are three types of these filegroups—primary, user-defined, and default. You always have a primary filegroup in use; SQL Server creates this filegroup when the database is created. You use a filegroup to manage multiple data files spread across multiple disks. This is an advanced administration technique that allows you to create objects in a specific filegroup on a specific drive in order to achieve performance benefits. For example, you could place heavily queried tables of a database in one filegroup on one hard drive and place heavily modified tables in another filegroup located on another hard drive.

Note: *Transaction logs are never part of a filegroup. Follow the instructions later in this section for optimization techniques with the transaction log.*

You create filegroups and specify their data files using the **CREATE DATABASE** command. This example creates the Revenue database and uses the primary filegroup and two user-defined filegroups to distribute the data across physical disks:

```
CREATE DATABASE Revenue
ON PRIMARY
( NAME = Rev_dat,
   FILENAME = 'd:\sqldata\revdat.mdf',
   SIZE = 10,
   MAXSIZE = 50,
   FILEGROWTH = 15% ),
( NAME = Rev_dat2,
   FILENAME = 'e:\sqldata\revdat2.ndf',
   SIZE = 10,
   MAXSIZE = 50,
   FILEGROWTH = 15% ),
FILEGROUP RevGroup1
( NAME = Rev_dat3,
   FILENAME = 'f:\sqldata\revdat3.ndf',
   SIZE = 10,
   MAXSIZE = 50,
   FILEGROWTH = 5 ),
( NAME = Rev_dat4,
   FILENAME = 'f:\sqldata\revdat4.ndf',
   SIZE = 10,
   MAXSIZE = 50,
   FILEGROWTH = 5 ),
FILEGROUP RevGroup2
( NAME = Rev_dat5,
   FILENAME = 'g:\sqldata\revdat5.ndf',
   SIZE = 10,
   MAXSIZE = 50,
   FILEGROWTH = 5 ),
( NAME = Rev_dat6,
   FILENAME = 'g:\sqldata\revdat6.ndf',
   SIZE = 10,
   MAXSIZE = 50,
   FILEGROWTH = 5 )
LOG ON
( NAME = 'Rev_log',
   FILENAME = 'h:\sqldata\revlog.ldf',
   SIZE = 5MB,
   MAXSIZE = 25MB,
   FILEGROWTH = 5MB )
```

In order to later view information about filegroups, you should use the **sp_helpfilegroup** stored procedure. When later creating your tables for a database, you can assign them to specific user-defined filegroups and, therefore, specify their storage location.

In addition to using filegroups to achieve performance enhancements, you can also use filegroups to simplify and enhance the effectiveness of your server maintenance. For example, you can use filegroups to backup and restore individual files, or you can group tables with similar maintenance requirements together.

The Transaction Log

An excellent and simple way to improve the performance of your database and dramatically improve the recoverability of the data is to place the transaction log on a separate physical disk from the data files. To further experience the performance and recoverability enhancements, you should also dedicate a hard drive to the sole purpose of hosting the transaction log. You should also consider mirroring this drive using RAID level 1, thus enhancing recoverability even further.

Tempdb

Moderate performance enhancements can be realized by placing the tempdb system database on its own dedicated hard drive as well. Because this database is built each time SQL Server 2000 starts, you should not worry about RAID for increasing recoverability.

Viewing Database Information

In this chapter, you have already learned how to view information regarding database options relevant to SQL Server 2000. In this section, you learn how to gain additional information about your user databases using a variety of different methods.

System Tables

Remember, SQL Server 2000 is managed by system databases and system tables. The system tables that run SQL Server 2000 are divided into two groups—the system catalog and the database catalog.

The System Catalog

The system catalog consists of the tables that manage SQL Server 2000 itself. These tables exist solely in the master database. These tables contain information about all databases, users, and system configurations for the system as a whole. Table 7.5 lists the tables that make up the system catalog and describes the function of each of these tables.

Table 7.5   Tables in the system catalog.

Table Name	Function
sysaltfiles	Stores information for each data or log file storing each database
syscachedobjects	Stores information detailing how the cache memory is used
syscharsets	Stores information for the character sets and sort orders used in SQL Server 2000
sysconfigures	Stores information regarding server configurations, both dynamic and manually assigned
syscurconfigs	Stores information regarding the current server configuration
sysdatabases	Stores information regarding each database stored on SQL Server
sysdevices	Stores information regarding permanent backup devices
syslanguages	Stores information for each language used in SQL Server
syslockinfo	Stores information regarding resource locks in SQL Server
syslogins	Stores information for each login account on the server
sysmessages	Stores information for each system error message or warning
sysoledbusers	Stores information for each user and password mapping for the specified linked server
sysperfinfo	Stores information regarding the internal performance counters in Performance Monitor
sysprocesses	Stores information about processes running on SQL Server
sysremotelogins	Stores information for each remote user allowed to call remote stored procedures
sysservers	Stores information for each server that SQL Server can access as an OLE DB data source

The Database Catalog

The database catalog also consists of system tables. These system tables are located in each database stored on SQL Server 2000, and are used to manage a particular database. Table 7.6 lists the system tables that make up the database catalog and describes the function of each.

Querying System Tables Directly

One method for viewing key information regarding your user databases involves querying the system tables that make up the system catalog and the database catalog directly. You can use Enterprise Manager, Query Analyzer, or Transact-SQL scripts to do so easily.

Warning! Understand that if you create Transact-SQL scripts for this process, these scripts might not function with later versions of SQL Server. This is because Microsoft tends to make changes to the system tables with each software revision.

Table 7.6   Tables in the database catalog.

Table Name	Function
syscolumns	Stores information for every column in every table and view, and for each parameter in a stored procedure
syscomments	Stores information for each view, rule, default, trigger, **CHECK** constraint, **DEFAULT** constraint, and stored procedure
sysconstraints	Stores information mapping constraints to the objects that own the constraints
sysdepends	Stores information regarding dependencies between objects and the objects contained in their definition
sysfilegroups	Stores information for each filegroup in a database
sysfiles	Stores information for each file in a database
sysforeignkeys	Stores information regarding the **FOREIGN KEY** constraints that are in table definitions
sysfulltextcatalogs	Stores information regarding the full-text catalogs
sysindexes	Stores information for each index and table in the database
sysindexkeys	Stores information for the keys or columns in an index
sysmembers	Stores information for each member of a database role
sysobjects	Stores information for each object created within a database
syspermissions	Stores information about permissions granted and denied to users, groups, and roles in the database
sysprotects	Stores information about permissions that have been applied to security accounts with the **GRANT** and **DENY** statements
sysreferences	Stores information regarding mappings of **FOREIGN KEY** constraint definitions to the referenced columns
systypes	Stores information for each system-supplied and each user-defined data type
sysusers	Stores information for each user, or SQL Server role in the database

Here is an example of using Enterprise Manager to view the information in **sysaltfiles** of the system catalog:

1. Select Start|Programs|Microsoft SQL Server|Enterprise Manager.

2. In the left pane, expand your server and expand the databases node.

3. Expand the master database node.

4. Select the Tables node and right-click **sysaltfiles** in the right pane.

5. Choose Open Table|Return All Rows from the shortcut menu in order to view the contents of this table (see Figure 7.17).

Using Query Analyzer is just as simple for viewing this information. In this example, you use the graphical tools of Query Analyzer to view the information stored in the sysdatabases system catalog system table:

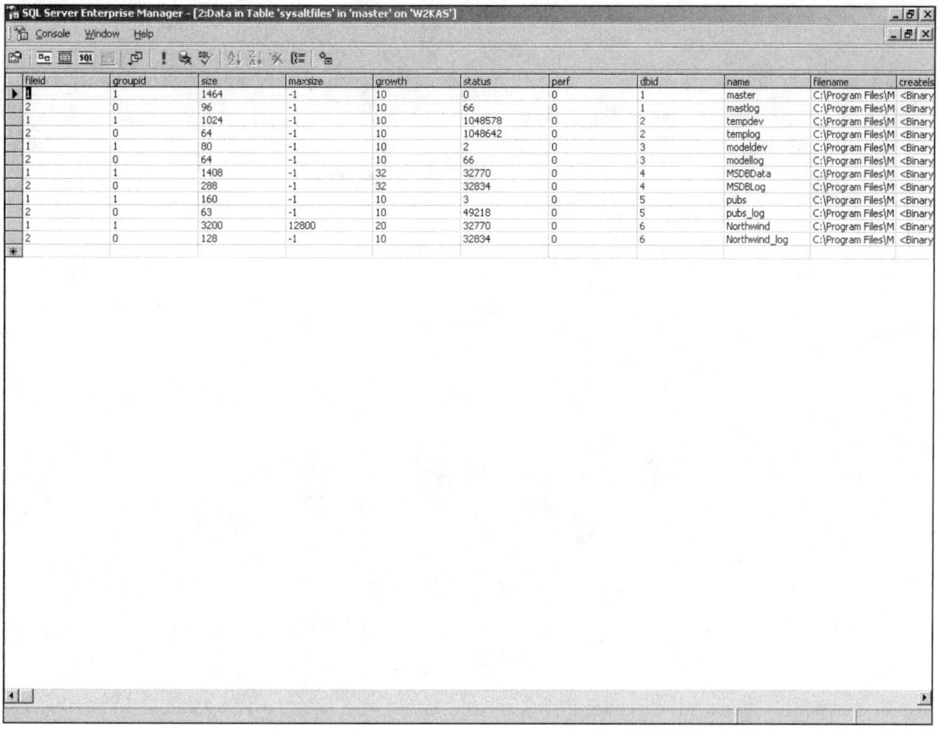

fileid	groupid	size	maxsize	growth	status	perf	dbid	name	filename	createls
1	1	1464	-1	10	0	0	1	master	C:\Program Files\M	<Binary
2	0	96	-1	10	66	0	1	mastlog	C:\Program Files\M	<Binary
1	1	1024	-1	10	1048578	0	2	tempdev	C:\Program Files\M	<Binary
2	0	64	-1	10	1048642	0	2	templog	C:\Program Files\M	<Binary
1	1	80	-1	10	2	0	3	modeldev	C:\Program Files\M	<Binary
2	0	64	-1	10	66	0	3	modellog	C:\Program Files\M	<Binary
1	1	1408	-1	32	32770	0	4	MSDBData	C:\Program Files\M	<Binary
2	0	288	-1	32	32834	0	4	MSDBLog	C:\Program Files\M	<Binary
1	1	160	-1	10	3	0	5	pubs	C:\Program Files\M	<Binary
2	0	63	-1	10	49218	0	5	pubs_log	C:\Program Files\M	<Binary
1	1	3200	12800	20	32770	0	6	Northwind	C:\Program Files\M	<Binary
2	0	128	-1	10	32834	0	6	Northwind_log	C:\Program Files\M	<Binary

Figure 7.17
Viewing the contents of **sysaltfiles**.

1. Select Start|Programs|Microsoft SQL Server|Query Analyzer.
2. Choose OK in the Connect to SQL Server dialog box.
3. Choose the Tools menu and select Object Browser|Show/hide to make certain the Object Browser is visible inside Query Analyzer.
4. In the Object Browser, expand the master database node, and then expand the System Tables node (see Figure 7.18).
5. Select the **dbo.sysdatabases** object and choose the Tools menu.
6. From the Tools menu, choose Object Browser|Open to open this table and view the information stored there.

Creating Transact-SQL scripts to access this information is just as easy. The following script is intended for use in the osql utility. The script displays the information stored in the **sysdatabases** system table:

```
USE master
SELECT * FROM sysdatabases
GO
```

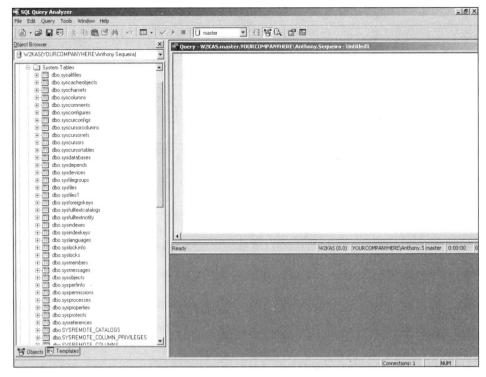

Figure 7.18
Using the Object Browser in Query Analyzer.

Stored Procedures

Although you can access the information about your databases by querying the system tables directly, you can also use one of many system stored procedures provided by Microsoft to assist you in obtaining the information you need. Table 7.7 provides a list of the most commonly used system stored procedures for obtaining database information.

For example, if you would like to view information regarding the pubs database on your SQL Server 2000 system, access an appropriate client tool and enter the following statement:

```
EXEC sp_helpdb pubs
```

This query displays information about the database itself and the physical data and log files that make up the database. This is a very convenient and efficient method for gaining this information, and notice it does not involve querying the tables directly.

Table 7.7 System stored procedures for viewing database information.

Stored Procedure Name	Function
sp_configure	Changes or displays SQL Server 2000 configuration settings
sp_dboption	Changes or displays database option settings
sp_help	Displays information regarding a particular database or other object
sp_depends	Displays information about object dependencies
sp_helpdb	Displays information about a particular database
sp_helpfile	Displays physical file information for a database
sp_lock	Displays information about current locks
sp_spaceused	Displays critical information regarding storage space used by databases
sp_statistics	Displays information about all indexes and statistics on a table or view
sp_who	Displays information about current SQL Server 2000 users

System Functions

As you learned in Chapter 3, Microsoft also provides a large number of system functions that assist you in querying information stored in the system and database catalogs. Table 7.8 presents the most commonly used functions and their exact purpose.

Table 7.8 System functions used for viewing database information.

System Function Name	Purpose
DATABASEPROPERTYEX	Displays database option settings
DB-ID	Displays the ID number for a database
DB_NAME	Displays the name of a database
FILE_ID	Displays the ID of a logical file name
FILE_NAME	Displays the logical file name of a database file
FILEPROPERTY	Displays a value for a particular file property
GET DATE	Displays the current system date and time
HOST_NAME	Displays the name of a host computer
STATS_DATE	Displays the date statistics were updated
USER_ID	Displays the database ID of a user
USER_NAME	Displays the database name of a user

For example, the following query displays the number of data pages allocated to the pubs database:

```
USE pubs
SELECT FILEPROPERTY ('pubs', 'spaceused')
```

Information Schema Views

Perhaps one of the most powerful methods for viewing database information in SQL Server 2000 is to use the information schema views. These views are based on the underlying system and database catalogs. They are compliant with SQL-92 standards and offer yet another method of viewing information without relying on direct queries of the system tables. Table 7.9 lists the information schema views of SQL Server 2000.

Here is an example of using an information schema view to look at all of the tables you have permission to access in the Northwind database:

```
USE Northwind
SELECT * FROM INFORMATION_SCHEMA.TABLES
```

Summary

It is obviously critical for you to master database creation techniques and issues. After all, this is where it all begins for the database administrator. Remember, you have different methods available to you for creating these user databases. There are also various maintenance tasks for you to perform and different ways to accomplish them. Finally, as you learned in this chapter, you have many methods for obtaining information about your databases, including queries, stored procedures, and information schema views.

Although this chapter was of obvious importance, the next chapter is also extremely important because it covers all aspects of securing your SQL Server 2000 implementation. This includes securing access to the server itself, as well as access to specific data in specific database locations.

Table 7.9   The information schema views of SQL Server 2000.

Information Schema View	Purpose
INFORMATION_SCHEMA.CHECK_CONSTRAINTS	Displays information about **CHECK** constraints in the database
INFORMATION_SCHEMA.COLUMN_DOMAIN_USAGE	Displays information about user-defined data types in the database
INFORMATION_SCHEMA.COLUMN_PRIVILEGES	Displays privileges in the current database
INFORMATION_SCHEMA.COLUMNS	Displays information on each accessible column in the current database
INFORMATION_SCHEMA.CONSTRAINT_COLUMN_USAGE	Displays information about constraints in the current database
INFORMATION_SCHEMA.CONSTRAINT_TABLE_USAGE	Displays information about tables that have constraints
INFORMATION_SCHEMA.DOMAIN_CONSTRAINTS	Displays information about user-defined data types with rules bound to them
INFORMATION_SCHEMA.DOMAINS	Displays user-defined data types that the current user can access from the current database
INFORMATION_SCHEMA.KEY_COLUMN_USAGE	Displays information about the columns used as key fields
INFORMATION_SCHEMA.PARAMETERS	Displays information about parameters of user-defined functions or stored procedures accessible to the current user in the current database
INFORMATION_SCHEMA.REFERENTIAL_CONSTRAINTS	Displays information about each foreign constraint in the current database
INFORMATION_SCHEMA.ROUTINES	Displays information about each stored procedure and function accessible to the current user in the current database
INFORMATION_SCHEMA.ROUTINE_COLUMNS	Displays information for each column returned by the table-valued functions accessible to the current user in the current database
INFORMATION_SCHEMA.SCHEMATA	Displays information for each database the current user has permissions for
INFORMATION_SCHEMA.TABLE_CONSTRAINTS	Displays information about each table constraint in the current database
INFORMATION_SCHEMA.TABLE_PRIVILEGES	Displays each table privilege granted to or by the current user in the current database
INFORMATION_SCHEMA.TABLES	Displays information about each table in the current database for which the current user has permissions
INFORMATION_SCHEMA.VIEW_COLUMN_USAGE	Displays information about each column in the database used in a view definition
INFORMATION_SCHEMA.VIEW_TABLE_USAGE	Displays information for tables used in views in the current database
INFORMATION_SCHEMA.VIEWS	Displays information about views accessible to the current user in the current database

7

Part III

Administering and
Optimizing SQL
Server 2000

Configuration Deployment
Planning
Troubleshooting

Chapter 8

Securing SQL Server 2000

Welcome to one of the most important topics this book presents—how to secure your SQL Server 2000 installation. In addition to being one of the most important topics, it is also one of the most complex. This is because SQL Server 2000 uses a multilayered security approach that is also very effective, and it is most often installed on Windows 2000 or Windows NT 4, which also features a multilayered approach to security. Follow the instructions presented in this chapter, however, and you can construct a powerful security fortress around your mission-critical SQL Server data.

An Overview of SQL Server Security

The security model of SQL Server 2000 is quite complex. First, you need to successfully secure the operating system that SQL Server 2000 functions upon. You should consult the *Windows 2000 Security Little Black Book* by Ian McLean for the appropriate steps required for securing the Windows 2000 operating systems.

Beyond the underlying operating system, in order for you to provide effective SQL Server security you must first control access to the SQL Server 2000 services. Then, as an additional level of security, you must control access to the particular databases users may access. Finally, you must construct the specific permissions users are to have within these databases.

These multiple layers of SQL Server security guarantee not only a high level of security, but also make sure you have a high degree of granularity when administering the system. While your administrative workload can be a bit high, the payoff—a secure relational database management system—is well worth the price.

SQL Server Authentication

SQL Server 2000 must authenticate user accounts that desire access to the RDBMS. This is certainly where it all begins from a security perspective for SQL Server 2000. Remember (from Chapter 4 of this book) that there are two options for authenticating these users—relying on the Windows operating system for the authentication, or having SQL Server 2000 itself perform the authentication. Decision Tree 8.1 summarizes the information from Chapter 4 to help you make this choice quickly and easily.

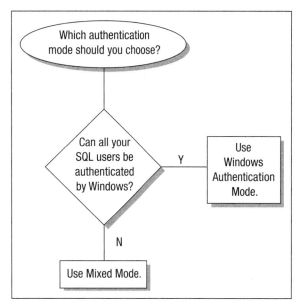

Decision Tree 8.1
Choosing your SQL Server authentication mode.

Although you were forced to select an authentication model used by SQL Server 2000 during installation, you can switch models later using the following steps:

1. Select Start|Programs|Microsoft SQL Server|Enterprise Manager.

2. Expand the nodes in the left pane to view your SQL Server instance.

3. Right-click your server and choose Properties from the shortcut menu.

4. Choose the Security tab (see Figure 8.1). Notice how you are able to switch authentication modes in the Authentication area. Notice also how Mixed Mode appears as SQL Server and Windows in this interface. Also notice the auditing area on this tab. The next section details these options for authentication.

Auditing Authentication

In a high security environment, you may need to audit the login activity against your server and the results of authentication. You configure this auditing activity on the Security tab of the server Properties window, which permits you the following options for logging SQL Server authentication activity:

- *None*—Choosing this option disables auditing. This is the default setting for auditing and places no additional overhead on the authentication process.

- *Success*—Choosing this option causes SQL Server 2000 to audit successful login attempts. Log records for these events appear in the Windows application log of Event Viewer (see Figure 8.2) and the SQL Server error log. Selecting this option requires you to stop and restart the server in order for logging to begin.

8

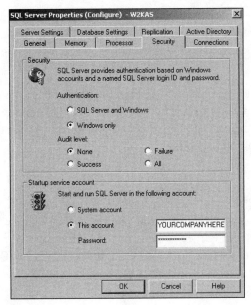

Figure 8.1
Configuring the authentication mode for SQL Server 2000.

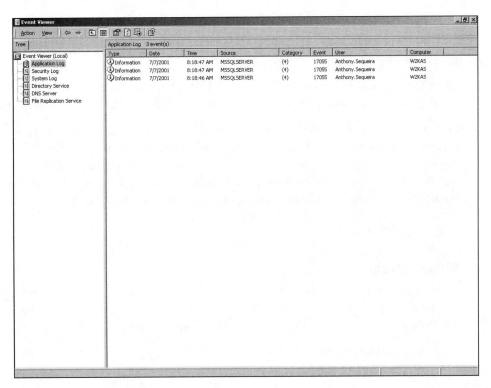

Figure 8.2
Viewing authentication events in the Event Viewer.

- *Failure*—Selecting this option causes SQL Server 2000 to audit failed login attempts. Log records for these events appear in the Windows application log of Event Viewer and the SQL Server error log. Selecting this option requires you to stop and restart the server in order for logging to begin.

- *All*—Selecting this option causes SQL Server 2000 to audit both successful and failed login attempts. Log records for these events appear in the Windows application log of Event Viewer and the SQL Server error log. Selecting this option requires you to stop and restart the server in order for logging to begin.

Windows Authentication

If your SQL Server 2000 users are being authenticated by a Windows operating system (either NTDS or Kerberos authentication mechanisms), you should consider using Windows Authentication as your login security mechanism, because of the reduced administrative workload it offers. You do not have to create separate logins within SQL Server for these users; you can rely upon the accounts already created within Windows for those users that desire access to your RDBMS.

Here are the steps SQL Server 2000 follows when you select Windows Authentication as your authentication mode:

1. A user attempts to connect to SQL Server 2000.

2. The client application opens a trusted connection to SQL Server and passes the user's Windows security credentials to the server.

3. SQL Server checks the **sysxlogins** system table for the Windows user account or a group the user account belongs to. If an appropriate entry is found, the connection is accepted.

Remember, choosing Windows Authentication Mode has many advantages. Users love it because they do not have to provide additional login credentials to access the SQL Server. You can quickly add entire groups of users to SQL Server by mapping Windows groups in SQL Server, and you can take advantage of additional security features—including secure validation and encryption of passwords, auditing, password expiration, minimum password length requirements, and account lockouts rules. All of these additional features are provided by Windows directory services.

Mixed Mode

If you must accommodate user accounts that have not been validated by a Windows directory service, you must use Mixed Mode authentication. Here are the steps SQL Server 2000 follows when you select Mixed Mode authentication as your authentication mode:

1. A user attempts to connect to SQL Server 2000.

2. If no trusted connection is established for Windows Authentication, SQL Server 2000 challenges the user for a valid user account and password.

3. SQL Server checks the login account and password against the entries in the **sysxlogins** table.

4. If there is not a matching entry in the table, the user is denied access to the server.

Realize that the single advantage Mixed Mode authentication provides you is the ability to accommodate non-Windows NT/2000 clients, such as Unix or Internet clients who do not log on against Windows systems anywhere in your network infrastructure.

Security Account Delegation

In order to increase the capabilities of your SQL Server 2000 implementation, the product supports security account delegation. One of your SQL Server 2000 installations can connect to others using the security credentials of the original logon. In order to take advantage of this feature, make sure the following conditions are met:

- All SQL Server systems must be participating in Windows 2000 domains supporting both Kerberos and Active Directory.

- The user account must not have the following option selected in Windows 2000— "Account is sensitive and cannot be delegated."

- The user account must have this option selected in Windows 2000—"Account is trusted for delegation."

- The computer running SQL Server 2000 must have the following option selected in Windows 2000—"Computer is trusted for delegation."

- SQL Server 2000 must be running the TCP/IP protocol.

- You must assign a Service Principal Name (SPN) to the SQL Server 2000 system. Delegation enforces mutual authentication, and the SPN proves that SQL Server is verified on the particular server, at the particular socket address, by you as the Windows 2000 account domain administrator. You can establish an SPN for SQL Server using the setspn utility. This utility can be found in the Windows 2000 Resource Kit. Use the following code at a command prompt to create the SPN:

```
setspn -A MSSQLSvc/Host:port serviceaccount
```

For example:

```
setspn -A MSSQLSvc/sqlsrv1.acme.com sqlaccount
```

Impersonation

SQL Server 2000 has the ability to impersonate the client when it needs to access resources on the network. For example, if SQL Server needs to access file resources protected by

NTFS security, SQL Server presents the security credentials of the logged-on user. Fortunately, SQL Server 2000 supports this ability by default, and no further configuration is required.

SQL Server Encryption

Remember that SQL Server 2000 helps to protect your mission-critical data using *encryption*. Encryption is the process of making data unreadable as it is transmitted or stored on a network device. SQL Server 2000 automatically encrypts passwords stored in system tables, preventing all users from viewing this important security information. SQL Server also has the ability to encrypt the Transact-SQL definition of objects stored in the **syscomments** system table. Finally, SQL Server 2000 encrypts data as it is transferred across the network, thanks to network encryption mechanisms. See Chapters 4 and 5 of this book for more information regarding enabling this level of encryption.

Managing Logins

Obviously, a critical step in your mastery of SQL Server security is the successful management of logins. Whether you are using Windows Authentication Mode or Mixed Mode security, you must properly create and manage logins so that users can access the server. This is the first of several layers of security you must properly maintain.

Creating Logins

There are many methods for creating logins in SQL Server 2000. You have a wizard, the graphical tools of Enterprise Manger, and Transact-SQL options. This section covers all of these for you.

Perhaps the simplest (yet not the fastest) method for creating SQL Server 2000 login accounts is to use the SQL Server Create Login Wizard. You may use this wizard for creating logins in both authentication modes. Here are the steps for using the wizard to create a SQL Server login account when using Windows Authentication:

1. Select Start|Programs|Microsoft SQL Server|Enterprise Manager.

2. Expand the nodes in the left pane to view your SQL Server instance.

3. From the Tools menu, choose Wizards.

4. In the Select Wizard window, expand the Databases node.

5. Select the Create Login Wizard option and choose OK.

6. Select Next in the Welcome page of the wizard.

7. In the Select Authentication Mode For This Login page (see Figure 8.3), indicate whether you are creating a login for your Windows authenticated account, or creating a SQL Server login account for authentication by SQL Server 2000. For these steps, select the Windows Account Information... option to create a login for a Windows-authenticated account. Choose Next.

8. In the Authentication With Windows page (see Figure 8.4), provide the domain name and the account name for the Windows account. Then, in the Security Access area, choose whether access to the server should be permitted or denied. When you have completed these selections, choose Next.

9. In the Grant Access To Security Roles page (see Figure 8.5), select which server roles the user account should be added to. Server roles permit special abilities for the account, and this chapter covers these roles in detail in a later section appropriately titled "Roles." Choose Next when finished making your selections.

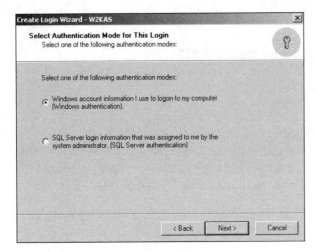

Figure 8.3
The Select Authentication Mode For This Login page.

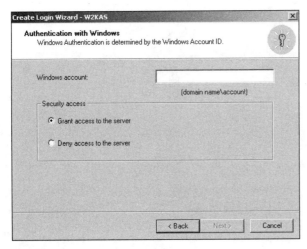

Figure 8.4
The Authentication With Windows page.

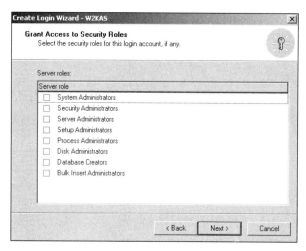

Figure 8.5
The Grant Access To Security Roles page.

10. In the Grant Access To Databases page (see Figure 8.6), select which databases you need to enable the login account to access. This creates a database user account in the appropriate databases, and this level of security also receives coverage later in this chapter in the "Database Users" section. Choose Next when finished.

11. In the Completing The Create Login Wizard page, review the options you provided and choose Finish when you are ready to create the login.

12. Select OK in the Wizard Complete! dialog box.

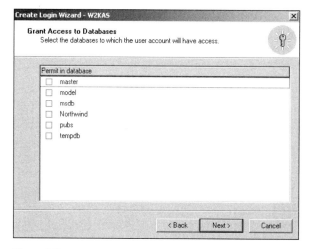

Figure 8.6
The Grant Access To Databases page.

You should follow these steps for using the Create Login Wizard for creating login accounts that SQL Server 2000 provides the authentication for:

1. Select Start|Programs|Microsoft SQL Server|Enterprise Manager.

2. Expand the nodes in the left pane to view your SQL Server instance.

3. From the Tools menu, choose Wizards.

4. In the Select Wizard window, expand the Databases node.

5. Select the Create Login Wizard option and choose OK.

6. Select Next in the Welcome page of the wizard.

7. In the Select Authentication Mode For This Login page, indicate whether you are creating a login for your Windows authenticated account, or creating a SQL Server login account for authentication by SQL Server 2000. For these steps, select the SQL Server Login Information... option. Choose Next.

8. In the Authentication with SQL Server page (see Figure 8.7), provide the Login ID (name) and password, and confirm the password for this account. Choose Next when finished.

9. In the Grant Access To Security Roles page, select which server roles the user account should be added to. Choose Next when finished making your selections.

10. In the Grant Access To Databases page, select which databases you need to enable the login account to access. Choose Next when finished.

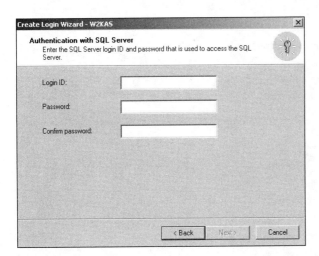

Figure 8.7
The Authentication With SQL Server page.

11. In the Completing The Create Login Wizard page, review the options you provided and choose Finish when you are ready to create the login.

12. Select OK in the Wizard Complete! dialog box.

You can also create logins for SQL Server 2000 using tools in Enterprise Manager that are not wizard based. Obviously, these logins may serve Windows Authentication Mode, or SQL Server 2000 authentication in Mixed Mode. Follow these steps for creating a Windows Authentication Mode login or a SQL Server 2000 authenticated login in Enterprise Manager directly:

1. Select Start|Programs|Microsoft SQL Server| Enterprise Manager.

2. Expand the nodes in the left pane to view your SQL Server instance.

3. Expand the Security node. Notice the Logins object inside this node.

4. Right-click the Logins object and choose New Login from the shortcut menu. Notice that the SQL Server Login Properties - New Login window appears (see Figure 8.8).

5. On the General tab, complete the Login name. Notice that you may use the ellipses button to browse a Windows directory service for the name if you are using Windows Authentication Mode. Notice also that you have the opportunity to select a default database for the user account to connect to and a default language for the user account using this method of account creation. When you are finished with these options, choose the Server Roles tab.

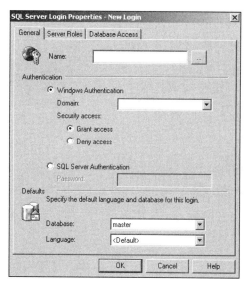

Figure 8.8
The SQL Server Login Properties - New Login window.

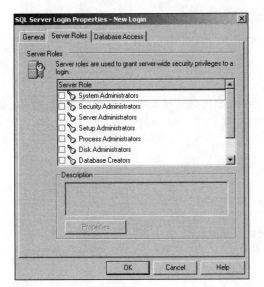

Figure 8.9
The Server Roles tab of the SQL Server Login Properties - New Login window.

6. Use the Server Roles tab (see Figure 8.9) to select any server roles for the login. When you are finished, choose the Database Access tab to configure specific database access for the login account.

7. When you are finished, choose OK.

8. If you are creating a SQL Server authenticated login account, you must confirm the password in the Confirm Password dialog box that appears and choose OK.

Fortunately, Microsoft also provides the ability to create these SQL logins using Transact-SQL syntax. This is often the most effective and efficient method for creating large numbers of logins quickly.

You use the stored procedure **sp_grantlogin** to add a Windows account to SQL Server 2000 and permit this account to participate in Windows Authentication on the server. Remember that this account can be a Windows group account, thus permitting large numbers of users access to the server with this single administrative operation. The full syntax of the **sp_grantlogin** procedure follows:

```
sp_grantlogin [@loginame =] 'login'
```

Here the **@loginname** argument simply provides the name of the Windows account, using the domain name\account name syntax. For example, the command

```
EXEC sp_grantlogin 'Acme\JohnJ'
```

creates a login for the JohnJ account of the Acme windows domain. The following example creates a login account for the entire Managers group of this same domain:

```
EXEC sp_grantlogin 'Acme\Managers'
```

In order to add logins for authentication by SQL Server 2000, you use the **sp_addlogin** stored procedure. The complete syntax for this procedure follows:

```
sp_addlogin [ @loginame = ] 'login'
    [ , [ @passwd = ] 'password' ]
    [ , [ @defdb = ] 'database' ]
    [ , [ @deflanguage = ] 'language' ]
    [ , [ @sid = ] sid ]
    [ , [ @encryptopt = ] 'encryption_option' ]
```

These syntax elements are as follows:

- **[@loginame =]**—Specifies the name of the login account.

- **[@passwd =]**—Specifies the password for the account.

- **[@defdb =]**—Specifies the default database for the user to enter upon logon.

- **[@deflanguage =]**—Specifies the default language assigned when a user logs on to SQL Server.

- **[@sid =]**—Specifies the Security Identifier for the account and is optional since SQL Server 2000 can automatically generate this value.

- **[@encryptopt =]**—Specifies whether the password is encrypted when stored in the system tables.

For example, this code creates a new login account named TamiS with a password of supersecret and a default database of corporate:

```
EXEC sp_addlogin 'TamiS', 'supersecret', 'corporate'
```

Although there are many methods for creating your SQL Server logins, there are not nearly as many for planning for these accounts.

Modifying Logins

There are various modifications you may need to make to SQL Server logins after you create them. These modifications include changing passwords, changing default databases, or changing default languages these logins use. This section examines making these modifications using Enterprise Manager, as well as Transact-SQL.

Password changes are inevitable within the security system of SQL Server 2000. Fortunately, these changes are simple for you to make. Follow these steps for changing the login password for an account using Enterprise Manager:

1. Select Start|Programs|Microsoft SQL Server|Enterprise Manager.

2. Expand the nodes in the left pane to view your SQL Server instance.

3. Expand the Security node.

4. Select the Logins object in the left pane; notice that the logins appear in the right pane.

5. Right-click the login you need to change the password for and choose Properties from the shortcut menu (see Figure 8.10).

6. In the SQL Server Login Properties window, use the Password field on the General tab to change the password for the account. Remember, if you select the Properties for a Windows Authentication account, you cannot change the password for the account from within SQL Server. This is because the password property is controlled from within the Windows operating system. In the case of Windows 2000, use the Active Directory Users And Computers console in order to change the password.

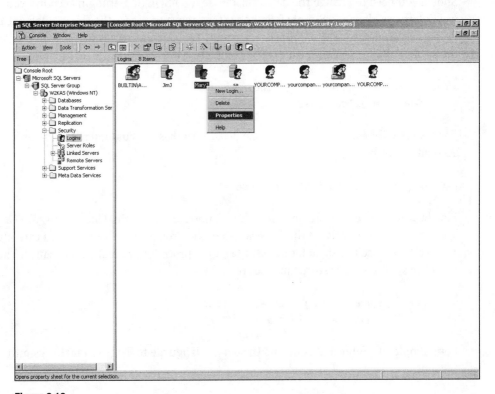

Figure 8.10
Accessing the Properties for a login account.

Note: One of the first tasks you should accomplish as a SQL Server administrator is to protect the system administrator (sa) login by assigning a complex, thus difficult-to-hack, password to this account. This is because this very important account has no password set by default. Use the steps described above to accomplish this. It is frightening to think about how many SQL Server installations in production still have no password set on the most powerful account in SQL Server.

Fortunately, you can also change the password property for a login using the Transact-SQL stored procedure **sp_password**. The complete syntax for this stored procedure follows:

```
sp_password [ [ @old = ] 'old_password' , ]
    { [ @new =] 'new_password' }
    [ , [ @loginame = ] 'login' ]
```

Obviously, this simple syntax needs no explanation. Here is an example that changes the password for the JJJames account from password to supersecret:

```
EXEC sp_password 'password', 'supersecret', 'JJJames'
```

Should you need to change the default database for a SQL Server login account, you can use Enterprise Manager. Simply follow the steps above to access the General tab of the Properties window for the appropriate account. You can also use Transact-SQL thanks to the **sp_defaultdb** stored procedure. The complete syntax for this procedure follows:

```
sp_defaultdb [ @loginame = ] 'login' ,
    [ @defdb = ] 'database'
```

For example, the following code sets the default database as **customers** for the user account MSmith:

```
EXEC sp_defaultdb 'MSmith', 'customers'
```

Finally, you may need to change the default language for a login. Once again, you can accomplish this easily using the General tab of the Properties window, or you can rely on Transact-SQL. Use the **sp_defaultlanguage** stored procedure to make this change. The complete syntax for this stored procedure follows:

```
sp_defaultlanguage [ @loginame = ] 'login'
    [ , [ @language = ] 'language' ]
```

For example, the following code sets the default language to English for the ASmith account:

```
EXEC sp_defaultlanguage 'ASmith', 'english'
```

Viewing Login Information

As you have seen earlier in this chapter, you can use Enterprise Manager to easily view login information. You can also use Transact-SQL to efficiently view this information. To do this, use the **sp_helplogins** stored procedure. The complete syntax for this procedure follows:

```
sp_helplogins [ [ @LoginNamePattern = ] 'login' ]
```

For example, the following code lists all logins for a particular instance of SQL Server 2000:

```
EXEC sp_helplogins
```

If you are interested in viewing login information for a specific login account, you may specify the login name with the stored procedure. For example, the following code provides information specific to the MaryJ account:

```
EXEC sp_helplogins 'MaryJ'
```

Removing Logins

In order to maintain proper security in your data environment, you should consistently remove SQL Server login accounts that are no longer needed. These may represent users that are no longer with your enterprise, or that no longer require access to your SQL Server 2000 installation.

You may use Enterprise Manager to remove these accounts using the following steps:

1. Select Start|Programs|Microsoft SQL Server|Enterprise Manager.

2. Expand the nodes in the left pane to view your SQL Server instance.

3. Expand the Security node.

4. Select the Logins object in the left pane; notice that the logins appear in the right pane.

5. Select the login you need to remove, right-click the account and choose Delete from the shortcut menu that appears.

6. Select Yes from the warning dialog box that indicates removing the login also removes all associated database users.

Note: *You can select multiple accounts for deletion by holding the control key down on the keyboard as you select various accounts. You can also use the shift key while selecting accounts to highlight multiple, contiguous accounts. Right-clicking any of the highlighted accounts and choosing delete, deletes all of the selected accounts.*

You can also remove SQL Server login accounts using Transact-SQL thanks to the **sp_droplogin** stored procedure. The complete syntax for this procedure follows:

```
sp_droplogin [ @loginame = ] 'login'
```

For example, the following command deletes the account JimJ from SQL Server 2000:

```
EXEC sp_droplogin 'JimJ'
```

Default Login Accounts

SQL Server 2000 features two default login accounts you do not need to create—BUILTIN\ADMINISTRATORS and sa. Any Windows 2000 administrators are automatically mapped to the BUILTIN\ADMINISTRATORS SQL account. This account has all rights within SQL Server 2000 and in all of its databases.

Note: If you do not desire this configuration, you may remove this group.

The system administrator account (sa) also has all rights within SQL Server and all of its databases. This account is used when you are running in Mixed Mode authentication and is a non-Windows account. As you read previously, it is critical that you protect this account with a strong password, as it has no password by default. This account is provided for backwards compatibility with previous versions of SQL Server, and you should instead use a Windows 2000 administrator account for when you need such powerful access to SQL Server.

Database Users

After creating login accounts to allow Windows users or non-Windows users to access your SQL Server, you also need to create database user accounts to allow access to specific SQL Server 2000 user databases. You may have noticed how easy it is to create these accounts as you create your login accounts using Enterprise Manager or the Create Login Wizard of Enterprise Manager. Fortunately, it is also easy to create these accounts following initial login creation.

There are two different—and simple—methods for creating these database user accounts in Enterprise Manager. The first method involves modifying the properties of an existing login. Follow these steps:

1. Select Start|Programs|Microsoft SQL Server|Enterprise Manager.

2. Expand the nodes in the left pane to view your SQL Server instance.

3. Expand the Security node.

4. Select the Logins object in the left pane; notice that the logins appear in the right pane.

5. Right-click the login you need to assign database access and choose Properties from the shortcut menu.

6. In the Properties window, select the Database Access tab. Select the Permit checkbox for the database the account needs to access. Notice how you can also assign the account to a database role from this tab as well. This chapter covers database roles in detail in the "Roles" section.

7. Choose OK to complete the configuration and create the database user account or accounts.

You can also create database user accounts from within the context of a database in Enterprise Manager. To do so, follow these steps:

1. Select Start|Programs|Microsoft SQL Server|Enterprise Manager.

2. Expand the nodes in the left pane to view your SQL Server instance.

3. Expand the server, and then expand the Databases node.

4. Expand the database you need to add a database user in and choose the Users object. Notice that user accounts in the database display in the right pane.

5. Right-click within the right pane and choose New Database User from the short-cut menu. Notice the Database User Properties - New User window appears (see Figure 8.11).

6. In the Login Name drop-down list, choose the SQL Server login account that requires access to the database. Once again, notice how easy it is to assign the account to a particular database role.

7. Choose OK when finished.

You can also use Transact-SQL to create your database user accounts thanks to the **sp_grantdbaccess** stored procedure. Here is the complete syntax for this stored procedure:

```
sp_grantdbaccess [@loginame =] 'login'
    [,[@name_in_db =] 'name_in_db' [OUTPUT]]
```

In this syntax, **[@loginame =]** is the name of the login for the new security account in the current database and **[@name_in_db =]** *'name_in_db'* **[OUTPUT]]** is the name for the security account in the database.

For example, this code creates a database user account named JohnS for the Windows 2000 user account of JohnS in the Windows 2000 domain of Acme:

```
EXEC sp_grantdbaccess 'Acme\JohnS', 'JohnS'
```

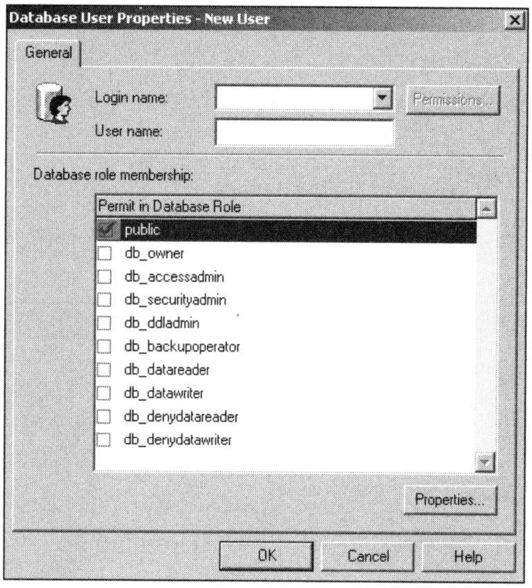

Figure 8.11
The Database User Properties - New User window.

Just as you must often remove SQL Server logins to make certain that accounts no longer have access to SQL Server 2000, you must also remove database user accounts to ensure users no longer have access to certain databases. You can remove these database user accounts using Transact-SQL or Enterprise Manager. To do so with Enterprise Manager, follow these steps:

1. Select Start|Programs|Microsoft SQL Server|Enterprise Manager.

2. Expand the nodes in the left pane to view your SQL Server instance.

3. Expand the server, and then expand the Databases node.

4. Expand the database from which you need to remove the database user account and choose the Users object. Notice that user accounts in the database display in the right pane.

5. Right-click the database user you want to delete and choose Delete from the shortcut menu.

6. Choose Yes in the warning dialog box.

To use Transact-SQL to remove database user accounts from a database, you can use the **sp_revokedbaccess** stored procedure. The complete syntax for this command follows:

```
sp_revokedbaccess [ @name_in_db = ] 'name'
```

For example, the following code removes the Georgia database user account from the **pubs** database:

```
USE pubs
EXEC sp_revokedbaccess 'Georgia'
```

Yet another powerful stored procedure you may use when managing your database users in SQL Server 2000 is **sp_change_users_login**. As its name implies, this stored procedure allows you to change the relationship between a SQL login account and a database user account. This stored procedure also allows you to create a report listing all the database users in a particular database not linked to any SQL Server login. The complete syntax for this stored procedure is:

```
sp_change_users_login [ @Action = ] 'action'
    [ , [ @UserNamePattern = ] 'user' ]
    [ , [ @LoginName = ] 'login' ]
```

The options in this stored procedure are as follows:

- **[@Action =]**—Indicates the action the stored procedure is to perform. There are three possibilities—**Auto_Fix**, **Report**, and **Update_One**. You use **Auto_Fix** to link user entries in the **sysusers** table in the current database to logins of the same name in **syslogins**. You use **Report** to lists database users, and their corresponding security identifiers (SID), that are in the current database yet not linked to any login. Finally, you use **Update_One** to link a specified database user to a specific login account.

- **[@UserNamePattern =]**—Allows you to specify the name of the database user.

- **[@LoginName =]**—Allows you to specify the name of the SQL login.

For example, this code produces a report of all the database users in the current database not mapped to SQL logins:

```
EXEC sp_change_users_login 'Report'
```

This example maps a database user named JohnS to a SQL Server login named JohnSequeira:

```
EXEC sp_change_users_login 'Update_One', 'JohnS', 'JohnSequeira'
```

Permissions

As you have learned, it is not enough to allow access to SQL Server 2000. You must also specify exactly which databases a user may access. But this is also not enough in the multi-level security model of SQL Server. You also must be certain that the database user account has appropriate permissions within the database. These permissions might include the rights to create objects, execute certain Transact-SQL statements, insert data into tables, or view data in these tables. This section examines the various permissions available in SQL Server 2000 and the mechanisms available for granting these permissions.

Mechanisms for Granting User Permissions

There are many mechanisms for assigning these permissions within SQL Server 2000. Some of these include:

- *Database owner (dbo)*—the database owner (dbo) is a special database user that has the implied permissions to perform any activities in the database whatsoever. Any member of the **sysadmin** fixed server role (including sa) who uses a database is mapped to this special user account to make sure they have adequate permissions to perform any activity. The **sysadmin** fixed server role is described later in this chapter in the "Roles" section. Also, any object created by any member of the **sysadmin** fixed server role belongs to this special dbo account automatically. The dbo user cannot be deleted and is always present in every database. As a member of the **sysadmin** role, you can change the owner of a database using the **sp_changedbowner** system stored procedure.

- *User*—As you have seen, you can create database user accounts based upon your SQL Server logins. These logins can be Windows users or non-Windows users as long as you are running Mixed Mode authentication. Database user accounts are then assigned specific permissions within databases.

- *Guest user*—The guest user account allows one or more of your SQL Server 2000 login accounts to access a database without an explicit database user account created for them. If a user tries to access a database, they will automatically assume the identity of this guest account if they have a valid SQL Server login account, they have no specific database user account, and there is a valid guest account in the database. You can even apply permissions to the guest user account as if it were any other database user account. You can add or delete a guest user account to all databases except **master** and **tempdb**, where it must always exist. By default, a guest user account is not created in your newly created databases, but adding one later is a simple matter. Just use the **sp_grantdbaccess** stored procedure that you learned earlier. For example:

```
USE Customers
GO
EXECUTE sp_grantdbaccess guest
```

- *Public role*—the public role is a convenient database role that automatically contains all users and groups defined as database users. It is comparable to the Everyone group in Windows NT or Windows 2000 in that it is a simple "catch-all" object that is convenient for you to use when you would like to assign a certain set of permissions to all users of a particular database. Because all users and groups within a database belong to this role already, you cannot assign these objects to this role. This special role exists in all databases (including system databases) and cannot be dropped.

- *Fixed database role*—These objects contain predefined rights within a database to perform select database-wide activities.

- *User-defined database role*—You can create these roles within a database to ease the assignment of permissions. You would do this if the fixed database roles do not meet your specific needs.

- *Statement permissions*—These are permissions to execute administrative statements against the database.

- *Object permissions*—These are permissions to access database objects.

- *Application role*—This allows you to grant permissions for database object and statement access to an application as opposed to users or groups.

Most of these mechanisms for the assignment of permissions in SQL Server 2000 are given further coverage in this section.

Statement Permissions

In order to create databases or objects within databases your users must possess sufficient statement permissions. These permissions allow your users to execute particular Transact-SQL statements against the server. In order to grant such permissions, the grantor must be a member of the **sysadmin**, **db_owner**, or **db_securityadmin** roles. These roles are covered in detail later in this chapter in the "Roles" section. Typical Transact-SQL statements that require these special permissions are:

- **BACKUP DATABASE**
- **BACKUP LOG**
- **CREATE DATABASE**
- **CREATE DEFAULT**
- **CREATE FUNCTION**
- **CREATE PROCEDURE**
- **CREATE RULE**
- **CREATE TABLE**

- **CREATE TRIGGER**

- **CREATE VIEW**

Chain of Ownership Issues

One major issue that arises when you grant these statement permissions to individual database user accounts is known as the chain of ownership issue. Here is a step-by-step example of how this issue arises and the problems it can cause:

1. You grant the ability to create tables in your database to the database user account JohnS.

2. JohnS creates a table named **Invoices** (without specifying a non-default table owner) and is considered by SQL Server as the owner of the table.

3. Mary issues the following query against your database and receives an error because she does not specify the owner of the table (the correct query should be **SELECT * FROM JohnS.Invoices**):

```
SELECT * FROM Invoices
```

4. To make matters worse (and further demonstrate chain of ownership issues), suppose the MaryS database user later creates a view based upon John's table. When users try to access this view, SQL Server 2000 must check permissions separately on each object in the chain. If your ownership chain is very long and complex, this can dramatically affect server performance, and it can make troubleshooting errors a nightmare for you.

The solution to the chain of ownership issue is to make sure that all users creating objects in your database specify the **dbo** role as the owner of the object. This enforces consistent ownership across all objects and dramatically simplifies the security model of SQL Server.

In order to implement this solution, users that you grant statement permissions to should be members of the **sysadmin**, **db_owner**, or **db_ddladmin** fixed database roles, and they should specify **dbo** as the owner in the statement as follows:

```
CREATE TABLE Customers.dbo.Regions
    ( RegionID nchar (5), RegionName nvarchar (20) )
```

Based on this information, you may find it necessary to change the owner of a database object. You can do so using the **sp_changeobjectowner** stored procedure. This procedure uses the following syntax:

```
sp_changeobjectowner [ @objname = ] 'object' , [ @newowner = ] 'owner'
```

For example, this code changes the ownership of the **Regions** table from JohnS of the Acme domain to **dbo**:

```
EXEC sp_changeobjectowner 'Acme\JohnS', 'dbo'
```

Granting Statement Permissions

As you might guess, SQL Server 2000 provides simple methods for granting statement permissions to your database users. You have graphical user interface methods thanks to Enterprise Manager, and you have Transact-SQL options.

In order to grant statement permissions using Enterprise Manager, follow these steps:

1. Select Start|Programs|Microsoft SQL Server|Enterprise Manager.

2. Expand the nodes in the left pane to view your SQL Server instance.

3. Expand your server and then expand the Databases container.

4. Right-click the database you need to grant statement permissions within, and choose Properties from the shortcut menu.

5. In the database Properties window, select the Permissions tab (see Figure 8.12).

6. Use the checkboxes to grant the appropriate permissions for the appropriate database user accounts. When you are finished with your selections, click OK.

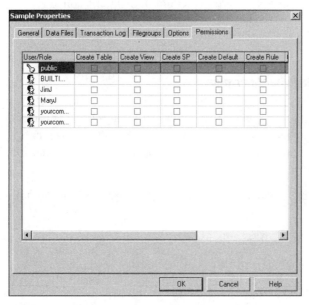

Figure 8.12
Granting statement permissions within a database.

In order to grant statement permissions to a database user account using Transact-SQL, use the **GRANT** statement. The complete syntax for this statement follows:

```
GRANT { ALL | statement [ ,...n ] }
TO security_account [ ,...n ]
```

The complete list of statements you may use with this command follows:

- **BACKUP DATABASE**

- **BACKUP LOG**

- **CREATE DATABASE**

- **CREATE DEFAULT**

- **CREATE FUNCTION**

- **CREATE PROCEDURE**

- **CREATE RULE**

- **CREATE TABLE**

- **CREATE VIEW**

For example, this statement grants multiple statement permissions to the users JohnS, MaryS, and the Designers Windows 2000 group account of the Acme domain:

```
GRANT CREATE DATABASE, CREATE TABLE
TO JohnS, MaryS, [Acme\Designers]
```

Denying and Revoking Statement Permissions

You may find yourself in the position of needing to deny or revoke certain statement permissions that you have granted to particular database user accounts. This is a simple matter. Keep in mind that explicitly denying a user account the ability to execute a particular statement is very powerful and overrides any other permissions they may have from other group or role membership.

In order to revoke or deny statement permissions using Enterprise Manager, follow these steps:

1. Select Start|Programs|Microsoft SQL Server|Enterprise Manager.

2. Expand the nodes in the left pane to view your SQL Server instance.

3. Expand your server and then expand the Databases container.

4. Right-click the database you need to grant statement permissions within, and choose Properties from the shortcut menu.

5. In the database Properties window, select the Permissions tab.

6. Notice that clicking a checkbox that is checked (permission granted) replaces the green check mark with a red X (see Figure 8.13). This denies the statement permission for the user account or group. Clicking the red X clears the checkbox, thereby revoking the statement permission, and at the same time eliminates the denial of the statement permission.

Denying statement permissions is also quite simple using the Transact-SQL **DENY** statement. The complete syntax for this statement follows:

```
DENY { ALL | statement [ ,...n ] }
TO security_account [ ,...n ]
```

Obviously, the possible statements used in this syntax matches the list of possible statements that you can grant access to. This example denies the **CREATE DATABASE** and **CREATE TABLE** statement permissions for JohnS, MaryS, and the Designers Windows 2000 group account of the Acme domain:

```
DENY CREATE DATABASE, CREATE TABLE
TO JohnS, MaryS, [Acme\Designers]
```

Revoking statement permissions using Transact-SQL is just as simple. Use the **REVOKE T-SQL** statement, which has the following syntax:

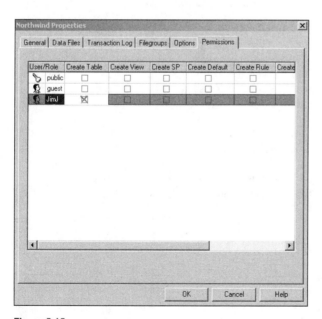

Figure 8.13
Denying statement permissions in Enterprise Manager.

```
REVOKE { ALL | statement [ ,...n ] }
FROM security_account [ ,...n ]
```

For example, the following statement revokes the **CREATE DATABASE** and **CREATE TABLE** statement permissions for JohnS, MaryS, and the Designers Windows 2000 group account of the Acme domain:

```
REVOKE CREATE DATABASE, CREATE TABLE
TO JohnS, MaryS, [Acme\Designers]
```

Viewing Statement Permissions

Obviously, it is simple to view statement permissions for a particular database in Enterprise Manager. Just follow the above steps for granting statement permissions in Enterprise Manager to access the Permissions dialog for a particular database. You can view the settings in this window, and select Cancel when you are finished.

You can also view statement permission settings using the Transact-SQL **sp_helprotect** stored procedure. The syntax for this procedure follows:

```
sp_helprotect [ [ @name = ] 'object_statement' ]
    [ , [ @username = ] 'security_account' ]
    [ , [ @grantorname = ] 'grantor' ]
    [ , [ @permissionarea = ] 'type' ]
```

Here is an explanation of the key arguments used in this syntax:

- **[@name =]**—Indicates the name of an object in the current database, or a statement, you would like to appear in the report. If you set this value to **NULL**, all statement permissions for all objects are reported for the current database.

- **[@username =]**—Specifies the name of the security account for which permissions are returned.

- **[@grantorname =]**—Specifies the name of the security account that has granted permissions.

- **[@permissionarea =]**—This value is a character string indicating whether to display object permissions (o), statement permissions (s), or both (o s).

For example, the following statement lists all of the statement permissions in the current database:

```
EXEC sp_helprotect NULL, NULL, NULL, 's'
```

Object Permissions

Chances are all of your database users are going to require object permissions. Object permissions allow your users to perform actions on tables, views, functions, and stored procedures. Database object owners, members of the **sysadmin** role, or members of the

db_securityadmin role can grant, revoke, or deny these object permissions to users for specific objects.

As a database administrator, the most common object permissions you deal with are database object permissions, described in Table 8.1.

Note: *In many interfaces within SQL Server 2000, the **REFERENCES** object permission appears as the abbreviation **DRI**. This stands for declarative referential integrity.*

Granting Object Permissions

Granting object permissions is possible using both Enterprise Manager and Transact-SQL syntax. In order to use Enterprise Manager to grant these permissions, follow these simple steps:

1. Select Start|Programs|Microsoft SQL Server|Enterprise Manager.

2. Expand the nodes in the left pane to view your SQL Server instance.

3. Expand your server and then expand the Databases container.

4. Expand the database that contains objects you need to specify object permissions for. For example, expand the Northwind database and then select the **Tables** object.

5. In the right pane, right-click the **Customers** table and choose Properties. The Table Properties - Customers window appears (see Figure 8.14).

6. Choose the Permissions button to view the object permissions set on this object (see Figure 8.15). Selecting a checkbox places a green checkmark in the box indicating the permission is granted.

7. Notice the Columns button for this object. Because tables consist of columns, you can set object permissions even at the column level. Choose the Columns button to view the Column Permissions window (see Figure 8.16). Notice how you can easily specify which specific columns a user can access.

8. When you have made all of your modifications to object permissions, choose OK in each of the configuration screens to accept your changes.

Granting object permissions can be very efficient if you use Transact-SQL methodologies. Doing so requires the use of the **GRANT** statement. The syntax changes a bit when you use the **GRANT** statement to grant object permissions as opposed to statement

Table 8.1   Database object permissions.

Permission	Description
DELETE	Allows users to delete data from tables or views.
EXECUTE	Allows users to run stored procedures and functions.

(continued)

Table 8.1   Database object permissions _(continued)_.

Permission	Description
INSERT	Allows users to add new data to tables or views.
REFERENCES	Allows users to refer to a table with a **FOREIGN KEY** constraint without having **SELECT** permissions to the table.
SELECT	Allows users to view information in tables, views, columns, or functions.
UPDATE	Allows users to update data in tables, columns, or views.

permissions. The complete syntax for the **GRANT** statement when assigning object permissions follows:

```
GRANT
    { ALL [ PRIVILEGES ] | permission [ ,...n ] }
    {
        [ ( column [ ,...n ] ) ] ON { table | view }
        | ON { table | view } [ ( column [ ,...n ] ) ]
        | ON { stored_procedure | extended_procedure }
        | ON { user_defined_function }
    }
TO security_account [ ,...n ]
[ WITH GRANT OPTION ]
[ AS { group | role } ]
```

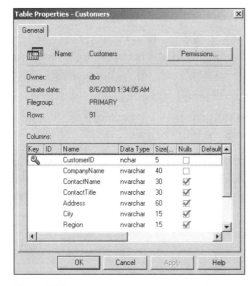

Figure 8.14
The Table Properties-Customers window.

Notice there are some additional syntax elements used with the **GRANT** statement now that require explanation. The *permission* argument allows you to specify the permission or permissions you are granting. These include:

- **DELETE**

- **EXECUTE**

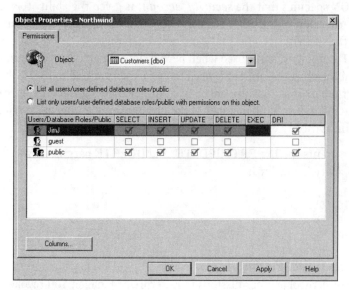

Figure 8.15
Setting permissions for an object.

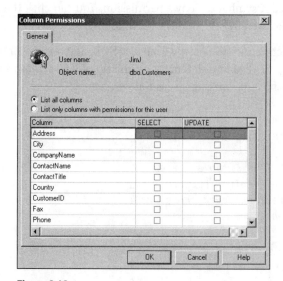

Figure 8.16
The Column Permissions window.

- **INSERT**
- **REFERENCES**
- **SELECT**
- **UPDATE**

WITH GRANT OPTION specifies that the **security_account** is given the ability to grant the specified object permission to the other security accounts. **AS {group|role}** specifies the optional name of the security account in the current database that has the authority to execute the **GRANT** statement. **AS** is used when permissions on an object are granted to a group or role, and the object permissions need to be further granted to users who are not members of the group or role. Because only a user, rather than a group or role, can execute a **GRANT** statement, a specific member of the group or role grants permissions on the object under the authority of the group or role.

The following example grants the **INSERT**, **UPDATE**, and **DELETE** permissions to the database users JohnS, MaryS, and JimJ:

```
GRANT INSERT, UPDATE, DELETE
ON authors
TO JohnS, MaryS, JimJ
```

Denying and Revoking Object Permissions

You can easily revoke or deny object permissions in Enterprise Manager. You revoke permissions in order to remove permissions you have previously granted. Just use the steps for granting object permissions to access the appropriate Properties window, and then click a checkbox to add the red X symbol to deny a permission. You can click the checkbox again to clear all symbols, thereby revoking the permission.

You can also deny and revoke object permissions using Transact-SQL, and once again the syntax differs slightly from denying or revoking statement permissions. The syntax of the **DENY** statement when used with object permissions is as follows:

```
DENY
    { ALL [ PRIVILEGES ] | permission [ ,...n ] }
    {
        [ ( column [ ,...n ] ) ] ON { table | view }
        | ON { table | view } [ ( column [ ,...n ] ) ]
        | ON { stored_procedure | extended_procedure }
        | ON { user_defined_function }
    }
TO security_account [ ,...n ]
[ CASCADE ]
```

Notice this syntax follows closely the **GRANT** statement when used to grant object permissions. There is one major difference, and that is the **CASCADE** option: [**CASCADE**] specifies that permissions are denied from *security_account* as well as any other security accounts granted permissions by *security_account*.

The following example denies the **SELECT**, **INSERT**, **UPDATE**, and **DELETE** object permissions on the invoices table for the database users JohnS, MaryS, and JimJ:

```
DENY SELECT, INSERT, UPDATE, DELETE
ON invoices
TO JohnS, MaryS, JimJ
```

Finally, the syntax for the **REVOKE** statement when used with object permissions follows. Notice it closely follows the syntax for both the **GRANT** and **DENY** statements when used with object permissions:

```
REVOKE [ GRANT OPTION FOR ]
    { ALL [ PRIVILEGES ] | permission [ ,....n ] }
    {
        [ ( column [ ,....n ] ) ] ON { table | view }
        | ON { table | view } [ ( column [ ,....n ] ) ]
        | ON { stored_procedure | extended_procedure }
        | ON { user_defined_function }
    }
{ TO | FROM }
    security_account [ ,....n ]
[ CASCADE ]
[ AS { group | role } ]
```

One new argument you find in this syntax is the **[GRANT OPTION FOR]** argument, which you use when you need to specify that **WITH GRANT OPTION** permissions are being revoked as well.

In the following example, the **REVOKE** statement removes the **SELECT** object permissions on the **customers** table for the database user Mary:

```
REVOKE SELECT ON customers TO Mary
```

Viewing Statement Permissions

You can view statement permissions easily using Enterprise Manager. Simply access the Properties window for an object and use the Permissions button to view the permission settings for a particular object.

You can also use the **sp_helprotect** stored procedure to view these permissions using Transact-SQL. For example, this statement displays all of the object permissions for the **Invoices** table of the current database:

```
EXEC sp_helprotect 'Invoices'
```

Predefined Permissions

In addition to statement and object permissions there are also predefined permissions in SQL Server 2000. These are permissions possessed by database object owners or members of fixed roles. This chapter examines roles in the next section, and you should recall that database object owners possess the ability to make any change to the object they own. For example, if you have a database user that owns a table in the database, that user can view, add, or delete data, or they can alter the table definition as well as control the permissions for other users of the table.

Roles

Now that you fully understand the various permission levels within SQL Server 2000, it is time to acquaint yourself with the single largest administrative time saver you have in the security model: roles. Roles allow you to assemble users into a single unit. This single unit possesses certain permissions to the server, databases, and/or database objects. Roles are analogous to groups in the Windows NT or Windows 2000 operating system. There are fixed roles provided by Microsoft already in SQL Server 2000 for your use, or you can create your own roles to increase flexibility when assigning permissions.

You should always try to use roles when assigning permissions. Using roles reduces your administrative workload considerably, just as using groups to assign permissions helps you in the Windows 2000 operating system. Roles makes it simple to assign additional permissions as new database users are created in your SQL Server environment and when database users must receive new permissions due to a job change.

Fixed Server Roles

Fixed server roles allow you to grant specific permissions to specific individuals that require rights on the SQL Server 2000 installation. This is excellent if you have other users that you would like to assist you in administering the server. For example, if you have a user that is going to help you with the creation and management of databases on the server, you can simply add that user to the **dbcreator** fixed server role and the appropriate permissions are automatically granted to the account. Table 8.2 describes the fixed server roles present in SQL Server 2000.

The exact Transact-SQL statements each fixed server role may execute vary from role to role, obviously. The following list details these exact assignments:

- **bulkadmin**—BULK INSERT
- **dbcreator**—ALTER DATABASE, CREATE DATABASE, RESTORE
- **diskadmin**—only has permissions for certain stored procedures
- **processadmin**—KILL

Table 8.2   Fixed server roles.

Role	Permission
bulkadmin	Allows the user to execute **BULK INSERT** statements
dbcreator	Allows the user to create and alter databases
diskadmin	Allows the user to manage disk files
processadmin	Allows the user to manage SQL Server processes
securityadmin	Allows the user to manage and audit server logins
serveradmin	Allows the user to configure server-wide settings
setupadmin	Allows the user to install replication
sysadmin	Allows the user to perform any activity upon the server

- **securityadmin**—DENY, GRANT, REVOKE

- **serveradmin**—DBCC, RCONFIGURE, SHUTDOWN

- **setupadmin**—only has permissions for certain stored procedures

- **sysadmin**—all Transact-SQL statements

Remember, you can easily place a SQL Server login account in the appropriate fixed server roles when you create the account. Or you can follow the steps below to assign a user or group to the roles at a later time using Enterprise Manager:

1. Select Start|Programs|Microsoft SQL Server|Enterprise Manager.

2. Expand the nodes in the left pane to view your SQL Server instance.

3. Expand the Security container and select the Logins object.

4. Right-click the login and choose Properties from the shortcut menu.

5. Select the Server Roles tab and choose the fixed server roles the user account requires membership in (see Figure 8.17).

6. When you are finished making the selections, choose the OK button.

As you might guess, you can also use Transact-SQL to assign a login account to a fixed server role. This is done by using the **sp_addsrvrolemember** stored procedure. The complete syntax for this procedure follows:

```
sp_addsrvrolemember [ @loginame = ] 'login'
    , [ @rolename = ] 'role'
```

The possible role names you may use with this syntax are:

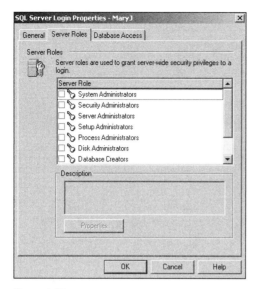

Figure 8.17
Adding a login to fixed server roles.

- **bulkadmin**
- **dbcreator**
- **diskadmin**
- **processadmin**
- **securityadmin**
- **serveradmin**
- **setupadmin**
- **sysadmin**

For example, the following code adds the HelenS account of the Acme domain to the **diskadmin** fixed server role:

```
EXEC sp_addsrvrolemember 'Acme\HelenS', 'diskadmin'
```

If you should need to remove a user from a fixed server role, you can use the appropriate Properties window within Enterprise Manager, or you can use the **sp_dropsrvrolemember** system stored procedure. The complete syntax for this procedure follows:

```
sp_dropsrvrolemember [ @loginame = ] 'login' , [ @rolename = ] 'role'
```

For example, this code removes a user named MaryS from the **securityadmin** fixed server role:

```
EXEC sp_dropsrvrolemember 'MaryS', 'securityadmin'
```

Fixed Database Roles

Just as fixed server roles provide you with a simple method for assigning permissions that allow users to manage server wide settings, fixed database roles permit you to easily assign permissions within databases. Table 8.3 describes the various fixed database roles within SQL Server 2000.

The exact Transact-SQL statements each fixed database role may execute vary from role to role. The list below details these exact assignments:

- **db_accessadmin**—only has permissions for certain stored procedures

- **db_backupoperator**—**BACKUP, CHECKPOINT, DBCC**

- **db_datareader**—**READTEXT, SELECT**

- **db_datawriter**—**DELETE, INSERT, UPDATE, UPDATETEXT, WRITETEXT**

- **db_ddladmin**—**ALTER DATABASE, ALTER FUNCTION, ALTER PROCEDURE, ALTER TABLE, ALTER TRIGGER, ALTER VIEW, CREATE DEFAULT, CREATE FUNCTION, CREATE INDEX, CREATE PROCEDURE, CREATE RULE, CREATE TABLE, CREATE TRIGGER, CREATE VIEW, DROP, REFERENCES, TRUNCATE TABLE**

- **db_denydatareader**—members are explicitly denied the ability to view data

- **db_denydatawriter**—members are explicitly denied the ability to change data

- **db_owner**—**ALTER DATABASE, ALTER FUNCTION, ALTER PROCEDURE, ALTER TABLE, ALTER TRIGGER, ALTER VIEW, BACKUP, CHECKPOINT, CREATE DEFAULT, CREATE FUNCTION, CREATE INDEX, CREATE PROCEDURE, CREATE RULE, CREATE TABLE, CREATE TRIGGER, CREATE VIEW, DBCC, DELETE, DENY, DENY** on object, **DROP, EXECUTE, GRANT, GRANT** on object, **INSERT, READTEXT, REFERENCES, RESTORE, REVOKE, REVOKE** on object, **SELECT, SETUSER, TRUNCATE TABLE, UPDATE, UPDATE STATISTICS, UPDATETEXT, WRITETEXT**

Table 8.3   Fixed database roles in SQL Server 2000.

Role	Description
db_accessadmin	Allows the user to add or remove database users, groups, or roles
db_backupoperator	Allows the user to backup the database
db_datareader	Allows the user to read data from any table
db_datawriter	Allows the user to change, add, or delete data from any table

(continued)

Table 8.3   Fixed database roles in SQL Server 2000 *(continued).*

Role	Description
db_ddladmin	Allows the user to add, modify, or drop database objects
db_denydatareader	Prohibits the user from reading data from any table
db_denydatawriter	Prohibits the user from changing data in any table
db_owner	Allows the user to perform any database activity
db_securityadmin	Allows the user to assign statement and object permissions
public	Contains all database users and can be used to assign default permissions

- **db_securityadmin—DENY, GRANT, REVOKE**

- **public—BEGIN TRANSACTION, COMMIT TRANSACTION, PRINT, RAISERROR, ROLLBACK TRANSACTION, SAVE TRANSACTION, SET**

You can easily place a SQL Server login account in the appropriate fixed database roles when you create the account. Or you can follow the steps below to assign a user or group to the roles at a later time using Enterprise Manager:

1. Select Start|Programs|Microsoft SQL Server|Enterprise Manager.

2. Expand the nodes in the left pane to view your SQL Server instance.

3. Expand the Security container and select the Logins object.

4. Right-click the login and choose Properties from the shortcut menu.

5. Select the Database Access tab and choose the fixed database roles that the user account requires membership in (see Figure 8.18).

6. When you are finished making the selections, choose the OK button.

You can also add users to fixed database roles using Transact-SQL. You can do this with the **sp_addrolemember** stored procedure. The complete syntax for this command follows:

```
sp_addrolemember [ @rolename = ] 'role' ,
   [ @membername = ] 'security_account'
```

For example, this code adds the user JohnS to the fixed database role of **db_datareader**:

```
EXEC sp_addrolemember 'JohnS', 'db_datareader'
```

Removing a user from a fixed database role is simple in Enterprise Manager. Just access the appropriate Properties window and use the checkbox to remove the account. You can also use the **sp_droprolemember** stored procedure. The complete syntax follows:

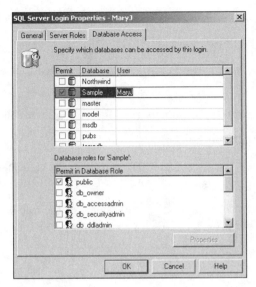

Figure 8.18
Adding a login to fixed database roles.

```
sp_droprolemember [ @rolename = ] 'role' ,
    [ @membername = ] 'security_account'
```

For example, this code removes the user AllisonS from the **db_datawriter** role:

```
EXEC sp_droprolemember 'Acme\AllisonS, 'db_datawriter'
```

User-defined Roles

You should find yourself relying on the fixed server and fixed database roles heavily in SQL Server 2000. You should also find that often you will have a large number of people that all need the same permissions and that there are no fixed roles that provide the suitable permissions. This is when you can create your own user-defined roles in SQL Server.

For example, say that you need to allow the Accounting Clerks access to a single table in the Accounting database. You can create a user-defined role named **AcctgClerks** and assign this role the appropriate access. As you add users to this role, they inherit the appropriate permissions.

In order to use Enterprise Manager to create a user-defined role, follow these steps:

1. Select Start|Programs|Microsoft SQL Server|Enterprise Manager.

2. Expand the nodes in the left pane to view your SQL Server instance.

3. Expand your server instance and then expand the Database container.

4. Expand the database you need to add a user-defined role to and right-click the Roles object.

5. Choose New Database Role from the shortcut menu.

6. In the Database Role Properties - New Role window, provide a name for your new role in the name field (see Figure 8.19).

7. Use the Add button to add the appropriate database users to the user-defined role.

8. Choose the OK button to create the user-defined role.

9. To modify the permissions this role possesses, right-click the role in the right-pane and choose Properties from the shortcut menu.

10. Use the Permissions button to assign the appropriate permissions for the role (see Figure 8.20). Notice the Columns button, which allows you to apply permissions to this specific level of access.

11. Choose OK twice in order to close all Windows and finish the permissions assignments.

You can use the **sp_addrole** stored procedure to create a user-defined role using Transact-SQL. The syntax for this procedure follows:

```
sp_addrole [ @rolename = ] 'role'
    [ , [ @ownername = ] 'owner' ]
```

For example, the following code creates a new role named **Managers** in the current database:

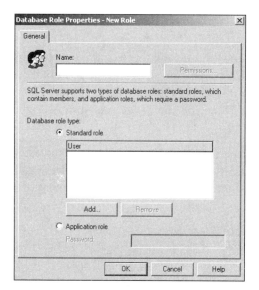

Figure 8.19
The Database Role Properties - New Role window.

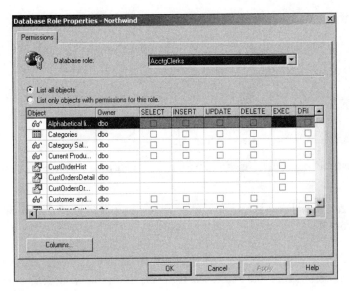

Figure 8.20
Setting permissions for the role.

```
EXEC sp_addrole 'Managers'
```

You can add members to this role easily using the **sp_addrolemember** stored procedure. Note that this is the same stored procedure you used earlier to add database users to fixed database roles. You can also use the **sp_droprolemember** stored procedure to remove accounts from these new roles you create.

Application Roles

Another method for controlling security in your SQL Server environment is to use application roles. Application roles allow applications to access the SQL Server data and maintain permissions you select for the application. For example, you can create an application for the Accounting Clerks and provide this application with the permissions necessary for updating certain tables within the Accounting database. If the Accounting Clerks attempt to update data using any other method, such as using a SQL Server client tool, they are denied access.

Application roles are unique in that they have no members. This works out well for you as an administrator because you do not have to grant permissions to user accounts directly. You simply create the application role, grant it the necessary permissions, and then be sure the application uses the role. Application roles are also unique in that they require a password for activation.

Follow these instructions for creating an application role in SQL Server 2000 using Enterprise Manager:

1. Select Start|Programs|Microsoft SQL Server|Enterprise Manager.

2. Expand the nodes in the left pane to view your SQL Server instance.

3. Expand your server instance and then expand the Database container.

4. Expand the database you need to add an application role to and right-click the Roles object.

5. Choose New Database Role from the shortcut menu.

6. In the Database Role Properties - New Role window, provide a name for your new role in the name field.

7. Choose the Application Role radio button and provide a password for the application role in the password field.

8. Choose the OK button to create the application role.

9. To modify the permissions this role possesses, right-click the role in the right-pane and choose Properties from the shortcut menu.

10. Use the Permissions button to assign the appropriate permissions for the role. Notice the Columns button, allowing you to apply permissions to this specific level of access.

11. Choose OK twice in order to close all Windows and finish the permissions assignments.

You can also use the **sp_addapprole** stored procedure to create your new application role using Transact-SQL. The syntax for this procedure follows:

```
sp_addapprole [ @rolename = ] 'role'
    , [ @password = ] 'password'
```

This example creates an application role named **AppRole** with a password of supersecret:

```
EXEC sp_addapprole 'AppRole', 'supersecret'
```

Your application developers must use the **sp_setapprole** stored procedure in their application to activate the application role and pass the password. This password may be encrypted in the application.

Summary

Securing your SQL Server 2000 system properly may be one of your most important jobs as a SQL Server administrator. Remember to properly secure the sa account by assigning a difficult to decipher password—and do this right away. Also, be sure you understand the various levels of security and how to properly configure them. You must set up access to the server itself for your users, then you must specify which databases they may access.

Finally, you must be very specific regarding which Transact-SQL statements these users may execute within a particular database.

You should use roles to simplify the assignment of these permissions in your SQL Server 2000 implementation. Fixed server roles, fixed database roles, user-defined roles, and application roles all can work together to make certain that you have permissions configured appropriately for your users.

The next chapter of this book is equally important. You must be able to back up data and restore this data in the event of an emergency of any kind.

8

Chapter 9

Backing Up and Restoring SQL Server 2000

Are regular backups of your SQL Server data really that important? Absolutely they are! In fact, securing the information contained in both your system and user databases is one of the most critical responsibilities you have as a database administrator. The importance of backups is often overlooked, which in turn costs companies millions of dollars every year.

Data loss is one of the biggest concerns of most Information Technology (IT) experts. However, with a thorough understanding of the backup-and-restore process—and a well-planned and designed backup-and-restore strategy—you can avoid losing SQL Server data.

Reasons for Performing Backups

A backup-and-restore strategy should be designed for recovery from disasters, fault tolerance, sharing of data, and optimizing your database activities. A proper backup strategy provides you the ability to utilize the restore process in any of these situations, therefore improving productivity.

Disaster Recovery

You should develop a backup-and-restore strategy that encompasses every possible disaster. Disasters can range from an accidental modification of data to a natural disaster. The following list contains many of the common disasters that can occur, prompting the need to restore data:

- Loss of a hard drive that contains your system files
- Loss of a hard drive that contains a data file
- Loss of a hard drive that contains a transaction log file
- Operating system failure
- Loss, theft, or destruction of your entire server
- Faulty backup media
- Faulty restoration device
- Theft of your backup media

- Accidental or malicious deletion of data

- Accidental or malicious update of data

- Natural disaster (earthquake, fire, or flood)

A properly designed backup-and-restore strategy provides a quick and efficient recovery process from any of these disasters. However, if the amount of data is so large that it takes an unacceptable amount of time to recover, you may need to configure multiple database environments to implement a fault-tolerance environment.

Fault Tolerance

A fault-tolerant SQL Server environment is implemented to make certain that SQL Server is always available even if you experience hardware failures. RAID 1, RAID 5, or RAID 10 can be used to provide fault tolerance for your disk subsystem. You use uninterruptible power supply (UPS) devices, perform system backups regularly, use reliable hardware, and prepare yourself for the loss of your entire server when planning your faul-tolerance strategy in SQL Server 2000.

Copying Data From One SQL Server to Another

Using a backup and restore strategy is one way you can move databases from one SQL Server 2000 system to another. Although there are other methods for moving your databases, the backup and restore strategy is known for its reliability and relative simplicity. All methods for transferring data from one system to another are presented in this book.

Monitoring Your Database

The backups you create in SQL Server can also be used for monitoring your database in an effort to proactively detect problems and resolve them before they occur. Furthermore, you can configure databases so that your users only have read-only access to the information.

One of the numerous tasks you have to perform as a database administrator is maintaining the consistency of your data. This is most commonly accomplished by monitoring your databases using Database Consistency Checker (DBCC) commands to make sure of their physical and logical consistency. For instance, you can back up the data on your production SQL server and restore it on a second SQL server. After restoring the data on the second SQL server, you can issue your DBCC commands on that database to detect and optionally correct problems they discover. You can also set performance condition alerts on the databases on the second SQL server to notify you of potential problems, such as running low on free space.

Read-only Databases

After restoring data on a second SQL server you can direct users that require only read access to data to that server. This strategy improves performance by minimizing contention for the data for the users who are performing the read-only requests and the users who are performing data modifications on your primary SQL server.

Understanding Backup and Restore Terminology

It is important to have a thorough understanding of the different terms and concepts used when discussing database backups and restorations. With a clear understanding of the different terms and concepts, you will be able to easily design an optimal backup-and-restore strategy that you can use for any of the aforementioned reasons.

Backup Devices

When performing a backup of your data you can choose to back up to either disk or tape for your backup media. The SQL Server 2000 backup program supports local (attached to the computer) tape drives, local disk drives, network disk drives, and named pipes.

Note: We'll talk more about backup devices later in this chapter.

Disk

In SQL Server 2000 you can perform a backup to a hard drive that resides locally or remotely. You can specify the path name to the local or remote hard drive when performing the backup operation or you can create a logical name for the hard drive and specify the logical name during the backup operation.

Tape

In SQL Server 2000 you can also perform a backup to a local tape drive. Unlike the disk media type, a backup cannot be written to a remote tape drive. Furthermore, the local tape device attached to your machine must be supported by Windows NT or Windows 2000. To be sure the tape device is supported by SQL Server 2000, verify that the tape drive exists on the Hardware Compatibility List (HCL) for your operating system.

Named Pipes

Named Pipes functionality is included with SQL Server to provide you the capability to perform backups using third-party software backup solutions. The functionality of the SQL Server 2000 backup software is based on your operating system's backup utility. For example, if you are running SQL Server 2000 on Windows 2000 and you are backing up to a local tape device, you may experience some limitations. If you want to overcome those limitations, you can purchase third-party backup software that allows additional backup functionality.

Backup Media Terms

Table 9.1 contains a list and description of many terms that you will see throughout this chapter and that you will use when discussing SQL Server Backups.

Now that you understand the different backup devices available to you and you are familiar with some of the terms you will be seeing and using, it is time to take a look at the permissions required to perform the backup and restore operations.

Table 9.1   Backup terminology.

Term	Description
Backup	A full or partial copy of a database, file, filegroup, or transaction log that creates a backup set. A backup set is stored on backup media (disk or tape) using a backup device (physical file name or a tape drive name).
Backup Device	The physical file (D:\mssql\backups\FullBack.bak) or specific tape \\.\Tape1 that you use to store a backup on backup media.
Backup File	A file that contains a backup set.
Backup Media	The actual physical media (disk or tape) used to store a backup set using a backup file. Backup media can contain multiple backup sets.*
Backup Set	The backup from a single backup operation located on a backup media. The backup set can reside on an individual backup media, a media family, or a media set.
Continuation Media	The backup media used when the initial media becomes full. The continuation media allows the backup process to continue even after the initial media is totally consumed.
Initial Media	The first media in a media family.
Media Family	All media (disk or tape) contained in a media set that was written by a single backup device for a single backup set.
Media Header	Contains information about the contents of the backup media. This header must be written before a backup set can be recorded on the backup media. This is also referred to as initializing the backup media.
Media Set	All media involved in a single backup operation. Some examples of media sets include: a single file, a single tape, a set of tapes written to by one backup device, or a set of tapes written by more than one backup device. For example, if four tape backup devices are used when creating a database backup and there are three tapes per tape backup device used to store the devices, then the media set contains twelve tapes.

*Backup media can contain multiple SQL Server 2000 backups and Windows 2000 backups.

Securing Your Backup Operations

As with all other aspects of SQL Server 2000, it is imperative to understand the security options available to you when you are implementing your backup strategy. By default you can successfully execute the **BACKUP LOG** or **BACKUP DATABASE** commands if you are a member of one of the following roles:

- **Sysadmin** fixed server role

- **Db_owner** fixed database role

- **Db_backupoperator** fixed database role

Additionally, you can grant **BACKUP DATABASE** and **BACKUP LOG** in Query Analyzer to individual users or groups using the following command:

```
GRANT BACKUP DATABASE, BACKUP LOG
TO Don, Thelma, [Corporate\Brian]
```

You are now also able to specify passwords for a backup set, media set, or both. This provides an additional layer of security when performing backup and restore operations by preventing unauthorized appends of backup sets to media sets and unauthorized restores of the backup.

Using the Password Option on a Media Set

After you apply a password to a media set, you are required to supply the password during the backup operation in addition to having the appropriate **BACKUP** permissions. You define the password for your backup set or media set by supplying an optional parameter when you execute the **BACKUP** command.

Note: The media set password is set when the media header is written and cannot be altered.

Although this prevents unauthorized appending of data it does not prevent the contents from being overwritten when the **FORMAT** command is used. Although passwords are used to prevent unauthorized access to media contents using SQL tools, it does not prevent unauthorized access by programs specifically created for accessing and destroying the data.

Note: Passwords do not encrypt the data in any way.

Using the Password Option on a Backup Set

A password on a backup set only protects that specific backup set. You can set different backup-set passwords on your media. Your backup-set password is set and written to the media when defined. After setting your backup-set password you will have to supply it when you perform a restore operation.

Ownership and Permissions

You can also control access to your backup devices with the use of the permissions and ownership on the device's physical file. SQL Server 2000 must be able to read and write to the device; the account that is used to start the SQL Server service must have write permissions. However, the **sp_addumpdevice** system stored procedure adds an entry for each device in the master database **sysdevices** system table without checking file access permissions.

Backup Device Types

You already know there are really two primary types of backup devices—disk and tape. With each of the two backup device types there are considerations you need to be aware of. When referencing a disk or tape device, you can specify either the physical name or the logical name of the device.

Physical and Logical Devices

When creating and referencing your backup devices, you can use either a physical or logical device name. Sometimes the physical and logical device names are referred to as permanent and temporary device names, respectively.

Physical Device Names

A physical device name is the name used by the operating system to identify the actual physical backup device. It includes the directory path name and the actual file name. For example, D:\mssql\backups\sales\backup.bak is used to reference the physical device name of these backup devices during the backup and restore operations.

The following backup example uses a physical device name:

```
BACKUP DATABASE Accounting
TO DISK = 'D:\MSSQL\Backups\Accounting\Acct.bak'
```

Logical Device Names

A logical device name is an alias or common name used to reference the physical device name. After defining the logical device name, information regarding the logical device is stored in the system tables within SQL Server. Often the logical device name is simpler and shorter to refer to than the physical device name. For example, a physical device name of D:\mssql\backups\Acct\backup.bak can be associated with a logical device name of Accounting_BU.

The following backup example uses a logical device name:

```
BACKUP DATABASE Accounting
      TO Accounting_BU
```

Note: When you are backing up or restoring a database, you can specify either the physical or logical device name.

Disk Devices

Remember, in SQL Server 2000 you can perform a backup to a hard drive that resides locally or remotely. You specify the path name to the hard drive when you start the backup operation or you create a logical name for the hard drive and specify the logical name during the backup operation. In either scenario, if the hard drive is on a remote machine, you can specify the remote location using the Universal Naming Convention (UNC). For instance, if you were performing a backup to a network share called backups on a computer called Server1, you would specify \\Server1\backups\filename.bak as the physical path name to that remote machine.

Tip: During the backup of your data over the network, you can experience network errors. Be sure to verify the backup operation after it completes.

When using disk devices, take the following facts into consideration:

- These files are handled like any other operating system files.

- The size of your backup file is determined by the data being backed up.

- The maximum size of a disk device is equivalent to the amount of free space on the drive that contains the disk device.

- The appropriate permissions are needed for the SQL Server service user account to read or write to the file on the remote disk.

Warning! Backing up your data to a file on the same physical disk as the database is NOT recommended. If the disk containing the database fails, there is no way to access the backup.

Tape Devices

In SQL Server 2000 you can also perform a backup to a local tape drive. Remember, the local tape device attached to your machine must be supported by your operating system. To ensure the tape device is supported, verify that the tape drive exists on the HCL for your operating system.

Note: When a tape backup device fills up during a backup operation, but you still have additional data to back up, SQL Server will prompt you for a new tape before it can continue the backup operation.

Tape Backup Formats

SQL Server 2000 backups conform to the Microsoft Tape Format (MTF) that is also used by the Windows NT and Windows 2000 operating system tape backups. This means your SQL Server backups can coexist on the same tape as non-SQL Server backups (foreign backup sets) provided that the backups use MTF.

Tip: To guarantee interoperability, the tape should be formatted using the NTBackup program.

Integrating your SQL Server and non-SQL Server backups onto a single tape reduces your backup media storage requirements, costs, and administrative overhead because you can store different backups from different applications on the same tape media.

All backup media begin with a media header that describes the media. The media header information is used to track each piece of media. The media header can contain a media name that is assigned by the first person using the media. This name is used to help identify the media and can prevent errors.

Note: Usually, the media header is written once and then remains on the media for the life of the media.

Using the Console Utility

You can use a command prompt utility called console to display backup and restore messages when you are backing up or restoring from your tape devices. This utility is run by the operator performing the backup or restore operation.

Warning! The console utility must be running before a backup or restore operation to a tape device will proceed.

You should run the console workstation on the same machine that is running the instance of SQL Server because it displays prompts and messages for the operator during the backup or restore operation.

Tip: If the console utility has been started but appears to be unusable, wait for a minute and try it again. SQL Server may be in the process of repairing a broken console connection.

If you are using two tapes for a backup or restore operation, you only need one console. The console program was designed to print messages one at a time and waits for a response before displaying the next prompt. To help the operator differentiate between the multiple tapes being used, the console program messages include the name of the physical drive for each tape device.

Note: To stop a backup or restore operation, you can enter "n" in response to any prompt asking you to mount a new tape.

Managing Your Backup Devices

If you want to utilize logical disk or tape devices, you must first create them before you specify them in your backup and restore operations. These backup devices can be created using Enterprise Manager or with a system stored procedure called **sp_addumpdevice**.

*Note: Only members of the **sysadmin** and **diskadmin** fixed server roles have permissions to execute the **sp_addumpdevice** system stored procedure.*

Understanding the sp_addumpdevice System Stored Procedure

The **sp_addumpdevice** system stored procedure is used to add a new disk or tape logical backup device to the **master.dbo.sysdevices** table. After executing this stored procedure, with the required parameters, you can refer to the logical device in your backup and restore operations.

Note: sp_addumpdevice cannot be executed inside a SQL Server transaction.

Let's discuss the syntax and arguments available with the **sp_addumpdevice** system stored procedure. After you become familiar with these arguments, you will be able to create a logical device that meets your specific needs.

The following code lists the **sp_addumpdevice** syntax and the available arguments described in Table 9.2:

```
sp_addumpdevice [ @devtype = ] 'device_type' ,
    [ @logicalname = ] 'logical_name' ,
    [ @physicalname = ] 'physical_name'
    [ , { [ @cntrltype = ] controller_type
            | [ @devstatus = ] 'device_status'
        }
    ]
```

Now that you are familiar with the numerous arguments available with the **sp_addumpdevice** system stored procedure, it is time to take a look at the steps required to create the different logical backup devices using both Enterprise Manager and Transact SQL syntax.

*Note: You can specify either **device_status** or **controller_type**, but not both.*

Creating a Local Disk Backup Device Using Enterprise Manager

You can easily create a local disk backup device through the Enterprise Manager using the following steps:

Table 9.2 Sp_addumpdevice arguments.

Argument	Datatype	Default	Description
devtype	varchar (20)	None	Specifies the type of backup device. There are three possible values; **disk**, **pipe**, and **tape**.
logicalname	sysname	None	Specifies the logical name of your backup device used in your backup and restore statements. This value cannot be **NULL**.
physicalname	nvarchar(260)	None	Specifies the physical name of the backup device. Your physical names are specified in the same format as any operating-system file name, or if it is a remote server, you specify the Universal Naming Convention (UNC) name.
cntrltype	smallint	Null	Specifies the controller type; it is not required when creating backup devices, but used when writing scripts. There are three possible values; **2** for **disk**, **5** for **tape**, and **6** for **pipe**.
Devstatus	varchar(40)	noskip	Specifies whether ANSI tape labels are read (noskip) or ignored (skip)

1. After opening Enterprise Manager, expand the server group that contains the server that you want to create the local disk backup device on, as shown in Figure 9.1.

2. Expand the Management option, right-click on the Backup option, and then click New Backup Device to display the New Backup Device Properties dialog box.

3. Type a name for the new local backup device in the Name box of the New Backup Device Properties dialog box, as shown in Figure 9.2

4. Click the File Name radio button and perform one of the following steps:

   • Type the name of the backup device used to reference the local disk backup device.

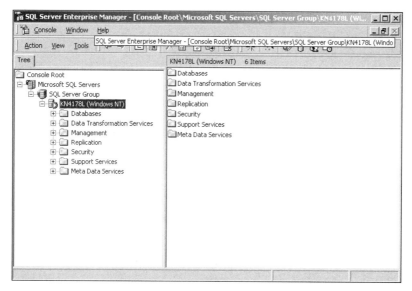

Figure 9.1
Enterprise Manager with expanded SQL Server.

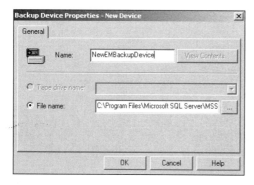

Figure 9.2
New Backup Device Properties dialog box.

- Click the Browse (…) button to display the Backup Device Location dialog box shown in Figure 9.3, and then choose the local file used by the disk backup device.

Creating a Local Disk Backup Device Using Transact-SQL

You can also create a local disk backup device using the **sp_addumpdevice** system stored procedure within Query Analyzer. The following Transact-SQL statement connects to the master database and then creates a local disk backup device called NewTSDiskBackup with the physical name and location of 'D:\sqldata\backups\NewTSDiskBackup.bak':

```
USE master
EXEC sp_addumpdevice 'disk', 'NewTSDiskBackup',
'D:\sqldata\backups\NewTSDiskBackup.bak'
```

Creating a Network Disk Backup Device Using Enterprise Manager

You can easily create a network disk backup device through the Enterprise Manager using the following steps:

1. After opening Enterprise Manager, expand the server group that contains the server that you want to create the network disk backup device on, as shown in Figure 9.4.

2. Expand the Management option, right-click on the Backup option, and then click New Backup Device to display the New Backup Device Properties dialog box.

3. Type a name for the new network backup device in the Name box of the New Backup Device Properties dialog box, as shown in Figure 9.5.

Figure 9.3
Backup Device Location dialog box.

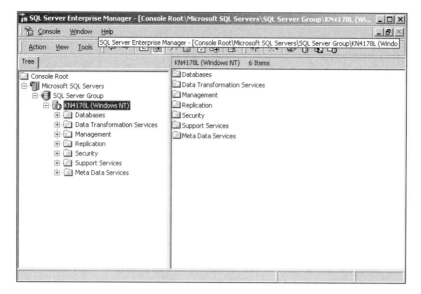

Figure 9.4
Enterprise Manager with expanded SQL Server.

4. Click the File Name radio button and perform one of the following steps:

- Type the name of the backup device used to reference the network disk backup device.

- Click the Browse (…) button to display the Backup Device Location dialog box shown in Figure 9.6, and then choose the network file used by the disk backup device.

Creating a Network Disk Backup Device Using Transact-SQL

You can also create a network disk backup device using the **sp_addumpdevice** system stored procedure within Query Analyzer. The following Transact-SQL statement connects to the

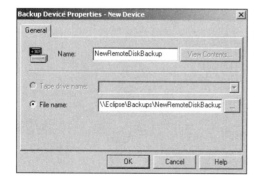

Figure 9.5
New Backup Device dialog box for network disk backup.

Figure 9.6
Backup Device Location dialog box.

master database and then creates a network disk backup device called NewTSRemoteBackup
with the physical name, '\\Eclipse\Backups\NewRemoteDiskBackup.bak':

```
USE master
EXEC sp_addumpdevice 'disk', 'NewTSRemoteBackup',
'\\Eclipse\Backups\NewRemoteDiskBackup.bak'
```

Note: *The name of the account used to start the SQL Server service must have permissions to the remote file.*

Creating a Tape Backup Device Using Enterprise Manager

You can easily create a logical tape backup device through Enterprise Manager using the
following steps:

1. After opening Enterprise Manager, expand the server group that contains the server
   in which you want to create the logical disk backup device.

2. Expand the Management option, right-click on the Backup option, and then click
   New Backup Device to display the New Backup Device Properties dialog box.

3. Type a name for the new backup device in the Name box of the New Backup Device
   Properties dialog box.

4. Click the Tape Drive Name radio button and then use the drop-down menu to choose
   the name of the tape device you want to use as the tape backup device.

Note: *If no tape devices are listed, then SQL Server is not detecting any tape devices on the local computer. If you want to add a tape device to your operating system so SQL Server will detect and list it, see the Microsoft Windows NT 4 and Windows 2000 operating system documentation.*

Creating a Tape Backup Device Using Transact-SQL

You can also create a logical tape backup device using the **sp_addumpdevice** system stored procedure within Query Analyzer. The following Transact-SQL statement connects to the master database and then creates a logical tape backup device called NewTSTapeBackup with the physical name of '\\.\tape1':

```
USE master
EXEC sp_addumpdevice 'tape', 'NewTSTapeBackup', '\\.\tape1'
```

Deleting a Logical Backup Device Using Enterprise Manager

After creating a backup device, you may at some point need to remove the tape or disk backup device from your computer. This can be done from within Enterprise Manager or by using Transact-SQL statements. You can delete a logical backup device from within Enterprise Manager using the following steps:

1. After opening Enterprise Manager, expand the server group that contains the server in which you want to create the logical disk backup device.

2. Expand the Management option, and then click on Backup.

3. In the details pane of Enterprise Manager, locate and right-click on the specific backup device that you want to delete to open the shortcut menu shown in Figure 9.7.

4. Click Delete on the shortcut menu, and then click Yes in the SQL Server Enterprise Manager confirmation box shown in Figure 9.8 to delete the logical backup device.

Deleting a Logical Backup Device Using Transact-SQL

Deleting a logical device through Query Analyzer is accomplished using the **sp_dropdevice** system stored procedure. This procedure is used to delete the backup device from SQL Server and remove the information about the backup device from the

Figure 9.7
Shortcut Menu used to delete logical disk backup devices.

Figure 9.8
SQL Server Enterprise Manager confirmation box.

sysdevices table in the master database. The **sp_dropdevice** system stored procedure can also be used to delete database devices that were used in earlier versions of SQL Server.

*Note: **sp_dropdevice** cannot be executed inside a SQL Server transaction.*

The following code lists the **sp_dropdevice** syntax and arguments followed by Table 9.3 describing the arguments associated with **sp_dropdevice**:

```
sp_dropdevice [ @logicalname = ] 'device'
    [ , [ @delfile = ] 'delfile' ]
```

The following example drops the **NewTSTapeBackup** tape dump device from SQL Server:

```
sp_dropdevice 'NewTSTapeBackup'
```

By default, members of the **sysadmin** and **diskadmin** fixed server roles have the required permissions to execute the **sp_dropdevice** system stored procedure.

Setting the Media Retention Option

After creating a backup media device using one of the preceding options, you can control how long to retain the backup medium after you have performed either a database or transaction log backup to that backup media device. Media retention helps protect your backups from being accidentally overwritten by specifying a number of days before they can be overwritten.

You can set the system-wide media retention option to define a default length of time to retain your backups so you don't have to specify this information each time you perform a backup. If you use the backup medium before the specified number of days

Table 9.3   Sp_dropdevice arguments.

Argument	Datatype	Default	Description
Logicalname	**sysname**	None	The name assigned to the backup device, and listed in the name field of the **sysdevices** table of the master database.
Delfile	**varchar**(7)	N/A	Determines whether or not the physical backup device file is deleted. If you specify delfile, the physical backup device disk file is deleted from your hard drive.

has passed, SQL Server will issue a warning message to help you prevent an accidental overwrite of data. However, if you leave the default setting of 0 days, SQL Server will not issue the warning message.

Tip: *The system-wide media retention setting can be overridden by using the **RETAINDAYS** option with the* **BACKUP** *command.*

The media retention option is an advanced option that can be set using the **sp_configure** system stored procedure. However, the media retention option can only be modified if you have set the Show Advanced Options to 1.

Note: *After you set the Show Advanced Options to 1, you must stop and restart the MSSQLSERVER service for it to take effect.*

As with most other aspects of SQL Server, you can use either Enterprise Manager or Transact-SQL statements to set the system-wide backup media retention option.

Setting the Media Retention Option Using Enterprise Manager

You set the backup media retention option through Enterprise Manager using the following steps:

1. After opening Enterprise Manager, locate and expand the server group that contains the SQL server where you want to set the backup retention duration option.

2. Right-click the SQL Server, and then click Properties on the drop-down menu, shown in Figure 9.9.

3. After opening the SQL Server Properties dialog box, click the Database Settings tab to display the Database Settings of the SQL Server.

Figure 9.9
SQL Server Properties shortcut menu.

4. Type or use the spin-dial to set the number of days the backup medium will be retained after you perform a database or transaction log backup. Figure 9.10 shows a media retention period of 14 days.

Setting the Media Retention Option Using Transact-SQL

The system stored procedure **sp_configure** is used to display or modify system-wide configuration settings for the SQL server you have connected to. **Sp_configure** is used for configuring numerous settings including the media retention period.

*Tip: Dynamic options, such as media retention, can be installed immediately, without stopping and restarting the MSSQLSERVER service, by executing the **RECONFIGURE** command.*

The following code lists the **sp_configure** syntax and arguments:

```
sp_configure [ [ @configname = ] 'name' ]
    [ , [ @configvalue = ] 'value' ]
```

Table 9.4 describes the arguments associated with **sp_configure**.

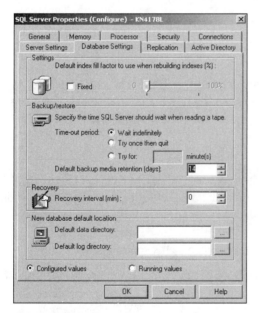

Figure 9.10
SQL Server Properties Database Settings dialog box.

Table 9.4 Sp_configure arguments.

Argument	Datatype	Default	Description
Configname	**varchar(35)**	Null	Is the name of the configuration option, for instance; media retention. If no value is specified, it returns all possible configuration options.
Configvalue	**int**	Null	Is the new configuration setting

The following example sets the system-wide media retention period to 14 days using the **sp_configure** system stored procedure. It then executes the **RECONFIGURE** statement to install the new value for the media retention option. Here is the code:

```
sp_configure 'media retention', '14'
Reconfigure
```

By default, anyone can execute the **sp_configure** stored procedure with no permissions or with just the first argument. However, also by default, in order to execute **sp_configure** with both arguments, therefore changing a configuration option, you must be a member of the **sysadmin** or **serveradmin** fixed server roles.

*Warning! To execute the **RECONFIGURE** command, you must also be a member of the **sysadmin** or **serveradmin** fixed server role.*

After creating your backup devices and configuring your media retention period, you are ready to create backups of your data. However, there are numerous types of backups available to you, and it is imperative to choose the correct one to make sure you are creating a useful backup.

Knowing Your Recovery Models

SQL Server 2000 supports three recovery models that are directly associated with your individual databases. The recovery model you choose for your database greatly affects the performance of your backup and restore operations. Furthermore, the recovery model also has an impact on what actions are taken when a checkpoint occurs.

Note: A checkpoint is an operation performed by the database engine to write dirty buffer pages to your data files on disk. Dirty pages are pages that have been modified, but for which the modifications have not yet been written to disk. Each checkpoint operation writes all pages to disk that were dirty since the last checkpoint and that still have not been written to disk. Checkpoints occur periodically based on the number of log records generated by data modifications, or when requested by a user or a system shutdown.

We'll begin with a review of the three different recovery models, and then we'll discuss how to switch between the various recovery models.

What Is a Recovery Model?

Each database you create in SQL Server 2000 can use one of three recovery models—Simple, Full, or Bulk-Logged. Your choice of recovery model determines how your data is backed up and defines the level of exposure to data loss.

Tip: The recovery model of each new database you create is determined by the recovery model of the model database. If you have a preferred recovery model for new databases, be sure to set that recovery model on the model database.

The three recovery models are used to:

- Simplify your recovery plan.

- Simplify your backup and restore procedures.

- Clarify the tradeoffs between your system's operational requirements.

Each of the recovery models addresses different aspects of performance, disk and tape space, and protection of data loss. When choosing a recovery model, you must consider the tradeoffs of the following business requirements:

- Level of data loss exposure.

- Performance of large-scale operations (bulk loads, index creation).

- Simplicity of your backup and restore procedures.

- Amount of transaction log space consumed.

As already mentioned, you can implement multiple recovery models; you are not restricted to a specific one. After deciding which recovery model or models you wish to implement, you can plan your backup and restore procedures.

You can use Table 9.5 as a quick reference guide to determine the benefits and implications of the three recovery models.

Table 9.5   SQL Server 2000 recovery models.

Recovery Model	Benefits	Allows Recovery To
Simple	Small transaction log size	Last database backup; you lose changes since last database backup
Full	No loss of work due to damaged or lost data file; can recover to a point in time	Any point in time
Bulk-Logged	Small transaction log size	End of any backup; you must redo bulk operations since last backup

Simple Recovery Model

In the Simple Recovery model you can recover data only up to the point of the most recent full or differential database backup. Although this model requires the least amount of administration, it is at the expense of a higher level of data loss if one of your data files is damaged.

Warning! Your transaction log is purged regularly. Therefore, this model is NOT an appropriate choice for a production database from which you cannot afford to lose recent data modifications.

This model prevents you from restoring your database to the point of failure or to a specific point of time. If your backup strategy includes the ability to restore to either of those conditions, you will have to implement either the Full Recovery or the Bulk-Logged Recovery model

Note: The Simple Recovery model is similar to setting the Truncate Log On Checkpoint database option in previous versions of SQL Server.

Full Recovery Model

The Full Recovery model provides you the capability to recover a database to an earlier point in time or to a point of failure. This capability is available because all operations, including bulk operations such as **SELECT INTO**, bulk loading of data, and creating indexes are fully logged in your transaction log.

This model uses your database and transaction log backups to provide complete protection against media failure. Even if multiple data files are damaged or lost, you can recover all committed transactions.

Warning! To make sure that you can recover all transactions under this model, your transaction log should be protected against damage. We strongly recommend that you store your transaction logs on fault-tolerant disks.

Bulk-Logged Recovery Model

The Bulk-Logged Recovery model provides higher performance and smaller transaction log files. Specific operations—**SELECT INTO**, creating indexes, or bulk copy, are not fully logged in the transaction log.

Warning! Unlike the Full Recovery model, you are not able to recover up to a specific point in time.

Without the full logging of these large-scale operations, you increase the chance of losing data that was created with these operations. These operations are minimally logged when in this recovery model, and this logging action cannot be controlled during the performance of individual operations.

Warning! *Backing up a transaction log that contains bulk-logged operations requires access to all data files associated with the database. If any of your files are inaccessible, you will not be able to back up the latest transaction log, and all committed transactions contained in the transaction log will be lost.*

Switching Between Recovery Models

The choice you make when you implement a recovery model is not permanent. You can easily switch from one recovery model to another to meet your business needs. For instance, you may have an OLTP database using Full Recovery, but occasionally you create indexes on it. When creating indexes, you want to increase performance—by not logging every action, and you want to reduce the required size of the transaction log. You can switch to Bulk-Logged Recovery before creating the index and then switch back to Full Recovery.

Tip: *You can switch recovery models during a bulk load operation and the bulk operation performs the appropriate logging.*

Use Table 9.6 to determine what action to take when switching from one recovery model to another.

Table 9.6   How to switch between recovery models.

Current Model	Desired Model	Action	Description
Full Recovery	Bulk-Logged	None	Requires no change in backup strategy
Full Recovery	Simple	Optionally, back up the transaction log	Stop executing transaction log backups
Recovery Bulk-Logged	Full	None	No change in backup strategy, back up transaction log for point in time recovery
Bulk-Logged Recovery	Simple	Optionally back up the transaction log	Stop executing transaction log backups
Simple Recovery	Full	Back up the database	Start executing database and transaction log backups
Simple Recovery	Bulk-Logged	Back up the database	Start executing database and transaction log backups

Understanding the Types of Backups in SQL Server 2000

SQL Server 2000 supports numerous types of backups that can be used separately or in combination. The recovery model you choose for your database greatly affects your overall backup strategy, including the decision of what backup type or types to use.

Table 9.7 introduces the different backup types and provides a brief description of them. The sections following the table provide in-depth information regarding the different backup types available in SQL Server 2000.

Table 9.7   SQL Server database backup types.

Backup Type	Description
Full database backup	Copy of all data files associated with the database
Differential backup	Copy of all modified data pages since performing last full database backup
File backup	Copy of a specific database file
Filegroup backup	Copy of all data files in the specified database filegroup
Differential file backup	Copy of all modified data pages in a specified database file since last full database backup
Differential filegroup backup	Copy of all modified data pages in a specified database filegroup
Snapshot backup	Copy of all data files associated with a database that is performed in a very short period of time using third-party hardware and/or software
Transaction log backup	Copy of all committed transactions and purge out the active portion of the transaction log

Database Backups (Full or Normal)

A full database backup, sometimes called a normal backup, creates a copy of all data files associated with the database being backed up. This backup also includes data modifications being made when the backup operation is taking place (see dynamic backups later in this chapter).

Tip: SQL Server full database backups can be performed when users are accessing the data. However, it is recommended that you perform your full database backups during off-peak hours when the database is not being heavily used.

After a full database backup completes, it will contain all user data and database objects including the system tables, user-defined tables, and indexes. A full database backup generally takes more time and space to perform than any other backup type available in SQL Server 2000.

Full database backups are the starting point for a complete database restoration when such a data restoration is required. Full database backups should be performed:

- After you create your database.

- Immediately after you populate your database.

- After creating indexes on tables within your database.

Additionally, full database backups should be performed on a scheduled basis. The frequency of your full database backups depends on the size of your database and how often the data changes. However, as a general rule we recommend you perform a full database backup as frequently as once a day, and no less than once a week.

Tip: If the size of your database is too large to perform a full database backup regularly, we suggest you consider performing file and filegroup backups.

Differential Database Backups

A differential backup is a copy of all data files that contain changes that have occurred since the last full database backup. This backup also includes data modifications being made when the differential backup operation is being performed.

A differential backup records only the most recent changes made to a data record if there is a data record that has had multiple changes made to it since the last full database backup. A differential backup takes less time and space than a full database backup, which in turn reduces the data restoration time. This reduction of space and time can also permit you to perform differential backups more often, thereby reducing the risk of losing data.

To improve the performance of a differential database backup, SQL Server 2000 tracks all extents that have changed since the last full database backup using a Differential Changed Map (DCM) page. The differential backup operation scans the DCM page to locate and back up the extents that have changed. If the bit for an extent is 1, the backup operation knows the extent contains modified data.

Note: *A full database backup operation changes the bit for the changed extents back to 0.*

You should consider using differential database backups when:

- You are using the Simple Recovery model and want to perform more frequent backups, but don't want to perform lengthy full database backups.

- You are using the Full or Bulk-Logged Recovery model and want to minimize the time it takes to roll forward transaction log backups when performing a database restoration.

- You have added a relatively small portion of modified data to the database since the last database backup.

Tip: *Differential backups are particularly efficient if the same data changes several times.*

A recommended process for implementing differential database backups in your backup strategy is:

- Create regular full database backups.

- Create a differential backup periodically between your full database backups.

- Create transaction log backups more frequently than your differential backups when using the Full or Bulk-Logged Recovery models.

Transaction Log Backups (Incremental)

A transaction log backup is a copy of a sequential record of all transactions recorded in the transaction log since the last transaction log backup. Transaction log backups are only available with the Full and Bulk-Logged Recovery models. This type of backup can be used to recover your database to a point of failure or to a specific point in time, such as prior to accidentally modified data.

Transaction log backups generally take less time and space than any other backup type. Because of this, you can create them more frequently than other types of backups. With the more frequent backups, you reduce the risk of losing data.

Warning! Sometimes your transaction log backup is larger than your database backup. For instance, if a database has a high transaction rate —therefore causing the transaction log to grow quickly—you will want to back up your transaction log more often to truncate it.

Your transaction log backups cannot take place during a full backup or a differential backup. However, you can back up your transaction log when performing a database file backup. You should not back up the transaction log:

- Until you perform a database or file backup, because the transaction log contains the changes made to the database after the last backup was done.

- If the transaction log has been manually truncated, unless you have performed a database or differential backup since you truncated the transaction log.

File and Filegroup Backups

A file backup is a copy of a specific data file associated with a database, whereas a filegroup backup is a copy of each data file in a single filegroup associated with a database. These backups also include data modifications being made when the backup operation is being performed.

File and filegroup backups take less time and space than a full database backup. File and filegroup backups are generally implemented when you are using Very Large Databases (VLDB)s that require too much time to perform a full database backup.

When working with VLDBs, you can design the database so that certain filegroups contain data that changes frequently and other filegroups contain data that changes infrequently, or not at all. With the size of the database reduced into smaller chunks, you are able to perform backups of these smaller chunks of data as needed. For instance, the data that is changing frequently can be backed up more often than the data that isn't changing as often.

Warning! File and filegroup backups require a thorough analysis and planning to make sure you implement a backup strategy to back up related data and indexes together.

File and Filegroup Differential Backups

A differential file or filegroup backup is a copy of all changes that have occurred to a file or filegroup since the last file or filegroup backup. These backups also include data modifications being made during the time that the backup operation is being performed.

Differential file and filegroup backups are conceptually the same as differential database backups. They take less time and space than copying the entire file or filegroup and also reduce the amount of time required to perform the restore process.

Snapshot Backups

A snapshot backup is a copy of a database that uses third-party hardware and software vendor backup and restore technologies. Snapshot backups are used to minimize or eliminate the use of your server resources during the backup operation. These types of backups are especially beneficial for moderate-to-large databases that require high-availability.

The primary benefits of snapshot technology are:

- A backup can be created in a very short period of time, typically in seconds, with minimal or no impact to your server.

- A restore can be quickly achieved from a disk backup.

- A backup to tape can be achieved by another system with no impact on your production system.

- A copy of your production database can be created and used for reporting or testing.

Snapshot backups, like all other backups, can be created for individual files or entire databases and are tracked in the msdb database. These backups provide the same functionality as your full database and file backups in that you can use them to roll forward transactions using full, differential, and transaction log backups.

The difference is that the backup-and-restore functionality is achieved through the use of third-party software and/or hardware vendors. However, the vendors are using features of SQL Server designed to create the snapshot in minimal time.

Note: *For more information on creating snapshot backups, see the SQL Server page at the Microsoft Web site, or contact your enterprise storage vendor and/or backup software vendor.*

Understanding the Effects of a Backup

Now that you are familiar with the types of backup media you have available to you and the different backup types you can choose from, it is time to become familiar with the backup operation itself.

As mentioned numerous times before, your users can be accessing your SQL Server databases while you are performing a backup operation. However, there are some activities that cannot take place during a backup operation. Furthermore, when performing a backup operation, you should be familiar with the numerous system tables that are updated, in the event you need to troubleshoot your backup process.

Understanding the Backup Process

The ability to perform a database backup while users are accessing it provides you a wealth of flexibility when it comes to scheduling your backup. Of course, as you have already seen, you don't want to perform a database backup during peak usage, or your users and the backup operation will experience performance degradation.

There are many things that are going on behind the scenes during a backup operation in SQL Server 2000:

- Dynamic backups allow your users to continue to work when you are performing a backup operation in SQL Server 2000. However, there are some restrictions discussed in the next section.

- The backup operation backs up the original files and records their physical location. The completed backup will contain the following information:

  - The schema and file structure.

  - The data.

  - The portion of the transaction log that contains the database activity that was occurring during the backup operation.

Note: SQL Server uses the previous information to recreate the database files, objects, and data in their original locations during a restore operation.

The dynamic backup process is achieved because SQL Server is performing the following steps behind the scenes:

- Issuing a checkpoint on the database and recording the Log Sequence Number (LSN) of the oldest active transaction log record.

- Writing all data pages to the backup media from the disks directly, bypassing the buffer cache.

- Writing all transaction log records being written during the backup process. Specifically, it is writing the records from the recorded LSN through the end of the transaction log.

All of these activities are going on behind the scenes to make the backup operation dynamic and to provide you the ability to recover the database activity that was taking place during the backup operation. However, there are certain tasks that cannot be performed during a backup operation.

Activities Restricted During a Backup

Almost all SQL Server activities can occur during a SQL Server backup. However, there are some SQL Server operations that cannot be performed while you are backing up your databases. The following list contains the SQL Server activities that cannot be performed on a database that is being backed up:

- Using an **ALTER DATABASE** statement to create or delete files associated with the database.

- Truncating a file caused by a manual or automatic shrink operation.

If a backup is started when one of these operations is being performed, the backup waits for the conflicting operation to end and then proceeds. However, if a backup operation is in progress and someone begins a conflicting operation, the conflicting operation fails and the backup continues.

System Tables Updated

SQL Server 2000 includes backup history tables that are used to track your backup activity. Depending on the backup activity, the respective table located in the msdb database will be appropriately modified.

These backup history tables, the number of columns in the table, and a description of the table are listed in Table 9.8.

Warning! These table names are new to SQL Server 2000; therefore backups created with SQL Server 2000 cannot be restored to earlier versions of SQL Server.

Table 9.8   Backup history tables.

Table Name	Number of Columns	Description
Backupfile	13	Contains one row for each database or log file that is backed up.
Backupmediafamily	8	Contains one row for each media family you create.
Backupmediaset	8	Contains one row for each backup media set created.
Backupset	40	Contains one row for each backup set you create.

Note: These backup history tables are also modified when performing a restore operation in SQL Server 2000.

Performing Database Backups

You now have the information required to actually create a backup. However, as you know, there are three ways to back up your data in SQL Server 2000: using the **BACKUP** command, using Enterprise Manager, or using the Create Database Backup Wizard.

Understanding the **BACKUP** Command

We'll begin with an explanation of the **BACKUP** command that you use in Query Analyzer (or a related T-SQL tool) to back up your entire database, changes to your database, the transaction log, or one or more of your database files or filegroups. The following basic syntax is used to perform a backup of a database:

```
BACKUP DATABASE database_name
TO backup_device
```

The **BACKUP** command has many arguments that can be used to customize your backup. It is important to understand the most commonly used **BACKUP** command arguments, and in what backup operations they are used. Table 9.9 contains a list of the most commonly used **BACKUP** command arguments.

Table 9.9 BACKUP command arguments.

Argument	Backup Type	Description
DATABASE	All except transaction log	Specifies the name of the database to back up. If you include a list of files and filegroups, only those files and filegroups are backed up. If you include with **DIFFERENTIAL**, only the changes made to the database since the last full backup are backed up.
WITH DIFFERENTIAL	File, filegroup, full	Specifies the backup should consist only of the changes made to the database, file, or filegroup since the last full, file, or filegroup backup respectively.
LOG	Transaction log	Specifies to only back up the transaction log.
BACKUP DEVICE	All	Specifies the logical or physical backup device used to store the copy of the data being backed up. If backing up to a physical backup device, you must specify backup media type of disk or tape in the **BACKUP** statement using the **TO DISK** or **TO TAPE** arguments.
DESCRIPTION	All	Specifies a description of the backup set. This can contain a maximum of 255 characters.
EXPIREDATE	All	Specifies the date when the backup set expires and can be overwritten by another backup operation.
RETAINDAYS	All	Specifies the number of days that must pass before the backup media set can be overwritten by another backup operation.
PASSWORD	All	Specifies a password on the backup set that must be supplied when performing a restore of the backup set.
FORMAT	All	Specifies that the media header information should be written, or overwritten if it already exists, on all volumes used for the backup operation.
INIT	All	Specifies that all backup sets should be overwritten, but does not overwrite the media header information.
NOINIT	All	Specifies that the backup set is appended to the existing backup sets on the backup media.

(continued)

Table 9.9 **BACKUP** command arguments *(continued)*.

Argument	Backup Type	Description
MEDIANAME	All	Specifies a name for the entire backup media set. This can contain a maximum of 128 characters.
NAME	All	Specifies the name of the backup set. This can contain a maximum of 128 characters.
NOREWIND	All	Specifies that SQL Server keep the tape open and available after the backup operation completes.
REWIND	All	Specifies that SQL Server releases and rewinds the tape after the backup operation completes.
NOSKIP	All	Specifies that the **BACKUP** statement checks the expiration date of all backup sets on the backup media before allowing them to be overwritten.
SKIP	All	Specifies that the **BACKUP** statement ignore the check of the expiration date of the backup sets on the backup media.
NOUNLOAD	All	Specifies that SQL Server does not automatically rewind and unload the tape from the tape drive after the backup operation completes.
UNLOAD	All	Specifies that SQL Server automatically rewinds and unloads the tape from the tape drive after the backup operation completes.
RESTART	All	Specifies that SQL Server restart an interrupted backup operation from the point of interruption.*
STATS	All	Specifies that backup display a message each time another percentage completes. Used to guage progress
FILE	File	Specifies the name of one or more files to be backed up.
FILEGROUP	Filegroup	Specifies the name of one or more filegroups to be backed up.

*This option can only be used for backups being performed to multiple tape volumes.

Tip: Your database and transaction log backups can be written to the same disk or tape backup device, allowing them to be stored in one physical location. This can reduce the amount of time required to perform a restore operation.

The **BACKUP** command is very powerful and as you can see provides numerous options that can be used to back up your SQL Server data. It is now time to take a look at how to create a backup using the **BACKUP** command.

Creating a Full or Differential Database Backup Using Transact-SQL

After accessing Query Analyzer you can use the following steps to perform a full or differential database backup in SQL Server:

1. Execute the **BACKUP DATABASE** statement and specify the following arguments:

   - The name of the database that you want to back up.

   - The name of the backup device that you want to store the copy of the database on.

2. Optionally, you can specify any of the following:

- The **INIT** clause to overwrite the existing backup sets, making the current backup operation the first backup set on the backup media.

- The **SKIP** and **INIT** clause to overwrite the backup media, even if there are backup sets that have not expired, or if the media name does not match the name on the backup media.

- The **FORMAT** clause when you are using the backup media for the first time and you want to initialize the media and overwrite any existing media header information.

Warning! *When using the* ***INIT*** *or* ***FORMAT*** *option with the* ***BACKUP*** *command use extreme caution, as this will destroy any existing backup sets that reside on the backup media.*

The following code is an example of a full database backup. This backup operation will overwrite any existing media header information and backup sets on the disk called NewDiskBackup, before copying the Northwind database to the backup media:

```
USE Northwind
GO
BACKUP DATABASE Northwind
  TO NewDiskBackup
  WITH FORMAT
```

The following code is an example of a differential database backup. This backup operation will retain existing media header information and backup sets on the file called NewDiskBackup, and then copy the Northwind database changes to the file:

```
USE Northwind
GO
BACKUP DATABASE Northwind
  TO NewDiskBackup
  WITH DIFFERENTIAL
```

The **BACKUP** command provides a plethora of options to customize your backup operation to suit your specific needs. However, there are easier ways to create your backups, using either Enterprise Manager or the Create Database Backup Wizard.

Creating a Full or Differential Database Backup Using Enterprise Manager

SQL Server also provides you the capability to create a full database backup using Enterprise Manager. The following steps can be used to create a full database backup through Enterprise Manager:

1. After opening Enterprise Manager, expand the server group and the SQL Server that contains the database that you want to back up.

2. Expand the Databases option and right-click on the database to open the shortcut menu and choose All Tasks to display another shortcut menu, and then click the Backup Database option as shown in Figure 9.11 to open the SQL Server backup dialog box.

3. Type the name of the backup set in the Name box, and optionally type in a description of the backup set.

4. Under Backup, click Database—Complete.

Note: *If you were performing a differential backup, you would click Database—Differential in this step.*

5. Under Destination, click Disk or Tape to identify your backup media type, and then specify your backup destination.

Note: *If no backup destinations appear, click Add to create a new backup destination or to select an existing backup destination.*

6. Under Overwrite, perform one of the following:

   - Click Append To Media to append the backup to any existing backup sets on your backup device.

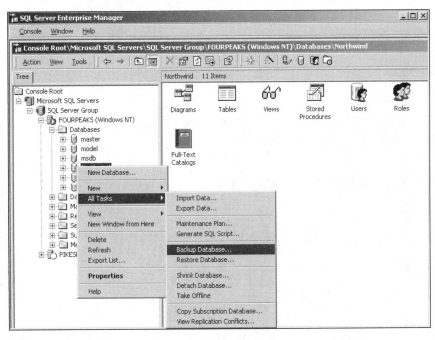

Figure 9.11
All Tasks shortcut menu to choose the Backup Database option.

- Click Overwrite Existing Media to overwrite any existing backup sets on your backup device.

7. Optionally, you can click the Schedule checkbox to create a schedule for the backup operation for later or recurring execution and complete the General tab of the Backup dialog box, as shown in Figure 9.12.

8. Optionally, you can click the Options tab shown in Figure 9.13 and choose one or more of the following options:

- Click the Verify Backup Upon Completion checkbox to verify the backup when completed.

- Click the Eject Tape After Backup checkbox to verify that the tape is ejected when the backup operation completes.

Note: This option is only available with tape devices.

- Click the Check Media Set Name And Backup Set Expiration checkbox to make sure the backup media is checked before overwriting. Type the name of the media you want to use for the backup operation in the Media Set name box.

9. If you are using this backup media for the first time, or if you want to change the existing media label, select the Initialize And Label Media checkbox and type the name and description of the media set.

Note: This option is only available when you are overwriting the media.

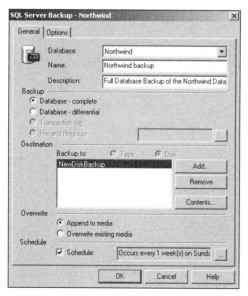

Figure 9.12
Completing the General tab of the Backup dialog box.

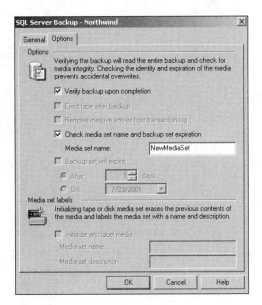

Figure 9.13
Completing the Options tab of the Backup dialog box.

Creating a Full, Differential, or Transaction Log Backup Using the Create Database Backup Wizard

If creating the database backup through the Enterprise Manager is not easy enough, you can use a wizard called Create Database Backup Wizard to perform the backup operation in SQL Server 2000.

Use the following steps to back up your database using the Wizard:

1. After opening Enterprise Manager, expand the server group and the SQL Server that contains the database that you want to back up.

2. Locate and click Wizards on the Tools menu.

3. Expand Management in the Select Wizard dialog box as shown in Figure 9.14.

4. Double-click on Backup Wizard to begin the Create Database Backup Wizard and open the Create Database Backup Wizard welcome screen. After reading the explanation of the Wizard, click Next.

5. Using the drop-down menu on the Select Database To Backup screen shown in Figure 9.15, locate and select the database that you want to back up and then click Next.

6. Type the name of the backup, and optionally a description, in the Name and Description boxes of the Type The Name And Description For Backup dialog box shown in Figure 9.16, and then click Next.

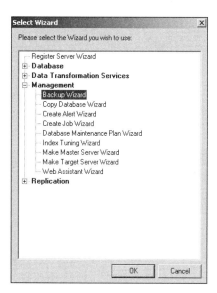

Figure 9.14
Starting the Create Database Backup Wizard.

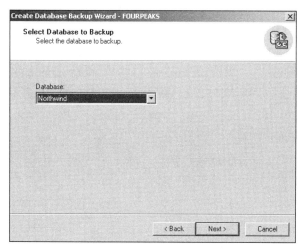

Figure 9.15
Selecting the database to backup.

7. Click one of the radio buttons in the Select Type Of Backup dialog box shown in Figure 9.17 to specify your backup type and then click Next.

Note: *You can choose a full database backup, differential backup, or transaction log backup in this dialog box.*

8. Select the backup device type and name using the radio buttons and drop-down menus on the Backup Destination And Action dialog box shown in Figure 9.18.

9

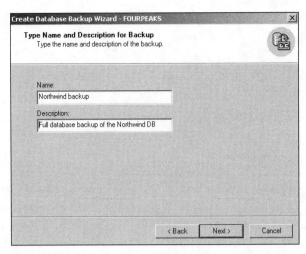

Figure 9.16
Specifying the name and description of the database backup.

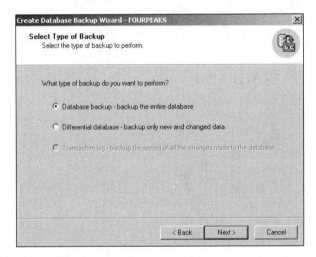

Figure 9.17
Specifying the type of backup.

Note: *You can choose a tape backup device, temporary backup device, or permanent backup device by choosing Tape, File, or Backup Device respectively. After choosing your type of device, you can select an existing backup device or create a new one from within this dialog box.*

9. Also on the Backup Destination And Action dialog box, you specify the actions that you want to take place under the Properties section shown in Figure 9.18.

10. After you click Next, the Backup Verification And Scheduling dialog box is displayed as shown in Figure 9.19. You can set the media set label and backup set expiration date and time to avoid accidental overwrites. Furthermore, you can click the checkbox next to the Schedule option to create a schedule for the backup operation.

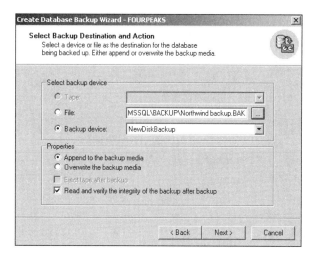

Figure 9.18
Specifying the backup device and actions.

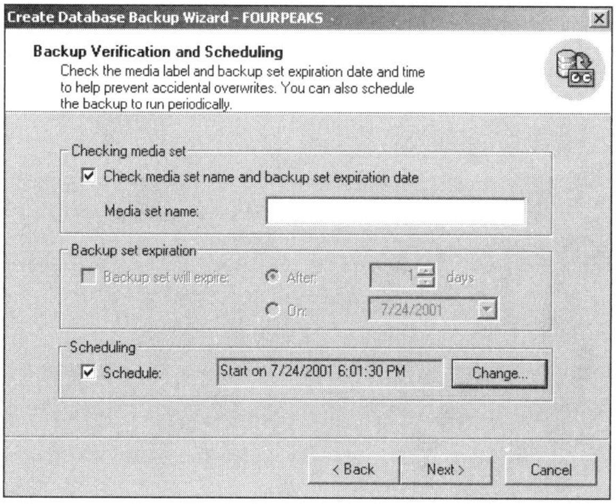

Figure 9.19
Setting the schedule and verification options of the backup.

Note: You can click Change to modify the schedule of the backup operation.

11. After clicking Next on the Backup Verification And Scheduling dialog box, you receive a summary page of the responses you supplied. Click Finish to complete the Wizard and create the backup.

Tip: If you want to modify a response you can click the Back button to go back to the screen you want to modify and make the modifications. After making your modifications click Next the required number of times to return you to the summary screen and then click Finish to complete the Wizard.

Backing Up Files and Filegroups Using Transact-SQL

After accessing Query Analyzer, you can execute the **BACKUP DATABASE** statement to perform a file or filegroup backup in SQL Server. You will need to specify the following arguments:

- The name of the database that you want to back up.

- The name of the backup device that you want to store the copy of the database on.

- The file clause for each file you are backing up.

- The filegroup clause for each filegroup you are backing up.

The following code is an example of a file and filegroup backup. This backup operation will copy the specified files and filegroups to the backup device called FileBackups:

```
USE Northwind
GO
BACKUP DATABASE Northwind
  FILE = 'Northwind_Data',
  FILEGROUP = 'Northwind_Report'
  TO FILEBACKUPS
```

The following code is an example of a differential file and filegroup backup. This backup operation will copy the changes that were made on the file and filegroup to the backup device called FileDiffBackups:

```
USE Northwind
GO
BACKUP DATABASE Northwind
  FILE = 'Northwind_Data',
  FILEGROUP = 'Northwind_Report'
  TO FILEDIFFBACKUPS
  WITH DIFFERENTIAL
```

Now let's see how we can perform the same file and filegroup backups using Enterprise Manager.

Backing up Files and Filegroups Using Enterprise Manager

SQL Server allows you to create file and filegroup backups using Enterprise Manager. The following steps can be used to create a file or a filegroup backup through the Enterprise Manager:

1. After opening Enterprise Manager, expand the server group and the SQL Server that contains the database that you want to back up.

2. Expand the Databases option and right-click on the database to open the shortcut menu. Choose All Tasks to display another shortcut menu, and then click the Backup Database option to open the SQL Server backup dialog box.

3. Type the name of the backup set in the Name box, and optionally type in a description of the backup set.

4. Under Backup, click File and filegroup and then click the elipses (...) button to open the Specify Filegroups and Files dialog box shown in Figure 9.20.

5. Select a Backup checkbox for each file or filegroup you want to back up.

Note: By selecting a filegroup, all the files within the filegroup are automatically selected.

6. Under Destination, click Disk or Tape to identify your backup media type, and then specify your backup destination.

Note: If no backup destinations appear, click Add to create a new backup destination or to select an existing backup destination.

7. Under Overwrite, perform one of the following:

- Click Append To Media to append the backup to any existing backup sets on your backup device.

- Click Overwrite Existing Media to overwrite any existing backup sets on your backup device.

8. Optionally, you can click the Schedule checkbox to create a schedule for the backup operation for later or recurring execution and complete the General tab of the backup dialog box.

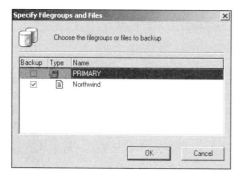

Figure 9.20
Selecting your files and filegroups.

9. Optionally, you can click the Options tab and choose one or more of the following options:

   - Click the Verify Backup Upon Completion checkbox to verify the backup when backed up.

   - Click the Eject Tape After Backup checkbox to make sure the tape is ejected when the backup operation completes.

   Note: *This option is only available with tape devices.*

   - Click the Check Media Set Name And Backup Set Expiration checkbox to be sure the backup media is checked before overwriting. Type the name of the media you want to use for the backup operation in the Media Set Name box.

10. If you are using this backup media for the first time, or if you want to change the existing media label, select the Initialize And Label Media checkbox and type the name and description of the media set.

   Note: *This option is only available when you are overwriting the media.*

Now that you are familiar with the different ways to create a database backup, you can actually perform a database backup of your system databases and your user databases using any of the numerous ways discussed. The next section will take a look at the considerations and steps required to back up your system databases.

Backing up Your System Databases

Your system databases need to be backed up so you can rebuild them in the event of a system or database failure such as a hard drive failure. It is important to perform regular backups of the following system databases:

- master

- msdb (if automating jobs, or configuring replication)

- model (if modified)

- distribution (if the server is configured as a replication Distributor)

Note: *It is not possible to back up the tempdb system database. This system database is rebuilt each time you start an instance of SQL Server 2000. When the instance of SQL Server is stopped, all data in tempdb is permanently deleted.*

Backing up the Master Database

Backing up the master database is an extremely important task that must be performed regularly. If the master database is damaged in any way, for example, because of a media failure, an instance of SQL Server may not start.

If you are unable to start an instance of SQL Server because the master database is corrupt, it is necessary to rebuild the master database, and then perform a restore from the master database backup. You rebuild the master database using the rebuildm.exe utility that is discussed later in this chapter.

Note: Only a full database backup can be performed on the master database.

You should consider backing up your master database after executing any statement or system procedure that changes information in the master database. For example, if you change a server-wide configuration option that updates the master database, you will want to back up the master database. If you don't back up the master database after changing it and you have to restore the master database from a previous backup, the changes you made will be lost.

Note: We highly recommend you avoid creating user objects in the master database; otherwise you will need to back up the master database more often than when you make a system-wide change.

The following list contains the types of operations that cause the master database to be updated, and therefore will require you to back up the master database:

• Creating or deleting a user database.

Note: If a user database expands automatically, or if you delete a file or filegroup associated with a user database, the master database is not affected.

• Adding user logins or other login security-related operations.

Note: Database security operations such as adding a new user to the database do not affect the master database.

• Changing any SQL Server configuration or database configuration option.

• Creating or removing logical backup devices.

• Configuring SQL Server for linked servers or remote logins when using distributed queries or remote procedure calls.

The other system databases we need to be concerned about are the msdb, model, and the distribution databases. These databases should be backed up in the same way you perform your user database backups. Like your user databases these system databases are regularly backed up, but under different conditions or for different reasons.

Note: The msdb, model, and distribution databases support all recovery models.

Backing up the Msdb Database

The msdb database is used by SQL Server, SQL Server Agent, and the Enterprise Manager to store data. This data includes information about scheduling, jobs, alerts, operators, and backup and restore history information.

The msdb database contains online information about your backups and restores that is automatically maintained by SQL Server. This information, stored in the system tables discussed earlier, includes:

- Who performed the backup operation.

- What time the backup operation took place.

- Which devices or files the backup information is stored in.

The information about your backups that is stored by SQL Server is used by the SQL Server Enterprise Manager to recommend a plan for restoring your database and for applying your transaction log backups.

The information contained in this database is for all backup events, including those that were created with custom applications or third-party tools. If you use the backup-and-restore information stored in the msdb database when recovering your databases, be sure to use the Full Recovery model for the msdb database. You should also place the msdb transaction log on fault-tolerant storage.

Warning! *If the msdb database is damaged and there is no current backup available, then all scheduling information used by the SQL Server Agent is lost and needs to be re-created manually. Furthermore, your backup-and-restore history information is also lost.*

The following list contains the types of operations that cause the msdb database to be automatically updated, and require that you back it up:

- Scheduling tasks.

- Storing Data Transformation Services (DTS) packages that were created with the DTS Import/Export Wizard.

- Maintaining online backup and restore history information.

- Replication configuration.

Note: As with the master database, we highly recommend you avoid creating user objects in the msdb database; otherwise you will need to back up the msdb database more frequently. Also, these user objects compete with the system objects for space in the database.

Backing up the Model Database

The model database is the database used as a template by SQL Server to create a new database. When you are creating a new database, the entire contents of the model database and settings are copied to the new database. This database is modified only by specific user changes. The following information is automatically included in the new database:

- User-defined objects (tables, views, etc.).

- User-defined data types.

- Database options (read-only, single-user, etc.).

Warning! If the model database is damaged, and there is no current backup available, all user-supplied information added to the model database is lost and needs to be re-created manually.

Backing up the Distribution Database

The distribution database is only used by the replication components of SQL Server. This system database is not available until you configure the server to participate as either a combined Publisher/Distributor or as a remote distribution server.

The distribution database is used to store such data as transactions, synchronization status, snapshot jobs, and replication history information. If this database is damaged and there is no current backup available, all replication information must be re-created manually.

Tip: We recommend you use the Full Recovery model on the distribution database. This provides you the highest possibility of recovering all the data stored in the database.

The following list contains the replication components that automatically update the distribution database, and will require that you back it up:

- The Replication Distribution Agent utility.

- The Replication Log Reader Agent utility.

- The Replication Snapshot Agent utility.

- The Replication Merge Agent utility.

Note: As with the master and model database, we highly recommend you avoid creating user objects in the distribution database; otherwise you will need to back up the distribution database more frequently. Also, these user objects compete with the system objects for space in the database.

Backing Up Your Transaction Logs

A critical part of creating a backup strategy that allows you to recover most, if not all, of your data involves backing up your transaction logs. To create a complete set of backups, you typically create a database backup at periodic intervals, such as daily, and then create transaction log backups at shorter intervals, such as every four hours.

You must have at least one full database backup, or a set of file backups, in order to utilize your transaction log backups. Your decision of how often to back up your transaction log is determined by the criticality of your data and the workload of your server.

If your transaction log is damaged, you will lose transactions written since the most recent full database backup or file backup. With this said, you see how important it is to perform regularly scheduled backups of your transaction logs. Furthermore, you see how important it is to implement a fault-tolerant strategy when deciding where to place your transaction log files.

You have three ways to perform a transaction log backup: using Transact-SQL, Enterprise Manager, or the Create Database Backup Wizard that was explained earlier in this chapter. Let's take a look at creating a transaction log using Transact-SQL and Enterprise Manager.

Creating a Transaction Log Backup Using Transact-SQL

After accessing Query Analyzer you can use the following steps to back up your transaction log in SQL Server:

1. Execute the **BACKUP LOG** statement and specify the following arguments:

   - The name of the database that contains the transaction log that you want to back up.

   - The name of the backup device on which you want to store the copy of the transaction log.

2. Optionally, you can specify any of the following:

   - The **INIT** clause to overwrite the existing backup sets, making the current backup operation the first backup set on the backup media.

   - The **SKIP** and **INIT** clause to overwrite the backup media, even if there are backup sets that have not expired, or if the media name does not match the name on the backup media.

   - The **FORMAT** clause when using the backup media for the first time and you want to initialize the media and overwrite any existing media header information.

Warning! Use the INIT or FORMAT option with the BACKUP command with extreme caution, as this will destroy any existing backup sets that reside on the backup media.

The following code is an example of a transaction log backup. Use the following code to overwrite any existing media header information and backup sets on the disk called NewTLogBackup, before copying the Northwind transaction log to the backup media:

```
USE Northwind
GO
BACKUP LOG Northwind
 TO NewTLogBackup
 WITH FORMAT
```

Creating a Transaction Log Backup Using Enterprise Manager

You can also create a transaction log backup using Enterprise Manager by following these steps:

1. After opening Enterprise Manager, expand the server group and the SQL Server that contains the database that you want to back up.

2. Expand the Databases option and right-click on the database to open the shortcut menu, choose All Tasks to display another shortcut menu, and then click the Backup Database option to open the SQL Server backup dialog box.

3. Type the name of the backup set in the Name box, and optionally type in a description of the backup set.

4. Under Backup, click the Transaction log radio button.

Note: If this option is dimmed out, make sure that the Full Recovery or Bulk-Logged Recovery model is configured on the database by right-clicking on the database, and choosing Properties. Click on the Options tab, and use the drop-down menu to set the model under Recovery.

5. Under Destination, click Disk or Tape to identify your backup media type, and then specify your backup destination.

Note: If no backup destinations appear, click Add to create a new backup destination or to select an existing backup destination.

6. Under Overwrite, perform one of the following:

   - Click Append To Media to append the backup to any existing backup sets on your backup device.

   - Click Overwrite Existing Media to overwrite any existing backup sets on your backup device.

7. Optionally, you can click the Schedule checkbox to create a schedule for the backup operation for later or recurring execution and complete the General tab of the backup dialog box.

8. Optionally, you can click the Options tab and choose one or more of the following options:

   - Click the Verify Backup Upon Completion checkbox to verify the backup when completed.

   - Click the Eject Tape After Backup checkbox to verify that the tape is ejected when the backup operation completes.

Note: This option is only available with tape devices.

- Click the Check Media Set Name And BackupSet Expiration checkbox to verify that the backup media is checked before overwriting. Type the name of the media you want to use for the backup operation in the Media Set Name box.

9. If you are using this backup media for the first time, or if you want to change the existing media label, select the Initialize And Label Media checkbox and type the name and description of the media set.

Note: This option is only available when you are overwriting the media.

Backing Up the Transaction Log When Your Database is Damaged.

Backing up the transaction log using Transact-SQL, Enterprise Manager, or the Create Database Backup Wizard is useful when the database and the transaction log are both available. However, if the database associated with the transaction log— each of which should be on separate hard drives—becomes damaged or is deleted, your transaction log backup steps change slightly.

Warning! This procedure can only be used to back up your transaction log if the transaction log is accessible and undamaged.

After accessing Query Analyzer, you can use the following steps to back up a damaged database transaction log:

1. Execute the **BACKUP LOG** statement and specify the following arguments:

   - The name of the database that contains the transaction log that you want to back up.

   - The name of the backup device that you want to store the copy of the transaction log on.

   - The **NO_TRUNCATE** option to back up the transaction log without purging the information that is being backed up.

2. Optionally, you can specify any of the following:

   - The **INIT** clause to overwrite the existing backup sets, making the current backup operation, the first backup set on the backup media.

   - The **SKIP** and **INIT** clause to overwrite the backup media, even if there are backup sets that have not expired, or if the media name does not match the name on the backup media.

   - The **FORMAT** clause when using the backup media for the first time and you want to initialize the media and overwrite any existing media header information.

*Warning! Use the **INIT** or **FORMAT** option with the **BACKUP** command with extreme caution, as this will destroy any existing backup sets that reside on the backup media.*

The following code is an example of a transaction log backup that you would perform on a database that is damaged or inaccessible if your transaction log is not damaged and is accessible. Use the following code to copy the contents of the transaction log to a backup set on the disk called NewTLogBackup, without truncating the contents of the Northwind database transaction log:

```
USE Northwind
GO
BACKUP LOG Northwind
  TO NewTLogBackup
  WITH NO_TRUNCATE
```

Note: *The primary reason for not purging the contents of the transaction log is to avoid disrupting your scheduled transaction log backup.*

As you can see, there are numerous ways to perform backups in SQL Server 2000, with many variables to consider. However, if you properly plan and design a backup strategy you will be successful at reducing or avoiding loss of data.

Creating a Backup Strategy

Designing the appropriate backup strategy involves identifying the requirements for the availability of your data. Your overall backup strategy defines the type and frequency of your backups as well as the nature and speed of the hardware required to perform the backups.

Warning! It is STRONGLY recommended that you thoroughly test your backup-and-recovery process. Testing your strategy helps to guarantee you have the required backups necessary to recover from various failures. Furthermore, it will help make certain that your procedures execute smoothly and quickly in the event of a failure.

The design of your backup strategy needs to take many factors into consideration, but the two primary considerations are the time to restore the data and the amount of data you can, or cannot, afford to lose. The time to perform the backup should not be a factor when you're designing your backup strategy.

The efficiency and cost of the restore operation should be the two key factors influencing your backup strategy.

There are three primary areas of concern that you need to consider when you are designing your backup strategy: assessing availability and recovery requirements, planning for disaster recovery, and selecting a recovery model. Each of these primary areas should be thoroughly researched and discussed when planning your backup strategy.

Analyzing Availability and Recovery Requirements

You must research and gain an understanding of when your data needs to be accessible and the potential impact of data loss to your business. To assist you in analyzing your availability and recovery requirements, ask the following questions:

- What are your data availability requirements? What hours of each day must your database be available to your users?

- What is the financial loss when your database is unavailable?

- What is the acceptable period of unavailability in the event you experience a media failure?

- What is the acceptable period of unavailability in the event of a natural disaster?

- How critical is it that you never lose data modifications?

- How easy would it be to re-create lost data modifications?

- Does your company employ database and system administrators?

- Who is responsible for performing your backup and restore operations?

After answering the previous questions, you also need to ask the following questions to help you choose the appropriate hardware, techniques, and tools for your site:

- How large is each database you are responsible for maintaining?

- How frequently does the data change in the database?

- What are your daily critical database production periods?

- When are your peak times for data modifications?

- How often are you truncating your transaction logs?

- Do you perform bulk data operations to load data into your database?

- Is your database part of a SQL Server failover cluster?

It is also recommended that your backup plan include a process for managing your backup media. For instance, consider implementing the following media management recommendations:

- A tracking plan for storing, rotating, and recycling your backup sets.

- A schedule for overwriting your backup media.

- In a multiserver environment, a decision whether to use centralized or distributed backups.

- A plan for tracking the lifespan of your backup media.

- A procedure to minimize the effects if you lose a backup set or backup media.

- A decision to store a copy of your backup sets offsite, and how this will affect your overall recovery time.

Planning for Disaster Recovery

You must establish a disaster recovery plan to guarantee that all of your systems and data can be easily and quickly restored to a normal state of operation in the event you experience a natural disaster.

To assist you in planning your disaster recovery plan, include the following information:

- A plan to acquire the required hardware.

- A plan to communicate the recovery process.

- A list of people that have to be notified in the event of a disaster.

- Instructions on how to contact the people involved in the recovery process.

- Information regarding who is responsible for administering the plan.

When creating your plan to recover from a disaster, be sure to include the following actions:

- Perform regularly scheduled database and transaction log backups to minimize the amount of lost data.

- Maintain operating system and SQL Server logs in a secure area. These logs should contain information regarding service pack installations, network libraries, security mode, and the password for the sa account.

- Assess the steps you need to take to quickly and easily recover from a disaster by performing them on another SQL Server. Modify any steps that you consider to be inefficient or time-consuming.

Selecting a Recovery Model

The Recovery model you choose to implement has a direct impact on your recovery process and time. Be sure you are very familiar with the recovery models discussed earlier in this chapter.

Optimizing Your Backups

You can implement several methods to increase the speed of your backups and restores in SQL Server 2000. A few of these methods include:

- Using multiple backup devices to increase throughput by allowing your backups to be written to multiple backup devices in parallel. Similarly, you can use multiple devices in parallel when restoring the data from the backup devices.

Note: The increased throughput is in proportion to the number of devices involved in the backup or restore operation.

- Using a combination of full database, differential database, and transaction log backups to minimize the time required to recover from a database failure. Differential backups reduce the number of transaction logs that must be used to recover the database.

Tip: A combination of database backup types is normally faster than creating and restoring full database backups.

- Using Logged and Minimally Logged Bulk Copy Operations will also reduce the amount of data stored in the transaction log, therefore reducing the time it takes to perform your backup and restore operations.

The options discussed earlier in this chapter under Creating Your Backup Strategy, along with the information provided in Chapter 13, provides additional information on optimizing your SQL Server backups.

Viewing Information about Your Backups

After creating your backups, you may need to view information about your backups. Information that you may want to view includes:

- The database and transaction log files contained in a specific backup set.
- The backup header information for all backup sets on your backup media.
- The media header information on your backup media.

Table 9.10 lists the **RESTORE** options that you can use to view different information about your backups. You can use the table as a quick reference when deciding what option will return the information you are looking for.

Table 9.10 RESTORE Options used for viewing backup information.

Command	Description
RESTORE FILELISTONLY	Displays a list of the database and log files contained on the backup set.
RESTORE HEADERONLY	Displays the backup header information for all backup sets on the specified backup device.
RESTORE LABELONLY	Displays the backup media identified by the given backup device. This includes information such as: media name, media set id, media description, and media date.
RESTORE VERIFYONLY	Verifies the backup set, but does not restore the backup. Used to make sure the backup set is complete and all volumes are readable before you perform the restore operation.

Let's take a look at what information is provided when you are viewing your backup sets and backup media.

Listing Database and Transaction Log Files on a Backup Set

Information that is displayed when you are viewing database and transaction log backups using the **RESTORE FILELISTONLY** command includes the following:

- Logical name

- Physical name

- Backup type (database or transaction log)

- Filegroup membership

- File size (in bytes)

- Maximum file size allowed

- File growth size (in bytes)

All of this information can be used to determine the names of the files stored on a database backup, prior to performing the restore operation. This information can be useful when:

- You have lost a hard drive containing one or more of your files for a database.

Note: You can determine which files were affected on the hard drive, then view the files on your backup to be certain you restore the correct ones.

- You are restoring a database from one SQL Server to another SQL Server that contains a different directory structure and drive mapping.

Note: You can list the files on the backup to determine where their original location was. You can then determine what parameters you will need to specify in order to successfully restore the backup set.

Viewing the Backup Header Information

You can display the backup header information to view the information about the SQL Server and foreign backup sets on a specific backup media using the **RESTORE HEADERONLY** statement. Some of the information that you will receive includes:

- Types of backup devices.

- Types of backups (full, differential, or transaction log).

- Backup start and stop dates and times.

- Database creation date.

This information can be used to determine which backup sets reside on the backup media, allowing you to choose the backup set you want to restore.

Note: Viewing backup header information can take a long time for your high-capacity tapes because your entire media set is scanned for information about each backup set on the backup media.

As you have probably already determined, this is a great way to review your backup media information before performing a restore. After determining that you have located the correct backup set, you also will want to familiarize yourself with the restore operation in SQL Server 2000.

Understanding the Restore Operation

As we have mentioned previously, your backup and restore operations work hand-in-hand and both will have an impact on your backup and restore strategies. To implement an effective restore strategy, you must understand the SQL Server 2000 recovery process. There are two recovery processes in SQL Server 2000: an automatic process that occurs every time you start SQL Server and a manual process that you initiate. We'll begin by looking at the automatic recovery process, which in turn will help you understand the manual process.

RECOVERY versus NORECOVEREY When Restoring a Backup

When performing restore operations in SQL Server 2000, you must be familiar with how the restore operations affect the status of your database availability. During your restore operation, you can specify **RECOVERY** or **NORECOVERY**.

When you specify the **NORECOVERY** option during a restore operation, it instructs SQL Server to not roll back any uncommitted transactions and also indicates that the database is unusable in this state. You specify this restore option when performing all restore operations except the very last restore.

*Note: If you do not specify **NORECOVERY** or **RECOVERY**, the option will default to **RECOVERY**.*

When you apply the very last backup using a restore operation, you specify the **RECOVERY** option. The **RECOVERY** option instructs SQL Server to roll back any uncommitted transactions and make the database usable. You specify this option when performing the very last restore operation in a series of restores.

Automatic Recovery Process

The automatic recovery process is used to guarantee that after SQL Server is started, the data in each of your databases is logically consistent, regardless of how or why SQL Server was stopped.

SQL Server uses the transaction log to perform the automatic recovery process by reading the active portion of the transaction log for each of your databases. The recovery process examines all transactions that have occurred since the most recent checkpoint. During this examination process it identifies all committed transactions and rolls them forward (applies them to the database).

However, if it identifies uncommitted transactions, it will roll them back (remove any partially written transactions from the database). This process ensures you have a logically consistent database before you start working with it.

The master database is the first database on which SQL Server 2000 performs the automatic recovery process when you start SQL Server. This database is recovered first because it contains all of the information required to locate, open, and recover the remaining databases.

The model, msdb, and distribution (if it exists) databases are recovered next. After your system databases are recovered, it recovers your user databases. Finally, it clears and starts the tempdb database.

Tip: You can examine the restoration process by reviewing the SQL Server error log, similar to what is shown in Figure 9.21.

The automatic recovery process cannot be controlled directly. However, you can define the maximum amount of time SQL Server should take to perform the automatic recovery process. The default value is **0**, indicating SQL Server will dynamically determine how often to issue a checkpoint.

Note: The more frequently a checkpoint is issued, the smaller the active portion of the transaction log is, therefore reducing the number of transactions that need to be rolled forward or rolled back.

Manual Recovery Process

The manual recovery process involves restoring one or more of your database backups, and then manually recovering them completely or to a specific point in time. This recovery process may include restoring:

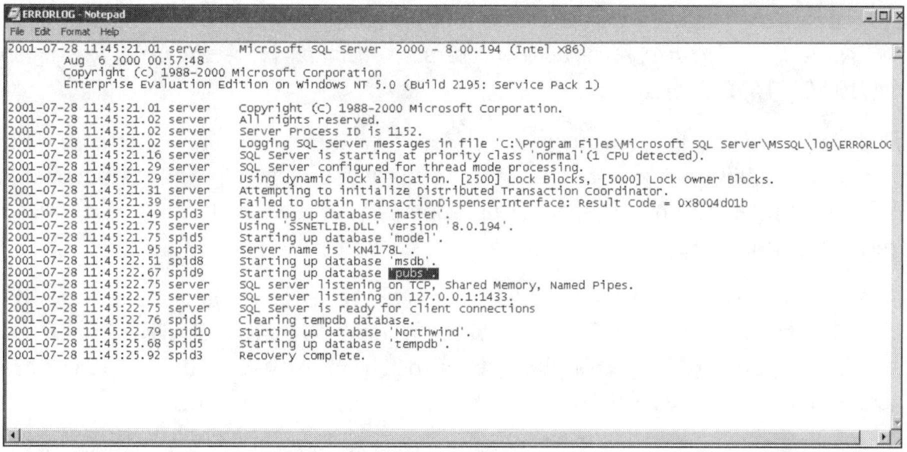


```
2001-07-28 11:45:21.01 server    Microsoft SQL Server  2000 - 8.00.194 (Intel X86)
        Aug  6 2000 00:57:48
        Copyright (c) 1988-2000 Microsoft Corporation
        Enterprise Evaluation Edition on Windows NT 5.0 (Build 2195: Service Pack 1)

2001-07-28 11:45:21.01 server    Copyright (C) 1988-2000 Microsoft Corporation.
2001-07-28 11:45:21.02 server    All rights reserved.
2001-07-28 11:45:21.02 server    Server Process ID is 1152.
2001-07-28 11:45:21.02 server    Logging SQL Server messages in file 'C:\Program Files\Microsoft SQL Server\MSSQL\log\ERRORLOG
2001-07-28 11:45:21.16 server    SQL Server is starting at priority class 'normal'(1 CPU detected).
2001-07-28 11:45:21.29 server    SQL Server configured for thread mode processing.
2001-07-28 11:45:21.29 server    Using dynamic lock allocation. [2500] Lock Blocks, [5000] Lock Owner Blocks.
2001-07-28 11:45:21.31 server    Attempting to initialize Distributed Transaction Coordinator.
2001-07-28 11:45:21.39 server    Failed to obtain TransactionDispenserInterface: Result Code = 0x8004d01b
2001-07-28 11:45:21.49 spid3     Starting up database 'master'.
2001-07-28 11:45:21.75 server    Using 'SSNETLIB.DLL' version '8.0.194'.
2001-07-28 11:45:21.75 spid5     Starting up database 'model'.
2001-07-28 11:45:21.95 spid3     Server name is 'KN4178L'.
2001-07-28 11:45:22.51 spid8     Starting up database 'msdb'.
2001-07-28 11:45:22.67 spid9     Starting up database 'pubs'.
2001-07-28 11:45:22.75 server    SQL server listening on TCP, Shared Memory, Named Pipes.
2001-07-28 11:45:22.75 server    SQL server listening on 127.0.0.1:1433.
2001-07-28 11:45:22.75 server    SQL Server is ready for client connections
2001-07-28 11:45:22.76 spid5     Clearing tempdb database.
2001-07-28 11:45:22.79 spid10    Starting up database 'Northwind'.
2001-07-28 11:45:25.68 spid5     Starting up database 'tempdb'.
2001-07-28 11:45:25.92 spid3     Recovery complete.
```

Figure 9.21
Recovery Process Information in the SQL Server error log.

- A full database backup.
- Optionally a differential backup.
- A series of transaction log backups.

During the restoration process of each of these backups, your database is not available to your users. However, you can restore a database to stand-by (read-only) mode so you can view the state of the data after each restoration to identify the point in the transaction log where the data restoration should stop.

After restoring all the applicable database and transaction logs, you need to specify the recovery option to roll forward and roll back the appropriate transactions and bring the database online in a logically consistent state.

Warning! *The recovery option is only used with the last restore you perform. After using the recovery option, no further restorations can occur.*

Securing Your Restore Operations

As with all other aspects of SQL Server 2000, it is imperative to understand the security options available to you when you are implementing your restore strategy. By default you can successfully execute the **RESTORE LOG** or **RESTORE DATABASE** commands if you are a member of one of the following roles:

- **Sysadmin** fixed server role
- **Db_creator** fixed server role
- Owner of the database

9

*Warning! Because fixed database roles can only be checked when the database is accessible, which is not always the case when you are performing a restore operation, members of the **db_owner** fixed database role do not have **RESTORE** permissions.*

You are now also able to specify passwords for a backup set, media set, or both. This provides an additional layer of security when performing backup and restore operations by preventing unauthorized appends of backup sets to media sets and unauthorized restores of the backup.

After you apply a password to a media set, you are required to supply the password during the restore operation in addition to having the appropriate **RESTORE** permissions. You specify the password for your backup set or media set by supplying an optional parameter when you execute the **RESTORE** command.

Note: The media set password is set when the media header is written and cannot be altered.

Although passwords are used to prevent the unauthorized access of media using SQL tools, they do not prevent unauthorized access by programs specifically created for accessing and destroying the data. Furthermore, the password option does not encrypt the data in any way.

Understanding the Types of Restores in SQL Server 2000

SQL Server 2000 supports numerous types of restores that can be used separately or in combination. The recovery model you choose for your database greatly affects your overall restore strategy, including the decision of what restore type or types are used to recover your database.

Table 9.11 introduces the different restore types and provides a brief description of them. The sections following the table provide in-depth information regarding the different restore operations available in SQL Server 2000.

Table 9.11   SQL Server database restore types.

Restore Type	Description
Full database restore	Restore the entire database using your full database backup, your most recent differential backup (if any), and all transaction log backups in the same chronological order that you performed the transaction log backups since your most recent differential backup.
File or Filegroup restore with full recovery	Restore the entire file or filegroup using a file or filegroup backup, the most recent differential file or filegroup backup (if any), and all transaction log backups in the same chronological order that you performed the transaction log backups since the most recent differential file or filegroup backup.
Recovery to a point in time	Restore the entire database to a specified earlier point in time using your full database backups, differential backups, file and filegroup backups, and your transaction log backups.
Recovery to a named transaction	Restore the entire database to a specified named mark (immediately before or after a specific transaction) using your full database backups, differential backups, file and filegroup backups, and your transaction log backups.

Note: You can also perform a partial restoration of a database to extract specific data by restoring the required filegroups of a database. This is normally done to a secondary SQL Server.

Full Database Restore

When you want to restore a database to its most current status you need to perform the following restore operations:

1. Full database restore—specifying **NORECOVERY**.

Note: You can restore an entire database to any SQL Server instance, not just the instance of SQL Server that the backups were created on.

2. Differential restore (if any)—specifying **NORECOVERY**.

3. Transaction logs restore (in chronological order since last differential backup) specifying **RECOVERY** on the restore of the latest transaction log.

Tip: If your most recent differential backup is damaged or is inaccessible, you can restore all transaction logs in chronological order since your full database backup. Therefore, it is recommended you maintain all transaction log backups since your last full backup to provide a fault tolerant backup strategy when you are using differential backups.

File or Filegroup Restore with Full Recovery

When you are restoring a file or filegroup, you begin with the most recent backup of your file or filegroup. This most recent backup can be from a file or filegroup backup, or a full database backup. However, restoring a single file from a full database backup will take longer than restoring the file from a file backup.

When you want to restore a file or filegroup to its most current status you need to perform the following restore operations:

1. File or filegroup restore specifying **NORECOVERY**.

2. Differential file or filegroup restore (if any)—specifying **NORECOVERY**.

3. Transaction logs restore (in chronological order since last file or filegroup differential backup) specifying **RECOVERY** on the restore of the latest transaction log.

Warning! Unlike a full or differential database backup, your file or filegroup backups must have transaction log backups applied to them to make the restored file or filegroup consistent with the rest of your database.

Recovery to a Point in Time

Sometimes you may want to recover to an earlier point in time because of incorrect data being inserted. You can achieve this by recovering your database to a specific point in time of the transaction log or to a named transaction within the transaction log.

To recover to a specific point in time in SQL Server 2000, you need to perform the following steps:

1. Full database restore—specifying **NORECOVERY.**

2. Differential restore (if any)—specifying **NORECOVERY**.

3. Transaction logs restore (in chronological order since last differential backup) specifying the exact point in time along with the **RECOVERY** option on the restore of the latest transaction log.

Recovery to a Named Transaction

In SQL Server 2000 you can insert a mark into the transaction log to identify a location of a specific transaction. The mark you insert is recorded in the **logmarkhistory** table of the msdb database and is used to determine what transactions to restore in that transaction log.

To restore to a named transaction, you use the same steps as you use when you are recovering to a point in time. You simply supply the named transaction and whether or not you want to recover to the mark, and either include or exclude the mark.

Warning! *You can recover to a specific point in time or to a named transaction if the last transaction log backup that you want to restore contains a bulk-logged transaction that was logged using the Bulk-Logged Recovery model.*

Understanding the Effects of a Restore

Now that you are familiar with the restore options you have available to you, it is time to become more familiar with the restore operation itself.

Unlike the dynamic backup operation—where your users can access the database during the time the backup is being performed, your restore operation is not dynamic. Users cannot access the database when you are performing the restore.

The data in the current database is replaced by the data being restored during the restore operation. When the restore operation is being performed, the backup history tables listed in Table 9.8 are modified. Furthermore, the restore history files listed in Table 9.12 are also updated during a restore operation.

Warning! *These table names are new to SQL Server 2000; therefore backups created with SQL Server 2000 cannot be restored to earlier versions of SQL Server.*

Table 9.12   Restore history tables.

Table Name	Number of Columns	Description
Restorefile	4	Contains one row for each restored file, including the files restored indirectly by filegroup name.
Restorefilegroup	2	Contains one row for each restored filegroup.
Restorehistory	12	Contains one row for each restore operation performed.

When restoring a database, the restorable database options (which are all the settable options of the **ALTER DATABASE** statement except the **merge publish**, **published**, and **subscribed replication** options) are reset to the settings that were in force at the time the backup operation completed.

*Note: The user access option setting can be overridden by specifying the **WITH RESTRICTED_USER** option.*

Restoring Your Databases

You now have the information required to actually perform a restore operation from one of your SQL Server 2000 backups. However, as you know, there are a couple of ways to restore your data in SQL Server 2000—using the **RESTORE** command or using Enterprise Manager.

Understanding the **RESTORE** Command

We'll begin with an explanation of the **RESTORE** command that you use in Query Analyzer to restore your full database backups, differential database backups, transaction logs, or one or more of your database files or filegroups. The following basic syntax is used to perform a restore of a database:

```
RESTORE DATABASE database_name
FROM backup_device
```

The **RESTORE** command has many arguments that can be used to customize your restore operation. It is important to understand the most commonly used **RESTORE** command arguments, and in what restore operations they are used. Table 9.13 contains a list of the most commonly used **RESTORE** command arguments.

Table 9.13   RESTORE command arguments.

Argument	Restore Type	Description
DATABASE	All except transaction log	Specifies the name of the database to restore. If you include a list of files and filegroups, only those files and filegroups are restored.
LOG	Transaction log	Specifies the transaction log to be restored.

(continued)

Table 9.13 RESTORE command arguments *(continued)*.

Argument	Restore Type	Description
BACKUP DEVICE	All	Specifies the logical or physical backup device from which to restore the backup. If restoring from a physical backup device you must specify backup media type (disk or tape) in the **RESTORE** statement using the **FROM DISK** or **FROM TAPE** arguments.
FILE	All	Specifies the backup set to be restored from the backup medium, where 1 is the first backup set, 2 is the second, etc.
RESTRICTED_USER	All	Specifies that the newly restored database can only be accessed by **db_owner**, **dbcreator**, or **sysadmin** role members. This option is used with the **RECOVERY** argument.
PASSWORD	All	Specifies the password set on the backup set when it was created. This password must be supplied when performing the restore from the backup set.
MEDIANAME	All	Specifies the name of the media set. If provided, the name specified with the **RESTORE** command must match the name supplied when the backup was created.
MOVE...TO...	All	Specifies the location to restore the backup, if different than the location that the database was originally backed up from.
REPLACE	All	Specifies that SQL Server should restore the specified database and its related files even if another database with the same name already exists, thereby deleting the existing database.
NORECOVERY	All	Specifies to not make the database usable after the restore operation of the backup set completes.
RECOVERY	All	Specifies to make the database usable after the restore operation of the backup set completes.
STANDBY	All	Specifies the undo file name that you can use to undo changes made to a standby server. Allows a database to be configured for read-only access, while still allowing transaction logs to be restored.
NOREWIND	All	Specifies that SQL Server keep the tape open and available after the restore operation completes.
REWIND	All	Specifies that SQL Server releases and rewinds the tape after the restore operation completes.
NOUNLOAD	All	Specifies that SQL Server does not automatically rewind and unload the tape from the tape drive after the restore operation completes.
UNLOAD	All	Specifies that SQL Server automatically rewinds and unloads the tape from the tape driver after the restore operation completes.
RESTART	All	Specifies that SQL Server restart an interrupted restore operation from the point of interruption.*
STATS	All	Specifies that SQL Server displays progress in a percentage of the restore operation.

(continued)

Table 9.13 RESTORE command arguments *(continued).*

Argument	Restore Type	Description
STOPAT	Transaction log	Specifies that SQL Server only restore the transactions within the transaction log up to the specified date and time. Transactions after the specified date and time are not applied to the database.
STOPATMARK	Transaction log	Specifies that SQL Server only restore the transactions within the transaction log up to and including the marked transaction. Transactions after the marked transaction are not applied to the database.
STOPBEFOREMARK	Transaction log	Specifies that SQL Server only restore the transactions within the transaction log up to but not including the marked transaction. Transactions after the marked transaction are not applied to the database.

*This option can only be used for restores being performed from multiple tape volumes.

Restoring a Full or Differential Database Backup Using Transact-SQL

After accessing Query Analyzer, you can use the following steps to restore a full or differential database backup in SQL Server:

1. Execute the **RESTORE DATABASE** statement and specify the following arguments:

   - The name of the database that you want to restore.

   - The name of the backup device that you want to retrieve the database backup from.

   - If this is not the last restore operation for this recovery process you specify the **NORECOVERY** option, otherwise you specify the **RECOVERY** clause.

2. Optionally, you can specify the **FILE** argument to identify the backup set on a backup media that contains multiple backup sets.

Warning! The system administrator performing the restore operation must be the only person currently connected to the database you are restoring.

The following code is an example of a full database restore. This restore operation will restore the backup of Northwind located on the backup device called NewDiskBackup. Immediately following this restore, a differential database restore will be performed, prompting the need to specify the **NORECOVERY** option.

```
USE master
GO
RESTORE DATABASE Northwind
 FROM NewDiskBackup
 WITH NORECOVERY
GO
```

The following code is an example of a differential database restore. This restore operation takes place after performing the full database restore operation just discussed. The differential backup is the second backup set on the same backup device (NewDiskBackup) as the full database backup and is the last restore operation to be performed.

```
USE Northwind
GO
RESTORE DATABASE Northwind
       FROM NewDiskBackup
       WITH FILE = 2
       RECOVERY
GO
```

The **RESTORE** command provides numerous options to customize your restore operation to suit your specific needs. However, it is easier to restore your backups using Enterprise Manager.

Restoring a Full or Differential Database Backup Using Enterprise Manager

SQL Server allows you to restore a full or differential database backup using Enterprise Manager. The following steps can be used to restore a full or differential database backup through Enterprise Manager:

1. After opening Enterprise Manager, expand the server group and the SQL Server that contains the database that you want to restore.

2. Expand the Databases option and right-click on the database to open the shortcut menu, choose All Tasks to display another shortcut menu, and then click the Restore Database option as shown in Figure 9.22 to open the SQL Server Backup dialog box.

3. Type or select the name of the database to restore in the Restore As Database box of the Restore Database dialog box.

Tip: If restoring a backup to a new database name, type a new name in this box.

4. Click the Database radio button to select the Restore operation type.

5. Locate and click the backup set you want to restore in the First Backup To Restore drop-down menu.

6. In the Restore list, click the full database backup that you want to restore to complete the Restore Database dialog box shown in Figure 9.23.

Note: If you are performing a differential database restore, then click the differential backup that you want to restore.

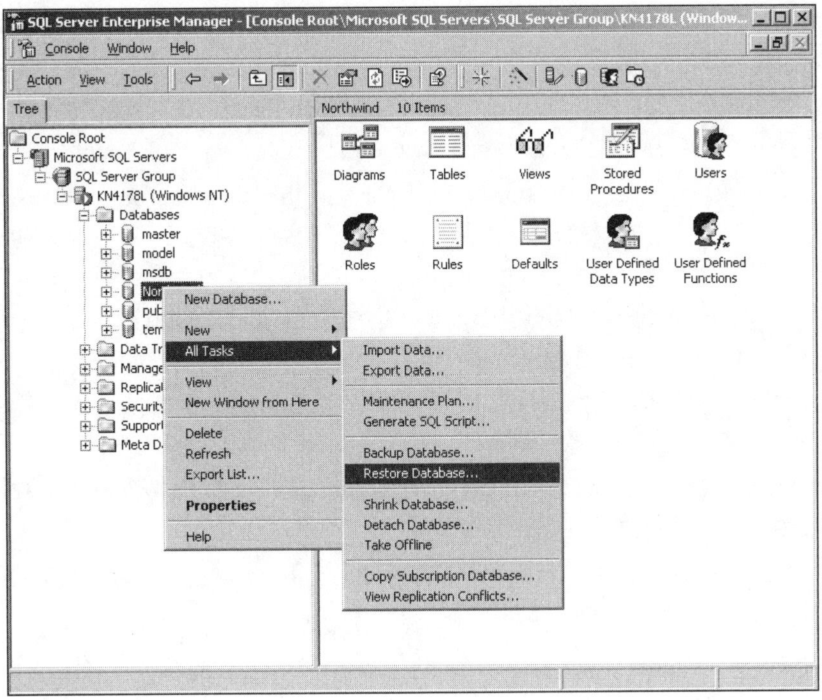

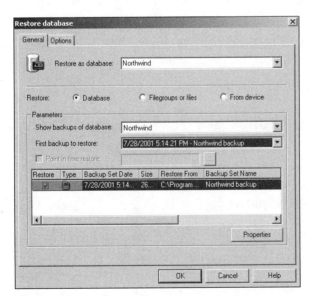

Figure 9.22
All Tasks shortcut menu to choose the Restore Database option.

Figure 9.23
Specifying the database to restore.

9

7. You can also click on the Options tab shown in Figure 9.24 and choose any of the following options:

- Click the Eject Tapes (If Any) After Restoring Each Backup checkbox to eject your tapes as your backups complete.

- Click the Prompt Before Restoring Each Backup checkbox to prompt the user before restoring each backup. This can prevent a user from accidentally restoring the wrong backup.

- Click the Force Restore Over Existing Database checkbox to force the restore over the existing database on your SQL Server.

- Click Leave Database Operational. No Additional Transaction Logs Can Be Restored, if no other backups are going to be restored.

*Note: This is the equivalent of the **RECOVERY** option you specify with the **RESTORE DATABASE** and **RESTORE LOG** commands.*

- Click Leave Database Nonoperational But Able To Restore Additional Transaction Logs, if you will be restoring other backups.

*Note: This is the equivalent to the **NORECOVERY** option you specify with the **RESTORE DATABASE** and **RESTORE LOG** commands.*

- Click Leave Database Read-only And Able To Restore Additional Transaction Logs to leave the database in read-only mode, but still allow you to restore additional transaction logs.

*Note: This is equivalent to the **STANDBY** option you specify with the **RESTORE DATA-BASE** and **RESTORE LOG** commands.*

8. Click OK to perform the restore operation.

Restoring Files and Filegroups

File and filegroups are used to reduce the amount of time it takes to back up large databases or databases that contain some data that is frequently changing and some that rarely changes.

To restore file or filegroup backups, you start by restoring the most recent backup of the file or filegroup. After performing the restore of the file or filegroup, you restore the most recent file or filegroup differential, and finally you complete the recovery process by restoring the transaction logs in chronological order.

Restoring Files and Filegroups Using Transact-SQL

After accessing Query Analyzer, you can use the following steps to restore a file or filegroup backup in SQL Server:

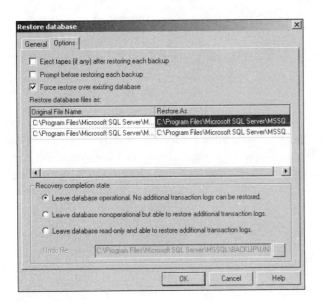

Figure 9.24
Choosing the Restore options.

1. Execute the **RESTORE DATABASE** statement to restore the file or filegroup, and specify the following arguments:

   - The name of the database that you want to restore.

   - The name of the backup device that you want to retrieve the database backup from.

   - The **FILE** clause for each file you are restoring.

   - The **FILEGROUP** clause for each filegroup you are restoring.

   - If this is not the last restore operation for this recovery process you specify the **NORECOVERY** option, otherwise you specify the **RECOVERY** clause.

*Note: If you are restoring the file or filegroup over existing files that have the same name and location, you must also use the **REPLACE** clause.*

2. Optionally, if the file or filegroup has been modified since the backup was created, execute the **RESTORE DATABASE** statement to apply the latest differential backup, and the **RESTORE LOG** statement to apply the appropriate transaction log backups.

Warning! The system administrator performing the restore operation must be the only person currently connected to the database you are restoring.

The following code is an example of a file restore. This restore operation will restore the specified file from the backup device called FileBackups and set the database to an unusable status:

```
USE master
GO
RESTORE DATABASE Northwind
 FILE = 'Northwind_Data'
 FROM FILEBACKUPS
 WITH NORECOVERY
```

The following code is an example of a differential file and filegroup restore. This restore operation will restore the changes that were made to the file and filegroup from the backup device called FileDiffBackups to the Northwind database and set the database to a usable status:

```
USE Northwind
GO
RESTORE DATABASE Northwind
 FILE = 'Northwind_Data'
 FILEGROUP = 'Northwind_Report'
 FROM FILEDIFFBACKUPS
 WITH RECOVERY
```

The **RESTORE** command provides numerous options to customize your restore operation to suit your specific needs. However, it is easier to restore your backups using Enterprise Manager.

Restoring Files and Filegroups Using Enterprise Manager

The following steps can be used to restore a file or filegroup backup using Enterprise Manager:

1. After opening Enterprise Manager, expand the server group and the SQL Server that contains the database that you want to restore.

2. Expand the Databases option and right-click on the database to open the shortcut menu, choose All Tasks to display another shortcut menu, and then click the Restore Database option to open the SQL Server Restore dialog box.

3. Type or select the name of the database to restore in the Restore As Database box of the Restore Database dialog box.

4. Click the Filegroups or Files radio button to select the Restore operation type.

5. In the Restore list, locate and select each file and filegroup backup that you want to restore to complete the Restore Database dialog box shown in Figure 9.25.

Note: If you are performing a differential file or filegroup restore, click the differential backup that you want to restore.

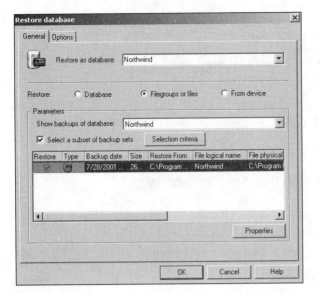

Figure 9.25
Specifying the file and filegroups to restore.

6. If you have numerous backup sets and you want to narrow the number of backup sets displayed, you can click the Select A Subset Of Backup Sets checkbox to display the Filter Backup Sets dialog box shown in Figure 9.26.

7. Alternatively, you can click on the Options tab and choose either of the following options:

   • If no other backups are going to be restored, click Leave Database Operational. No Additional Transaction Logs Can Be Restored.

Figure 9.26
Filtering your backup sets.

*Note: This is the equivalent of the **RECOVERY** option you specify with the **RESTORE DATABASE** and **RESTORE LOG** commands.*

- Click Leave Database Nonoperational But Able To Restore Additional Logs, if you will be restoring other backups.

*Note: This is the equivalent to the **NORECOVERY** option you specify with the **RESTORE DATABASE** and **RESTORE LOG** commands.*

8. Click OK to perform the restore operation.

Restoring Files and Filegroups Over Existing Files Using Enterprise Manager

By default, SQL Server performs a safety check that prevents you from overwriting an existing database that resides in the same location as the database that you are trying to restore. To override this safety check and perform the restore of a file or filegroup using Enterprise Manager use the following steps:

1. After opening Enterprise Manager, expand the server group and the SQL Server that contains the database that you want to restore.

2. Expand the Databases option and right-click on the database to open the shortcut menu, choose All Tasks to display another shortcut menu, and then click the Restore Database option to open the SQL Server Restore dialog box.

3. Type or select the name of the database to restore in the Restore As Database box of the Restore Database dialog box.

4. Click the From Device radio button, and then click the Select Devices button to open the Choose Restore Devices dialog box shown in Figure 9.27.

5. Under the Restore From area, click Disk or Tape and then locate and select a device from which to restore.

Note: If no backup devices appear, click Add to create a new backup device or to select an existing backup device. However, the backup device must reference the backup device files that were created at the primary server.

6. In the Restore Database dialog box, click View Contents and choose the backup set you want to restore from the Select Backup dialog box shown in Figure 9.28.

7. Under the Restore Backup set area, click File or Filegroup, and then type in the names of the files that you want to restore and complete the General tab of the Restore Database dialog box shown in Figure 9.29.

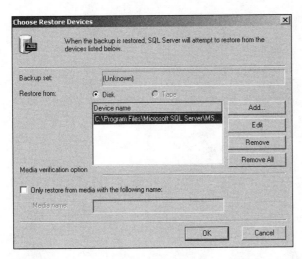

Figure 9.27
Choosing the backup device to restore from.

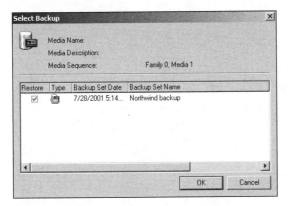

Figure 9.28
Selecting the backup set to restore.

8. Click the Options tab and then click the Force Restore Over Existing Database checkbox.

9. Under the Recovery Completion State, choose one of the following options:

   • If no other backups are going to be restored, click Leave Database Operational. No Additional Transaction Logs Can Be Restored.

   • Click Leave Database Nonoperational But Able To Restore Additional Logs, if you will be restoring other backups.

10. Click OK to perform the restore operation.

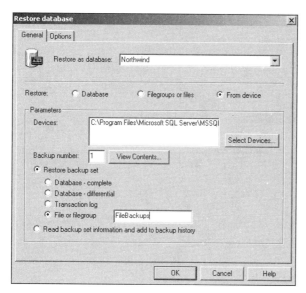

Figure 9.29
Completed Restore Database dialog box.

Restoring Your System Databases

The loss of your system databases can be detrimental and can greatly impact the time it takes to recover your system. Be sure you are familiar with restoring your system databases to ensure that your procedure is efficient and timely.

Restoring the Master Database

The master database contains system-wide configuration information. Any changes made to the master database after you back it up are lost in the event you lose access to the database and restore the backup of the database. Therefore, it is necessary to re-create those changes manually after restoring the master database. These changes are re-created by executing the statements necessary to re-create the missing changes.

Note: The master database can only be restored from a backup that was created on an instance of SQL Server 2000. SQL Server 2000 does not support restoring master database backups that were created in previous versions of SQL Server.

For instance, let's say you create SQL Server logins for three new employees, and you lose the master database before you back it up. After restoring the master database from the last backup, you are going to have to create those three logins.

Tip: You can re-create the logins by using Enterprise Manager, or if you used a script to create the logins you can re-execute that script.

If you create user databases after you backed up your master database, SQL Server 2000 will not recognize them. In order to make them available to your users, you will have to perform one of the following tasks:

- Attach the user databases to SQL server using one of the following options:

  - **sp_attach_db** system stored procedure.

  - Attach Database option on the All Tasks shortcut menu on a specific database. (Right click on the database to open the All Tasks shortcut menu.)

*Note: Attaching a database to SQL Server re-creates the system table entries (**sysdatabases**) and makes the database available in the same state it was before you restored the master database.*

- Restore the user databases from their backups.

Tip: It is recommended that you attach your database because it generally takes less time than performing a restore operation.

After running the rebuildm.exe command prompt utility, you will also have to restore the master database. The rebuildm.exe is used to create a new, but empty, master, model, and msdb database. If you do not want to re-create the missing data manually, you can restore the master database from the most recent database backup.

After restoring the master database, the instance of SQL Server that you restored it to is automatically stopped. Therefore, if you wish to make further repairs and want to prevent more than a single connection to SQL Server, you should start SQL Server in single-user mode again.

Tip: If you start SQL Server in single-user mode, all other SQL services and utilities, such as the SQL Server Agent, may still try to access SQL Server. Therefore, you should stop all SQL services and utilities.

After determining that you need to restore the master database, you can do so using Enterprise Manager or Transact-SQL. You can follow the steps provided in the "How to Restore a Full and Differential Database Backup Using Enterprise Manager" section in this chapter to restore the master database through Enterprise Manager.

You can use the following steps to restore the master database using Transact-SQL:

1. Start SQL Server in single-user mode using the following command-line syntax:

```
C:\ sqlservr.exe -c -m
```

Note: You must switch to the directory that contains the instance of SQL that you want to start in single-user mode before issuing this command.

2. Execute the **RESTORE DATABASE** statement to restore the master database backup from the backup device containing the master database.

The following code is used to restore the master database from a logical backup device called MasterBackup:

```
USE master
GO
RESTORE DATABASE master
 FROM MasterBackup
GO
```

Restoring the Model Database

The other system databases can be restored using either Enterprise Manager or Transact-SQL. However, you should be aware of certain facts and considerations before restoring the model, msdb, or distribution system databases. If the model database is damaged and you have made modifications to it since you installed SQL Server, you can restore it from your database backups. Modifications generally made to the model database include:

- User-defined objects (tables, views, etc.).

- User-defined data types.

- Database options (read-only, single-user, etc.).

The model database can only be restored from backups that were created on SQL Server 2000.

Note: *After running the rebuildm.exe utility to rebuild the master database, you will have to restore the model database as well. Rebuildm.exe also creates a new model database during its execution.*

Restoring the Msdb Database

If the msdb database is damaged and you have made modifications to it since you installed SQL Server, you can restore it from your database backups. Modifications generally made to the msdb database include:

- Jobs, alerts, and operators.

- Scheduling of jobs.

- Backup and restore history information.

- Meta Data Services.

The msdb database can only be restored from backups that were created on SQL Server 2000.

Note: After running the rebuildm.exe utility to rebuild the master database, you will have to restore the msdb database as well. Rebuildm.exe also creates a new msdb database during its execution.

Restoring the Distribution Database

If the distribution database is damaged and you have made modifications to it since you configured replication in SQL Server, you can restore it from your database backups or attach the database to SQL Server. If neither of these options is available to you, your SQL Server replication utilities will not run until you manually reconfigure your replication environment.

Note: Most of your replication configuration information is stored in the distribution database.

Only one user can access the database while a restore operation is in process. Your replication utilities that are used to maintain the replication process may try to access the distribution database when your restore operation is running. Before restoring the distribution database, you should verify that the following replication utilities are stopped:

- The Log Reader Agent

- The Distribution Agent

- The Snapshot Agent

- The Merge Agent

Note: In contrast to the procedure for working with the other system databases, after running the rebuildm.exe utility to rebuild the master database, you do not have to restore the distribution database. Rebuildm.exe does not create a new distribution database during its execution.

Restoring Your Transaction Logs

Usually the last step required to complete the restoration of your backups is to restore the backups of your transaction logs. This is the most critical step when recovering a database in SQL Server 2000.

When preparing to restore your transaction logs, note the conditions listed below that will prevent the transaction log from being restored:

- The database or differential database backups preceding the transaction log backup have not been restored.

- A preceding transaction log that was created after the full and differential database backups has not been applied.

Note: Transaction logs must be restored in the exact order they were backed up. If one of them becomes corrupt or missing, all subsequent backups cannot be restored.

- The database has already been recovered and all outstanding transactions have been rolled back or rolled forward.

*Note: The database may already have been recovered if the **RECOVERY** option has already been specified during one of the previous restore operations.*

After restoring your full database, file, filegroup, and differential backups, you can restore your transaction log backups. Unlike all other types of backups you can restore the entire backup, or up to a specific area of the transaction log, based on time or an explicitly named mark in the transaction log.

Restoring Your Transaction Log Backup Using Transact-SQL

You can restore a transaction log backup using Transact-SQL after opening Query Analyzer. You will execute the **RESTORE LOG** statement to restore the transaction log and specify the following arguments:

- The name of the database that you want the transaction log applied to.

- The name of the backup device that you want to retrieve the transaction log backup from.

- If this is not the last restore operation for this recovery process you specify the **NORECOVERY** option, otherwise you specify the **RECOVERY** clause.

Note: You repeat this procedure for each transaction log that you want to restore.

The following code is an example of multiple transaction logs being restored. This restore operation will restore the specified transaction log from the backup device called NWBackupLogs and set the database to an unusable status:

```
RESTORE LOG Northwind
  FROM NWBackupLogs
  WITH NORECOVERY
```

The following code is an example of a second and final transaction log restore. This restore operation will restore the specified transaction log from the backup device called NWBackupLogs_2 and set the database to a usable status:

```
RESTORE LOG Northwind
  FROM NWBackupLogs_2
  WITH RECOVERY
```

The **RESTORE** command provides numerous options to customize your restore operation to suit your specific needs. However, it is easier to restore your backups using Enterprise Manager.

Restoring Your Transaction Log Backup Using Enterprise Manager

Follow these steps to restore a transaction log backup using Enterprise Manager:

1. After opening Enterprise Manager, expand the server group and the SQL Server that contains the database of the transaction log that you want to restore.

2. Expand the Databases option and right-click on the database to open the shortcut menu, choose All Tasks to display another shortcut menu, and then click the Restore Database option to open the SQL Server Backup dialog box.

3. Type or select the name of the database to restore in the Restore As Database box of the Restore Database dialog box.

4. Click the Database radio button.

5. Locate and click the backup set you want to restore in the First Backup To Restore drop-down menu.

6. In the Restore list, click the transaction log backup that you want to restore and complete the Restore Database dialog box shown in Figure 9.30.

7. Alternatively, you can click on the Options tab and choose either of the following options:

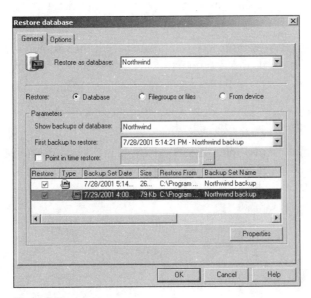

Figure 9.30
Specifying the transaction log to restore.

- If no other backups are going to be restored, click Leave Database Operational. No Additional Transaction Logs Can Be Restored.

*Note: This is the equivalent of the **RECOVERY** option you specify with the **RESTORE DATABASE** and **RESTORE LOG** commands.*

- Click Leave Database Nonoperational But Able To Restore Additional Logs if you will be restoring other backups.

*Note: This is the equivalent to the **NORECOVERY** option you specify with the **RESTORE DATABASE** and **RESTORE LOG** commands.*

8. Click OK to perform the restore operation.

Restoring Your Transaction Log to a Specific Point in Time Using Transact-SQL

After opening Query Analyzer, use the following steps to restore a transaction log backup to a specific point in time using Transact-SQL:

1. Execute the **RESTORE LOG** statement to restore the transaction log and specify the following arguments:

- The name of the database that you want the transaction log applied to.

- The name of the backup device that you want to retrieve the transaction log backup from.

- The **RECOVERY** and **STOPAT** clauses to specify when to quit the restore operation based on the time of the records in the transaction log, and to put the database in a usable status.

*Note: If your transaction log does not contain the time specified with the **STOPAT** clause, a warning is generated and the database remains unrecovered.*

The following code is an example of multiple transaction logs being restored. This restore operation will restore the specified transaction log from the backup device called NWBackupLogs and set the database to an unusable status:

```
RESTORE LOG Northwind
  FROM NWBackupLogs
  WITH NORECOVERY
```

The following code is an example of a second and final transaction log restore. This restore operation will restore the specified transaction log from the backup device called NWBackupLogs_2, but ends the restore operation at 11:00p.m. on July 29th. It also sets the database to a usable status. Here is the code:

```
RESTORE LOG Northwind
 FROM NWBackupLogs_2
 WITH RECOVERY,
       STOPAT = 'Jul 29, 2001 11:00 PM'
```

The **RESTORE** command provides numerous options to customize your restore operation to suit your specific needs. However, it is easier to restore your backups using Enterprise Manager.

Restoring Your Transaction Log to a Specific Point in Time Using Enterprise Manager

The following steps can be used to restore a transaction log backup to a specified time using Enterprise Manager:

1. After opening Enterprise Manager, expand the server group and the SQL Server that contains the database of the transaction log that you want to restore.

2. Expand the Databases option and right-click on the database to open the shortcut menu, choose All Tasks to display another shortcut menu, and then click the Restore Database option to open the SQL Server Backup dialog box.

3. Type or select the name of the database to restore in the Restore As Database box of the Restore Database dialog box.

4. Click the Database radio button.

5. Locate and click the backup set you want to restore in the First Backup To Restore drop-down menu.

6. In the Restore list, click the Full Database Backup and the transaction log backup that you want to restore and open the Point In Time Restore dialog box shown in Figure 9.31.

Tip: If you have selected a transaction log backup the Point in Time checkbox becomes available. If this is dimmed, then you have not selected a transaction log backup to restore and will not be able to specify a point in time.

7. If no other backups are going to be restored, click on the Options tab and then click Leave Database Operational. No Additional Transaction Logs Can Be Restored.

*Note: This is the equivalent of the **RECOVERY** option you specify with the **RESTORE DATABASE** and **RESTORE LOG** commands.*

8. Click OK to perform the restore operation.

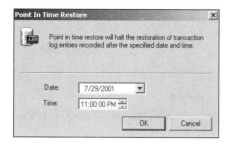

Figure 9.31
Specifying a point in time to restore.

Specifying Named Marks in Your Transaction Log

You can insert named marks into the transaction log so that you can later recover to that specific mark. These marks are transactional and will only be written in the transaction log if their associated transaction commits. After inserting the mark, you can recover to a point that includes or excludes the marked transaction.

Before using marked transactions in your transaction log, consider the following:

- Use transaction marks on transactions that play a significant role in your database recovery strategy to avoid consuming transaction log space.

- The **logmarkhistory** table of the msdb database is updated when a marked transaction is committed.

- If a marked transaction spans multiple databases on the local or on remote servers, the marks must be inserted in all affected databases.

You insert a named mark in your transaction log by using the **BEGIN TRANSACTION WITH MARK** statement. You must supply a name for your transaction, which will also be used as the name of the mark.

After applying a named transaction, SQL Server records the name, description, database, user, datetime information, and the Log Sequence Number (LSN) in the **logmarkhistory** table of the msdb database. The names of these marks do not have to be unique, which allows them to be reused.

Restoring Your Transaction Log to a Specific Named Transaction Using Transact-SQL

After opening Query Analyzer, you use the following steps to restore a transaction log backup to a named mark in the transaction log using Transact-SQL:

1. Execute the **RESTORE LOG** statement to restore the transaction log and specify the following arguments:

    - The name of the database that you want the transaction log applied to.

- The name of the backup device that you want to retrieve the transaction log backup from.

- Specify one of the following clauses:

  - **WITH STOPATMARK**—causes SQL Server 2000 to roll forward to the mark and include the transaction that contains the mark.

  - **WITH STOPBEFOREMARK**—causes SQL Server 2000 to roll forward to the mark, but to exclude the transaction that contains the mark.

*Note: Optionally, you can specify the **AFTER DATETIME** clause to instruct SQL Server 2000 to stop the recovery at the first mark with the specified name on or after the time specified in the **DATETIME** clause.*

Restoring Your Transaction Log to the Point of Failure Using Transact-SQL

After experiencing a problem with a database, you may be able to recover up to the time the database failed. For instance, if you have your database files on one hard drive and your transaction log files on a separate hard drive and you lose the hard drive that contains your database files, you can still salvage the transactions contained in the transaction log.

After replacing the bad hard drive and opening Query Analyzer, take the following steps to restore a transaction log backup to the point of failure using Transact-SQL:

1. Execute the **BACKUP LOG** statement with the **NO_TRUNCATE** option to back up the currently active transaction log without purging the information that is being backed up.

2. Restore the full database backup using the **RESTORE DATABASE** statement with the **NORECOVERY** option.

3. Restore the most recent differential backup (if any) using the **RESTORE DATABASE** statement with the **NORECOVERY** option.

4. Restore all transaction log backups, except the one created in Step 1, using the **RESTORE LOG** statement with the **NORECOVERY** option.

5. Restore the transaction log you created in Step 1, using the **RESTORE LOG** statement with the **RECOVERY** option.

The following code is an example of how to perform the recovery process described above. You will begin by backing up the current transaction log to a temporary backup device, but will not purge the transactions. Here is the statement:

```
BACKUP LOG northwind
 TO DISK = 'd:\SQLBackup\CriticalBU.BAK'
 WITH NO_TRUNCATE
```

Your next step is to restore the full database and differential backups (if any) using the following statements:

```
RESTORE DATABASE northwind
  FROM NWBackups
  WITH NORECOVERY

RESTORE DATABASE northwind
  FROM NWDiffBackups
  WITH NORECOVERY
```

Your next step is to restore all of your transaction log backups in the order they were backed up without making the database accessible:

```
RESTORE LOG Northwind
  FROM NWBackupLogs_1
  WITH NORECOVERY

RESTORE LOG Northwind
  FROM NWBackupLogs_2
  WITH NORECOVERY
```

Your final step is to restore the transaction log you created when you discovered the database was inaccessible. Furthermore, because this is the last restore operation in your recovery process, you will make the database accessible using the following statement:

```
RESTORE LOG northwind
  FROM DISK = 'd:\SQLBackup\CriticalBU.BAK'
  WITH RECOVERY
```

Creating a Restore Strategy

The design of your restore strategy is directly affected by your backup strategy. Your backup strategy defined the type and frequency of your backups as well as the nature and speed of the hardware required to perform the backups. This same hardware will most likely be used if you have to perform a recovery process in SQL Server 2000. Verify that your recovery process is not restricted by your hardware.

Warning! *It is STRONGLY recommended that you thoroughly and frequently test your recovery process. Testing your restore strategy helps to ensure that you have the required backups necessary to recover from various failures. Furthermore, it will help you make certain that your recovery procedures execute smoothly and quickly in the event of a failure.*

After testing your restore strategy and ensuring it works as designed, you should also be prepared to recover from a disaster. After acquiring and replacing the troubled hardware, use the following steps to recover from a disaster:

1. Install Windows NT 4 or Windows 2000 and apply the required service pack. Verify that the operating system is functioning properly.

2. Install SQL Server 2000 and apply the required service pack. Restore the master database and restart SQL Server.

3. Restore the msdb, model, and distribution (if applicable) databases from your backups.

4. Configure SQL Server for the appropriate network libraries and security mode.

5. Confirm that SQL Server is running properly by checking SQL Server Service Manager, your SQL Server error logs, and the Windows application log.

6. If the computer name has changed, use the **sp_dropserver** and **sp_addserver** system stored procedures to match it with the SQL Server computer name.

7. Restore each user database according to your recovery plan.

8. Verify the availability of SQL Server by connecting to it using; a graphical user interface (Enterprise Manager), a command-line utility (osql), and, if available, an outside application (VB application).

Optimizing Your Restore Operation

Normally, when you are performing a restore operation, you are going to be under the gun; the pressure is going to be on you to get the system up and running and allow the users back into SQL Server. Along with testing the restore strategy, there are other steps you can take to make sure your restore process runs quickly and efficiently.

The first thing you want to do is have an understanding of what is involved with restoring the different types of backups. Each of them takes a different amount of time and may also have a different number of steps.

Restoring a full or differential database backup usually consists of four steps:

1. Creating the database and transaction log files if they are unavailable.

2. Copying the data from your backup devices to your database files.

3. Copying the transaction logs from your transaction log backup devices.

4. Rolling the transaction log forward and restarting the recovery process, if necessary.

Applying a transaction log backup usually consists of two steps:

1. Copying data from your backup devices to the transaction log file.

2. Rolling forward the committed transactions contained in the transaction log.

Restoring a database file usually consists of two steps:

1. Determining that you have missing files and re-creating the missing files.

2. Copying the data from your backup devices to your database files.

The process of creating your database and transaction log files and initializing them requires very high throughput. It is recommended that you spread these files evenly across all available logical drives to achieve the highest performance.

Performance increases linearly with the number of backup devices used in a backup or restore operation. It is recommended you back up and restore your database and transaction log to as many devices as you deem beneficial.

Improving Performance of Your Tape Backup Devices

When you are analyzing the performance of your tape devices, keep in mind the following three variables that can affect the overall performance:

- Software data block size

- Number of tape devices that are sharing a Small Computer System Interface (SCSI) bus

- Type of tape device

SQL Server can improve performance of both the backup and restore operations by adding more tape devices. The performance will roughly scale linearly as more tape devices are added. However, it is recommended that you dedicate a SCSI bus for each tape device being used to reap the full benefit of your faster tape devices.

Note: For more information about your tape drive's performance, see the tape drive vendor's documentation.

Improving Performance of Your Disk Backup Devices

When analyzing the performance of your disk backup devices, the raw I/O speed of the disk allows SQL Server backup and restore operations to roughly scale linearly as multiple disk devices are added.

The use of Redundant Array of Independent Disks (RAID) as a disk backup device should be carefully analyzed. For instance, RAID 5 has low write performance because of the need to maintain the parity information. Careful configuration of your hardware is likely to improve performance.

Note: For more information about settings that affect your disk drive's performance, see the disk drive vendor's documentation.

Troubleshooting Your Backup and Restore Operations

As much as you would like to believe that there will be no problems when performing your backups and restores, it most likely just isn't going to be that simple. Listed below are some of the common problems and the associated error number that you may encounter when backing up and restoring your databases in SQL Server 2000:

- Symptom: (Error #156) A syntax error occurred when using the **BACKUP** or **RESTORE** command, indicating that the database is in SQL Server 6.5 compatibility mode. **BACKUP** and **RESTORE** commands are only compatible with SQL Server 7 and SQL Server 2000 databases.

  Resolution: Set the SQL Server compatibility level to 80 before using the **BACKUP** or **RESTORE** commands.

- Symptom: (Error #3023) The **BACKUP** command cannot be executed at the same time as creating and deleting database files.

  Resolution: Reissue the command after the conflicting operation completes.

- Symptom: (Error #3036) A standby database cannot be backed up if it hasn't been recovered yet.

  Resolution: Use the backups from your primary server until operations have switched to the standby server.

- Symptom: (Error #3143) The backup being restored is a valid Microsoft Tape Format (MTF), but is not a SQL Server backup.

  Resolution: Use the **RESTORE HEADERONLY** command to determine the contents of the backup.

- Symptom: (Error #3154) The backup set is a backup of a database with the same name as the database you are restoring to.

  Resolution: Either restore the backup set to a different database name or overwrite the existing database.

- Symptom: (Error #3256) The backup operation that created the backup set did not complete successfully.

  Resolution: Either restore the next transaction log, if error occurs when you are restoring a transaction log, or restore a different database backup if you are restoring a database backup.

- Symptom: (Error #4208) Some commands are not allowed when using Simple Recovery model.

  Resolution: Use **ALTER DATABASE** to change the recovery model mode.

9

- Symptom: (Error #4306) No further restore operations may be performed after a database is recovered.

  Resolution: Restart the restore sequence and use the **NORECOVERY** option on all but the last **RESTORE** command.

Summary

A well-planned and thoroughly tested backup strategy is critical to successfully recovering from unexpected lost or damaged data. It is imperative that your system and user databases are using the appropriate recovery model and are backed up regularly. This will guarantee that you are able to recover your system to the state it was prior to the discovery of the lost or damaged database.

Generally, a combination of full database, differential database, and transaction log backups provide you the best opportunity to recover all data that is lost or damaged if you experience media failure. However, in order to implement the designed restore strategy, it is critical that your database files and transaction log files are stored on separate physical drives on your computer.

Your backup strategy is going to be determined by the amount of data you can or cannot afford to lose, and the amount of down time you can or cannot afford. Furthermore, your backup strategy should take your restore strategy into consideration. The biggest difference between the implementation of your backup and restore strategy is that your backup strategy can be automated.

Chapter 10 will provide information that you will need to automate your backup process as well as other routine administrative tasks. Automating your routine administrative tasks will reduce the number of problems caused during a manual operation and it also creates additional free time for you to perform other tasks, such as optimization.

Chapter 10

Automating Administrative Tasks

You can configure SQL Server 2000 to be practically maintenance-free, thereby greatly reducing the amount of time required to perform your common DBA tasks. You also can easily automate your recurring mundane DBA tasks that consume a large portion of your administrative time.

This additional free time can be spent on activities such as designing databases and assisting programmers on correct coding techniques to ensure their database applications are running as efficiently as possible.

Reasons to Automate

The automation features available to you in SQL Server 2000 are not limited to database administration tasks. You can also automate the business practices that your databases support. Furthermore, you can use SQL Server automation functionality to create a proactive database management environment to reduce or prevent problems with your databases.

SQL Server 2000 automation can be used to perform the following recurring tasks:

- *Backups*—Your database backups should be one of the first things you automate after configuring SQL Server 2000. Backups are one of the most critical tasks you perform as a database administrator and can consume a significant amount of time.

- *Importing and exporting data*—This task is often performed to share data between heterogeneous database environments, SQL Servers, or even from database to database. The ability to automate this task and avoid performing it interactively will greatly reduce the amount of time required to move data throughout your enterprise.

- *Scheduled database maintenance*—You can automate maintenance commands, such as **DBCC CHECKDB** and **DBCC DBREINDEX**, to run during off-peak hours.

- *Respond to potential problems*—You can proactively prepare for potential problems by configuring SQL Server to respond to SQL Server application errors, performance conditions, or operating system errors.

Understanding the SQL Server Automation Process

Before you can take advantage of the automation features in SQL Server, you need to be familiar with the different components that comprise the process that allows you to automate your tasks.

The SQL Server components described briefly below all work together to allow a hands-off, proactive automated environment in SQL Server 2000:

- *SQL Server service*—The MSSQLSERVER service enters errors, messages, and events to the Windows application log.

- *SQL Server Agent service*—The SQLSERVERAGENT service must be running in order for the automation process to function. It monitors the Windows application log for SQL Server events written to it by the SQL Server service.

- *Windows application log*— The Windows application log found in the Windows Event Viewer is used to store the events written by the MSSQLSERVER service and all other applications running on the computer.

After verifying that the required SQL Server components are configured correctly, you need to look at the SQL Server Agent components that are required to enable the automation functionality in SQL Server. All of the following automation components are stored in the msdb system database:

- *Jobs*—A defined series of operations or tasks performed sequentially by the SQL Server Agent. You create jobs to define your administrative tasks that can be executed one or more times and monitored for success or failure every time the jobs execute. Jobs can execute:

  - On a local server or on multiple remote servers.

  - According to one or multiple schedules.

  - By one or multiple alerts.

- *Alerts*—Signals an operator that an event has occurred, or executes a predefined job. You determine and define the conditions for which the alert is generated. You also define which of the following actions the alert takes:

  - Notify one or more operators.

  - Forward the event to another SQL Server.

  - Execute a predefined job.

- *Operators*—The individuals responsible for the maintenance of SQL Server or individuals who should be notified on the success or failure of a job. Operators are notified of alerts using one or more of the following:

  - *Email*—You can define the email alias of an individual operator or a group of operators. It is recommended that you use a group rather than notify numerous operators individually.

- *Pager*—Sent through email.

- *Net send*—Executed at the command prompt.

Note: *Jobs, alerts, and operators are explained in much greater depth later in this chapter beginning with "Understanding Job Characteristics" and ending with "Introducing the Database Maintenance Plan Wizard."*

Preparing to Automate

After making the decision to automate your recurring tasks or to configure an environment to proactively respond to potential problems, it is important to make sure your SQL Server environment is configured to respond as expected. This means you have to configure the key components necessary for an automated administrative environment.

There are numerous aspects involved with the configuration of SQL Server to perform automated tasks. Let's take a look at each of these required components that will make your SQL Server automated environment run consistently, effectively, and efficiently.

Understanding the SQL Server Agent Service

The SQL Server Agent service is a Windows service that must be running in order to execute your automated jobs and fire your defined alerts. A correct configuration of this service is extremely important if you are expecting a hands-off, trouble-free automated SQL Server environment.

Note: *The service name of SQLServerAgent only applies to the SQL Server Agent service associated with the default instance of SQL Server. Named instances of SQL Server 2000 use the SQL Server Agent service associated with that named instance using the format of SQLAgent$InstanceName. For instance, a named instance of SQL Server called SQLOLTP, will have a SQL Server Agent service name of SQLAgent$SQLOLTP.*

SQL Server Agent is responsible for:

- Running scheduled SQL Server tasks at specific times or intervals.

- Detecting specific predefined conditions, such as a task that addresses the condition, or notifying someone through email or pager.

- Running predefined replication tasks.

Choosing the Appropriate SQL Server Agent Service Logon Account

The account you use to start your SQL Server Agent service greatly impacts which tasks you can perform within SQL Server 2000. Specifically, if you are required to perform remote administration of SQL Server you have to make certain your SQL Server Agent service is started with an account that has the appropriate permissions.

There are two types of accounts that can be used to start the SQL Server Agent Service:

- *Local system account*—Choosing this account may restrict your SQL Server 2000 installation from interacting with other SQL Servers. In Windows 2000, this account has network access rights. However, in Windows NT 4, it does not have network access rights, therefore preventing remote interaction with other SQL Server machines.

- *Domain user account*—Choosing this account configures SQL Server to use Windows Authentication to set up and connect to SQL Server.

Note: *By default, the domain user account you are logged in to when setting up and installing SQL Server is used by the SQL Services.*

Assigning an Account to the SQL Server Agent Service through Enterprise Manager

Follow these steps to assign a login account to the SQL Server Agent service:

1. After opening Enterprise Manager, expand the server group that contains the SQL Server Agent service that you want to configure.

2. Expand the Management option by clicking on the plus sign or double-clicking on the Management option.

3. Right-click SQL Server Agent and choose Properties on the shortcut menu.

4. Click the General tab of the SQL Server Agent Properties dialog box shown in Figure 10.1.

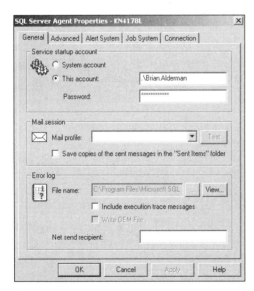

Figure 10.1
Using the General tab of the SQL Server Agent Properties dialog box.

5. Enter the desired account and password information under the Service Startup Account box.

6. Click OK to apply your changes and close the SQL Server Agent Properties dialog box.

Tip: We suggest that you create one Windows account that can be used to start all SQL Server services. This will help when you are troubleshooting a problem with your services.

Assigning an Account to the SQL Server Agent Service through Services

Alternatively, you can configure the account used to start your SQL Server Agent service through the Services option using the following steps:

1. Open Services from within Administrative Tools.

2. Locate the SQLSERVERAGENT service and right-click it and then click Properties on the shortcut menu.

3. Click the Log On tab of the SQLSERVERAGENT Properties dialog box shown in Figure 10.2.

4. Choose the Local System Account or This Account and then specify the domain user account and password to assign the account that will be used to start the service.

5. Click OK to apply your changes and close the SQLSERVERAGENT Properties dialog box.

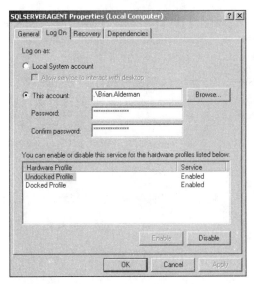

Figure 10.2
Configuring the account used to start your SQL Server Agent service.

Tip: These steps can be used to configure the startup account of any service in Windows 2000. Simply choose the appropriate service (instead of SQLSERVERAGENT) in Step 2 and follow the remaining steps to complete the startup account configuration for the service.2

Configuring SQL Server Agent to Start Automatically

Because the availability of the SQL Server Agent service is so important to your automated environment, you need to make sure it is always running. It is recommended that you configure the service to start automatically under the following two conditions:

• While starting your operating system.

• If the SQL Server Agent service should stop unexpectedly.

Note: The SQL Server Agent application is also supported on the Microsoft Windows 98 operating system, but the SQL Server Agent cannot be used with Windows Authentication when running on Windows 98.

Configuring the SQL Server Agent Service to Start During System Bootup

After creating tasks that require the SQL Server Agent to run, you will want the service to automatically start when the operating system starts. This will prevent you from having to manually start the service. There are three ways to configure the service to start automatically when the operating system is starting; through Enterprise Manager, SQL Server Service Manager, or Windows Services. Follow these steps in Enterprise Manager to configure the SQL Server Agent service to start automatically:

1. After opening Enterprise Manager, right-click the SQL Server for which you want to configure the SQL Server Agent Service, which will open the shortcut menu shown in Figure 10.3. Click Properties.

2. Click the General tab of the SQL Server Properties (Configure) To Display The Configuration Properties dialog box.

Figure 10.3
Shortcut menu of your SQL Server.

10

Figure 10.4
SQL Server Properties dialog box.

3. Under Autostart Policies When The Operating System Starts, click the Autostart SQL Server Agent checkbox as shown in Figure 10.4 to configure the service to start automatically.

4. Click OK to apply the changes and close the dialog box.

Alternatively, the service can be configured to start automatically through the SQL Server Service Manager using the following steps:

1. Click Start|Programs|Microsoft SQL Server|Service Manager to open the SQL Server Service Manager dialog box.

2. Use the Services drop-down menu shown in Figure 10.5 to locate the SQL Server Agent service, and click SQL Server Agent.

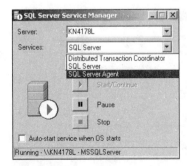

Figure 10.5
Using the SQL Server Service Manager to configure SQL Server Agent to start automatically.

Figure 10.6
Configuring the SQL Server Agent Service to start automatically.

3. Click the Auto-start Service When OS Starts checkbox in the SQL Server Service Manager dialog box as shown in Figure 10.6 to configure the service to start automatically when your operating system starts.

4. Click the close button (x) to close the SQL Server Service Manager dialog box and apply the change.

The third and final way to configure the SQL Server Agent service to start automatically is accomplished using the following steps:

1. Click Start|Programs|Administrative Tools|Services to open the Services dialog box shown in Figure 10.7.

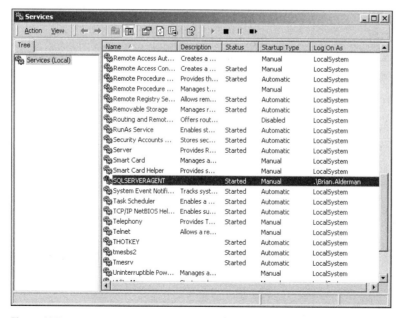

Figure 10.7
Windows 2000 Services dialog box.

2. Locate and right-click the SQLSERVERAGENT service, and click Properties to open the SQLSERVERAGENT Properties dialog box.

3. Click the Startup Type drop-down menu to choose the Automatic option as shown in Figure 10.8.

4. Click OK to apply the changes and close the SQLSERVERAGENT Properties dialog box.

Any of the methods discussed above will configure the SQL Server Agent service to start automatically when you start your operating system. However, your SQL Server Agent service may unexpectedly stop after the operating system starts.

10

Configuring the SQL Server Agent Service to Automatically Start If It Stops Unexpectedly

You can also configure the SQL Server Agent service to start automatically in the event it stops unexpectedly after you start your operating system. This is yet another way to guarantee that this service is always available for your automated procedures. Use the following steps to configure the SQL Server Agent to restart automatically if it stops unexpectedly:

1. After opening Enterprise Manager, expand the server group and then expand the server for which you want to configure the SQL Server Agent Service to start automatically.

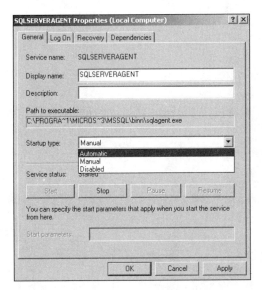

Figure 10.8
Choosing the Automatic Startup option.

2. Expand the Management option. Right-click SQL Server Agent, and then click Properties on the shortcut menu.

3. Click the Advanced tab of the SQL Server Agent Properties dialog box. Check the Auto Restart SQL Server Agent If It Stops Unexpectedly checkbox as shown in Figure 10.9.

4. Click OK to apply the changes and open the SQL Server Agent Properties confirmation dialog box shown in Figure 10.10.

5. Click Yes in the SQL Server Agent Properties dialog box that asks if you want to stop the service to apply the changes. This will stop the SQL Server Agent service and restart it with the new configuration settings.

6. Click OK in the confirmation dialog box to close all open SQL Server Agent service dialog boxes.

As previously mentioned, you can define operators to be notified when an event occurs. However, in order to use the email or the pager notification process, you need to configure SQL Server to use email.

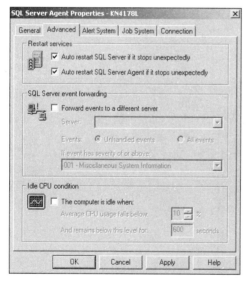

Figure 10.9
Advanced tab of the SQL Server Agent Properties dialog box.

Figure 10.10
Confirming that you want to stop the SQL Server Agent Service.

Using Email with SQL Server

In order to use the functionality that allows you to send and receive email or notify pagers, you need to configure SQL Server to use email. SQL Server can communicate with any Post Office Protocol 3 (POP3) server to send and receive email after configuring two different services: SQL Mail and SQLAgentMail.

However, in order for these services to function correctly, both of them require a Messaging Application Programming Interface (MAPI) messaging profile and a client application (such as Microsoft Outlook) on the SQL Server 2000 computer. The MAPI messaging profile requires the use of a domain user account.

10

Note: For administrative convenience, you can configure SQL Mail and SQLAgentMail to use the same domain user account for their MAPI messaging profile.

Understanding SQL Mail

SQL Mail is the mail service used by the SQL Server service to execute **xp_sendmail** extended stored procedures to send email from any of the following components:

- Transact-SQL batches

- Scripts

- Stored Procedures

- Triggers

The following code uses the **xp_sendmail** extended stored procedure to send an email message to Roland concerning the current performance of SQL Server 2000:

```
EXEC xp_sendmail 'RolandA@briana.org',
@subject = 'Current SQL Server Performance Information',
@query = 'SELECT * FROM master.dbo.sysperfinfo'
```

Tip: To keep Roland current on the performance of SQL Server, you could schedule this command to run periodically.

Your email messages can contain any of the following:

- A Transact-SQL statement or batch job for execution.

- A result set from a query already executed.

- A message string.

- A page for an electronic pager.

SQL Server can use any of the following stored procedures to process email sent to the domain user account assigned to the SQL Server service:

- **sp_processmail**
- **xp_findnextmsg**
- **xp_readmail**
- **xp_deletemail**

Tip: To automatically process your email, you should create a scheduled job to run periodically.

Understanding SQLAgentMail

SQLAgentMail is the mail service used by the SQL Server Agent service to send email and electronic pager notifications to previously defined operators. These notifications are usually a direct result of a failed or successfully completed job or in response to the triggering of an alert. This mail session is automatically started when the SQL Server Agent service is started.

Configuring the MAPI Message Profile

After installing your MAPI client application required by SQL Mail and SQLAgentMail on your SQL Server 2000 computer, you next need to create a messaging profile. This profile will be created for the domain user account or accounts assigned to your SQL Server and SQL Server Agent services.

If you plan to mail stored procedures or send notifications to operators by email or pager you must:

- Have a mail server that is extended MAPI-compliant.

- Create a messaging profile for the domain user account used to start the MSSQLSERVER service (if mailing stored procedures) and the SQLSERVERAGENT service (if using email or pager notification).

- Have a mail server and the hardware required to communicate with your pagers.

Use the following steps to create a mail profile for the domain user account assigned to your SQL Server 2000 services:

1. Log on to your Windows 2000 or Windows NT server using the domain user account and password assigned to the SQL Server 2000 services.

2. Click Start|Settings|Control Panel to open Control Panel.

3. Click the Mail icon to create and configure the mail profile.

4. Select the appropriate mail service that will be used to interact with your mail host.

5. Enter a name for the profile that will be used by the recipient to help identify the messages.

6. On the instance of SQL Server you are configuring the profile for, start the mail client using the new mail profile.

7. Test the configuration by sending a message to the profile name ensuring the mail client, mail profile, and email service are all working properly.

Note: If your message does not appear, click Deliver Now on the Tools menu to establish mail synchronization.

Setting up SQL Mail through Enterprise Manager

After creating your messaging profile for SQL Mail you can now configure it by performing the following steps:

1. After opening Enterprise Manager, expand the server group and then expand the server for which you want to configure SQL Mail.

2. Expand Support Services, and then right-click SQL Mail and choose Properties on the shortcut menu.

3. Type the profile name in the Profile Name field, or select the name of the profile from the drop-down menu in the SQL Mail Configuration dialog box shown in Figure 10.11.

4. Click Test to verify that you are able to start and stop mail client services with the mail profile entered.

5. Click OK to apply the changes and close the SQL Mail Configuration dialog box.

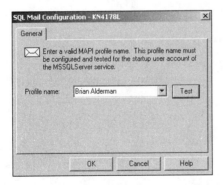

Figure 10.11
Selecting the SQL mail profile.

Setting up SQLAgentMail through Enterprise Manager

After creating your messaging profile for SQLAgentMail you can now configure it using the following steps:

1. After opening Enterprise Manager, expand the server group and then expand the server for which you want to configure SQL Mail.

2. Expand Management, and then right-click SQL Server Agent and choose Properties on the shortcut menu.

3. In the Profile Name field, select the name of the profile from the drop-down menu in the Mail Session box of the SQL Server Agent Properties dialog box shown in Figure 10.12.

4. Click Test to verify that you are able to start and stop mail client services with the mail profile entered.

5. Click OK to apply the changes and close the SQL Server Agent Properties dialog box.

After creating your mail profiles and testing the connection between all of the components involved in the SQL Server Mail environment, you are ready to begin creating your automated tasks.

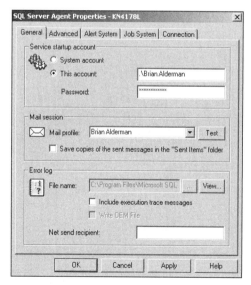

Figure 10.12
Selecting the SQLAgentMail profile.

Understanding Job Characteristics

In SQL Server 2000 you can create a job to perform a specified series of tasks sequentially. The SQL Server Agent is responsible for performing these tasks that can include the following activities:

- Running Transact-SQL scripts

- Executing command-line applications

- Executing Microsoft ActiveX scripts

Jobs are often created to perform recurring tasks that you can schedule, and they can be configured to automatically notify users of the job status by generating alerts. Each job contains job steps that define what action is to be performed during each portion of the job.

If you discover that there are so many jobs that it is difficult for you to manage them, you can categorize them to help ease administration. We'll begin with a discussion on how to create jobs in SQL Server 2000. We'll then take a look at creating job categories and assigning jobs to these categories. We'll then look at the steps required to schedule the jobs and also ways to review the history of the jobs that have run.

Creating and Scheduling a Job Using Transact-SQL

To create and schedule a job using Transact-SQL you have to execute three system stored procedures sequentially. You use the system stored procedure in Step 1 to create a job, add one or more job steps to the job, and then create a schedule for the job. Here are the steps:

1. Execute **sp_add_job**, which adds a new job to be executed by the SQLServerAgent service. The **sp_add_job** stored procedure has numerous arguments that are used to customize the new job being created. The following code sample is used to create a job called **DailyMasterBackup**:

```
USE msdb
EXEC sp_add_job @job_name = 'DailyMasterBackup'
```

*Note: You can use **sp_update_job** and **sp_delete_job** to modify and delete an existing job, respectively.*

2. Execute **sp_add_jobstep**, which adds a step (task to be performed) to a job you have created. This stored procedure also has numerous arguments available for you to use to customize each job step as you are adding them. The subsystems listed in Table 10.1 are used by the SQL Server Agent service to execute the step. The following code

Table 10.1   Job step subsystems.

Subsystem	Type of Step
Activescripting	Active script (VBScript or JavaScript)
Cmdexec	An executable program or an operating-system command
Distribution	Replication Distribution Agent job step
Logreader	Replication Log Reader job step
Merge	Replication Merge Agent job step
Snapshot	Replication Snapshot Agent job step
Tsql	Transact-SQL statement (this is the default)

sample is used to add a job step called **BackupMasterDB** to the job we created in the previous step by executing the Transact-SQL **BACKUP** command:

```
USE msdb
EXEC sp_add_jobstep @job_name = 'DailyMasterBackup',
   @step_name = 'BackupMasterDB',
   @subsystem = 'TSQL', --
   @command = 'BACKUP DATABASE master to MasterBUDevice'
```

*Note: You can use **sp_update_jobstep** and **sp_delete_jobstep** to modify and delete existing job steps, respectively.*

3. Execute **sp_add_jobschedule**, which creates a schedule after creating a job and its job steps. This stored procedure also has numerous arguments available for you to use to customize the recurring schedule when you define it. The following code sample is used to create a schedule for the job called **DailyMasterBackup** that we created in Step 1. This job is scheduled to run every day at 1:00 A.M., beginning on Sunday:

```
USE msdb
EXEC sp_add_jobschedule @job_name = 'DailyMasterBackup',
   @name = 'ScheduledMasterBackup',
   @freq_type = 4, -- daily
   @freq_interval = 1,
   @active_start_time = 010000 -- using a 24-hour clock in the format of
HHMMSS
```

*Note: You can use **sp_update_jobschedule** and **sp_delete_jobschedule** to modify and delete an existing job schedule, respectively.*

These three system stored procedures together create and schedule a job for you in SQL Server 2000. I grouped them together so you can see how the information from the previous task was used in the subsequent tasks. Now it is time to look at creating a job using a GUI and a wizard. After you see how to create the jobs we will look at creating the different types of job steps through Enterprise Manager and how to schedule the job through Enterprise Manager.

Creating and Scheduling a Job Using Enterprise Manager

Using the Enterprise Manager to create a job, the steps of the job, and a schedule for the job is much easier and more efficient than using the system stored procedures listed above. Lets take a look at the different parts required to create a job using Enterprise Manager in SQL Server 2000.

10

Creating a Job Using Enterprise Manager

The following steps will create a job in Enterprise Manager:

1. After opening Enterprise Manager, expand the server group and then expand the server for which you want to create a new job.

2. Expand Management, and then expand SQL Server Agent.

3. Right-click Jobs, and then click New Job on the shortcut menu.

4. Type a name for the job in the Name box on the General tab of the New Job Properties dialog box.

Tip: If you are creating a job that you do not want to execute after you create it, clear the check mark in the Enabled box. This disables the job until you add the check mark.

5. Use the drop-down menu of the Category box to specify the category that this job falls under.

6. Under the Source area, choose one of the following:

   • *Target Local Server*—If the job is to run only on the local machine.

   • *Target Multiple Servers*—If the job should run on a remote machine.

Note: Target Multiple Servers is only available if the machine is configured as a master server, which is discussed later in this chapter under "Defining Your Master Server."

7. If you chose Target Multiple Servers in the previous step, perform the following steps:

   a. Click Change to open the Change Job Target Servers dialog box.

   b. Click on the Available Servers tab and click on a server.

   c. Click the right arrow to move the server to the Selected Target Servers list.

   d. Click OK to return to the New Job Properties dialog box.

8. Select a user to be the owner of the job in the Owner list.

9. Enter a description of what the job does, up to a maximum of 512 characters, in the Description box to complete the General tab of the New Job Properties dialog box shown in Figure 10.13.

Warning! *Every job must have at least one step. You must create a step before the job can be saved.*

10. Click the Steps tab to create a step for this job.

Note: *If you click OK before adding a step, you will receive the New Job Properties error message shown in Figure 10.14.*

The second part of creating a job using Enterprise Manager is to create the specific job steps that define what action that the job takes on a database or a server. You decide what action you want SQL Server Agent to take when you create the job step.

Creating Your Job Steps Using Enterprise Manager

The type of job step that you want to run determines the sequence of screens you see when you create the job step. Lets discuss the different screens you will encounter when you use Enterprise Manager to create a CmdExec job step, Transact-SQL job step, ActiveX scripting job steps, and replication job steps.

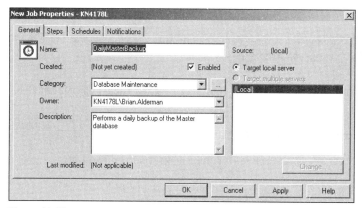

Figure 10.13
Completing the New Job Properties dialog box.

Figure 10.14
New Job Properties error message if no steps exist for the job.

Adding a CmdExec Job Step Using Enterprise Manager

CmdExec job steps run executable programs ending with BAT, CMD, COM, or EXE and also run operating system commands. When you create a CmdExec job step, you must specify the following characteristics:

- The entire physical pathname for the program being run and any required parameters of the **CmdExec** command (for example, D:\Program Files\Microsoft SQL Server\80\Tools\Binn\bcp.exe Northwind.dbo.categories out Categories.txt–Usa).

- The process exit code you want returned if the program ran successfully.

Take these steps to create a CmdExec job step using Enterprise Manager:

1. After opening Enterprise Manager, expand the server group and then expand the server that you want to create a new job on.

2. Expand Management, and then expand SQL Server Agent.

3. Create a new job, or locate and right-click an existing job and click Properties on the shortcut menu to open the Job Properties dialog box.

4. Click the Steps tab in the Job Properties dialog box to display the Steps tab shown in Figure 10.15.

5. Click on the New button to open the New Job Step dialog box.

6. Type the name of the job step in the Step Name box. This can be up to 128 characters.

7. Click Operating System Command (CmdExec) from the Type drop-down menu.

8. Enter a value between 0 and 999999 in the Process Exit Code Of A Successful Command box.

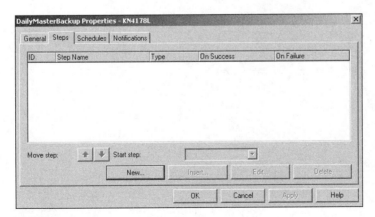

Figure 10.15
Displaying the Steps tab of the Job Properties dialog box.

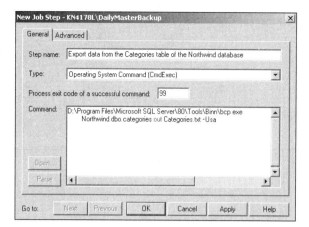

Figure 10.16
Completing the New CmdExec Job Steps Properties dialog box.

9. Enter the entire operating system command that you want to execute in the Command box to complete the New Job Step dialog box as shown in Figure 10.16.

10. Click OK to close the New Job Step dialog box and return to the Jobs Properties dialog box.

11. Click the Advanced tab to configure the following advanced options shown in Figure 10.17:

  • *On Success Action*—Specify the action to perform when the step successfully completes.

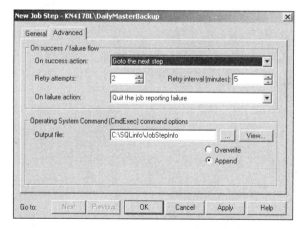

Figure 10.17
Completing the Advanced tab of the New Job Step dialog box.

- *Retry Attempts*—Specify the number of times to retry the step if it fails. This number can be between 0 and 9999.

- *Retry Interval*—Specify how long to wait before attempting to retry the step. This number can be between 0 and 9999.

- *On Failure Action*—Specify the action to perform if the step fails (after performing the specified number of retries).

- *Output File*—Specify the name of the file to store the results of the Transact-SQL or CmdExec job step. Click the Browse (...) button to search for a location to store the file.

12. Choose one of the following radio buttons:

- *Overwrite*—Specify whether or not you should overwrite the contents of the existing file with the new results.

- *Append*—Specify whether or not you should add the results to the end of the existing file.

Note: *Click the View button to display the contents of the specified output file.*

13. Click OK to apply the changes and close the New Job Step dialog box.

Adding a Transact-SQL Job Step Using Enterprise Manager

Transact-SQL job steps run Transact-SQL statements, batches, and stored procedures. When you create a Transact-SQL job step, you must specify the following characteristics:

- The database in which to execute the job.

- The Transact-SQL, stored procedure, or extended stored procedure.

Tip: *If the statements you want to execute are fairly lengthy, create a Transact-SQL script file that you can import.*

These steps will create a Transact-SQL job step using Enterprise Manager:

1. After opening Enterprise Manager, expand the server group and then expand the server on which you want to create a new job.

2. Expand Management, and then expand SQL Server Agent.

3. Create a new job, or locate and right-click an existing job and click Properties on the shortcut menu to open the Job Properties dialog box.

4. Click the Steps tab in the Job Properties dialog box.

5. Click on the New button to open the New Job Step dialog box.

6. Type the name of the job step in the Step Name box. This can be up to 128 characters.

7. Click Transact-SQL Script (TSQL) from the Type drop-down menu.

8. Use the Database drop-down menu to choose the database to which the actions of this step will be applied.

9. In the Command box, type the Transact-SQL statements or batches, or click the Open button to locate and select a Transact-SQL file containing the SQL statements.

*Note: A Transact-SQL job step can contain multiple batches separated by the **GO** statement.*

10. After entering the required information to complete the New Job Step dialog box, click the Parse button shown in Figure 10.18 to make sure that you have entered the syntax correctly.

Note: The Parse button does not check to see if the objects specified in the statements exist. It also does not execute the command; it only checks for syntactical errors.

11. Click OK to close the New Job Step dialog box and return to the job's Properties dialog box.

12. Click the Advanced tab to configure the advanced options discussed in Step 11 of Adding a CmdExec Job Step Using Enterprise Manager; there are two additional options:

   - *Append Output To Step History*—Appends the results of your Transact-SQL job step to the existing history information for this step.

   - *Run As User*—Allows the system administrator to execute the Transact-SQL step on behalf of another database user.

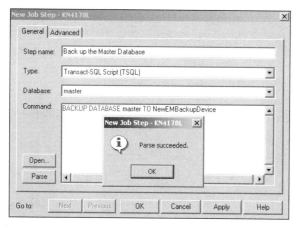

Figure 10.18
Parsing the syntax entered in the Command box.

Adding an ActiveX Script Job Step Using Enterprise Manager

ActiveX Script job steps run VBScript or JavaScript programs. When you create an ActiveX Script job step you must perform the following tasks:

- Specify the scripting language in which the job step is written.

- Write the ActiveX script.

Note: *Alternatively, you can externally compile an ActiveX script using something like Microsoft Visual Basic and then run it as a **CmdExec** step.*

Take these steps to create an Active Script job step using Enterprise Manager:

10

1. After opening Enterprise Manager, expand the server group and then expand the server that you want to create a new job on.

2. Expand Management, and then expand SQL Server Agent.

3. Create a new job, or locate and right-click an existing job and click Properties on the shortcut menu to open the Job Properties dialog box.

4. Click the Steps tab in the Job Properties dialog box.

5. Click on the New button to open the New Job Step dialog box.

6. Type the name of the job step in the Step Name box. This can be up to 128 characters.

7. Click ActiveX Script from theType drop-down menu.

8. Click the radio button of the scripting language you are using, shown in Figure 10.19. If you click Other, enter the name of the Microsoft ActiveX scripting language in which the command was written.

9. In the Command box, type the source for the job step.

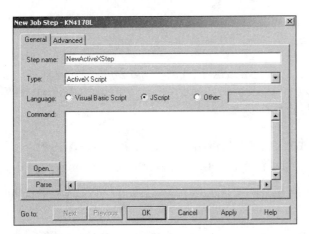

Figure 10.19
Specifying the type of ActiveX script used in the job step.

10. After entering the required information to complete the New Job Step dialog box, click the Parse button to make sure that you have entered the syntax correctly.

11. Click OK to close the New Job Step dialog box and return to the job's Properties dialog box.

12. Click the Advanced tab to configure the following advanced options:

    - *On Success Action*—Specify the action to perform when the step successfully completes.

    - *Retry Attempts*—Specify the number of times to retry the step if it fails. This number can be between 0 and 9999.

    - *Retry Interval*—Specify how long to wait before attempting to retry the step. This number can be between 0 and 9999.

    - *On Failure Action*—Specify the action to perform if the step fails (after performing the specified number of retries).

13. Click OK to apply the changes and close the New Job Step dialog box.

Scheduling Your Job Using Enterprise Manager

The best part of creating jobs is that you can then schedule them to automatically run for you without you having to start the job manually. You can schedule multiserver jobs and local jobs to run automatically. Your jobs can be run manually or you can schedule them to run under the following conditions:

- When the SQL Server Agent service starts.

- One time, when a specific date and time is reached.

- When the CPU utilization of your computer reaches a predefined threshold.

- On a predefined recurring schedule.

- In response to a predefined alert.

Note: You cannot run simultaneous instances of a job. For example, if you execute a job manually and one of the conditions above attempts to start the job, SQL Server will refuse to start the scheduled job.

Defining a Schedule for a Job Using Enterprise Manager

Take these steps to define a schedule for an existing job in SQL Server Enterprise Manager:

1. After opening Enterprise Manager, expand the server group and then expand the server on which you want to create a new job schedule.

2. Expand the Management node and then expand SQL Server Agent to display the Jobs node.

3. Click on the Jobs node to display the list of existing jobs.

4. In the Details pane, locate and right-click the job that you want to define a new schedule for and click Properties on the shortcut menu to open the jobs Properties dialog box.

5. Click on the Schedules tab to open the Job Schedule dialog box shown in Figure 10.20.

6. Click on the New Schedule button to open the New Job Schedule dialog box shown in Figure 10.21.

7. Type in a name for the new schedule in the Name box.

8. If you do not want the schedule to be effective immediately, clear the Enabled checkbox.

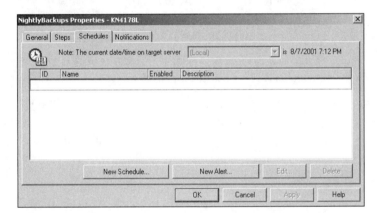

Figure 10.20
Job Schedule dialog box.

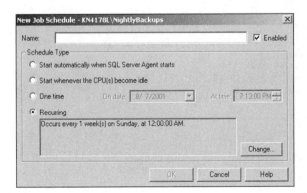

Figure 10.21
New Job Schedule dialog box.

9. Under the Schedule type, choose one of the following:

- *Start Automatically When SQL Server Agent Starts*—Defines a schedule that causes the job to run when the SQL Server Agent service is started.

- *Start Whenever The CPU(s) Become Idle*—Defines a schedule that causes the job to run when the CPU(s) reaches a predefined idle threshold.

Note: *The default idle threshold is set to a CPU(s) usage of less than 10 percent for longer than 600 seconds. However, this can be configured on the Advanced tab of the SQL Server Agent Properties dialog box shown in Figure 10.22.*

- *One Time*—Defines a schedule that causes the job to run one time only at the specified date and time. To specify the date and time, enter values in the On Date and At time boxes, shown in Figure 10.21, respectively.

- *Recurring*—Defines a schedule that causes the job to run repeatedly. To set the recurring schedule, click the Change button, and then complete the Edit Recurring Job Schedule dialog box shown in Figure 10.23.

Note: *The default recurring schedule is shown in Figure 10.23. It is once a week, on Sunday, at 12:00 A.M., beginning with the current date, with no end date.*

By default, a job is enabled to run according to the schedule you define for it. If you decide that you do not want a job to run according to its schedule, you can disable the schedule for the job by clearing the Enabled checkbox of the Schedule dialog box.

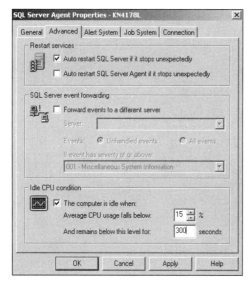

Figure 10.22
Configuring the CPU(s) idle time setting.

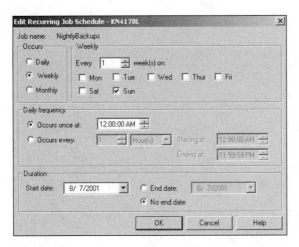

Figure 10.23
Edit Recurring Job Schedule dialog box.

SQL Server Agent automatically disables schedules if:

- They are defined to run one time at a specific date and time and that time has passed.

- They are defined to run on a recurring schedule that has a defined end date and that end date has passed.

Using the Enterprise Manager is much easier than using Transact-SQL system stored procedures, but there is an even easier way; using the Create Job Wizard.

Creating and Scheduling a Job Using the Create Job Wizard

Using the Create Job Wizard to create a job is much easier and more efficient than creating and scheduling a job using the different tabs in Enterprise Manager. Follow these steps to create a job using the Create Job Wizard:

1. After opening Enterprise Manager, expand the server group and then click on the server that you want to create a new job on.

2. Click on Wizards located on the Tools menu to open the Select Wizard screen.

3. Expand Management and then double-click Create Job Wizard to open the Create Job Wizard Welcome screen. Click Next to open the Select Job Command Type screen shown in Figure 10.24.

4. Select one of the following three radio buttons and then click Next:

   - *Transact-SQL Command*—Runs T-SQL statements or stored procedures.

   - *Operating-System Shell Command*—Runs applications or batch scripts.

   - *Active Script*—Runs VBScript or JavaScript.

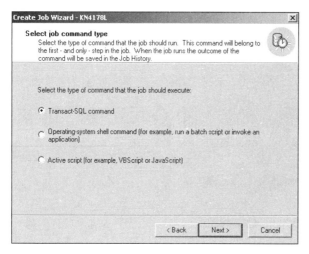

Figure 10.24
Select Job Command Type Wizard screen.

5. Your choice in Step 4 will determine which of the following screens is displayed and which actions you take:

    *   *Transact-SQL*—Use the Database Name drop-down menu to select the database that you are creating the job in. Enter the Transact-SQL statements or stored procedures in the Transact-SQL Statement box and then click the Parse button to check for syntactical accuracy as shown in Figure 10.25.

    *   *Operating System Shell*—Enter the Operating System shell command that you want this job to execute.

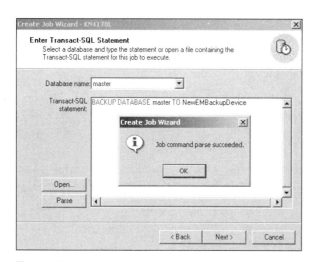

Figure 10.25
Completing the Enter Transact-SQL Statement dialog box.

- *Active Script*—Type the name of the Visual Basic script in the Visual Basic script box or use the Open button to open the file containing the script that you want this job to execute.

6. Click Next after supplying the required information in Step 5 to open the Specify Job Schedule dialog box shown in Figure 10.26, and choose one of the following schedule options:

- *Now*—Will execute immediately after the wizard is completed.

- *One time*—Will execute on the date and at the time you specify.

- *Automatically When The SQL Server Agent Starts*

- *When The Computer Is Idle*

- *On A Recurring Basis*—Will execute repeatedly using the schedule you define after clicking the Schedule button.

Note: *The On A Recurring Basis option will open the Edit Recurring Job Schedule dialog box previously shown in Figure 10.23.*

7. Click Next to open the Job Notifications dialog box shown in Figure 10.27, which allows you to optionally supply an operator that can be notified using a net send and/or an email address you specify using the respective drop-down menus.

Warning! *You must create your operators before you start the wizard in order to specify them on this screen. This process is discussed later in this chapter under "Creating Your SQL Server Operators."*

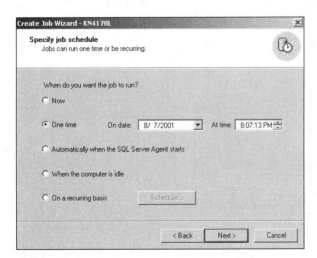

Figure 10.26
Specify Job Schedule dialog box.

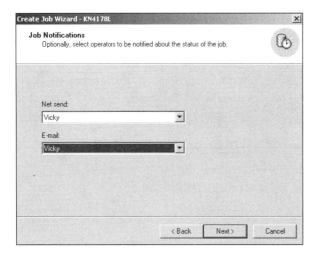

Figure 10.27
Specifying the operators to notify.

8. Click Next to go to the Completing The Create Job Wizard dialog box shown in Figure
   10.28 and accept the default name or enter a name for the job in the Job Name box.
   Click the Finish button to complete the Create Job Wizard and create the job with the
   configuration settings you specified. Click OK in the informational box advising you
   the job was created successfully.

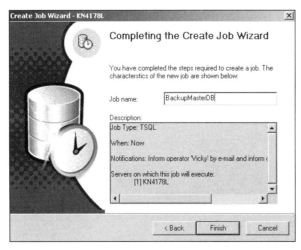

Figure 10.28
Completing the Create Job Wizard dialog box.

Creating a Transact-SQL Script to Re-create Your Existing Jobs

If you have a problem and lose all of your existing SQL Server jobs, you will have to re-create them. This can be done very easily using scripts. Follow these steps to generate Transact-SQL Scripts for your jobs using Enterprise Manager:

1. After opening Enterprise Manager, expand the server group and then expand the server on which you want to create a new job schedule.

2. Expand the Management node and then expand SQL Server Agent to display the Jobs node.

3. Right-click Jobs, point to All Tasks, then click Generate SQL Script to open the Generate SQL Script dialog box shown in Figure 10.29.

4. Enter a name for the script in the File Name box.

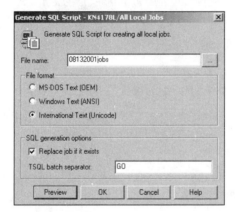

Figure 10.29
Generating a script to re-create your jobs.

5. Choose one of the following under File Format:

- Click MS-DOS Text (OEM) to save the script to a file in OEM format.

- Click Windows Text (ANSI) to save the script to a file in ANSI format.

- Click International Text (Unicode) to save the script to a file in Unicode format.

6. Optionally, you can perform one or both of the following:

- If you want to include the commands required to delete existing jobs that have the same name, check the Replace Job If It Exists checkbox.

- If you are in a multiserver environment and you want to include the script commands for your target server assignments, check the Include Target Server checkbox.

7. Enter a Transact-SQL batch separator in the TSQL Batch Separator box.

Tip: *To preview the script file before you create it, click the Preview button to display the code, which will be similar to that shown in Figure 10.30.*

8. Click OK to generate the SQL script and close the Generate SQL Script dialog box.

Deleting a Job Using Enterprise Manager

After creating a job, you may discover you no longer need the job and that you want to delete it from SQL Server. Follow these steps to delete a job from SQL Server using Enterprise Manager:

1. After opening Enterprise Manager, expand the SQL Server group and then expand the server on which you want to delete the job.

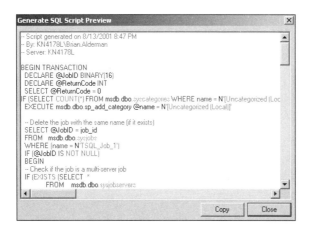

Figure 10.30
Previewing the SQL script code.

2. Expand Management, and then expand SQL Server Agent.

3. Click Jobs, and then in the detail pane locate and right-click the job that you want to delete.

4. Click Delete on the shortcut menu to delete the job.

5. Click Yes in the Delete Job confirmation box.

You may create a job and decide that you want the job to execute only once and then automatically delete itself. Follow these steps to configure Enterprise Manager to automatically delete the job under specific conditions:

1. After opening Enterprise Manager, expand the SQL Server group and then expand the server on which you want to delete the job.

2. Expand Management, and then expand SQL Server Agent.

3. Click Job. In the detail pane, locate and right-click the job that you want to have automatically deleted and then click Properties to open the Properties dialog box.

4. Click the Notifications tab shown in Figure 10.31 and click the Automatically Delete Job checkbox. Choose one of the following from the drop-down menu:

    • *When The Job Succeeds*—Deletes the job when it completes successfully.

    • *When The Job Fails*—Deletes the job when it completes unsuccessfully.

    • *Whenever The Job Completes*—Deletes the job when it completes regardless of the completion status.

5. Click OK to apply the changes and close the Properties dialog box.

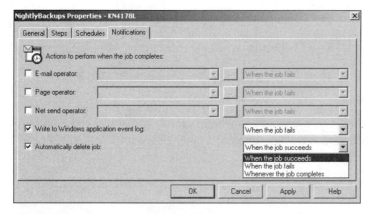

Figure 10.31
Scheduling a job to be deleted automatically.

Creating Job Categories

Job categories help you organize and filter your jobs, making it easier to locate the different types of jobs. For instance, you can use the Database Maintenance category to store all the jobs that:

- Perform database and transaction log backups.

- Use DBCC commands to maintain the consistency of your databases.

- Create or rebuild indexes.

You can also create your own job categories to group job types. You can use Transact-SQL or Enterprise Manager to create job categories in SQL Server 2000.

Creating a Job Category Using Transact-SQL

To create a job category with Transact-SQL, use the **sp_add_category** system stored procedure. The **sp_add_category** stored procedure has numerous arguments that can customize the new category being created.

The **sp_add_category** must be executed in the msdb database, (where all jobs, alerts, and operators are stored) and can only be executed by members of the **sysadmin** fixed server role, and members of the **db_owner** fixed database role.

*Note: The **sp_add_category** is also used to add alert and operator categories.*

The following code sample is used to create a local job category called **DataTransferJobs**:

```
USE msdb
EXEC sp_add_category 'JOB', 'LOCAL', 'DataTransferJobs'
```

*Note: You can use **sp_update_category** and **sp_delete_category** to modify and delete an existing category, respectively.*

Creating a Job Category Using Enterprise Manager

To create a job category using Enterprise Manager, follow these steps:

1. After opening Enterprise Manager, expand the server group that contains your SQL Server, and then expand the SQL Server in which you want to create the new job category.

2. Expand the Management node and then expand the SQL Server Agent to display the Jobs node.

3. Right-click Jobs, point to All Tasks, and then click Manage Job Categories to open the Job Categories dialog box shown in Figure 10.32.

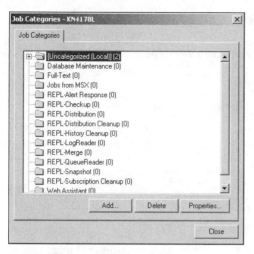

Figure 10.32
Job Categories dialog box.

4. Click Add in the Job Categories dialog box to open the New Job Category Properties dialog box.

Note: *To delete an existing job category you would select the job category in this dialog box and click Delete.*

5. Type a name for the new job category in the Name box of the New Job Category Properties window as shown in Figure 10.33.

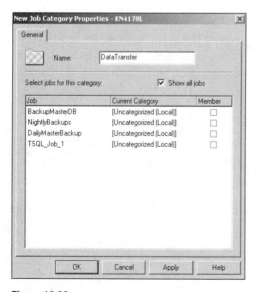

Figure 10.33
New Job Category Properties dialog box.

Tip: *Optionally, you can click the Show All Jobs checkbox to show all currently defined jobs.*

6. Click OK to close the New Job Category Properties dialog box, and click Close to close the Job Categories dialog box.

Assigning a Job to a Job Category Using Transact-SQL

After creating your job categories, you can add existing jobs to the categories to help you easily identify the types of jobs you have created. This can be accomplished using Transact-SQL or Enterprise Manager.

Use the **sp_add_job** system stored procedure to add a job to a job category with Transact-SQL. The **sp_add_job** system stored procedure has numerous arguments, including one that specifies the category to which you want to add the job.

The following code sample is used to add the local job **BcpCustomersTable** to an existing category called **DataTransferJobs**:

```
USE msdb
EXEC sp_add_job @job_name = 'BcpCustomersTable',
          @category_name = 'DataTransferJobs'
```

*Note: You can use **sp_update_job** to change the membership of a job category.*

Assigning a Job to a Job Category Using Enterprise Manager

An easier way to add a job to a job category is using Enterprise Manager. Just follow these steps:

1. After opening Enterprise Manager, expand the server group that contains your SQL Server, and then expand the SQL Server in which you want to modify the job properties.

2. Expand the Management node and then expand the SQL Server Agent to display the Jobs node.

3. Click on the Jobs node to display the existing jobs in the detail pane of Enterprise Manager.

4. Locate and right-click the job you want to add to a category, and then click Properties on the shortcut menu to open the Jobs Properties dialog box.

5. Select the job category that you want to assign the job to from within the Category drop-down menu.

6. Click OK to assign the job category and close the Job Properties dialog box.

Warning! Your job must have at least one step defined for each job or you will not be able to save the job.

Changing the Membership of a Job Category Using Enterprise Manager

After assigning a job to a job category, you may decide you want to change the membership of the job category. Use the following steps to modify the membership of a job category using Enterprise Manager:

1. After opening Enterprise Manager, expand the server group that contains your SQL Server, and then expand the SQL Server in which you want to modify the job category membership.

2. Expand the Management node and then expand the SQL Server Agent to display the Jobs node.

3. Right-click the Jobs node, and point to All Tasks, and then click the Manage Job Categories option to open the Job Categories dialog box.

4. Locate and select a job category, and then click the Properties button.

5. Click the Show All Jobs checkbox.

6. Select or clear the Member checkbox in the Select Jobs For This Category list as shown in Figure 10.34.

7. Click OK to close the Categories Properties dialog Box, then Close to close the Job Categories dialog box.

After creating your jobs, adding the job steps, and scheduling your jobs, you may want to monitor the activity of the job. You can monitor the activity of a job by reviewing and configuring the job history.

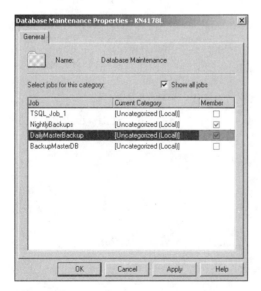

Figure 10.34
Selecting the job category.

Reviewing the History of Your Jobs

After your job has run, or if you are experiencing problems with a job, you can review the history of the job using the details pane of the Jobs container in SQL Server Enterprise Manager.

The following information regarding the history of each job is displayed:

- Name
- Category
- Enabled (Yes or No)
- Runnable (Yes or No)
- Scheduled (Yes or No)
- Status (for instance; Executing or Not Running)
- Last Run Status (Succeeded, Failed, Unknown, etc..)
- Next Run Date

Use the following steps to view the history of a job using Enterprise Manager:

1. After opening Enterprise Manager, expand the server group that contains your SQL Server, and then expand the SQL Server in which you want to modify the job category membership.

2. Expand the Management node and then expand SQL Server Agent to display the Jobs node. Click on the Jobs node to display the defined jobs in the detail pane.

3. Locate and right-click a job in the details pane and perform one of the following:

   - Click View Job History to open the Job History dialog box shown in Figure 10.35 and view the history of the local job.

   - Click Job Status to view the history of a multiserver job.

4. If you clicked Job Status in the Multiserver Job Execution Status dialog box, perform the following steps:

   - Click the Job button.

   - Click a Job name.

   - Click View Remote Job History.

Note: To manually update the job history, click the Refresh button.

5. Click the Close button to close the Job History dialog box.

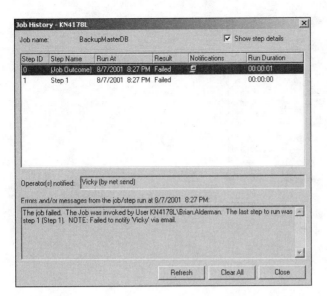

Figure 10.35
Job History dialog box.

Configuring the Size of Your Job History Log

You can control the size of the job history log using the Job System tab of the SQL Server Agent Properties dialog box. By default, the size of a job history log is 100 rows, and 1000 rows for all defined jobs combined. However, if you discover that either of these is inadequate, you can enter in a different job history size using the following steps:

1. After opening Enterprise Manager, expand the server group that contains your SQL Server, and then expand the SQL Server in which you want to modify the job category membership.

2. Expand the Management node, right-click the SQL Server Agent, and click Properties.

3. Click the Job System tab, and click the Limit Size Of Job History Log checkbox.

4. Enter the maximum number of rows the job history log should allow in the Maximum Job History Log Size (Rows) box.

5. Enter the maximum number of rows allowed for a job in the Maximum Job History Rows Per Job with the new values as shown in Figure 10.36.

6. Click OK to apply your changes and close the SQL Server Agent Properties dialog box.

Note: You can click the Clear Log button to clear the entire history log.

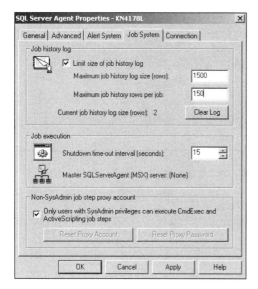

Figure 10.36
Job System tab of the SQL Server Agent dialog box.

If you want to edit or review the properties of a specific job, you can right-click the job in the details pane of the Enterprise Manager and click Properties.

Introducing SQL Server Operators

Operators are individuals who are notified that an event has occurred. After defining your operators, you notify them by defining alerts and associating an operator or multiple operators to be notified when the alert is fired.

You can use Transact-SQL and Enterprise Manager to create, manage, view, and delete your operators. Operators can be notified via Net Send, email, or pager. However, for each notification process, you must supply the information required to notify them.

Tip: We recommend that you create your operators before you define your alerts. This will streamline the process of assigning operators to alerts because you can assign and test the notification process for your operators while defining your alerts.

When defining your operators, there are two primary attributes you must supply in order for them to be notified:

- *Name*—A unique name to identify the operator. This name cannot be longer than 128 characters.

- *Notification method(s)*—One or more of the following notification attributes:

  - *Email*—A MAPI-1-compliant email client used to notify a user or distribution group. Examples of a MAPI-1 client includes Microsoft Outlook and Microsoft Exchange client.

- *Pager*—Pager information that is used by third-party software and/or hardware to page the operator.

- *Net send*—Name or computer that can be notified using the **net send** command on computers running Windows NT 4 or Windows 2000.

Understanding the Operator Notification Process

In order to notify your operators using the three notification methods listed in the preceding section, you need to be familiar with how the operators are contacted using these methods. Lets take a look at how each of these notification methods are implemented using SQL Server 2000:

10

- *Email notification*—Your SQL Server Agent service establishes its own mail session of the email profile you supplied in the SQL Server Agent Properties dialog box.

- *Net send*—Your net send notification specifies the recipient (computer or user) of the network message when running Windows NT 4 or Windows 2000.

- *Pager notification*—Your paging notification is implemented using the email configuration you have established. To utilize the pager notification process, you must install and configure pager notification software that processes inbound email and converts it to a pager message. Depending on the software installed, the pager notification process will use one of the following approaches:

  - Forward the email to a remote email server at the pager provider's site.

  - Route the email using the Internet to a mail server at a pager provider's site. (This is similar to the first approach, but uses a different path to reach the pager provider.)

  Note: This process requires that the pager provider offer this service, although the software required is generally part of the email system.

  - Process the inbound email and establish a connection to the pager provider by dialing using an attached modem.

  Note: The required software for paging is proprietary to your pager service provider. The software acts as an email client that periodically processes its inbox by matching the email address to a pager number using a translation table, or by interpreting all or part of the email address information as a pager number.

If you have multiple operators that share a pager provider, you can use Enterprise Manager to specify any special email formatting required by the pager-to-email system with the following prefix or suffix formatting options:

- To line

- Subject line

- CC line

Note: You can shorten the length of the text sent by excluding the error text from the pager notification if you are limited to a specific number of characters, for instance, if your alphanumeric paging system can only send 64 characters.

After reviewing your paging provider's special pager-to-email formatting instructions, follow these steps to configure SQL Server to understand the pager addresses:

1. After opening Enterprise Manager, expand the server group and the SQL Server that contains the operators that require the special pager addresses.

2. Expand Management, then open the Properties dialog box of the SQL Server Agent by right-clicking on SQL Server Agent.

3. Click the Alert System tab to display the SQL Server Agent Alert System dialog box shown in Figure 10.37.

4. Enter the pager address prefix or suffix in the To Line and CC Line boxes.

5. Enter the subject line prefix or suffix in the Subject box.

6. Click the Include Body Of Email In The Notification Page checkbox to include the entire email message with the pager message (instead of only the subject line text).

7. Click OK to apply the changes and close the SQL Server Agent Properties dialog box.

Creating Your SQL Server Operators

After determining the notification methods you want to assign for each operator and retrieving the required information about your operators, you can use Transact-SQL or Enterprise Manager to create the operators.

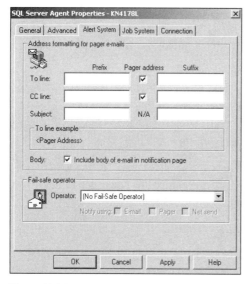

Figure 10.37
SQL Server Agent Alert System dialog box.

Creating an Operator Using Transact-SQL

To create an operator with Transact-SQL, use the **sp_add_operator** system stored procedure. The **sp_add_operator** stored procedure has numerous arguments that are used to configure the new operator.

The **sp_add_operator** procedure must be executed in the msdb database, (where all jobs, alerts, and operators are stored) and can only be executed by members of the **sysadmin** fixed server role.

The following code sample is used to create an operator called Linda W. with an email address of LindaW@briana.org, and a pager address of 4567890@pagerprov.com. She will be available for notification immediately after her account is created. Here is the code:

```
USE msdb
EXEC sp_add_operator @name = 'Linda W.',
 @email_address = 'LindaW@briana.org',
 @pager_address = '4567890@pagerprov.com',
        @enabled = 1
```

*Note: You can use **sp_update_operator** and **sp_delete_operator** to modify and delete an existing operator, respectively.*

Creating an Operator Using Enterprise Manager

To create an operator using Enterprise Manager, follow these steps:

1. After opening Enterprise Manager, expand the SQL Server group and then expand the server for which you want to create a new operator.

2. Expand Management, and then expand SQL Server Agent.

3. Right-click Operators, and then click New Operator on the shortcut menu.

4. Type a name for the operator in the Name box on the General tab of the New Operator Properties dialog box.

5. To define the notification methods for the operator, perform one or more of the following:

   - Enter the operator's email address in the E-mail Name box to notify the operator by email.

   - Enter the operator's pager address in the Pager E-mail Name box to notify the operator by pager. Also click the checkbox next to the days the operator is supposed to receive pager notifications.

Note: Use the Workday Begin and Workday End boxes to enter the time frame within which the operator should be notified by pager.

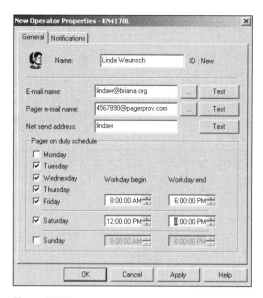

Figure 10.38
Completing the New Operator's dialog box.

- Enter the operator's net send address in the Net Send Address box to notify the operator using the **net send** command.

6. After completing the New Operators dialog box as shown in Figure 10.38, click OK to create the operator and close the dialog box.

As you can see, there are a couple of ways to create an operator in SQL Server 2000. It is always best to be prepared when you decide to create an operator, regardless of how you choose to create them.

Creating a Transact-SQL Script to Re-create Your Existing Operators

If you have a problem and lose all of your existing SQL Server operators, you will have to re-create them. This can be done very easily if you generate scripts that you can execute to re-create the operators. Follow these steps to generate Transact-SQL Scripts for your operators using Enterprise Manager:

1. After opening Enterprise Manager, expand the server group and then expand the server on which you want to create a new job schedule.

2. Expand the Management node and then expand SQL Server Agent to display the Operators node.

3. Right-click Operators and point to All Tasks, then click Generate SQL Script to open the Generate SQL Script dialog box.

4. Enter a name for the script in the File Name box.

5. Choose one of the following under File Format:

   • Click MS-DOS Text (OEM) to save the script to a file in OEM format.

   • Click Windows Text (ANSI) to save the script to a file in ANSI format.

   • Click International Text (Unicode) to save the script to a file in Unicode format.

6. Optionally, you can perform one or both of the following:

   • If you want to include the commands required to delete existing operators that have the same name, check the Replace Operator If It Exists checkbox.

   • If you want to include the script commands necessary to generate the alert assignments for your operators, check the Include Notifications Sent By Alerts To The Operator checkbox.

7. Enter a Transact-SQL batch separator in the TSQL Batch Separator box.

8. Click OK to generate the SQL script and close the Generate SQL Script dialog box.

Updating and Viewing Operator Information

After creating an operator and assigning tasks and jobs to it, you will most likely need to update the operators' information. After creating an operator, you can:

• *View their information*—View the alerts they are responsible for as well as the dates of the most recent attempts by SQL Server to notify them.

• *Edit their information*—Edit their addresses, pager schedules, assigned alerts, and notification methods.

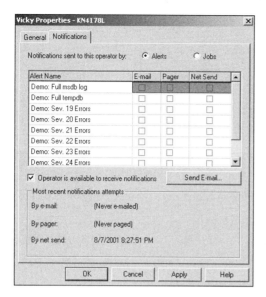

Figure 10.39
Enabling or disabling an operator's availability.

- *Change their availability*—Enable and disable their availability by selecting or deselecting the Operator Is Available To Receive Notifications checkbox on the Notifications tab of the Properties for the operator as shown in Figure 10.39.

- *Delete an operator*—Delete an operator when it no longer has operator responsibilities.

Configuring SQL Server to Notify Your Operators of a Job's Status

After creating both your jobs and your operators, you can configure SQL Server to notify your operators of a job's status. You can configure your operators to be notified when the job:

- Completes successfully

- Completes unsuccessfully

- Completes either successfully or unsuccessfully

Use the following steps to notify an operator of a job status using Enterprise Manager:

1. After opening Enterprise Manager, expand the SQL Server group and then expand the server that contains the job that you want to modify.

2. Expand Management, and then expand SQL Server Agent and click the Jobs node to list the jobs in the detail pane.

3. Locate and right-click the job for which you want to configure the operator to be notified of the job status, and click Properties on the shortcut menu.

4. Click the Notifications tab in the Job Properties dialog box.

5. Choose one or more of the following notification methods:

   - Email operator
   - Page operator
   - Net send operator

Note: *If the operator does not exist and you want to create a new one, you can choose the New Operator option from within the notification method drop-down menu.*

10

6. Within each notification method you chose, select one of the following job status options:

   - *When The Job Succeeds*—Notify the operator that the job completed successfully.
   - *When The Job Fails*—Notify the operator that the job did not complete successfully.
   - *Whenever The Job Completes*—Notify the operator that the job finished regardless of whether it was successful or unsuccessful.

7. After configuring the desired notification methods as shown in Figure 10.40, click OK to apply the changes and close the Jobs Properties dialog box

Note: *You also have the opportunity to choose if the job status is written to the event log, and under which condition it is written, by clicking the Write To Windows Application Event Log checkbox.*

After you configure job notification for your operators, you may also want to configure a fail-safe operator.

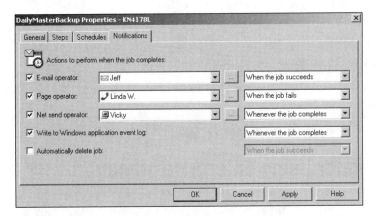

Figure 10.40
Configuring the operators to be notified of a job's status.

Configuring a Fail-Safe Operator Using Enterprise Manager

A fail-safe operator creates a safety net in case you are unable to page all of your designated pager operators. For instance, if you have assigned pager notifications to four operators and none of them can be paged, the fail-safe operator is notified.

Note: The fail-safe operator only applies to pager notifications, not email or net send notifications.

The fail-safe operator is notified under the following circumstances:

- The operator(s) responsible for the job could not be paged because of an incorrect address, or because all operators are off-duty.

- The SQL Server Agent is unable to access the system tables in the msdb database to determine whom to notify.

Warning! You cannot delete the operator designated as the fail-safe operator. If you want to do so, you must first reassign the fail-safe duty to another operator or delete the fail-safe assignment.

After determining who your fail-safe operator is going to be, follow these steps to designate the fail-safe operator using Enterprise Manager:

1. After opening Enterprise Manager, expand the server group and server that contain the operator that you want to designate as the fail-safe operator.

2. Expand Management, and right-click SQL Server Agent to open a shortcut menu that contains Properties.

3. Click Properties, and then click the Alert System tab to display the SQL Server Agent Properties dialog box.

4. Under the Fail-Safe Operator box, use the Operator drop-down menu to select the operator you want to assign as the fail-safe operator.

5. Click one or more notification methods to specify how the operator will be notified, as shown in Figure 10.41.

6. Click OK to apply the changes and close the SQL Server Agent Properties dialog box.

Deleting an Operator Using Enterprise Manager

After creating operators, you may need to delete them from your SQL Server notification process. You can follow these steps to delete an operator from SQL Server using Enterprise Manager:

1. After opening Enterprise Manager, expand the SQL Server group and then expand the server for which you want to delete the operator.

2. Expand Management, and then expand SQL Server Agent.

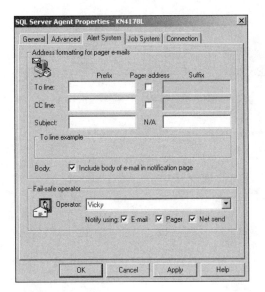

Figure 10.41
Designating the fail-safe operator.

3. Click on Operators, and then in the detail pane locate and right-click the operator that you want to delete.

4. Click Delete on the shortcut menu to delete the operator.

5. If the Delete Operator dialog box shown in Figure 10.42 appears, perform one of the following:

   - If you want another operator to receive the alert and job notifications currently being sent to the operator you are deleting, click the operator to receive the notifications in the Reassign To list. Click Reassign.

   - If you want to delete the operator without assigning the alert and job notifications assigned to the operator you are deleting, click Delete Without Reassigning.

Note: The Delete Operator dialog box will only appear if the operator that you are deleting has alert and job notifications assigned to it.

Introduction to Alerts

The third component used to automate your administrative tasks is an alert. Alerts integrate your jobs and operators in an automated SQL Server environment. Alerts are used to determine what actions to take, such as running a job or notifying an operator, when specific events occur, such as:

- Specific error messages.

- Errors of certain severity.

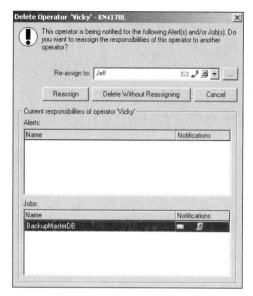

Figure 10.42
Reassigning jobs in the Delete Operator dialog box.

- Database characteristics reaching a specified threshold (e.g., free space available).

Your alerts can be defined to take any of the following actions:

- Send an email message.

- Page an operator.

- Run a predefined job to address the problem.

Types of Alerts

When creating an alert, you specify the name of the alert and the event or performance condition specification. There are also user-defined messages that can be created and associated with an alert.

Event-Specific Alerts

You can specify that an alert fire in response to one or multiple events. You define the event(s) that cause SQL Server Agent to fire an alert using the following options:

- *Error number*—A specific error occurs.

- *Message string*—Diagnostic information regarding the cause of the error.

- *Severity*—Any error with specific severity occurs (lower severity numbers indicate informational messages, higher numbers indicate serious errors).

- *Database*—Database in which the event must occur to cause the alert to fire.

Performance Condition Alerts

You can define performance condition alerts that fire in response to a performance threshold being reached. SQL Server includes numerous performance objects and counters that you can use to set performance condition alerts. To define a performance condition alert you must supply the following information:

- *Object*—Area of SQL Server that you want to monitor.

- *Counter*—Attribute within the area that you want to monitor.

- *Instance*—Specific instance (if multiple instances) of the counter that you want to monitor.

- *Behavior*—The condition the counter instance must exhibit to cause the alert to fire. This includes: equal to, greater than, or less than a specified value.

User-Defined Message Alerts

You can create event messages to track special events that are not addressed by the default SQL Server event messages. User-defined messages have an error number greater than 50,000. You can also assign them a severity level so an alert will fire based on the severity level.

Each of the user-defined event messages must be unique and must have a unique number assigned to it. Furthermore, if you are running a multiple language SQL Server environment, you have to create your user-defined message in each of the languages your SQL Server supports.

Understanding the Alert Process

Alerts respond to errors, events, or messages generated by SQL Server and written to the Window's application log. The SQL Server Agent reads the application log and compares the events written to it with alerts you have defined.

After SQL Server Agent finds a match between the two, it fires the alert. SQL Server has included the following SQL Server events and automatically writes them to the Windows application log:

- Error messages contained in the **sysmessages** table with a severity level of 19 or higher.

- **RAISERROR** statements invoked using the **WITH LOG** syntax.

- Applications logged using the **xp_logevent** extended stored procedure.

Warning! *To avoid losing SQL Server event information, be sure the Windows application log is of sufficient size.*

Creating Your Alerts

After determining what alerts you need to create within each type, you need to decide which method you are going to use to create the alert. You can use Transact-SQL or Enterprise Manager to create the alerts.

Creating an Alert Using Transact-SQL

Transact-SQL creates all the different types of alerts using the **sp_add_alert** system stored procedure. The **sp_add_alert** stored procedure has numerous arguments that are used to configure the new alert being created.

The **sp_add_alert** must be executed in the msdb database, (where all jobs, alerts, and operators are stored) and can only be executed by members of the **sysadmin** fixed server role.

The following code sample is used to create an alert called Backup Completed with a severity level of 0, message number of 55000, and a notification message of "Database backup completed successfully":

```
USE msdb
EXEC sp_add_alert @name = 'Backup Completed',
 @Severity = 0,
        @message_id = '55000',
 @notification_message = 'Database backup completed successfully'
```

*Note: You can use **sp_update_alert** and **sp_delete_alert** to modify and delete an existing alert, respectively. However, **sp_update_alert** will only modify the alert settings for which the parameter values are passed. If a parameter value is not passed, the current setting is retained.*

Creating an Alert Using an Error Number in Enterprise Manager

You must take different steps for the different types of alerts when creating alerts in Enterprise Manager. Follow these steps to create an alert using an error number:

1. After opening Enterprise Manager, expand the SQL Server group and then expand the server for which you want to create a new alert.

2. Expand Management, and then expand SQL Server Agent.

3. Right-click Alerts, and then click New Alert on the shortcut menu.

4. Enter the name for the alert in the Name box.

5. Check the Enabled checkbox to enable the alert to run immediately after creating it.

6. Click Error Number, and then enter a valid error number for the alert or click the ellipses (…) button to open the Manage SQL Server Messages dialog box.

Note: When the error number is found in the **sysmessages** table, the associated text is displayed. Otherwise, "Not a valid error number" is displayed.

7. To restrict the alert to a specific database, use the Database Name drop-down menu to select the appropriate database.

8. Enter a keyword or character string in the Error Message Contains This Text box to restrict the alert to a particular character sequence.

Note: The maximum number of characters allowed in the Error Message Contains This Text box is 100.

9. After supplying all required information shown in Figure 10.43, click OK to create the alert and close the New Alert Properties dialog box.

Creating an Alert Using a Severity Level in Enterprise Manager

Creating an alert using a severity level is similar to creating an alert using an error number in Enterprise Manager. Alerts defined using severity levels are not as specific as alerts created using error numbers and will be used more frequently.

Follow these steps to create an alert using severity levels in Enterprise Manager:

1. After opening Enterprise Manager, expand the SQL Server group and then expand the server for which you want to create a new alert.

2. Expand Management, and then expand SQL Server Agent.

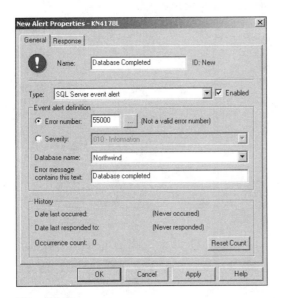

Figure 10.43
Creating an alert using an error number.

3. Right-click Alerts, and then click New Alert on the shortcut menu.

4. Enter the name for the alert in the Name box.

5. Check the Enabled checkbox to enable the alert to run immediately after creating it.

6. Click Severity, and then use the drop-down menu to locate and click a valid severity level for the alert.

*Note: Severity levels 19 through 25 automatically send a SQL Server message to the Windows application log to trigger an alert. Events with severity levels less than 19 will only trigger an alert if you have used **sp_altermessage**, **xp_logevent**, or **RAISERROR WITH LOG** to write the event to the Windows application log.*

7. To restrict the alert to a specific database, use the drop-down menu of the Database Name box to select the appropriate database.

8. Enter a keyword or character string in the Error Message Contains This Text box to restrict the alert to a particular character sequence.

Note: The maximum number of characters allowed in the Error Message Contains This Text box is 100.

9. After supplying all the required information shown in Figure 10.44, click OK to create the alert and close the New Alert Properties dialog box.

Warning! *If you define an alert for an error number and also have an alert defined for the severity level of the error number generated, the error number alert will fire as it is the more specific one.*

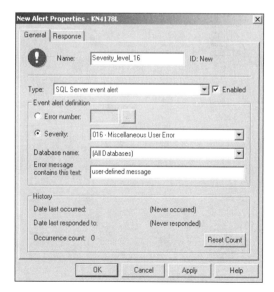

Figure 10.44
Creating an alert using a severity level.

Configuring a SQL Server Database Alert Using System Monitor

You create SQL Server database alerts to be fired when a threshold value for a System Monitor counter has been reached. You can configure System Monitor to launch a custom application written to handle the alert condition. For example, you can create an alert to execute a job that performs a backup of the transaction log when the amount of free space in a transaction log drops below the defined threshold.

*Warning! Performance condition alerts can only be defined for the first 99 databases. Databases created after the first 99 databases will not be included in the **sysperfinfo** system table, and using the **sp_add_alert** stored procedure will return an error message.*

10

Follow these steps to configure a database alert in SQL Server 2000 using Enterprise Manager:

1. Click Start|Programs|Administrative Tools|Performance to open the Windows 2000 Performance window.

2. Expand the Performance Logs And Alerts node as shown in Figure 10.45.

3. Right-click Alerts and click New Alert Settings.

4. Type a name in the New Alert Settings dialog box and click OK to open the dialog box of the new alert shown in Figure 10.46.

5. Click Add to open the Select Counters dialog box.

6. Select a SQL Server object from the Performance Object drop-down menu shown in Figure 10.47.

7. Select a counter from the drop-down menu of the Select Counters From List box shown in Figure 10.48.

Note: If you want this alert to be applied to all instances, click the All Instances radio button; otherwise, select the specific instance for which you want this alert defined. For instance, to apply the alert to all databases, click all instances.

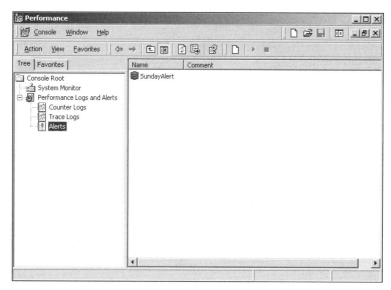

Figure 10.45
Locating and expanding the Performance Logs And Alerts node.

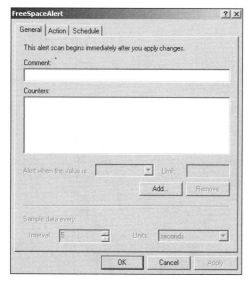

Figure 10.46
Configuring the General tab of the New Alert Settings dialog box.

8. Click Add to add the selected counter. Repeat this step for all counters you want to add for the selected object and then click Close to return to the Alert dialog box.

9. In the Alert When The Value Is section of the General tab, choose either Over or Under from the drop-down menu. Enter the threshold value for the alert.

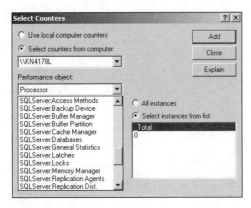

Figure 10.47
Selecting the SQL Server performance object.

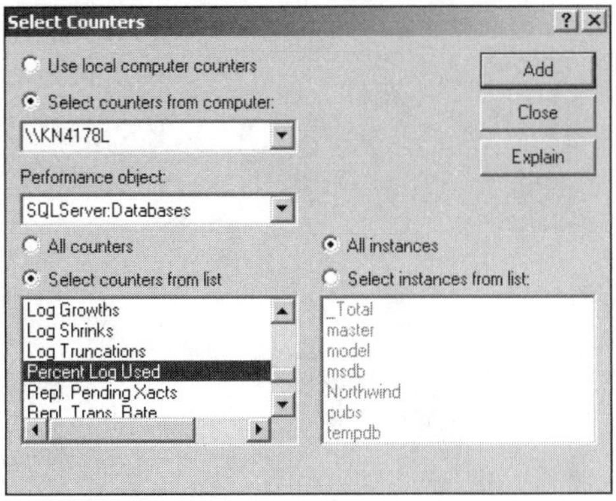

Figure 10.48
Selecting the SQL Server performance counter.

Note: This step must be performed for every entry in the Alert box before you can apply the settings or move to another tab.

10. Set the sampling frequency by specifying the Interval and Units values in the Sample Data Every box to complete the General tab as shown in Figure 10.49.

11. Click the Action tab shown in Figure 10.50 to configure the actions you want to occur when the alert threshold is reached.

12. Click the Schedule tab shown in Figure 10.51, and define when to start the alert scan in the Start Scan box and when to end the alert scan in the Stop Scan box. Or click Manually to fire the alert interactively using the shortcut menu.

13. Click OK to create the SQL Server database performance alert and close the New Alert Settings dialog box.

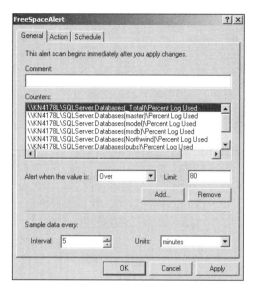

Figure 10.49
Completing the General tab of the New Alert Settings dialog box.

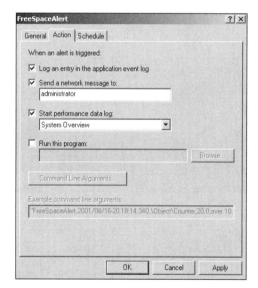

Figure 10.50
Configuring the Action tab of the New Alert Settings dialog box.

Assigning Alerts to an Operator Using Enterprise Manager

After creating your severity level and error number alerts, you need to assign them to the operator that you want notified when the alert is fired. Follow these steps to assign an alert to an operator:

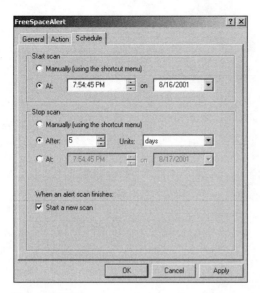

Figure 10.51
Configuring the Schedule tab of the New Alert Settings dialog box.

1. After opening Enterprise Manager, expand the SQL Server group and then expand the server that contains the alert and operator that you want to associate.

2. Expand Management, expand SQL Server Agent, and then click Operators.

3. Locate and right-click the operator you want to associate an alert with in the details pane. Click Properties and then click the Notifications tab to open the Operator's Properties dialog box.

4. Under the Notifications Sent To This Operator By box select one or more of the following checkboxes to define the notification method for each alert listed:

   - E-mail

   - Pager

   - Net Send

5. To enable the selected notification methods, click the Operator Is Available To Receive Notifications checkbox to complete the association of the alerts to the operator, as shown in Figure 10.52.

6. Click OK to apply the changes and close the Operators Properties dialog box.

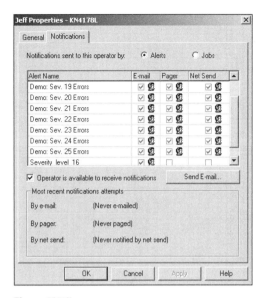

Figure 10.52
Assigning alerts to an operator.

Creating an Alert Using the Create Alert Wizard

Using the Create Alert Wizard to create an alert is much easier and more efficient than creating an alert using the different tabs in Enterprise Manager. Follow these steps to create an alert using the Create Alert Wizard:

1. After opening Enterprise Manager, expand the server group and then click the server that you want to create a new alert on.

2. Click Wizards located on the Tools menu to open the Select Wizard screen.

3. Expand Management and then double-click Create Alert Wizard to open the Create Alert Wizard Welcome screen. Click Next to open the Define The Alert screen shown in Figure 10.53.

4. Click one of the following radio buttons under the Raise This Alert box:

   • *Only If This Error Occurs*—To enter or search for the desired error message and description for the alert.

   • *For Any Error Of Severity*—To use the drop-down menu to specify a severity level for the alert.

5. Click Next to display the Specify A Database Or Error Keywords wizard screen.

6. Optionally, use the drop-down menu to locate a specific database for this alert, and supply keywords that the error message must contain, as shown in Figure 10.54.

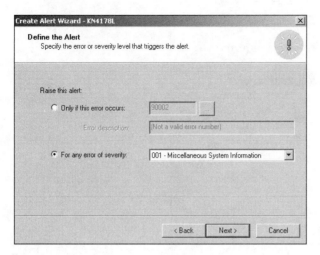

Figure 10.53
Define the Alert Wizard screen.

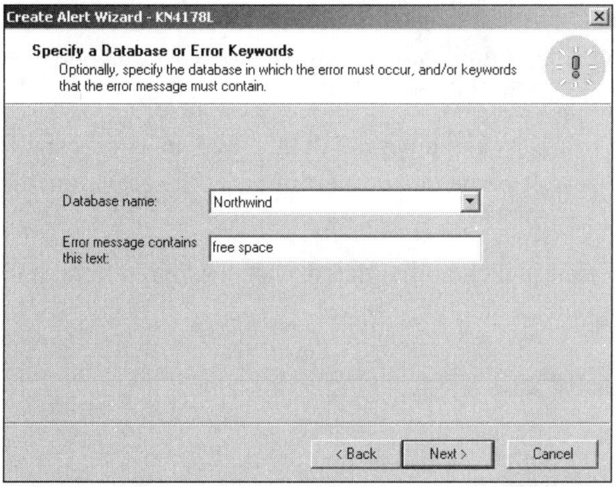

Figure 10.54
Specifying the database(s) for the alert.

7. Click Next to display the Define Alert Response wizard screen.

8. Optionally, select the job to execute and the operator(s) and notification method(s), as shown in Figure 10.55.

Note: You can create a new job from this screen by selecting the New Job option in the drop-down menu of the Job To Execute box. This opens the New Job Properties dialog box discussed earlier in this chapter under Creating a Job Using Enterprise Manager.

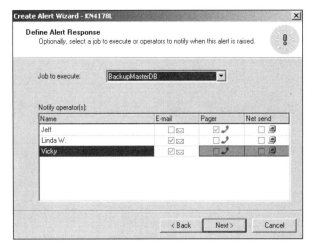

Figure 10.55
Specifying the jobs, operators, and notification methods for the alert.

9. Optionally, specify text that you want to send to the operator, and whether or not to send the error message text in the notification method(s) by selecting one or more of the notification methods as shown in Figure 10.56.

10. Click Next to display the summary screen of the Create Alert Wizard as shown in Figure 10.57. Accept the default name for the alert or enter the desired name for the alert.

11. Click Finish to create the alert and close the wizard, which will present an informational box informing you that the alert was created.

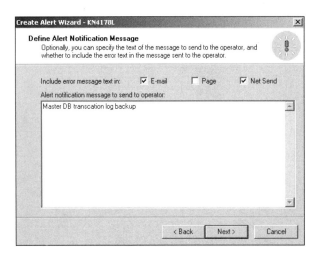

Figure 10.56
Specifying the text received by the operator.

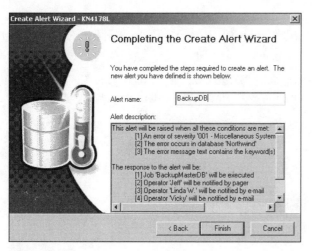

Figure 10.57
Completing the Create Alert Wizard.

Creating a Transact-SQL Script to Re-create Your Existing Alerts

If you have a problem and lose all of your existing SQL Server alerts, you will have to re-create them. This can be done very easily if you generate scripts that you can execute to re-create the alerts. Follow these steps to generate Transact-SQL Scripts for your alerts using Enterprise Manager:

1. After opening Enterprise Manager, expand the server group and then expand the server that you want to create the script file of your alerts.

2. Expand the Management node and then expand SQL Server Agent to display the Alerts node.

3. Right-click Alerts and point to All Tasks. Click Generate SQL Script to open the Generate SQL Script dialog box.

4. Enter a name for the script in the File Name box.

5. Choose one of the following under File Format:

   • Click MS-DOS Text (OEM) to save the script to a file in OEM format.

   • Click Windows Text (ANSI) to save the script to a file in ANSI format.

   • Click International Text (Unicode) to save the script to a file in Unicode format.

6. Optionally, you can perform one or both of the following:

   • If you want to include the commands required to delete existing alerts that have the same name, check the Replace Alert If It Exists checkbox.

- If you want to include the script commands necessary to generate the alert assignments for your operators, check the Include Notifications Sent By Alerts To The Operators checkbox.

- If you want to include the name of the job that is executed by the alert, check the Include The Name Of The Job Executed By The Alert checkbox

7. Enter in a Transact-SQL batch separator in the TSQL Batch separator box to complete the Generate SQL Script dialog box shown in Figure 10.58

8. Click OK to generate the SQL script and close the Generate SQL Script dialog box.

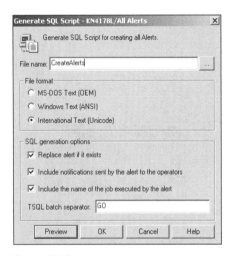

Figure 10.58
Completing the Generate SQL Script dialog box for your alerts.

Editing and Viewing Alerts Using Enterprise Manager

After creating an alert, you may want to view its properties—or even modify its behavior. You can perform either of these tasks through Enterprise Manager using the following steps:

1. After opening Enterprise Manager, expand the server group and then expand the server that contains the alert that you want to edit or view.

2. Expand the Management node and then expand SQL Server Agent to display the Alerts node.

3. Click Alerts to display the Alerts in the detail pane.

4. To view information about an alert, locate and right-click the alert and click Properties. Review the history of the alert under the History box of the General tab. View the actions of the alert on the Response tab.

5. To edit the alert, locate and right-click the alert and click Properties. Update the desired information on the General and Response tabs of the alert.

Deleting an Alert Using Enterprise Manager

At some point you may need to delete an alert from your SQL Server environment. Follow these steps to delete an alert from SQL Server using Enterprise Manager:

1. After opening Enterprise Manager, expand the SQL Server group and then expand the server that contains the alert that you want to delete.

2. Expand Management, and then expand SQL Server Agent.

3. Click on Alerts, and then in the detail pane, locate and right-click the alert that you want to delete.

4. Click Delete on the shortcut menu to delete the alert.

5. Click Yes in the Delete Alert confirmation box to confirm the deletion.

Introducing the Database Maintenance Plan Wizard

One of the primary responsibilities of a database administrator is to maintain the databases, guaranteeing that they are optimized and recoverable in the event of a problem.

Maintaining your databases can be accomplished using the information provided throughout the chapters of this book. However, the Database Maintenance Plan Wizard provides an easy way to set up a schedule for your core maintenance tasks. The wizard creates a SQL Server job that performs maintenance tasks at scheduled intervals. The tasks that can be automated include:

• Backing up your database and transaction logs and retaining the backups for a specified amount of time. This backup history can be used if you need to restore a database to a time earlier than the last database backup.

• Compressing your data files by removing unused database pages.

• Configuring log shipping. Log shipping allows the transaction logs from the source database to be constantly fed to the destination database when maintaining a standby server. The standby server is used to provide fault tolerance of your primary SQL Server, and can be configured as a read-only database that can generate reports.

• Performing internal consistency checks of the data and data pages. Consistency checks verify that the data has not been damaged by the system or software.

• Reorganizing the data and index pages by rebuilding your indexes with the specified fill factor. Creating data and index pages with a low fill factor ensures that database pages contain an equally distributed amount of data and free space on the data and index pages. This free space is essential for improving performance when inserting data.

- Updating your index statistics to be certain that the SQL Server query optimizer has current information about the distribution of data values in the tables. Up-to-date statistics allows the query optimizer to make a better decision about the best way to access the data stored in the database.

Note: Periodically, SQL Server automatically updates the index statistics; however, this option can force the statistics to be updated immediately.

These maintenance tasks generate results that can be written as a report to:

- A text file.

- An HTML file.

- The **sysdbmaintplan_history** tables in the msdb database.

- An email message sent to an operator.

After becoming familiar with the different options available to you in the Database Maintenance Plan Wizard, your next step is to create a maintenance plan for your databases.

Tip: Prior to using the Database Maintenance Plan Wizard to schedule a maintenance task, perform a test run to become familiar with the various options available to you.

After deciding you want to use the wizard to create a maintenance plan for one or more of your databases, follow these steps to start the Database Maintenance Plan Wizard and create a maintenance plan job:

1. After opening Enterprise Manager, expand the server group, and then click the SQL Server that contains the database for which you want to create a maintenance plan.

2. Click Database Maintenance Planner on the Tools menu to display the welcome screen of the Database Maintenance Plan Wizard.

3. After reading the information presented, click Next to display the Select Databases window, as shown in Figure 10.59. Choose one of the following options:

   - *All Databases*—Create a plan that runs the defined maintenance tasks against all databases.

   - *All System Databases (Master, Model, Msdb)*—Create a plan that runs only the defined maintenance tasks against each of the system databases.

   - *All User Databases (All Databases Other Than Master, Model, and Msdb)*—Create a plan that runs only the defined maintenance tasks against all user-created databases.

   - *These Databases*—Create a plan that runs only the defined maintenance tasks against the databases you checked.

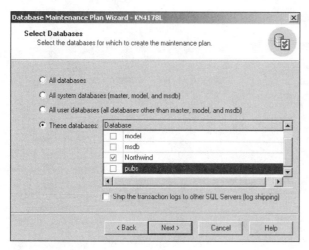

Figure 10.59
Selecting the Databases of the Maintenance Plan.

Note: You must check at least one database before you can continue.

4. Optionally, you can choose the Ship The Transaction Logs To Other SQL Servers (Log Shipping) to automate the log shipping to your standby server.

Note: If you are using the Simple Recovery Model for the database or are creating a plan for multiple databases, the log shipping option will be dimmed out.

5. Click Next to display the Update Data Optimization Information window shown in Figure 10.60. Choose one or more of the following options:

   • *Reorganize Data And Index Pages*—Specifies that you want the indexes on the tables in the database to be dropped and re-created using the specified **FILLFACTOR**.

   • *Reorganize Pages With The Original Amount Of Free Space*—Specifies that the indexes on the table in the database be dropped and re-created using the **FILLFACTOR** that was specified when the indexes were created.

   • *Change Free Space Per Page Percentage To*—Specifies that you want the indexes on the tables in the database to be dropped and re-created using a new **FILLFACTOR**. The new **FILLFACTOR** is determined by the free-space value that you supply.

*Note: A higher free-space value indicates a lower **FILLFACTOR** value. You can specify a value between 0 and 100.*

   • *Update Statistics Used By Query Optimizer*—Specifies that you want to regenerate the distribution statistics of each index on your user tables in the database.

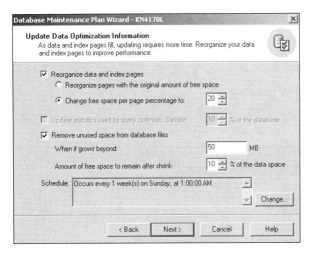

Figure 10.60
Specifying your optimization information.

- *Sample % Of The Database*—Used with the Update Statistics Used By Query Optimizer option to specify the amount of data to sample to determine the new statistics.

- *Remove Unused Space From Database Files*—Removes any unused space from the database files, thereby allowing the data files to shrink.

- *When It Grows Beyond*—Used with the Remove Unused Space From Database Files to specify the size that the database has to exceed before it attempts to remove any unused space.

- *Amount Of Free Space To Remain After Shrink*—Used with the Remove Unused Space From Database Files to determine how much free space should remain in the database after the shrink is performed.

- *Schedule*—Specifies how often to perform the optimization portion of the maintenance plan.

- *Change*—Used to modify the default schedule of every Sunday at 1:00 A.M.

6. Click Next to open the Database Integrity Check window shown in Figure 10.61 and choose one or more of the following options:

- *Check Database Integrity*—Runs the **DBCC CHECKDB** Transact-SQL statement to check the allocation and structural integrity of the user and system tables in the database.

- *Include Indexes*—Used with the Check Database Integrity option if you want the **DBCC CHECKDB** command to also check the allocation and structural integrity of the indexes.

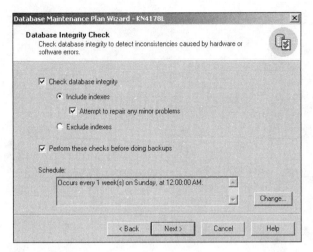

Figure 10.61
Specifying the Database Integrity options.

- *Attempt To Repair Any Minor Problems*—Used with the Include Indexes option if you want SQL Server to automatically attempt to correct any minor problems detected during the database integrity check.

- *Exclude Indexes*—Used to specify that you don't want to check the allocation and structural integrity of the user and system table indexes when the **DBCC CHECKDB** command is running.

- *Perform These Tests Before Doing Backups*—Specifies that the selected data integrity tests are to be executed before backing up the database or transaction log.

- *Schedule*—Specifies how often to perform the database integrity portion of the maintenance plan.

- *Change*—Used to modify the default schedule of every Sunday at 12:00 am.

7. Click Next to open the Specify the Database Backup Plan window shown in Figure 10.62 and choose one or more of the following options:

- *Back Up The Database As Part Of The Maintenance Plan*—Specifies that you want to back up the entire database as part of the maintenance tasks.

- *Verify The Integrity Of The Backup When Complete*—Ensures that the backup set is complete and all volumes are accessible by executing the **RESTORE VERIFYONLY** Transact-SQL command after the backup has completed.

- *Tape*—Specifies the backup media that you will use is a tape device. The tape device has to be attached to the computer containing the database.

- *Disk*—Specifies the backup media that you will use is a disk.

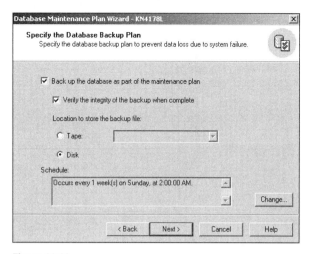

Figure 10.62
Specifying your Database Backup options.

- *Schedule*—Specifies how often to perform the database backup portion of the maintenance plan.

- *Change*—Used to modify the default schedule of every Sunday at 2:00 A.M.

8. Click Next to open the Specify Backup Disk Directory window shown in Figure 10.63 if you chose Disk as your backup media. If you chose to backup to tape, the Specify Backup Disk Directory displays the Specify the Transaction Log Backup Plan window shown in Figure 10.64. Choose one or more of the following options on the Specify Backup Disk Directory:

- *Use The Default Backup Directory*—Specifies that you want to back up your database to the default backup directory located on the computer that contains the database. By default, this is the \MSSQL\BACKUP directory.

- *Use This Directory*—Specifies that you want to back up your database to the location you specify.

- *Create A Subdirectory For Each Database*—Specifies that you want to create a subdirectory for each database of this maintenance plan under the directory location you specified for your backup.

- *Remove Files Older Than*—Specifies when to automatically delete your database backups from the directory location you specified.

Tip: *Be sure to keep a history of backups in the event that the database must be restored to an earlier point of time than the last database backup.*

- *Backup File Extension*—Specifies the file extension applied to the file that contains the database backup. The default extension is BAK.

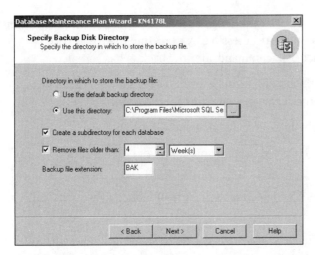

Figure 10.63
Specifying your Backup Disk options.

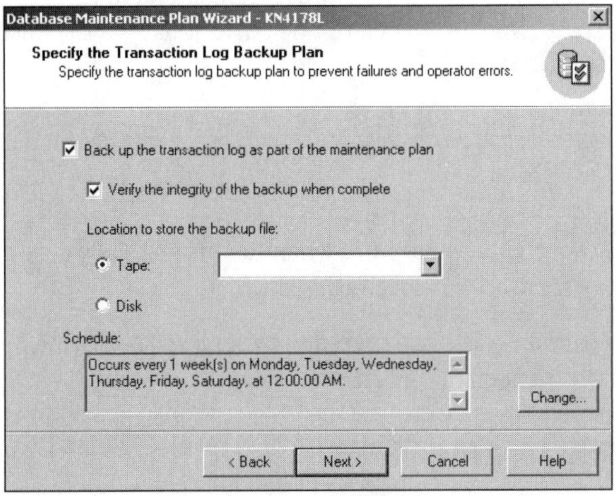

Figure 10.64
Specifying your Transaction Log Backup options.

Note: The file names are automatically generated using a timestamp. For instance, a backup of the transaction log for the Northwind database executed on 08/18/2001 would be called northwind_tlog_200108180203.

9. Click Next to open the Specify The Transaction Log Backup Plan window shown in Figure 10.64 and choose one or more of the following options:

   - *Backup The Transaction Log As Part Of The Maintenance Plan*—Specifies that you want to back up the transaction log as part of the maintenance plan.

- *Verify The Integrity Of The Backup When Complete*—Ensures that the backup set is complete and all volumes are accessible by executing the **RESTORE VERIFYONLY** Transact-SQL command after the backup has completed.

- *Tape*—Specifies that the backup media you will use is a tape device. The tape device has to be attached to the server that contains the database.

- *Disk*—Specifies that the backup media that you will use is a disk.

- *Schedule*—Specifies how often to perform the transaction log backup portion of the maintenance plan.

- *Change*—Used to modify the default schedule of Monday through Friday at 12:00 A.M.

10. Click Next to open the Reports To Generate window shown in Figure 10.65 and choose one or more of the following options:

    - *Write Report To A Text File In Directory*—Specifies the full path and name of the text file that will contain the report being generated. The generated reports maintain version information by adding a suffix using the current date to the file name in the format of YYYYMMDDHHMM.

Tip: *This is a great tool to assist you in troubleshooting any problems that may occur with the database maintenance plan.*

    - *Delete Text Report Files Older Than*—Specifies when to automatically delete your reports from the directory location you specified.

    - *Send E-mail Report To Operator*—Use the drop-down menu to specify the operator that you want to receive the generated report.

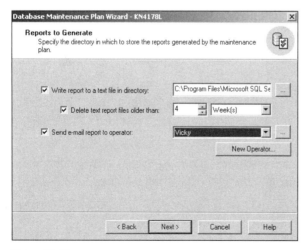

Figure 10.65
Specifying your Report Generation options.

Tip*: After selecting the operator of your choice, you can click the browse (…) button to modify their properties.*

- *New Operator*—If you decide you want to send the reports to an operator that does not currently exist, you can create a new operator.

11. Click Next to open the Maintenance Plan History window shown in Figure 10.66 and choose one or more of the following options:

- *Write History To The msdb.dbo.sysdbmaintplan_history Table On This Server*— Specifies that your report information will be written to the tables in the local msdb database.

- *Limit Rows In The Table To*—Specifies the maximum number of rows in the table that will contain history data for this plan. If you reach the maximum number of rows, the older information is deleted to allow space for the newer information.

- *Write History To The Server*—Specifies that your report information will be written to the **msdb.dbo.sysdbmaintplan_history** table on the remote server you specify. You can click the browse (…) button to open the Select Server dialog box containing a list of active servers on your network.

- *Limit Rows In The Table To*—Specifies the maximum number of rows in the remote table that will contain history data for this plan. If you reach the maximum number of rows, the older information is deleted to allow space for the newer information.

12. Click Next to display the summary screen shown in Figure 10.67. Enter a name for the maintenance plan in the Plan Name box. Review the plan using the scroll bar on

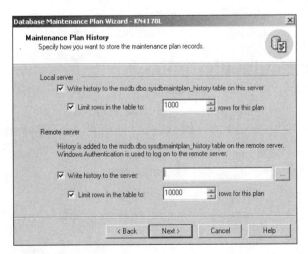

Figure 10.66
Specifying where your plan history information is stored.

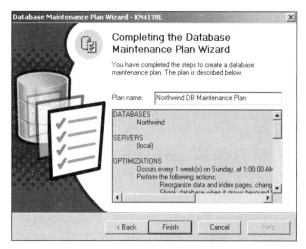

Figure 10.67
Completing the Database Maintenance Plan Wizard.

the right side of the window, then click Finish to create the database maintenance plan and display the informational message indicating you have successfully created the database maintenance plan. Click OK to close the informational box and complete the Database Maintenance Plan Wizard.

Note: After reviewing the summary for the current plan, you can modify the plan by clicking the Back button until you reach the screen window that contains the information you want to modify. After making the modification, click Next the required number of times to return to the summary screen.

When creating a job in SQL Server 2000, you can define it to run on only your local server or on multiple SQL Servers running on your network. This eliminates the need to create the same job multiple times on each SQL Server instance in your network.

Introducing Multiserver Administration

Multiserver administration reduces the amount of administrative overhead involved in creating and maintaining administrative tasks in your SQL Server environment. Multiserver administration centralizes your job status information on one SQL Server.

Multiserver administration is created when you automate the administration of SQL Server 2000 across multiple instances of SQL Server. You can use multiserver administration if you:

• Schedule information to be exchanged between enterprise servers for data warehousing.

• Manage multiple SQL Servers on your network.

There are two primary components involved with administering a multiserver job:

- *Master server*—Configures and distributes the multiserver jobs and receives the status information about your jobs.

- *Target servers*—Executes the jobs and reports status information to the master server.

Consider the following facts when creating a multiserver environment in SQL Server 2000:

- The master and target servers must be running Windows NT 4 or Windows 2000 operating systems.

- Your target servers can only report to one master server. To change the master server of an existing target server, you must defect the target server from the current master server and then enlist it into a different master server.

- When modifying the name of a target server, you must defect it from the master server, modify the name, and then reenlist the target server into the master server.

- If you decide to remove the multiserver configuration, you must defect all target servers from the master server.

Defining Your Master Server

To implement multiserver administration, you must first create a master server. You can use Transact-SQL or Enterprise Manager to create a master server. However, this is one of those administrative tasks that is handled much more easily using the Make Master Server Wizard in Enterprise Manager.

Note: *Use the* **sp_msx_enlist** *to define your master and target servers and enlist target servers using Transact-SQL.*

The Make Master Server Wizard takes you through the following steps:

- Checks the security settings for the SQL Server service and the SQL Server Agent service on all target servers.

- Creates a master server operator called **MSXOperator** on the master server. This operator receives all notifications for multiserver jobs.

- Starts the SQL Server Agent service on the master server.

- Enlists one or more target servers.

Tip: *If you have a large number of target servers, we recommend that you define the master server on a non-production SQL Server to improve performance.*

After opening Enterprise Manager, follow these steps to create a master server in SQL Server 2000:

1. Expand the server group that contains the instance of SQL Server that you want to establish as a master server.

2. Expand the Management node and right-click SQL Server Agent.

3. Select Multi Server Administration, and then click Make This A Master to display the welcome screen of the Make MSX Wizard. After reviewing the description of the wizard's functionality click Next to display the Create 'MSXOperator' screen shown in Figure 10.68.

Note: Only computers running Windows NT 4 or Windows 2000 can be master servers.

4. Enter the operator that is to be notified when the multiserver jobs complete in the following fields:

   - E-mail Address
   - Pager Address
   - Net Send Address

Tip: To make sure the notification method is configured properly, click the Test button after each notification method you configured.

5. Click Next to display the Select Servers To Enlist screen shown in Figure 10.69 and specify the target servers for your multiserver administration. Click the checkbox next to each server you want to list.

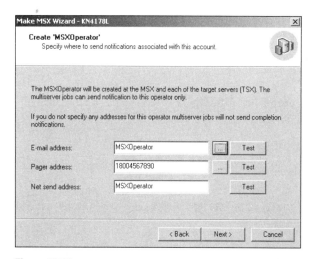

Figure 10.68
Specifying the operator notification methods.

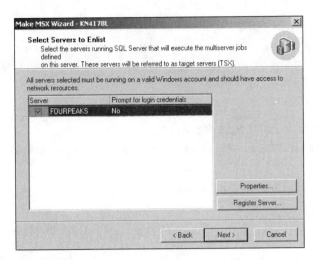

Figure 10.69
Selecting the target servers to enlist.

6. Click Next to display the Provide Target Server Description shown in Figure 10.70. Optionally, click in the Description column and enter a description for each server.

7. Click Next to display the summary screen of the Make MSX Wizard. Click Finish to enlist the servers specified and close the Make MSX Wizard summary screen.

Note: After reviewing the summary for the current target servers, you can modify any of the details you specified earlier by clicking the Back button until you reach the screen that contains the information you want to modify. After making the modification, click Next the required number of times to return to the summary screen.

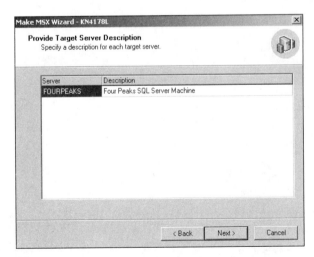

Figure 10.70
Providing a description of your target servers.

Defining Your Targets Servers

Your target servers periodically connect to the master server for a list of the current multiserver jobs. After downloading the new jobs from the master server, the target server executes them according to the schedule defined by the master server and sends status information to the master server.

Creating a Target Server Using Enterprise Manager

After opening Enterprise Manager, take these steps to create a target server in SQL Server 2000:

1. Expand the server group that contains the instance of SQL Server that you want to establish as a master server.

2. Expand the Management node and right-click SQL Server Agent.

3. Select Multi Server Administration and then click Make This A Target to display the welcome screen of the Make TSX Wizard.

Note: *Only computers running Windows NT 4 or Windows 2000 can be target servers.*

4. Click Next to open the Specify Master Server And Target Server Locations dialog box shown in Figure 10.71.

5. Enter the name of the master server in the Master Server (MSX) box, and optionally enter the physical location of the target server in the Physical Location Of *'Computer Name'* box.

6. Click Next to open the summary screen of the Make TSX Wizard.

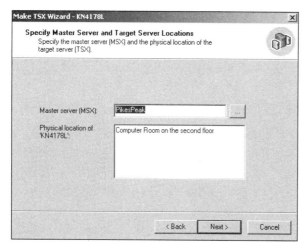

Figure 10.71
Specifying the master server and target server locations.

7. After confirming that the appropriate target servers are listed, click Finish to create the target server and close the wizard.

Note: After reviewing the summary screen of the target wizard, you can modify the list of servers you are enlisting by clicking the Back button to return to the Specify Master Server and Target Server Locations screen. After making the required modifications, click Next to return to the summary screen.

Enlisting a Target Server Using Enterprise Manager

After you have created your master server using the Make Master Server Wizard and you decide to enlist additional target servers, you can perform the following steps in Enterprise Manager:

1. After opening Enterprise Manager, expand the server group that contains the SQL Server configured as the master server.

2. Expand the Management node and right-click SQL Server Agent.

3. Select Multi Server Administration, and then click Add Target Servers.

4. Select one or more of the registered servers displayed and click Enlist.

5. Click OK to close the Add Target Servers dialog box.

Note: After creating your master server and enlisting your target servers, use the steps discussed in Creating A Job Using Enterprise Manager to configure the multiserver jobs.

Defecting a Target Server From a Master Server Using Enterprise Manager

After enlisting a target server, you may decide you no longer want to maintain it in a multiserver environment. Removing the target server from the master server is referred to as *defecting*. To defect a target server from the master server using Enterprise Manager take these steps:

*Note: Use the **sp_msx_defect** to remove a target server from your multiserver operations using Transact-SQL.*

1. After opening Enterprise Manager, expand the server group that contains the target server that you want to defect.

2. Expand the Management node and right-click the SQL Server Agent.

3. Select Multi Server Administration, and then click Defect From MSX.

4. In the confirmation dialog box, click Yes to confirm that you want to defect the selected target server from the master server.

Note: If you receive an error message preventing you from performing the defect, click the Force Defection checkbox to force the target server to defect even if it cannot contact the master server.

Troubleshooting SQL Server Automation

You may experience problems when automating your administrative tasks in SQL Server 2000. Most often, you will want to take one or more of the following actions when troubleshooting problems with SQL Server and the required services:

- Ensure that the SQL Server Agent service is started and is using a domain user account.

- Ensure that the SQL Server service is started and is using a domain user account.

- Ensure that the Eventlog service is running.

- Ensure that the event is being written to the Windows Event Viewer application log.

- Ensure that the job, operator, and alert are all enabled.

- Ensure that the history values are updated.

- Ensure that the counter threshold values are maintained for at least 20 seconds.

- Test the operator's notification methods configuration.

- Check the operator's schedule.

- Ensure that you have configured a fail-safe operator.

Summary

Automating your routine tasks requires some strategic planning. After determining which jobs can be automated, who is responsible for the jobs, and how they are going to be notified, you have to create the three components to implement the automated process.

We recommend that you create your jobs first, because they can be kicked-off manually until you create your operators and alerts. After creating your jobs, you should define your operators and their schedules. Finally, you should create your alerts and associate the appropriate operator with the alerts.

If you have multiple instances of SQL Server, you can further ease the administration of your SQL Server environment by creating multiserver jobs that are propagated from a defined master server to the defined target servers in your network. This reduces the number of jobs that have to be created, along with centralizing the job status information.

Chapter 11

Configuring SQL Server for Availability

You can configure SQL Server 2000 so that data is available 99.999 percent of the time. In order to achieve this goal of "five 9s" reliability, you must master the techniques and configurations presented in this chapter. You may implement a single solution presented here, or you may use a variety of these solutions blended together. Your choice is directly dependent upon your budget, administrative capabilities, and desired level of failover support. In order to help you choose which high availability method is right for you, complete Decision Tree 11.1.

Failover Clustering

Enterprise Edition of SQL Server 2000 features an extremely powerful method to make sure your SQL Server 2000 data is always available. This method is known as failover clustering. Failover clustering enables a second server to automatically begin servicing requests from clients in the event the primary server fails for any reason, hardware or otherwise. This is obviously one of the most powerful ways in which you can guarantee your SQL Server 2000 data is always available in the network. The failover cluster consists of two or more SQL Server 2000 Enterprise Edition installations. These installations are referred to as *nodes* when they are installed in a cluster configuration. Collectively they form a Virtual Server. The number of nodes you may install is limited by the operating system used to support SQL Server 2000. Table 11.1 shows the number of nodes supported in each operating system.

Table 11.1   SQL Server 2000 cluster nodes supported by OS.

Operating System	Nodes Supported
NT 4.0 Enterprise	2
Windows 2000 Advanced Server	2
Datacenter Server	4

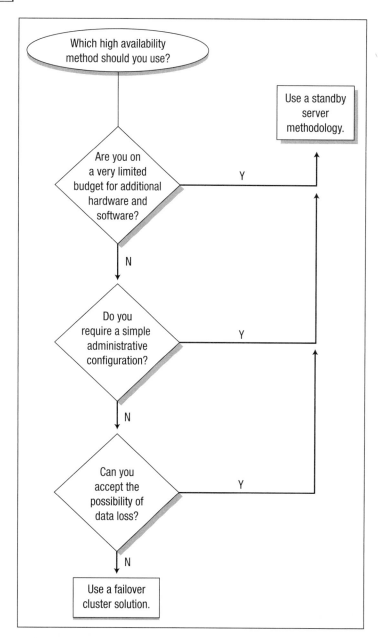

Decision Tree 11.1
Choosing a high availability method.

In order to create a SQL Server 2000 cluster successfully, you must check some obvious configurations before you begin. First, each SQL Server 2000 system must possess an independent network link, and each system should have another independent network link that connects them to each other. Second, each system must be able to access a shared set of SCSI disks or a RAID array. This shared set of disks shares the cluster data provided by the SQL Server cluster. Finally, you need to combine the resources shared by the cluster into a resource group and assign this group a primary node. This node functions as the default node for access by clients.

A critical component of Microsoft Cluster Service is the Resource Monitor. This component handles communications between the nodes in the cluster and makes sure that applications and data are always available. If SQL Server 2000 fails because of a crash, the Resource Monitor notifies the Cluster Service and the service responds with an attempt to restart SQL Server 2000. If this restart fails, Cluster Service then uses SQL Server 2000 in the other node, moving SQL Server's resources for use on this node as well.

Active/Passive versus Active/Active Configurations

You have two options when you are creating your failover clusters with SQL Server 2000—active/passive or active/active configurations. In an active/passive configuration, only one node in the cluster is active for servicing client requests. The other node or nodes are passive and only become active in the event of a failure with the active node. This option provides for availability by presenting a failover solution and at the same time ensuring that a certain performance level is always maintained. Be sure you configure the following criteria when you are creating a failover cluster in the active/passive configuration:

- Each node must be running identical versions of Windows 2000 Advanced Server or Windows 2000 Datacenter Server.

- Windows Clustering must be installed on each node.

- SQL Server 2000 must be installed on the SCSI disk or RAID array shared by each node.

- The nodes must be connected by an independent network connection.

- A virtual server must be created that represents all nodes.

You may also choose to configure an active/active failover cluster configuration. In an active/active configuration, each node runs one or more copies of SQL Server 2000 that may act as a primary server for one virtual server, and at the same time act as a secondary server for another virtual server. This configuration provides failover and improved performance, yet at the cost of overall performance, which declines in the event of a server failure. You must meet the following criteria should you decide to set up an active/active failover cluster:

- Each node must be running identical versions of Windows 2000 Advanced Server or Windows 2000 Datacenter Server.

- Windows Clustering must be installed on each node.

- Two shared SCSI disk systems or RAID systems must exist on a shared SCSI bus.

- SQL Server 2000 must be installed on each of the shared disks.

- At least two independent network connections must link the nodes.

- Two virtual servers must exist, each representing a composite of the nodes you created.

Planning Issues

There are a number of issues you should consider prior to creating your failover cluster:

- If you have configured a minimum memory setting for a particular node, you must make sure the failover node has sufficient memory capacity to effectively failover.

- If you are using Windows 2000 Address Windowing Extensions (AWE) on one of your nodes, you should ensure that all nodes feature the same amount of AWE. You must also be sure that the total value of the max server memory setting for all instances is less than the lowest amount of physical memory available in any of the nodes in the cluster.

- Be sure the recovery interval is set to zero, allowing SQL Server to establish the recovery interval.

- Be sure service account passwords are identical on all nodes.

- Disable caching on all internal disk controllers.

- Consider external disk controllers certified for relational database system usage.

- If Windows NT 4 is the operating system used throughout the cluster, make sure the domain user account used for SQL services is a member of the local Administrators group on each node.

- If you are using replication, use the shared disk system for the snapshot files.

Installing Failover Clustering Support

In order to take advantage of SQL Server Failover Clustering, you must install Windows NT 4 Enterprise Edition, Windows 2000 Advanced Server, or Windows 2000 Datacenter Server on each node that is to participate in the cluster. You cannot mix and match versions of Windows; they must be identical across the cluster. Regardless of which operating system you choose, you must also install Microsoft Cluster Services (MSCS).

Remember, each node of your cluster is going to require at least two network cards because an independent network connection between nodes is needed. One of these cards connects to the network that clients are operating on; the other network card is the private "cluster-only" card. In order to configure the network adapter that is private to the cluster, follow these steps:

1. Right-click My Network Places and choose Properties from the shortcut menu.

2. Right-click the Local Area Connection 2 icon and choose Properties from the shortcut menu.

Note: *These instructions assume your private network connection is installed as Local Area Connection 2. This is true if you install and configure this additional card following the installation of your first, "public" card.*

3. In the Properties window for the connection, select Configure.

4. Choose Advanced to display the network adapter for the connection.

5. Choose Transmission Control Protocol/Internet Protocol (TCP/IP) and then choose Properties.

6. Choose Use The Following IP Address and provide an appropriate private IP address such as, for example, 10.10.10.10. Also provide a subnet mask such as, for example, 255.255.0.0.

7. Select the WINS tab and choose Disable NetBIOS Over TCP/IP.

8. Click OK when finished.

Because this text focuses on SQL Server 2000 Enterprise Edition running on Windows 2000 Advanced Server, follow these steps to make sure that you are properly configured for SQL Server 2000 Failover Clustering:

1. Install Windows 2000 Advanced Server in a default configuration.

2. Choose Start|Programs|Administrative Tools|Configure Your Server (see Figure 11.1).

3. Select the Advanced option in the left pane, and then choose Cluster Service.

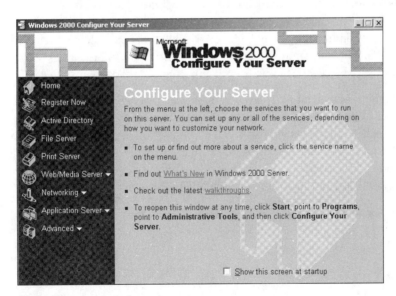

Figure 11.1
The Windows 2000 Configure Your Server interface.

4. Follow the instructions provided for installing Microsoft Cluster Service on the system.

5. Following your successful installation of Microsoft Cluster Service, you must make sure that MS DTC (Distributed Transaction Coordinator) is configured to run on a cluster. In order to do this, choose Start|Programs|Administrative Tools|Cluster Administrator.

6. In the Cluster Administrator, choose View Groups|Cluster Group. If the group contains your MS DTC resource, your system requires no further configuration and you are ready to install SQL Server 2000 as a cluster node.

7. If your MS DTC resource does not appear in the group, run the comclust.exe utility from a command prompt.

Following the installation of the Microsoft Cluster Service on at least two nodes in your network, you should verify that the installation of your cluster was successful. To do so, follow these steps:

1. Choose Start|Programs|Administrative Tools|Cluster Administrator.

2. Look for the presence of two nodes—this is verification that your installation of the Cluster Service was successful.

3. You can further verify the cluster by right-clicking a disk group and choosing Move from the shortcut menu. This allows you to move a group and its resources to another node.

Once you have verified that the underlying Windows operating system is configured properly by using the preceding steps, you are ready to begin cluster installations of SQL Server 2000. These additional nodes of SQL Server 2000 that you install are referred to as virtual servers. Each of your failover clusters can contain one or more of these virtual servers. Obviously, to be effective for failover you need more than one installed.

During installation, each of your virtual servers is given a network name to make certain you can connect to the server for administration purposes. Each is also assigned an IP address or multiple IP addresses. It is an excellent strategy to assign servers multiple IP addresses covering several subnets within your organization, so that users can still access SQL Server 2000 data even in the event of a router failure. Follow these steps to create your failover cluster and install a SQL Server 2000 virtual server:

1. Insert the SQL Server 2000 installation CD-ROM.

2. To begin the SQL Server 2000 Setup Wizard, choose Install Database Server from the SQL Server 2000 Install Components dialog box. This causes the Welcome page of the Wizard to appear.

3. Choose Next from the Welcome page of the Wizard.

4. On the Computer Name page, verify that Virtual Server is selected and enter a virtual server name for your node. This name must be unique across all virtual servers in the failover cluster. Choose Next when you are finished with this page.

5. Enter your name and company information in the User Information page and choose Next.

6. Choose Yes in the Software License Agreement window.

7. Use the Failover Clustering page to specify the IP addresses and subnets the virtual server responds to. Do this using the Add button. When finished, choose Next.

8. On the Cluster Disk Selection page, choose the cluster disk grouping where your data files are to placed by default. Choose Next when finished.

9. On the Cluster Management page, review the cluster definition provided by SQL Server 2000. Notice all available nodes are selected by default. Remove any nodes you do not want in the definition for the virtual server you are creating. Choose Next when finished.

10. On the Remote Information page, enter appropriate login credentials for any cluster nodes you selected on the previous page. The account you provide must have administrator privileges on these other system(s). Choose Next.

11. On the Instance Name page, make the selection to create a default instance or a named instance. If you are creating a named instance, provide a name for this instance and choose Next.

12. On the Setup Type page, choose the installation type. You may use the Browse button if you need to specify a path on a clustered drive resource. The drive must be a member of the cluster group you previously selected. Choose Next when finished.

13. On the Services Accounts page, choose the service account(s) that you want to run in the failover cluster. Choose Next.

14. On the Authentication Mode page, choose the authentication mode to use with this installation. Choose Next.

11

15. On the Start Copying Files page, choose Next.

16. On the Setup Complete screen, click Finish.

In order to install additional nodes in your SQL Server 2000 failover cluster, simply run the SQL Server Setup application again and select the appropriate choices during virtual server installation.

Note: *You also use the Setup program to recover from node failures. Run the Setup program to remove the failed node, and then run it again to reinstall the node when you have fixed the problem.*

Administering Failover Clusters

The following tools, features, and components are all supported for use with failover clusters, yet you should be aware of the included usage considerations:

- *Microsoft Search Service*—Full-text queries only function on failover clusters if the same security account is used on all nodes. You must use Enterprise Manager if you change this account in any way.

- *Multiple Instances*

- *SQL Server Enterprise Manager*—While creating and altering databases, you can only view the cluster disks for the local virtual server; if you restart the SQL Server service, the full text and SQL Server Agent services are not automatically brought back online. You must start those services manually using the Windows Cluster Administrator utility.

- *Service Control Manager*—You cannot use Service Control Manager to pause a clustered instance of SQL Server.

- *Replication*

- *SQL Profiler*—Traces running on virtual servers must be restarted in the event of failover.

- *SQL Query Analyzer*—Queries run against virtual servers must be restarted in the event of failover.

- *SQL Mail*—SQL Mail relies upon the same security account in use on all nodes across the failover cluster. Also, each failover node must have a Messaging Application Programming Interface (MAPI) profile with identical settings.

Removing a Node from a Failover Cluster

You can remove a node from the failover cluster at any time, for any reason, and you can even place the node back in the cluster at a later time. In order to properly remove a node, follow these instructions:

1. Insert the SQL Server 2000 installation CD-ROM.

2. To begin the SQL Server 2000 Setup Wizard, choose Install Database Server from the SQL Server 2000 Install Components dialog box. This causes the Welcome page of the Wizard to appear.

3. Click Next in the Welcome page of the Setup Wizard.

4. On the Computer Name page, verify that Virtual Server is selected and specify the name of the server you want to remove from the cluster. Choose Next.

Note: You may receive an error message stating that the node or the cluster is not available—this is most likely to occur if the node is damaged. You may still remove the node, however, so choose the OK button in the warning dialog.

5. On the Installation Selection page, choose Advanced Options and then click Next.

6. On the Advanced Options page, choose Maintain A Virtual Server For Failover Clustering and choose Next.

7. On the Failover Clustering page, choose Next.

8. On the Cluster Management page, select the node you need to remove and choose the Remove button. Click Next when finished.

9. On the Remote Information page, provide the login credentials with administrator privileges for the nodes of the cluster and choose Next.

10. Click Finish in the Setup Complete page.

Note: Be sure to restart any nodes that SQL Server instructs you to restart. Failure to do so may cause failures in the future when running the Setup program to manage nodes.

Recovering from Failures within Failover Cluster

There are two main scenarios that can lead to a failure within the failover cluster. You may have a hardware failure in the first node of a two node cluster, or you may simply have one of the nodes go offline. In order to recover from either case, you must first remove the failover cluster using the following steps:

1. Insert the SQL Server 2000 installation CD-ROM.

2. To begin the SQL Server 2000 Setup Wizard, choose Install Database Server from the SQL Server 2000 Install Components dialog box. This causes the Welcome page of the Wizard to appear.

3. Click Next in the Welcome page of the Setup Wizard.

4. On the Computer Name page, choose Virtual Server and specify the name of the server from which to remove a clustered instance. Click Next when finished.

5. On the Installation Selection page, choose Upgrade, Remove, Or Add Components To An Existing Instance Of SQL Server. Choose Next.

6. On the Instance Name page, for a default instance, click Default. For a named instance, specify the name of the instance to remove. Click Next when finished.

7. On the Existing Installation page, click Uninstall Your Existing Installation. Click Next when finished.

8. On the Remote Information page, provide the login credentials with administrator privileges for the nodes of the cluster and choose Next.

9. Click Finish in the Setup Complete page.

Note: Be sure to restart any nodes that SQL Server instructs you to restart. Failure to do so may cause failures in the future when running the Setup program to manage nodes.

Perhaps the most common failure situation in a failover cluster is a hardware failure in the first node of a two-node cluster. Perhaps the drive system this node relies upon fails. Obviously, following this failure, the cluster fails over to your second node of the cluster by design, and users experience no interruption of data access. Follow these steps to recover from this scenario:

1. Use the preceding steps to remove the failover cluster instance that has failed.

2. From your second node, use the Cluster Administrator utility to evict the failed node from the cluster. In order to do this, right-click the failed node and choose Evict Node from the shortcut menu.

3. Replace hardware or make whatever repairs are necessary in the failed node; this may include re-installing the operating system and Microsoft Cluster Service.

4. From the previously failed node, rejoin the cluster using Microsoft Cluster Service.

5. Run the SQL Server Setup program on your second node in order to add the previously failed node back to the failover cluster.

Another possible failure scenario is that a node in your cluster simply goes offline. Often this is not because of a hardware failure, but is caused by some problem with the operating system. Once again, thanks to the failover cluster, your second node begins servicing client requests and users experience no disruption of data access. Obviously, attempt to fix minor problems without disrupting the configuration of the failover cluster. If the problem is more serious, however, follow these steps:

1. Run SQL Server 2000 setup and remove the failed node.

2. Resolve the problem with this failed node.

3. Ensure that the Microsoft Cluster Service cluster is functioning properly and all nodes are online.

4. Run the SQL Server Setup program on the second node and add the previously failed node back to the failover cluster.

Failover Cluster Troubleshooting

There are a number of common problems and issues you might experience with creating and maintaining SQL Server 2000 failover clusters. Here are some common problems and solutions:

- *SQL Server 2000 does not start properly after joining a new cluster*. Be sure to check the user account assigned to the SQL Server services. Remember, the account credentials must be identical across all nodes for a cluster to function properly. If you need to change user account information after your cluster is established, be sure to use Enterprise Manager—this ensures that the information changes consistently throughout the cluster.

- *SQL Server cannot access the cluster disks*. Often, this is because a cluster node failed and you have not configured the shared disks with the same drive letter on each and every node in the cluster. Be sure you use the same drive letter to map to the shared cluster disks on each node.

- *Your cluster installation keeps failing over to another node simply because the full-text search service or the SQL Server Agent is failing*. Use the Cluster Administrator in Windows to access the properties for the service or services that are causing the unnecessary failover. In the Advanced tab of the Properties window, clear the Affect The Group checkbox.

- *SQL Server 2000 is no longer starting automatically when you are participating in a cluster*. This is expected behavior. You must use Cluster Administrator in Windows to automatically start a failover cluster.

- *You see an error message during SQL Server Setup that states "No compatible resource groups found".* This error occurs because of the MS DTC setup on Windows NT 4 Enterprise Edition. To troubleshoot this error, you must be certain that MS DTC has a group containing a network name, IP address, and shared cluster disk owned by the local node when the Setup program is run. You should use Cluster Administrator to determine there is a group meeting these requirements and owned by the local node. If you find there is none, you can simply move a disk into the cluster group that already contains a network name and IP address.

- *You see an error message during SQL Server Setup that states "All cluster disks available to this virtual server are owned by other node(s)".* This message results when you select a drive and path for the installation of data files and the local node does not own the drive you have selected. You should move the disk to the local node using Cluster Administrator to resolve the issue.

- *You see an error message during SQL Server Setup that states "Unable to delete SQL Server resources. They must be manually removed. Uninstallation will continue".* This message displays if SQL Server Setup cannot delete all of the SQL Server resources. You should enter Control Panel and uninstall the instance you were trying to remove on every node.

- *You cannot enable the clustering operating system error log.* This log is used by Cluster Service to record information about the cluster. In order to enable this log, be sure to set the environment variable **CLUSTERLOG=<path to file>**.

- *You change an IP address assigned to an interface in the cluster and the cluster no longer functions.* This is by design. Unfortunately, changing any assigned IP address in the cluster requires breaking the cluster for the re-assignment, and then re-clustering the environment following the change.

- *The Network Name is offline and you cannot connect using TCP/IP.* You should try to connect using Named Pipes. Do this by creating an alias using the Client Network Utility to connect to the appropriate computer. To do so, follow these steps:

1. Using the Cluster Administrator, determine the node the instance of SQL Server is running on.

2. Start the SQL Server service on that computer using the **net start** command.

3. Start the SQL Server Network Utility on the computer and note the pipe name the server is listening on.

4. On the client computer, start the Client Network Utility.

5. Create an alias to connect via Named Pipes using the pipe name recorded above.

Standby Servers

The next best thing to a failover cluster is to employ the use of a standby server. As its name implies, this server waits until a problem with the primary server occurs, and then steps in and takes the place of the primary system. However, you are responsible for bringing the standby server up in place of the primary; it does not feature the automatic failover that you have with clustering. SQL Server 2000 makes the creation, maintenance, and general implementation of a standby server much easier than it was in previous versions.

Note: As you soon will learn, successfully implementing a standby server requires knowledge of backup and restore processes for SQL Server 2000. See Chapter 9 if you need help with these processes.

The secret to the success of a standby server methodology is to keep the standby system data up-to-date with the primary server data. This involves making periodic truncation log backups on the production system and restoring them on the standby server. SQL Server 2000 automates this process for you through a feature called *log shipping*. Keep in mind that, because it is up to date with the primary system, a standby server does not just have to sit there useless, waiting for you to one day bring it online as the primary system. A standby system can be used to run reports on data, or any other intensive tasks that you do not want to bog down the production system with.

In order to create the standby server initially, simply perform a full database backup for the data that you need available on the standby system. Restore this full database backup on the standby system using either the **NORECOVERY** or the **STANDBY** restoration option. By doing this, you make sure the restored database is left in a mode that permits additional transaction logs to be applied. Remember, this is how you are to keep the standby database up-to-date with the production system.

If a problem with your production server develops—or should you need to down it for any other reason—you simply promote the standby server to become the new primary server. Your SQL users do not know the data is coming from another server, and you have far less downtime. Obviously, before you promote the standby system, be sure to apply all transaction logs from the primary system, and you should go to the production system and back up the active portion of the transaction log and apply this last backup to the standby system. Hopefully, you are using a RAID solution on the production system so that you can in fact back up the transaction log one last time. You should restore this last transaction log backup on the standby system using the **RECOVERY** option. This sets the standby system in a ready state for the users that will soon be accessing it.

To further facilitate your primary server/standby server plan, you should back up the active portion of the transaction log on the primary server using the **NORECOVERY** option. This allows you to restore transaction log backups from the standby system to the production system once you have this production system back online. This helps your failover plans dramatically; you should be just as concerned about the amount of time it takes to get your primary system back up and running and in production as you are about how long it takes to get your standby system in production when the primary system fails.

How do users start using the standby server once the primary server fails? When you promote the standby server, you must either change the name of this server to the name of the primary server, or you must redirect users to the standby system. Typically, the simplest solution is to rename the standby server. You can rename the Windows 2000 system using the Network Identification tab of the Properties window of My Computer. Use the SQL Server Setup program to rename your SQL Server 2000 installation.

To successfully implement the standby server and make it useful in production, you must ensure the appropriate user logins exist on the standby system. The creation of these accounts can be accomplished in one of three simple ways. First, you can script these logins on the primary server and run the scripts on the standby server. Second, you can use the **sp_resolve_logins** stored procedure (covered later in this chapter). Finally, you can use Data Transformation Services. DTS features the DTS Transfer Logins Task in the DTS Designer, allowing you to fully automate the copying of the user logins from one system to another. Chapter 14 covers DTS in detail.

Automated Log Shipping

In order to make the process of maintaining a standby server much, much easier, you should consider implementing the automation of log shipping. Remember, the bulk of your administrative effort for successfully configuring and maintaining a standby server hinges upon your ability to back up transaction logs on the primary server and restore these logs on the standby system. This process is often referred to as log shipping. SQL Server 2000 makes it simple for you to automate these tasks by creating jobs that back up, copy, and restore these transaction logs for you. The simplest method for automating log shipping in your SQL Server environment is to use the Database Maintenance Planner Wizard in Enterprise Manager. The steps for doing so are as follows:

1. Choose Start|Programs|Microsoft SQL Server|Enterprise Manager.

2. Expand your server in the left pane.

3. Expand the Databases container in the left pane.

4. Right-click the database you need to configure log shipping for and choose All Tasks from the shortcut menu, then Maintenance Plan. Notice the Database Maintenance Plan Wizard appears open at the Welcome page.

5. Choose Next in the Welcome page.

6. On the Select Databases page, make sure that the appropriate database is selected. This should be the database you are interested in making available at all times, and it should be a copy of the database on the primary server. Choose the Ship The Logs To Other SQL Servers (Log Shipping) checkbox (see Figure 11.2) to select it and choose Next.

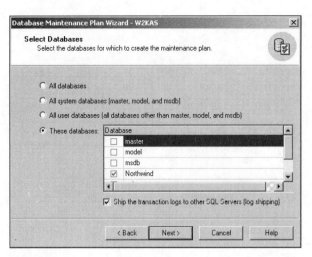

Figure 11.2
Selecting the Log Shipping option.

7. Because in this example you are only interested in using the Wizard to configure log shipping, choose Next in the Update Data Optimization Information page.

8. Choose Next in the Database Integrity Check page.

9. On the Specify The Database Backup Plan page, clear the checkbox that indicates Back Up The As Part Of The Maintenance Plan and choose Next.

10. On the Specify Transaction Log Backup Disk Directory page, verify that the Use The Default Backup Directory option is selected.

11. Select the Remove Files Older Than checkbox to enable this feature and choose 1 in the spin box and Hour(s) in the drop-down list box (see Figure 11.3). Click Next when finished.

12. On the Specify The Transaction Log Share page of the Wizard, provide the path to the share on your network where you will store the transaction log backups. This share must offer read and write access for the primary server and read access for the standby server. Specifically, the account used to run the SQL Server agent service must possess these permissions. When you are finished, choose Next.

13. On the Specify The Log Shipping Destinations page, use the Add button to add the destination server—the destination server is your standby server. Use the Server Name drop-down list to select this server (see Figure 11.4).

14. On the Database Load State area, select the Standby Mode option and select Terminate Users In Database (Recommended) check box. Also choose the Allow Database To Assume Primary Role check box.

15. On the Directory text box, provide the path to a share that exists on the destination (standby) server that acts as a repository for the shipped logs. Click OK when finished.

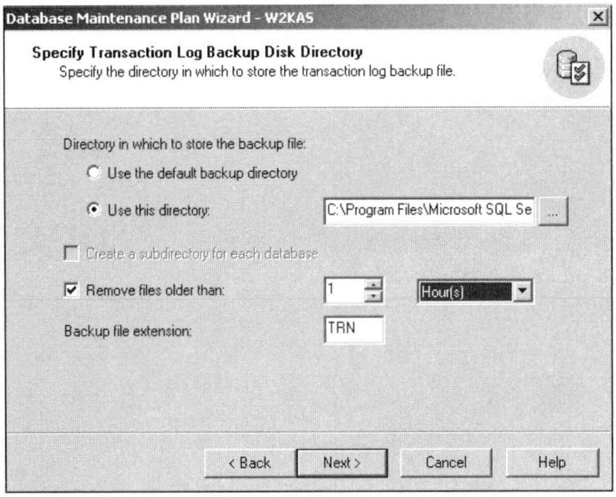

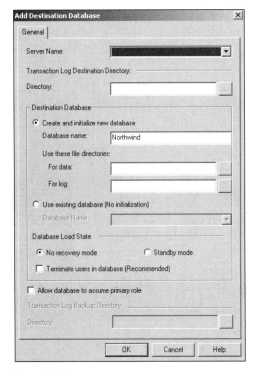

Figure 11.3
The Specify Transaction Log Backup Disk Directory page.

Figure 11.4
Adding a destination server.

16. Choose Next in the Specify The Log Shipping Destinations page.

17. In the Initialize The Destination Databases page, verify that the Perform A Full Database Backup Now option is selected and choose Next.

18. In the Log Shipping Schedule page, specify the exact schedule you need for updating the standby server with transaction logs from the primary server. This schedule is directly related to how often data changes on the primary server, and how many resources you are prepared to dedicate to the log shipping process. This also will have an impact on the amount of time it takes to get your standby server online as the primary server when it fails. Choose Next when finished.

19. In the Log Shipping Thresholds page, select the Log Shipping Threshold and the Out Of Sync Alert Threshold appropriate for your environment and choose Next.

20. In the Specify The Log Shipping Monitor Server Information page, make sure the appropriate server is selected and choose Next. Monitoring log shipping is covered in detail in the next section of this chapter.

21. Choose Next in the Reports To Generate page.

22. Choose Next in the Maintenance Plan History page.

23. In the Database Maintenance Plan Wizard Summary page, provide a name for the plan and choose Next.

24. Choose the Finish button in the Completing The Database Maintenance Plan Wizard page.

25. Choose OK in the dialog box informing you the plan was created successfully.

Monitoring Log Shipping

Monitoring the status of log shipping in your environment is simple with Enterprise Manager. Simply launch Enterprise Manager on the server you designated to monitor log shipping and open the Management container. Select the Log Shipping Monitor object in this container. Notice that details regarding the status of log shipping display in the right pane. Status information includes:

- Data and time of the last backup

- The current backup threshold setting

- The most recent copy of the transaction log backup in the backup share

- The most recent restore of the transaction log backup on the standby server

- The synchronization status

You can also use the Log Shipping Monitor object to view history information and change the settings for log shipping. Simply right-click the log shipping pair and choose the appropriate option from the shortcut menu.

Bringing the Standby Server Online

In the event your primary server fails, or you must bring this server offline for any reason, you must bring the standby server online to take the place of the primary server. This is a fairly straightforward and simple process, but be sure to follow these steps to do so properly:

1. Run the **sp_change_primary_role** stored procedure on the primary server. The complete syntax for this procedure follows:

```
sp_change_primary_role [ @db_name = ] 'db_name'
    , [ @backup_log = ] backup_log
    , [ @terminate = ] terminate
    , [ @final_state = ] final_state
    , [ @access_level = ] access_level
```

The arguments used in this syntax are as follows:

- **@db_name**—Used to specify the name of the database.

- **@backup_log**—Allows you to specify a backup of the current transaction log on the server.

- **@terminate**—Allows you to specify a rollback of all incomplete transactions should take place.

- **@final_state**—Specifies the recovery state for the database— either **RECOVERY**, **NO RECOVERY**, or **STANDBY**.

- **@access_level**—Specifies the access level for the database after the completion of the stored procedure with the argument. This includes **MULTI_USER**, **RESTRICTED_USER**, or **SINGLE_USER**.

*Note: Although running **sp_change_primary_role** on the primary server is ideal for ensuring your change of roles includes all data, it may be impossible if the primary server failure is catastrophic. The use of a standby server, therefore, is not foolproof, and may result in some data loss. You should consider this when deciding between a clustering solution and a standby server solution.*

2. Run the **sp_change_secondary_role** stored procedure on the secondary server. The complete syntax for this command follows:

```
sp_change_secondary_role [ @db_name = ] 'db_name'
    , [ @do_load = ] do_load
    , [ @force_load = ] force_load
    , [ @final_state = ] final_state
    , [ @access_level = ] access_level
```

```
, [ @terminate = ] terminate
, [ @keep_replication = ] keep_replication
, [ @stopat = ] stop_at_time
```

Notice the arguments are almost identical to those used in the **sp_change_primary_role** with the exception of the following:

- **@do_load**—Used to specify that any pending transaction logs be copied and restored before converting **db_name** to a primary database.

- **@force_load**—Used to specify that the **Force_Load** option be used in restoring any pending transaction logs to the secondary database.

- **@keep_replication**—Specifies that replication settings be preserved when restoring any pending transaction logs on the secondary database.

- **@stopat**—Used to specify that when applying any pending transaction logs, the secondary database be restored to the state it was in as of the specified date and time.

3. You may run the **sp_change_monitor_role** stored procedure to switch the respective roles for the log shipping monitor server. The complete syntax follows:

```
sp_change_monitor_role [ @primary_server = ] 'primary_server'
    , [ @secondary_server = ] 'secondary_server'
    , [ @database = ] 'secondary_database'
    , [ @new_source = ] 'new_tlog_source_directory'
```

4. You may use the **sp_resolve_logins** stored procedure to be sure the user login accounts exist on the standby server. The syntax for this stored procedure is:

```
sp_resolve_logins [ @dest_db = ] 'dest_db'
    , [ @dest_path = ] 'dest_path'
    , [ @filename = ] 'filename'
```

The **@dest_db** parameter indicates the name of the new primary database, and **@dest_path** and **@filename**, respectively, specify the path and name of the bulk copy of the **syslogins** table from the original database. You can use DTS to create this file.

5. Do not forget to change the name of the standby server and the SQL instance to those of the primary server so that users will connect to the new system seamlessly.

Summary

If you are concerned about increasing the amount of time data is available for your SQL users, you should choose between a standby server methodology and the use of failover clusters. It is also possible you will use both of these strategies in different areas of your implementation. Use the decision tree seen earlier in this chapter to help you determine which strategy might be right for you.

Failover clustering requires a much larger financial commitment as well as a larger administrative workload, yet this solution ensures the highest level of data availability possible. The use of standby servers reduces both the workload you face and the investment you must make for the solution. Obviously, this solution does not provide the same degree of availability, however.

No matter which method you choose to ensure your data is always available, it is going to be your responsibility to consistently monitor SQL Server 2000. Doing this guarantees you are maintaining a server and its databases that meet the performance needs of your users, and also helps to maintain constant availability. The next chapter of this book examines the monitoring of SQL Server 2000 in detail.

Chapter 12

Monitoring and Optimizing SQL Server 2000

As a SQL Server 2000 database administrator, you must master the ability to monitor key performance measures of the server and optimize the server as a result of these measurements. There are a variety of methods for monitoring the server, and there are a number of tools you can use to accomplish these tasks. This chapter explores all of these aspects of monitoring and optimizing SQL Server 2000.

Strategies and Approaches to Optimization

In this chapter, the focus is on improving the performance of SQL Server 2000. But this leads to the obvious question—what really measures performance in SQL Server? There are actually two primary indicators of performance in the relational database management system (RDBMS):

- *Response time*—This indicator of performance measures the amount of time required to return the first row of a result set.

- *Throughput*—This indicator measures the total number of queries a server can handle in a given time frame.

Notice that both of these performance indicators help measure server performance as well as performance of the SQL Server application designed to retrieve data from the server. It is critical that you consider both when you are seeking to improve performance.

The approaches you take to optimizing both of these performance indicators include:

- Tuning the client application. This includes making sure that queries are composed that limit database searches; ensuring that useful indexes are created; minimizing lock contention and avoiding deadlocks; using stored procedures that reduce contention; and offloading data and processing from the server.

- Tuning the database through logical and physical redesigns.

- Tuning SQL Server itself by evaluating storage designs or changing key configuration options on the server.

- Tuning the hardware configuration by increasing network performance, or adding memory, processors, faster disk systems, or additional computers.

Common Monitoring and Optimization Tasks

Because SQL Server 2000 runs as services within the Windows operating system, monitoring can be quite complex. In order to successfully monitor SQL Server 2000, you must also monitor the underlying operating system, and there are a number of interrelated factors you must consider.

Establishing a Baseline and Detecting Bottlenecks

You must realize it is critical when monitoring the server to establish baselines for performance. Without these, it is almost impossible to detect performance problems and areas for enhancing system performance. First, you must realize that there are five key factors that can influence the performance of your relational database management system. These five factors are presented in Table 12.1.

You should keep these areas in mind as you are monitoring performance and establishing your baselines. You should use the tools presented later in this chapter to establish and document these baselines. You should create measurements to determine peak and off-peak hours of database activity, query or batch command response times, and database backup and restore times.

Once you have established performance baselines, you can compare current performance measurements gathered from SQL Server 2000 to these baselines to determine if performance issues exist that might warrant your attention. Obviously, monitoring results that deviate greatly from the baseline deserve scrutiny.

Baselines help you dramatically in detecting bottlenecks. Bottlenecks are areas of server activity that negatively impact performance. For example, if your SQL Server 2000 system is having difficulty reading information from disk because of the contention on your single disk hard drive system, the disk system has resulted in a bottleneck on the server. This bottleneck can negatively affect a wide variety of other systems and result in unacceptable server response times for users.

Sadly enough, your server is never in perfect equilibrium when it comes to the finite resources it maintains. These resources are always approaching a bottleneck state (albeit

Table 12.1   Factors affecting server performance.

Factor	Description
Workload	Volume of server activity
Throughput	Total number of queries in given time period
System resources	Physical capacity of hardware
Optimization	Application and database design
Contention	Competition for data

sometimes very slowly). It is your job to detect these bottlenecks and correct them before substantial performance problems result.

In order to properly catch bottlenecks before they become a problem, you should monitor memory usage, CPU usage, disk I/O performance, user connections, and locks. You should also know the acceptable range of performance you are looking for. The baseline that you establish should help you significantly in this area. You should also simulate loads on the server where appropriate, using the tools presented in this chapter. Simulating large amounts of server activity can assist you dramatically in tracking down bottlenecks.

System-Level Monitoring

When you are attempting to catch bottlenecks before they inhibit your SQL Server's performance, you should monitor at three levels—system-level, SQL Server-level, and query-level. In fact, you should consider monitoring these levels in the order presented.

As mentioned earlier, monitoring at the system level is critical because SQL Server 2000 relies upon the underlying operating system so considerably. This level of monitoring includes not only the operating system, but also the raw hardware resources this operating system is installed upon.

In order to most effectively monitor at this level, you should use the Windows 2000 Event Viewer and the Windows System Monitor. Each of these tools is covered in greater detail later in this chapter.

SQL Server Monitoring

You should also carefully monitor performance at the SQL Server level, including the amount of SQL Server activity and the data consistency resulting from end user interactions with the various databases hosted on the server. Key factors to consider when monitoring at this level include the amount of locking and contention for specific data hosted.

To monitor at this level, you should consider using the Current Activity Window, Transact-SQL statements and stored procedures, and the SQL Profiler. You may also use Database Consistency Checker (DBCC) statements or the Windows System Monitor.

Query Monitoring

Finally, you should also monitor specific query performance factors. These include index usage, CPU time, and actual I/O statistics. You should consider using SQL Profiler and SQL Query Analyzer for these tasks.

Monitoring Tools

You have a large variety of tools to use for monitoring SQL Server and the system that hosts it. These tools are either included in the operating system (such as Event Viewer and System Monitor), or they are included in SQL Server 2000 (such as Profiler and

Query Analyzer). Keep in mind that you should not run these tools simply for the sake of running them, as all of the tools consume varying amounts of system resources. The last thing that you want to do is actually create bottlenecks on your server because you are running monitoring tools for no good reason.

Windows 2000 Event Viewer

Windows 2000 Event Viewer is a critical monitoring tool-not only for SQL Server 2000 installations, but for anyone running any version of Windows 2000. As its name implies, this tool is used to capture events that could affect system performance.

Event Viewer consists of the following logs described in Table 12.2.

As a SQL Server database administrator, you primarily will concern yourself with two Event Viewer logs—the Application Log and the Security Log. The steps below demonstrate how you can use the Application Log to monitor your SQL Server 2000 installation:

1. Select Start|Programs|Administrative Tools|Event Viewer.

2. Select the Application Log object in the left pane (see Figure 12.1).

3. Notice the Application Log contains many entries that are unrelated to SQL Server 2000. You can easily filter the view in the Application Log to pinpoint events dealing with a particular service. Select the Action menu and choose Properties.

4. In the Properties window for the Application Log, select the Filter tab (see Figure 12.2).

5. Clear the Information check box in the Event Types area. This ensures only Warnings, Errors, and audit information is displayed in the log.

6. Use the Event Source drop-down list to select the MSSQLSERVER service. Note that you may select any of the other services that make up SQL Server should you need to.

7. Note the other options available on the Filter tab and choose OK when finished.

Table 12.2   Event Viewer logs.

Log	Description
Application	Records events logged by applications
Security	Records security related operating system events
System	Records events generated by OS components
Directory Service	Records events generated by Active Directory services
DNS Server	Records events generated by the DNS service
File Replication Service	Records events generated by the File Replication Service

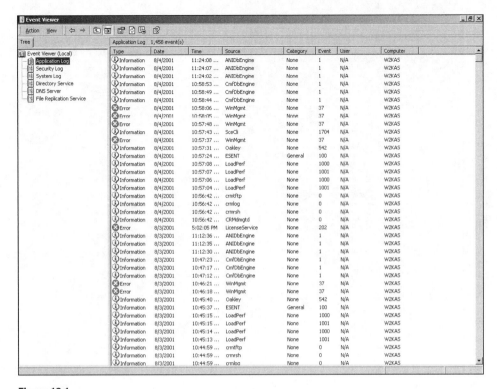

Figure 12.1
The Application Log of Event Viewer.

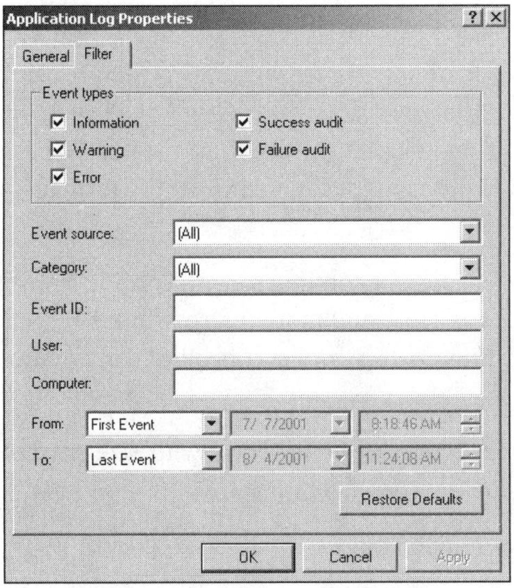

Figure 12.2
Filtering events in the Application Log.

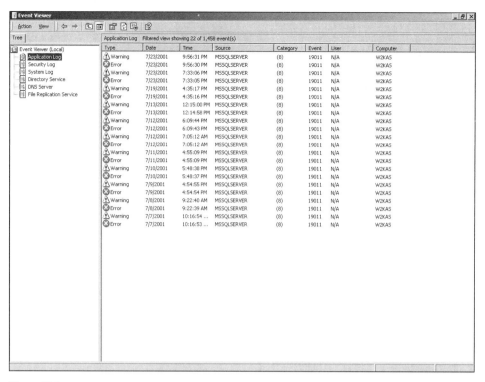

Figure 12.3
The Application Log after filtering.

8. Notice the change in the display of the Application Log (see Figure 12.3). Only Warnings and Errors appear in the display.

9. Select the Action menu again. Notice that you can use the New Log View menu item to create another view of the Application Log. Also notice the Save Log File As menu selection. This option allows you to easily save the log in a variety of formats for use in other applications.

It is important to realize that Event Viewer logs are configured with specific settings that by default affect the behavior of these logs as more and more information is logged there. Specifically, each log can grow no larger than 512KB, and events older than 7 days are automatically overwritten by default.

You may find these settings are not to your liking, or do not meet your security requirements. These settings are easily changed using these steps:

1. Make sure you are in the Event Viewer application.

2. With the appropriate log selected in the left pane, select the Action menu and choose Properties.

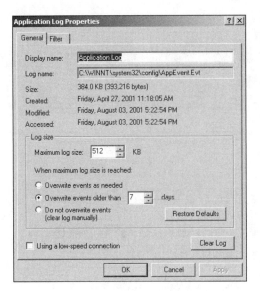

Figure 12.4
Setting the General properties for the Application Log.

3. Note the possible settings for configuring the log properties on the General tab (see Figure 12.4).

Windows System Monitor

Perhaps the most powerful (and unfortunately underused) tool for monitoring SQL Server 2000 is the Windows System Monitor. This application, included within the Windows NT or 2000 operating system, permits you to view performance data from a wide variety of sources in real time. You may also use it to generate sophisticated reports regarding historical performance for the system.

System Monitor functions using preexisting counters installed in the application by the Windows operating system. These counters measure particular resources on the system. Counters are grouped in collections known as performance objects. Fortunately, the System Monitor architecture is extensible and additional performance objects and counters may be installed by applications running within Windows at any time. For example, when you install SQL Server 2000, new performance objects are added to System Monitor for monitoring SQL Server specific information. These SQL Server counters enable you to monitor SQL I/O, memory usage, user connections, locking, and replication. Table 12.3 lists these additional performance objects and their functions. Notice you can even create your own counters to monitor other aspects of SQL Server's performance or usage, such as stored procedure utilization.

12

Table 12.3 SQL Server 2000 performance objects.

Object	Function
SQLServer:Access Methods	Measures access to SQL Server database objects—often used to measure query efficiency
SQLServer:Backup Device	Measures backup and restore performance
SQLServer:Buffer Manager	Measures the utilization of the memory buffer—often helps to indicate additional memory requirements
SQLServer:Buffer Partition	Also measures specifics regarding memory buffer pages
SQLServer:Cache Manager	Measures the use of memory used for caching stored procedures, T-SQL statements, and triggers
SQLServer:Databases	Measures database activity, including active transactions, bulk copy throughput, and transaction log activities
SQLServer:General Statistics	Provides counters for general server-wide activity, such as user connections and logins
SQLServer:Latches	Measures internal SQL Server resource locks
SQLServer:Locks	Provides counters for the monitoring of locks, including lock timeouts and deadlocks
SQLServer:Memory Manager	Measures overall memory usage
SQLServer:Replication Agents	Measures the number of replication agents currently running
SQLServer:Replication Dist.	Measures key replication statistics regarding the Distributor/Subscriber relationship
SQLServer:Replication Logreader	Helps to measure the key statistics regarding the Publisher/Distributor relationship
SQLServer:Replication Merge	Measures key information regarding merges during replication between the Publisher and the Subscriber
SQLServer:Replication Snapshot	Measures the amount of snapshot replication information delivered to the Distributor
SQLServer:SQL Statistics	Contains counters that help measure server performance by examining T-SQL queries and batches
SQLServer:User Settable	Contains custom counters you can use to monitor custom information such as product inventory information

In order to use System Monitor successfully, you need to be aware of several steps. In the following step-by-step example, you use System Monitor to examine real-time statistics regarding memory usage on a SQL Server 2000 system:

1. Select Start|Programs|Administrative Tools|Performance to launch the Performance Console of Windows 2000 (see Figure 12.5).

2. Select the Add button on the System Monitor toolbar in the right pane. Notice that this launches the Add Counters dialog box (see Figure 12.6).

3. In the Performance object drop-down box, choose the Memory performance object.

4. Choose Select Counters From List and select the Available MBytes counter. Choose the Add button to add this counter to the chart view of System Monitor.

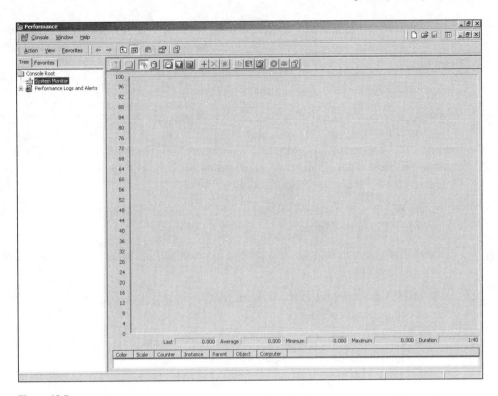

Figure 12.5
The Performance Console of Window 2000.

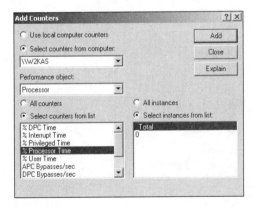

Figure 12.6
The Add Counters dialog box of System Monitor.

5. In the Performance Object drop-down menu, choose the **SQLServer:Memory Manager** object.

6. In the Select Counters From List box, choose Target Server Memory (KB). Choose the Add button to add this counter to the chart view of System Monitor.

Note: *This is the total amount of dynamic memory SQL Server 2000 is able to consume. You can compare this number against the total amount of memory available on the server.*

   7. Choose Close from the Add Counters dialog box.

As you can clearly see, the chart view of System Monitor is very useful for examining data in real-time. You may want to log data "behind the scenes" using System Monitor, and then view this data using any of the available views in System Monitor. You could also examine this logged data in other applications compatible with the log format. Follow these steps to log data using System Monitor:

1. Select Start|Programs|Administrative Tools|Performance to launch the Performance Console of Windows 2000.

2. Double-click the Performance Logs And Alerts object in the left pane of the Performance Console.

3. Right-click the Counter Logs object in the left pane and choose New Log Settings from the shortcut menu.

4. In the New Log Settings window, provide a name for the new log settings and choose OK. For this example, we'll use SQL Memory.

5. In the SQL Memory window (see Figure 12.7), note the location and name of the actual log file on your system.

6. Use the Add button to add counters to be collected in the log.

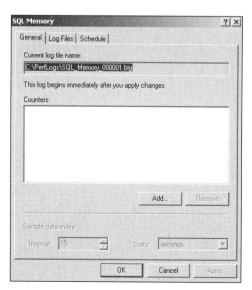

Figure 12.7
Configuring the log settings.

7. In the Performance Object drop-down box, choose the Memory performance object.

8. Choose Select Counters From List and select the Available MBytes counter and select the Add button.

9. In the Performance Object drop-down box, choose the SQLServer:Memory Manager object.

10. In the Select Counters From List drop-down, choose Target Server Memory (KB) and choose the Add button.

11. Choose Close from the Add Counters dialog box.

12. In the Sample Data Every area, choose the Units drop-down list to select Minutes. Notice that you are now collecting the log information every 15 minutes.

13. Choose the Log Files tab and review the possible configuration settings you can make here (see Figure 12.8).

14. Finally, choose the Schedule tab (see Figure 12.9) and review your options for starting and stopping the logging of the counters you selected.

15. When you are finished reviewing the settings, click the OK button to create the new log settings. Notice your log object appears in the right pane of the Performance Console. When the log begins collecting data, the icon turns green; when the logging stops, the icon appears red.

16. To manually stop logging, simply right-click the object and choose Stop from the shortcut menu.

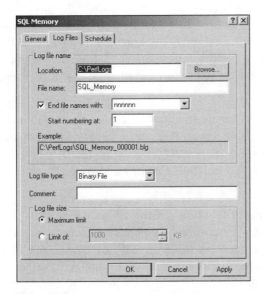

Figure 12.8
Log Files options for logging performance counters.

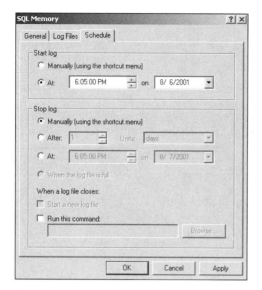

Figure 12.9
Setting a schedule for the starting and stopping of logging.

It is simple to view log results in the Performance Console. Simply open the System Monitor and use the View Log File Data button to navigate to the log file on your system and open it for viewing.

Monitoring Memory

As you have learned in previous chapters, SQL Server 2000 requires quite a bit of memory in a busy production environment. In fact, the more memory you provide the server, the better performance you can receive. SQL Server 2000 requires memory to run its services and perform basic server tasks, and memory is also needed for its data cache. This area of memory is also known as the buffer cache and dramatically impacts the performance of queries, because results can be stored in memory for faster presentation upon subsequent queries.

In its default configuration, SQL Server dynamically adjusts the amount of memory used for the buffer cache based upon the available resources on the system and the amount of competition for resources on the server. SQL Server 2000 always attempts to leave 4 to 10MB of memory free on the server to make sure that Windows 2000 operates properly and does not need to use paging.

Thanks to the many useful memory-related counters available in System Monitor, you should be able to easily monitor available memory and memory usage on your server to guarantee an optimal configuration. In order to provide you with guidance, Table 12.4 lists the most important counters for general memory monitoring and even provides specifics regarding values you should look for.

Table 12.4   Key counters for monitoring memory.

Counter	Description	Guideline
Memory:Available Bytes	Amount of physical memory available to processes running on the computer	Should always be greater than 5,000KB
Memory:Pages/sec	Number of pages read from or written to disk to resolve hard page faults, which occur when a process requires code or data that is not in its working set or elsewhere in physical memory and must be retrieved from disk	Should never be consistently greater than zero
Process:Page Faults/sec/SQL Server Instance	The rate at which page faults occur in the threads executing in the specified process	This number should never grow excessively high
Process:Working Set/SQL Server Instance	Current number of bytes in the working set of the specified process. The working set is the set of memory pages touched recently by the threads in the process	This should always be greater than 5,000KB
SQL Server:Buffer Manager: Buffer Cache Hit Ratio	Percentage of pages that were found in the buffer pool without having to incur a read from disk	This should be greater than 90 for maximum performance
SQL Server:Buffer Manager: Total Pages	Number of pages in the buffer pool (includes database, free, and stolen)	Lower numbers indicate memory may be running low
SQL Server:Memory Manager: Total Server Memory	Total amount of dynamic memory the server is currently consuming	Should not be consistently high in comparison to the amount of physical memory available

12

Monitoring the Processor

As you know, SQL Server 2000 is also processor intensive. In fact, complex queries or large data transfers can actually utilize 100 percent of the available processor. Use the counters listed in Table 12.5 to determine if your processor is up to the task of maintaining your SQL Server 2000 system. If you are using multiple processors, be sure to use the Instance area when selecting your counters to be certain you are examining all processors.

Table 12.5   Key counters for monitoring the processor.

Counter	Description	Guideline
Processor:% Processor Time	Percentage of time that the processor is executing a non-idle thread	Should be less than 90 percent over time; some installations will require a substantially lower figure
System:Context Switches/sec	Combined rate at which all processors on the computer are switched from one thread to another	Should not reach 8000 with Processor: % Processor Time over 90 percent
System:Processor Queue Length	Number of threads in the processor queue	Should never be consistently greater than 2
Processor:% Privileged Time	Percentage of non-idle processor time spent in privileged mode	If this number trends high and physical hard disk counters are high, consider improving the performance of hard disk systems
Processor:% User Time	Percentage of non-idle processor time spent in user mode	Can be used to indicate that other processes or applications are executing and preventing SQL Server operations

Monitoring Hard Disk Activity

Hard disk performance is critical for your SQL Server implementation. Your SQL Server may need to access data from the drive system so often that these needs exceed the capabilities of this drive system. Remember, however, that shortages of memory may produce an excessive amount of hard disk I/O as a result of increased paging of information to disk from memory.

You should use the counters presented in Table 12.6 when using System Monitor to monitor hard disk activity:

Table 12.6   Key counters for monitoring the disk system.

Counter	Description	Guideline
PhysicalDisk:% Disk Time	The percentage of elapsed time that the selected disk drive is busy servicing read or write requests	This should always be less than 90 percent
PhysicalDisk:Avg. Disk Queue Length	The average number of both read and write requests that were queued for the selected disk during the sample interval	This counter should be no more than 2 times the number of spindles
PhysicalDisk:Disk Reads/Sec	The rate of read operations on the disk	Should be consistently less than the capacity of your hard drive system
PhysicalDisk:Disk Writes/sec	Monitors the rate of write operations	Should be consistently less than the capacity of your hard drive system

Current Activity Window

Another tool available to you for monitoring SQL Server 2000 is the Current Activity window. This tool is built into SQL Server; in fact, it appears in the SQL Server Enterprise Manager console. Follow these steps to access this monitoring tool:

1. Select Start|Programs|Microsoft SQL Server|Enterprise Manager to launch the Enterprise Manager console.

2. Expand your appropriate server instance in the left pane.

3. Expand the Management object, then expand the Current Activity object (see Figure 12.10).

4. Select a particular object in the left pane of the Current Activity object in order to view details for that object in the right pane.

12

Notice the Current Activity window allows you to view information about current user connections and locks on resources. You may also view the process number, status, locks, and statements that active users are running.

In order for you to effectively interpret the Current Activity window information, you should use the following tables that explain the objects and parameters you see displayed. First, Table 12.7 displays the icons found in the Current Activity window and their meaning.

When you are examining process information in the Current Activity window, you should note how many fields of information are displayed. The explanation of this information is provided in Table 12.8, which describes the process information fields.

Notice also that the Current Activity window provides information regarding locks in SQL Server 2000. Table 12.9 describes the lock information that may be presented.

As a system administrator, you can also use the Current Activity window to send a message to a user who is connected currently to SQL Server, or terminate a selected process. Follow these steps to use the Current Activity window to send a message to a connected user:

1. Select Start|Programs|Microsoft SQL Server|Enterprise Manager.

2. Expand the appropriate server instance in the left pane.

3. Expand the Management object, then expand the Current Activity object.

4. Choose Process Info in the left pane. Notice that the current server activity displays in the right pane.

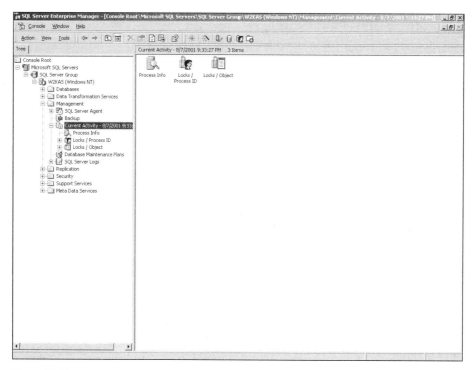

Figure 12.10
The Current Activity options in Enterprise Manager.

5. Right-click the Process ID associated with the user you need to communicate with and click Send Message.

Note: It is not possible to send a message to a user when SQL Server Enterprise Manager is running on Windows 98.

6. In the Message dialog box, type the message you would like to send to the SQL user. Note that you may also select Using Hostname, and enter the computer name in order to send the message to a specific computer.

As you probably noticed during the above steps for sending a message to a SQL user, killing a process is just as simple. Follow the above steps, and when you right-click a Process ID, choose Kill Process from the shortcut menu.

Transact-SQL Tools

This section will explore many Transact-SQL tools available to you for monitoring SQL Server 2000 performance. If you need to review the use of Transact-SQL, be sure to revisit Chapter 3 of this book.

Table 12.7   The icons of the Current Activity window.

Icon	Description
	Current Activity gives process and lock information at a designated time
	Process Info provides information about the current connections and activity in a system
	Running process that is waiting for a lock or user input
	Sleeping process that is waiting for a lock or user input
	Background process that wakes up periodically to execute work
	Process (SPID) that is blocking one or more connections
	Process (SPID) that is blocked by another connection
	Running process that is not blocking or being blocked
	Process that is not blocking or being blocked
	Table lock
	Database lock

Table 12.8   Process Information fields of the Current Activity window.

Item	Explanation
Process ID	SQL Server Process ID
Context ID	Execution context ID used to uniquely identify the subthreads operating on behalf of a single process
User	ID of the user who executed the command

(continued)

Table 12.8   Process Information fields of the Current Activity window *(continued)*.

Item	Explanation
Database	Database currently being used by the process
Status	Status of the process
Open Transactions	Number of open transactions for the process
Command	Command currently being executed
Application	Name of the application program being used by the process
Wait Time	Current wait time in milliseconds
Wait Type	Indicates the name of the last or current wait type
Wait Resources	Textual representation of a lock resource
CPU	Cumulative CPU time for the process
Physical IO	Cumulative disk reads and writes for the process
Memory Usage	Number of pages in the procedure cache that are currently allocated to this process
Login Time	Time at which a client process logged into the server
Last Batch	Last time a client process executed a remote stored procedure call or an **EXECUTE** statement
Host	Name of the workstation
Network Library	Column in which the client's network library is stored
Network Address	Assigned unique identifier for the network interface card on each user's workstation
Blocked By	Process ID (SPID) of a blocking process
Blocking	Process ID (SPID) of processes that are blocked

Table 12.9   Lock information found in the Current Activity window.

Item	Type	Description
spid	spid	Server process ID of the current user process
ecid	ecid	Execution context ID
Lock type	RID	Row identifier
	KEY	A row lock within an index
	PAG	Data or index page
	EXT	Contiguous group of eight data pages or index pages
	TAB	Entire table including all data and indexes
	DB	Database
Lock mode	Shared (S)	Used for operations that do not change or update data (read-only operations), such as a **SELECT** statement

(continued)

Table 12.9   Lock information found in the Current Activity window *(continued)*.

Item	Type	Description
	Update (U)	Used on resources that can be updated
	Exclusive (X)	Used for data modification operations, such as **UPDATE**, **INSERT**, or **DELETE**
	Intent	Used to establish a lock hierarchy
	Schema	Used when an operation dependent on the schema of a table is executing
	Bulk update (BU)	Used when bulk copying data into a table and the TABLOCK hint is specified
	RangeS_S	Shared range, shared resource lock; serializable range scan
	RangeS_U	Shared range, update resource lock; serializable update scan
	RangeI_N	Insert range, null resource lock. Used to test ranges before inserting a new key into an index
	RangeX_X	Exclusive range, exclusive resource lock. Used when updating a key in a range
Status	GRANT	Lock was obtained
	WAIT	Lock was blocked by another process
	CNVT	Lock is being converted to another lock
Owner	Owner	The lock owner
Index	Index	The index associated with the resource
Resource	RID	Row identifier of the locked row within the table
	KEY	Hexadecimal number used internally by SQL Server
	PAG	Page number
	EXT	First page number in the extent being locked
	TAB	No information is provided because the **Objld** column already contains the object ID of the table
	DB	No information is provided because the **dbid** column already contains the database ID of the database

System Stored Procedures

Remember, stored procedures are objects that can contain multiple T-SQL statements that execute on the server together as a batch, which results in optimal performance and assists in administration and server usage. Many of these procedures, described in Table 12.10 are designed to assist you in monitoring the server.

This example demonstrates using the osql utility to quickly and efficiently access current SQL Server statistics:

12

1. Select Start|Programs|Accessories|Command Prompt.

2. In the Command Prompt, type "osql -E" and press Enter to start the osql utility in the context of the currently logged on user.

3. At the first line prompt for osql, type "EXEC sp_monitor" and press Enter.

4. At the second line prompt, type "GO" and press Enter to execute the query.

5. Note that the results of the query display in the command prompt (see Figure 12.11).

Global Variables

There are many global variables in Transact-SQL that you may use to query specific SQL Server 2000 statistics that measure performance. Table 12.11 details these global variables for you.

In the following example, you use Query Analyzer and global variables to monitor SQL Server 2000:

1. Select Start|Programs|Microsoft SQL Server|Query Analyzer in order to launch the SQL Server Query Analyzer.

2. Select OK to log on to the server using Windows Authentication.

3. In the query window, type the following query:

```
SELECT @@servername
SELECT @@idle
```

4. Press the F5 key on the keyboard to execute the query.

Table 12.10   System stored procedures for monitoring SQL Server 2000.

Procedure	Usage
sp_who	View current SQL Server users and processes
sp_who2	Another view of current users and their processes but with additional information reported
sp_lock	View current locks
sp_spaceused	View amount of disk space a table or database uses
sp_helpdb	View databases and their objects
sp_monitor	View SQL Server statistics including CPU usage and idle time
sp_helpindex	View indexes on a table
sp_statistics	View all indexes on a specific table

5. Note the results displayed in the Grids area of the query pane (see Figure 12.12). The query provides the name of the local computer running SQL Server and the time in milliseconds that the processor has been idle.

Transact-SQL Statements

There are several Transact-SQL statements that are critical for successful monitoring of your SQL Server installation. Table 12.12 details these statements for you.

This example demonstrates the use of **SET SHOWPLAN_ALL** in Query Analyzer:

1. Select Start|Programs|Microsoft SQL Server|Query Analyzer in order to launch the SQL Server Query Analyzer.

2. Select OK to log on to the server using Windows Authentication.

3. In the query window, type the following query:

```
USE pubs
GO
SET SHOWPLAN_ALL ON
GO
SELECT au_id
FROM authors
WHERE au_id = '409-56-7008'
GO
SET SHOWPLAN_ALL OFF
```

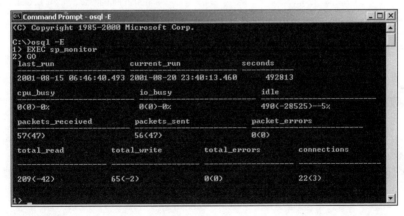

Figure 12.11
Using a system stored procedure to monitor SQL Server 2000.

Table 12.11   Global variables for gathering performance statistics.

Global variable	Usage
@@connections	Displays view the number of logins or attempted logins since SQL Server was last started
@@error	Shows the error number for the last T-SQL statement executed
@@spid	Shows the server process ID of the current user process
@@procid	Shows the stored procedure ID of the current procedure
@@cpu_busy	Displays the time in milliseconds that the processor has spent working
@@idle	Shows the time in milliseconds that the processor has been idle
@@io_busy	Shows the time in milliseconds that SQL Server has spent performing input and output operations
@@pack_received	Shows the number of input packets read from the network
@@pack_sent	Shows the number of output packets written to the network
@@packet_errors	Shows the number of network packet errors that have occurred on connections
@@total_errors	Displays the number of disk read/write errors encountered
@@total_read	Shows the total number of disk reads
@@total_write	Shows the total number of disk writes
@@cursor_rows	Returns the number of qualifying rows currently in the last cursor opened on the connection
@@fetch_status	Returns the status of the last cursor **FETCH** statement issued against any cursor currently opened by the connection
@@lock_timeout	Returns the current lock timeout setting, in milliseconds, for the current session
@@max_connections	Returns the maximum number of simultaneous user connections allowed on a SQL Server
@@remserver	Returns the name of the remote SQL Server database server as it appears in the login record
@@rowcount	Returns the number of rows affected by the last statement
@@servername	Returns the name of the local server running SQL Server
@@servicename	Returns the name of the registry key under which SQL Server is running
@@trancount	Returns the number of active transactions for the current connection
@@version	Returns the date, version, and processor type for the current installation of SQL Server

4. Notice that the results from this query display how the query will execute and the estimated resources used (see Figure 12.13).

DBCC

DBCC statements also help you to monitor SQL Server. DBCC stands for Database Consistency Checker and more and more of these statements have been built for SQL Server over the years with the intent of allowing you to more effectively monitor the server and its health. Table 12.13 describes these statements.

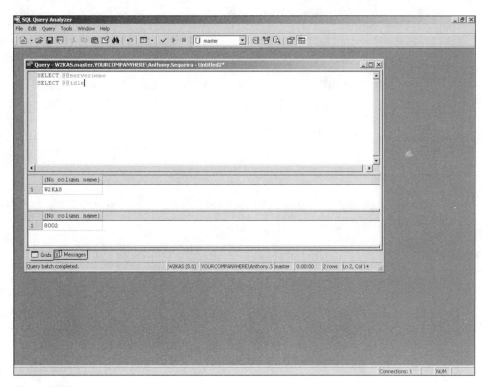

Figure 12.12
Using global variables to monitor the server.

Table 12.12   Transact-SQL statements for monitoring the server.

Statement	Usage
set statistics IO	Displays information regarding the amount of disk activity T-SQL statements generate
set statistics time	Shows the number of milliseconds required to parse, compile, and execute each statement
set statistics profile	Displays a result set after each executed query representing a profile of the execution of the query
set showplan_text on/off	Causes SQL Server not to execute the query and returns detailed information about how the statements are executed
set noexec	Compiles a query but does not execute it
set showplan_all	Causes SQL Server not to execute the T-SQL statements, returns detailed information about how the statements are executed, and provides estimates of the resource requirements for the statements
set forceplan	Causes the SQL Server query optimizer to process a join in the same order as tables appear in the **FROM** clause of a **SELECT** statement only

You should consult Books Online for the specific parameters to use with any of these DBCC commands. Here is an example of using the **DBCC SQLPERF** command to view transaction log information for all of the databases currently installed on your server:

1. Select Start|Programs|Accessories|Command Prompt.

2. In the command prompt, type "osql -E" and press Enter to start the osql utility in the context of the currently logged on user.

3. At the first line prompt for osql, type "DBCC SQLPERF (LOGSPACE)" and press Enter.

4. At the second line prompt, type "GO" and press Enter to execute the query.

5. Notice that the results of this query are displayed in the command prompt window (see Figure 12.14).

Note: Alternatively, you can execute the DBCC commands within Query Analyzer.

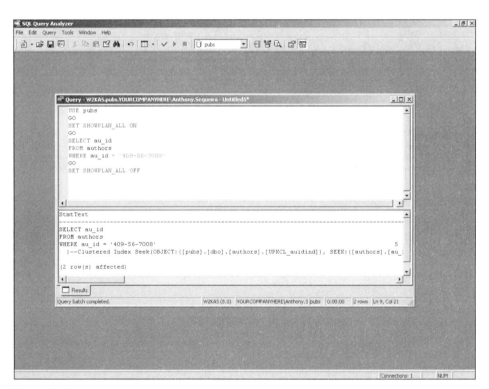

Figure 12.13
Using the **SET SHOWPLAN_ALL** statement.

Trace Flags

You use trace flags to temporarily set specific server characteristics or to switch off a particular behavior. For example, if you set trace flag 3205, hardware compression for tape drivers is disabled. You can use these trace flags to diagnose performance issues or to debug stored procedures. Table 12.14 presents some popular trace flags for use with SQL Server 2000.

Table 12.13   DBCC statements.

Statement	Usage
DBCC CHECKALLOC	Checks the consistency of disk space allocation structures for a specified database
DBCC CHECKCATALOG	Chocks for consistency in and between system tables in the specified database
DBCC CHECKCONSTRAINTS	Checks the integrity of a specified constraint or all constraints on a specified table
DBCC CHECKDB	Checks the allocation and structural integrity of all the objects in the specified database
DBCC CHECKFILEGROUP	Checks the allocation and structural integrity of all tables (in the current database) in the specified filegroup
DBCC CHECKIDENT	Checks the current identity value for the specified table and, if needed, corrects the identity value
DBCC CHECKTABLE	Checks the integrity of the data, index, text, ntext, and image pages for the specified table or indexed view
DBCC CLEANTABLE	Reclaims space for dropped variable length columns and text columns
DBCC CONCURRENCYVIOLATION	Displays statistics on how many times more than five batches were executed concurrently on SQL Server 2000 Desktop Engine or SQL Server 2000 Personal Edition
DBCC DBREPAIR	Drops a damaged database
DBCC DBREINDEX	Rebuilds one or more indexes for a table in the specified database
DBCC *dllname* (FREE)	Unloads the specified extended stored procedure dynamic-link library (DLL) from memory
DBCC DROPCLEANBUFFERS	Removes all clean buffers from the buffer pool
DBCC FREEPROCCACHE	Removes all elements from the procedure cache
DBCC HELP	Returns syntax information for the specified DBCC statement
DBCC INDEXDEFRAG	Defragments clustered and secondary indexes of the specified table or view
DBCC INPUTBUFFER	Displays the last statement sent from a client to SQL Server
DBCC NEWALLOC	Checks the allocation of data and index pages for each table within the extent structures of the database
DBCC OPENTRAN	Displays information about the oldest active transaction and the oldest distributed and nondistributed replicated transactions, if any, within the specified database
DBCC OUTPUTBUFFER	Returns the current output buffer in hexadecimal and ASCII format for the specified system process ID (SPID)
DBCC PINTABLE	Marks a table to be pinned, which means SQL Server does not flush the pages for the table from memory

12

(continued)

Table 12.13   DBCC statements *(continued)*.

Statement	Usage
DBCC PROCCACHE	Displays information in a table format about the procedure cache
DBCC ROWLOCK	Used for SQL Server version 6.5, enabling Insert Row Locking (IRL) operations on tables
DBCC SHOWCONTIG	Displays fragmentation information for the data and indexes of the specified table
DBCC SHOW_STATISTICS	Displays the current distribution statistics for the specified target on the specified table
DBCC SHRINKDATABASE	Shrinks the size of the data files in the specified database
DBCC SHRINKFILE	Shrinks the size of the specified data file or log file for the related database
DBCC SQLPERF	Provides statistics about the use of transaction-log space in all databases
DBCC TRACEOFF	Disables the specified trace flag(s)
DBCC TRACEON	Turns on (enables) the specified trace flag(s)
DBCC TRACESTATUS	Displays the status of trace flags
DBCC UNPINTABLE	Marks a table as unpinned
DBCC UPDATEUSAGE	Reports and corrects inaccuracies in the **sysindexes** table, which may result in incorrect space usage reports by the **sp_spaceused** system stored procedure
DBCC USEROPTIONS	Returns the **SET** options active (set) for the current connection

You can use the **DBCC TRACEON** command to enable any of these traces. For example, the following code turns on trace flag 3205:

```
DBCC TRACEON (3205)
```

SNMP

You may also use Simple Network Management Protocol (SNMP) to monitor SQL Server 2000. SNMP is an application protocol that offers network management services. Thanks to this powerful protocol, you can monitor an instance of SQL Server from many other operating system platforms, including Unix and other non-Windows NT based systems.

SNMP works with SQL Server because SQL Server 2000 is equipped with the Microsoft SQL Server Management Information Base (MSSQL-MIB). Thanks to this SNMP Management Information Base, you can use SNMP applications to monitor the status of SQL Server installations, including the monitoring of performance information, database access information, and server and database configuration parameters. The MSSQL-MIB is implemented using the following file—C:/ProgramFiles/MicrosoftSQLServer/MSSQL/Binn/Mssql.mib.

SQL Server 2000 is also equipped with an SNMP Agent. This SQL Server SNMP agent exists as a Dynamic Link Library (DLL) file called Sqlsnmp.dll, located in the same directory as the mssql.mib. This DLL extends the functionality of the SNMP service

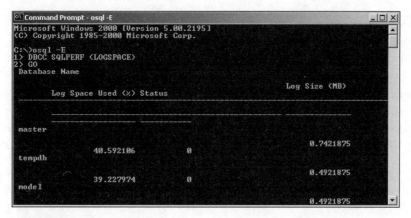

Figure 12.14
Using a DBCC command to monitor SQL Server 2000.

12

Table 12.14   Trace flags.

Trace Flag	Usage
260	Prints version information about extended stored procedure dynamic-link libraries (DLLs)
1204	Returns the type of locks participating in the deadlock and the current command affected
2528	Disables parallel checking of objects by **DBCC CHECKDB**, **DBCC CHECKFILEGROUP**, and **DBCC CHECKTABLE**
3205	Disables hardware compression for tape drivers

running within SQL Server and processes requests for data and data objects that reside on the local server.

SNMP support for SQL Server 2000 is enabled automatically for you as long as the operating system you install SQL on has SNMP support properly configured. This support must be configured properly upon installation of SQL Server 2000 or SNMP support will not be properly implemented in SQL Server.

For SNMP applications to successfully monitor the status of a SQL Server installation, you must place a copy of MSSQL-MIB (remember this is implemented in Mssql.mib) on the monitoring workstation, and this copy must be loaded into the SNMP application. Mssql.mib is a text file that contains the definitions of objects available to SNMP workstations. This file consists of read-only variables for monitoring general performance counters and monitoring the status of SQL Server installations and databases. The variables also provide limited discovery of configuration options and database files.

You will need to check the documentation of your specific SNMP monitoring application for any other steps that may be necessary.

SQL Profiler

You can use SQL Profiler to closely monitor stored procedures and Transact-SQL batches. This application functions by intelligently capturing events from SQL Server 2000 and saving them in a trace file. You can later analyze or replay a specific series of steps when diagnosing performance problems. You can use SQL Profiler for such activities as stepping through problematic queries to find the cause of the issue or monitoring the performance of SQL Server to tune workloads. You can also use SQL Profiler for auditing the actions performed on instances of SQL Server. These audits record security-related actions for your review.

Before you can fully master the use of Profiler, you should become familiar with the following terminology:

- *Template*—A Profiler template defines the criteria for each event you want to monitor. Once you define a template, you can use it to start a trace anytime you need to monitor those specific events defined in the template. Profiler templates use a .tdf file extension.

- *Trace*—The trace is the main component of SQL Profiler. You use a trace to gather specific events you need to monitor. Often you create the trace based upon a template you created in Profiler. Once you create a trace, you can analyze it immediately, or you can save it and replay it at any time for analysis.

- *Filter*—When you create a trace or template, you typically define criteria to filter the data collected. If you do not use a filter, you collect much more data than is useful, and you can seriously impede the performance of SQL Server 2000.

- *Event Category*—Event categories define the way events are grouped. For example, all lock events classes are grouped within the Locks event category.

- *Event*—Events are actions generated within the SQL Server engine. All of the data that is generated as a result of an event is displayed in the trace in a single row. This row contains columns of data called event classes that describe the event in detail. Examples of events include login connections, failures, and disconnections; Transact-SQL **SELECT**, **INSERT**, **UPDATE**, and **DELETE** statements; the start or end of statements within stored procedures; or an error written to the SQL Server error log. There are many more examples to provide robust monitoring capabilities.

- *Event Class*—An event class is the column that describes the event that was produced by the server. The event class determines the type of data collected. Keep in mind that not all data columns are applicable to all event classes. Examples of event classes include **SQL:BatchCompleted** which indicates the completion of a SQL batch; the name of the computer on which the client is running; and the ID of the object affected by the event, such as a table name.

• *Data Column*—Data columns describe the data collected for each of the event classes captured in the trace. Default data columns are populated automatically for all event classes.

As you can see from the above definitions, you should definitely consider creating Profiler templates for efficient monitoring with the tool. In fact, you should consider the following trace templates:

• *Long-running queries*—This template should capture all data columns related to TSQL and Stored Procedure event classes and then be grouped by Duration and filtered by length of time.

• *Stored procedure performance*—This template should capture all data columns related to the selected Stored Procedure event classes and then should be grouped by **ClientProcessID**.

• *Cause of a deadlock*—This template should capture all data columns related to selected TSQL and Stored Procedure event classes, and then group by **EventClass**. The **Database ID** event allows you to limit the analysis to a specific database.

• *Login and logouts*—This template should capture the **EventClass**, **EventSubClass**, **LoginSID**, and **Login** data columns for the Security Audit/Audit Login event class.

• *Individual user activity*—This template should capture all data columns related to the Sessions/ExistingConnection and TSQL event classes and should group these by **DBUserName**.

Obviously, in order to build effective Profiler templates, you must understand the event categories and event classes available to you. Refer to Table 12.15 for this information.

Follow these steps to create a template in SQL Server Profiler:

1. Select Start|Programs|Microsoft SQL Server|Profiler (see Figure 12.15).

2. Choose the File|New|Trace Template (see Figure 12.16).

3. Use the Save As button on the General tab to save the template in a particular location and name the template.

4. Select the Events tab and in the Available event classes area, expand the Stored Procedures node.

5. Select the **RPC:Completed** event class and choose the Add button. Do the same for the **SQL:BatchCompleted** event class of the TSQL category (see Figure 12.17).

6. Select the Data Columns tab, choose Duration in the Unselected Data area and use the Add button to add this column to the Selected Data area (see Figure 12.18).

Table 12.15   Profiler event classes.

Event Category	Event Classes	Description
SQL Profiler Default	**Audit Login Event**	Collects all new connection events since the trace was started
	Audit Logout Event	Collects all new disconnect events since the trace was started
	ExistingConnection	Detects activity by all users connected to an instance of SQL Server before the trace was started
	RPC:Completed	Indicates that a remote procedure call (RPC) has completed
	SQL:BatchCompleted	Indicates that a transact-SQL batch has completed
Cursors	**CursorClose**	Indicates a cursor previously opened on a T-SQL statement by ODBC, OLE DB, or DB-Library is closed
	CursorExecute	Indicates a cursor previously prepared on a T-SQL statement by ODBC, OLE DB, or DB-Library is executed
	CursorImplicitConversion	Indicates a cursor on a T-SQL statement is converted by SQL Server from one type to another
	CursorOpen	Indicates a cursor is open on a T-SQL statement by ODBC, OLE DB, or DB-Library
	CursorPrepare	Indicates a cursor on a T-SQL statement is prepared for use by ODBC, OLE DB, or DB-Library
	CursorRecompile	Indicates that a cursor is open on a T-SQL statement by ODBC or that a DB-Library has been recompiled either directly or indirectly due to a schema change
	CursorUnprepare	Indicates that a prepared cursor on a T-SQL statement is deleted by ODBC, OLE DB, or DB-Library
Database	**DataFileAutoGrow**	Indicates that the data file grew automatically
	DataFileAutoShrink	Indicates that the data file has been shrunk
	LogFileAutoGrow	Indicates that the log file grew automatically
	LogFileAutoShrink	Indicates that the log file has been shrunk
Errors and Warnings	**Attention**	Collects all attention events, such as client-interrupt requests or broken client connections
	ErrorLog	Error events have been logged in the SQL Server error log
	EventLog	Events have been logged in the Windows application log
	Exception	Exception has occurred in SQL Server
	Execution Warnings	Any warnings that occurred during the execution of a SQL Server statement or stored procedure
	Hash Warning	Hashing operation may have encountered a problem
	Missing Column Statistics	Column statistics for the query optimizer are not available
	Missing Join Predicate	Executing query has no join predicate

(continued)

Table 12.15 Profiler event classes *(continued)*.

Event Category	Event Classes	Description
	OLEDB Errors	OLE DB error has occurred
	Sort Warnings	Sort operations do not fit into memory
Locks	**Lock:Acquired**	Acquisition of a lock on a resource, such as a data page, has been achieved
	Lock:Cancel	Acquisition of a lock on a resource has been canceled
	Lock:Deadlock	Two concurrent transactions have deadlocked each other by trying to obtain incompatible locks on resources that the other transaction owns
	Lock:Deadlock Chain	This event is produced for each of the events leading up to the deadlock
	Lock:Escalation	A finer-grained lock has been converted to a coarser-grained lock
	Lock:Released	A lock on a resource, such as a page, has been released
	Lock:Timeout	A request for a lock on a resource, such as a page, has timed out due to another transaction holding a blocking lock on the required resource
Objects	**Auto Stats**	Indicates when the automatic creation and updating of statistics has occurred
	Object:Closed	Indicates when an open object has been closed
	Object:Created	Object has been created
	Object:Deleted	Object has been deleted
	Object:Opened	Indicates when an object has been accessed
Performance	**Degree Of Parallelism1**	Describes the degree of parallelism assigned to the SQL statement; if you are tracing a SQL Server 7 server, this event will trace an **INSERT** statement
	Degree of Parallelism2	Describes the degree of parallelism assigned to the SQL statement; if you are tracing a SQL Server 7 server, this event will trace an **UPDATE** statement
	Degree of Parallelism3	Describes the degree of parallelism assigned to the SQL statement; if you are tracing a SQL Server 7 server, this event will trace a **DELETE** statement
	Degree of Parallelism4	Describes the degree of parallelism assigned to the SQL statement; if you are tracing a SQL Server 7 server, this event will trace a **SELECT** statement
	Execution Plan	Displays the plan tree of the SQL statement being executed
	Show Plan All	Displays the query plan with full compile-time details of the SQL statement being executed

12

(continued)

Table 12.15   Profiler event classes *(continued).*

Event Category	Event Classes	Description
	Show Plan Statistics	Displays the query plan with full run-time details, including actual number of rows passing through each operation of the SQL statement that was executed
	Show Plan Text	Displays the query plan tree of the SQL statement being executed
Scans	**Scan: Started**	Table or index scan has started
	Scan: Stopped	Table or index scan has stopped
Security Audit	**Audit Add DB User Event**	Records the addition and removal of database users
	Audit Add Login to Server Role Event	Records the addition or removal of logins to and from a fixed server role for **sp_addsrvrolemember** and **sp_dropsrvrolemember**
	Audit Add Member to DB Role Event	Records the addition and removal of members to and from a database role (fixed or user-defined) for **sp_addrolemember**, **sp_droprolemember**, and **sp_changegroup**
	Audit Add Role Event	Records add or drop actions on database roles for **sp_addrole** and **sp_droprole**
	Audit Addlogin Event	Records add and drop actions on SQL Server logins for **sp_addlogin** and **sp_droplogin**
	Audit App Role Change Password Event	Records changes to the password of an application
	Audit Backup/Restore Event	Records **BACKUP** and **RESTORE** events
	Audit Change Audit Event	Records **AUDIT** modifications
	Audit DBCC Event	Records **DBCC** commands that have been issued
	Audit Login Event	Collects all new connection events since the trace was started
	Audit Login Change Password Event	Records SQL Server login password changes
	Audit Login Change Property Event	Records modifications on login property, except passwords for **sp_defaultdb** and **sp_defaultlanguage**
	Audit Login Failed Event	Indicates that a login attempt to an instance of SQL Server from a client has failed
	Audit Login GDR Event	Records **GRANT**, **REVOKE**, and **DENY** actions on Windows NT 4 or Windows 2000 account login rights for **sp_grantlogin**, **sp_revokelogin**, and **sp_denylogin**
	Audit Logout Event	Collects all new disconnect events since the trace was started, such as when a client issues a disconnect command

(continued)

Table 12.15   Profiler event classes (continued).

Event Category	Event Classes	Description
	Audit Object Derived Permission Event	Records when a **CREATE**, **ALTER**, or **DROP** command is issued for the specified object
	Audit Object GDR Event	Records permissions events for **GRANT**, **DENY**, **REVOKE** objects
	Audit Object Permission Event	Records the successful or unsuccessful use of object permissions
	Audit Server Starts and Stops Event	Records shut down, start, and pause activities for services
	Audit Statement GDR Event	Records permission events for **GRANT**, **DENY**, **REVOKE** statements
	Audit Statement Permission Event	Records the use of statement permissions
Sessions	**ExistingConnection**	Detects activity by all users connected to SQL Server before the trace was started
Stored Procedures	**RPC Output Parameter**	Displays information about output parameters of a previously executed remote procedure call (RPC)
	RPC:Completed	Occurs when an RPC has been completed
	RPC:Starting	Occurs when an RPC has started
	SP:CacheHit	Procedure is found in the cache
	SP:CacheInsert	Item is inserted into the procedure cache
	SP:CacheMiss	Stored procedure is not found in the procedure cache
	SP:CacheRemove	Item has been removed from the procedure cache
	SP:Completed	Stored procedure has completed
	SP: ExecContextHit	Execution version of a stored procedure has been found in the cache
	SP:Recompile	Stored procedure has been recompiled
	SP:Starting	Stored procedure has started
	SP: StmtCompleted	Statement within a stored procedure has completed
	SP:StmtStarting	Statement within a stored procedure has started
Transactions	**DTCTransaction**	Tracks Distributed Transaction Coordinator (MS DTC) coordinated transactions between two or more databases
	SQLTransaction	Tracks Transact-SQL **BEGIN**, **COMMIT**, **SAVE**, and **ROLLBACK TRANSACTION** statements
	TransactionLog	Tracks when transactions are written to the transaction log
TSQL	**Exec Prepared SQL**	Indicates when a prepared SQL statement or statements have been executed by ODBC, OLEDB, or DB-Library

12

(continued)

Table 12.15 Profiler event classes *(continued).*

Event Category	Event Classes	Description
	Prepare SQL	Indicates when SQL statement or statements have been prepared for use by ODBC, OLEDB, or DB-Library
	SQL:BatchCompleted	Transact-SQL batch has completed
	SQL:BatchStarting	Transact-SQL batch has started
	SQL:StmtCompleted	Transact-SQL statement has completed
	SQL:StmtStarting	Transact-SQL statement has started
	Unprepare SQL	Indicates when a prepared SQL statement or statements have been unprepared by ODBC, OLEDB, or DB-Library
User Configurable	**UserConfigurable (0-9)**	Event data defined by the user

7. Select the Filters tab and expand the DatabaseName node, then expand the Like node.

8. Type Northwind in the Like text box and press Enter (see Figure 12.19).

Figure 12.15
Microsoft SQL Server Profiler.

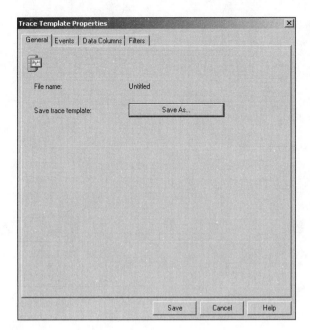

Figure 12.16
The Trace Template Properties window.

9. Expand the Duration node and then the Greater Than Or Equal node.

10. Type 100 in the text box and press Enter.

11. Choose Save in the Trace Template Properties window to save your trace template.

Now you should practice using your trace template to actually create a trace in SQL Profiler. But first, follow these steps to create sample T-SQL batches to run against Northwind in order to effectively test your trace template:

1. Select Start|Programs|Microsoft SQL Server|Query Analyzer.

2. Select OK in the Connect To SQL Server dialog box in order to connect to SQL Server using Windows authentication.

3. Input the following queries in the empty query window that appears:

```
USE Northwind
SELECT * FROM Products
GO
--
SELECT ProductName, UnitPrice, UnitsInStock
FROM Products
```

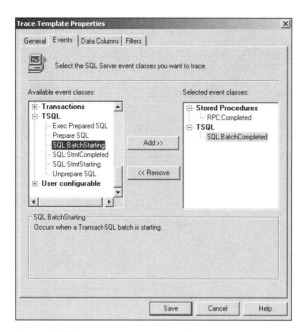

Figure 12.17
Configuring the events for your trace template.

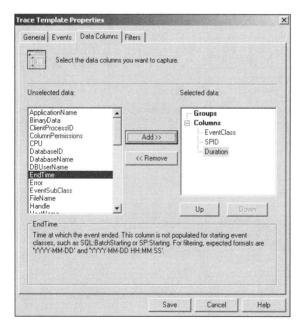

Figure 12.18
Choosing the data columns for your trace template.

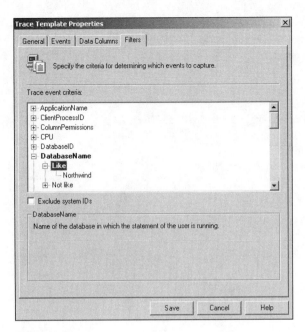

Figure 12.19
Completing the Filters tab.

```
WHERE ProductName LIKE 'D%'
GO
--
SELECT CompanyName, ContactName, Phone
FROM Customers
WHERE CustomerID = 'FOLKO'
GO
--
SELECT ProductName, UnitPrice
FROM Products
WHERE UnitPrice >= 1
GO
--
SELECT c.CompanyName, p.ProductName, SUM(d.Quantity * d.UnitPrice)
FROM Customers c JOIN Orders o ON c.CustomerID = o.CustomerID
JOIN [Order Details] d ON o.OrderID = d.OrderID
JOIN Products p ON d.ProductID = p.ProductID
WHERE p.ProductID in (6, 9, 12)
GROUP BY c.CompanyName, p.ProductName
GO
--
```

```
SELECT p.ProductName, SUM(d.Quantity * d.UnitPrice)
FROM [Order Details] d JOIN Products p
ON d.ProductID =  p.ProductID
GROUP BY p.ProductName
GO
--
SELECT e.LastName, e.FirstName, COUNT(o.OrderID)
FROM Employees e JOIN Orders o
ON e.EmployeeID = o.EmployeeID
GROUP BY e.LastName, e.FirstName
GO
--
EXEC sp_help
GO
--
EXEC sp_monitor
GO
--
EXEC sp_lock
GO
```

4. Notice that there are a variety of queries in this batch that should take varying amounts of time to execute against the Northwind database. Remember, your trace template is constructed to report on queries or stored procedures executed against the Northwind database that take longer than 100 milliseconds to execute.

5. Do not execute the scripts in this query window yet. You are first going to launch a trace based upon your trace template, and then you will execute the query in order to view the trace results.

In order to create and run a trace based on your trace template, follow these steps:

1. Select Start|Programs|Microsoft SQL Server|Profiler.

2. Choose File|New|Trace.

3. Choose OK in the Connect To SQL Server dialog box.

4. In the Trace Properties window, provide a name for the trace in the Trace Name field (see Figure 12.20) and select the Profiler template you created earlier in the Template Name drop-down list.

5. Choose the Run button to begin the trace. Notice the trace window that appears and notice the entry indicating your trace has started (see Figure 12.21).

6. Switch to the Query Analyzer and press the F5 key to execute the queries you entered earlier.

7. Switch back to the Profiler. Notice that the queries that took longer than 100 milliseconds to execute (see Figure 12.22) are displayed in the trace along with the exact time of execution.

8. Use the Stop button on the toolbar to stop the trace. Notice you can use the File menu to save the trace in a number of formats in case you need this information later.

SQL Query Analyzer

By this point in the book, you have used Query Analyzer many times. As you know, this important graphical tool allows you to test and execute queries against SQL Server. But many do not realize the powerful abilities this tool has for monitoring query performance and helping to optimize server activities.

Query Analyzer is able to perform these tasks thanks to the following features:

• *Show Query Execution Plan*—Displaying the execution plan for your queries allows you to view the actual data retrieval methods used by the query optimizer when it executes your queries. This provides a detailed definition of the exact sequence in which source tables are accessed and the methods used to extract data from each table.

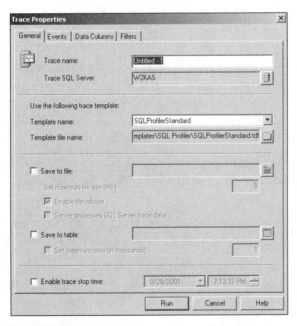

Figure 12.20
Completing the Trace Properties.

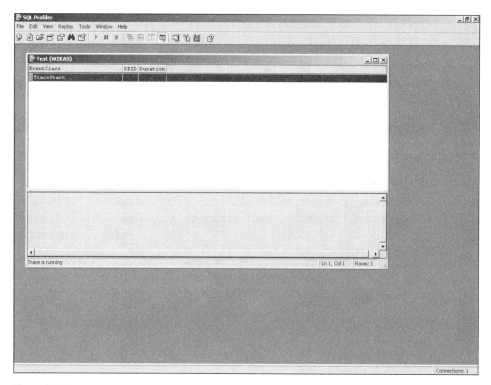

Figure 12.21
Your trace after starting.

- *Show Server Trace*—This feature of Query Analyzer provides you with access to information you may use to determine the server-side impact of a query. If you enable this feature, when you execute your query, a trace pane in Query Analyzer provides information about the event class, subclass, integer data, text data, database ID, duration, start time, reads and writes, and CPU usage associated with the query.

- *Show Server-Side Statistics*—You can help determine the performance of your database queries by using **SET** statements to enable the **SHOWPLAN**, **STATISTICS IO**, and **STATISTICS TIME** options.

- *Show Client-Side Statistics*—You can use the **SHOW CLIENT STATISTICS** command to provide detailed information about client-side statistics for execution of your query.

- *Index Tuning Wizard*—Using the Index Tuning Wizard allows you to view suggestions for additional indexes and statistics on nonindexed columns. Often, these suggestions, if followed, improve the ability of the query optimizer to process queries efficiently.

Follow these steps to view an example of using the Server Trace feature of Query Analyzer to view key performance information regarding your queries:

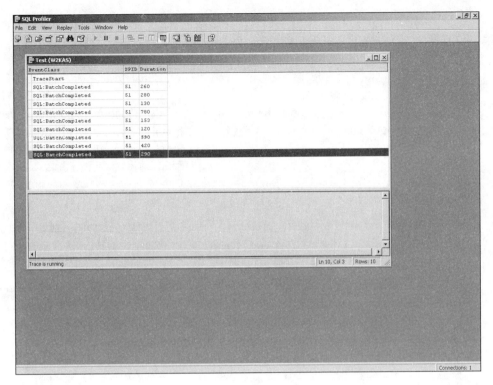

Figure 12.22
Viewing the results of your trace.

1. Select Start|Programs|Microsoft SQL Server|Query Analyzer.

2. Select OK in the Connect To SQL Server dialog box to connect to SQL Server using Windows authentication.

3. Input the following query in the empty query window that appears:

```
USE Northwind
GO
SELECT c.CompanyName, p.ProductName, SUM(d.Quantity * d.UnitPrice)
FROM Customers c JOIN Orders o ON c.CustomerID = o.CustomerID
JOIN [Order Details] d ON o.OrderID = d.OrderID
JOIN Products p ON d.ProductID = p.ProductID
WHERE p.ProductID in (6, 9, 12)
GROUP BY c.CompanyName, p.ProductName
```

4. Use the Query menu option to select Show Server Trace.

5. Press the F5 key to execute the query.

6. Select the Trace tab in the results area to view the server trace information for the query just executed (see Figure 12.23).

Summary

Consistently monitoring and optimizing your SQL Server 2000 implementation is critical for the prolonged success of your server. Although initially resources might be near-perfectly allocated and users of the system will be extremely pleased, eventually performance begins to slip and bottlenecks begin to develop. It is one of your jobs as a SQL Server administrator to make certain that this situation is not allowed to develop to the point where performance becomes an issue for users.

Be sure to use the tools and advice presented in this chapter to carefully monitor key performance statistics of the server and respond as necessary to bring key resources back in line with baselines you have established.

The next chapter presents another important task you may face as a SQL Server administrator: The proper implementation and maintenance of English Query. This component actually allows users to submit queries to the server in plain English, so that the server can convert these queries into the proper T-SQL commands.

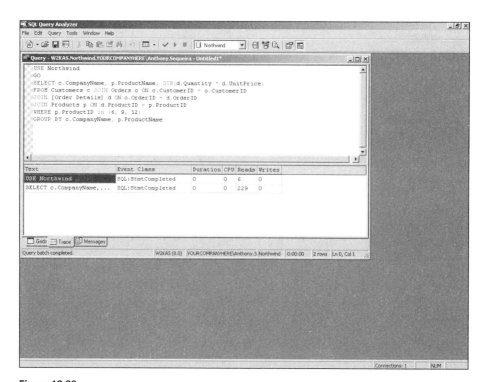

Figure 12.23
Analyzing the server trace results in Query Analyzer.

Chapter 13

English Query

There is a very good chance that not all of your SQL Server end users are going to know Transact-SQL. In fact, the average user is not only ignorant when it comes to T-SQL statements, he would deem learning T-SQL to issue queries as time not well spent. English Query is your answer for customizing SQL Server 2000 to satisfy users that do not know T-SQL, or to appease users that would rather not use it.

English Query permits SQL users to present questions to the server in plain English and have the server convert these questions into the appropriate T-SQL syntax. If you think this sounds amazing, you should also consider the fact that, thanks to speech recognition capabilities, users may also physically speak their questions to the server!

Installing English Query

English Query possesses its own set of software requirements that you must provide prior to installation. These requirements are:

- The underlying Operating System must be Windows 95, Windows 98, Windows NT 4 (Service Pack 6 or later), or Windows 2000.

- You must have 40MB of free disk space.

- You must be running Internet Explorer 5 or later (build 2615 or later is required for the display of large models and other user interface elements if running on a Windows 98 system).

You should also consider the following prior to installing English Query:

- Although there is documentation regarding English Query found in SQL Server 2000 Books Online, this documentation is limited. For a full set of documentation, you should consult English Query Books Online, which you may install when you install English Query. English Query Books Online appears in the English Query group. This group is located in the Microsoft SQL Server group.

- English Query is compiled with XML 2, whereas SQL Server 2000 uses XML 2.6. To prevent compilation errors, you should select XML 2 in the References section of your English Query project.

- Installing English Query when the SQL Server 7 OLAP Services service is running may break connectivity to the local OLAP Client. This does not occur when SQL Server 2000 Analysis Services is running.

- If you are running OLAP Services 7, OLAP Manager must not be running during installation. If OLAP Manager is running, English Query Setup cannot copy the files needed for English Query OLAP support.

- Uninstalling English Query breaks SQL Server 7 OLAP Services and vice versa. If you have installed SQL Server 7 OLAP Services, and you uninstall English Query, you must reinstall OLAP Services. Note that this does not occur with Analysis Services.

- Microsoft Internet Information Server (IIS) must not be running with an English Query application during installation. If you are using English Query in a Web page and you are about to install English Query, be sure to shut down IIS prior to the installation.

You should follow these steps for installing English Query:

1. Insert the SQL Server 2000 installation CD-ROM.

2. In the SQL Server Automenu window, select SQL Server 2000 Components (see Figure 13.1).

3. In the Install Components window, choose Install English Query (see Figure 13.2).

4. Choose Continue in the Microsoft English Query 2000 Setup window.

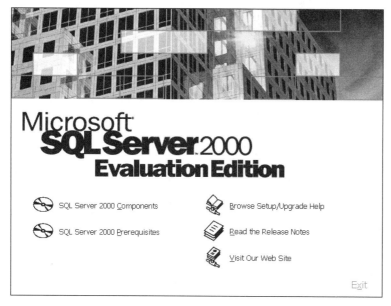

Figure 13.1
The SQL Server Automenu window.

Figure 13.2
The Install Components window.

5. Choose I Agree in the Microsoft English Query 2000 window.

6. In the next Microsoft English Query 2000 Setup window that appears, choose the Complete button to install all English Query components. Notice that you may also control the folder used to store the files that make up English Query from this window (see Figure 13.3).

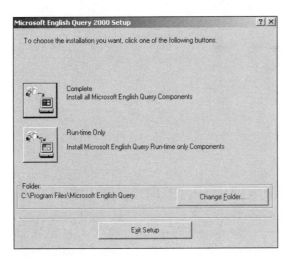

Figure 13.3
Selecting the type of installation you want to perform.

7. Choose OK in the next Microsoft English Query 2000 Setup window that appears to complete the installation.

To verify that the installation completed successfully, you should use the Start menu to navigate to the Microsoft SQL Server group and make certain the English Query group is inside.

To make English Query work for you, you must first use the SQL Project Wizard to create a new English Query Project and Model (see Figure 13.4). After the basic model is created, you can refine, test, and compile it into an English Query application (*.eqd) and then deploy it. Most often, you deploy the application to the Web using Internet Information Server (IIS) as your Web server platform, as this product is built into Windows 2000.

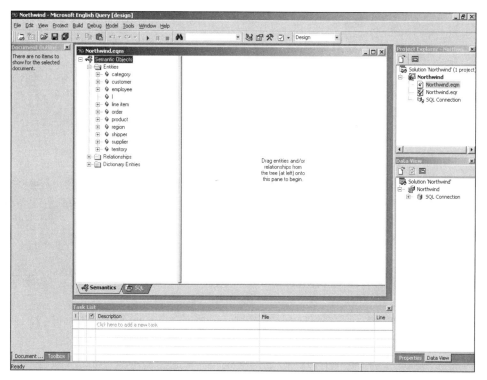

Figure 13.4
An English Query project and model.

English Query Components and Terminology

By far the best way to master an English Query implementation is to step through an example using the product. Before you do this, however, you should review the following key English Query components and terminology:

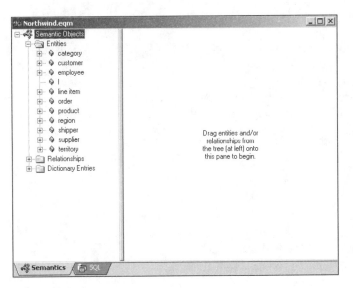

Figure 13.5
The English Query Model Editor.

- *English Query Model Editor*—You use this graphical user interface to view and create relationships used by English Query to build T-SQL queries (see Figure 13.5). The editor consists of two tabs, Semantics and SQL. The Semantics tab allows you to graphically drag and drop entities and relationships to build your English Query model. The SQL tab lists the tables in the database. You can expand the view here to access both fields and joins. This allows you to further modify your English Query Model.

- *Project Explorer*—You use the Project Explorer to navigate through the different components of your English Query Project (see Figure 13.6). Note that English Query projects contain an .eqm file, an .eqr file, and the SQL connection to the database you are dealing with. The .eqm file is your module file and is related to the panes of the Model Editor window. The .eqr file is a regression test file. Double-clicking the .eqr file displays the Regression Test file, which is empty until you add test questions for your project.

Figure 13.6
The Project Explorer of English Query.

Figure 13.7
The Data View window of English Query.

- *Data View*—The Data View window (see Figure 13.7) provides a graphical view of the database objects that reside in the selected database on your SQL Server. Although the Data View window provides a view of the selected database, you do not necessarily need it to create your English Query model or application. It can be quite useful, however, for remembering exact objects and structures in the source database.

- *Task List*—the Task List window (see Figure 13.8) allows you to easily list tasks that you need to complete in the construction of your English Query application. This grid allows you to prioritize tasks and also mark their completion.

- *Entities and relationships*—You use wizards in English Query to create the semantic objects that make up your English Query application. Mainly, these semantic objects consist of entities and relationships. Entities represent real world objects that your database describes. For example, in a Customers database, entities might be Orders, Addresses, and Regions. Relationships describe how entities interact with each other. For example, Customers place Orders that consist of Products.

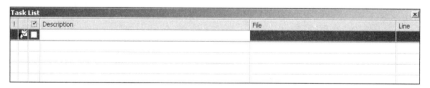

Figure 13.8
The Task List window of English Query.

- *Active Server Pages (ASP)*—When deploying your English Query application for distribution via the Web using Internet Information Server, Active Server Pages provide the interface for the users.

In order to easily explore the various components of English Query, begin by viewing a sample project completed for you by Microsoft. Follow these steps for opening and viewing an English Query project:

1. Select Start|Programs|Microsoft SQL Server|English Query|Microsoft English Query.

2. In the New Project window (see Figure 13.9) choose the Existing tab and use the Look In drop-down menu to browse to the SAMPLES subdirectory of the Microsoft English Query directory.

3. Double-click the Models folder and then the Northwind folder.

4. Select the Northwind.eqp file and choose the Open button.

5. Use the Project Explorer window in the top right corner to explore the various components of this sample project.

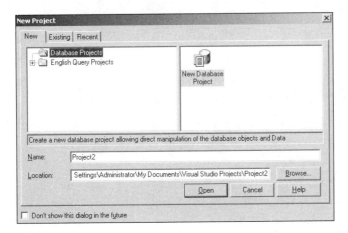

Figure 13.9
The New Project window of English Query.

Building a Sample English Query Application

Remember, the best way to master the use of English Query is to build a sample application. In this section, you do just that. This application allows plain English queries to be used against the Northwind sample database.

Building the Basic Model

Follow these steps to create a new sample project and a basic model to use for your first English Query application:

1. Select Start|Programs|Microsoft SQL Server|English Query|Microsoft English Query.

2. In the New Project dialog box, choose the English Query Projects node in the left pane. In the right pane, choose the SQL Project Wizard.

3. In the Name field, provide a name for your sample project—note the default location for new projects in the Location field (see Figure 13.10). When you are finished, click the Open button.

4. In the Data Link Properties window (see Figure 13.11), choose Select Microsoft OLE DB Provider For SQL Server, and then click Next.

5. In the first step, use the drop-down menu to select your SQL Server system. If your server name does not appear, provide it.

6. In the second step, indicate you wish to Use Windows NT Integrated Security.

7. In the third step, use the drop-down menu to select the Northwind database on the server (see Figure 13.12).

8. Use the Test Connection button to make sure your connection is successful.

9. Once you have successfully tested the connection, use the OK button to create the Data Link.

10. In the New Database Tables And Views window, use the double arrow button to select all the tables and views of the database (see Figure 13.13) and choose OK.

11. Note that the SQL Project Wizard displays an alphabetical list of the potential entities available for your model based on the tables present in the database (see Figure 13.14).

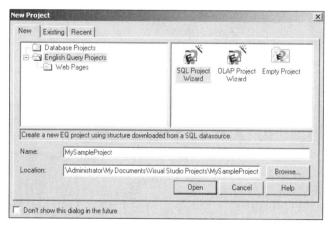

Figure 13.10
Creating a new project using the SQL Project Wizard.

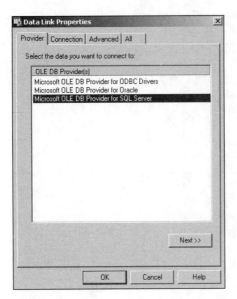

Figure 13.11
The Data Link Properties window of the SQL Project Wizard.

13

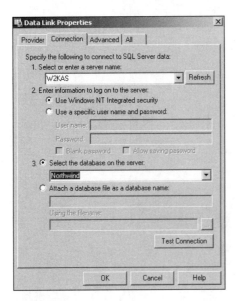

Figure 13.12
Supplying the details for your connection in the Data Link Properties window.

Note also that you can remove any entities using the checkboxes. For this example, you should use all the entities.

12. In order to view the relationships created by the wizard, expand the employee entity (see Figure 13.15).

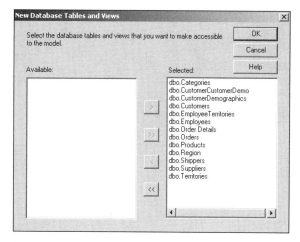

Figure 13.13
Selecting the tables and views for use in your model.

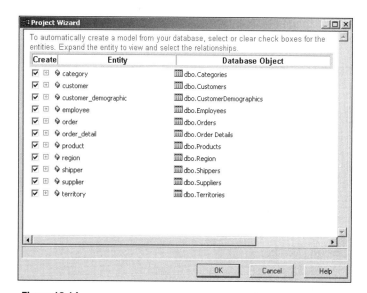

Figure 13.14
The entities for your model as selected by the wizard.

13. When you are finished exploring the entities and their relationships as defined by the wizard, choose OK.

14. Notice that the English Query Model Editor window appears, awaiting further modifications to your English Query Model.

15. In order to save your sample model, choose File|Save All.

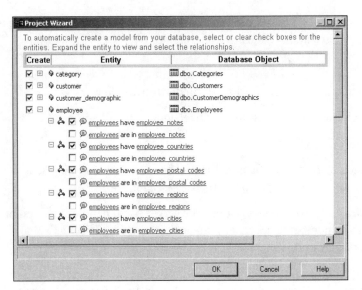

Figure 13.15
The relationships of the employee entity.

Expanding the Basic Model

Now that you have created a basic English Query Model, it is time to expand upon it. Realize at this point, however, that your model would successfully respond to a wide variety of plain English queries. For example, SQL Server 2000 could respond appropriately to the following:

- Who are all the customers?

- What are the addresses of all the customers?

- What are the addresses and cities of all the customers?

- What are all the products?

- Which products start with "A"?

- What are the territory descriptions?

- What are the home phones for all employees?

- What is the home phone for Andrew Fuller?

You should test one of the above queries against your server to verify that it does in fact work. Follow these steps for testing your English Query Model. You should note that these steps assume you have completed the steps to create the simple model and that you have saved your model and closed English Query:

1. Select Start|Programs|Microsoft SQL Server|English Query|Microsoft English Query.

2. In the New Project dialog box, choose the Recent tab. Double-click the EQP file for the project you created and saved earlier.

3. Select the Debug menu and choose Start.

4. Type your question in the Query field of the Model Test window.

5. Select the View Results button just below this field.

6. Select the Submit Query button.

7. Note the results that display confirming the proper operation of English Query and the success of your model for the question posed (see Figure 13.16).

Although there are many, many more questions the server could handle at this point, you can always increase the number supported by enhancing your English Query Model, using the techniques that follow in this chapter.

First, let's add some synonyms to some of our entities to dramatically increase the success percentage of plain English queries. For example, notice in the questions shown in Figure 13.16 regarding home phone numbers, you had to very specifically ask about "home phones" as the name of the related entity is **employee_home_phone**. If someone were the ask the question, "What are the home phone numbers for all employees?" the query would fail as SQL Server 2000 would not know what to make of the word "numbers" in the query. Again, the solution is very simple and merely involves adding synonyms using the following steps:

1. Open English Query and verify that your project is loaded.

2. Ensure your English Query Model window is displayed. Double-click the EQM file in the Project Explorer window if it is not.

3. Expand the employee entity in the left pane of the Semantics tab.

4. Double-click the **employee_home_phone** attribute of the employee entity to launch the Entity dialog box (see Figure 13.17).

5. Click the ellipses button next to the Words field to view the synonyms for this attribute.

6. Click in the Words field and add the following synonyms:

   • phone number

   • home phone number

   • home number

   • home telephone number

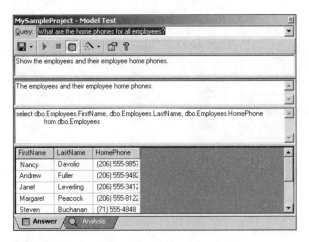

Figure 13.16
Testing your English Query Model.

- telephone number

7. Click OK.

8. You can now use the Debug window to test your English Query Model with any of the following questions:

   - What are the home phone numbers for all employees?

   - What is the home number for Andrew Fuller?

   - What is the telephone number for Nancy Davolio?

In addition to adding synonyms to increase the effectiveness of English Query, you can also add relationships to your model. For example, English Query cannot answer the question "Who sells Boston Crab Meat?" because the relationships of suppliers actually *selling* products is not made clear in the database schema. This is easy to solve. The SQL Project Wizard already created a relationship named **products have suppliers** thanks to the existing database schema. You will simply add the relationship of suppliers selling products to this relationship with the steps below:

1. In the left pane of the Semantics tab of the Model Editor window, expand Relationships and double-click **products have suppliers**.

2. In the Relationship window (see Figure 13.18), select the Add button.

3. In the Select Phrasing window, double-click Verb Phrasings to launch the Verb Phrasing window (see Figure 13.19).

4. In the Sentence Type dropdown menu, select Subject Verb Object.

Figure 13.17
Examining the **employee_home_phone** attribute.

5. In the Subject dropdown menu, select Suppliers.

6. In the Verb field, type "sell".

7. Choose Products in the Direct Object drop-down menu.

8. Choose OK to close the Verb Phrasing window, and then click OK again to close the Relationship window.

9. You can now test your new relationship by posing the question, "Who sells Boston Crab Meat?"

Using the Model Test Window to Make Modifications

The Model Test window is much more useful than it might appear at first. In fact, this Test Window includes a powerful wizard called the Suggestion Wizard to aid you in creating a near perfect English Query Model. Follow these steps for using the advanced features of this tool:

1. With your sample model loaded in English Query, use the Debug menu to start a new debug process.

2. Type the following plain English into the Query field, "What is the price of Boston Crab Meat?"

3. Verify that the View Results button is selected and click the Submit Query button.

4. Notice English Query responds with the following statement, "I haven't been given any information on prices." This is because the products table contains a Unit Price entity and English Query does not recognize this as "prices".

5. Select the Suggestion Wizard in the Model Test window. Notice that the Suggestion Wizard window appears (see Figure 13.20).

Figure 13.18
Adding a new relationship to the model.

Figure 13.19
The Verb Phrasing window.

6. In the Boston Crab Meat Refers To A(n) . . . area, select Product from the dropdown list.

7. Scroll down and select **product_unit_price** in the dropdown menu in the Price Refers To A(n) . . . area.

8. Select OK to alter your model based on the results of the Suggestion Wizard.

9. Select Start from the Debug menu and run your query again. The correct result is now returned (see Figure 13.21).

Advanced Query Model Modification Techniques

There are additional Query Model techniques you should master that are a bit more advanced. Let's examine those in this section.

Displaying Help Text

Perhaps you would like some explanatory text displayed when users query about certain objects. This is actually quite simple thanks to the Help Text field in the Properties area for entities. Follow these steps to add Help Text:

1. In the Model Editor window, expand the Entities node in the left pane.

2. Expand the product entity.

3. Double-click the **product_id** entity and enter the following in the Help Text field: This is a unique identifier used to distinguish different products from each other.

4. Choose OK.

Displaying Remote Fields

If you ask the following question of your model

What are all the products?

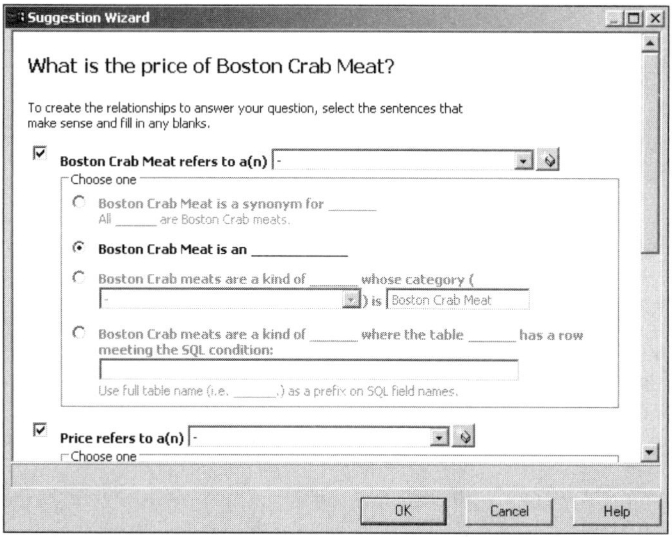

Figure 13.20
The Suggestion Wizard of English Query.

English Query returns a list of all the **ProductNames** from the Products table. But what if you would also like the Product Category returned with such a query? This is problematic for English Query, especially considering the **CategoryName** entity is not part of the Products table. Follow these instructions to add a remote field to be returned in this case, and cases like it:

1. Expand the Entities node in the left pane of the Model Editor window.

2. Double-click the product entity.

3. In the Entity dialog box, click the Advanced button to display the Advanced Entity Properties dialog (see Figure 13.22).

4. In the Advanced Entity Properties dialog box, use the Add Field button in the Display Properties area.

5. In the Select Remote Fields dialog box (see Figure 13.23), select the **Categories** table and the **CategoryName** field and choose Add.

6. Choose OK in the Select Remote Fields dialog box.

7. Choose OK in the Advanced Entity Properties dialog box.

8. Choose OK in the Entity dialog box.

9. Use the Start option on the Debug menu to test the following query: "What are all the products?"

Be sure to use the View Results button when testing the query. Ensure that both products and their product categories are reported.

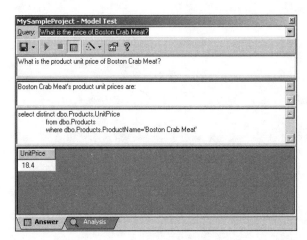

Figure 13.21
Your Model Test window following the use of the Suggestion Wizard.

Using Views in your Query Model

Several of the products the Northwind database stores are not current products that it sells. In fact, there is a view constructed in the database that displays only the current products for Northwind. You can easily incorporate this view into your English Query Model. In this section, you perform this task and create the necessary model objects and relationships to answer the question: What are the current products?

1. Ensure that your model is loaded and the Model Editor window is open.

2. Click the Model menu, and select Import Tables.

3. In the New Database Tables and View window, double-click **dbo.Current Product List** to move it to the Selected area and choose OK.

4. Next, you will add a primary key to the view in order to join it to the **Products** table. Select the SQL tab in the Model Editor window.

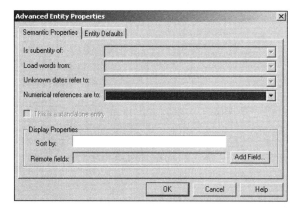

Figure 13.22
The Advanced Entity Properties dialog box.

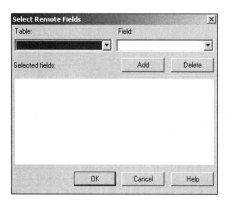

Figure 13.23
The Select Remote Fields dialog box.

5. Double-click **dbo.Current Product List**.

6. In the **Table: dbo.Current Product List** window (see Figure 13.24), right click the first cell in the ProductID row, choose Primary Key from the shortcut menu, and choose OK.

7. Next, you need to create a join between the **Current Product List** view and the **Products** table. Choose the Model menu, select Add Database Object, and choose Add Join.

8. In the New Join window (see Figure 13.25), select **dbo.Products** in the Source drop-down menu and select **dbo.Current Product List** in the Destination drop-down menu.

9. Click the Add button.

10. Select ProductID in both the From Source Table Field and To Destination Table Field dropdown menus and choose OK.

13

11. Choose OK in the New Join window.

12. Next, you need to set **CurrentProducts.ProductName** as a denormalized field of **Products.ProductName**. Double-click **dbo.Current Product List**.

13. Select the ProductName row and then select the Advanced tab in the **Table: dbo.Current Product List** window.

14. In the Denormalized fields, choose the **dbo.Products** table and the ProductName field. Choose OK.

15. Next, you enable the limiting of items that are loaded to only those in the Current Product List. Select the Semantics tab.

16. Expand Product in the Entities list, and then double-click **product_name**.

17. In the Entity dialog box, click Add Values Of Entity To Model.

18. Click the Advanced button.

19. In the Advanced Entity Properties dialog box, choose **dbo.Current Product List** in the Load Words From field.

20. Choose OK in the Advanced Entity Properties dialog box and choose OK in the Entity dialog box.

21. Next, you create a new adjective relationship that shows "some products are current."

22. From the left pane of the Semantics tab, drag Product to the Canvas pane.

23. In the Canvas pane, right-click Product and select Add Relationship from the shortcut menu.

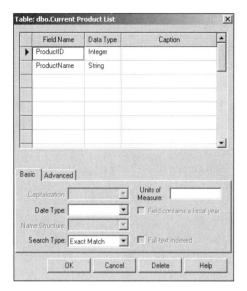

Figure 13.24
Adding a primary key.

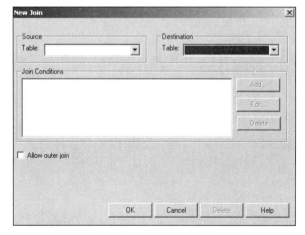

Figure 13.25
Creating a new join.

24. In the New Relationship dialog box click Add in the Phrasings area.

25. In the Select Phrasing dialog box, double-click Adjective Phrasing.

26. In the Adjective Phrasing dialog box, type "current" in the An Adjective That Describes Subject field and press Enter.

27. Click OK in the Adjective Phrasing dialog box.

28. Next, you need to add a SQL condition that identifies which products are current. To do so, select the Database tab, select This Relationship Is True Only When The Following SQL Condition Is True, and type "dbo.Products.Discontinued=0".

29. Click OK in the New Relationship dialog box.

30. Finally, test your query model by testing the following plain English query: "What are the current products?"

Building your Application

Once you are satisfied with the performance of your English Query Model, you can build the English Query application your users will query against. Doing so is very simple. First, you set the project properties to permit sample data to be viewed by users, then you build the application. Follow these steps:

1. Select the Project menu and select the Properties menu item for your sample project.

2. In the Project Properties window (see Figure 13.26), select the Sample Data checkbox. Notice the other properties configured for your English Query Model. When you are finished, choose OK.

3. After saving your English Query Model using the File menu, select the Build menu.

4. From the Build menu, choose the Build option.

5. In the lower left corner of the English Query interface, check for the success of your application build.

Deploying your Application

Once you have built your application, you should be ready to deploy it. This section guides you through the most common method of deployment—deploying your application to the Web.

Note: *In order to deploy your application to the Web, you must have write permissions to the root of the Web server. You must also be listed as an operator for that Web server.*

Although you could also deploy your application in a Visual Basic or Visual C++ application, realize that deployment to the Web is quite convenient and makes your English Query application available to the widest number of possible users.

Warning! *It is necessary to have Visual InterDev installed to create Web projects. English Query uses the Web Project Wizard in Visual InterDev to deploy English Query applications to the Web.*

Follow these steps to deploy your application to the Web:

1. Ensure that your English Query Model is open and built using the steps in "Building Your Application."

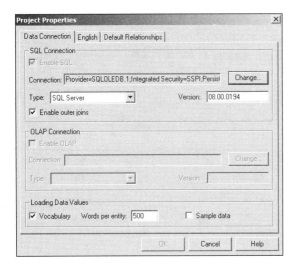

Figure 13.26
The Project Properties window.

2. Select the Project menu, then select Deploy To Web. This launches the Web Project Wizard (see Figure 13.27).

3. Select your server in the What Server Do You Want To Use? field. If your server does not appear in the list, type in the name.

4. In the What Mode Do You Want To Work In? area, choose Master Mode. Choose Next to continue in the wizard.

5. On the Specify Your Web page (see Figure 13.28), choose Create A New Web Application and provide the name you would like. Clear the Create Search.htm To Enable Full Text Searching option and choose Next.

6. In the Apply A Layout page (see Figure 13.29), choose Bottom 1 and click Next.

7. In the Apply A Theme page, choose a theme for your application and choose Finish when done.

8. In the SQL Connection Properties window (see Figure 13.30), provide the appropriate credentials for making a connection to SQL Server in design time or run time and choose OK.

Once the wizard has finished building your application, note the files that were created to build the Web application in the Project Explorer. You are now ready to view and test your application via a Web browser!

Open your browser and visit the following location to view your deployed application (see Figure 13.31):

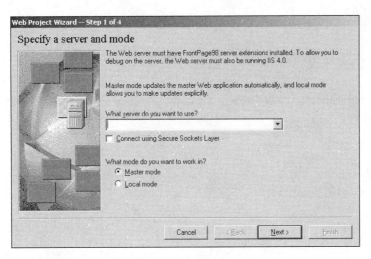

Figure 13.27
The Web Project Wizard.

```
http://yourservername/yourprojectname
```

Guidelines for English Query Usage

You should keep the following guidelines in mind as you are creating your English Query models:

- You should strive for the normalization of data in the database that you are using with English Query.

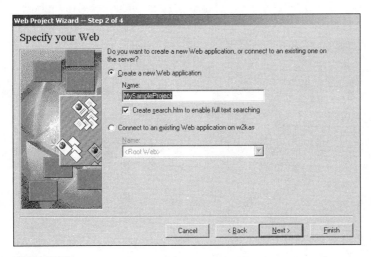

Figure 13.28
The Specify Your Web page of the wizard.

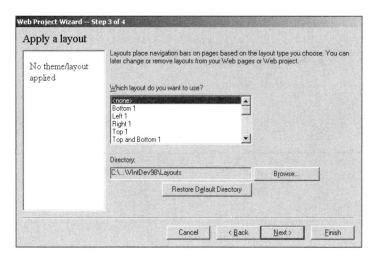

Figure 13.29
Specifying a layout.

- You should always provide sample questions for your English Query users. These sample questions will permit users to construct their own questions more efficiently and will increase the chances that your model can provide sufficient and correct responses.

- You should save and analyze any questions that could not be answered by English Query. Encourage your users to send these questions to you. Analyzing these questions is the number one method for you to use to improve your English Query Model.

- Avoid the use of the word "name" to describe an entity in English Query. This word is considered a key word and generates an error in the compile and testing modes.

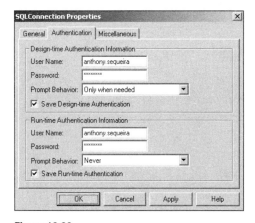

Figure 13.30
The SQL Connection Properties window.

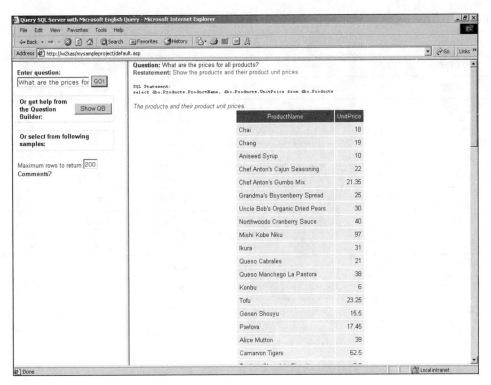

Figure 13.31
Viewing your deployed application.

- Strive to use active voice, and guide your English Query users to use active voice. Although English Query understands both active and passive voice, it functions more efficiently with active voice.

- You should educate your users to avoid the use of the prepositions "by" and "to." These tend to confuse English Query and may cause the engine to return unexpected results.

- You should avoid using **NULL** data elements in English Query entities. Your results for some questions may not return the results you expect due to **NULL** massing in the **WHERE** clause of the query returned by the English Query engine.

- Do not mix the cases of words when describing entities. You should use all lowercase letters for describing words unless they are submitted in uppercase or mixed case.

- At times you may need to create duplicate entities to support the relationships needed to answer some plain English queries. For example, the question "Which manager reports to another manager?" is one such query.

- There is a list of verbs you must be careful of when using them in English Query Models. These verbs can cause problems in command relationships. Table 13.1 lists these problematic verbs.

Table 13.1   Verbs that can cause problems in command relationships.

achieve	add	add up	adjust	alphabetize	ascent	attain
average	base	begin	break down	calculate	call	cease
change	chart	commerce	compare	compute	contain	contract
correlate	count	decline	decrease	describe	display	divide
drop	end	enlarge	equal	exceed	expand	fetch
fill	find	find out	finish	gain	go down	go up
graph	grow	help	identify	improve	increase	include
keep	know	list	locate	look up	lose	magnify
meet	mention	merge	miss	multiply	name	order
plot	print	print out	quit	raise	rank	rate
reach	reduce	relate	report	reprint	reshow	rise
save	search	search	search out	select	sequence	show
shrink	sort	stack	stack up	start	stop	store
subcount	subtotal	subtract	sum	sum up	tell	total
total	up	unview	vary	view	widen	

Summary

English Query allows your users to submit queries to the server in plain English. This shields users from any knowledge of Transact-SQL syntax. You use the English Query application to compose an English Query Model. The easiest way to do this is by using the wizards that ship with English Query. The English Query Model you create contains all the entities and relationships used in potential plain English queries. You can debug and test the model to make sure your application answers as many questions correctly as possible. You can enhance your model by adding synonyms and relationships.

Once your English Query Model is designed and debugged to your satisfaction, you can build the application with a simple menu item selection. Once the application is built, you can then easily deploy your application to the Web using the Web Project Wizard, although this option is only available if you have Visual InterDev installed.

The next chapter of this book deals with efficiently and effectively moving data in and out of SQL Server 2000. You might be interested in exporting a large amount of data to another RDBMS, or perhaps you need to import massive amounts of data in from another system or even a text file. All this is possible with SQL Server 2000 thanks to Data Transformation Services and a number of special commands and utilities.

Part IV

Using SQL Server 2000

Deployment

Troubleshooting Configuration Planning

Configuration Deployment
Planning
Troubleshooting

Chapter 14

Transferring and Transforming Data

Surely, at some point during your career as a SQL Server 2000 administrator, you will need to transfer large amounts of data into or out of SQL Server 2000. Perhaps you will need information added to your database from an electronic spreadsheet program, or perhaps you will need data transferred from another relational database management system like Oracle. There are several options for performing these operations in SQL Server 2000. Thanks to Data Transformation Services (DTS), you also have the ability to manipulate data as it is imported or exported from SQL Server 2000. This chapter explores all these tools and opportunities in detail.

BCP

The Bulk Copy Program (BCP) is a command-prompt utility that imports and exports native SQL Server 2000 data, ASCII text files, or Unicode data. In earlier versions of SQL Server, this utility was the main method for transferring data, and now has been largely replaced by Data Transformation Services. There are still reasons for using BCP, however. Consider these:

- BCP features backward compatibility with other SQL Server versions.

- BCP features improved performance over DTS, thanks to optimization hints you may enable.

- BCP causes minimal overhead on the SQL Server 2000 system.

- Many administrators are familiar with BCP from earlier versions and prefer to use it.

- BCP can be easily automated.

Here is the syntax for BCP:

```
BCP {[[database_name.][owner].]{table_name | view_name} | "query"}
    {in | out | queryout | format} data_file
    [-m max_errors] [-f format_file] [-e err_file]
    [-F first_row] [-L last_row] [-b batch_size]
    [-n] [-c] [-w] [-N] [-V (60 | 65 | 70)] [-6]
```

```
[-q] [-C code_page] [-t field_term] [-r row_term]
[-i input_file] [-o output_file] [-a packet_size]
[-S server_name[\instance_name]] [-U login_id] [-P password]
[-T] [-v] [-R] [-k] [-E] [-h "hint [,...n]"]
```

Note: *The switches used in the above syntax are case sensitive.*

Although some of the above syntax is somewhat self-explanatory, much of it is not. Here is an explanation of all syntax elements:

- **database_name**—Provides the name of the database you are copying information into or out of. If no database is specified, the default database for the user executing BCP is used.

- **owner**—Specifies the owner of the table or view you are copying data into or out of. If no owner is specified, the user running BCP must be the owner of the table or view.

- **table_name**—Allows you to specify the name of the destination table when copying data into SQL Server, or the source table name when copying data from SQL Server.

- **view_name**—Allows you to specify the name of the destination view when copying data into SQL Server, or the source view name when copying data from SQL Server.

- **"query"**—Allows you to specify a T-SQL query to select specific data for import or export. If your query returns multiple result sets, such as a **SELECT** statement that specifies a **COMPUTE** clause, only the first result set is copied to the data file; subsequent result sets are ignored. You must use double quotation marks around the query and single quotation marks around anything embedded in the query.

- **in|out|queryout|format**—Permits you to specify the direction of the bulk copy. **in** copies from a file into the database table or view, and **out** copies from the database table or view to a file. **queryout** must be specified only when bulk copying data from a query. **format** creates a format file based on the option specified (**-n**, **-c**, **-w**, **-6**, or **-N**) and the table or view delimiters. If **format** is used, the **-f** option must be specified as well.

- **data_file**—Allows you to specify the full path of the data file used when bulk copying a table or view to or from a disk. The path can have from 1 to 255 characters.

- **-m max_errors**—Specifies the maximum number of errors that can occur before the bulk copy operation is canceled. Each row that cannot be copied by BCP is ignored and counted as one error. If you do not include this option, the default is **10**.

- **-f format_file**—Specifies the full path of the format file that contains stored responses from a previous use of BCP on the same table or view. You can use this option when using a format file created with the format option to bulk copy data in or out. After prompting you with format questions, BCP prompts you whether to save the answers in a format file. The default file name is Bcp.fmt. BCP can refer to a format file when bulk copying data; therefore, reentering previous format responses interactively is not necessary. If this option is not used and **-n**, **-c**, **-w**, **-6**, or **-N** is not specified, BCP prompts for format information.

- **-e err_file**—Allows you to provide the full path of an error file used to store any rows BCP is unable to transfer from the file to the database.

- **-F first_row**—Allows you to specify the number of the first row to bulk copy. Obviously, the default is **1**, indicating the first row in the specified data file.

- **-L last_row**—Allows you to specify the number of the last row to bulk copy. The default for this value is **0**, indicating the last row in the specified data file should be copied.

- **-b batch_size**—Allows you to specify the number of rows per batch of data copied. Each batch is copied to the server as one transaction. SQL Server commits (or rolls back, in the case of failure) the transaction for every batch. By default, all data in the specified data file is copied in one batch. You should not use this option in conjunction with the **-h "ROWS_PER_BATCH = bb"** option.

- **-n**—Causes the bulk copy operation to be performed using the native (database) data types of the data.

- **-c**—Causes the bulk copy operation to be performed using a character data type. This option uses **char** as the storage type, no prefixes, **\t** (tab character) as the field separator, and **\n** (newline character) as the row terminator.

- **-w**—Causes the bulk copy operation to be performed using Unicode characters. This option uses **nchar** as the storage type, no prefixes, **\t** (tab character) as the field separator, and **\n** (newline character) as the row terminator. You cannot use this option with SQL Server version 6.5 or earlier.

- **-N**—Causes the bulk copy operation to be performed using the native (database) data types of the data for noncharacter data, and Unicode characters for character data. This option offers a higher performance alternative to the **-w** option, and is intended for transferring data from one SQL Server to another using a data file. You should consider using this option when you are transferring data that contains ANSI extended characters and you want to take advantage of the performance of native mode. You cannot use this option with SQL Server version 6.5 or earlier.

- **-V (60|65|70)**—Causes the bulk copy operation to be performed using data types from an earlier version of SQL Server. You use this option in conjunction with character (**-c**) or native (**-n**) format. For example, to bulk copy date formats supported by the BCP utility provided with SQL Server 6.5 (but no longer supported by ODBC) into SQL Server 2000, use the **-V 65** parameter. Understand, however, that when you are bulk copying data from SQL Server into a data file, the BCP utility does not generate SQL Server 6 or SQL Server 6.5 date formats for any **datetime** or **smalldatetime** data, even if **-V** is specified. Dates are always written in ODBC format. Additionally, null values in bit

14

columns are written as the value **0** because SQL Server versions 6.5 and earlier do not support nullable bit data.

- **-6**—Causes the bulk copy operation to be performed using SQL Server 6 or SQL Server 6.5 data types. This option is provided for backward compatibility only; you should use the **-V** option instead of this option.

- **-q**—Executes the **SET QUOTED_IDENTIFIERS ON** statement in the connection between the BCP utility and an instance of SQL Server. You should use this option to specify a database, owner, table, or view name that contains a space or a quotation mark. Enclose the entire three-part table or view name in double quotation marks (" ").

- **-C code_page**—Specifies the code page of the data in the data file. **code_page** is relevant only if the data contains **char**, **varchar**, or **text** columns with character values greater than 127 or less than 32. The code page values that may be used are as follows:

  - **ACP**—ANSI/Microsoft Windows (ISO 1252).

  - **OEM**—Default code page used by the client. This is the default code page used by BCP if **-C** is not specified.

  - **RAW**—No conversion occurs from one code page to another. This is the fastest option because no conversion occurs.

  - **<value>**—specific code page number, for example, 850. This option is provided for backward compatibility only; you should specify a collation name for each column in the format file or in interactive BCP.

- **-t field_term**—Allows you to specify the field terminator. The default is **\t** (tab character). You can use this parameter to override the default field terminator.

- **-r row_term**—Allows you to specify the row terminator. The default is **\n** (newline character). You can use this parameter to override the default row terminator.

- **-i input_file**—Allows you to specify the name of a response file, which contains the responses to the command prompt questions for each field when performing a bulk copy using interactive mode (**-n**, **-c**, **-w**, **-6**, or **-N** not specified).

- **-o output_file**—Allows you to specify the name of an output file, which receives output from BCP redirected from the command prompt.

- **-a packet_size**—Allows you to specify the number of bytes, per network packet, sent to and from the server. Although this setting can be set with a server configuration option in Enterprise Manager (or the **sp_configure** system stored procedure), this server configuration option can be overridden on an individual basis by using this option in BCP. **packet_size** can be from 4096 to 65535 bytes; the default is 4096. Increased packet size can enhance the performance of bulk copy operations. If a larger packet is requested but cannot be granted, the default is used. The performance statistics generated by BCP show the packet size used.

- **-S server_name[\instance_name]**—Allows you to specify the instance of SQL Server that BCP should connect to. You can specify **server_name** to connect to the default instance of SQL Server on that server, or you can specify **server_name\instance_name** to connect to a named instance of SQL Server 2000 on that server. If no server is specified, BCP connects to the default instance of SQL Server on the local computer. This option is required when executing BCP from a remote computer on the network.

- **-U login_id**—Allows you to specify the login ID used to connect to SQL Server.

- **-P password**—Allows you to specify the password for the login ID. If you do not use this option, BCP prompts for a password. If you use this option at the end of the command prompt without a password, BCP uses the default password (NULL).

- **-T**—Allows you to specify that BCP connects to SQL Server with a trusted connection, using the security credentials of the network user. Obviously, when you use this option **login_id** and **password** are not required.

- **-v**—Causes BCP to produce a report providing the utility version number and copyright information.

- **-R**—Allows you to specify that currency, date, and time data is bulk copied into SQL Server using the regional format defined for the local setting of the client computer. By default, regional settings are ignored.

- **-k**—Allows you to specify that empty columns should retain a null value during the bulk copy operation, rather than have default values for the columns inserted.

- **-E**—Allows you to specify that values for an identity column are present in the file being imported. If you do not provide the **-E** option, the identity values for this column in the data file being imported are ignored, and SQL Server 2000 automatically assigns unique values based on the seed and increment values specified during table creation. If the data file does not contain values for the identity column in the table or view, use a format file to specify that the identity column in the table or view should be skipped when importing data; SQL Server 2000 automatically assigns unique values for the column.

- **-h "hint [,...n]"**—Allows you to specify the hint(s) to be used during a bulk copy of data into a table or view. You cannot use this option when bulk copying data into SQL Server 6.*x* or earlier. The hints you may specify include the following:

  - **ORDER (*column* [ASC | DESC] [,...*n*])**—Allows you to specify the sort order of the data in the data file. Bulk copy performance is improved if the data being loaded is sorted according to the clustered index on the table. If the data file is sorted in a different order, or there is no clustered index on the table, the **ORDER** hint is ignored. The names of the columns you supply must be valid columns in the destination table. By default, BCP assumes the data file is unordered.

14

- **ROWS_PER_BATCH = *bb***—Specifies the number of rows of data per batch (as *bb*). You can use this hint when **-b** is not specified, resulting in the entire data file being sent to the server as a single transaction. The server optimizes the bulk load according to the value *bb*. By default, **ROWS_PER_BATCH** is unknown.

- **KILOBYTES_PER_BATCH = *cc***—Specifies the approximate number of kilobytes (KB) of data per batch (as *cc*). By default, **KILOBYTES_PER_BATCH** is unknown.

- **TABLOCK**—Specifies that a table-level lock is acquired for the duration of the bulk copy operation. This hint significantly improves performance because holding a lock only for the duration of the bulk-copy operation reduces lock contention on the table. A table can be loaded concurrently by multiple clients if the table has no indexes and **TABLOCK** is specified. By default, locking behavior is determined by the table option table-lock on bulk load.

- **CHECK_CONSTRAINTS**—Specifies that any constraints on the destination table are checked during the bulk-copy operation. By default, constraints are ignored.

- **FIRE_TRIGGERS**—Specified with the **in** argument, causes any insert triggers defined on the destination table to execute during the bulk-copy operation. If **FIRE_TRIGGERS** is not specified, no insert triggers will execute. **FIRE_TRIGGERS** is ignored for the **out**, **queryout**, and **format** arguments.

By default, the BCP command-prompt utility is not protected with any special permissions, but in order to import data into a table using the utility you must have **INSERT** permissions for the target table. Also, if you are exporting data out of a table, you must have **SELECT** permissions for the source table.

As you may have also noticed from the discussion above regarding the options for use with BCP, the utility can work with data in either character file format, or native format. You use the **-c** switch to specify character mode and use ASCII text, while the **-n** switch features native mode. Native mode features the use of special formatting characters internal to SQL Server to represent data. You should only consider this mode when transferring data between SQL Server tables.

Interactive BCP

BCP automatically enters an interactive mode in which it prompts the user for necessary information should any of the following switches be omitted:

- **-n**

- **-N**

- **-c**

- **-f**

- **-w**

Running in interactive mode, BCP prompts you with plain English questions regarding the import and export specifications for the task you would like to perform. At a minimum, BCP prompts you for four pieces of information:

- File storage type

- Prefix length

- Field length

- Field and row terminators

Figure 14.1 demonstrates BCP running in interactive mode. Notice the BCP statement used to produce the results shown in this example.

Interactive BCP asks about the file storage type for each column of data. File storage type specifies the data types used to read and write to data files. The following are valid storage types you may specify:

- **char**

- **varchar**

- **nchar**

- **nvarchar**

- **text**

- **ntext**

- **binary**

- **varbinary**

- **image**

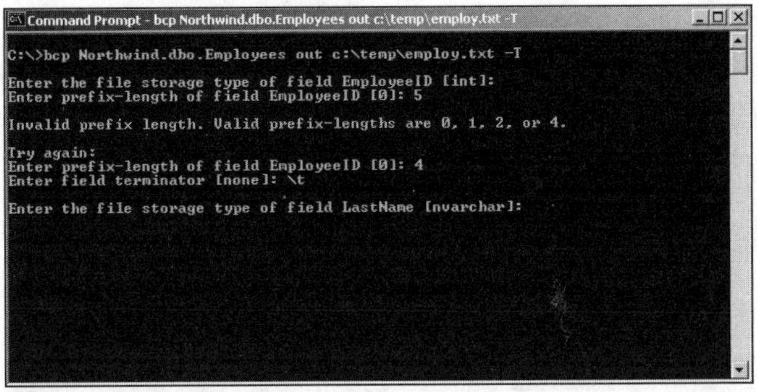

Figure 14.1
BCP in interactive mode.

- **datetime**
- **smalldatetime**
- **decimal**
- **numeric**
- **float**
- **real**
- **int**
- **smallint**
- **tinyint**
- **money**
- **smallmoney**
- **bit**
- **uniqueidentifier**
- **timestamp**

Although you have such a wide variety of choices for file storage type, remember, when working with ASCII files you should set all the file storage types to **char**, regardless of the data types in use within the source table.

Interactive BCP also prompts you for prefix length for each column of data. SQL Server 2000 uses this prefix-length value to store compacted data. When you are working in native mode, you should accept the default values whenever possible, but when you are working with fixed-width ASCII data, you should always set the prefix length to **0**.

When you are prompted for field length, BCP wants you to specify the number of bytes required to store a SQL Server data type. You should consider using default lengths whenever possible to avoid data truncation or overflow errors. When you are importing and exporting ASCII fixed-width data files, you sometimes need to modify the field length to match your import/export specification. For example, to export a **char(10)** column as a 20-byte piece of data, you can specify a field length of **20**. This pads the data length to 20 bytes. Table 14.1 provides the default field lengths for the various data types.

Table 14.1   Default field lengths.

Data Type	Length
bigint	19
binary	Column length + 1
bit	1

(continued)

Table 14.1   Default field lengths *(continued)*.

Data Type	Length
char	Column length
datetime	24
decimal	41
float	30
image	0
int	12
money	30
nchar	2 times column length
ntext	0
numeric	41
nvarchar	2 times column length
real	30
smalldatetime	24
smallint	7
smallmoney	30
text	0
timestamp	17
tinyint	5
uniqueidentifier	37
varbinary	2 times column length + 1
varchar	Column length

14

You must also specify the field terminator for use with BCP in interactive mode. This value controls how field data is delimited, also known as *separated*. The default delimiter is for no field terminator to be used whatsoever. Table 14.2 provides the possible field terminators for use with BCP.

Table 14.2   Valid field terminators.

Terminator Type	BCP Syntax
Tab	\t
Newline	\n
Carriage return	\r
Backslash	\\
NULL Terminator	\0
User-defined terminator	Character (such as ^, &, %, •, etc.)

At the end of your interactive BCP session, you are prompted to save the format information in a file. Should you do so, you can later specify the file using the **-f** switch to automatically reuse the formatting information you provided during the interactive session.

BCP Examples

Perhaps the simplest way to master the use of the BCP utility is to work with examples that use the utility. This section presents many examples that range from simple to complex. All these examples use the **Employees** table of the Northwind database. The structure of the **Employees** table is presented in Table 14.3.

This **Employees** table consists of nine rows of data (see Figure 14.2). Here are two examples of data rows stored in this table:

Table 14.3   The Employees table.

Name	Data Type	Size (Precision, Scale)
EmployeeID	int	4
LastName	nvarchar	20
FirstName	nvarchar	10
Title	nvarchar	30
TitleOfCourtesy	nvarchar	25
BirthDate	datetime	8
HireDate	datetime	8
Address	nvarchar	60
City	nvarchar	15
Region	nvarchar	15
PostalCode	nvarchar	10
Country	nvarchar	15
HomePhone	nvarchar	24
Extension	nvarchar	4
Photo	image	16
Notes	ntext	16
ReportTo	int	4
PhotoPath	nvarchar	255

Figure 14.2
The **Employees** table of Northwind.

```
EmployeeID      1
LastName Davolio
FirstName       Nancy
Title    Sales Representative
TitleOfCourtesy Ms.
BirthDate       12/8/1948
HireDate 5/1/1992
Address  507 - 20th Ave. E.
City     Seattle
Region          WA
PostalCode      98122
Country  USA
HomePhone       (206) 555-9857
Extension       5467
Photo    <Binary>
Notes    Education includes a BA in psychology from Colorado State University
in 1970. She also completed "The Art of the Cold Call." Nancy is a member of
Toastmasters International.
ReportTo 2
PhotoPath       http://accweb/emmployees/davolio.bmp


EmployeeID      2
```

```
LastName Fuller
FirstName       Andrew
Title    Vice President, Sales
TitleOfCourtesy Dr.
BirthDate       2/19/1952
HireDate 8/14/1992
Address  908 W. Capital Way
City     Tacoma
Region   WA
PostalCode       98401
Country  USA
HomePhone        (206) 555-9482
Extension        3457
Photo    <Binary>
Notes    Andrew received his BTS commercial in 1974 and a Ph.D. in
international marketing from the University of Dallas in 1981. He is fluent in
French and Italian and reads German. He joined the company as a sales
representative, was promoted to sales manager in January 1992 and to vice
president of sales in March 1993. Andrew is a member of the Sales Management
Roundtable, the Seattle Chamber of Commerce, and the Pacific Rim Importers
Association.
ReportTo <NULL>
PhotoPath        http://accweb/emmployees/fuller.bmp
```

Simple Import

The following example uses BCP to import data stored in a text file into the **Employees** table of the Northwind database (see Figure 14.3). The complete contents of the text file (addemploy.txt) are displayed:

```
Sequeira        Allison CEO     Mrs.    11/22/1958      2/12/1989       100
North Ave       Worcester       MA      01562   USA     (508) 555-5498 5214
        Allison received her Masters from Harvard where she studied
Accounting and Law.             http://accweb/emmployees/allisons.bmp
Sequeira        Amy     CIO     Mrs.    5/4/1960        8/17/1989       1435 Main
St      Worcester       MA      01654   USA     (508) 456-4567 3456
Amy
 possesses every major computer certification including MCSE, CCIE, and
Oracle.
        http://accweb/emmployees/amys.bmp
Sequeira        Brian   Director of Marketing  Mr.     6/12/1972       1/23/1990
356 Willow Dr   Shrewsbury      MA      06524   USA     (508) 657-
2345    5674            Brian obtained his Masters degree from Yale. 17
 http://accweb/emmployees/brians.bmp
Sequeira        David   President       Mr.     7/30/1950       5/12/1978
345
North Main      Memphis TN      56412   USA     (456) 456-2968 5832
        David obtained his Masters from Stanford.       17
 http://accweb/emmployees/davids.bmp
```

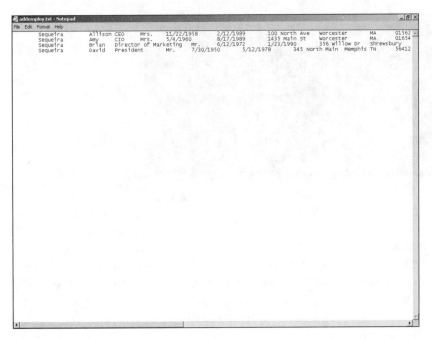

Figure 14.3
The addemploy.txt file.

The following use of BCP takes the tab-delimited (default) text file contents above and imports them into the **Employees** table (see Figure 14.4):

```
bcp Northwind.dbo.Employees in c:\temp\addemploy.txt -c -T
```

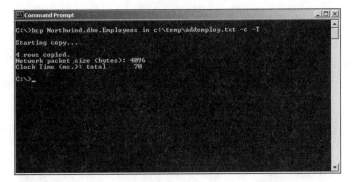

Figure 14.4
Performing a simple import using BCP.

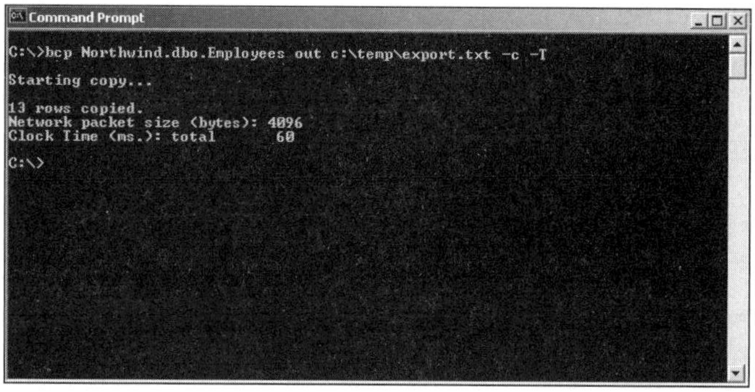

Figure 14.5
Performing a simple export with BCP.

Simple Export

Now let's try a simple export using BCP. Here we use the **-c** switch again to verify that we are working with character mode. Because we are not specifying any formatting options, tab-delimited fields are used by default with newline-delimited rows. Notice how we are performing the export using a view. This view eliminates the Photo field, for this field contains binary information of an image data type. The BCP syntax used follows (see Figure 14.5):

```
bcp Northwind.dbo.Employees_Export out c:\temp\export.txt -c -T
```

Partial results of this export follow:

```
1 Davolio Nancy   Sales Representative   Ms.     1948-12-08
 00:00:00.000   1992-05-01 00:00:00.000       507 - 20th Ave. E.
Apt. 2A  Seattle WA     98122   USA     (206) 555-9857 5467
 Education includes a BA in psychology from Colorado State University in
 1970.  She also completed "The Art of the Cold Call."  Nancy is a member of
 Toastmasters International.   2     http://accweb/emmployees/davolio.bmp
2 Fuller  Andrew  Vice President, Sales  Dr.     1952-02-19 00:00:00.000
 1992-08-14 00:00:00.000       908 W. Capital Way     Tacoma  WA     98401
USA
 (206) 555-9482 3457    Andrew received his BTS commercial in 1974 and
 a Ph.D. in international marketing from the University of Dallas in 1981.  He
 is fluent in French and Italian and reads German.  He joined the company as a
 sales representative, was promoted to sales manager in January 1992 and to
 vice president of sales in March 1993.  Andrew is a member of the Sales
 Management Roundtable, the Seattle Chamber of Commerce, and the Pacific Rim
 Importers Association.        http://accweb/emmployees/fuller.bmp
3 Leverling      Janet   Sales Representative   Ms.     1963-08-30
 00:00:00.000   1992-04-01 00:00:00.000       722 Moss Bay Blvd.     Kirkland
WA
 98033   USA     (206) 555-3412 3355    Janet has a BS degree in
 chemistry from Boston College (1984).  She has also completed a certificate
program in food retailing management.  Janet was hired as a sales associate in
```

1991 and promoted to sales representative in February 1992. 2
http://accweb/emmployees/leverling.bmp

Comma-Delimited Export

Here we perform a comma-delimited export of the **Employees_Export** view to a file named Export_Comma.txt. Note the use of the **-t** switch to specify a comma delimiter, and the use of the **-r\n** switch to note newline row delimiters. The syntax for this export follows:

```
bcp Northwind.dbo.Employees_Export out c:\temp\Export_Comma.txt -c -t, -r\n -T
```

Figure 14.6 shows this syntax and its execution results.

Here are partial results for this export:

```
1,Davolio,Nancy,Sales Representative,Ms.,1948-12-08 00:00:00.000,1992-05-01
 00:00:00.000,507 - 20th Ave. E.
Apt. 2A,Seattle,WA,98122,USA,(206) 555-9857,5467,Education includes a BA in
psychology from Colorado State University in 1970.  She also completed "The
Art
of the Cold Call."  Nancy is a member of Toastmasters
International.,2,http://accweb/emmployees/davolio.bmp
2,Fuller,Andrew,Vice President, Sales,Dr.,1952-02-19 00:00:00.000,1992-08-14
 00:00:00.000,908 W. Capital Way,Tacoma,WA,98401,USA,(206) 555-
9482,3457,Andrew
received his BTS commercial in 1974 and a Ph.D. in international marketing
from
 the University of Dallas in 1981.  He is fluent in French and Italian and
reads German.  He joined the company as a sales representative, was promoted
to
sales manager in January 1992 and to vice president of sales in March 1993.
 Andrew is a member of the Sales Management Roundtable, the Seattle Chamber of
Commerce, and the Pacific Rim Importers
Association.,,http://accweb/emmployees/fuller.bmp
3,Leverling,Janet,Sales Representative,Ms.,1963-08-30 00:00:00.000,1992-04-01
00:00:00.000,722 Moss Bay Blvd.,Kirkland,WA,98033,USA,(206) 555-
3412,3355,Janet
has a BS degree in chemistry from Boston College (1984).  She has also
completed a certificate program in food retailing management.  Janet was hired
as a sales associate in 1991 and promoted to sales representative in February
 1992.,2,http://accweb/emmployees/leverling.bmp
```

Modes of Operation

During the import of data, BCP offers two modes of operation—fast mode and slow mode. Fast mode offers performance enhancements over slow-mode BCP because fast mode bypasses the transaction log process of SQL Server 2000.

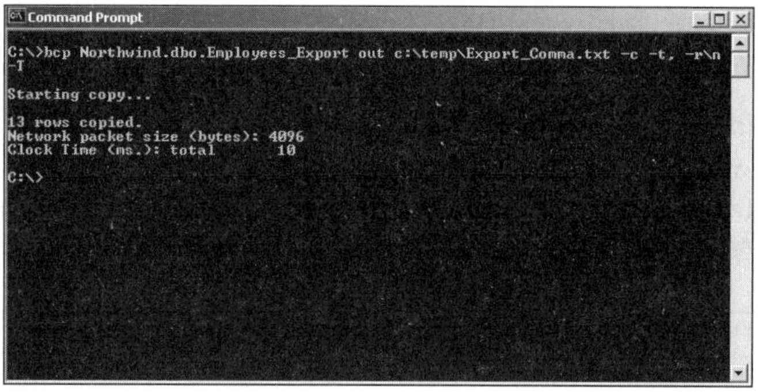

Figure 14.6
Performing a comma-delimited export.

When you run BCP, SQL Server 2000 automatically determines which BCP mode to run in. The factors that determine whether or not BCP runs in fast mode deal with **SELECT INTO/BULKCOPY** and indexes. In order for BCP to run in fast mode, the following four conditions must be true:

- The database option **SELECT INTO/BULKCOPY** must be equal to **TRUE.**

- Indexes must not exist on the target table.

- Triggers must not exist on the target table.

- The target table must not be replicated.

Should any of the above conditions prove to be **FALSE**, BCP runs in slow mode.

Table 14.4 presents the advantages and disadvantages to fast- versus slow-mode BCP.

BCP and Triggers, Rules, Defaults, Constraints, and Unique Indexes

If you have triggers, rules, defaults, constraints, and/or unique indexes configured on your SQL Server 2000 destination table during the use of BCP, it is important to realize that some of these objects are not enforced. Table 14.5 indicates the behavior of these objects during BCP utilization.

Table 14.4   Fast- versus slow-mode BCP.

Mode	Advantages	Disadvantages
Fast	Increased speed	Zero recoverability
	Transaction log does not fill	Full database backup required following BCP
		Indexes must be rebuilt following BCP
Slow	Maximum recoverability	Slower speeds
		Transaction log may become filled

Table 14.5   Object enforcement and BCP.

Object	Enforcement(Yes/No)
Default	Yes
Unique index	Yes
Unique constraint	Yes
Primary key constraint	Yes
Foreign key constraint	Yes
Check constraint	No
Rule	No
Trigger	No

There are some exceptions to the above default behaviors you should be aware of. Although you see that check constraints are not enforced by default with BCP, you can enable constraint checking. Use the **CHECK_CONSTRAINTS** hint when running BCP in order to force this behavior. You can also override the default behavior so that defaults are not processed with BCP. Use the **-k** option when importing data to keep defaults from being processed.

Note: Because triggers, check constraints, and rules are not processed by default when using BCP, you should consider running data integrity checks on your data before importing it into your SQL Server database.

BCP Best Practices

You should consider using the following best practices when using BCP to be certain you are getting the most out of this utility:

- Consider using BCP hints in your syntax.

- Be sure to locate source files for import or destination files for import or export locally on your SQL Server system. Copying data over the network to or from these files can impede performance dramatically.

- Use BCP in parallel on separate machines for very large import/export operations.

- Use views in order to restrict the data that you are exporting using BCP or to change the format that data is presented in using the **CONVERT** function.

- Capture BCP output and errors to a text file when you are troubleshooting. Use the **-o** switch to capture BCP's output. Use the **-e** switch to capture BCP's error messages.

- If you have imports and exports that must occur periodically, consider creating stored procedures that call your BCP syntax, and schedule these stored procedures using the SQL Server Agent.

BULK INSERT

The **BULK INSERT** Transact-SQL statement provides the fastest method for copying large amounts of data from a text file into SQL Server 2000. Keep in mind, however, that you cannot perform data transformations with this method. If you need to transform data as it is imported, you should consider using Data Transformation Services, which is covered later in this chapter.

Here is the syntax for the **BULK INSERT** statement:

```
BULK INSERT [ [ 'database_name'.] [ 'owner' ].] { 'table_name' FROM
'data_file'
 }
    [ WITH
       (
              [ BATCHSIZE [ = batch_size ] ]
              [ [ , ] CHECK_CONSTRAINTS ]
              [ [ , ] CODEPAGE [ = 'ACP' | 'OEM' | 'RAW' | 'code_page' ] ]
              [ [ , ] DATAFILETYPE [ =
                  { 'char' | 'native'| 'widechar' | 'widenative' } ] ]
              [ [ , ] FIELDTERMINATOR [ = 'field_terminator' ] ]
              [ [ , ] FIRSTROW [ = first_row ] ]
              [ [ , ] FIRE_TRIGGERS ]
              [ [ , ] FORMATFILE = 'format_file_path' ]
              [ [ , ] KEEPIDENTITY ]
              [ [ , ] KEEPNULLS ]
              [ [ , ] KILOBYTES_PER_BATCH [ = kilobytes_per_batch ] ]
              [ [ , ] LASTROW [ = last_row ] ]
              [ [ , ] MAXERRORS [ = max_errors ] ]
              [ [ , ] ORDER ( { column [ ASC | DESC ] } [ ,...n ] ) ]
              [ [ , ] ROWS_PER_BATCH [ = rows_per_batch ] ]
              [ [ , ] ROWTERMINATOR [ = 'row_terminator' ] ]
              [ [ , ] TABLOCK ]
        )
    ]
```

The explanations for this syntax follow:

- **database_name**—Allows you to specify the name of the database where the table or view resides. If you do not specify a database, the current database is assumed.

- **owner**—Specifies the name of the table or view owner. The **owner** argument is optional if you own the specified table or view. If **owner** is not specified and you or the user performing the bulk copy operation does not own the specified table or view, SQL Server returns an error message, and the bulk copy operation is canceled.

- **table_name**—Specifies the name of the table or view to bulk copy data into. You can only specify views in which all columns refer to the same base table, however.

- **data_file**—Specifies the full path of the data file that contains data to copy into the specified table or view. **BULK INSERT** can copy data from a disk (including network disks, floppy disks, local hard disks, etc). Remember, this element must specify the full path, which means using a local path if the file is stored on the system running SQL Server 2000, or using a Universal Naming Convention (UNC) path if the file is remote.

- **BATCHSIZE [= batch_size]**—Allows you to specify the number of rows in a batch. Each batch is copied to the server as one transaction. SQL Server commits (or rolls back, in the case of failure) the transaction for every batch. By default, all data in the specified data file is one batch.

- **CHECK_CONSTRAINTS**—Allows you to specify that any constraints on **table_name** be checked during the bulk copy operation. By default, constraints are ignored.

- **CODEPAGE [= 'ACP' | 'OEM' | 'RAW' | 'code_page']**—Allows you to specify the code page of the data in the data file. **CODEPAGE** is relevant only if the data contains **char**, **varchar**, or **text** columns with character values greater than 127 or less than 32. The default is **OEM**. The possible values are as follows:

  - **ACP**—Columns of **char**, **varchar**, or **text** data type are converted from the ANSI/Microsoft Windows code page (ISO 1252) to the SQL Server code page.

  - **OEM**—Columns of **char**, **varchar**, or **text** data type are converted from the system **OEM** code page to the SQL Server code page.

  - **RAW**—No conversion from one code page to another occurs; this is the fastest option.

  - **code_page**—Specific code page number, for example, 850.

- **DATAFILETYPE [= { 'char' | 'native'| 'widechar' | 'widenative' }]**—allows you to specify that **BULK INSERT** performs the copy operation using the specified default. The default value for this parameter is **char**. The possible values are as follows:

  - **char**—Performs the bulk copy operation from a data file containing character data.

  - **native**—Performs the bulk copy operation using the native (database) data types. The data file to load is created by bulk copying data from SQL Server using the BCP utility.

  - **widechar**—Performs the bulk copy operation from a data file containing Unicode characters.

  - **widenative**—Performs the same bulk copy operation as **native**, except **char**, **varchar**, and **text** columns are stored as Unicode in the data file. The data file to be loaded was created by bulk copying data from SQL Server using the BCP utility. This option offers you a higher performance alternative to the **widechar** option, and is intended for transferring data from one computer running SQL Server to another by using a data file. You should use this option when transferring data that contains ANSI extended characters in order to take advantage of native mode performance.

14

- **FIELDTERMINATOR [= 'field_terminator']**—Allows you to specify the field terminator to be used for **char** and **widechar** data files. The default is **\t** (tab character).

- **FIRSTROW [= first_row]**—Allows you to specify the number of the first row to bulk copy. Obviously, the default is **1**, indicating the first row in the specified data file.

- **FIRE_TRIGGERS**—Specifies that any insert triggers defined on the destination table will execute during the bulk copy operation. If you do not specify **FIRE_TRIGGERS**, no insert triggers will execute.

- **FORMATFILE = 'format_file_path'**—This option specifies the full path of a format file. You use a format file to describe the data file that contains stored responses created using the BCP utility on the same table or view. You should use a format file when the data file contains greater or fewer columns than the table or view, or the columns are in a different order. This file should also be used when the column delimiters vary, or there are other changes in the data format. You typically create format files using the BCP utility and modify them with a text editor as needed.

- **KEEPIDENTITY**—Allows you to specify that the values for an identity column are present in the file imported. If you do not specify **KEEPIDENTITY**, the identity values for this column in the data file imported are ignored, and SQL Server automatically assigns unique values based on the seed and increment values specified during table creation. If your data file does not contain values for the identity column in the table or view, you should use a format file to specify that the identity column in the table or view should be skipped when importing data.

- **KEEPNULLS**—Specifies that empty columns should retain a **NULL** value during the bulk copy operation, rather than have any default values for the columns inserted.

- **KILOBYTES_PER_BATCH [= kilobytes_per_batch]**—Specifies the approximate number of kilobytes (KB) of data per batch. By default, **KILOBYTES_PER_BATCH** is unknown.

- **LASTROW [= last_row]**—Allows you to specify the number of the last row to bulk copy. The default for this value is **0**, indicating the last row in the specified data file should be copied.

- **MAXERRORS [= max_errors]**—Specifies the maximum number of errors that can occur before the bulk copy operation is canceled. Each row that cannot be copied by the **BULK INSERT** process is ignored and counted as one error. If you do not include this option, the default is **10**.

- **ORDER ({ column [ASC | DESC]**—Specifies how the data in the data file is sorted. You can improve bulk copy operation performance if the data loaded is sorted according to the clustered index on the table. If the data file is sorted in a different order, or there is no clustered index on the table, the **ORDER** clause is ignored. The column names supplied must be valid columns in the destination table. By default, the bulk insert operation assumes the data file is unordered.

- **ROWS_PER_BATCH [= rows_per_batch]**—Specifies the number of rows of data per batch (as **rows_per_batch**). You use this option when **BATCHSIZE** is not specified, resulting in the entire data file being sent to the server as a single transaction. The server optimizes the bulk load according to **rows_per_batch**. By default, **ROWS_PER_BATCH** is unknown.

- **ROWTERMINATOR [= 'row_terminator']**—Specifies the row terminator to be used for **char** and **widechar** data files. The default is **\n** (newline character).

- **TABLOCK**—Specifies that a table-level lock is acquired for the duration of the bulk copy operation. A table can be loaded concurrently by multiple clients if the table has no indexes and **TABLOCK** is specified. By default, locking behavior is determined by the table option table-lock on bulk load. Holding a lock only for the duration of the bulk copy operation reduces lock contention on the table, significantly improving performance.

In this example, you use the contents of a text file named addsupp.txt to add several suppliers to the **Suppliers** table of the Northwind database. The text file consists of tab-delimited columns with newline row-delimiters. The contents of this file appear here:

```
AJS Ent.        Anthony Sequeira      Manager 23 Thomas Rd.   Phoenix
AZ      85268   USA     (480)546-6784 (480)867-4572  http://www.main.com
Thomas Foods    Jim Gardner     Owner   100 Main St.    Tempe   AZ      78658
USA
(602)567-3456           http://www.thomas.com
TFG Foods       John Smith      President       234 Swallow Dr.     El Cajon
CA      86745   USA     (567)342-5682 (567)245-6798  http://www.tfg.com
```

The syntax you use for the **BULK INSERT** follows:

```
BULK INSERT Northwind.dbo.Suppliers
FROM 'c:\temp\addsupp.txt'
```

This sample **BULK INSERT** syntax imports the contents of sample.txt into the **Order Details** table of the Northwind database. This txt file uses the **|** as a field terminator and **\n** as the row terminator. This query also specifies that any insert triggers defined on the **Order Details** table will execute during the bulk copy operation:

```
BULK INSERT Northwind.dbo.[Order Details]
   FROM 'f:\orders\sample.txt'
   WITH
   (
       FIELDTERMINATOR = '|',
       ROWTERMINATOR = '|\n',
   FIRE_TRIGGERS
     )
```

Here is another **BULK INSERT** example that uses high performance options to perform a character data import:

```
BULK INSERT Northwind.dbo.Customer
FROM 'c:\temp\customer.txt'
WITH (ORDER(customer_id), TABLOCK)
```

DTS Overview

If your organization is like most organizations, it has data stored in many different places and in many different formats. Data Transformation Services (DTS) in SQL Server 2000 allows you to easily import, export, and transfer this data to and from SQL Server 2000 using graphical tools and wizards.

DTS provides the ability to:

- Import and export data between different OLE DB, ODBC, or text file sources

- Transform the data as it is transferred

- Transfer database objects between databases in SQL Server 2000 systems

- Create custom transformation objects you can integrate into third-party products

- Build data warehouses and data marts

- Access applications by using third-party OLE DB providers

At some point in your enterprise operations, you are going to need to move or copy data from one application to another. This process usually involves identifying a particular data source, specifying the destination for the data, and manipulating or transforming the data as it is transferred.

Why might you need to transform data as it is moved or copied from a source to the destination? Here are some of the more common reasons:

- *Change the format of data*—Perhaps your source stores a particular data value as **TRUE** or **FALSE** and your receiving application needs this information stored as **1** or **0**. Another common example is that you need to change the date format as you are transferring the data.

- *Transform and map data*—Oftentimes, you need to combine data from different sources into a single dataset at the destination.

- *Make data consistent*—Perhaps you need to make the entries in a **Company Name** column consistent because you notice the same company is listed several different ways in the column, for example, AJS Industries, AJS Ind., and simply AJS.

- *Validate data*—You need to verify the accuracy of data as it is transferred. For example, using DTS you can easily verify that data meets a specific condition before it is included with your destination data.

- *Schedule the operation*—DTS allows you to schedule data moves, copies, and transformations. This capability allows you to address situations in which you periodically need to transfer and transform data.

- *Import and export between heterogeneous environments*—This situation occurs often in enterprises. For example, you may need to periodically transfer information from an Oracle RDBMS to your SQL Server 2000 RDBMS.

DTS Components

It probably does not surprise you that something as powerful as DTS comprises components. This section examines the components that make up the service. Knowledge of these components is critical for your mastery of DTS.

DTS Package

Without a doubt, the DTS package is the core component of Data Transformation Services. You create and execute packages to actually carry out DTS tasks. All the other components that make up DTS are children to this parent object. See Figure 14.7 for a

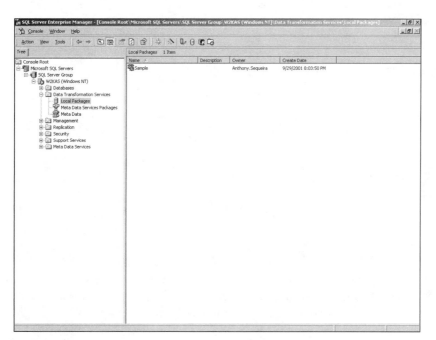

Figure 14.7
A sample DTS package in Enterprise Manager.

glimpse of a sample DTS package in Enterprise Manager. Notice the location of this package in the object hierarchy in the left pane of Enterprise Manager.

You can create DTS packages using the DTS Designer, a graphical user interface tool for designing DTS packages, or you can use two core DTS-related wizards. You can save your DTS packages to the local SQL Server, the Microsoft Repository, Visual Basic files, or COM-structured files. You also have the ability to create your package and execute it once, without actually saving the package. This strategy works just fine if you never intend to use the package again, or you are not going to schedule the package for periodic execution.

A DTS package consists of four major components. These components are Connections, Tasks, Steps, and Global Variables. Your packages typically consist of one or more of these objects. All these child objects of packages are explored in this section.

Connections

As mentioned earlier, you can use DTS to connect to any OLE DB-compliant data source in the interest of transferring and/or transforming data. Without any additional software, DTS can connect to the following data providers:

- SQL Server
- Microsoft Access
- Microsoft Excel
- Visual FoxPro
- Paradox
- dBase
- Text files
- HTML files
- Oracle
- Microsoft Data Link files

You can easily expand the above list by downloading the appropriate drivers and files from Microsoft. You should visit **www.microsoft.com/data** for more information. You can also obtain the appropriate driver directly from the specific vendor.

Tasks

Tasks allow your packages to actually accomplish specific objectives. Without tasks, your DTS packages are not worth their weight in code. The 17 built-in tasks in SQL Server 2000 are listed below:

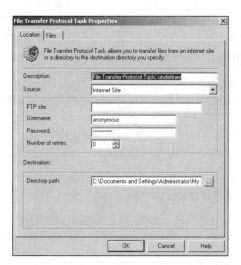

Figure 14.8
The Properties for the File Transfer Protocol Task.

14

- *File Transfer Protocol Task*—New to SQL Server 2000, this task allows the user to receive files from internal or external servers using the FTP protocol. Figure 14.8 shows you the Properties window for this task and the configuration options available.

- *ActiveX Script Task*—This task opens up the possibilities for DTS to an almost unlimited degree. You can add any ActiveX scripts to your package by using this task to perform a number of different functions not explicitly defined by other built-in or custom tasks. Figure 14.9 shows the available Properties for this task.

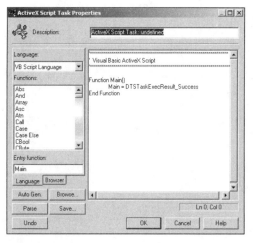

Figure 14.9
The Properties for the ActiveX Script Task.

- *Transform Data Task*—This powerful task allows you to transform data from any OLE DB data source to any other OLE DB data source. This task is also known as the Data Pump Task—not only by SQL Server 2000 programmers, but also in some Microsoft documentation. Just a few of the features of this task include the ability to:

  - Automatically map columns between the source and the destination data stores.

  - Narrow the source rowset by running a query you specify.

  - Setup row-level restartability that causes the entire step to fail should one attempted insertion fail.

  - Allow for events to execute before and after the transformation.

  - Configure row-by-row level handling of data, allowing you to execute customized procedures.

  Figure 14.10 shows you the Properties available with this powerful task.

- *Execute Process Task*—This task allows you to execute any Windows compatible program or batch file.

- *Execute SQL Task*—This task allows you to execute any Transact-SQL statement within your DTS Package. For example, you might need to run maintenance tasks following the import of data.

- *Data Driven Query Task*—This task allows DTS to scan through the source data row by row and perform a query dynamically, based on the data that is received. For example, you could have this task examine each record in a source Customers file and only insert

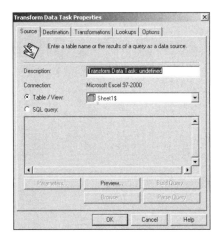

Figure 14.10
The Properties for the Transform Data Task.

Figure 14.11
The Properties for the Data Driven Query Task.

14

those customers that do not exist in the destination database. Figure 14.11 shows the Properties available for this powerful task.

- *Copy SQL Server Objects Task*—This task allows you to copy SQL Server database objects from one database to another. For example, perhaps you need to copy triggers from one database to another; this operation is accomplished easily using this task.

- *Send Mail Task*—This task allows you to send email to a recipient. Often you use this task to alert an operator to the success or failure of a task.

- *Bulk Insert Task*—As its name implies, this task relies on the **BULK INSERT** Transact-SQL statement to perform high-speed data transfers into SQL Server 2000. This task has strict rules that must be met. These rules include:

  - SQL Server must be the destination.

  - Data column mappings in the source must be identical in the destination.

  - The number of columns in the source and the destination must be identical.

- *Execute Package Task*—New to SQL Server 2000, this task allows one package to call and execute another package. This capability permits you to divide very large and complex DTS jobs into multiple packages.

- *Message Queue Task*—New to SQL Server 2000, this task allows your package to communicate with other applications using Microsoft Message Queue Server as the communications medium.

- *Transfer Error Messages Task*—New to SQL Server 2000, this task allows you to transfer user-specified error messages from one SQL Server system to another.

- *Transfer Databases Task*—New to SQL Server 2000, this task allows you to transfer a database from SQL Server 7 or SQL Server 2000 to another SQL Server 2000 server. As you might guess, the Copy Database Wizard relies upon this task.

- *Transfer Master Stored Procedures Task*—New to SQL Server 2000, this task allows you to transfer stored procedures from the Master database of a SQL Server 7 or 2000 server to another SQL Server 2000 system. The Copy Database Wizard relies upon this task. See Figure 14.12 for a glimpse of the configuration options for this task.

- *Transfer Jobs Task*—New to SQL Server 2000, this task allows you to transfer jobs from one SQL Server system to another. The destination server must be running SQL Server 2000, however. The Copy Database Wizard relies upon this task.

- *Transfer Logins Task*—New to SQL Server 2000, this task allows you to transfer logins from one SQL Server to another. The destination server must be running SQL Server 2000, however. The Copy Database Wizard relies upon this task.

- *Dynamic Properties Task*—New to SQL Server 2000, this task allows you to dynamically set DTS objects to a value received from an INI file, environment or global variable, query, constants, or a data file. This task is very powerful, allowing you to design one package and use it for a variety of circumstances, thanks to its ability to respond to a changing variable. Figure 14.13 shows the Properties of this task.

Steps

Steps allow you to carry out tasks in your package in a sequential order. You can also use steps to set precedence constraints on tasks. For example, you could have an Execute SQL Task that creates a new table in your database. You could then have a task that populates this table, but you could make sure this task does not run until the successful completion of the create table task. Each task in your package will have one step associated with it that can execute in either sequential or parallel order.

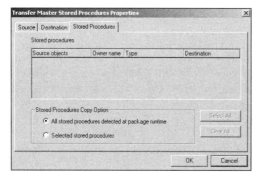

Figure 14.12
The Properties of the Transfer Master Stored Procedures Task.

Figure 14.13
The Properties of the Dynamic Properties Task.

Global Variables

Global variable objects dramatically increase the dynamic nature of your DTS packages. Thanks to these objects, your package can set a variable in a single area and use the variable over and over again throughout the package.

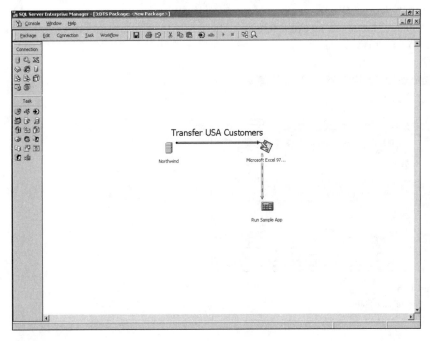

Figure 14.14
A simple package in the DTS Designer.

A Simple Package Example

You can employ two wizards to use DTS services. Most often, however, you will use the powerful DTS Designer. Figure 14.14 shows a simple package in this designer. You will build this package later in the chapter using the designer.

As you can see, this package accomplishes the following:

- The package makes a connection to the Northwind database on a SQL Server system.

- It then makes a connection to an Excel 2000 spreadsheet.

- The package then transfers only those customers in Northwind from the USA to a new sheet in the Excel workbook.

- If the transfer is successful, the package executes a sample application—in this case, the Windows calculator.

Using the DTS Wizards

Two SQL Server 2000 wizards rely heavily upon the functionality of DTS—the Import/Export Wizard and the Copy Database Wizard. This section guides you through the use of these wizards.

Import/Export Wizard

The Import/Export Wizard is extremely powerful, guiding you through the steps to create DTS packages and even save and schedule these packages for execution. Follow the steps below to use this wizard:

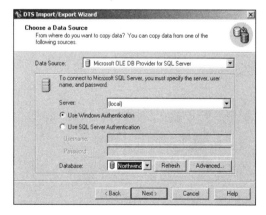

Figure 14.15
Choosing your data source.

1. Select Start|Programs|Microsoft SQL Server|Import And Export Data to launch the DTS Import/Export Wizard.

2. Choose Next in the Welcome screen of the wizard.

3. In the Choose a Data Source page (see Figure 14.15), select the Northwind database in the Database drop-down menu. Notice the other options on this page. Choose Next when you are finished reviewing them.

4. In the Choose A Destination page, select the Destination drop-down menu and choose Text File.

5. Open the Windows Explorer and create a text file in your temp folder named sample.txt.

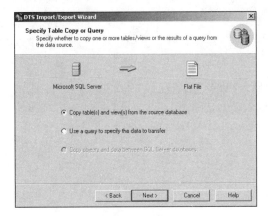

Figure 14.16
Choosing the manner in which data will be copied.

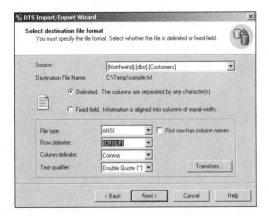

Figure 14.17
Selecting a destination file format.

6. In the Choose A Destination page, provide the file name and path in the File name field and choose Next.

7. In the Specify Table Copy or Query page, choose Next to accept the default selection. You would like to Copy Table(s) and View(s) from the Source Database (see Figure 14.16).

8. In the Select Destination File Format page, choose [Northwind].[dbo].[Customers] in the Source drop-down menu. Notice the options for creating a delimited file that appear on this page (see Figure 14.17). Choose Next when you are finished reviewing these options.

9. In the Save, Schedule, And Replicate Package page, select the Save DTS Package check box and choose Next.

10. In the Save DTS Package page, name your package Export Customers To Text using the Name field.

11. In the Description field, type "This package exports the Customers table to a comma-delimited text file".

12. Choose Next in the Save DTS Package page.

13. Review the choices you selected in the Completing page and choose Finish when you are ready to perform the export and save the DTS package.

14. The Executing Package window appears, providing you with status information regarding each step of your package. See Figure 14.18.

15. Choose Done in the Executing Package window.

16. Use the Windows Explorer to open the sample.txt file and review the results (see Figure 14.19).

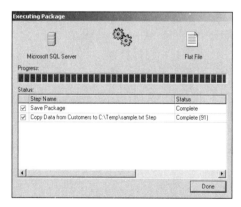

Figure 14.18
The Executing Package window.

Figure 14.19
The sample.txt file populated by the Import/Export Wizard.

You should also use Enterprise Manager to view the package that you created and saved using the Import/Export Wizard of DTS.

Copy Database Wizard

In this section, you explore the use of the Copy Database Wizard. Follow the steps below to leverage the power of this important tool:

1. Select Start|Programs|Microsoft SQL Server|Enterprise Manager to launch the Enterprise Manager graphical tool.

2. Expand the hierarchy in the left pane and select your server with a left mouse click.

3. From the Tools menu in Enterprise Manager, choose Wizards.

4. In the Select Wizard window, expand the Management node and double-click the Copy Database Wizard.

5. Choose Next in the Welcome page.

6. Choose Next in the Select A Source Server page to select your local server as the source.

7. In the Select A Destination Server page, use the ellipses button to browse to and select the destination server for the copy operation. When you are finished, choose Next.

8. In the Select The Databases To Move Or Copy screen, use the checkboxes in the Move or Copy columns to select those databases you would like to move or copy. Choose Next when you are finished.

9. In the Database File Location page, choose Next after you are certain there are no file name conflicts at the destination. File name conflicts appear with a red X.

10. In the Select Related Objects page, choose the objects you would like moved with the database. These options include SQL Server logins, shared stored procedures, jobs, and user-defined error messages. After you have made your selections, choose Next.

11. In the Schedule The DTS Package page, indicate whether or not you would like the package to run immediately, run once at a specified time, or be scheduled to run later. When you have finished, choose Next.

12. Review your selections in the Completing page and choose Finish when you are ready to either run or save the package.

Using the DTS Designer

Although the DTS wizards are certainly powerful, and they make it easy for you to perform many common data transfer and transformation tasks, there is no substitute for the powerful DTS Designer. The designer allows you to take advantage of every possible task Data Transformation Services has to offer. In the steps that follow, you will use the DTS Designer to design the package shown earlier:

1. Select Start|Programs|Microsoft SQL Server|Enterprise Manager to launch the Enterprise Manager graphical tool.

2. Expand the hierarchy in the left pane and expand your server to view the Data Transformation Services node. Expand this node and right-click to view the shortcut menu. Select New Package from the shortcut menu to launch the DTS Designer.

3. In the Connection area of the toolbar in the left of the designer, choose the Microsoft OLE DB Provider For SQL Server icon to add this connection to your designer pane.

4. In the Connection Properties window, name the connection Northwind and choose the Northwind database in the Database drop-down menu. When you have finished with these selections, choose OK. Notice that your connection appears in the designer pane.

5. In the Connection area of the toolbar, choose the Microsoft Excel 97-2000 icon.

6. Use Windows Explorer to create an Excel file named sample.xls in your temp folder.

7. In the Connection Properties window, name the new connection Excel and use the ellipses button to browse to the Excel file you just created in Step 6. Choose OK when you are finished.

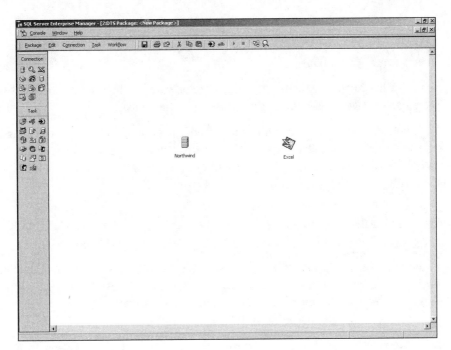

Figure 14.20
Placing your connection objects.

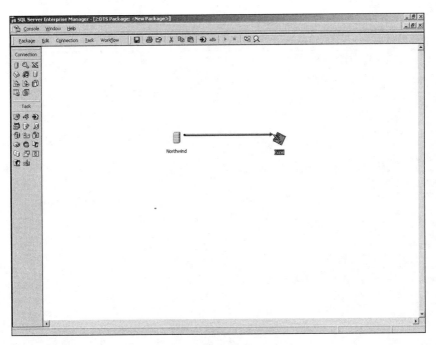

Figure 14.21
Creating the Transform Data Task.

8. Click and drag the connection objects to move them to the center of the DTS Designer pane. Make sure there is enough space between these objects to add other objects (see Figure 14.20).

9. Left-click the Northwind connection object to be sure it is highlighted and choose the Transform Data Task icon in the Task area of the toolbar.

10. Move your mouse pointer back into the designer pane and notice the "Select destination connection" message. Click the Excel connection and notice the arrow that appears from one connection to the other. Notice also that the arrow is pointing to Excel from the Northwind connection (see Figure 14.21).

11. Left-click the Transform Data Task arrow in order to select it. Right-click the object and choose Properties from the shortcut menu.

12. In the Transform Data Task Properties window, enter the following in the Description field "Transfer all Customers from the USA." Choose the SQL Query radio button and then choose the Build Query button to launch the Data Transformation Services Query Designer window (see Figure 14.22).

13. Drag [Northwind].[dbo].[Customers] from the left pane into the top pane of the Query Designer. Notice that the query is being completed for you in the bottom pane of the Query Designer. Select the All Columns checkbox in the Customers window.

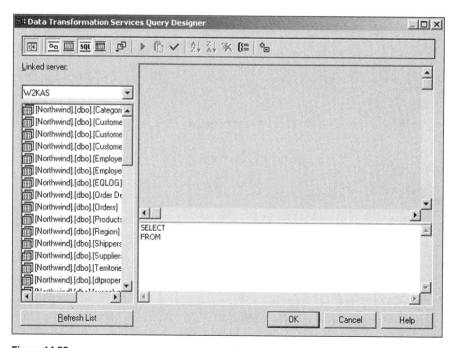

Figure 14.22
The Data Transformation Services Query Designer window.

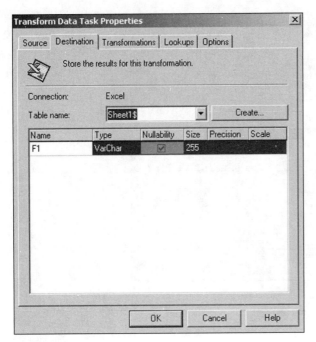

Figure 14.23
The Destination tab of the Transform Data Task Properties window.

14. Click after Customers in the **FROM** clause in the bottom pane and press Enter to being a new line. Type "WHERE Country = 'USA'" to finish the query. Choose OK in the Query Designer.

15. Choose the Parse Query button to verify that the query is constructed properly.

16. Choose the Destination tab in the Transform Data Task Properties window (see Figure 14.23). Choose the Create button. Replace the name of the table (currently New Table) with Customers and choose OK in the Create Destination Table window.

17. Choose OK in the Transform Data Task Properties window to complete the properties for this task.

18. In the Task area of the toolbar, choose the Execute Process Task icon.

19. In the Execute Process Task Properties window (see Figure 14.24), type "Run sample application" in the Description field. Use the ellipses button to navigate to the application you would like to execute. For this example, choose Calc.exe. When you have finished, choose OK.

20. Click and drag the Run Sample Application task to place it under the Excel connection.

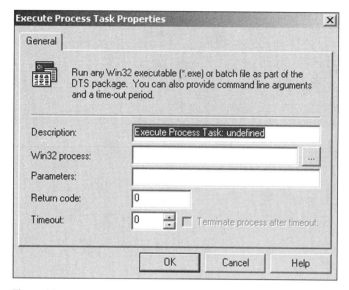

Figure 14.24
The Execute Process Task Properties window.

21. Left-click the Excel connection object, hold down the shift key and select the Run Sample Application task in order to select both objects. Right-click one of the objects and choose Workflow|On Success from the shortcut menu. Notice the Precedence Constraint that is added to the Designer (see Figure 14.25).

22. Choose the Package menu in the DTS Designer and choose Save As.

23. Name your package Export Customers and choose OK in the Save As window.

24. Run your DTS package using the Execute button in the top toolbar of the DTS Designer. Notice that the Calculator launches following the successful transfer of data. Choose Done in the Executing Package window.

DTS Packages

Packages are obviously the key to DTS. Packages and the objects they contain allow Data Transformation Services to function. This section provides you with more information regarding saving, scheduling, and maintaining your packages.

Saving Packages

Remember, there are many options for saving your DTS packages. Each option offers its own unique advantages and disadvantages. Your options for saving DTS packages include the following:

• *Meta Data Services (Repository)*—Without a doubt, this is the most powerful option for saving your packages. When you save packages to the Repository, they are stored in the

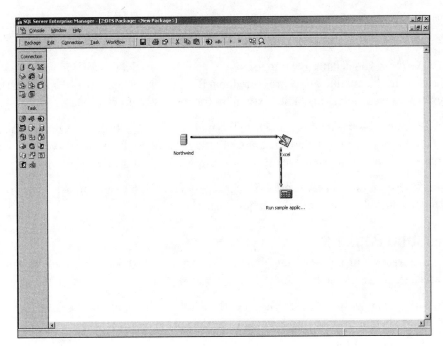

Figure 14.25
Adding a Precedence Constraint.

msdb system database of SQL Server 2000. The tremendous advantage this method offers is your ability to save package meta data and execution information. This is known as the *lineage data* for the package.

Table 14.6   Advantages and disadvantages of each save method.

Save Method	Advantages	Disadvantages
Repository	Audit trails possible	Slowest to execute
	Lineage data available	
	Easy backup of packages	
COM-Structured File	Packages are portable	Version control is more difficult
	Faster saves and loads	No lineage data available
	Performance gains due to caching	Separate backup and recovery strategy for packages
SQL Server	Faster save than Repository	Slow execution compared to COM
	Simplified backup of packages	No lineage data available
Visual Basic File	Simple programmability	More difficult editing
		Lacks version control

- *COM-Structured Storage File*—Provides the fastest way to save or load your package. The package is stored with a .DTS extension.

- *SQL Server*—The default location for saving your DTS packages. Should you save your packages in this manner, they are stored in a Binary Large Object (BLOB) field in the **sysdtspackages** table. This table is stored in the msdb system database.

- *Visual Basic File*—Saving the package in this manner creates a .BAS file. Although this option allows you to further enhance and edit the package using Visual Basic, it is no longer simple to open and edit your package using the graphical tools of SQL Server 2000.

So just where should you save your DTS packages? Table 14.6 helps you decide by presenting the advantages and disadvantages of each method.

Executing Packages

Once you create your DTS Package, there are a variety of methods for actually executing the package. These methods include:

- Executing from within the DTS Designer. This is possible thanks to the Execute button on the toolbar, or by choosing Execute from the Package menu.

- Scheduling the DTS Package for execution using the SQL Server Agent.

- Executing from a command-line environment using the dtsrun utility or from Windows using the dtsrunui utility.

- Using a custom application with the Execute method in the DTS package object.

- Executing from within Enterprise Manager by right-clicking a package and choosing Execute Package.

dtsrun

The dtsrun.exe utility is a simple command-prompt utility you can use for executing DTS packages. The complete syntax for this command follows:

```
dtsrun
[/?] |
[
    [
        /[~]S server_name[\instance_name]
        { {/[~]U user_name [/[~]P password]} | /E }
    ]
    {
        {/[~]N package_name }
        | {/[~]G package_guid_string}
        | {/[~]V package_version_guid_string}
    }
    [/[~]M package_password]
```

```
    [/[~]F filename]
    [/[~]R repository_database_name]
    [/A global_variable_name:typeid=value]
    [/L log_file_name]
    [/W NT_event_log_completion_status]
    [/Z] [/!X] [/!D] [/!Y] [/!C]
]
```

The explanations for these syntax elements follow:

- **/?**—Allows you to display the option for running dtsrun.

- **~**—Specifies that the parameter to follow is hexadecimal text representing the encrypted value of the parameter. You can use this indicator with the **/S, /U, /P, /N, /G, /V, /M, /F,** and **/R dtsrun** options. If you use encrypted values you increase the security of the command used to execute the DTS package because the server name, password, and so on, are not visible. You can use **/!Y** to determine the encrypted command.

- **/S server_name[\instance_name]**—Allows you to specify the instance of SQL Server to connect to. You need to specify **server_name** to connect to the default instance of SQL Server on that server or specify **server_name\instance_name** to connect to a named instance of SQL Server 2000 on that server.

- **/U user_name**—Allows you to specify a login ID used to connect to an instance of SQL Server.

- **/P password**—Allows you to specify a user-specified password used with a login ID.

- **/E**—Allows you to specify that a trusted connection should be used to connect to SQL Server 2000. (A password is not required when connecting in this manner.)

- **/N package_name**—Specifies the name assigned to a DTS package when the package was created.

- **/G package_guid_string**—Allows you to specify the package ID assigned to the DTS package when it was created. The package ID is a GUID (Globally Unique Identifier).

- **/V package_version_guid_string**—Allows you to specify the version ID assigned to the DTS package when it was first saved or executed. A new version ID is assigned to the DTS package each time it is modified. The version ID is a GUID.

- **/M package_password**—Allows you to specify an optional password assigned to the DTS package when it was created.

- **/F filename**—Allows you to specify the name of a structured storage file containing DTS packages. If **server_name** is also specified, the DTS package retrieved from SQL Server is executed and that package is added to the structured storage engine.

- **/R repository_database_name**—Allows you to specify the name of the repository database containing DTS packages. If no name is specified, the default database name is used.

- **/A global_variable_name:typeid=value**—Allows you to specify a package global variable, where **typeid** is the type identifier for the data type of the global variable. The entire argument string can be quoted. This argument can be repeated to specify multiple global variables. To set global variables with this command switch, you must have either Owner permission for the package or the package must have been saved without DTS password protection enabled. If you do not have Owner permission, you can specify global variables, but the values used will be those set in the package, not those specified with the **/A** command switch.

- **/L log_file_name:**—Allows you to specify the name of the package log file.

- **/W Windows_Event_Log**—Allows you to specify whether or not to write the completion status of the package execution to the Windows Application Log. You specify **True** or **False** for this value.

- **/Z**—allows you to specify that the command-line information for dtsrun is encrypted using SQL Server 2000 encryption.

- **/!X**—Allows you to block execution of the selected DTS package. Use this command parameter when you want to create an encrypted command line without executing the DTS package.

- **/!D**—Allows you to delete the DTS package from an instance of SQL Server. The package is not executed. It is not possible to delete a specific DTS package from a structured storage file. The entire file needs to be overwritten using the **/F** and **/S** options.

- **/!Y**—Allows you to display the encrypted command used to execute the DTS package without actually executing it.

- **/!C**—Allows you to copy the command used to execute the DTS package to the Windows clipboard. This option can also be used in conjunction with **/!X** and **/!Y**.

For example, the following syntax allows you to execute a DTS package saved as a COM-structured storage file:

```
dtsrun /Ffilename /Npackage_name /Mpackage_password
```

This syntax example executes a DTS package saved in the SQL Server msdb database:

```
dtsrun /Sserver_name /Uuser_nName /Ppassword /Npackage_name /Mpackage_password
```

Finally, this example executes a DTS package saved in the Repository:

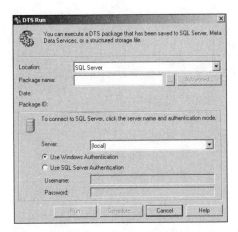

Figure 14.26
Running the dtsrunui.exe utility.

14

```
dtsrun /Sserver_name /Uuser_name /Ppassword /Npackage_name /Mpackage_password
/Rrepository_name
```

dtsrunui

The dtsrunui.exe utility allows you to quickly write a **DTSRUN** statement and automates the process of passing parameters to the package. By default, you can find this utility in the following location on your server:

```
c:\Program Files\Microsoft SQL Server\80\Tools\Binn
```

When you execute this utility, the graphical user interface appears as depicted in Figure 14.26.

As you can see, executing a package using this utility is simple. First, select the source of the package using the Location drop-down menu. This represents the type of save location you choose. Notice that this utility allows you to run packages saved to the following locations:

• Meta Data Services (Repository)

• SQL Server

• Structured Storage File

When you have finished selecting the location of your saved package, use the ellipses button to select the specific package you would like to execute. Notice that there is a Schedule button at the bottom of the interface. This allows you to schedule your package for later—or even periodic—execution. More information is provided later in this section regarding scheduling your packages for execution. It is much more common to make these configuration changes using Enterprise Manager.

Figure 14.27
The Advanced DTS Run window.

Once you have selected the package, you may access the Advanced button. The Advanced button permits you to enter configuration information in the Advanced DTS Run window (see Figure 14.27).

Notice that the Advanced DTS Run window allows you to pass the values of global variables to the package. As you know, your packages can contain global variables that make them extremely flexible, allowing you to create a single package to service many potential needs.

You should also notice the Generate button in the Advanced DTS Run window. This button causes dtsrunui.exe to automatically generate the appropriate command-line syntax for the dtsrun utility. For example:

```
DTSRun /S "(local)" /N "Export Customers to Text "
/G "{139BEE44-CED2-455D-B1D5-4AEEDA8B9970}" /W "0" /E
```

This function is a great way to make sure that your command-line syntax is 100 percent accurate.

Scheduling your Package

In this section, you schedule the package named Export Customers that you created earlier in this chapter. Follow these steps to do so:

1. Select Start|Programs|Microsoft SQL Server|Enterprise Manager to launch the Enterprise Manager interface.

2. Expand the hierarchy in the left pane and expand your server to view the Data Transformation Services node. Expand this node and left-click the Local Packages node to view the packages stored on your server in the right pane.

3. Right-click the Export Customers package and select Schedule Package from the shortcut menu (see Figure 14.28).

4. In the Edit Recurring Job Schedule window (see Figure 14.29), select the job schedule that meets your needs and choose OK when finished.

You should certainly be familiar with the Edit Recurring Job Schedule window from

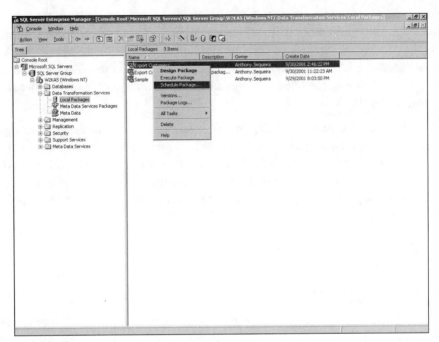

Figure 14.28
Scheduling your package for execution.

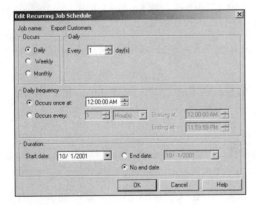

Figure 14.29
Creating a Recurring Job Schedule.

Chapter 10 of this book, where you learned to automate routine administrative tasks. The scheduling of packages relies upon the internal job system of the SQL Server Agent. As you might guess, for the job (package) to actually execute on the recurring basis that you specify, the SQL Server Agent service must be properly configured and actually running. Should you not have the SQL Server Agent running, you can still schedule jobs; they will wait in queue and execute the next scheduled time after the service does, in fact, start.

When you schedule a package for execution in the manner specified above, there is a powerful advantage over other methods of scheduling package execution. The advantage is that the package execution is carried out in an encrypted fashion by default. The password used to execute the package is stored in an encrypted form. The jobs that actually make up these scheduled packages are stored in the **sysjobs**, **sysjobschedules**, and the **sysjobsteps** tables.

You could also create a job manually for the execution of your packages by navigating to the Jobs node in the Management folder of Enterprise Manager. Right-click this node and choose New Job from the shortcut menu. For the step that you are going to have your job perform, choose to perform an operating system command in order to execute your package. For the operating system command, simply use the appropriate **DTSRUN** syntax.

Tip: Remember, you can use the dtsrunui utility to generate the appropriate syntax for you.

Logging DTS Activity

Data Transformation Services offers its own logging capability. Because this logging can create massive amounts of overhead—and can cause your msdb system database to grow to a very large size—you should use your ability to log DTS activity very sparingly. One approach is to enable logging on a package only when you suspect there might be problems and you are debugging. Once you are satisfied that your package is constructed properly and there will not be any issues, you should immediately disable the logging behavior.

Follow the steps below to enable logging for a particular package, create logging activity, and view the results of logging:

1. Select Start|Programs|Microsoft SQL Server|Enterprise Manager to launch the Enterprise Manager interface.

2. Expand the hierarchy in the left pane and expand your server to view the Data Transformation Services node. Expand this node and left-click the Local Packages node to view the packages stored on your server in the right pane.

3. Right-click the Export Customers package and choose Design Package from the shortcut menu.

4. From the Package menu of the DTS Designer, choose Properties.

5. In the DTS Package Properties:Export Customers window, select the Logging tab (see Figure 14.30).

6. In the Logging area, choose the Log Package Execution To SQL Server check box. Notice that the Delete Logs button becomes available. Selecting this button helps reduce the size of the msdb database, at any point when logging package activity, by clearing the logs for this particular package.

7. Choose OK in the DTS Package Properties:Export Customers window.

8. In order to create activity with the package, click the Execute button on the toolbar in the DTS Designer. Choose Done in the Executing Package window.

9. Close the DTS Designer using the close button and opt to save the changes to your package.

14

10. In the Local Packages node of Enterprise Manager, right-click the Export Customers package and choose Package Logs from the shortcut menu.

11. In the DTS Package Logs window (see Figure 14.31), expand the node in the DTS Package Versions and Log Tree area to view the logs.

12. After selecting a log, choose the Open Log button to actually view the log information in the Log Detail window (see Figure 14.32).

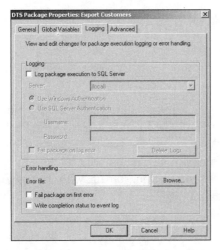

Figure 14.30
Setting logging options for a package.

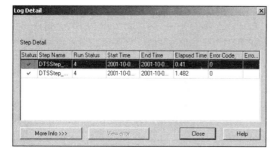

Figure 14.32
Viewing the log information.

Figure 14.31
Accessing the log information.

Advanced DTS Tasks

Most DTS tasks are quite self-explanatory and easy to configure and build into your packages. These tasks include the Bulk Insert Task, the Execute Process Task, the Execute SQL Task, the Copy SQL Server Objects Task, and so on. Other DTS tasks are so complex and powerful that they warrant further explanation to guarantee you can take full advantage of their power. This section details these tasks for you, starting with the most used and powerful of all tasks, the Transform Data Task.

Transform Data Task

The Transform Data Task has undergone dramatic improvements since previous versions of DTS. This task can now perform the following:

- Add logic to the task for custom error handling.

- Initialize and free your own COM components.

- Use ActiveX Data Objects and similar technologies.

- Maintain "success points" in the transformation process for easier restarts at a later time.

- Improve data-cleansing capabilities.

- Improve data-awareness capabilities.

- Greatly improve multi-phase data-pump design architecture.

In order to take advantage of the multi-phase data-pump design architecture, you actually must be certain that it is enabled in DTS. Follow these steps to verify that this functionality is enabled:

1. Make sure any DTS Designers that you might have open on your system are closed.

2. Select Start|Programs|Microsoft SQL Server|Enterprise Manager to launch the Enterprise Manager interface.

3. Expand the hierarchy in the left pane and expand your server to view the Data Transformation Services node.

4. Right-click the Data Transformation Services node and choose Properties.

5. In the Package Properties window, select the checkbox for Show multi-phase Pump In DTS Designer (see Figure 14.33).

Note: *You should also notice the Turn On Cache checkbox. This enables faster loading of the DTS Designer thanks to the caching of DTS Tasks, Transforms, and OLEDB Providers information.*

6. Click OK in the Package Properties window.

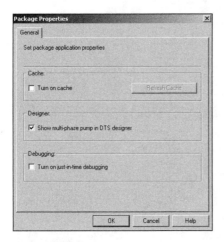

Figure 14.33
Enabling the multi-phase behavior.

Once you have enabled multiphase data pump behavior in your Data Transformation Services application, you are ready to discover the power this behavior brings to your fingertips. The Transform Data Task will now operate using six distinct phases of execution:

1. *Pre Source Data*—This phase executes once at the beginning of the data transformation. Functions you have performed in this phase occur before the first row of data is retrieved from the source. This is very useful if you need to execute simple but critical T-SQL tasks against your target data store. For example, perhaps you need to truncate a particular table.

2. *Row Transform*—All your transformations use this critical phase to transfer data from the source to the destination.

3. *Post Row Transform*—This phase occurs for each row that is transformed during the transfer. It consists of three sub-phases: Transform Failure, Insert Success, and Insert Failure. This phase provides you with the opportunity to address the quality of data, correct data issues, maintain counters, and respond to the state of individual rows.

4. *On Batch Complete*—As its name implies, this phase executes for each batch processed by the Transform Data Task. By default, only a single batch is processed per usage of the task. You can control the size of batches, however, using the Insert Batch Size field of the Options tab of the Transform Data Task Properties window (see Figure 14.34).

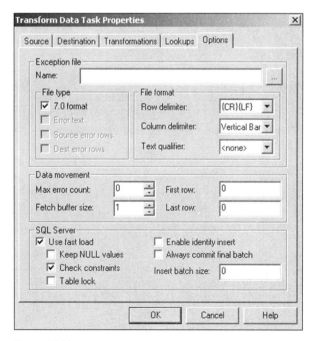

Figure 14.34
Changing the batch size.

5. *On Pump Complete*—This phase executes after all the rows have been transformed.

6. *Post Source Data*—This phase executes after the transformation of all rows, but is unique in that it can access data.

The key to the functionality of the Transform Data Task is held in the Transformations tab of the Properties window for a task. Figure 14.35 demonstrates this important tab for a sample data transfer task.

Notice the Phases Filter drop-down menu and how easy it is to select the particular phase you would like to configure. Also notice that the first row is selected for a transformation to be configured. This is given the default name of DTSTransformation_1.

Note: *Notice how the arrow between the ProductID in the Source area and the Destination area is highlighted. This represents your transformation. If you double- click this arrow, or choose the Edit button with it highlighted, you can edit the transformation.*

14

In the example in Figure 14.35, the transformation for this first row is currently a simple copy column. If you choose the Edit button, the Transformation Options window appears (see Figure 14.36).

The real power of this window is accessed with the Properties button within the Transformation Options window. The Properties for each of the different possible transformations vary dramatically. For example, choosing the New button on the Transformation tab allows you to select a new transformation from the Create New Transformation window (see Figure 14.37).

If you were to select an ActiveX Script to perform the transformation, and then select the Properties button in the Transformation Options window, you would see the ActiveX

Figure 14.35
The Transformations tab.

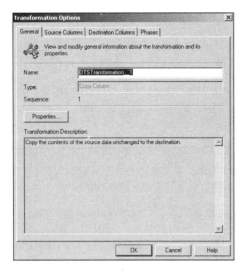

Figure 14.36
The Transformation Options window.

Figure 14.37.
The Create New Transformation window.

Script Transformation Properties window. Notice in Figure 14.38 how this window assists you with the possible syntax for your VB Script or JScript assisted transformation. You can also parse and test your code in this very sophisticated interface.

You should experiment with the various transformation tasks that are available to you. The possibilities are nearly limitless.

Tip: Consider using the tempdb system database as your source data connection when you are experimenting with DTS. This is great for experimentation because this database is purged of all its contents each time SQL Server 2000 restarts.

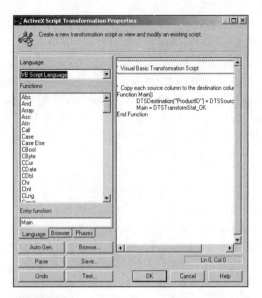

Figure 14.38
The ActiveX Script Transformation Properties window.

Data Driven Query Task

Although the Transform Data Task is quite powerful, it only gives you the ability to insert records directly. The Data Driven Query Task, however, supports the insertion, deletion, and updating of records in response to the data transformations. This task also has the ability to support user commands such as stored procedures. This function is extremely powerful as

Figure 14.39
The Queries tab of the Data Driven Query Task Properties window.

well. Thanks to the architecture of the Data Driven Query Task, this task has the ability to scan source records row by row and perform actions against a target data source.

The key to the functionality of the Data Driven Query Task is your ability to perform **INSERT**, **UPDATE**, **DELETE**, and related queries while data is being transferred and/or transformed. This functionality is brought to DTS thanks to the Queries tab of the Data Driven Query Task Properties window (see Figure 14.39). This interface allows you to specify various query types and provides you with assistance in building the queries, thanks to a robust query builder accessible via the Build button.

Message Queue Task

Microsoft Message Queue Server is a powerful server application that allows any application to communicate with any other application using a powerful queue system. This application ensures that messages are delivered to the intended recipient properly even if the transmission medium is an extremely unreliable Internet connection. Another great advantage that Message Queue Server presents is allowing applications written in completely different languages and running on completely different platforms to communicate successfully.

Specifically within DTS, the DTS Message Queue Task allows you to:

• Send messages between packages (including packages located on different server).

• Communicate with other applications relying on Microsoft Message Queue Server for messaging functions.

• Cause packages to wait for other packages to communicate before proceeding.

• Divide very large and complex packages into smaller packages and distribute these packages across multiple servers.

Obviously this task adds to the power of DTS dramatically, especially its ability to integrate with other applications and servers in your enterprise.

Advanced Package Options

In addition to the advanced tasks we examined in the previous section of this chapter, there are some other advanced options that merit special attention. These are options you can set that affect the way packages and their tasks are handled as a whole.

Each package that you create in DTS has its own properties window associated with it. Each of the windows has an Advanced tab containing advanced options that control package behavior (see Figure 14.40).

Note: Remember, you access the Properties for a package by loading the package into the DTS Designer and choosing Properties from the Package menu.

The advanced options you have available to you for a package are as follows:

Figure 14.40
Advanced package options.

14

- *Lineage*—When enabled, this feature allows you to audit the individual activities performed by a task within the package. The package actually has the ability to track— for a piece of data—exactly what transformations have occurred. This ability is only possible when the package has been saved to Meta Data Services (Repository). Selecting Show Lineage Variables As Source Columns turns data auditing on, and Write Lineage To Repository causes this audit information to be stored in Meta Data Services.

- *Scanning*—The scanning options available in DTS allow you to build upon your ability to store lineage information. Specifically, by using the Resolve Package References To Scanned Catalog Meta Data check box in the Scanning Options window, you have the ability to track column-level lineage for your package.

Table 14.7 Creating standalone packages.

Filename	Function
Axscphst.dll Axscphst.rll	Manages ActiveX scripting
Dtsffile.dll Dtsffile.rll	OLE DB flat-file provider used in the DTS Package Designer and Wizards
Dtspkg.dll Dtspkg.rll	Manages the package
Dtspump.dll Dtspump.rll	Holds the ActiveX constants for the Transform Data Task
Sqlresld.dll	Used for loading satellite resource files

(continued)

Table 14.7   Creating standalone packages *(continued)*.

Filename	Function
Dtsrun.exe Dtsrun.rll	Command file for executing DTS packages
Custtask.dll	Handles any custom tasks
Sqlwoa.dll Sqlwid.dll	Unicode and ANSI translation for SQL Server
Sqlredis.exe	Includes all necessary client components

- *Transactions*—These settings allow you to control the behavior of the package as a transaction. As you know, if the package is treated as a transaction, each part of the package must succeed in order for the entire package to succeed. You also have the ability to affect the transaction isolation-level that the package adheres to. This level determines to what extent changes outside the package are visible to the package. Your isolation level options are chaos, read committed, read uncommitted, repeatable read, and serializable.

- *OLE DB*—This option instantiates the OLE DB provider data source objects using the OLE DB service components. If you clear this option, the data source objects must be instantiated directly using **CoCreateInstance**.

DTS Interoperability

As was mentioned earlier, DTS can function independently of SQL Server 2000. Although you certainly need SQL Server 2000 to run the DTS designer, as long as you save your packages as COM-structured files you can access them using the freely distributed DTS engine. If your package connects to a SQL Server, you *do* need a Client Access License (CAL).

In order to be sure your DTS package is truly "standalone", you need several files. All these files are found in the \x86\binn directory of the SQL Server 2000 CD-ROM. Table 14.7 lists these files and their functions.

If you need to make database connections using your package, you also need the appropriate connectivity files for MDAC 2.6, which you will find on the CD-ROM.

To help you with this fairly complex set of procedures for creating standalone packages, Microsoft incorporates several pre-developed samples on the CD-ROM including:

- DTS Packages

- DTS custom applications

- ActiveX scripts

These samples are compressed in the following file on the CD-ROM:

```
\DevTools\Samples\DTS\Unzip_DTS.exe
```

Summary

SQL Server 2000 does not exist in a vacuum when it comes to data storage in your enterprise. You often need to transfer and transform data to and from your SQL Server 2000 systems. BCP is a simple, but powerful command line utility that allows you to very quickly and efficiently perform bulk imports and exports of data. **BULK INSERT** is another simple method for doing so, but with **BULK INSERT** you are limited to imports. **BULK INSERT** has the advantage of being a native Transact-SQL command.

If you need the most sophisticated data transfer and transformation capabilities, use Data Transformation Services (DTS). In fact, you need to use the DTS Designer of DTS. This tool provides access to a large number of connection, task, and step objects that you build together to form a powerful package capable of intense transfers and transformations.

It is no coincidence that the next chapter of this book also deals with moving data from system to system. Yet the method of data transfer we cover in Chapter 15 is much more sophisticated. The process is called *replication* and it allows us to decentralize data storage in a multiple SQL Server environment.

14

Chapter 15

Distributing Data Using Replication

Replication provides a set of technologies for copying and distributing data and database objects from a source database to one or more destination databases. Furthermore, replication provides the capability to synchronize the data between databases, therefore maintaining consistency between the two.

You should consider using the information presented in Chapter 10 to automate the distribution of data. After configuring replication on the source and destination databases, you allow it to run like any other automated tasks you have configured.

You can distribute data using one or more of the following connectivity options:

• Over a local area network (LAN).

• Over the Internet.

• Using a dial-up connection.

Replication can also be used to enhance application performance by distributing database processing across multiple servers.

Replication Benefits

Replication offers numerous benefits, depending on the type of replication and the options you choose to implement. However, the primary benefit of SQL Server 2000 replication is the availability of data when and where it is needed. Other benefits of SQL Server replication include:

• Allowing multiple locations to keep copies of the same data. This improves performance for the users who are generating reports specific to their location.

• Separating OLTP and DSS data for improved read performance when using online analytical processing (OLAP) databases, data marts, or data warehouses.

• Allowing greater site autonomy. Users are able to modify the data locally and then propagate their changes to the other databases configured in the replication process.

- Improving aggregate read performance.

- Bringing data closer to the users or groups of users, thus reducing conflicts when multiple users are modifying the data.

- Separating data that is to be browsed by end users, for example, data that is accessed using Web-based applications.

- Using replication as part of your standby server strategy.

Note: Along with replication, you can use log shipping and failover clustering to provide copies of your data in the event your SQL Server fails.

Deciding When to Use Replication

With many replication options available, and the support of diverse hardware as well as software applications, it becomes more and more necessary to maintain redundant copies of your SQL Server data. Furthermore, multiple applications that are accessing your data have different needs for the consistency and autonomy of the data.

You may decide to use replication for data distribution when you need to:

- Allow multiple users and locations to make changes to the data and then merge the changes together, identifying and resolving conflicts.

- Build data applications that need to be used in both offline and online environments.

- Build Web-based applications where users browse a large amount of data.

- Copy and distribute data to one or more locations.

- Distribute data modifications to other servers.

- Distribute copies of data at regularly scheduled times.

Replication Terms and Concepts

In order to properly implement replication in SQL Server 2000, you need to be certain that you have a thorough understanding of the replication architecture and the different terms and concepts used when discussing replication.

Here are the primary concepts you need to be familiar with when working with replication:

- Publisher-Subscriber metaphor

- Replication types

- Replication topologies

- Replication options

- Replication agents

Each of these concepts uses different terms to define the functionality, capabilities, and configuration options available to them. The next few sections explain the terms and concepts you will need to understand all aspects of replication in SQL Server 2000.

Publisher-Subscriber Metaphor

The implementation of replication used to distribute data requires the following three components:

- *Publisher*—Contains the source of the data that is published to one or more databases. The Publisher defines one or more *articles* that are created from a table or other database object. One or more articles from one database are organized into a *publication*. Publications are convenient ways to group database objects that you want to replicate together.

- *Subscriber*—Contains a copy of the distributed data replicated from the Publisher. The Subscriber creates a *subscription* to the publication on the Publisher. The subscription specifies when the Subscriber receives an update of information from the Publisher. The subscription also defines the database, tables, and other database objects on the Subscriber machine that is going to store the information received.

- *Distributor*—Performs the various tasks involved when replicating data from the Publisher to the Subscribers. The actual tasks performed by the Distributor depend on the type of replication being performed.

Note: *Often the Publisher and Distributor are located on the same computer. However, if the computer acting as the Publisher is heavily tasked, you can locate the Distributor on another computer to improve performance.*

SQL Server 2000 supports replication to and from heterogeneous data sources. Subscribers using OLE DB or ODBC can subscribe to SQL Server publications. SQL Server can also receive data being replicated from data sources other than SQL Server, including:

- Microsoft Access
- Oracle
- DB2
- Microsoft Exchange

Types of Subscriptions

You can create subscriptions using two primary methods in SQL Server; a *pull subscription* or a *push subscription*. The method you choose determines the amount of work required by the Publisher and the processor overhead on the Publishing SQL Server.

Note: *You can also use an anonymous subscription that is a type of pull subscription.*

Push Subscriptions

Push subscriptions are used to reduce the number of tasks required by the subscriber to subscribe to a publication. Push subscriptions centralize subscription administration because you do not have to configure each Subscriber individually.

Push subscriptions increase the overhead on the Distributing SQL Server because the Distribution Agent or Merge Agent runs on the Distributor. The push subscriptions are created at the Publisher, and the replication agents propagate the data and the modifications to the Subscriber without waiting for a request.

You should use push subscriptions when:

- Data is typically synchronized on a frequently recurring schedule or on demand.
- You want centralized subscription administration.
- Higher processor overhead at the Publisher with a local Distributor is not a concern.
- Your publications require near-realtime replication of data.

You can create a push subscription using Transact-SQL or Enterprise Manager. When creating a push subscription, you have to provide the following information:

- Name of the Subscriber.
- Name of the subscription database.
- Location where the Distribution Agent or Merge Agent will run (Distributor or Subscriber).
- How often the Distribution Agent or Merge Agent runs (scheduled or on demand).
- If and how the initial snapshot will be applied to the Subscriber.
- If you are going to use the immediate updating or queued updating functionality and the options for them.
- Priority value for merge replication.
- Services that need to be started to create the subscription.

Push subscriptions take the responsibility and overhead away from the subscribers and centralize the administration of the replication process. However, if you are busy and are not concerned about the overhead on your Distributor, you can offload the responsibility of the subscriptions to the Subscriber.

Pull Subscriptions

Pull subscriptions are used to reduce the number of tasks required by the Publisher to create subscriptions to a publication. Pull subscriptions decentralize subscription administration because you do not have to configure each Subscriber individually. The Subscribers decide which publications they want and create the subscriptions.

Pull subscriptions also allow the Subscriber to determine how often to receive changes made to the data, either using a schedule or on demand.

You should use pull subscriptions when:

- You want decentralized subscription administration.

- High processor overhead on the Distributor is a concern and you want to minimize the number of agents running on the Distributor.

- Subscribers will determine when they connect to Publisher/Distributor to synchronize changes.

- Subscribers are mobile, often offline, and/or autonomous.

You can create a pull subscription using Transact-SQL or Enterprise Manager. When creating a pull subscription, you have to provide the following information:

- Name of the subscription database.

- If and how the initial snapshot will be applied to the Subscriber.

- Location of the snapshot files to apply to the Subscriber.

- Priority value for merge replication.

- If you are going to use the immediate updating or queued updating functionality and the options for them.

- How often the Distribution Agent or Merge Agent runs (continuously, scheduled, or on demand).

- Services that need to be started to create the subscription.

Warning! *When creating a pull subscription to a publication for which you already have a push subscription , you will receive an error message informing you that the push subscription already exists. You must drop the push subscription before you can create the pull subscription.*

Anonymous Subscriptions

A variation on pull subscriptions is anonymous subscriptions. However, the detailed information about the subscription and the Subscriber are not stored anywhere. This type of subscription is initiated at the Subscriber as all other pull subscriptions are, but the Subscriber is responsible for keeping the data synchronized.

Types of Replication

There are three basic types of replication used to distribute data in SQL Server 2000. However, there are variations of these replication types that can be implemented to customize your replication configuration.

The three basic types of replication are:

- *Snapshot*—Copies the data or database object exactly as it exists at the time the replication occurs. This replication type is normally scheduled at a specific time and is used to maintain a copy of a published article as it existed the last time it was replicated to the Subscriber. Snapshot replication is used when the data is not modified often, the amount of data being replicated is small, and the Subscribers are content with the data being slightly out of date.

- *Transactional*—Copies of the data or database objects from the source database are first synchronized with the Publisher, typically using a snapshot of the data, and then the Subscriber is periodically updated with the changes made to the data on the Publisher. Transactional replication is used when the data must be replicated to your Subscribers every time the data is modified on the Publisher. This requires that the Publisher and Subscribers are reliably and/or frequently connected through the network.

- *Merge*—Copies of the data or database objects from the source database are first synchronized with the Publisher, typically using snapshot replication, and changes made to the data at both the Subscriber and Publisher are tracked and merged to form a single version of the data on the Publisher. If multiple changes are made to the same data, defined conflict-resolvers are used to determine how to resolve the conflict. Merge replication is used when the data must be modified on both the Subscriber and Publisher.

Along with these three basic types of replication, there is also a variation of the snapshot and transactional replication types that is implemented using Immediate Updating Subscribers:

- *Immediate Updating Subscribers*—Uses the initial process of synchronizing the data and database objects using the snapshot replication type. After the data is synchronized, the data can be modified on the Subscriber and the modification is immediately distributed to the Publisher using a two-phase commit protocol. After the change is made on the Publisher, the modification is replicated to all other Subscribers. The Immediate Updating Subscribers feature is used when the data does not change frequently, and when all servers have a reliable network connection.

Note: *The two-phase commit protocol ensures that all changes occur immediately on all servers participating in the transaction. Otherwise, the modification is not made on any server participating in the replication.*

Many times people are unsure whether to use merge replication or use replication with updating subscribers, whether it be immediate updating or queued updating. There is a difference in the two implementations and Table 15.1 explains when you should use merge replication and when you should use the updatable subscription options.

You can use Decision Tree 15.1 to assist you in determining whether to use merge replication or updating subscribers when implementing your replication strategy.

Table 15.1   Choosing merge replication or updating subscribers.

Use Merge Replication	Use Updating Subscribers
Data is read and updated at Subscriber	Data is mostly read-only
Publisher and Subscriber are rarely connected	Subscriber, Distributor, and Publisher are often connected. (This is not necessary for queue updates)
Conflicts caused by multiple updates are resolved	Conflicts caused by multiple updates are rare
Updates are propagated row-by-row and resolved at the row level	Transactional updates are propagated, causing the entire transaction to be committed or rolled back

15

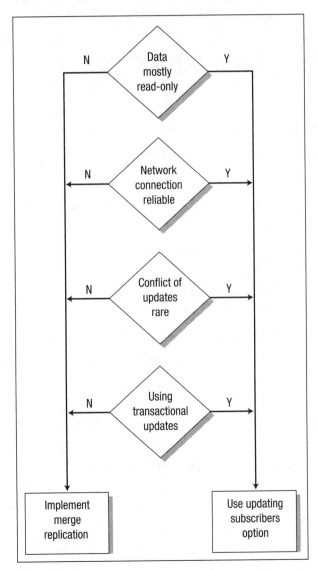

Decision Tree 15.1
Determining whether to use merge replication or the updating subscribers option.

Understanding the different replication types available in SQL Server will assist you in determining which type you should implement in your SQL Server environment. The type of replication you choose determines how the replication will occur, but you also have to be familiar with the different replication models available to you.

Replication Topologies

A replication topology is used when implementing replication to distribute data in SQL Server 2000. The topology defines the relationship between the servers and copies of data, as well as the logic that determines how the synchronization occurs.

The replication topology determines the following three characteristics of your replication:

- How long it takes for changes to get from the Publisher to the Subscribers

- Whether the failure of an update to one Subscriber prevents other Subscribers from being updated

- The order in which updated information arrives at the Subscriber

When determining your replication topology, consider the following:

- The physical replication model

- Where your snapshot files will be located and how initial synchronization will occur between your Publisher and Subscriber

- Whether the Distributor will be local or remote, and whether you will share the distribution database among several Publishers

- Whether multiple Publishers will share a Distributor, will share a distribution database, or will use their own distribution databases on the Publisher

- The type of replication and the required options to use

- Whether you are going to use push or pull subscriptions

Note: The replication topology is not just the physical connections between servers; it also includes the data paths between copies of the data. For example, a Subscriber can receive multiple copies of data from different Publishers, and all of those copies can be on one server.

There are four replication models you can choose to implement in SQL Server 2000:

- Central Publisher

- Central Publisher with Remote Distributor

- Central Subscriber

- Republisher

To make certain you implement the appropriate physical model for your SQL Server replication process, you need to be familiar with the replication models discussed in the next sections.

Central Publisher

The easiest replication topology model to implement in SQL Server is the Central Publisher. This model creates one Publisher and one Distributor on the same server and a single Subscriber on a separate server. The only complexity to this model occurs if you add Subscribers to the Publisher/Distributor. The Publisher owns the data and is responsible for managing the changes made to the data.

A Central Publisher is often used to distribute master data, lists, or reports from the Central Publisher to one or more Subscribers.

Note: *The role of Publisher and Subscriber are not exclusive. SQL Server can perform both roles simultaneously. For instance, SQLServerA can be publishing PublicationA to SQLServerB and at the same time subscribing to PublicationB on SQLServerB.*

Central Publisher with Remote Distributor

As the publishing server becomes more active with publishing and performing other replication-related tasks as well as nonreplication-related tasks, you may experience performance degradation.

To improve performance for SQL Server replication and other applications on the Publisher, you can place the Publisher and the Distributor on separate servers. Creating a Distributor separate from the Publisher reduces disk usage and local processing on the Publisher. However, if you create a Distributor separate from the Publisher, you are going to increase the overall traffic.

The Central Publisher with Remote Distributor is similar to the Central Publisher model, except that you now have separate computers performing the publishing and distributing tasks. This replication model is beneficial when the Publisher is a heavily used OLTP server.

Warning! *The Publisher and Distributor should be connected by a reliable, high-speed communication link.*

Central Subscriber

In the Central Subscriber model, numerous Publishers replicate information to a single destination table at the Subscriber. The destination table is partitioned horizontally and the primary key contains location-specific information. Each of the Publishers replicates rows of data specific to its location.

The Central Subscriber model can be used to:

• Roll up inventory data from a number of remote SQL Servers into a centralized database at corporate headquarters.

- Consolidate order processing from branch offices.

- Roll up information from autonomous business divisions within your company.

Republisher

This model uses two SQL Servers to publish the same data. In this scenario, the Publisher sends data to a Subscriber, which then republishes the data to one or more Subscribers. This scenario is beneficial when you are publishing data to your Subscribers over a slow or expensive communication link.

If most of your Subscribers are on the other side of a slow or expensive link, using a Republisher reduces the distribution load from the Publisher by shifting the publication tasks to the Republisher.

Note: *Any server can act as both a Publisher and a Subscriber, making all of these scenarios possible.*

Replication Options

Replication options are used to customize your replication solution with the different types of replication available. These options provide greater flexibility and control of your replication process in your applications.

SQL Server 2000 replication options include:

- Filtering published data

- Publishing database objects

- Publishing schema objects

- Updatable subscriptions

- Transforming or manipulating published data

- Alternating synchronization servers

Filtering Published Data

Filtering data allows you to replicate only the data needed by the Subscriber. You can filter data horizontally (by row), or vertically (by column) or a combination of both. When using merge replication, you can create dynamic and join filters.

With all types of replication, you can choose to replicate an entire table or a subset of a table, using filtering.

Filtering published data allows you to publish a subset of data, thereby:

- Reducing network bandwidth consumption

- Reducing the amount of storage space on the Subscriber

- Managing publications and applications for individual Subscribers

- Avoiding or reducing conflicts

Horizontal and vertical partitioning can be used with snapshot, transactional, and merge publications. Horizontal filtering is implemented using the **WHERE** clause, where vertical filtering is achieved by specifying only the required columns in the **SELECT** clause.

Dynamic and join filters are used to extend the capabilities of merge replication in SQL Server 2000. Dynamic filters are horizontal filters that use a function to retrieve a value from the Subscriber and filter the data based on that value. The dynamic filter is only defined once for a publication, but the value supplied by the Subscriber allows the Subscriber to customize the data to meet his needs.

Join filters define a relationship between two tables that will be enforced during the merge process. Join filters provide extended horizontal filtering capabilities from one published table to another.

Publishing Database Objects

You can publish objects contained within your database. The objects you choose to publish can be part of a data publication or can be contained in a separate publication. You can publish database objects such as:

- Tables

- Views

- Indexed views

- User-defined functions

- Stored procedure definitions

- Execution of stored procedures

Database objects can be published using the following replication types:

- Snapshot

- Transactional

- Merge

The database objects that can be published depend on the type of replication that you are using. Table 15.2 contains the database objects and the replication types that can be used to replicate the objects.

Table 15.2 Replication types and database objects.

Database Object	Snapshot	Transactional	Merge
Tables	Yes	Yes	Yes
Views	Yes	Yes	Yes
Indexed Views	Yes	Yes	Yes
Indexed View as Tables	Yes	Yes	No
User-Defined Functions	Yes	Yes	Yes
Stored Procedures (definition)	Yes	Yes	Yes
Stored Procedures (execution)	Yes	Yes	No

Publishing Schema Objects

You can publish objects contained in the schema of your published database. Furthermore, you can modify the destination table's data formats and owner names to assist you in optimizing SQL Server 2000 (or if you are using replication in a heterogeneous environment). SQL Server 2000 can replicate the following schema objects:

- Declared referential integrity such as primary key constraints, reference constraints, and unique constraints

- Clustered and nonclustered indexes

- User-defined triggers

- Collation settings

Updatable Subscriptions

You can also modify data at the Subscribers if you are using snapshot or transactional replication with the Updatable Subscription option. This option allows you to make changes to replicated data at the Subscriber and propagate those changes back to the Publisher and to other Subscribers. You can update your subscriptions using:

- *Immediate updating*—Allows your Subscribers to update the data on their machine if they are able to immediately propagate the changes to the Publisher. After the Publisher accepts them, it propagates the changes to the other Subscribers.

Warning! *Immediate updating requires that you have a continuous and reliable connection to the Publisher.*

- *Queued updating*—Allows your Subscribers to update data on their machine and store those modifications in a queue when disconnected from the Publisher. After the Subscriber reconnects to the Publisher, the changes are replicated to the Publisher. If the Publisher accepts the changes, they are replicated to other Subscribers.

Note: *These changes can be stored in a SQL Server 2000 queue or Microsoft Message Queue.*

- *Immediate updating with queued updating as a failover*—Allows you to try to update the Publisher immediately, but if a connection cannot be established, the updates are stored in the queue. After you establish a connection to the Publisher, the updates are sent to the Publisher from the queue and the queue is emptied.

Transforming Your Published Data

When you are using snapshot or transactional replication, you can utilize the scripting and transformation mapping capabilities of Data Transformation Services (DTS). This integration with DTS allows you to manipulate the data to the requirements of individual Subscribers. For example, a Subscriber may want different table names, data types, and column names than what the Publisher is using.

When transforming your published data, you can dynamically filter the data from one snapshot or transactional publication to Subscribers who require different slices of the data.

Alternate Synchronization Partners

When using merge replication, your Subscribers can synchronize with servers other than the original Publisher. This option allows Subscribers to synchronize data even if the original Publisher is unavailable.

This can be very beneficial for mobile Subscribers who have access to a faster more reliable network connection to an alternate Publisher than they have with the original Publisher.

The use of alternate synchronization partners has the following requirements:

- It is only available with merge replication.

- The alternate partner must have the requested schema and data.

- The publication on the alternate server should be a clone of the publication on the original Publisher.

- The publication properties must be configured to allow Subscribers to synchronize with other Publishers.

- Name subscriptions (non-anonymous) must have the Subscriber enabled at the alternate synchronization partner.

The different terms and concepts have been introduced, but you might be wondering what services or components manage the replication process. The next section discusses the different agents involved with making the entire replication process perform as expected.

Replication Agents

Agents are used by SQL Server 2000 replication to complete the tasks associated with copying and distributing the data. The following agents are used by SQL Server to carry out the entire replication process:

- SQL Server Agent

- Snapshot Agent
- Log Reader Agent
- Distribution Agent
- Merge Agent
- Queue Reader Agent
- Miscellaneous Agents

These agents all work together to successfully manage the replication process in SQL Server 2000. Each of them performs specific tasks that you should be familiar with when configuring and troubleshooting replication.

SQL Server Agent

The SQL Server Agent provides an easy way to run the replication agents by hosting and scheduling all the agents used by the replication process. Furthermore, SQL Server Agent controls and monitors many other operations outside of replication, such as:

- Monitoring the SQL Server Agent service
- Maintaining error logs
- Executing jobs
- Starting other processes required by SQL Server

Snapshot Agent

The Snapshot Agent is used with all replication types in SQL Server 2000. It typically runs under the SQL Server Agent at the Distributor and is managed through SQL Server Enterprise Manager. The Snapshot Agent is responsible for:

- Creating the schema and initial data files of published tables and stored procedures
- Storing the snapshot files
- Updating the distribution database with synchronization information

Log Reader Agent

The Log Reader Agent is used only with transactional replication in SQL Server 2000. Every database that publishes data using transactional replication has its own Log Reader Agent that runs on the Distributor and connects to the Publisher.

The Log Reader Agent moves transactions marked for replication from the publishing database transaction log to the distribution database, where it resides until the Distribution Agent performs its job.

Distribution Agent

The Distribution Agent is used with both transactional and snapshot replication. It moves the transactions and snapshot information stored in the distribution database to the Subscribers. The Distribution Agent runs at the:

- *Distributor*—for push subscriptions

- *Subscriber*—for pull subscriptions

Merge Agent

The Merge Agent is used only with merge replication in SQL Server 2000. Each merge subscription has its own Merge Agent that connects to both the Publisher and Subscriber to update both. The Merge Agent runs at the:

- *Distributor*—for push subscriptions

- *Subscriber*—for pull subscriptions

The Merge Agent normally uploads the changes from the Subscriber to the Publisher and then downloads changes from the Publisher to the Subscriber using a bi-directional merge. However, you can configure the Merge Agent to move changes in one direction. The Merge Agent performs the following tasks in merge replication:

- Applies the initial snapshot to the Subscriber

- Copies and reconciles incremental changes

Queue Reader Agent

The Queue Reader Agent is used with transactional and snapshot replication configured to use the queued updating option. It retrieves messages from the queue and applies them to the appropriate publication.

Note: *The Queue Reader Agent is also used if the immediate updating with queued updating as a failover option is enabled.*

This multithreaded agent only runs on the Distributor. Unlike the Distribution Agent and the Merger Agent, you need only one instance of the Queue Reader Agent to service all Publishers and publications for any given Distributor.

Miscellaneous Agents

There are also clean-up agents located in the Miscellaneous Agents folder in Replication Monitor that complete the scheduled and on-demand maintenance of replication. Table 15.3 provides the names, default schedules, and descriptions of the clean-up agents.

Table 15.3   Miscellaneous clean-up agents.

Clean-Up Agent Name	Default Schedule	Description
Agent History Clean Up	Distribution Every 10 minutes	Removes agent history from the distribution database
Distribution Clean Up	Distribution Every 10 minutes	Removes replicated transactions from the distribution database
Expired Subscription Clean Up	1:00am daily	Detects and removes expired subscriptions from publication databases
Replication Agents Checkup	Every 10 minutes	Detects replication agents that are no longer logging history
Reinitialize Subscriptions Having Data Validation Features	Disabled by default	Reinitializes all subscriptions that have encountered data validation failures

At this point, we have discussed all of the different concepts and terms you need to be familiar with when implementing, configuring, and maintaining replication. Let's take a look at the replication features available in the SQL Server 2000 editions.

Replication Features Supported by SQL Server 2000 Editions

There are numerous editions of SQL Server 2000 that you can choose to install. The edition you install impacts the replication functionality available to you when implementing and configuring replication. Table 15.4 provides a list of features and which SQL Server 2000 editions support them.

This table can be used to determine which SQL Server 2000 edition you should install to implement the replication topology required for your SQL Server 2000 configuration.

Table 15.4   Replication features supported in SQL Server 2000 editions.

Edition	Snapshot	Transactional	Merge	Immediate Updating	Queued Updating
Enterprise	Supported	Supported	Supported	Supported	Supported
Standard	Supported	Supported	Supported	Supported	Supported
Personal	Supported	Subscriber only	Supported	Supported	Supported
Developer	Supported	Supported	Supported	Supported	Supported
Desktop	Supported	Subscriber only	Supported	Supported	Supported
CE	N/A	N/A	Anonymous Subscriber only	N/A	N/A
Enterprise Evaluation	Supported	Supported	Supported	Supported	Supported

Stages of Replication in SQL Server 2000

After deciding which edition you should purchase and install based on our discussion of the concepts, terms, and features, you need to become familiar with the basic steps required to implement replication.

Here are the steps to follow when implementing snapshot replication and transaction replication:

1. *Configuring replication*—This stage is used to identify the Publisher, Distributor, and Subscribers in your topology. You can configure the Publisher, create the distribution database, and enable your Subscribers using any of the following tools:

   - SQL Server Enterprise Manager

   - SQL-DMO

   - Scripts

   - System stored procedures

2. *Publishing data and database objects*—After identifying the different players and their roles, you can create your publications. Your publications will contain the data and database object articles with the necessary filters applied to them.

3. *Subscribing to publications*—After you create your publications, you can create your push, pull, or anonymous subscriptions to define which publications you want replicated to your individual Subscribers and when the replication should take place.

4. *Applying the initial snapshot*—After creating your subscriptions, you are ready to perform the initial synchronization of data between the Publisher and Subscribers. During this step, you specify the following options:

   - Where to save the snapshot files and whether to compress them.

   - What scripts to execute before or after applying the initial snapshot.

   - When to apply the snapshot:

     - Immediately after creating the subscription

     - At a specified time

   - Whether you will apply the snapshot manually to the Subscribers by saving the snapshot to a network location or removable media, transporting it to the Subscribers, and applying them manually at the Subscribers.

5. *Synchronizing Data*—After the initial snapshot is applied, the synchronization of data occurs when the Snapshot, Log Reader, or Merge Agent runs and replicates the data from the Publisher to the Subscriber. This step is required to keep the

15

data synchronized, depending on the type of replication you have implemented. For instance:

- *Snapshot replication*—Snapshots are reapplied at the Subscriber.

- *Transaction replication*—Updated information is replicated to the Subscriber.

Note: *If you are using updatable subscriptions, with snapshot or transactional replication, the data is propagated from the Subscriber to the Publisher, and then replicated to the other Subscribers.*

- *Merge replication*—Updated information is synchronized during the merge process. When data changes at all servers and there are conflicts, these conflicts are detected and resolved.

Let's drill down into each of these steps to make sure you have a thorough understanding of what is involved at each stage of implementing replication.

Configuring Replication and Distribution

The first step requires you to do some research and planning to be certain you identify the Publishers, Distributors, and Subscribers across your entire enterprise. Use the following steps to configure replication in SQL Server 2000:

1. Identify a Distributor.

2. Create a distribution database or acquire access to an existing distribution database.

3. Enable the Publishers that will be using the Distributor.

4. Enable the databases for publishing.

5. Enable the Subscribers that will receive the published data.

After identifying your Distributor, you can acquire access to an existing database on the Distributor or create a new distribution database on your local machine or on a remote machine. You will then need to configure the Publishers, publications, and Subscribers to complete the process.

The configuration of replication in SQL Server 2000 can be completed using Enterprise Manager or using Transact-SQL statements.

Tip: *Although you have the option of using Transact-SQL statements to configure replication, we strongly recommend that you take advantage of the replication wizards in Enterprise Manager.*

Configuring Publishing and Distribution Using Transact-SQL

You can choose to use Transact-SQL to configure the Distributor, assign Publishers to the Distributor, and specify the databases that will be the publication database by executing several stored procedures. Only members of the **sysadmin** fixed server role can configure replication.

You apply stored procedures in the following order to configure the Distributor and the distribution database, and to identify the published databases:

1. **sp_adddistributor**—Executed in the master database on the server that you want to identify as the Distributor. It creates an entry containing the Distributors information in the **sysservers** table.

*Note: Use **sp_dropdistributor** and **sp_changedistributor_property** to uninstall the Distributor or modify the properties of the Distributor, respectively.*

2. **sp_adddistributiondb**—Executed in the master database on the Distributor. It creates the distribution database and the required tables and stored procedures to enable the replication distribution.

*Note: Use **sp_dropdistributiondb** and **sp_changedistributiondb** to drop the distribution database or modify the properties of the distribution database, respectively.*

3. **sp_adddistpublisher**—Executed on any database on the Distributor. It configures the Publisher to use the specified distribution database.

*Note: Use **sp_dropdistpublisher** and **sp_changedistpublisher** to drop the distribution publisher or modify the properties of the distribution publisher, respectively.*

4. **sp_replicationdboption**—Executed on any database on the Publisher. It turns the replication database option on when passing a value of **True**, therefore identifying the database as a published database.

*Note: Use **sp_replicationdboption** with a passed value of **false** to indicate that the database is no longer a published database.*

Configuring Publishing and Distribution Using Enterprise Manager

As you can see, it can be quite tedious to configure publishing and distribution using Transact-SQL. A much more efficient way to configure replication is to use the Configure Publishing And Distribution Wizard. You can do so by following these steps:

1. After opening Enterprise Manager, expand the SQL Server group that contains the server for which you want to configure replication.

2. Expand the server, right-click the Replication folder, and then click Configure Publishing, Subscribers, And Distribution to open the welcome screen of the Configure Publishing And Distribution Wizard.

Note: Alternatively, you can click on the server, click Tools|Wizards, expand Replication, and double-click on Configure Publishing And Distribution Wizard.

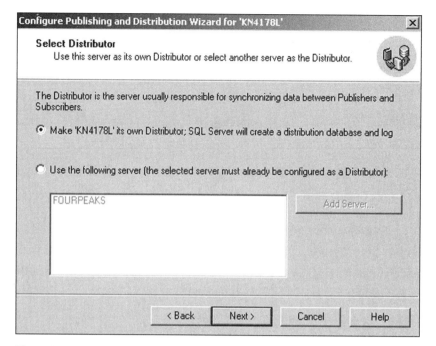

Figure 15.1
Selecting the distribution server.

3. Click Next to open the Select Distributor dialog box shown in Figure 15.1 and choose one of the following options:

- Make 'servername' Its Own Distributor; SQL Server Will Create The Distribution Database And Log to make the local server the Distribution server.

- Use The Following Server (The Selected Server Must Already Be Configured As A Distributor) to specify a remote server as the Distribution server.

Note: *If the remote server is not listed, click Add Server to open the Registered SQL Server Properties dialog box to register another SQL Server as a Distributor.*

4. Click Next to open the Specify Snapshot Folder dialog box shown in Figure 15.2 and specify the network path of the snapshot folder.

5. Click Next to open the Customize The Configuration dialog box shown in Figure 15.3 and choose one of the following options:

- *Yes, Let Me Set The Distribution Properties, Enable Publishers, Or Set The Publishing Settings*—if you want to Customize the Publishing and Distribution configuration.

- *No, Use The Following Default Settings*—if you want to use the default settings of the Publishing and Distribution configuration.

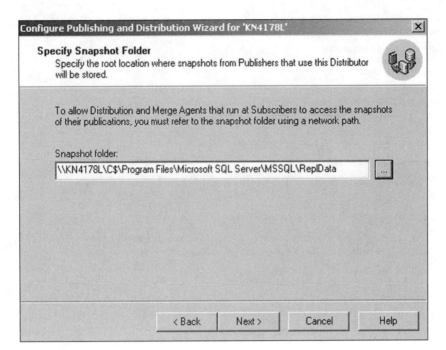

Figure 15.2
Specifying the snapshot folder.

6. Click Next to open one of the following dialog boxes:

   - If you chose not to customize the settings, you are presented with the Completing The Configure Publishing And Distribution Wizard screen.

   - If you chose to customize the settings, you are presented with the Provide Distribution Database Information screen shown in Figure 15.4.

7. In the Distribution Database name box, enter a name for the distribution database or use the default name. In the Folder For The Distribution Database File box, specify the location of the distribution database file. In the Folder For The Distribution Database Log File box, specify the location of the transaction log file. You can click the ellipses button to browse for a directory.

Note: The message at the bottom of this screen will state that you must specify a local path name if you chose the local server to be the Distributor in Step 3, or it will state that you must specify a remote path name if you chose a remote server to be the Distributor in Step 3.

8. Click Next to open the Enable Publishers dialog box shown in Figure 15.5. Click the box in the Registered servers to specify which Publishers are going to use this as their Distributor. You can click Enable All or Enable None if you want all servers listed to use this as their Distributor or none of them to use it as their Distributor, respectively. You can use the ellipses button to configure the Properties of a selected Publisher.

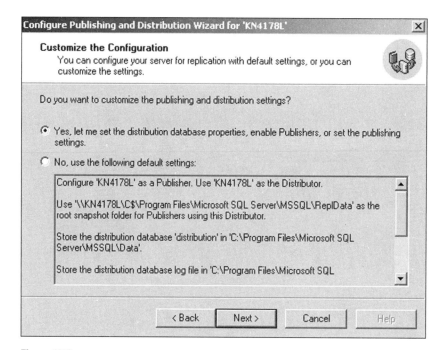

Figure 15.3
Choosing to customize the publishing and distribution configuration.

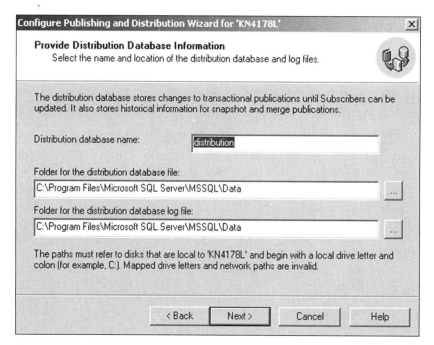

Figure 15.4
Specifying the distribution database information.

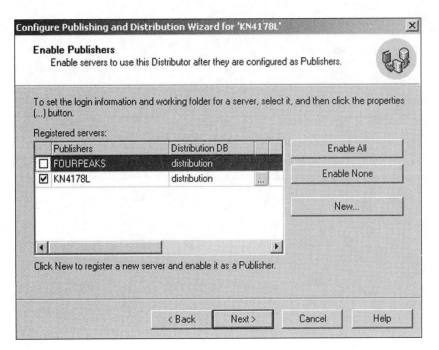

Figure 15.5
Specifying your publishers.

Note: *If a server is not listed, click New to open the Registered SQL Server Properties dialog box to register another SQL Server as a Publisher.*

9. Click Next to open the Enable Publication Databases dialog box shown in Figure 15.6. Click the box or boxes in the Databases area to specify which replication method or methods you are going to use for each database listed. You can click Enable All or Enable None if you want all databases listed to use transactional or merge replication, respectively.

Note: *There is an Enable All and an Enable None for each replication type. Be sure you click both of them if you want all databases to use both replication types.*

10. Click Next to open the Enable Subscribers dialog box shown in Figure 15.7. Click the box in the Registered Servers to specify which Subscribers are going to use this Publisher. You can click Enable All or Enable None if you want all servers listed to use this Publisher or none of them to use this Publisher, respectively. You can use the ellipses button to configure the Properties of a selected Subscriber.

Note: *If a server is not listed, click New to open the Registered SQL Server Properties dialog box to register another SQL Server as a Subscriber.*

11. Click Next to open the Completing The Configure Publishing And Distribution Wizard screen. Use the scroll bars to review the information about the choices you made. If you decide you want to modify an option, click Back to reach the dialog box

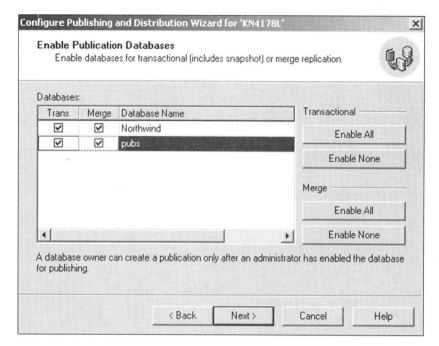

Figure 15.6
Specifying the databases to publish and replication type.

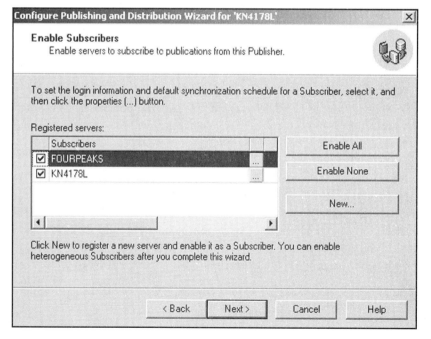

Figure 15.7
Specifying the subscribers of the Publisher.

you want to change. After making your modification, click Next the required number of times to return to the Completing The Configure Publishing And Distribution Wizard screen. Click Finish to begin installing Publishing and create the distribution database. You will receive a progress box as shown in Figure 15.8.

12. Click OK to close the information box stating that the Distributor was successfully enabled and open the information box shown in Figure 15.9 stating that the Replication Monitor was added to your system.

13. Click Close to close the information box and complete the Configure Publishing And Distribution Wizard.

After successfully creating your Distributor and Publisher, you need to create publications that your Subscribers can subscribe to.

Getting to Know the Distribution Database

The distribution database created on the Distributor stores the transactions generated when modifying data on your published databases. Transactional replication uses these transactions to update the Subscribers database. The transactions remain in the distribution database until all Subscribers have been successfully updated.

The distribution database acts as a store-and-forward database during the synchronization process. The database contains numerous system tables used to hold the information while waiting to forward it and waiting for a successful acknowledgement from each Subscriber that requires the transactions. The following are some of the system tables that comprise the distribution database:

• **MSdistribution_agents**—Stores information about the Distribution Agents.

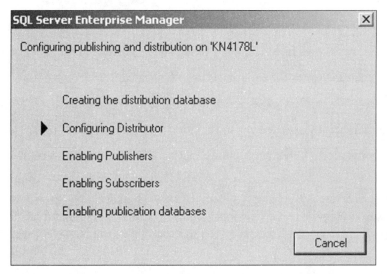

Figure 15.8
Progress box displayed during the installation of the Distributor, Publishers, and Subscribers.

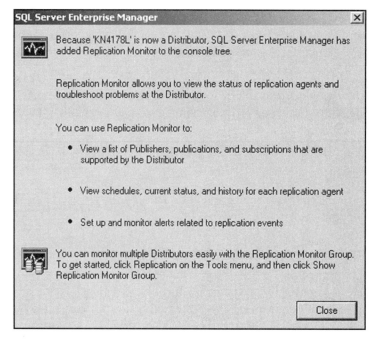

Figure 15.9
Learning that the Replication Monitor was installed.

- **MSdistribution_history**—Stores historical information about the Distribution Agents.

- **MSlogreader_agents**—Stores information about the Log Reader Agents on the local Distributor.

- **MSlogreader_history**—Stores historical information about your Log Reader Agents.

- **MSmerge_agents**—Stores information about the Merge Agents.

- **MSmerge_history**—Stores historical information about previous Subscriber updates.

- **MSrepl_commands**—Stores the commands to be replicated.

- **MSrepl_errors**—Stores information about failed replication processes.

- **MSrepl_transactions**—Stores a row of information for each replicated transaction.

- **MSrepl_version**—Stores a single row of information about the current version of the replication service installed.

The distribution database is treated as a system database when deciding the maintenance tasks and backup strategy. However, to modify the properties that are unique to the distribution database, you access the properties through Enterprise Manager using the following steps:

1. Click Tools|Replication|Configure Publishing, Subscribers, and Distribution.

2. Click the Distribution tab.

3. Locate and highlight the distribution database that you want to configure and click the Properties button.

After opening the Distribution Database Properties dialog box shown in Figure 15.10, you can configure the following options:

- *Transaction Retention*—Specifies in hours or days how long to retain the transactions in the Distribution database using the following options:

  - *Store Transactions At Least*—Configure the minimum length of time the transactions are retained.

  - *But Not More Than*—Configure the maximum length of time the transactions are retained.

Note: If you choose hours, the minimum value is 0 and the maximum value is 32767. If you choose days, the minimum value is 0 and the maximum value is 1365.

15

- *History Retention*—Specifies how long to retain the log history in the Distribution database using the following option:

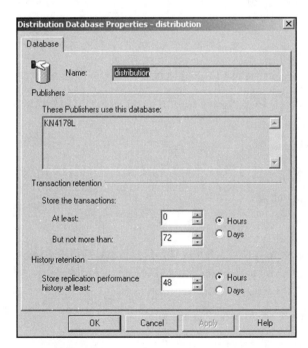

Figure 15.10
Configuring the Distribution Database Properties

- *Store Replication Performance History At Least*—Configure the minimum length of time the performance history is retained.

Tip: A shorter period of time will reduce the amount of disk space used on the Distributor.

Creating Your Publications and Articles

Your next step in configuring replication is to create the publications that contain one or more articles from one database. This collection of articles treated as a publication makes it easier to create a logically related set of data and database objects that you can replicate together. As with most tasks in SQL Server 2000, your publications and articles can be created using Transact-SQL or Enterprise Manager.

Creating a Publication and Articles Using Transact-SQL

There are numerous stored procedures that must be run in a specific order to create the publication and articles. Furthermore, the type of publication determines the stored procedures you will have to run to create the publication.

Creating a Snapshot or Transactional Publication

Transactional and snapshot publications can be created executing the following stored procedures:

1. If you haven't already enabled the database for publication, run **sp_replicationdboption** to enable publication on that database.

2. Run **sp_addpublication** and set the **repl_freq** parameter to **snapshot** to create the publication.

3. Run **sp_addpublication_snapshot** to:

   - Create the Snapshot Agent

   - Specify the publication **agent_id**

   - Copy the schema and data files into the replication working directory

Creating and Adding an Article to a Snapshot or Transactional Publication

After you create your publication, you can create and add your articles to the snapshot or transactional publication using the following stored procedures:

1. Run **sp_addarticle** one time for each article in the publication.

2. Run **sp_articlefilter** to horizontally partition the article.

3. Run **sp_articlecolumn** to vertically partition the article.

4. Run **sp_articleview** to create the synchronization object for an article that is horizontally or vertically partitioned.

Creating a Merge Publication

Merge publications can be created by executing the following stored procedures:

1. If you haven't already enabled the database for publication, run **sp_replicationdboption** to enable publication on that database.

2. Run **sp_addmergepublication** to create the publication.

3. Run **sp_addpublication_snapshot** to:

   - Create the Snapshot Agent

   - Copy the schema and data files into the replication working directory

Creating and Adding an Article to a Merge Publication

After you create your publication, you can create and add your articles to the merge publication using the following stored procedures:

1. Run **sp_addmergearticle** one time for each article in the merge publication.

2. Run **sp_addmergefilter** to create a partitioned article.

Creating a Publication and Articles Using Enterprise Manager

You might be thinking that is a lot of work just to create a publication and add articles to it. A much more efficient way to create a publication and its articles is to use the Create Publication Wizard.

Use the following steps to create a publication and its articles using the Create Publication Wizard:

1. After opening Enterprise Manager, expand the SQL Server group that contains the server for which you want to configure replication.

2. Expand the server, right-click the Replication folder, and then click New Publication to open the welcome screen of the Create Publication Wizard.

Note: Alternatively, you can click on the server, click Tools|Wizards, expand Replication, and double-click on Create Publication Wizard to open the Create and Manage Publications on 'servername' screen. Click Create Publication to open the Create Publication Wizard.

3. Click the Show Advanced Options In This Wizard box on the Welcome screen shown in Figure 15.11 if you want to configure updatable subscriptions or transformable subscriptions options.

4. Click Next to open the Choose Publication Database dialog box shown in Figure 15.12. Click on the database that contains the objects you want to publish.

5. Click Next to open the Select Publication Type dialog box shown in Figure 15.13 and choose one of the following:

   - *Snapshot Publication*—Periodic snapshots are replicated to the Subscriber.

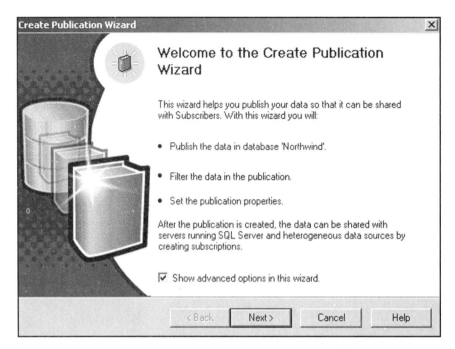

Figure 15.11
Displaying the advanced options of the Create Publication Wizard.

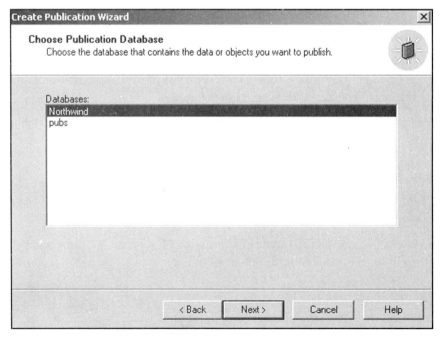

Figure 15.12
Selecting the database to publish.

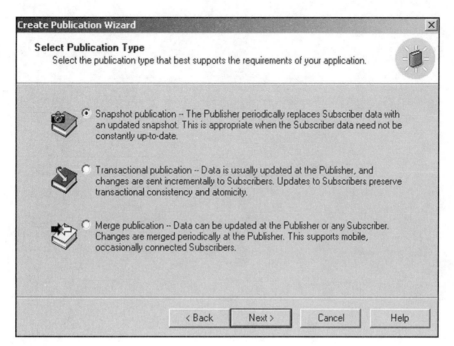

Figure 15.13
Selecting the publication type.

- *Transactional Publication*—After initial snapshot is applied at the Subscriber, changes made at the Publisher are sent to the Subscriber.

- *Merge Publication*—After initial snapshot is applied at the Subscriber, changes can be made at the Publisher or Subscriber and periodically merged at the Publisher.

6. Click Next to open the Updatable Subscriptions dialog box shown in Figure 15.14 and click the checkbox on one or both of the following options:

- *Immediate Updating*—Changes made at the Subscriber are immediately applied to the Publisher using a distributed transaction.

- *Queued Updating*—Changes made at the Subscriber are queued at the Subscriber until they can be applied at the Publisher.

Note: *If you choose both options, SQL Server will try the immediate update first. If unable to perform the update, it will use the queued update option. If you do not choose either option, the Transform Published Data dialog box is opened, allowing you to choose whether or not you want to manipulate the data before it is replicated to your Subscribers.*

7. Click Next to open the Specify Subscriber Types dialog box shown in Figure 15.15 and choose one or more of the following subscriber types:

- Servers Running SQL Server 2000

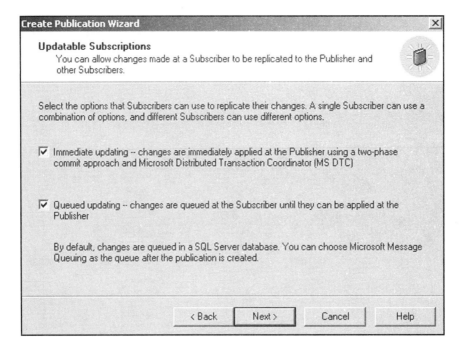

Figure 15.14
Selecting the Updatable Subscriptions options.

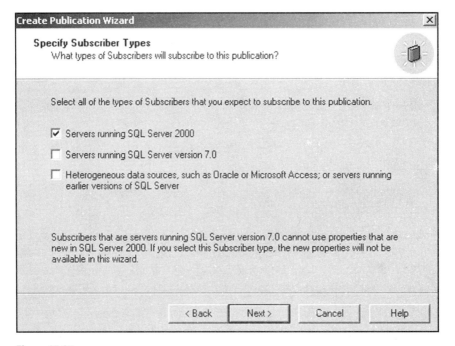

Figure 15.15
Specifying your subscriber types.

- Servers Running SQL Server Version 7

- Heterogeneous Data Sources, Such As Oracle Or Microsoft Access; Or Servers Running Earlier Versions Of SQL Server

Note: *If you are creating a merge publication, you will have an additional Subscriber type option of Devices Running SQL Server CE. Furthermore, the last option is listed as Heterogeneous Data Sources, Such As Microsoft Access*

8. Click Next to open the Specify Articles dialog box shown in Figure 15.16. Use the checkboxes to select the object types to display and to specify the objects to publish as articles. Click the ellipses button to view the Properties of a specific object.

Tip: *You can click the Publish All checkbox for a specific object if you want all the objects of that type to be published. For instance, if you want all the tables in the Northwind database, click the Publish All checkbox.*

9. Click Next to open the Article Issues dialog box shown in Figure 15.17. This list of issues notifies you that you may have to change any applications that access the table, because SQL Server is going to make changes to the table. Click each issue in the Issues box to receive a description of the issue in the Description box.

15

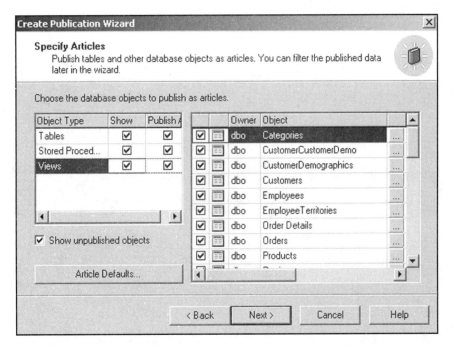

Figure 15.16
Specifying the objects to publish.

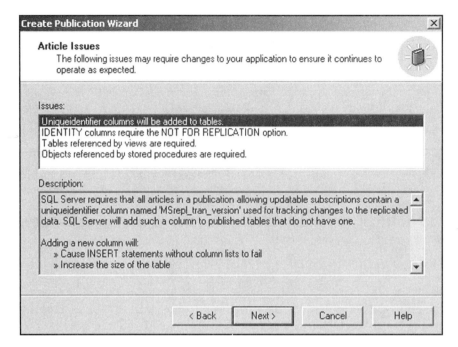

Figure 15.17
Reviewing the changes being made for the articles.

10. Click Next to open the Select Publication Name And Description dialog box shown in Figure 15.18. Type a name for the publication in the Publication Name box, and type a description of the publication in the Publication Description box. Click the List This Publication In Active Directory checkbox to include the publication in Active Directory.

11. Click Next to open the Customize The Properties Of The Publication dialog box shown in Figure 15.19 and choose one of the following options:

   • Yes, I Will Define Data Filters, Enable Anonymous Subscriptions, Or Customize Other Properties.

   • No, Create The Publication As Specified to open the Completing the Create Publication Wizard dialog box.

12. Click Next to open the Filter Data dialog box shown in Figure 15.20 and choose one or both of the following options:

   • Vertically, By Filtering The Columns Of Published Data

   • Horizontally, By Filtering The Rows Of Published Data

13. Click Next to open one or all of the following dialog boxes:

   • *Filter Table Columns*—(Shown in Figure 15.21, and shown only if you specified vertical filtering.) Highlight each table in the Tables In Publication box, and choose

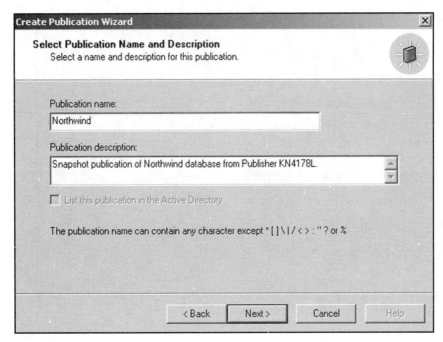

Figure 15.18
Specifying the publication name and description.

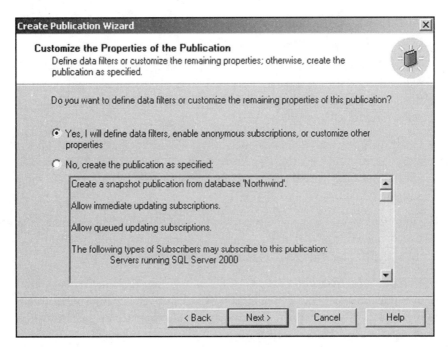

Figure 15.19
Choosing to further customize the publication.

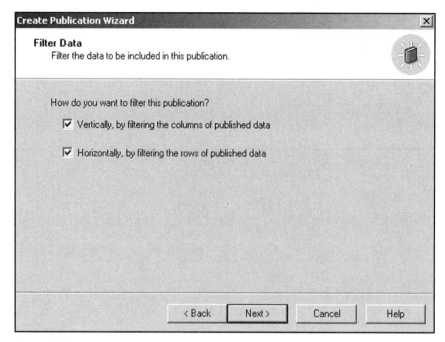

Figure 15.20
Specifying your filtering needs.

the columns you want published for the highlighted table in the Columns In Selected Table box.

- *Enable Dynamic Filters*—(Shown in Figure 15.22, and shown only with merge replication.) Click Yes, Enable Dynamic Filters to create a dynamic snapshot of only the data needed for a specific Subscriber. Click No, Use Static Filters to create a static filter for all Subscribers.

- *Generate Filters Automatically*—(Shown in Figure 15.23, and shown only with merge replication.) Use the dropdown menu to select the table that you want to filter. Enter the **WHERE** clause syntax to identify the rows in the table you want replicated.

- *Filter Table Rows*—(Shown if you specified horizontal filtering.) Highlight each table—one at a time—that you want to filter and click the ellipses button to open the Specify Filter dialog box as shown in Figure 15.24

- *Validate Subscriber Information*—(Shown in Figure 15.25, and shown only with dynamic filtering of merge replication.) Click Yes, Validate Subscriber Information to verify the Subscriber before each merge replication. Enter the function that will be used to verify the Subscriber in the Enter The Function(s) Used In Dynamic Filters For This Publication box. Click No, Do Not Validate Subscriber Information to skip the verification of the Subscriber before each merge replication.

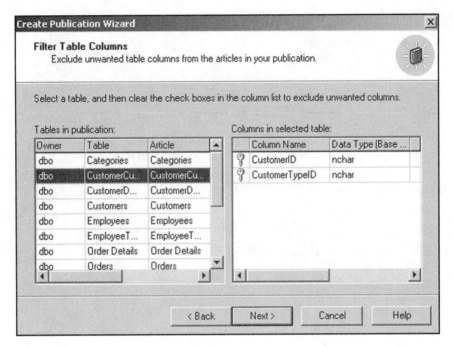

Figure 15.21
Specifying the columns to publish.

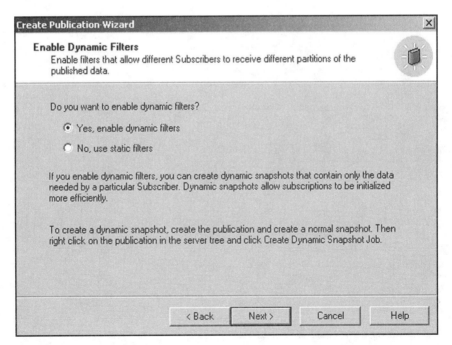

Figure 15.22
Enabling dynamic filtering.

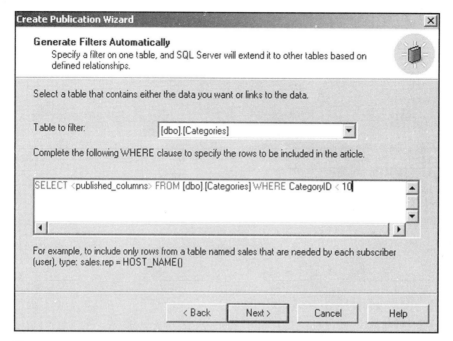

Figure 15.23
Specifying whether to automatically generate filters.

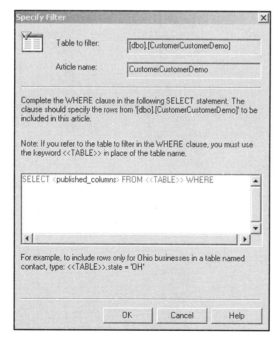

Figure 15.24
Specifying the horizontal filter criteria.

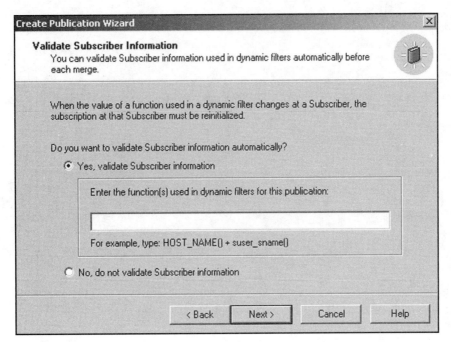

Figure 15.25
Specifying whether to validate subscriber information.

- *Optimize Synchronization*—(Shown in Figure 15.26, and shown only with merge replication.) Click Yes, Minimize The Amount Of Data to maintain additional data used by SQL Server to determine which filtered data should be sent to a specific Subscriber. Click No, Do Not Minimize The Amount Of Data to prevent SQL Server from filtering the data.

- *Allow Anonymous Subscriptions*—(Shown in Figure 15.27.) Click Yes, Allow Anonymous Subscriptions to allow anonymous subscriptions to your publication, or No, Allow Only Named Subscriptions to prevent anonymous subscriptions to your publication.

14. Click Next to open the Set Snapshot Agent Schedule dialog box shown in Figure 15.28 and clear the Create The First Snapshot Immediately checkbox to postpone the snapshot files creation. Click Change to open the Edit Recurring Job Schedule dialog box and change the default recurring schedule of the Snapshot Agent.

15. Click Next to open the Completing The Create Publication Wizard. Use the scroll bars to review the information about the choices you made. If you decide you want to modify an option, click Back to reach the dialog box you want to change. After making your modification, click Next the required number of times to return to the Completing The Create Publication Wizard screen. Click Finish to create the publication and display the progress box shown in Figure 15.29.

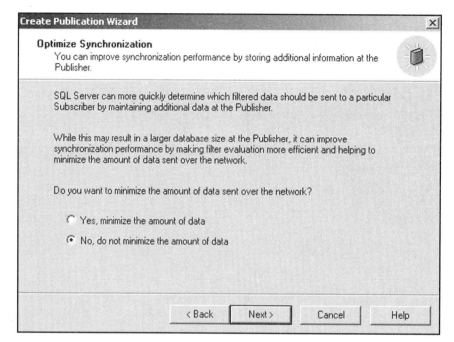

Figure 15.26
Specifying whether to optimize synchronization.

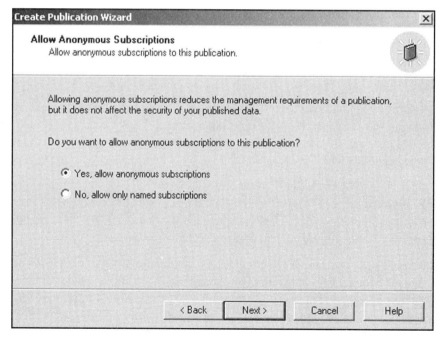

Figure 15.27
Specifying whether to allow anonymous subscriptions.

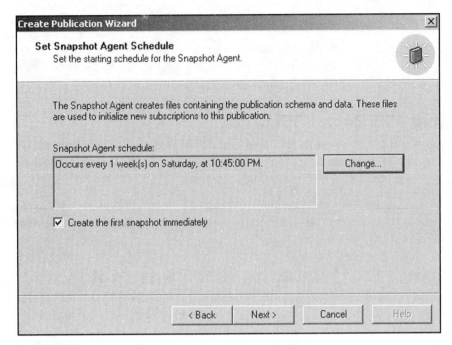

Figure 15.28
Setting the Snapshot Agent schedule.

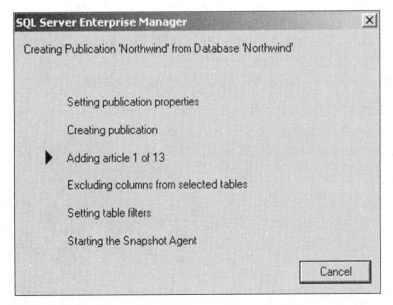

Figure 15.29
Progress box displayed when creating a new publication.

16. Click OK on the confirmation dialog box to close the Create Publication Wizard.

After creating your publications and articles, you need to allow your users to subscribe to them using pull subscriptions or anonymous subscriptions, or you can create the subscriptions from the Publisher using a push subscription.

Managing Your Subscriptions

Subscriptions are the requests for a copy of the published data or database objects using replication. The subscription defines which publications will be replicated, the location of the replicated data, and when the replication occurs.

You can configure the replication of the data using a push subscription, a pull subscription, or a combination of both. You can use either Transact-SQL or Enterprise Manager to create your subscriptions

Creating a Push Subscription Using Transact-SQL

To create a push subscription, you need to determine whether it is a snapshot publication, transactional publication, or merge publication. The following sections discuss how to create the different push subscriptions using Transact-SQL.

Note: Remember, a push subscription is performed from the Publisher. These stored procedures contain arguments that are used to identify the Publisher and Subscriber in the replication process.

Use the following system stored procedures in the following order to create a push subscription of a snapshot or transactional publication:

1. Run **sp_addsubscriber** to register the Subscriber at the Publisher.
2. Run **sp_addpublication** with the **allow_push** option set to **True** to enable the snapshot or transactional push subscription.
3. Run **sp_addsubscription** to create the subscription of the publication.

Use the following system stored procedures in the following order to create a push subscription of a merge publication:

1. Run **sp_addsubscriber** to register the Subscriber at the Publisher.
2. Run **sp_addmergepublication** with the **allow_push** option set to **True** to enable the push subscription.
3. Run **sp_addmergesubscription** to create the push subscription of the merge publication.

Viewing and Modifying a Push Subscription Using Transact-SQL

To view or modify an existing push subscription, you need to determine whether it is a snapshot publication, transactional publication, or merge publication. The following sections discuss how to view and modify the different push subscription using Transact-SQL.

Use the following system stored procedures in the following order to view a push subscription for snapshot or transactional publication:

1. Run **sp_helpsubscription** to list the information associated with a specific Subscriber, publication, article, or set of subscriptions.

2. Run **sp_helpsubscriberinfo** to list the information about a specific Subscriber.

To view a push subscription for a merge publication, run **sp_helpmergesubscription**. This procedure will list the information associated with a specific Subscriber, publication, article, or set of subscriptions.

Use the following system stored procedures in this order to modify a push subscription for a snapshot or transactional publication:

1. Run **sp_changesubscriber** to modify the Subscriber options.

2. Run **sp_changesubstatus** to modify the Subscriber status.

To modify a push subscription for a merge publication, run **sp_changemergesubscription**. This procedure will modify the Subscriber options.

Deleting a Push Subscription Using Transact-SQL

To delete an existing push subscription, you need to determine whether it is a snapshot publication, transactional publication, or merge publication. The following sections discuss how to delete the different push subscriptions using Transact-SQL.

Use the following system stored procedures to delete a push subscription for snapshot or transactional publication:

1. Run **sp_dropsubscription** to delete the push subscription.

2. Run **sp_dropsubscriber** to delete the Subscriber's registration entry.

*Note: You only need to run **sp_dropsubscriber** if you are dropping the last publication for that Subscriber.*

To delete a push subscription of a merge publication, run **sp_dropmergesubscription**.

As you can tell, there are numerous stored procedures available for you to manage your push subscriptions. But, as with most aspects of replication, it is much easier using Enterprise Manager to manage your push subscriptions.

Creating a Push Subscription Using Enterprise Manager

To create a push subscription, you need to determine whether it is a snapshot publication, transactional publication, or merge publication. The following sections discuss how to create the different push subscriptions using Enterprise Manager.

There are wizards available to help create your subscriptions using Enterprise Manager. To use these wizards, follow these steps:

1. After opening Enterprise Manager, expand the server group that contains the Publishing Server. Expand the Replication container and Publications folder, right-click the publication that you want to create the push subscription for, and click Push New Subscription, as shown in Figure 15.30.

2. Click the Show Advanced Options In This Wizard checkbox shown in Figure 15.31 to show all available push subscription options during the Wizard.

3. Click Next to open the Choose Subscribers dialog box shown in Figure 15.32. Click a group of Subscribers or an individual Subscriber for whom the push subscription is being created.

4. Click Next to open the Choose Destination Database dialog box shown in Figure 15.33. Type the name of the destination database or browse the Subscriber(s) server to locate the destination database of the subscription.

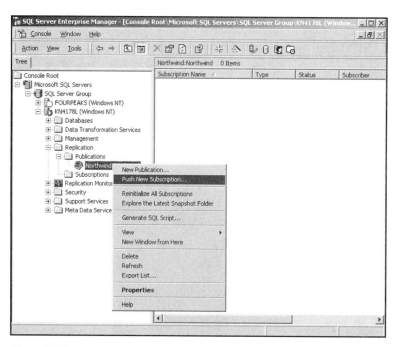

Figure 15.30
Starting the Push New Subscription Wizard.

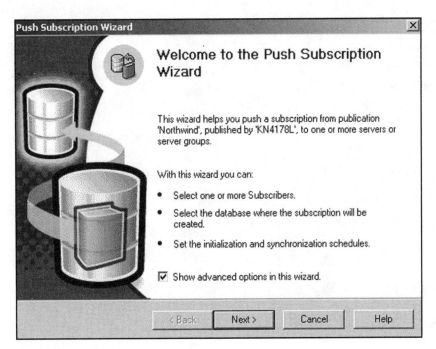

Figure 15.31
Choosing to view the advanced options.

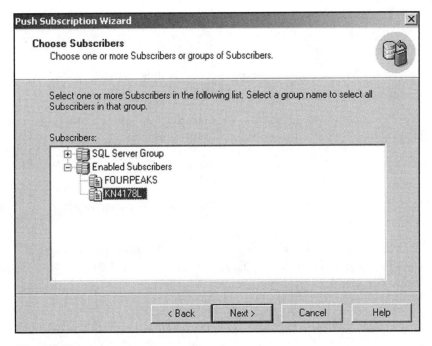

Figure 15.32
Selecting the Subscribers.

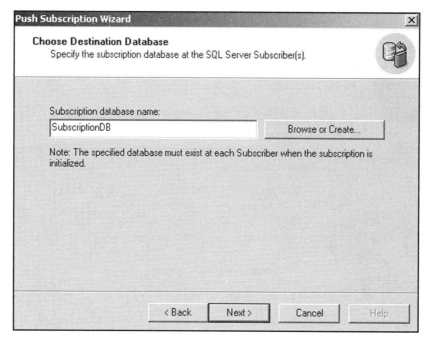

Figure 15.33
Specifying the destination database.

Note: If the database is not listed, click the Create New button on the Browse Databases
On 'servername' dialog box to open the Database Properties dialog box and supply the
new database information.

5. Click Next to open the Set Distribution Agent Schedule dialog box shown in Figure
   15.34 and choose one of the following options:

   - *Continuously*—Provides minimal latency between the time an action occurs at the
     Publisher and the time it is propagated to the Subscriber.

   - *Using The Following Schedule*—Click Change to modify the default schedule of
     every hour on every day.

6. Click Next to open the Initialize Subscription dialog box shown in Figure 15.35 and
   choose one of the following options:

   - *Yes, Initialize The Schema And Data*—Click the checkbox next to the Start The
     Snapshot Agent To Begin The Initialization Process Immediately if you want the
     snapshot created as soon as you complete the wizard. Otherwise, it will create the
     snapshot according to the schedule you defined.

   - *No, The Subscriber Already Has The Schema And Data*—Click this option if you
     have already done a manual load of the snapshot information.

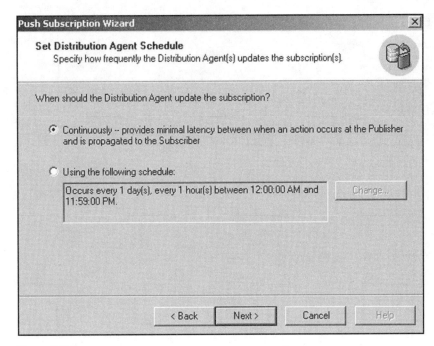

Figure 15.34
Specifying when replication occurs.

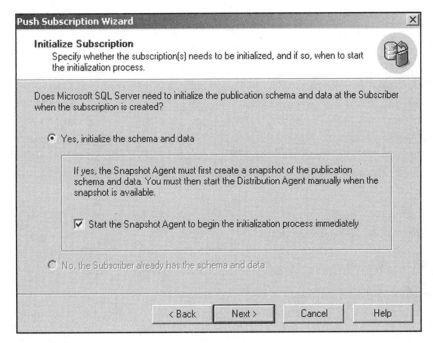

Figure 15.35
Specifying whether to create a snapshot on the Subscriber.

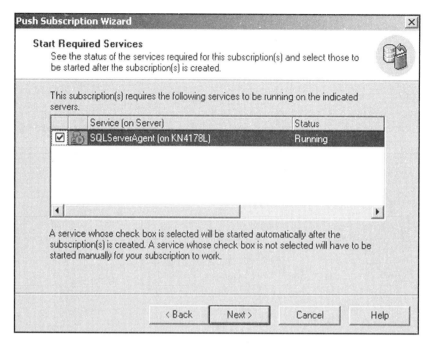

Figure 15.36
Configuring the services to start on the Subscriber.

7. Click Next to open the Start Required Services dialog box shown in Figure 15.36. Click the checkbox next to the services you want SQL Server to start on the Subscriber's machine after the subscription is replicated.

8. Click Next to open the Completing The Push Subscription Wizard screen. Use the scroll bars to review the information about the choices you made. If you decide you want to modify an option, click Back to reach the dialog box you want to change. After making your modification, click Next the required number of times to return to the Completing The Push Subscription Wizard screen. Click Finish to create the push subscription and display the progress box, and click Close when the subscription is created.

You can also create pull subscriptions using either Transact-SQL or Enterprise Manager as described in the following sections.

Viewing and Modifying a Push Subscription Using Enterprise Manager

To view the properties of a push subscription for a snapshot, transactional, or merge publication using Enterprise Manager, follow these steps:

1. After opening Enterprise Manager, expand the server group that contains the Publishing Server. Expand the Replication container and the Publications folder.

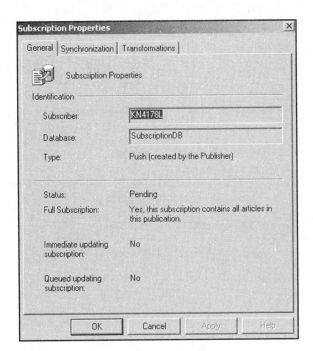

Figure 15.37
Viewing and modifying a push subscription.

2. Right-click the push subscription that you want to view and then click Properties to open the Subscription Properties dialog box shown in Figure 15.37. Click the General, Synchronization, and Transformations tabs to view the push subscriptions properties.

3. Make your changes on the different tabs and then click OK to save your changes and close the Subscription Properties dialog box.

Deleting a Push Subscription Using Enterprise Manager

Follow these steps to delete a push subscription for a snapshot, transactional, or merge publication using Enterprise Manager:

1. After opening Enterprise Manager, expand the server group that contains the Publishing Server. Expand the Replication container and the Publications folder.

2. Right-click the push subscription that you want to delete and then click Delete.

3. Click Yes in the SQL Server Enterprise Manager confirmation box to delete the push subscription.

Note: Remember, a push subscription is performed from the Subscriber. These stored procedures contain arguments that are used to identify the Publisher and Subscriber in the replication process.

Creating a Pull Subscription Using Transact-SQL

To create a pull subscription you need to determine whether it is a snapshot publication, transactional publication, or merge publication. The following sections discuss how to create the different pull subscriptions using Transact-SQL.

Use the following system stored procedures to create a pull subscription for a snapshot or transactional publication:

1. Run **sp_addpublication** with the **allow_pull** option set to **True** to enable the snapshot or transactional pull subscription at the Publisher.

2. Run **sp_addsubscriber** to register the Subscriber at the Publisher.

3. Run **sp_addsubscription** to create the subscription of the publication.

4. Run **sp_addpullsubscription** to create the pull subscription on the Subscriber.

5. Run **sp_addpullsubscription_agent** to schedule a job to run the Distribution Agent on the Subscriber.

Use the following system stored procedures to create an anonymous subscription for a snapshot or transactional publication:

1. Run **sp_addpublication** with the following options set to **True**:

   - **allow_pull**

   - **allow_anonymous**

   - **immediate_sync**

2. Run **sp_addpullsubscription** to create your anonymous subscription on the Subscriber.

3. Run **sp_addpullsubscription_agent** to schedule a job to run the Distribution Agent on the Subscriber.

Use the following system stored procedures to create a pull subscription for a merge publication:

1. Run **sp_addmergepublication** with the **allow-pull** option set to **True** to enable the pull subscription at the Publisher.

2. Run **sp_addsubscriber** to register the Subscriber with the Publisher.

3. Run **sp_addmergesubscription** to create the pull subscription for the merge publication.

4. Run **sp_addmergepullsubscription** to create the pull subscription at the Subscriber.

5. Run **sp_addmergepullsubscription_agent** to schedule a job to run the Distribution Agent at the Subscriber.

Use the following system stored procedures to create an anonymous subscription for a merge publication:

1. Run **sp_addmergepublication** with the following options set to **True**:

   - **allow_pull**

   - **allow_anonymous**

2. Run **sp_addmergepullsubscription** to create the anonymous subscription on the Subscriber.

3. Run **sp_addmergepullsubscription_agent** to schedule a job for the anonymous Merge Agent on the Subscriber.

Viewing or Modifying a Pull or Anonymous Subscription Using Transact-SQL

To view or modify a pull or anonymous subscription, you need to determine whether it is a snapshot publication, transactional publication, or merge publication. The following sections discuss how to view and modify the different pull and anonymous subscriptions using Transact-SQL.

Use the following system to view a pull or anonymous subscription for a snapshot or transactional publication:

1. Run **sp_helpsubscription** stored procedure to list the information associated with a specific Subscriber, publication, article, or set of subscriptions.

2. Run **sp_helppullsubscription** to view the information for one or many subscriptions on the Subscriber.

3. Run **sp_helpsubscriberinfo** to list the information about a specific Subscriber.

To view a pull or anonymous subscription for a merge publication, run **sp_helpmergepullsubscription**, which will list the information associated with a specific Subscriber, publication, article, or set of subscriptions.

Use the following system stored procedures to modify a pull or anonymous subscription for a snapshot or transactional publication:

1. Run **sp_changesubscriber** to modify the Subscriber options.

2. Run **sp_changesubstatus** to modify the Subscriber status.

To modify a push subscription of a merge publication, run **sp_changemergepullsubscription**.

Deleting a Pull Subscription Using Transact-SQL

To delete an existing pull subscription, you need to determine whether it is a snapshot publication, transactional publication, or merge publication. The following sections discuss how to delete the different pull subscription using Transact-SQL.

Use the following system stored procedures to delete a pull subscription for a snapshot publication:

1. Run **sp_dropsubscription** to delete the pull subscription.

2. Run **sp_dropsubscriber** to delete the Subscriber's registration entry.

Use the following system stored procedures to delete a pull subscription for a transactional publication:

1. Run **sp_dropsubscription** to delete the pull subscription.

2. Run **sp_dropsubscriber** to delete the Subscriber's registration entry.

3. Run **sp_droppullsubscription** on the Subscriber.

To delete a pull subscription for a merge publication, run **sp_dropmergepullsubscription**.

There are numerous stored procedures available for you to manage your pull subscriptions. But, as with most aspects of replication, it is much easier using Enterprise Manager to manage your pull subscriptions.

Creating a Pull or Anonymous Subscription Using Enterprise Manager

To create a pull or anonymous subscription, you need to determine whether it is a snapshot publication, transactional publication, or merge publication. The following sections discuss how to create the different pull or anonymous subscriptions using Enterprise Manager.

There are wizards available to you to create your subscriptions using Enterprise Manager. Use the following steps on the Subscriber to create a pull or anonymous subscription using Enterprise Manager:

1. After opening Enterprise Manager, expand the server group that contains the Publishing Server. Expand the Replication container, right-click the Subscriptions folder, and click New Pull Subscription, as shown in Figure 15.38.

2. Click the Show Advanced Options In This Wizard checkbox shown in Figure 15.39 to show all available pull subscription options throughout the wizard.

3. Click Next to open the Look For Publications dialog box shown in Figure 15.40 and choose one of the following options:

   - *Look At Publications From Registered Servers*—View all publications on the SQL Servers registered on the Subscriber.

   - *Look At Publications In The Active Directory Or Specify Publication Information*— View publications listed in Active Directory.

Note: This option is only available for Publishers running SQL Server 2000.

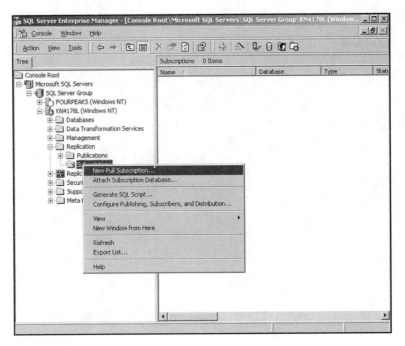

Figure 15.38
Starting the New Pull Subscription Wizard.

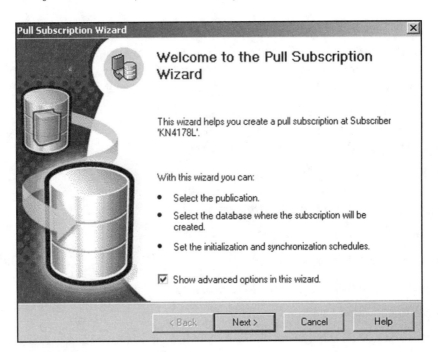

Figure 15.39
Choosing to view the advanced options.

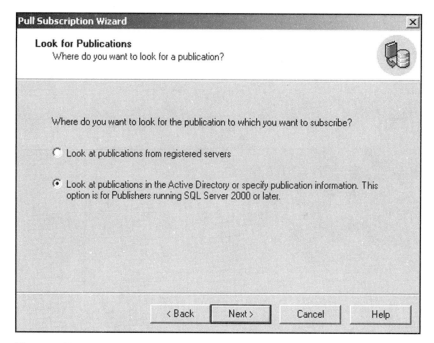

Figure 15.40
The Look For Publications dialog box.

4. Click Next to open one of the following dialog boxes:

- The Choose Publication dialog box shown in Figure 15.41 is displayed if you chose Look At Publications From Registered Servers in the previous step. Expand the server and click on the publication to which you want to subscribe.

Note: If the server containing the publication is not currently registered, you can click Register Server to open the Registered SQL Server Properties dialog box and provide the information required to register a new SQL Server.

- The Specify Publication dialog box shown in Figure 15.42 is displayed if you chose Look At Publications In Active Directory Or Specify Publication Information in the previous step. Provide the following information:

  - Publisher name

  - Publication database name

  - Publication name

  - Authentication type

Note: If you choose SQL Server Authentication, you must supply the Login and Password for the account that will be used to connect to the Publisher.

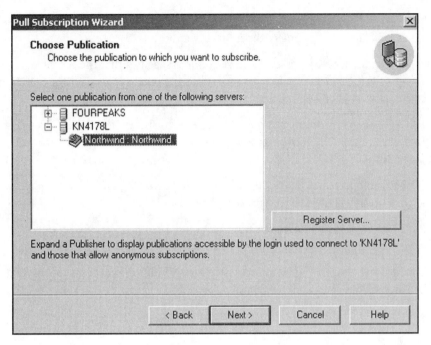

Figure 15.41
Selecting your publication from a registered server.

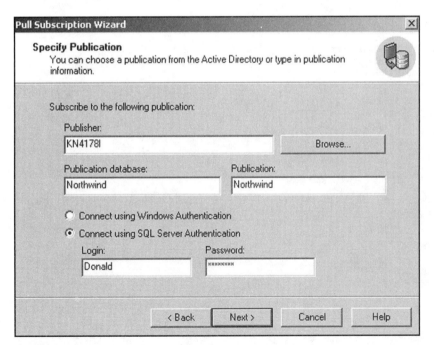

Figure 15.42
Selecting your publication from the Active Directory.

15

5. Click Next to open the Specify Synchronization Agent Login dialog box shown in Figure 15.43 and choose one of the following options:

- *Impersonate The SQL Server Agent Account*—Specifies that the Synchronization Agent uses the same domain user account as the one used to start the SQL Server Agent service when connecting to the Publisher and Distributor.

- *Use SQL Server Authentication*—Allows you to specify the SQL Server account to be used by the Synchronization Login to connect to the Publisher and Distributor.

6. Click Next to open the Choose Destination Database dialog box shown in Figure 15.44 and click on the database that will store the subscription.

Note: *If the destination database does not exist, click New to open the Database Properties dialog box and enter the information required to create a new database.*

7. Click Next to open the Allow Anonymous Subscriptions dialog box shown in Figure 15.45 and choose one of the following options:

- Yes, Make The Subscription Anonymous

- No, This Is A Named Subscription

Note: *Anonymous subscriptions can be used for Internet applications.*

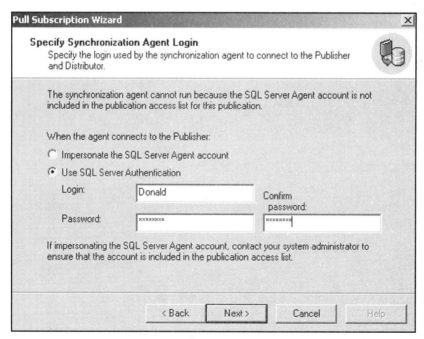

Figure 15.43
Specifying the Synchronization Agent login account.

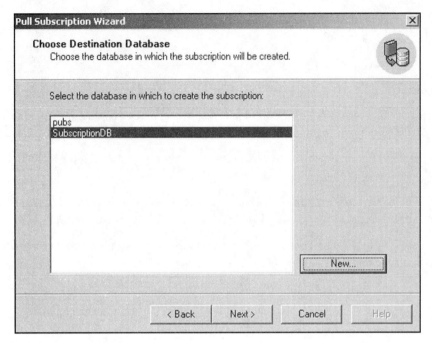

Figure 15.44
Specifying your destination database.

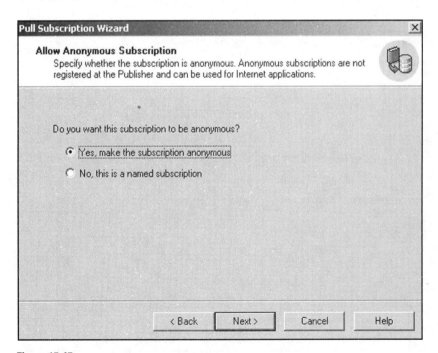

Figure 15.45
Specifying an anonymous subscription.

8. Click Next to open the Initialize Subscription dialog box shown in Figure 15.46 and choose one of the following options:

   • Yes, Initialize The Schema And Data

   • No, The Subscriber Already Has The Schema And Data

Note: *If you choose Yes, the Snapshot Agent has to create the schema and data used by the Distribution Agent to apply the snapshot when the Distribution Agent is available.*

9. Click Next to open the Snapshot Delivery dialog box shown in Figure 15.47 and choose one of the following options:

   • *Use Snapshot Files From The Default Snapshot Folder For This Publication*—Use the files found in \Program Files\Microsoft SQL Server\Mssql\ReplData

   • *Use Snapshot Files From The Following Folder*—Type the location of the folder that contains the snapshot files.

Note: *Alternatively, you can click the ellipses button to browse to the directory.*

10. Click Next to open the Set Distribution Agent Schedule dialog box shown in Figure 15.48 and choose one of the following:

    • *Continuously*—Provides minimal latency between the time a change occurs at the Publisher and the time it is propagated to the Subscriber.

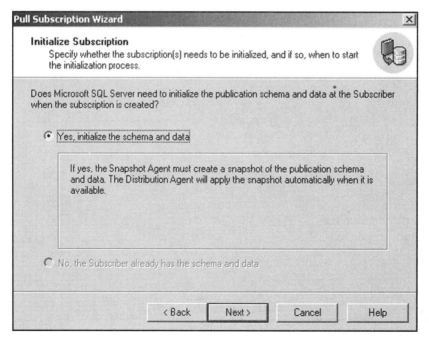

Figure 15.46
Specifying whether to initialize the schema and data.

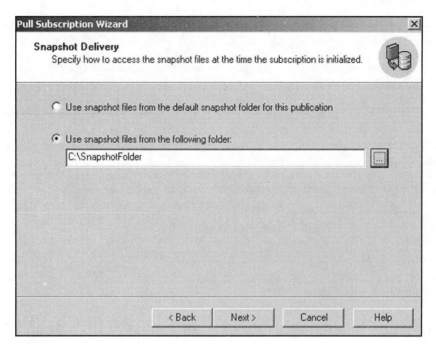

Figure 15.47
Specifying the location of your snapshot files.

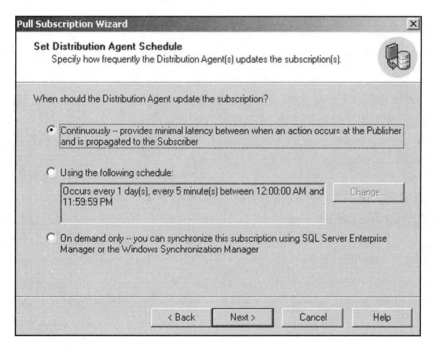

Figure 15.48
Specifying your synchronization schedule.

- *Use The Following Schedule*—Retains the default schedule of every five minutes every day of the week, or click the Change button to create a different schedule.

- *On Demand Only*—Synchronizes the subscription when you perform a manual synchronization using Enterprise Manager or the Windows Synchronization Manager.

11. Click Next to open the Start Required Services dialog box (if you chose Continuously or Use The Following Schedule in the previous step). Click in the checkbox of the services that you want SQL Server to start automatically if they are not started. If you chose On Demand Only, the dialog box in Step 12 is displayed.

12. Click Next to open the Completing The Pull Subscription Wizard screen. Use the scroll bars to review the information about the choices you made. If you decide you want to modify an option, click Back to reach the dialog box you want to change. After making your modification, click Next the required number of times to return to the Completing The Pull Subscription Wizard screen. Click Finish to create the pull subscription and display the progress box. Click Close when the subscription is created.

Viewing and Modifying a Pull or Anonymous Subscription Using Enterprise Manager

Use the following steps on the Subscriber to view the properties of a pull or anonymous subscription for a snapshot, transactional, or merge publication using Enterprise Manager:

1. After opening Enterprise Manager, expand the server group that contains the Subscriber's Server. Expand the Replication container and the Subscriptions folder.

2. Right-click the pull subscription that you want to view or modify and then click Properties. Click the General, Synchronization, and Transformations tabs to view or modify the pull or anonymous subscription's properties.

3. Make your changes on the different tabs and then click OK to save your changes and close the Subscription Properties dialog box.

Deleting a Pull or Anonymous Subscription Using Enterprise Manager

Follow these steps on the Subscriber to delete a pull or anonymous subscription for a snapshot, transactional, or merge publication using Enterprise Manager:

1. After opening Enterprise Manager, expand the server group that contains the Subscriber's server. Expand the Replication container and the Subscriptions folder.

2. Right-click the pull or anonymous subscription that you want to delete and then click Delete.

3. Click Yes in the SQL Server Enterprise Manager confirmation box to delete the pull or anonymous subscription.

Managing your subscriptions can be accomplished using Transact-SQL or Enterprise Manager. As you have seen, user-friendly wizards in SQL Server 2000 are a more efficient way to manage your subscriptions.

Applying the Initial Snapshot

After successfully creating your publications and subscriptions in SQL Server 2000, you need to create and transfer the initial snapshot of the source database schema, objects, and data to the destination database. This information is stored in snapshot files.

The following information is contained in the snapshot files:

- Data
- Constraints
- Extended properties
- Schema information
- System tables
- Triggers

All of the objects listed above are required to create the initial synchronization between the Publisher and the Subscriber. The type of replication and the articles within your publication determine the type of snapshot files used to apply the initial snapshot on the Subscriber. Table 15.5 contains a list of file types and the replication types that use them.

You can view the files before you apply the snapshot using Transact-SQL or Enterprise Manager.

Table 15.5   Snapshot file types.

File Type	Contents	Snapshot	Transactional	Merge
BCP	data	X	X	X
CFT	conflict tables			X
DRI	constraints/indexes	X	X	X
IDX	constraints	X	X	
SCH	schema	X	X	X
SYS	system data			X
TRG	triggers			X

Modifying Your Snapshot Files Working Directory

By default, the replication working directory is located in the root drive at Program Files\Microsoft SQL Server\Mssql\ReplData. However, you can use the following steps to modify the properties and location of a publication's snapshot file:

1. After opening Enterprise Manager, expand the server group that contains the Publishing Server. Expand the Replication container and the Publications folder.

2. Locate and right-click the publication for which you want to modify the snapshot directory properties and click Properties.

3. Click Generate Snapshots In The Following Location on the Snapshot Location tab as shown in Figure 15.49. Type in the Universal Naming Convention name for the new location or click the ellipses button to browse to a new location in the Generate Snapshots In The Following Location box.

4. Click the Compress The Snapshot Files In This Location checkbox to enable compression of your snapshot files.

5. Click the Subscribers Can Access This Folder Using FTP (File Transfer Protocol) if you are using FTP to transfer the snapshot files.

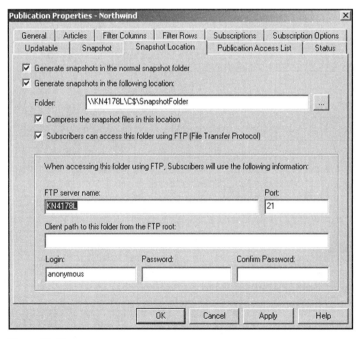

Figure 15.49
Modifying the snapshot files working directory.

Viewing Your Snapshot Files Using Transact-SQL

The type of publication determines which stored procedure to use when viewing the publication's snapshot files. Use one of the following system stored procedures to view the snapshot files using Transact-SQL:

- Execute **sp_browsesnapshotfolder** to browse the snapshot files associated with transactional or snapshot publications.

- Execute **sp_browsemergesnapshotfolder** to browse the snapshot files associated with merge publications.

Viewing Your Snapshot Files Using Enterprise Manager

Use the following steps to view the snapshot files using the Enterprise Manager Snapshot Explorer:

1. After opening Enterprise Manager, expand the server group that contains the Publishing Server. Expand the Replication container, and then expand the Publications folder.

2. Locate and right-click the publication for which you want to view the snapshot files.

3. Click the ExploreThe Latest Snapshot Folder option shown in Figure 15.50.

Note: If you attempt to view the snapshot files for a named Subscriber and they are not visible, they may have already been removed from the contents of the folder by the Distribution Clean Up Agent.

Figure 15.50
Viewing your snapshot files.

After the snapshot is created at the Publisher, the Subscriber has to be synchronized with the Publisher. The Subscriber will then be able to receive incremental changes from the Publisher. The initial snapshot contained in the snapshot files is used to create the schema, objects, and data on the Subscriber.

Applying the initial snapshot files can require additional time if you have a slow connection between the Publisher and Subscriber, or if you are transferring a large amount of data over the network. To combat this concern you can apply your snapshot files manually.

Manually Applying Your Initial Snapshot

If you choose to apply the initial snapshot manually, you can do so by loading the initial snapshot to removable media and shipping the media to the Subscriber. Removable media types include compact discs, tape devices, or any removable storage device the Subscriber is able to recognize.

SQL Server 2000 allows you to store snapshots in locations other than, or in addition to, the default location. As we discussed earlier, you can browse these snapshot files and you can also copy or move them.

To apply snapshots manually, you can:

• Base the initial snapshot on a database backup.

• Save the snapshot files to removable media and ship the media to the Subscriber.

After you create and ship the media to the Subscriber and it has loaded it on its machine, you can choose the No, The Subscriber Already Has The Schema And Data option on the Initialize Subscription page of the Create Push Subscription wizard or Create Pull Subscription wizard.

After the wizard is completed, the Distribution Agent and Merge Agent assume that the Publisher and Subscriber are already synchronized and start sending only data modifications to the Subscribers. However, if the snapshot has not been applied, SQL Server will wait until the Snapshot Agent schedule applies the snapshot to the Subscriber.

Automatically Applying Your Initial Snapshot

SQL Server 2000 has built-in functionality to automatically apply the initial snapshot to your Subscribers. When SQL Server applies the snapshot to the Subscriber the Distribution Agent (for snapshot and transactional replication) or the Merge Agent (for merge replication) applies the schema and data files to the Subscriber's destination database.

When working with transactional replication, SQL Server applies minimal locking behavior to make sure the snapshot is generated with a full, logical, and consistent set of data.

Warning! During the time the snapshot is being created, users are unable to update it. To reduce or eliminate the inconvenience to your users, schedule the snapshot creation when user updates are minimal.

For merge replication, SQL Server also applies a minimal number of locks when creating the snapshot. The tables are not locked during the bulk copy operation and updates at the Publisher are not prevented for the duration of the entire snapshot.

When automatically applying your initial snapshot through SQL Server, specify that SQL Server should initialize the schema and data on the Initialize Subscription Page of both the Create Push Subscription Wizard and Create Pull Subscription Wizard.

Executing Scripts When Applying Your Snapshot

SQL Server replication provides the capability to execute scripts on the Subscriber before applying the snapshot files, or immediately after applying the snapshot files. Reasons to execute a script file include:

- Creating a user-defined data type

- Creating user logins

- Updating statistics

After specifying the location of the script files and the script name, the Snapshot Agent maintains the script entry by copying the script files to the current snapshot folder each time snapshot processing occurs. The Distribution Agent or Merge Agent will run the pre-snapshot script files before applying an initial synchronization and the post-snapshot script files after the objects and data have been synchronized.

Note: *To test your script, you should run it from the command prompt using the osql utility. The pre-snapshot and post-snapshot scripts are actually launched using osql.*

Use the following steps in Enterprise Manager to execute scripts before or after the snapshot is applied:

1. After opening SQL Server Enterprise Manager on the Publishers, expand the Replication folder, and then expand the Publications folder.

2. Right-click the publication for which you want to apply the scripts and then click Properties to open the Publication Properties dialog box.

Warning! *You may receive an informational message, as shown in Figure 15.51, if the publication currently has subscribers or is currently disabled.*

3. Click the Snapshot tab to display the Publication Properties dialog box shown in Figure 15.52 and type the name of the script file in the Before Applying The Snapshot, Execute This Script or in the After Applying The Snapshot, Execute This Script, or both if you have a pre-snapshot script and post-snapshot script.

Tip: *Alternatively, you can browse for the script files by clicking the ellipses (...) button in each box.*

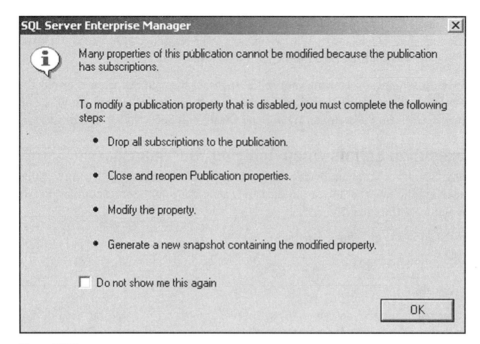

Figure 15.51
Publication properties informational message.

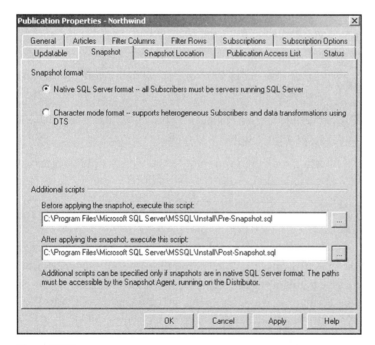

Figure 15.52
Specifying the script files in the Publication Properties dialog box.

4. Click OK to close the Publication Properties dialog box.

After applying the initial snapshot, you need to determine and configure the synchronization method you are going to use to keep the data synchronized between the Publisher and Subscriber.

Understanding Synchronization

Synchronizing data is the process of propagating data between the Publisher and Subscriber, keeping the data consistent. The method of synchronization depends on the type of replication you have implemented and whether the subscription has been marked for re-initialization.

The following replication types define how synchronization occurs on the Publisher and Subscriber in SQL Server 2000:

- *Snapshot replication*—Reapplies the entire snapshot of the schema and data on the Subscriber each time the synchronization occurs.

- *Transactional replication*—Distributes the data **INSERTS**, **UPDATES**, **DELETES**, and other modifications between the Publisher and Subscriber.

- *Merge replication*—Distributes data updates that occur at multiple sites and merges the updates after detecting and resolving any conflicts to determine the correct value.

Note: *The Distribution Agent and Merge Agent move the changes made on the Publisher to the Subscriber. SQL Server 2000 refers to this process as synchronization.*

Let's take a closer look at the three replication types available in SQL Server 2000 and see how the synchronization process occurs with each of them.

Snapshot Replication Synchronization

Snapshot replication propagates data exactly as it appears on the Publisher and does not monitor for updates to the data. When synchronization occurs, the entire snapshot is generated and propagated to the Subscribers.

Snapshot replication is most often used when:

- Your data is changed infrequently, and when it does change, it is more efficient to publish an entirely new copy to your Subscribers.

- It is acceptable to have copies of data on your Subscribers that are not synchronized with the Publisher for a period of time.

- Propagating a small amount of data during an entire refresh of the data is reasonable.

- The data is generally handled as read-only data by the Subscribers.

Note: If the data is changed on the Subscriber, the change must be immediately propagated to the Publisher using a two-phase commit protocol (2PC) implemented with the immediate updating feature of SQL Server.

Snapshot replication requires that you plan for the following areas:

- *Storing and transferring your snapshot files*—You have the option of storing the data in the default replication working directory or specifying an alternate directory. You also have the option of compressing the snapshot files. This option reduces the disk space usage and network bandwidth required to propagate the data, therefore reducing the time required to complete the replication.

- *Scheduling your snapshots*—To create an optimal schedule for propagating the snapshot files, you should determine the amount of time it will take the Snapshot Agent to complete the snapshot.

Tip: The snapshot is created using BCP. You can perform a test of the bulk copy of your data to determine how long the transfer will take.

Snapshot replication synchronization uses the Distribution Agent (using distrib.exe or the Distribution ActiveX Control) to apply the most recent snapshot on the Subscriber. If modifications were made to the data on the Publisher, new snapshot files are generated and placed in the replication working directory. These files are then copied and run on the Subscriber to synchronize the data between the Publisher and Subscriber.

Transactional Replication Synchronization

Transactional replication is implemented by applying an initial snapshot on the Subscribers. It then applies only the data modifications made on the Publisher to the Subscriber using the individual transactions that were captured on the Publisher.

Transactional replication is most often used when:

- You want to propagate incremental changes to your Subscribers as they occur.

- Your transactions must adhere to the ACID (Atomicity, Consistency, Isolation, and Durability) properties.

- Your Subscribers are frequently and/or reliably connected to the Publisher.

Transactional replication uses the transaction log of the published databases to capture the changes being made to the database. The Log Reader Agent monitors the published databases for **INSERT**, **UPDATE**, and **DELETE** statements or other modifications and stores the changes in the distribution database. The Distribution Agent monitors the distribution database for transactions and propagates them in the same order as they occurred to the Subscribers.

Transaction replication requires that you plan for the following areas:

- *Transaction log space for the published databases*—Published databases may require more transaction log space than databases that are not published. This statement is true if the transaction log records are not purged until after they have been moved to the distribution database. If the Log Reader Agent is not running, or if the distribution database is unavailable for a period of time, the transaction log of the published database will continue to grow. The transactions of the Published database bound for the distribution database cannot be removed until they are copied to the distribution database.

Tip: *It is recommended that you allow the transaction log of your published databases to autogrow to avoid running out of space.*

- *Disk space for your distribution database*—After creating a transactional publication and configuring the snapshot files to be immediately available to your Subscribers, the amount of space required for the distribution database increases. All transactions that occur after the snapshot files are created and retained until the snapshot files are applied to the Subscribers. At that point, the transactions that have occurred since the snapshot files were created will need to be synchronized with all Subscribers. Furthermore, the distribution database continues to store the transactions until the Snapshot Agent is run the second time (either manually or scheduled). After the Snapshot Agent runs the second time, the distribution database is cleaned up and reduced in size.

- *Primary keys for all tables being published*—All tables containing published data must contain a declared primary key. You can add a primary key to a published table using the **ALTER TABLE** statement.

- *Whether you will allow immediate updating and queued updating*—Allowing your Subscribers to perform updates to the data on their machine requires the implementation of a two-phase commit protocol.

- *Whether the data will be transformed*—Data that is going to be manipulated before it reaches the Subscriber requires Data Transformation Services (DTS) to be configured.

- **IDENTITY** *column ranges*—Data within an **IDENTITY** column requires the decision of whether new **IDENTITY** values will be generated on the Subscriber during replication, or the values stored on the Publisher will be replicated to the Subscriber.

- *Use of constraints and the* **NOT FOR REPLICATION** *option*—Triggers and constraints can also be configured to perform differently if the data is replicated versus being added using a regular transaction.

- *Replication* **of TEXT and IMAGE** *data types*—If you are replicating **TEXT** and **IMAGE** data types in a transaction publication, consider the following:

  - Subscribers cannot use **INSERT**, **UPDATE**, and **DELETE** statements to update text and image columns.

15

- Text or image columns published for replication using **WRITETEXT** and **UPDATETEXT** operations with the **WITH NO_LOG** option are not supported.

- **UPDATETEXT** operations are only supported if all Subscribers are running SQL Server 6 or later.

- Custom procedures containing modifications to multiple text columns cannot be used because the other text column values are not logged.

- Use the **max text repl** size parameter to control the maximum size in bytes of text and image data that can be published.

*Note: Use **sp_configure** to set the **max text repl** size parameter.*

- When publishing text and image columns, the text pointer used to locate the information should be retrieved in the same transaction as the **UDPATETEXT** or **WRITETEXT** operation.

Transactional replication uses the Distribution Agent to propagate the **INSERT**, **UPDATE**, and **DELETE** commands from the distribution database to the Subscriber. These are the same commands that were run on the Publisher to update the data there.

Merge Replication Synchronization

Merge replication is used to distribute data from the Publisher to the Subscribers, allowing both to make updates to the data, whether connected or disconnected from the network, and then merging the updates made by the Publisher and Subscribers when reconnected.

Merge replication allows different locations to work autonomously and merge the updates at a later time into a single result set. After the initial snapshot is applied at the Subscribers, SQL Server tracks the changes made to the data on the Publisher and the Subscribers. The data is synchronized between the participating servers using one of the following scheduling options:

- Continuously

- On Demand Only

- Using The Following Schedule

Because the same data can be updated in multiple locations, conflicts can occur when the data is merged. Conflict resolution must take place to determine the value that should be stored and propagated. The conflict resolution can take place using the default settings or custom settings.

Merge replication is most often used when:

- Numerous Subscribers need to modify the data at their location and propagate those changes to the Publisher and other Subscribers.

- Subscribers need to receive the data, modify it offline, and synchronize the modifications later with the Publisher and other Subscribers.

- You do not anticipate many conflicts when the data is modified at multiple locations. Furthermore, if conflicts do occur, ACID property violations are acceptable.

The Snapshot Agent and the Merge Agent are used to implement merge replication. As you already know, the Snapshot Agent is responsible for preparing the snapshot files, storing those files, and inserting the synchronization jobs in the publication database. The Snapshot Agent also creates replication-specific:

- *Stored procedures*—Used to update the Subscription database. There is one created for the **INSERT**, **UPDATE**, and **DELETE** statements. These stored procedures are used in place of the individual statements.

- *System tables*—Several system tables (such as **MSmerge_contents**, **MSmerge_tombstone**, **MSmerge_genhistory**, and **MSmerge_replinfo**) are added to the Publication database to support:

  - Data tracking

  - Synchronization

  - Conflict detection

  - Conflict resolution

  - Reporting

- *Tracking columns*—Columns are also added to the merge publication table to assist in the tracking of the merge replication, including:

  - **Conflict_type**

  - **Create_time**

  - **Origin_datasource**

  - **Pubid**

  - **Reason_code**

  - **Reason_text**

  - **Source_object**

  - **Tablenick**

- *Triggers*—Triggers are installed to track the changes to the data in each row or column. The triggers capture the changes made to the publishing table and enter the changes in the numerous merge system tables. The triggers created on the Publisher are created when the Snapshot Agent runs for the first time. The triggers created on the Subscriber are created when the snapshot is applied.

The Merge Agent applies the initial snapshot files to the Subscribers and also merges the incremental changes made on the Publisher or Subscriber after the initial snapshot was applied. Furthermore, it resolves any update conflicts based on the default conflict resolvers, or on custom resolvers you have configured.

Merge replication is completed when Publishers and Subscribers reconnect and their changes are propagated between locations. If necessary, conflicts are detected and resolved.

Replication is used to exchange data and modifications of data between two databases. Up to this point we have discussed replication in a SQL Server environment. Let's take a look at what replication options you have in a non-SQL Server environment.

Using Heterogeneous Data Sources With Replication

SQL Server 2000 presents the capability to replicate data to any heterogeneous data source that provides a 32-bit Open Database Connectivity (ODBC) or Object Linking and Embedding Database (OLE DB) driver on the following operating systems:

- Windows 2000

- Windows NT 4

- Windows 98

Additionally, SQL Server 2000 can receive data replicated from the following:

- Microsoft Access

- Microsoft Exchange

- Oracle

- DB2 Universal

- DB2/MVS

- DB2 AS400

Publishing to Heterogeneous Subscribers

The ability to publish to a variety of heterogeneous data sources provides SQL Server support for corporations that have acquired non-SQL Server databases. The easiest way to publish data to non-SQL Server data sources is by using ODBC or OLE DB along with a push subscription from the Publisher to the Subscriber via an ODBC or OLE DB interface.

Note: Alternatively, you can create publications and access them from an application with an embedded distribution control that implements a pull subscription from the Subscriber to the Publisher.

Although we have the support for heterogeneous Subscribers, you need to be aware of the following restrictions when replicating to heterogeneous Subscribers:

- Tables replicated to heterogeneous Subscribers inherit the table-naming convention of the heterogeneous data source.

- Schema files used to create files on a Subscriber do not include quotation marks around the table names, and the new table name is dependent on the Subscriber's behavior when they create the table. For instance, if you have a Subscriber using an Oracle database, and you pass the name Customer without quotation marks, Oracle will create a table name of **CUSTOMER**.

- Transactions applied to your heterogeneous Subscribers by the Distribution Agent contain quotation marks around the table names.

- ODBC Subscribers do not support batched statements.

- Because the Data Source Name (DSN) is stored in the **sysservers** table, it must conform to the SQL Server 2000 naming conventions.

- If the ODBC DSN is not a SQL Server DSN, the publication option to truncate is not supported.

- The setting of the quoted identified character of the target server is used to determine if quoted identifiers are allowed.

- ODBC Subscribers can only subscribe to publications that have chosen the character format bulk-copy method for synchronization.

- All heterogeneous Subscribers support **NULL**, **NOT NULL**, **IDENTITY**, and the constraint for **PRIMARY KEY** for **CREATE TABLE** options. Therefore, each time you add or remove an article from a publication, you must reinitialize the subscription.

SQL Server 2000 also provides replication support to Subscribers running different versions of SQL Server and also to Subscribers running Microsoft SQL Server 2000 Windows CE Edition. (See details in "Replicating to SQL Server CE").

To publish to heterogeneous Subscribers using Enterprise Manager, follow the steps listed earlier in this chapter under "Creating Publications and Articles Using Enterprise Manager." In Step 7, be sure to choose One Or More Subscribers Will Not Be SQL Servers.

After configuring the heterogeneous publication using steps listed earlier in this chapter under "Creating Publications and Articles Using Enterprise Manager," follow these steps to add the heterogeneous Subscribers from within Enterprise Manager:

1. Point to Replication on the Tools menu, and then click Configuring Publishing, Subscribers, And Distribution to open the Publisher And Distributor Properties dialog box. Click the Subscribers tab as shown in Figure 15.53.

15

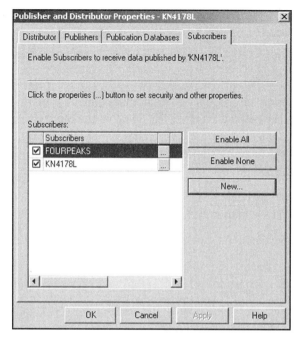

Figure 15.53
Opening the Subscribers option of the Publisher And Distributor Properties.

2. Click the New button to open the Enable New Subscriber dialog box shown in Figure 15.54.

3. Locate and click the type of data source and then click OK to open the Enable Subscriber - 'data source type' Data Source as shown in Figure 15.55.

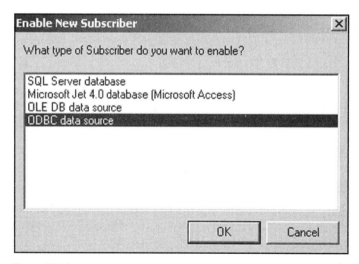

Figure 15.54
Opening the Enable New Subscriber dialog box.

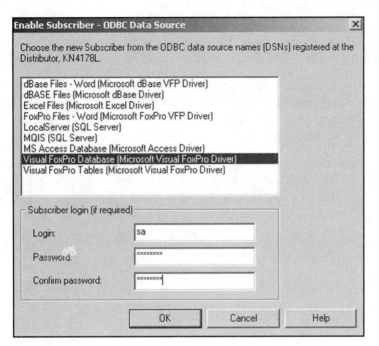

Figure 15.55
Specifying the heterogeneous data source and Subscriber login.

4. Locate and click the heterogeneous Subscriber. If necessary, enter the Subscriber's login information.

5. Click OK to create the heterogeneous Subscriber and close the Enable Subscriber - 'data source type' Data Source dialog box.

Subscribing to Heterogeneous Publishers

The ability to subscribe to a snapshot or transactional publication on an Oracle, DB2, Access, or other data sources allows companies to plan on deploying large databases or data warehouses in SQL Server, as well as intranet and Internet applications, to gain access to a variety of data sources.

Subscribing to snapshot and transactional replication publications on heterogeneous data sources is implemented through the use of third-party software or applications developed using SQL-DMO and the Replication Distributor Interface.

Replication Features of SQL Server 2000 Windows CE

You can also publish data to mobile devices running SQL Server 2000 Windows CE Edition using SQL Server 2000 and merge replication. Merge replication is great for Subscribers like CE users who are not continuously connected to the network.

Replication with SQL Server CE subscribes to a merge publication using an anonymous subscription. The Subscriber administers the subscription; therefore, no information about the subscription or the Subscriber is stored at the Publisher.

To configure this replication scenario, create a merge publication using the Create Publication Wizard. Select Servers Running SQL Server CE on the Specify Subscriber Types screen of the Wizard. After selecting this option, anonymous subscriptions are automatically enabled for the publication.

The SQL Server Merge Agent used to complete the synchronization is controlled by the SQL Server CE Replication Object within SQL Server CE. As with to all other merge publications, conflicts are resolved using the criteria you defined when you created the publication.

After configuring the numerous components of SQL Server 2000 replication, you may want to monitor the replication process. This is most easily accomplished using the Replication Monitor.

Monitoring Your Replication Process

The replication process in SQL Server 2000 contains many different areas that you may want to monitor in order to verify that they are performing as expected and meeting the needs of your organization.

As you are monitoring replication, you also can perform the following tasks:

• Manage replication agents from a central location.

• Set your agent profiles, properties, schedules, and notifications for the replication agents.

• Monitor and troubleshoot your agent activity, including when the agents last ran, specific activity that occurred, and performance.

• Receive notification using a replication alert when a specific event occurs on a replication agent.

• Re-initialize one or all subscriptions for a specific publication, if necessary.

• Verify your Subscriber's information to make certain the data values are consistent between your Publisher and Subscribers.

The primary tool used to monitor replication is the Replication Monitor that is automatically installed on the Distributor in Enterprise Manager during the installation of replication. The Replication Monitor shown in Figure 15.56 is designed to monitor the items listed above.

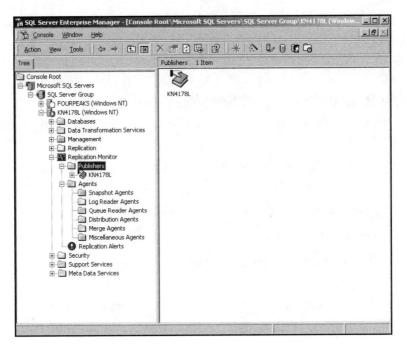

Figure 15.56
Locating and opening Replication Monitor.

Note: *You must be a member of the **sysadmin** fixed server role, or have been added to the* ***replmonitor*** *role of the distribution database to use Replication Monitor. However, members of **replmonitor** can only view information, whereas members of the **sysadmin** role can administer replication.*

The following sections list the steps required to monitor the replication agent performance, and replication agent session details.

Monitoring Replication Agent Performance

Follow these steps to configure Replication Monitor to monitor the performance of your replication agents:

1. Expand the server group that contains the server acting as your Distributor and then expand the Distributor Server.

2. After you right-click on Replication Monitor, click Performance Monitor to open up the System Monitor of Windows 2000, or the Performance Monitor of Windows NT 4.

3. Click Add To Chart on the Edit menu to open the Add Counters dialog box.

4. Using the Object list drop-down menu, locate and select the replication object you want to monitor.

5. Select the counter of the selected replication object from the Select Counters From List menu and click Add.

6. Click Close to close the Add Counters dialog box.

Monitoring Replication Agent Session Details

Follow these steps to configure Replication Monitor to monitor the session details of your replication agents:

1. Expand the server group that contains the server acting as your Distributor and then expand the Distributor Server.

2. Expand the Replication Monitor container, and then click Agents.

3. Click the agent you wish to monitor.

4. After you locate and right-click a row in the Details pane, click Agent History to open the Agent's history dialog box.

5. Locate and click on a session in the session list, and click Session Details.

6. After reviewing the details click Close.

Using Alerts to Automate Replication Notification

SQL Server 2000 also includes a set of predefined alerts specific to the replication process. These alerts can be configured to execute a task or notify an operator about the status of replication. Operators can configure an automated response to these alerts, or intervene manually. Table 15.6 provides a list of the predefined alerts in SQL Server 2000.

Table 15.6   Predefined alerts.

Error #	Alert Name	Cause For Alert to Fire	Updates sysreplicationalerts
14150	Replication: Agent success	agent successfully shut down	yes
14151	Replication: Agent failure	agent shut down with an error	yes
14152	Replication: Agent retry	agent shut down after unsuccessful retry of operation	yes
14157	Replication: Subscription cleaned up	deleted inactive subscription	no
20572	Replication: Subscription reinitialized after validation failure	Response to error 20574	no
20574	Replication: Subscriber has failed data validation	Distribution or Merge Agent fails data validation	yes
20575	Replication: Subscriber has passed data validation	Distribution or Merge Agent passed data validation	yes

Optimizing Replication

You need to make sure that the SQL Server 2000 replication component is running as efficiently as possible. You can enhance the overall performance of all types of replication in your application and on your network by implementing some or all of the following recommendations:

- Allocate a minimal amount of memory to SQL Server by setting the min server memory option to avoid low memory availability.

- Store your transaction log files and database files on separate disk drives for the publication, distribution, and subscription databases. Furthermore, create your snapshot folder on a separate drive as well.

- Add additional memory to your replication servers. You can use the **sp_configure** system stored procedure to assign additional memory to SQL Server.

- Use multiple processors on your replication servers. The replication agents can take advantage of multiple processors.

- Partition the published data to guarantee that only the data required is being published to your Subscribers.

- Schedule your snapshot files to be applied during off-peak hours, reducing the network bandwidth consumed and processor usage during peak hours. Compressing your snapshot files also reduces the amount of network bandwidth consumed, as well as disk space usage.

- Configure pull subscriptions instead of push subscriptions to offload the Distribution Agent and Merge Agent overhead to your Subscribers.

These options can be implemented in SQL Server 2000 to assist in optimizing replication performance and reduce the amount of time required to keep your data consistent throughout your SQL Server configuration.

Summary

The need to distribute data throughout your organization is often a time-consuming task. However, the ability to schedule the replication process and choose from a variety of implementations makes distribution much easier to manage.

Replication is a very powerful feature of SQL Server 2000 in that you can replicate to and from heterogeneous environments, partition the data vertically, horizontally, or both, and use Replication Monitor to monitor the efficiency of the replication process.

As your users look more and more for Web-based information, you will probably want to share your data on the Web in a dynamic and efficient method. SQL Server 2000 provides XML and other Internet-based features discussed in Chapter 16 to assist you in sharing your data on the Web.

15

Chapter 16

Configuring XML and
Internet Support

With today's constant drive toward Internet-based applications and solutions, more and more corporations require that you provide dynamic Web-based data for your clients. Generally, your Web-based clients only have the need to view the data, but there may be situations where your clients need to modify or delete data as part of database maintenance.

One common piece of software everyone has is a Web browser. The trick is to generate Web-based information for your clients regardless of what hardware, operating system, and browser they are running. This is where Extensible Markup Language (XML) comes into play. This industry-based standard provides a way to exchange structured data over the Internet in a platform-neutral environment.

The great thing about XML is that you don't have to toss out any of your existing techniques and technologies; instead, you retain your existing systems and integrate them with new ones. Even better, you're not limited to integrating with just your company's applications, you can also easily integrate applications with companies you're partnered with, regardless of what platform or system they are running.

XML is a technology that is new in SQL Server 2000, but it isn't the only means you have for sharing data on the Web. You can still share read-only data using the Web Assistant Wizard, which easily walks you through the configuration and maintenance of data you want others to view. This chapter will discuss both of these options, with most of the emphasis on the new technology, XML.

Note: *This chapter is not going to teach you how to use XML. It is going to introduce you to basic HTML and XML features in SQL Server 2000. There are books on how to use XML with SQL Server and other Web-based systems. To reap the benefits of this chapter, you should be familiar with the basic architecture and security concepts of SQL Server and the basic Transact-SQL statements such as* **INSERT**, **UPDATE**, *and* **DELETE**.

Introducing the Web Assistant Wizard

The Web Assistant Wizard, located in the Enterprise Manager, is used to generate standard HTML files from SQL Server data. The wizard generates HTML files using:

• Transact-SQL queries

• Stored procedures

• Extended stored procedures

The wizard can be used to generate an HTML file for a one-time execution or a regularly scheduled task. After creating the HTML files, you can use triggers to update the files when the data changes in the SQL Server database.

The Web Assistant Wizard allows you to:

• Schedule a task to automatically update the Web page containing the data contained in the SQL Server database.

• Publish and distribute management reports, such as:

  • Sales statistics

  • Resource allocations

  • Other SQL Server data

• Publish SQL Server reports containing information about who is accessing the server and who is holding a particular lock type.

• Use extended stored procedures to publish information outside of SQL Server.

• Use a table of favorite Web sites to publish a server jump list.

• Use the **sp_makewebtask** stored procedure to create an HTML file.

*Note: You can use **sp_dropwebtask** and **sp_runwebtask** to remove and execute, respectively, the tasks created using **sp_makewebtask**.*

Introducing XML Support in SQL Server 2000

SQL Server 2000 introduces new features that support the XML functionality to make SQL Server 2000 an XML-enabled database server. The new features include:

• The ability to use HTTP to access SQL Server.

• Support for XDR (XML-Data Reduced) schemas and the ability to execute Xpath queries to access these schemas.

• Enhancements to the OLE DB provider (SQLOLEDB) that allow XML documents to return results sets as a stream.

- The ability to access and write XML data:

  - Retrieve XML data using the **FOR XML** clause and the **SELECT** statement.

  - Write XML data using **OPENXML** rowset provider.

  - Access XML data using Xpath query statements.

Note: *For the latest information regarding SQL Server 2000 XML support, access the XML Developer Center on MSDN at* ***www.microsoft.com***.

Now that you have been introduced to the two different Internet-based options available in SQL Server 2000, let's examine each of them in more detail.

Becoming Familiar with XML

To take full advantage of the XML functionality available in SQL Server 2000, you have to be familiar with XML, URL syntax, and HTTP methods. You also need to be familiar with some of the terms most commonly used when referring to XML:

16

- *Element*—All the data located between the opening and closing tag.

- *Attribute*—Additional predefined information about the element.

- *Tag*—Code that identifies the type of element that follows and is used by the browser to parse and display information. They are often referred to as *markup tags*.

- *XML document*—A document containing XML elements and attributes.

- *Document Type Definition* (DTD)—A document containing code used to define the elements and attributes that can be used in an XML document.

- *Style sheet*—A document used to describe the way your data is formatted and displayed. XML documents commonly use Extensible Stylesheet Language (XSL).

- *Form*—A formatted document used to collect and submit the data to be processed.

- *Template*—An XML document containing one or more SQL statements. Template files are used to specify SQL and Xpath queries. These template files containing the queries are specified in the URL instead of the query itself.

- *Virtual root*—A location and name of a directory used to define and register a new virtual directory with the Internet Information Server (IIS). Using the Configure SQL XML Support in IIS utility in the SQL Server program group, you instruct IIS to create an association between the virtual directory and an instance of SQL Server.

Using tags, elements, and attributes to display data through a browser is not new with XML. Hypertext Markup Language (HTML) is the language of the Web and provided the foundation of XML.

Exploring HTML Sample Code

To get an understanding of the different elements used by HTML, and in turn by XML, lets take a look at some sample HTML code and walk through the end results of the code:

```
<P align="center">Welcome to an introduction to <STRONG> XML </STRONG>
support</P>
```

This HTML code contains two markup tags: **<P>** and **<STRONG>**. These two tags surround the text displayed when accessed by a browser. The closing tags **</P>** and **</STRONG>** indicate the end of the data for which the tags apply.

Note: *All the data between the opening tags and closing tags is referred to as the element.*

The following steps explain the results of the HTML code:

1. The **<P>** tag with the **align** attribute is used to start a new paragraph and center the text on the page when it is displayed by the browser.

2. The code will then display "Welcome to an introduction to".

3. The **<STRONG> XML </STRONG>** tag indicates to the browser to bold the word "XML". The **<STRONG>** begins the bolding, and the **</STRONG>** ends the bolding.

4. The code then displays the word "support".

5. The **</P>** ends the paragraph and indicates the end of the element.

The resulting formatted information is shown when displaying the text through your browser: "Welcome to an introduction to **XML** support".

The HTML parser must be able to locate the tags and understand how to implement the option within the tag.

Exploring XML Sample Code

The primary difference between HTML tags and XML tags is that HTML tags provide instructions on how to format the data, whereas XML tags provide the structure of the data itself. For example, an XML order document may look similar to this:

```
<Order OrderNum="9876">
        <OrderDate>09-20-2001</OrderDate>
        <CustomerFirstName>Brian</CustomerFirstName>
        <Item>
            <ProductNum>100</ProductNum>
            <Quantity>25</Quantity>
        </Item>
        <Item>
            <ProductNum>101</ProductNum>
```

```
        <Quantity>50</Quantity>
    </Item>
</Order>
```

Notice that there are no formatting instructions in the previous code sample; it contains only the data. This means the XML parser doesn't need to understand the meaning of the tags, only how to locate them and verify that the document is an XML document. Because the tags do not need to be predefined for the parser, you can use any tags you want. The *X* in XML stands for extensible—you can use any tags you choose, not just predefined tags recognized by the parser, as is the case with HTML tags.

Note: The attribute values in XML can be stored in either single or double quotation marks. For instance, <Order OrderNum="9876"> and <Order OrderNum='9876'> are both interpreted as being the same by the XML parser.

The following bullets explain the results of the XML code:

- The **Order** element contains an **OrderNum** attribute with a value of **9876** and the order contains child elements.

- The **OrderDate** child element contains the value **09-20-2001**.

- The **CustomerFirstName** child element contains the value of **Brian**.

- The first child **Item** element contains:

  - The child element of **ProductNum** with a value of **100**.

  - The child element of **Quantity** with a value of **25**.

- The second child **Item** element contains:

  - The child element of **ProductNum** with a value of **101**.

  - The child element of **Quantity** with a value of **50**.

To create an element that does not contain any data, you can generate an empty element with an opening element tag immediately followed by a closing element tag, as follows:

```
<Item>
        <ProductNum>100</ProductNum>
        <Quantity>25</Quantity>
         <ProductType></ProductType>
</Item>
```

Alternatively, to save time and space in your XML document, you can include only the closing tag, as follows:

```
<Item>
        <ProductNum>100</ProductNum>
```

16

```
        <Quantity>25</Quantity>
      </ProductType>
  </Item>
```

You can also have elements that contain attributes that do not hold values by using code similar to the following:

```
<Item>
      <ProductNum>100</ProductNum>
      <Quantity>25</Quantity>
      <PhoneNum="Home">480 5552121</PhoneNum>
      <PhoneNum="Work"/>
      <ProductType>="Personal</ProductType>
</Item>
```

Exploring an XML Document

Your XML documents must be created to meet two primary requirements—they must be well-formed and they must be valid. An XML document that is *well-formed* is correctly formatted, allowing the XML parser to interpret its contents correctly. The document must follow the rules so the XML parser can read it and identify the elements, attributes, and values.

Note: *A well-formed document just means it is correctly formatted so the parser can understand it. This does not guarantee it is going to be useful in your business process.*

A document is well-formed if it meets the following criteria:

• Contains a single root element encompassing all other elements in the document.

• Contains a corresponding closing tag for each opening tag.

• Contains case-sensitive opening and closing tags.

• Contains complete child elements within the parent elements of the root element.

A *valid* document is a document that is not only well-formed but also contains all the data required for a document of that type or class.

Let's take a look at the sample XML code we used earlier to make sure it meets the document requirements:

```
<Order OrderNum="9876">
      <OrderDate>09-20-2001</OrderDate>
      <CustomerFirstName>Brian</CustomerFirstName>
       <Item>
              <ProductNum>100</ProductNum>
              <Quantity>25</Quantity>
```

```
        </Item>
            <Item>
              <ProductNum>101</ProductNum>
            <Quantity>50</Quantity>
        </Item>
</Order>
```

The following list indicates whether our sample code addresses the XML document requirements:

- The **Order** element is the single root element that contains all the other elements in the code sample.

- Each element; **Order**, **OrderDate**, **CustomerFirstName**, **Item**, **ProductNum**, and **Quantity** has a corresponding closing tag.

- Each of the corresponding closing tags exactly matches the spelling and case sensitivity of the opening tag.

- None of the elements has an overlapping element. This means each element is closed with its appropriate closing tag before closing its parent element.

Adding Processing Instructions and Comments to Your XML Document

Optionally, you can add comments to your XML code and also processing instructions. Processing instructions inform the parser of your XML version and the name of the style sheet you may want to use.

We'll expand on the previous sample code to include the tags required to provide processing instructions and comments (information about the reason for the code) in your XML document:

```
<?xml version="1.0"?>
<!-- Customer order information --!>
<Order OrderNum="9876">
        <OrderDate>09-20-2001</OrderDate>
        <CustomerFirstName>Brian</CustomerFirstName>
        <Item>
              <ProductNum>100</ProductNum>
              <Quantity>25</Quantity>
        </Item>
<Item>
              <ProductNum>101</ProductNum>
              <Quantity>50</Quantity>
        </Item>
</Order>
```

Understanding the Namespace of Your XML Document

You need to be familiar with the names of the elements used when creating XML documents. There may be a situation where you have multiple element types with the same name in an XML document. This can cause confusion for your XML parser and create inaccurate results.

To avoid problems when you have multiple element names, you can use a *namespace*. A namespace associates elements or attributes with a unique identifier called a *Universal Resource Identifier (URI)*. This identifier can be a Universal Resource Locator (URL) or some other universally unique identifier used to establish uniqueness.

Implement a namespace by supplying an **xmlns** attribute within the element you want to uniquely identify. Again, we will expand on the previous code to include a namespace:

```
<?xml version="1.0"?>
<!-- Customer order information --!>
<Order OrderNum="9876">
      <OrderDate>09-20-2001</OrderDate>
      <Customer xmlns="http://www.knowledgenet.com/customer">
            <CustomerFirstName>Brian</CustomerFirstName>
      </Customer>
      <Item>
      <ProductNum>100</ProductNum>
      <Quantity>25</Quantity>              </Item>
      <Item>
      <ProductNum>101</ProductNum>
      <Quantity>50</Quantity>
  </Item>
</Order>
```

After adding the **Customer** opening and closing tags, the parser is able to uniquely identify the **CustomerFirstName** with the URI tag provided. If there were another **CustomerFirstName** that you were referencing in a different element, you would supply the unique URI tag within that element.

After creating your XML document, you will use an application to access the data. Your application needs to be able to navigate the XML document to retrieve the requested data, which is done using XML Path Language (XPath).

Using Xpath to Navigate Your XML Document

XPath is a graph navigation language used to select a set of nodes from an XML document. An XML document can consist of an element node, attribute node, text node, and so on. In the sample code we have been using, **Customer** is an *element node* and **CustomerFirstName** is an *attribute node*.

An XPath operator selects a node set based on the node set selected by a previous XPath operator. In our example the Xpath **Customer** node operator will use the **Order** node operator to retrieve all the orders for a customer.

Note: XPath is a standard navigation language defined by the W3C. For more information regarding the XPath language go to **www.w3.org/TR/1999/PR-xpath-19991008.html**.

Specifying Your XPath Location

XPath *location paths* can be provided using absolute or relative location paths—paths relative to the current selected node. Both methods begin by specifying the root of the document with a forward slash (/) and allow both forward and backward navigation through the nodes. Your Xpath location path can be specified using either abbreviated or unabbreviated syntax. The following code is the same code we have been using in the previous examples, but contains an additional node (**ProductInfo**) for the code location path code samples:

Note: The current selected node is known as the context node.

```
<Order OrderNum="9876">
 <OrderDate>09-20-2001</OrderDate>
 <CustomerFirstName>Brian</CustomerFirstName>
 <Item>
        <ProductInfo ProductNum=100>tea</ProductInfo>
        <Quantity>25</Quantity>
 </Item>
 <Item>
        <ProductInfo ProductNum=101>coffee</ProductInfo>
        <Quantity>50</Quantity>
 </Item>
</Order>
```

Using an Absolute Location Path

To specify an *absolute location path* when selecting the **Order** element node described in our earlier examples, use the following unabbreviated syntax:

```
/child::Order
```

The same absolute location specified using abbreviated syntax would appear as:

```
/Order
```

To take the same document and drill down further into the syntax, you would use the following unabbreviated Xpath expression:

```
/child::Order/child::Customer
```

16

The same abbreviated syntax would appear as follows:

```
/order/Customer
```

You must use the **attribute** keyword to retrieve an attribute node using unabbreviated syntax, or the **@** character to retrieve an attribute node using abbreviated syntax. For instance, to continue with the example syntax we have been using, you would use the following syntax to retrieve an attribute node:

```
/child::Order/attribute::OrderNum
```

The following syntax would be used to retrieve an attribute node using an abbreviated statement:

```
/Order/@OrderNum
```

You must use the descendant keyword to retrieve a *descendant node*—a node that appears further down in the hierarchy. You use two forward slashes (//) in abbreviated syntax. For example, you would use the following unabbreviated syntax to retrieve all of the **ProductInfo** nodes in the Order document:

```
/child::Order/descendant::ProductInfo
```

The following abbreviated syntax would also retrieve all of the **ProductInfo** nodes in the **Order** document:

```
/Order//ProductInfo
```

You can use wildcards to indicate names that aren't relevant in your XPath expressions. The asterisk (*) is used in both abbreviated and unabbreviated location paths to indicate that any node can be used. For example, the following unabbreviated code sample selects all the elements within **Order**:

```
/child::Order/child::*
```

The following abbreviated syntax selects the same elements within **Order**:

```
/Order/*
```

Using a Relative Location Path

You can also specify how to retrieve a node or set of nodes relative to the current node using *relative location paths*. For instance, if the first item in the **Order** document was the context node, you would use the following unabbreviated syntax to retrieve the **Quantity** element:

```
Child::Quantity
```

The same results would be returned using the following abbreviated syntax:

```
Quantity
```

To retrieve the **ProductNum** attribute of the **ProductInfo** element, use the following unabbreviated syntax:

```
Child::ProductInfo/attribute::ProductNum
```

Or you can use the following abbreviated syntax:

```
ProductInfo/@ProductNum
```

To access an element up the node tree, use the parent keyword in unabbreviated syntax, or double periods (..) in abbreviated syntax. For instance, if your context node is the **OrderDate** element, you can use the **OrderNum** element in the following relative location path:

```
Parent::Order/attribute::OrderNum
```

The abbreviated syntax would be:

```
../@OrderNum
```

Note: *Alternatively, you can use the **self** keyword or a single period to reference the context node.*

Specifying Criteria in Your Location Paths

You can restrict the number of nodes returned by your XPath query by including search criteria in your location path. Your *criteria specification* is appended to the location path in square brackets.

For instance, if you want to return all the **ProductInfo** elements with a **ProductNum** greater than 100, you can use the following unabbreviated syntax:

```
/child::Order/child::Item/child::ProductInfo[attribute::ProductNum>100]
```

The abbreviated syntax would be:

```
/Order/Item/ProductInfo[@ProductNum>100]
```

Now that you know how to use XPath expressions to locate data in your XML document, you need to become familiar with one of the most commonly used XML-related technologies, Extensible Stylesheet Language (XSL).

Introducing XSL Style Sheets

Extensible Stylesheet Language is used to transform your XML document into a different format such as HTML, Wireless Markup Language (WML), or an alternative XML representation.

Initially, XML was designed to present XML data as HTML, but it soon became evident that XML could be translated to any output format. Thus, an enhanced version—XSL Transformation (XSLT)—was developed.

XSL documents are used to define style sheets that you can apply to your XML documents. Your style sheet contains the instructions for your XML parser on how to generate an output document based on the XML document. Actually, the XSL style sheet is nothing more than a well-formed XML document containing XSL commands merged with literal output text.

The XML parser needs to recognize the commands in an XSL document, and to achieve this you must declare a namespace in the root element. This is usually declared using a prefix of **xsl**. You can use one of the following two common namespaces in a style sheet:

- Original XSL namespace

- XSLT namespace

Note: *The Microsoft XML parser version 3.0 (MSXML3) supports both namespaces. However, you need to install MSXML3 in Replace mode using xmlinst.exe to enable support for the XSLT namespace in Internet Explorer 5.x.*

The root element of your XSL document is usually the stylesheet element that contains one or more template elements that are matched to specific XML data in the XML document being processed. Because the XSL style sheet is an actual XML document, it must follow all rules for a well-formed XML document. The following sample XSL style sheet could be applied to the order document:

```
<?xml version="1.0"?>
<xsl:stylesheet xmlns:xsl="http://www.w3.org/1999/XSL/Transform"
version="1.0">
     <xsl:template match="/">
          <HTML>
          <HEAD>
                         <TITLE>Northwind Database Web Page</TITLE>
          </HEAD>
               <BODY>
                 <P>Customer Order</P>
```

```
            </BODY>
        </HTML>
    </xsl:template>
</xsl:stylesheet>
```

Note: This style sheet is based on the XSLT namespace and contains a single template that is applied to the root of the XML document and all elements within it. The template is nothing more than a series of HTML tags that appear in the output.

To merge XML data into the template, you need to use XSL commands. The following list contains the most commonly-used XSL commands found in a template.

- **xsl:apply-imports**—Processes the current node using only templates that were imported into the style sheet with the **xsl:import** command.

- **xsl:apply-templates**—Tells the processor to search and apply the highest-priority template contained within the style sheet that matches each node identified by the select attribute.

- **xsl:attribute**—Adds an attribute to an element in the result tree. This element can be an **xsl:element**, the child of an **xsl:attribute-set** element, or a literal result element.

- **xsl:attribute-set**—Defines a collection of attributes that can be applied to any element in the style sheet.

- **xsl:call-template**—Invokes a template by name.

- **xsl:comment**—Inserts a comment into the result tree.

- **xsl:copy**—Copies the current node from the source document into the output document.

- **xsl:element**—Inserts an element into the result tree with the name assigned by the **NAME** attribute.

- **xsl:for-each**—Iterates through the nodes identified by the **SELECT** attribute and applies the templates to each one.

- **xsl:if**—Contains a template that is used if the XPath expression contained in the **test** attribute is **True**.

- **xsl:import**—Imports the XSLT style sheet found at the URI given by the **href** attribute.

- **xsl:include**—Copies the contents of the **xsl:stylesheet** or **xsl:transform** element found at the URI given in the **href** attribute.

- **xsl:message**—Sends a message to the XSLT processor.

- **xsl:number**—Inserts a formatted integer into the result tree.

16

- **xsl:output**—Helps determine the exact formatting of the XML document produced when the result tree is stored in a file.

- **xsl:sort**—Appears as a child of either **xsl:apply-templates** or **xsl:for-each**.

- **xsl:stylesheet**—The root element for XSLT style sheets.

- **xsl:template**—The top-level element that is the key to all of XSLT.

- **xsl:text**—Indicates that its contents should be output as text.

- **xsl:value-of**—Computes the string value of an XPath expression and inserts it into the result tree.

- **xsl:variable**—Binds a name to a value of any type.

- **xsl:with-param**—Passes a named parameter to a template that expects it.

Applying Your Style Sheets

After you create your style sheets, your next step is to apply them to your XML document. You can do this by instructing your XML parser, either by including the processing instructions in the XML document itself or by using programmatic logic.

Applying Your Style Sheet within Your XML Document

The following example contains the sample code we have been using but includes the command required to apply the style sheet from within your XML document:

```
<?xml version="1.0"?>
<?xml - stylesheet type="text/xsl" href="Order.xsl"?>
<Order OrderNum="9876">
        <OrderDate>09-20-2001</OrderDate>
        <CustomerFirstName>Brian</CustomerFirstName>
        <Item>
                <ProductInfo ProductNum=100>tea</ProductInfo>
                <Quantity>25</Quantity>
        </Item>
        <Item>
                <ProductInfo ProductNum=101>coffee</ProductInfo>
                <Quantity>50</Quantity>
        </Item>
</Order>
```

When the XML parser reads the XML document, the **XML-stylesheet** command instructs the parser to apply the Order.xsl style sheet. The **type** attribute informs the parser of the type of style sheet that is being applied. The **href** attribute specifies either the absolute or relative path to the file containing the style sheet.

Applying Your Style Sheet Programmatically

The process used to apply your style sheet programmatically varies from parser to parser. However, if you use the Microsoft XML parser, the document is loaded into a **Microsoft.XMLDom** object and the **transformNode** method is used to apply the style sheet in another **XMLDom** object.

The following sample code could be used to apply the style sheet named Order.xsl to a XML document named Order.XML:

```
Dim objXML
Dim objXSL
Dim strFormat

'Load the XML document.
Set objXML = CreateObject("Microsoft.XMLDom")
ObjXML.Async = False
ObjXML.Load "C:\MSSQL\XML\Order.xml"

'Load the XSL style sheet.
Set objXSL = CreateObject("Microsoft.XMLDom")
ObjXSL.Asynch = False
ObjXSL.Load = "C:\MSSQL\XML\Order.XSL"

'Apply the style sheet.
StrFormat = objXML.transformNode(objXSL)
```

16

Validating Your XML Data Using XML Data Schemas

The definition for a particular type of XML document is stored in an XML document called the XML *data schema*. The XML data schema is used to validate the XML data.

For instance, when transferring data between two businesses you have to make certain the information being exchanged is valid based on common definitions of the data. Schemas provide a more flexible approach to document validation than do Document Type Definitions (DTDs).

Introducing an XDR Schema

An XML document containing declarations of the elements and attributes that can be used in an XML document is called an *XDR schema*. The schema can also contain the following information:

• Data types of elements and attributes.

• Order in which the elements and attributes appear.

• Minimum and maximum lengths of their values.

- Minimum and maximum occurrences of the elements and attributes.

- Whether additional elements and attributes can be included in the document.

The schema doesn't contain any declarations about the data, so you have to declare elements and attributes using the **ElementType** and **AttributeType** keywords. Elements are declared at the top level of the schema, and attributes are declared globally, allowing the reuse of your attributes with multiple elements.

The following sample code shows a schema that declares elements and attributes for the XML order document:

```
<?xml version="1.0"?>
<Schema name="orderschema"
 xmlns="urn:schemas-knowledgenet-com:xml-data">
    <ElementType name="OrderDate"/>
    <ElementType name="CustomerFirstName"/>
    <ElementType name="ProductInfo"/>
       <AttributeType name="ProductNum"/>
       <Attribute type ="ProductNum"/>
    </ElementType>

    <ElementType name="Quantity"/>
    <ElementType name="Item"/>
    <Element type ="ProductInfo"/>
    <Element type ="Quantity"/>
    </ElementType>

    <ElementType name="Order"/>
       <AttributeType name="OrderNum"/>
    <Attribute type ="OrderNum"/>
    <Element type ="OrderDate"/>
    <Element type ="CustomerFirstName"/>
    <Element type ="Item"/>
    </ElementType>
</Schema>
```

Specifying the Content of Your Schema

The capability to include elements and attributes in your document that are not defined in the schema makes the content model of the XDR schema open. The content model of each element is set in the schema by specifying the **model** attribute with a value of **open** or **closed**. The model attribute can be used to enhance the schema to restrict the possible elements and attributes by specifying a closed content model for each element, as shown in the following sample code:

```
<?xml version="1.0"?>
<Schema name="orderschema"
```

```
   xmlns="urn:schemas-knowledgenet-com:xml-data">
   <ElementType name="OrderDate" model="closed"/>
   <ElementType name="CustomerFirstName" model="closed"/>
   <ElementType name="ProductInfo" model="closed"/>
     <AttributeType name="ProductNum"/>
     <Attribute type ="ProductNum"/>
   </ElementType>

   <ElementType name="Quantity" model="closed"/>
   <ElementType name="Item" model="closed"/>
   Element type ="ProductInfo"/>
   <Element type ="Quantity"/>
   </ElementType>

   <ElementType name="Order" model="closed"/>
     <AttributeType name="OrderNum"/>
     <Attribute type ="OrderNum"/>
   <Element type ="OrderDate"/>
   <Element type ="CustomerFirstName"/>
   <Element type ="Item"/></ElementType>
</Schema>
```

This modification to the schema guarantees that any document based on the schema can only contain the elements and attributes defined in the schema.

Specifying Valid Data Types

The schema can also be used to define the data types of your elements and attributes in a valid XML document. This capability ensures that the data exchanged between XML documents is processed correctly, and minimizes the chance of errors caused by incorrect data types.

Use the **datatypes** namespace to specify the datatypes in your schema. The following list contains some of the XML and common datatypes supported for XML document elements:

- **boolean**
- **char**
- **datetime**
- **entity**
- **entities**
- **float**

- **id**

- **nmtoken**

- **notation**

- **string**

Validating Your XML Document

After creating your schema, you can make certain that an XML document is validated using the schema by referencing the schema in the document namespace using the *x-schema* keyword. The following code sample references a schema named Orderschema.xml:

```
<?xml version="1.0"?>
<Order OrderNum="9876 xmlns="x-schema:Orderschema.xml">
  <OrderDate>09-20-2001</OrderDate>
  <CustomerFirstName>Brian</CustomerFirstName>
  <Item>
        <ProductInfo ProductNum=100>tea</ProductInfo>
        <Quantity>25</Quantity>
  </Item>
  <Item>
        <ProductInfo ProductNum=101>coffee</ProductInfo>
        <Quantity>50</Quantity>
  </Item>
</Order>
```

You now know the basic concepts of XML documents, templates, style sheets, and schemas, all of which are used together to access, validate, and present data to you from your SQL Server database. Now it is time to look at how XML is integrated with SQL Server 2000.

Understanding XML and Relational Databases

Relational databases and XML are both concerned with representing your business entities, although they perform this representation differently. XML represents your business entities using XML documents, and relational databases represent your entities using tables.

An instance of an entity in an XML document is represented by an element, and an instance of an entity in a relational database is represented by a row in a table. In an XML document, an entity's characteristics are represented by an attribute. In a relational database, an entity's characteristics are represented by columns of a table. For further clarification, review Table 16.1.

Table 16.1   Customers table.

CustomerNum	FirstName	Company
10000	Brian	KnowledgeNet
10010	Don	Intel

This information would be represented in an XML document named Customers, containing two **Customer** elements. The columns of the table could be represented as attributes in the XML document as shown here:

```
<Customers>
  <Customer CustomerNum='10000' FirstName='Brian' Company='KnowledgeNet'/>
  <Customer CustomerNum='10010' FirstName='Don' Company='Intel'/>
</Customers>
```

Note: Alternatively, you can use element mappings, where the columns are returned as subelements of the element representing the table they belong to. Which method you choose is just a matter of style.

Using XML, SQL Server 2000 data is accessible over HTTP through a Universal Resource Locator (URL). You define a virtual root on a Microsoft Internet Information Services (IIS) server, providing HTTP access to the data and XML functionality of SQL Server 2000.

In SQL Server 2000, you can use ADO, OLE DB, or HTTP to work with the functionality of XML by:

- Defining XML views of SQL Server 2000 databases by annotating XML-Data Reduced (XDR) schemas that map the tables, views, and columns of the databases to the associated elements and attributes of the schema. Your XML views can then be referenced using XPath queries that retrieve the results from the database and return them as XML documents.

- Using the new **OPENXML** rowset function to expose the data from an XML document as a relational rowset. **OPENXML** can be used anywhere a rowset function can be used in a Transact-SQL statement, including in place of a table or view reference in a **FROM** clause. This provides you the capability to insert, update, or delete data in the tables of the database.

- Returning a result set from a **SELECT** statement as an XML document. The **SELECT** statement supports the **FOR XML** clause that specifies that the statement results are returned in the form of an XML document instead of a relational result set. More complex queries, or queries that you want to secure, can be stored as templates in an IIS virtual root directory and executed by referencing the template name.

Configuring an IIS Virtual Directory

After deciding you want to configure an IIS virtual directory for access to your SQL Server 2000 databases using HTTP, you can use the IIS Virtual Directory Management for SQL Server utility that is accessed from the Configure SQL XML Support in IIS option shown in Figure 16.1 to define and register a new virtual directory. This utility is located in the Microsoft SQL Server program group of the Programs option on the Start menu.

Note: The new virtual directory is also known as the virtual root on the computer running IIS.

After opening the IIS Virtual Directory Management for SQL Server, shown in Figure 16.2, you create the virtual directory to instruct IIS to create an association between the virtual directory and an instance of SQL Server 2000 using the following steps:

1. Right-click on Default Web Site or Administration Web Site and click New|Virtual Directory, as shown in Figure 16.3.

2. The New Virtual Directory Properties dialog box is displayed with the General tab selected.

3. Enter the name of the virtual directory in the Virtual Directory Name box. This is the name that will be used to access the SQL Server database.

4. Enter the full path to the physical directory associated with the virtual directory to complete the General tab shown in Figure 16.4. You can click the Browse button to locate the directory on the local machine.

5. Click the Security tab to open the Security Options dialog box shown in Figure 16.5 and specify the authentication method by choosing one of the following:

   • *Always Log On As*—Enter the user name and password of the SQL or Windows account that will be used to map the anonymous access scheme of the IIS authentication security. Be sure to specify the account type by clicking on either SQL Server or Windows.

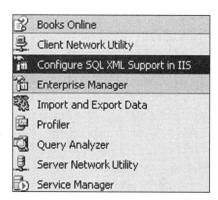

Figure 16.1
Opening the IIS Virtual Directory Management for SQL Server utility.

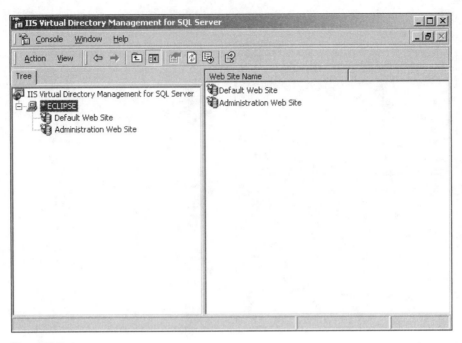

Figure 16.2
IIS Virtual Directory Management For SQL Server dialog box.

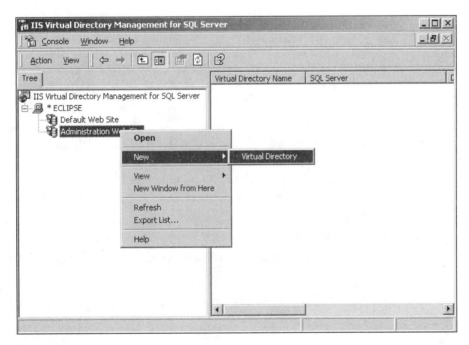

Figure 16.3
Creating a new virtual directory for SQL Server.

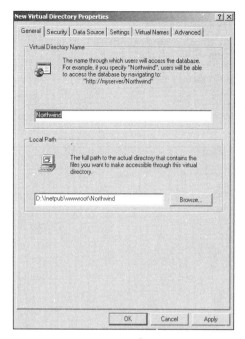

Figure 16.4
Completing the General tab of the New Virtual Directory Properties dialog box.

- *Use Windows Authentication*—Authenticates using Windows NT 4 or Windows 2000 user accounts to allow access to the virtual directory.

- *Use Basic Authentication (Clear Text) To SQL Server Account*—Prompts the user for a SQL Server login and password when she is connecting to the virtual directory.

6. Click the Data Source tab to specify the name of the server and database that you want to publish through this virtual directory. Enter the name of the server in the SQL Server box, or browse for the available servers by clicking the ellipses (...) button. To complete the Data Source tab shown in Figure 16.6, use the drop-down menu within the Database box to locate the database containing the data you are going to publish.

7. Click the Settings tab, shown in Figure 16.7, to specify the types of SQL Server 2000 access you want to provide through the virtual directory by choosing one or more of the following options:

- *Allow URL Queries*—Allow users to execute SQL queries through a URL.

- *Allow Template Queries*—Allow users to execute SQL queries defined in templates.

- *Allow XPath*—Allow users to execute XPath queries over SQL Views by mapping schemas.

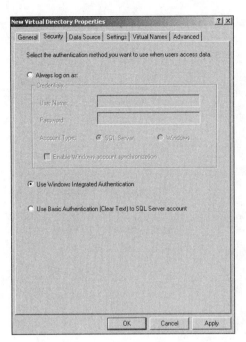

Figure 16.5
Completing the Security tab of the New Virtual Directory Properties dialog box.

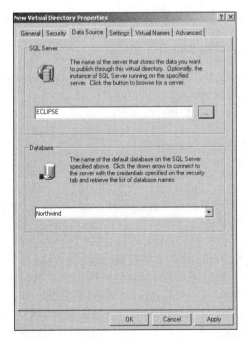

Figure 16.6
Completing the Data Source tab of the New Virtual Directory Properties dialog box.

16

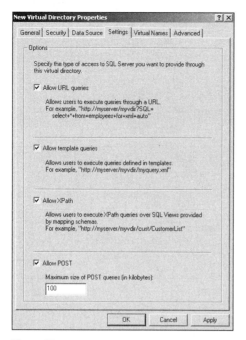

Figure 16.7
Completing the Settings tab of the New Virtual Directory Properties dialog box.

- *Allow POST*—Allow users to send data to the database. By default, they can only retrieve data. You also specify the maximum amount of data, in kilobytes, that can be sent to the server in a single query. The default is 100KB.

8. Click the Virtual Names tab shown in Figure 16.8 to create a virtual name that will be included in the URL to perform any of the following operations:

- Execute a template file

- Execute an XPath query against a mapping schema file

- Access a database object

Tip: *The location of the files and the information about what is being executed are not visible to the user if you provide them the capability to use virtual names in the URL.*

Click New to open the Virtual Name Configuration dialog box shown in Figure 16.9. After you enter the virtual name in the Virtual Name box, use the Type drop-down menu to specify the type of virtual name. Lastly, enter or browse for the directory in the Path box.

9. Click the Advanced tab shown in Figure 16.10, to specify the location of the ISAPI extension dynamic-link library (DLL). This file is Sqlisapi.dll for SQL Server 2000 and is required to access an instance of SQL Server 2000 through the virtual directory. By

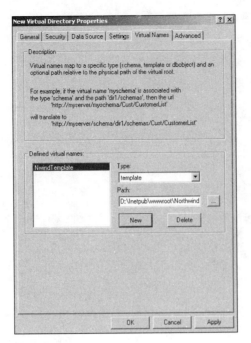

Figure 16.8
Completing the Virtual Name tab of the New Virtual Directory Properties dialog box.

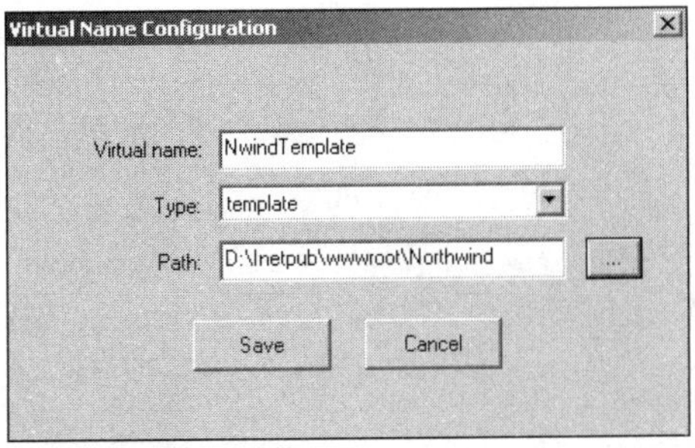

Figure 16.9
Completing the Virtual Name Configuration dialog box

default, this file is located in the %systemroot%\Program Files\CommonFiles\ System\ Ole DB directory.

Note: If you move Sqlisapi.dll to a different location, the Sqlisapi.rll must be moved to the same location.

16

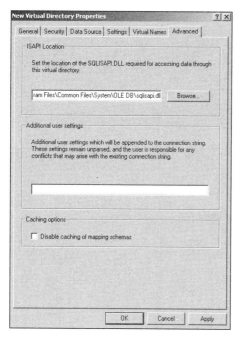

Figure 16.10
Completing the Advanced tab of the New Virtual Directory Properties dialog box.

After completing the Advanced tab, click OK to create the new virtual directory and close the New Virtual Directory Properties dialog box. The new virtual directory is located in the detail pane of the IIS Virtual Directory Management for SQL Server. To customize your virtual directory, right-click on it and choose Properties.

Note: For a step-by-step procedure on how to create and test a virtual directory for the Northwind database, see the "Creating the Nwind Virtual Directory" article in SQL Server 2000 Books Online.

Accessing SQL Server Data Using HTTP

After you've created your virtual root using the IIS Virtual Directory Management for SQL Server, you can access SQL Server 2000 using HTTP. When accessing data using HTTP, the name of the IIS server and the virtual directory are specified as part of the URL.

Using the Virtual Directory Information

The following information in the virtual directory is used to establish a connection to the database and execute the query:

- login
- password
- permissions

When accessing the virtual directory using the URL, you can specify that you want to:

- Directly access the database objects, such as tables and views

- Execute template files

- Execute XPath queries

You must specify the virtual name of the template file, mapping schema file, or database object as part of the URL using *template*, *schema*, and *dbobject* virtual names that you've already created. The virtual name specified in the URL is also used to determine the file type (template file or a mapping schema file) specified in the URL. For example, to access a SQL Server database using a template, enter the following URL:

```
http://IISserver/nwind/TemplateVirtualName/Template.xml.
```

Note: The TemplateVirtualName is the virtual name of the template file called Template.xml.

16

Choosing Your Access Method

You use variations of HTTP commands to access the SQL Server database. The command you use is determined by the method you have chosen to access the SQL Server database.

HTTP access to SQL Server allows you to:

- *Specify SQL Server queries in the URL*—For instance:

```
http://IISserver/Nwind?sql=SELECT+*+FROM+Employees+FOR+XML+AUTO&root=roots
```

Note: The **FOR XML** clause indicates to SQL Server to return the result set as an XML document instead of a standard rowset.

- *Specify templates in the URL*—Specifying templates is useful to present the data in a valid XML document using a statement similar to:

```
http://IISserver/nwind?template=<ROOT+xmlns:sql="urn:schemas-knowledgenet-
com:xml-sql"><sql:query>SELECT+*+FROM+Employees+FOR+XML+AUTO</sql:query></
ROOT>
```

- *Specify template files in the URL*—A template file is a valid XML document that contains your SQL statements and XPath queries. Supplying long SQL queries in the URL can be time consuming, and some browsers may have limitations on the amount of text that can be entered in the URL. A template file enhances security by removing the details of the query from the users. A template file is specified in the URL as follows:

```
http://IISserver/nwind/TemplateVirtualName/Northwindtemplate.xml
```

*Note: The **TemplateVirtualName** is a virtual name of the template type created using the IIS Virtual Directory Management for SQL Server utility.*

- *Writing XPath queries against your XDR schema*—Writing XPath queries against the schema is similar to creating views and then writing SQL queries against the view. For example:

```
http://IISserver/nwind/SchemaVirtualName/Northwindschema.xml/
Employees[@EmployeeID="1"]
```

*Note: The **SchemaVirtualName** is the virtual name of the schema type created using the IIS Virtual Directory Management for SQL Server utility. The **Employees[@EmployeeID="1"]** is the XPath query being executed against the **Northwindschema.xml** specified in the URL.*

- *Specify database objects directly in the URL*—Database objects, such as tables and views, are specified as part of the URL, and an XPath query is specified against the object. For instance:

```
http://IISserver/nwind/dbobjectVirtualName/XpathQuery
```

*Note: The **dbobjectVirtualName** is the virtual name of the **dbobject** that is also created using the IIS Virtual Directory Management for SQL Server utility.*

Accessing data using normal Transact-SQL statements (**SELECT**, **INSERT**, **UPDATE**, and **DELETE**) is quite easy using Query Analyzer. However, when you are accessing database information using XPath queries, you need to be aware of some SQL Server XPath query guidelines.

Guidelines for Using XPath Queries

SQL Server 2000 provides the functionality to use XPath queries by implementing a subset of the World Wide Web Consortium (W3C) Xpath specification located at **www.w3.org/TR/1999/PR-xpath-19991008.html**. However, the SQL Server 2000 implementation of XPath queries differs from the W3C specification in the following areas:

- *Cross-product queries*—SQL Server 2000 does not support cross-product XPath queries, such as **Customer [Order/@OrderDate=Order/@ShippedDate]**.

*Note: This query selects all customers with any order for which the order date equals the shipped date of any order. However, it does support a query which selects customers with any order for which the order date equals its shipped date using a query such as **Customer[Order[@OrderDate=@ShippedDate]]**.*

- *Data types*—SQL Server 2000 has limitations when implementing XPath **boolean**, **number**, and **string** data types.

- *Document order*—Document order is not always determined, meaning numeric predicates that use document order (such as **following**) are not implemented.

- *Reporting errors*—The W3C XPath specification does not define error conditions. XPath queries that fail to select any nodes return an empty node set. However, SQL Server 2000 can return many types of error messages, such as:

  - XPath: an unexpected internal error occurred. Not expected during typical processing.

  - XPath: unable to instantiate MSXML class factories.

  - XPath: the parsed XPath contains an unexpected value (%1). The version of msxml2.dll installed may be incompatible with sqlxmlx.dll. Not expected during typical processing.

Note: *Errors containing the message "not expected during typical processing" are usually caused by an installation problem. Check that your sqlxmlx.dll and msxml2.dll are the versions installed with SQL Server 2000.*

- *Root queries*—SQL Server 2000 does not support the root query (/). Every XPath query has to begin at the top level <element-type> in the schema.

As you have probably figured out, it is going to be much easier to use XML templates to specify your XPath queries, rather than supplying the actual queries in the URL.

Using XML Templates

XML templates are stored in a template file by creating a virtual name using the object type of **template**. You access the templates by specifying the template file name in the URL. However, to use template files you must configure the virtual directory that contains your virtual names to allow template queries. Use the following steps to do this:

1. Click Start|Programs|Microsoft SQL Server|Configure SQL XML Support In IIS

2. Locate the virtual directory in the detail pane of the Configure SQL XML Support In IIS dialog box by clicking the Default Web Site or Administrative Web Site option in the console tree.

3. Right-click the virtual directory and click Properties.

4. Click the Settings tab, and then click the Allow Template Queries option.

5. Click OK to enable template queries, and close the Configure SQL XML Support In IIS dialog box.

After you have configured the virtual directory to allow template queries, you can use a query similar to the following to retrieve data from the database:

```
http://IISserver/NWind/NorthwindTemplate/NorthwindTemp.xml
```

Retrieving and Writing XML Data

You can execute standard SQL queries to retrieve and write your XML data. This provides the ability to use syntax and processes that you are familiar with to maintain your XML data.

Retrieving Data Using the FOR XML Clause

You can execute SQL queries to return the results as XML rather than as the standard rowset. These types of queries can be executed directly or from within stored procedures. When retrieving database results directly, use the **FOR XML** clause of the **SELECT** statement and also specify an XML mode of:

- **RAW**—The easiest mode to use with the **FOR XML** clause, because it simply returns an XML element for each row in the resulting rowset. The XML element contains an attribute for each column retrieved. The following sample code is used to return XML data using the **FOR XML** clause in **RAW** mode:

```
USE Northwind
SELECT OrderID, ProductID, UnitPrice, Quantity
FROM [Order Details]
WHERE OrderID = 10248
FOR XML RAW
```

This query returns the following XML fragment:

```
<row OrderID="10248" ProductID="11" UnitPrice="14" Quantity="12"/>
<row OrderID="10248" ProductID="42" UnitPrice="9.8" Quantity="10"/>
<row OrderID="10248" ProductID="72" UnitPrice="34.8" Quantity="5"/>
```

- **AUTO**—Gives you the most control over the XML data returned. By default, each row in the result set is represented as an XML element named after the table it was selected from. The following sample code is used to return XML data using the **FOR XML** clause in **AUTO** mode:

```
USE Northwind
SELECT OrderID, CustomerID
FROM Orders
WHERE OrderID = 10248
FOR XML AUTO
```

This query returns the following XML fragment:

```
<Orders OrderID="10248" CustomerID="Vinet"/>
```

- **EXPLICIT**—Requires more complex query syntax but provides you the greatest control over the resulting XML data. This mode requires the use of a universal table consisting of a column for each piece of data you want returned and two additional columns to define the metadata for the XML fragment.

Note: We chose not to display sample code for this mode because it contains complex content not discussed in this chapter.

The modes used for these queries are valid for the specific query and are not maintained in subsequent queries. Therefore, you must include the mode in every statement containing the **FOR XML** clause.

Guidelines for Using the FOR XML Clause

Although the **FOR XML** clause is available for you to access your XML data using the **SELECT** statement, there are some limitations on the **SELECT** statement with the **FOR XML** clause. The following are some of the common limitations that apply to the **FOR XML** clause:

- **FOR XML** is not valid in subselections, including **INSERT**, **UPDATE**, **DELETE**, nested **SELECT** statements, or other statements (**SELECT INTO, ASSIGNMENT**).

- **FOR XML** is not valid for any selection that is used with a **COMPUTE BY** or **FOR BROWSE** clause.

- **FOR XML** is not valid in a **SELECT** statement with a view definition or a user-defined function that returns a rowset.

- **GROUP BY** and aggregate functions are currently not supported with **FOR XML AUTO**.

- **FOR XML** cannot be used in a stored procedure when called from within an **INSERT** statement.

- **FOR XML** cannot be used in a selection that requires additional processing in a stored procedure.

- **FOR XML** cannot be used with cursors.

Writing XML Data Using OPENXML

You can also use the Transact-SQL **OPENXML** function to insert data represented as an XML document. The **OPENXML** function is a rowset provider that acts similarly to a table or view by providing a rowset over in-memory XML documents.

The following sample code shows the use of **OPENXML** in **INSERT** and **SELECT** statements. This XML document consists of Customers and Orders and elements. The procedure begins by parsing the XML document, so **OPENXML** can refer to this parsed document and provide a rowset view of all or parts of the XML document. An **INSERT** statement using **OPENXML** can insert data from such a rowset into a database table. The sample code also shows a **SELECT** statement with **OPENXML** that retrieves **CustomerID** and **OrderDate** from the XML document. Here is the code:

```
DECLARE @hDoc int
EXEC sp_xml_preparedocument @hDoc OUTPUT,
     N'<ROOT>
          <Customers CustomerID="XYZAA" ContactName="Joe"
               CompanyName="Company1">
            <Orders CustomerID="XYZAA"
               OrderDate="2000-08-25T00:00:00"/>
            <Orders CustomerID="XYZAA"
               OrderDate="2000-10-03T00:00:00"/>
          </Customers>
          <Customers CustomerID="XYZBB" ContactName="Steve"
               CompanyName="Company2">No Orders yet!
          </Customers>
        </ROOT>'
-- Use OPENXML to provide rowset consisting of customer data.
INSERT Customers
SELECT ·
FROM OPENXML(@hDoc, N'/ROOT/Customers')
     WITH Customers
-- Use OPENXML to provide rowset consisting of order data.
INSERT Orders
SELECT ·
FROM OPENXML(@hDoc, N'//Orders')
     WITH Orders
-- Using OPENXML in a SELECT statement.
SELECT · FROM OPENXML(@hDoc, N'/ROOT/Customers/Orders') with (CustomerID
nchar(5) '../@CustomerID', OrderDate datetime)
-- Remove the internal representation of the XML document.
EXEC sp_xml_removedocument @hDoc
```

It is important to be able to import, export, and publish metadata in XML. *Metadata* is information about your data, including:

- Data type

- Length of a column

- Structure of the data

- Information about the design of objects, such as cubes and dimensions

Using XML in Meta Data Services

SQL Server 2000 supports XML encoding of information models—an object-oriented schema that defines metadata constructs that are used to specify the behavior and structure of an application, component, or process.

You can exchange your metadata between two *repositories*—a database that contains information models that manage the database, between an application and a repository database, or between two applications that are able to interpret the same XML format.

Note: *The term repository can also refer to an installation of the Meta Data Services.*

Your XML documents are encoded, exchanged, and decoded by the Meta Data Services of SQL Server 2000. The Meta Data Coalition (MDC) Open Information Model (OIM) XML Encoding format defines the XML format supported by Meta Data Services. This format defines the rules for generating XML based on an information model. Applying these rules enables Meta Data Services to create XML that corresponds to your information model. The same rules are also used to convert an XML document back into a repository instance.

You can use the Meta Data Services to import and export XML documents in SQL Server 2000.

Importing XML Documents in SQL Server 2000

Adding metadata to a target repository is achieved by importing an XML document in SQL Server 2000. You can import object data using the **Import** interface and the **Import** object. To import an XML document from memory, handle the document as a string. However, most often you will import an XML document from a file.

An import must meet the following conditions:

- XML documents being imported must be formatted to meet the MDC OIM XML Encoding.

- The type of information of the target repository or tool and the source objects or model must be identical. For example, if you are exporting objects from a Unified Modeling Language (UML) information model, an identical UML information model must reside in the target repository before the import operation. If they are not identical, you will lose data during the import operation.

Import operations return a collection of top-level objects that can be manipulated by your application. To view and manipulate your imported data in the repository database, the imported data must be related to the repository root object. After the information model of the target database is configured to correspond to the information model of the source database, a relationship to the root object can be established automatically.

Note: *To support navigation and define relationships with objects in other information models when your imported data is not related to the root object, you must programmatically add an object from the imported data to a collection of the root object.*

Exporting XML Documents in SQL Server 2000

Exporting XML using SQL Server 2000 Meta Data Services is the process of creating an XML document and populating it with metadata tagged as XML elements. You can export XML data as a string into memory or as an XML file. After exporting the XML data, you must import it into a repository database or make it available to another tool.

Automation and Component Object Model (COM) programmers can use the **Export** and **Lexport** interface provided by Meta Data Services to implement the dual interface required for exporting data.

You can export data for specific objects, or recursively through a set of related objects, to automatically create the XML document. When exporting data, you must, at a minimum, instantiate the **export** object and define the repository objects for which you want to export data. The methods you use directly affect whether the XML document is stored in memory or as an XML file.

You can also generate an XML Document Type Definition (DTD) that describes the exact XML produced. This XML DTD can be used to determine which XML structures you must support. The information model, which can be a version of the OIM or some other model that you create, determines the XML DTD generated.

The XML functionality in SQL Server 2000 provides you with a diverse, dynamic, and easy-to-use implementation of Web-based data sharing. SQL Server 2000 includes some sample files to give you the opportunity to install, configure, and manage XML in SQL Server 2000.

Installing and Using XML Sample Files

If you didn't install the XML sample files during the initial installation of SQL Server 2000, you will have to install them using the following steps:

1. Begin the SQL Server installation by inserting the Microsoft SQL Server 2000 compact disc and double-clicking autorun.exe in the root directory of the compact disc.

2. Select SQL Server 2000 Components|Install Database Server, and the setup program will prepare the SQL Server Installation Wizard. Click Next on the Welcome Screen.

3. Ensure that Local Computer is selected and the local computer name appears in the Edit box. Click Next on the Computer Name dialog box.

4. In the Installation Selection dialog box, click Upgrade, Remove, Or Add Components To An Existing Instance Of SQL Server, and then click Next.

5. Click Next in the Instance Name dialog box.

6. Select Add Components To Your Existing Installation on the Existing Installation dialog box and click Next.

7. Scroll down in the Components box of the Select Components dialog box shown in Figure 16.11 and select the Code Samples checkbox. Click Next.

8. Click Next on the Start Copying Files dialog box to begin the installation.

9. Click Finish to complete the installation of the sample code files.

Note: The default installation location is: C:\Program Files\Microsoft SQL Server\80\ Tools\Devtools\Samples\Xml\XMLDemo

Running the XML Demo

After installing the sample files on your machine, you are ready to demonstrate the SQL Server 2000 support for XML functionality. The first thing you have to do is install the *virtual roots*—also called the virtual directory—using the following steps:

1. Click Start|Programs|Microsoft SQL Server|Configure SQL XML Support In IIS.

2. Create a new virtual directory using the steps discussed earlier in this chapter under "Configuring an IIS Virtual Directory."

3. On the Virtual Names tab, configure the following three virtual names:

   • Dbobject with the type of **dbobject**

   • T with the type of **template**

   • S with the type of **schema**

4. On the Settings tab, check all query type checkboxes.

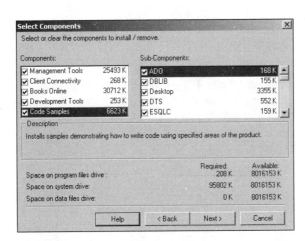

Figure 16.11
Choosing to install the code samples.

5. Save your virtual directory configuration.

6. Add a virtual root to the Web site name Demodir and configure it to point to the same physical location as your demo files. Save the configuration.

7. Do not edit the Demos virtual directory entry. You should now have access to the files of the Northwind database.

Your next task is to install the required stored procedure and table, using the following steps:

1. Click Start|Program Files|Microsoft SQL Server|Query Analyzer.

2. Using the drop-down menu, connect to the Northwind database.

3. Open the C:\Program Files\Microsoft SQL Server\80\Tools\DevTools\ Samples\xml\XMLDemo\Mycustomers.sql script.

4. Execute the query.

5. Open the C:\Program Files\Microsoft SQL Server\80\Tools\DevTools\Samples\ xml\XMLDemo\Mysproc.sql script.

6. Execute the query.

7. Leave Query Analyzer open so you can run the OpenXML demos.

8. To test the different sample queries, double-click C:\Program Files\ Microsoft SQL Server\80\Tools\DevTools\Samples\xml\XMLDemo\Url.htm file to open the Web page shown in Figure 16.12.

Using the XML Startup Exercises

You can also use the XMLStartup article discussed in the SQL Server 2000 Books Online to make SQL Server an XML-enabled database server. Follow the instructions in the C:\Program Files\Microsoft SQL Server\80\Tools\Devtools\Samples\Xml\Xmlstartup\Xmlstartup.doc to complete the following tasks:

• Configure IIS and SQL Server virtual directories

• Execute stored procedures and queries from a URL

• Execute template files

Making SQL Server 2000 an XML-enabled database server requires some planning and some configurations, but once configured, the ability to access your SQL Server data using XML technology is quite easy. If the features of XML are not required for your environment, you may want to generate HTML files using the Web Assistant Wizard.

Introducing the Web Assistant Wizard

The Web Assistant Wizard can be used to generate standard HTML files from data stored in SQL Server. The wizard generates HTML files using the following SQL Server features:

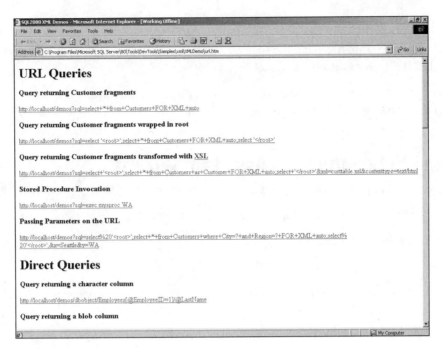

Figure 16.12
Testing the different sample queries.

- Transact-SQL queries

- Stored procedures

- Extended stored procedures

The Web Assistant Wizard can generate an HTML file for a single use or a regularly scheduled SQL Server task. You can also configure your HTML file to be updated using a trigger.

Note: *The Web Assistant Wizard is accessed from within Enterprise Manager.*

The Web Assistant Wizard can be used to:

- Schedule a task to automatically update your SQL Server Web page, providing you the capability to update your Web page when the data changes.

- Publish and distribute reports containing statistical information, resource allocation information, and other SQL Server data.

- Publish SQL Server informational reports regarding current locks and who holds them, along with who is currently accessing SQL Server.

- Use extended stored procedures to publish information outside of SQL Server.

- Use a table of favorite Web sites to publish server jump lists.

- Generate an HTML file using the **sp_makewebtask** system stored procedure to generate an HTML file from within a Transact-SQL program.

*Note: You can use **sp_dropwebtask** to delete a previously defined Web task. Also, **sp_runwebtask** can be used to execute a previously defined Web job to generate the HTML document.*

Preparing to Use the Web Assistant Wizard

Before you run the Web Assistant Wizard, there are a few tasks you must perform:

- Setting the required permissions

- Choosing the database to publish

- Creating the required queries

Before you run the Web Assistant Wizard, be certain the following permissions have been set:

- **CREATE PROCEDURE** permissions in the database being published.

- **SELECT** permissions on columns being published.

- Required permissions to create files in the user account in an instance of SQL Server 2000.

Choosing a Database to Publish

The Web Assistant Wizard works with databases created by SQL Server. During the execution of the wizard, you are prompted to choose the database to publish on the Web. If the server containing the database you want to publish is not available in Enterprise Manager, run the Register Server Wizard to register the server. After registering the server, click on it and then execute the Web Assistant Wizard.

Creating the Required Queries

The queries you enter will access the data in the database you specified when you ran the Web Assistant Wizard. You can run queries by:

- Specifying tables and columns

- Using a stored procedure to create result sets

- Using Transact-SQL statements to select the data

Note: The Web Assistant Wizard creates a job that will generate the HTML file. This job is assigned a default name, but you can give it a name to identify the reason and focus of the query.

Running the Web Assistant Wizard

After setting the appropriate permissions, deciding which database is going to be published, and determining the queries to use to create the job to generate the HTML file, you are ready to execute the Web Assistant Wizard. Follow these steps to run the Web Assistant Wizard in SQL Server 2000:

1. Click Start|Programs|Microsoft SQL Server|Enterprise Manager to open the Enterprise Manager interface.

2. Click the registered SQL Server—shown in Figure 16.13—containing the database that contains the data you want to publish.

3. Click Wizards on the Tools menu to open the Select Wizard dialog box.

4. In the Select Wizard dialog box, expand the Management option and double-click the Web Assistant Wizard shown in Figure 16.14 to open the Welcome screen of the Web Assistant Wizard.

5. After reviewing the explanation of the tasks the Web Assistant Wizard performs, click Next to open the Select Database screen.

16

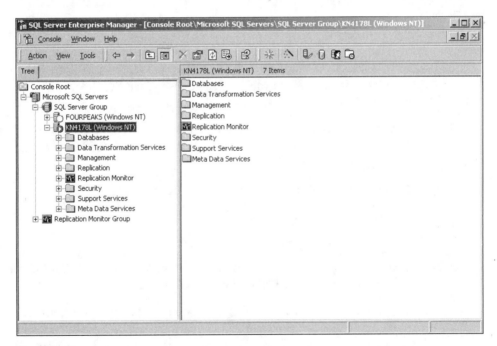

Figure 16.13
Selecting the SQL Server you want to publish.

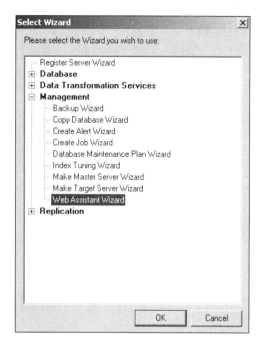

Figure 16.14
Starting the Web Assistant Wizard.

6. Use the Database Name drop-down menu—shown in Figure 16.15—to select the database that contains the data you want to publish. Click Next to open the Start A New Web Assistant Job screen.

7. In the Start A New Web Assistant Job screen shown in Figure 16.16, type a name for the Web Assistant job and specify which data you want to publish by choosing one of the following options and clicking Next:

   • Data From The Tables And Columns That I Select

   • Result Set(s) Of A Stored Procedure I Select

   • Data From The Transact-SQL Statement I Specify

8. The choice you make in Step 7 determines the next Web Assistant Wizard screen displayed in this step. Complete one of the following screens and click Next.

   • If you chose Data From The Tables And Columns That I Select, the Select A Table And Columns dialog box shown in Figure 16.17 is displayed. Use the Available Tables drop-down menu to choose the table containing the data you want to publish. After choosing the table, select the column(s) from the Table Columns box that you want to publish and then click Add. If you want all the columns of the table, click the Add All button.

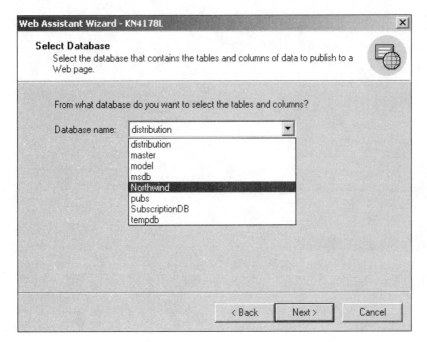

Figure 16.15
Selecting the database to publish.

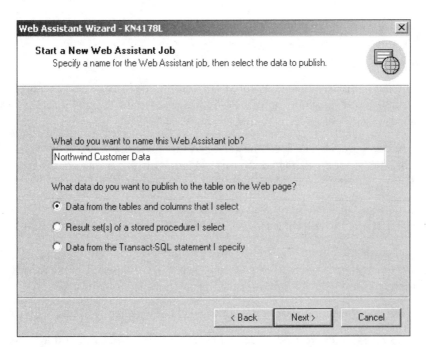

Figure 16.16
Specifying the name of the Web Assistant job.

16

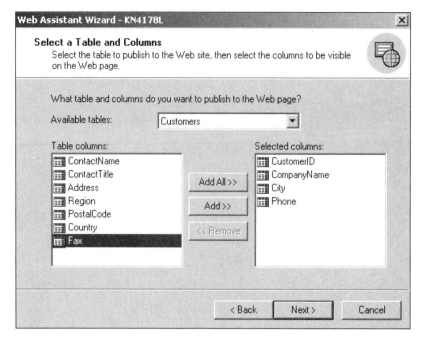

Figure 16.17
Specifying the tables and columns.

Note: After you click Add or Add All, the Selected Columns box will contain the columns that will be published. To prevent a column from being published, click the column in the Selected Columns box and click the Remove button.

- If you chose Result Set(s) Of A Stored Procedure I Select, the Select Stored Procedure dialog box shown in Figure 16.18 is displayed. In the Stored Procedures box, click the stored procedure you want to run that will create the result set to publish.

- If you chose Data From The Transact-SQL Statement I Specify, the Write A Transact-SQL Query dialog box shown in Figure 16.19 is displayed. Enter the Transact-SQL statement in the Transact-SQL Query box.

9. The choice you make in Step 7 also determines the screen that is displayed in Step 9. Complete one of the following screens and click Next:

- If you chose Data From The Tables And Columns That I Select in Step 7, the Select Rows dialog box shown in Figure 16.20 is displayed. Choose one of the following options to specify the rows of the table that are going to be published:

  - *All Of The Rows*—All rows of the table you chose will be displayed.

  - *Only Those Rows That Meet The Following Criteria*—Use the Column Name drop-down menu to specify the column. Use the Operator drop-down menu to specify the type of Operator you want to use with the column. Specify the Value

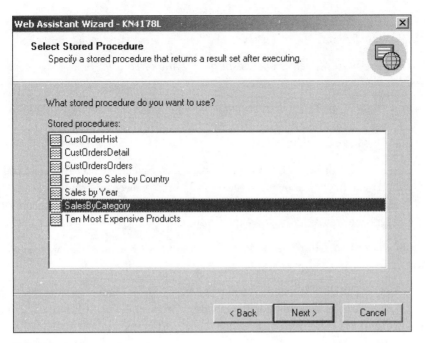

Figure 16.18
Specifying the stored procedures.

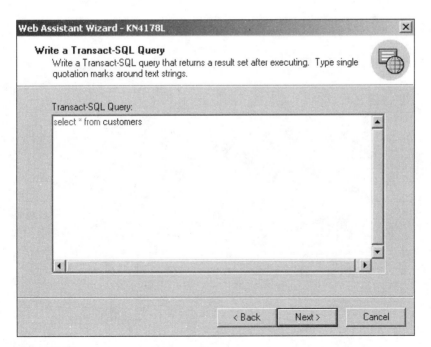

Figure 16.19
Specifying the Transact-SQL statement.

used with the operator and column. The combination of the Column, Operator, and Value generate the criteria used to determine what rows are published.

Note: You can use multiple selections by specifying And or Or and the Column, Operator, and Value for the second criteria.

- *Only Those Rows That Qualify Using The Following Transact-SQL* **WHERE** *Clause*—Specify the criteria in the **WHERE** clause that will be used to determine what rows are published.

- If you chose Result Set(s) Of A Stored Procedure I Select, the Set Stored Procedure Parameters dialog box shown in Figure 16.21 is displayed. Specify the Values for each stored procedure parameter. These values are used to define the criteria that will determine what data is going to be published.

- If you chose Data From The Transact-SQL Statement I Specify, the Schedule The Web Assistant Job dialog box is displayed as discussed in Step 10.

10. The Schedule The Web Assistant Job dialog box shown in Figure 16.22 is the next screen presented and is used to define when the Web Assistant will create the initial Web page, and when the Web page will be updated. Choose one of the following scheduling options:

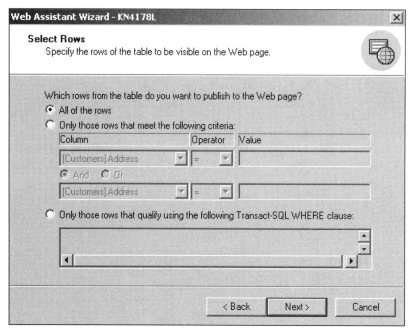

Figure 16.20
Specifying the rows to publish.

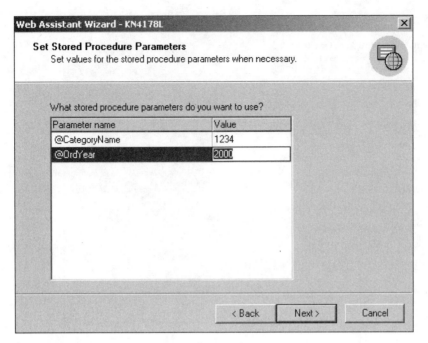

Figure 16.21
Specifying the stored procedure parameters.

- *Only One Time When I Complete This Wizard*—Executes the job to create the Web page upon completion of the Web Assistant Wizard.

- *On Demand*—Executes the job that creates and updates the Web page data when you manually start the job.

- *Only One Time At*—Executes the job that creates the Web page at the time you specify in the Time box on the date you specify in the Date box.

- *When The SQL Server Data Changes*—Executes the job when the data in the SQL Server database changes. Triggers are used to monitor the data for changes and perform the update of the changed data on the Web page.

- *At Regularly Scheduled Intervals*—Allows you to create a job that runs on a schedule you define in the Schedule The Update Interval screen of the Web Assistant Wizard.

Note: *By clicking the checkbox next to Generate A Web page when the wizard is completed, you are able to generate the Web page upon completion and use the options chosen here to determine when it is updated. However, this checkbox is grayed out if you chose Only One Time When I Complete This Wizard.*

11. The choice you make in Step 10 determines the screen that is displayed in Step 11. Complete one of the following screens and click Next:

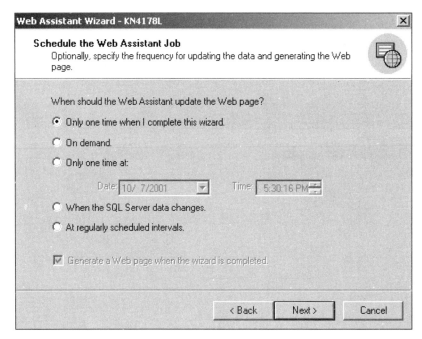

Figure 16.22
Scheduling the Web Assistant job.

- If you chose When The SQL Server Data Changes in Step 10, you are presented with the Monitor A Table And Columns dialog box shown in Figure 16.23, which allows you to specify the columns to monitor for changes, which in turn will fire the trigger that updates the Web page.

- Use the Available Tables drop-down menu to choose the table that contains the data you want to publish. After choosing the table, select the column(s) from the Table Columns box that you want to monitor and then click Add. If you want all the columns of the table, click the Add All button.

- If you chose At Regularly Scheduled Intervals in Step 10, you are presented with the Schedule The Update Interval screen shown in Figure 16.24. Create a schedule using the Periodically, Days Of Week, and Start Date And Time boxes.

Note: The Days Of Week configuration box is only available for configuration if you choose Weeks in the Periodically box.

- All other choices in Step 10 cause the Publish The Web Page screen to be displayed as discussed in Step 12.

12. The Publish The Web Page shown in Figure 16.25 is used to define the name of the Web page file and the directory where the Web page file will be stored. By default, the

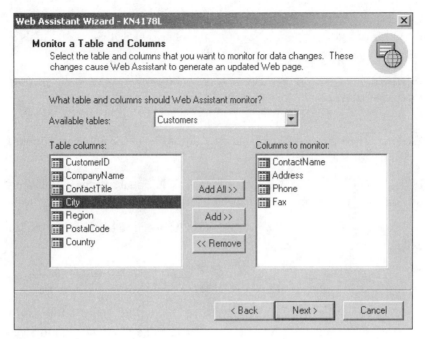

Figure 16.23
Specifying the tables and columns to monitor.

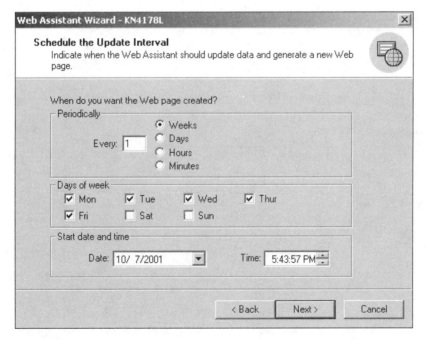

Figure 16.24
Scheduling the update interval.

first time you run the Web Assistant Wizard, The Web page file is named WebPage1.htm and stored in C:\Program Files\Microsoft SQL Server\80\Tools\ HTML\WebPage1.htm, but this can be modified.

Note: *Optionally, you can store the Web page on a network directory or FTP path that is accessible by SQL Server.*

13. After clicking Next on the Publish The Web Page screen, the Format The Web Page screen shown in Figure 16.26 is displayed. Choose one of the following options for formatting your Web page:

   • *Yes, Help Me Format The Web Page*—Displays additional screens in the Web Assistant Wizard to help you format the Web page.

   • *No, Use The Template File From*—Allows you to specify a template file that can be used to format your Web page.

Note: *Optionally, you can use the Use Character Set drop-down menu to specify a character set other than the default character set.*

14. If you chose Yes, Help Me Format The Web Page in Step 13, Steps 14 through16 need to be completed. If you chose No, Use The Template File From, proceed to Step 17.

   Use the Specify Titles screen shown in Figure 16.27 to:

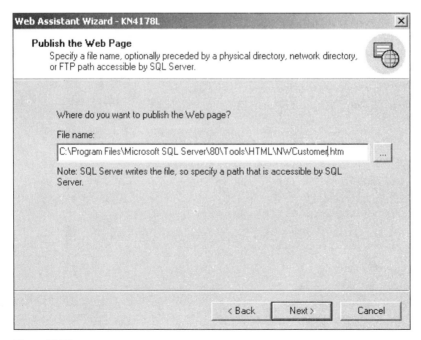

Figure 16.25
Defining the name of the published Web page .

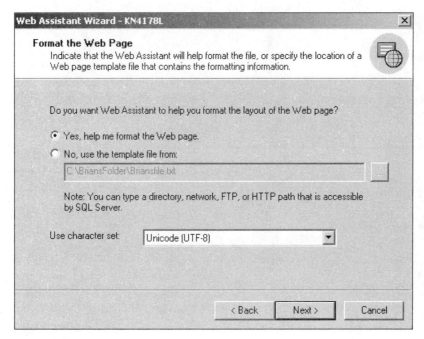

Figure 16.26
Choosing how to format your Web page.

- Specify the title of the Web Page.
- Specify the title of the HTML table that contains the data.
- Specify the table title font size.
- Specify whether to include the date and time on the Web page.

15. Click Next on the Specify Titles screen to display the Format A Table screen shown in Figure 16.28 and specify the following information:

- Whether to display the column names or just the data.
- Font characteristics.
- Whether to draw borderlines around the HTML table.

16. Click Next on the Format A Table screen to display the Add Hyperlinks To The Web Page screen shown in Figure 16.29 and choose one of the following options:

- *No*.
- *Yes, Add One Hyperlink*—Type the URL of the hyperlink and the name to be displayed on the SQL Server data Web page.
- *Yes, Add A List Of Hyperlink URLs. Select Them From A SQL Server Table With The Following SQL Statement*—Add multiple hyperlinks stored in a SQL Server table.

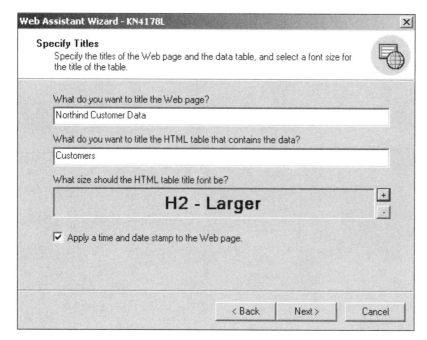

Figure 16.27
Formatting your Web page titles.

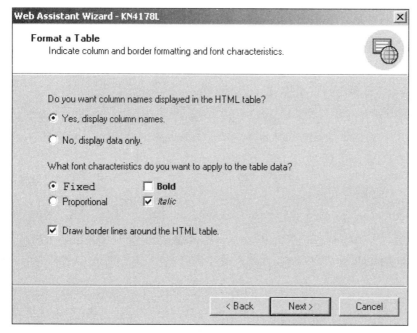

Figure 16.28
Formatting your table data.

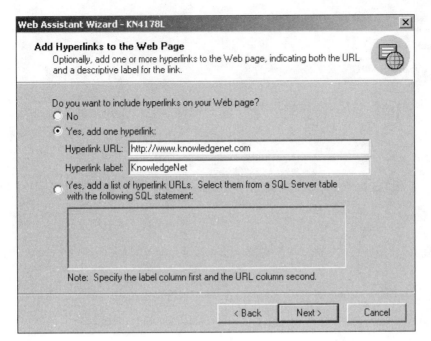

Figure 16.29
Specifying a hyperlink on your Web page.

17. Use the Limit Rows dialog box shown in Figure 16.30 to limit the total number of rows returned by SQL Server by choosing one of the following options:

    • *No, Return All Rows Of Data*—Returns all rows from the SQL Server table

    • *Yes*—Specify the maximum number of rows you want returned from SQL server in the Return The First ____ Rows Of Data box.

    To limit the number of rows displayed on a page, choose one of the following options:

    • *No, Put All Data In One Scrolling Page*

    • *Yes, Link The Successive Pages Together*—Supply a value in the Limit Each Page To ____ Rows Of Data box.

18. Click Next on the Limit Rows dialog box to display the Completing The Web Assistant Wizard screen shown in Figure 16.31. Click the Write Transact-SQL To File to save your choices to a script file so you can reuse them later. Click Finish to complete the wizard and create the Web page.

Note: *Use the scroll bar to review your choices. If you wish to change any choices, click the Back button the required number of times to return to the screen you want to modify. After making the modification, click Next to return to the Completing The Web Assistant Wizard.*

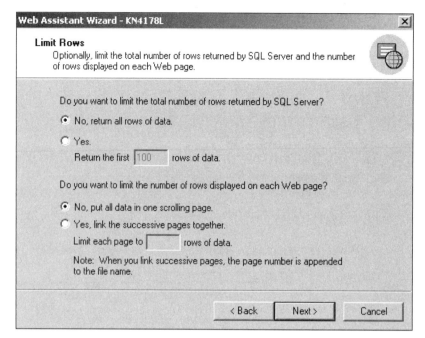

Figure 16.30
Specifying the amount of data to publish.

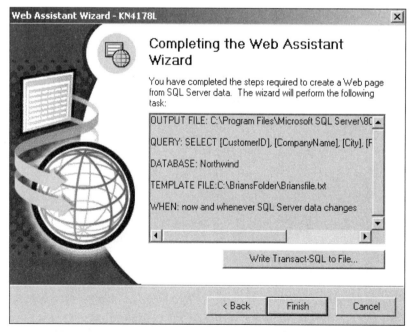

Figure 16.31
Completing the Web Assistant Wizard.

19. Use the following steps to view your Web page:

    1. Open Internet Explorer.

    2. Click File|Open to display the Open dialog box.

    3. Click the Browse button and locate your HTM file.

    4. Double-click the HTM file.

    5. Click OK in the Open dialog box to display it in Internet Explorer as shown in Figure 16.32.

These steps are used to generate HTML code to quickly create a Web page of SQL Server data that is either static or dynamic depending on the choices you made in the Web Assistant Wizard.

Summary

SQL Server 2000 provides the features and functionality to share data on the Web. If the data is shared correctly, it can be accessed by anyone using XML standards-based applications to access Web-based information. The great thing about XML documents is that they can be accessed using diverse hardware and browsers.

16

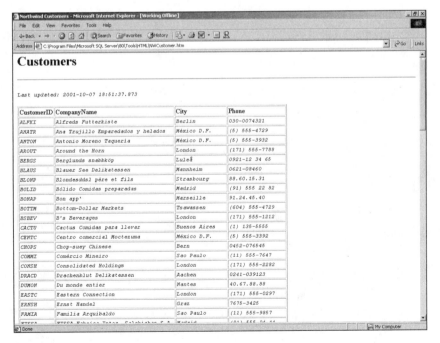

Figure 16.32
Viewing your Web page.

If XML is more than you need, you still have an opportunity to share data on the Web using the Web Assistant Wizard. This data can also be dynamic, but unlike XML, it is not standards-based and is updated using SQL Server triggers.

Glossary

active voice—Indicates the subject of the sentence is the entity that performs the action described by the verb. For example, "customers buy products" is in active voice, whereas "products are bought by customers" is in passive voice.

ActiveX Data Objects—An easy-to-use application programming interface (API) that wraps OLE DB for use in languages such as Visual Basic, Visual Basic for Applications, Active Server Pages, and Microsoft Internet Explorer Visual Basic Scripting.

adjective phrasing—A way of expressing a relationship in plain English in which an entity is described by an adjective (either a single word or another entity containing the adjective). For example, in the plain English phrasing "the orders are large", *large* is the adjective, and *orders* is the entity being described.

adverb—The part of speech modifying a verb, an adjective, or another adverb. In English Query, certain adverbs such as *very* and *recent* are interpreted correctly while other adverbs such as *rapidly* or *graciously* are not interpreted correctly.

aggregate function—An aggregate function performs a calculation on a column in a set of rows and returns a single value.

aggregate query—A T-SQL query that summarizes information from multiple rows by including an aggregate function, such as **SUM** or **AVG**.

alert—A user-defined response to a SQL Server event. An alert can either execute a defined task or send an email and/or pager message to a specified operator. You typically define alerts along with jobs that you create to automate the administration of SQL Server 2000.

alias—An alternate name for a table or column in expressions. You often use aliases to shorten the name for subsequent reference in code, prevent possible ambiguous references, or provide a more descriptive name in the query output.

American National Standards Institute (ANSI)—A private, non-profit organization that administers and coordinates the U.S. voluntary standardization and conformity assessment system. ANSI is one of the organizations that played a key role in the development of SQL standards.

anonymous subscription—A type of pull subscription in the replication system of SQL Server 2000. In this pull subscription, detailed information about the subscription and the Subscriber is not stored.

ANSI to OEM Conversion—The conversion of characters that must occur when data is transferred from a database that stores character data using a specific code page to a client application on a computer that uses a different code page.

application programming interface (API)—A set of routines available in an application for use by software programmers when designing an application interface. An excellent example is ADO. APIs make it simple for programmers to add powerful integration capabilities within an application. APIs shield programmers from many of the complexities of coding.

application role—A SQL Server role created to support the security needs of an application. Using application roles is an alternative to allowing users access to SQL Server 2000. You can create an application role and assign it to a particular application, allowing users who use the application to access SQL Server.

article—An object specified for replication. It is a component in a publication and can be a table, specified columns, specified rows, a stored procedure, a view definition, an indexed view, or a user-defined function.

atomicity—Atomicity is a feature provided by transactions. It is a principle that states either all of the transactions' data modifications are performed or none of them are performed.

authentication—A process that occurs as users attempt to log on to SQL Server 2000. This process verifies that the users are permitted to log on by checking their identity against a database of security accounts. There are two methods of authentication in SQL Server 2000—Mixed Mode authentication and Windows Authentication. Windows Authentication is recommended for all cases where all SQL Server 2000 users have the ability to log on initially in a Windows environment.

authorization—A security operation that verifies the permissions and access rights granted to a user account.

automatic recovery—A protection process built into SQL Server. This level of recovery occurs every time SQL Server is restarted. Automatic recovery protects your database in the event of a system failure.

autonomy—The independence one site has from other sites when you are performing modifications to data.

X

backup—A copy of a database, transaction log, file, or filegroup. Use this object to recover data after a system failure.

backup device—A tape or disk used in a backup or restore operation.

backup file—A file that stores a full or partial database, transaction log, or file and/or filegroup backup.

backup media—The tape, disk, or named pipe used to store a backup set.

backup set—The output of a single backup operation.

base data type—Any system-supplied data type. For example, **char**, **varchar**, **binary**, and **varbinary** are all base data types. You derive user-defined data types from base data types.

base table—A table stored permanently in a database. Base tables are referenced by views, cursors, SQL statements, and stored procedures.

batch—A set of SQL statements submitted together and executed as a group. A script is often a series of batches submitted one after the other.

BCP files—Files that store bulk copy data created by the bulk-copy utility or synchronization.

BCP utility—A command-prompt bulk copy utility that copies SQL Server data to or from an operating system file in a user-specified format.

bigint data type—An integer data type with a value from -2^{63} through $2^{63}-1$.

binary data type—A fixed-length binary data type with a maximum length of 8,000 bytes.

binary large object (BLOB)—A piece of binary data that has an exceptionally large size (such as pictures or audio tracks stored as digital data). In Transact-SQL, a BLOB is stored in an image column. Sometimes the term BLOB is also applied to large character data values, such as those stored in **text** or **ntext** columns.

bit data type—A data type that holds a value of either 1 or 0.

bitwise operation—An operation that manipulates a single bit, or tests whether a bit is on or off.

blocks—A series of Transact-SQL statements enclosed by **BEGIN** and **END**. You can nest **BEGIN**...**END** blocks within other **BEGIN**...**END** blocks.

Boolean—An operation or expression that can be evaluated only as either true or false.

built-in functions—A group of predefined functions provided as part of the Transact-SQL and Multidimensional Expressions (MDX) languages.

business rules—The logical rules that are used to run a business. Business rules can be enforced in the COM objects that make up the middle tier of a Windows DNA system. Business rules can also be enforced in a SQL Server database using triggers, stored procedures, and constraints.

cache aging—The mechanism of caching that determines when a cache row is outdated and must be refreshed.

calculated column—A column in a table that displays the result of an expression rather than stored data. For example, Cost = Price * Quantity .

calculated field—A field defined in a query that displays the result of an expression rather than stored data.

cascading delete—An operation that deletes a row containing a primary key value that is referenced by foreign key columns in existing rows in other tables.

cascading update—An operation that updates a primary key value that is referenced by foreign key columns in existing rows in other tables.

char data type—A character data type that holds a maximum of 8,000 characters.

character format—Data stored in a bulk copy data file using text characters.

character set—A character set determines the types of characters that SQL Server recognizes in the **char**, **varchar**, and **text** data types. Each character set is a set of 256 letters, digits, and symbols specific to a country or language

CHECK constraints—A **CHECK** constraint defines which data values are acceptable in a column. You can apply **CHECK** constraints to multiple columns, and you can apply multiple **CHECK** constraints to a single column. When a table is dropped, **CHECK** constraints are also dropped.

checkpoint—An event in which the database engine writes dirty buffer pages to disk. *Dirty pages* are pages that have been modified, but the modifications have not yet been written to disk. Each checkpoint writes to disk all pages that were dirty at the last checkpoint and still have not been written to disk. Checkpoints occur periodically based on the number of log records generated by data modifications, or when requested by a user or a system shutdown.

classification clause—In English Query, a classification clause is a sequence of related words within a sentence, having both a subject and a predicate and functioning as either an independent or a dependent unit. In Transact-SQL, a classification clause is a subunit of a SQL statement. A clause begins with a keyword.

clustered index—An index in which the logical order of the key values determines the physical order of the corresponding rows in a table.

X

code page—For character and Unicode data, a code page is a definition of the bit patterns that represent specific letters, numbers, or symbols.

collation—A set of rules that determines how data is compared, ordered, and presented. Character data is sorted using collation information, including locale, sort order, and case-sensitivity.

column—The area in each row that stores the data value for some attribute of the object modeled by the table.

column filter—In the replication system of SQL Server 2000, column filters restrict the columns to be included as part of a snapshot, transactional, or merge publication.

column-level collation—Column-level collation refers to the ability of SQL Server 2000 to support multiple collations in a single instance. This is a new and powerful feature. Databases can have default collations different from the default collation of the instance. Individual columns and variables can be assigned collations different from the default collation for the instance or database. Each column in a table can have a different collation.

column-level constraint—A constraint definition that is specified within a column definition when a table is created or altered. The constraint applies only to the associated column.

COM-structured storage file—A component object model (COM) compound file used by Data Transformation Services (DTS) to store the version history of a saved DTS package. This is one of several options you have for saving your DTS package.

commit—A commit operation saves all changes to databases made since the start of a transaction. A commit guarantees that all of the transaction's modifications are made a permanent part of the database. A commit also frees resources, such as locks, used by the transaction.

comparative form—A form of an adjective or adverb that refers to a comparison or that denotes a greater degree. Shorter adjectives and some adverbs typically form their comparative degree by adding -er, such as *young* and *younger*.

Component Object Model (COM)—COM is a Microsoft specification for developing component software. Several SQL Server and database application programming interfaces (APIs) such as SQL-DMO, OLE DB, and ADO are based on COM. Some SQL Server components, such as English Query, store objects as COM objects.

composite index—An index that uses more than one column in a table to index data.

composite key—A key composed of two or more columns.

computed column—A virtual column in a table whose value is computed at run time. The values in the column are not stored in the table, but are computed based on the expression that defines the column. An example of the definition of a computed column is: Cost as Price * Quantity.

concatenation—The process of combining two or more character strings or expressions into a single character string or expression. Concatenation also refers to combining two or more binary strings or expressions into a single binary string or expression.

concurrency—The process of allowing multiple users to access and change shared data at the same time. SQL Server uses locking to allow multiple users to access and change shared data at the same time without conflicting with each other.

conjunction—A part of speech (such as *and* or *although*) used to connect words, phrases, clauses, or sentences. Coordinating conjunctions *(and, but, or, nor, for, so, yet)* connect and relate words and word groups of equal grammatical rank.

connection—An interprocess communication (IPC) linkage established between a SQL Server 2000 application and an instance of SQL Server 2000.

constant—A group of symbols that represent a specific data value. The format of a constant depends on the data type of the value it represents. For example, **abc** is a character string constant, **123** is an integer constant, **December 16, 1999** is a **datetime** constant, and **0x02FA** is a binary constant.

constraint—A property assigned to a table column that prevents certain types of non-valid data values from being placed in the column.

continuation media—The backup media used when the initial medium becomes full, allowing continuation of the backup operation.

control-of-flow language—Transact-SQL keywords that control the flow of execution of SQL statements and statement blocks in triggers, stored procedures, and batches.

correlated subquery—A subquery that references a column in an outer statement. The inner query is executed for each candidate row in the outer statement.

CPU busy—A SQL Server 2000 statistic that reports the time, in milliseconds, the central processing unit (CPU) spent on a SQL Server task.

cursor—An entity that maps over a result set and establishes a position on a single row within the result set.

cursor data type—A special data type used to reference a cursor.

cursor library—A part of the ODBC and DB-Library application programming interfaces (APIs) that implements client cursors.

data connection—A collection of information required to access a specific database.

Data Control Language (DCL)—A subset of Transact-SQL statements. DCL is used to control permissions on database objects.

data definition—A data definition specifies the attributes, properties, and objects in a database.

Data Definition Language (DDL)—A subset of the Transact-SQL language. DDL is used to define all attributes and properties of a database, especially row layouts, column definitions, key columns (and sometimes keying methodology), file locations, and storage strategy.

data dictionary—A set of system tables stored in a catalog. A data dictionary includes definitions of database structures and related information, such as permissions.

data dictionary view—A data dictionary view is a system table.

data file—In bulk copy operations, the file that transfers data from the bulk copy out operation to the bulk copy in operation. Data files are also a critical part of SQL Server 2000 databases. Data files hold the data stored in the database. Every SQL Server 2000 database has at least one primary data file, and can optionally have multiple secondary data files to hold data that does not fit on the primary data file.

data integrity—Data integrity refers to a state in which all the data values stored in the database are correct.

data lineage—This information is used by Data Transformation Services (DTS) when it works in conjunction with Meta Data Services. This information records the history of package execution and data transformations for each piece of data.

data manipulation language (DML)—A subset of Transact-SQL. DML is used to retrieve and manipulate data.

data modification—An operation that adds, deletes, or changes information in a database, using Transact-SQL statements such as **INSERT**, **DELETE**, and **UPDATE**.

data pump—An OLE DB service provider that furnishes the infrastructure to import, export, and transform data between heterogeneous data stores using Data Transformation Services (DTS).

data source—In ADO and OLE DB, the location of a source of data exposed by an OLE DB provider.

data source name (DSN)—The name assigned to an ODBC data source.

data type—An attribute that specifies the type of information that can be stored in a column, parameter, or variable.

data-definition query—A SQL query that contains Data Definition Language (DDL) statements. As you know, Data Definition Language statements are statements that allow you to create or alter objects such as tables, indexes, or views.

database—A collection of information, tables, and other objects organized and presented to serve a specific purpose, such as searching, sorting, or recombining data.

database catalog—A database catalog contains the definition of all the objects in the database, as well as the definition of the database.

database file—One of the physical files that make up a database.

database language—A language used for accessing, querying, updating, and managing data in relational database systems. Transact-SQL is the language used for SQL Server 2000 and is a variation of the standard SQL.

database object—Any database component. It could be a table, index, trigger, view, key, constraint, default, rule, user-defined data type, or stored procedure in a database.

database owner—A member of the database administrator role of a database. For each database, there is only one database owner. The owner has full permissions in that database and determines the access and capabilities provided to other users.

database schema—Database schema refers to the names of tables, fields, data types, and primary and foreign keys of a database. Database schema is also known as the *database structure*.

database script—A collection of statements used to create database objects. Transact-SQL scripts are saved as files. These files usually ending with a .sql extension.

datetime data type—This SQL Server system data type stores a combined date and time value from January 1, 1753, through December 31, 9999. This system data type provides an accuracy of three-hundredths of a second, or 3.33 milliseconds.

deadlock—A situation in SQL Server 2000 when two users each have a lock on one piece of data and they attempt to acquire a lock on the other's piece of data. Each user would wait indefinitely for the other to release the lock, unless one of the user processes is terminated. SQL Server detects deadlocks and terminates one user's process.

decimal data type—Fixed precision and scale numeric data from -10^{38} -1 through 10^{38} -1.

decision support—A decision support system is designed to support the complex analytic analysis required to discover business trends. The information retrieved from these systems allows managers to make business decisions based on timely and accurate analysis of business trends.

declarative referential integrity (DRI)—**FOREIGN KEY** constraints defined as part of a table definition that enforce proper relationships between tables. The constraints ensure that proper actions are taken when **DELETE**, **INSERT**, and **UPDATE** statements remove, add, or modify primary or foreign key values.

default—A data value, option setting, collation, or name assigned automatically by the system if a user does not specify the value, option setting, collation, or name.

DEFAULT constraint—A property defined for a table column. The property specifies a constant to be used as the default value for the column. If any subsequent **INSERT** or **UPDATE** statement specifies a value of **NULL** for the column, or does not specify a value for the column, the constant value defined in the **DEFAULT** constraint is placed in the column.

default database—The database the user is connected to immediately after logging in to SQL Server. You can use Enterprise Manager to easily assign a default database for every user.

default instance—The copy of SQL Server that uses the computer name on which it is installed as its name.

default language—The language that SQL Server 2000 uses for errors and messages if a user does not specify a language. Each SQL Server 2000 login has a default language, which can be assigned to each user easily using Enterprise Manager.

DELETE query—This Transact-SQL query removes rows from one or more tables.

delimiter—A character that indicates the start and end of an object name. In SQL Server 2000, delimiters are either double quotation marks ("") or brackets ([]).

denormalize—The process of introducing redundancy into a table in order to incorporate data from a related table.

DENY—The **DENY** permission prevents an account from gaining permission through membership in groups or roles within the permission.

dependencies—The views and procedures that depend on the specified table or view.

dictionary entry—A defined word in the English Query dictionary. You can make additions to the dictionary through the English Query domain editor by specifying the word, its part of speech, and an optional irregular form.

differential database backup—This type of database backup records only those changes made to the database since the last full database backup. A differential backup is smaller, and is faster to restore than a full backup and has minimal effect on performance.

dirty pages—Dirty pages are buffer pages that contain modifications that have not been written to disk. See also "checkpoint."

dirty read—Reads that contain uncommitted data.

distribute—To distribute is to move transactions, or snapshots of data, from the Publisher to Subscribers, where they are applied to the destination tables in the subscription databases.

distributed query—A single query that accesses data from multiple data sources.

distribution database—A database on the Distributor that stores data for replication, including transactions, snapshot jobs, synchronization status, and replication history information.

distribution retention period—The distribution retention period determines the amount of information stored for a replication agent and the length of time subscriptions will remain active in the distribution database. When the distribution retention period is exceeded, the Distribution Clean Up Agent runs.

Distributor—A server that hosts the distribution database and stores history data and/or transactions and metadata.

domain—In the Windows 2000 security model, a domain is a collection of computers grouped for viewing and administrative purposes that share a common security database. In relational databases, a domain is a set of valid values allowed in a column.

domain integrity—Domain integrity enforces the validity of entries for a given column. The mechanism, such as the **CHECK** constraint, can restrict the possible data values by data type, format, or range of values allowed.

double-byte character set (DBCS)—A character set that generally uses two bytes to represent a character, allowing more than 256 characters to be represented. DBCSs are typically used in environments that use ideographic writing systems, such as Japanese, Korean, and Chinese.

DTS package—An organized collection of connections, Data Transformation Services (DTS) tasks, DTS transformations, and workflow constraints defined by the DTS object model and assembled either with a DTS tool or programmatically. You can save your packages to variety of places in a variety of formats.

DTS package template—A model Data Transformation Services (DTS) package. The template is used to help create and configure a particular type of package.

dynamic locking—SQL Server 2000 uses this process to determine the most cost-effective locks to use at any one time.

dynamic recovery—This process detects and/or attempts to correct software failure or loss of data integrity within a relational database management system (RDBMS).

dynamic snapshot—A snapshot of a merge publication, with dynamic filters, that is applied using bulk copy files to improve performance.

encrypted trigger—An encrypted trigger is created with an optional encryption parameter that encrypts the definition text and cannot be decrypted. Encryption makes the information indecipherable to protect it from unauthorized viewing or use.

encryption—A method for keeping sensitive information confidential by changing data into an unreadable form.

English Query—A SQL Server 2000 application that allows users to ask questions of the server in plain English. The alternative is to train SQL users in Transact-SQL.

English Query application—An application that accesses the English Query engine of SQL Server 2000. These applications allow users to submit queries in plain English.

X

entity—An entity is a real-world object, referred to by a noun (person, place, thing, or idea), such as people, products, shipments, cities, and so on. Entities are semantic objects used in English Query.

entity integrity—Entity integrity refers to a state in which all the rows in a database have a non-null primary key value, all tables have primary keys, and no table has any duplicate primary key values. Entity integrity ensures there are no duplicate entries for anything represented in the database.

enumeration—A data type of a property. Enumeration specifies that a property value should support a fixed set of constant strings or integer values.

error log—In SQL Server 2000, an error log is a text file that records system information from SQL Server.

error state number—A number associated with SQL Server 2000 messages that helps Microsoft support engineers find the specific code location that issued the message. This number can be helpful in diagnosing errors that may be generated from multiple locations in the SQL Server 2000 code.

exclusive lock—This type of lock prevents any other transaction from acquiring a lock on a resource until the original lock on the resource is released at the end of the transaction.

explicit transaction—A group of SQL statements enclosed within transaction delimiters. The first delimiter must be either **BEGIN TRANSACTION** or **BEGIN DISTRIBUTED TRANSACTION**, and the end delimiter must be one of the following—**COMMIT TRANSACTION, COMMIT WORK, ROLLBACK TRANSACTION, ROLLBACK WORK,** or **SAVE TRANSACTION**.

expression—A combination of symbols and operators that evaluate to a single data value. Simple expressions can be a constant, variable, column, or scalar function. Complex expressions are one or more simple expressions connected by operators. You use expressions in your Transact-SQL code.

extended stored procedure—A function in a dynamic link library (DLL) that is coded using the SQL Server 2000 Extended Stored Procedure API. The function can then be invoked from Transact-SQL using the same statements that are used to execute Transact-SQL stored procedures.

extent—The unit of space allocated to a SQL Server object, such as a table or index, whenever the object needs more space. In SQL Server 2000, an extent is eight contiguous pages.

field—An area in a window or record that stores a single data value.

field length—The maximum number of characters needed to represent a data item in a bulk copy character format data file. Field length is critical when you are performing bulk copy operations.

field terminator—One or more characters marking the end of a field or row, thus separating one field or row in the data file from the next. Field terminators are critical when you are performing bulk copy operations.

file—The basic unit of storage for a database. One database can be stored in several files. SQL Server uses three types of files: data files (which store data), log files (which store transaction logs), and backup files (which store backups of a database).

file DSN—A file DSN stores connection information for a database in a file that is saved on your computer. The file is a text file with the extension .dsn. The connection information consists of parameters and corresponding values that the ODBC Driver Manager uses to establish a connection.

file storage type—The file storage type defines the storage format used in the data file that transfers data from a bulk copy out operation to a bulk copy in operation. If you are using native mode files, all data is stored using the same internal structures that SQL Server 2000 uses to store the data in a database. If you are using character mode files, all data is converted to character strings.

filegroup—A named collection of one or more files that forms a single unit of allocation or for administration of a database. Filegroups allows you to engage in advanced administration techniques including the specific storage of particular objects on particular hard drives.

fill factor—Fill factor defines the amount of free space on each page of the index. You use fill factor when creating indexes. It accommodates future expansion of table data and reduces the potential for page splits.

filter—A set of criteria that controls the set of records returned as a result set. You can also use filters to define the sequence in which rows are returned.

filtering—Filtering refers to the ability to restrict data returned from a query based upon criteria set in the **WHERE** clause of a SQL statement. In the case of replication, filtering refers to acts you perform on table articles defined in a publication. When you filter in replication, you create partitions of data that can be published to Subscribers.

fixed database role—A predefined role that exists in each database. The scope of the role is limited to the database in which it is defined. You use fixed database roles to quickly define permissions within a particular database. Roles can be compared to groups in the Window NT/2000 operating systems.

fixed server role—A predefined role that exists at the server level. The scope of the role is limited to the SQL Server instance in which it is defined. Fixed server roles allow you to quickly assign permissions on the server to specific individuals. Roles can be compared to groups in the Window NT/2000 operating systems.

float data type—A float data type holds floating-point number data from $-1.79E + 308$ through $1.79E + 308$. Float, double precision, and float(n) are SQL Server float data types.

foreign key (FK)—A column or combination of columns whose values match the primary key (PK) or unique key in another table. The foreign key is also called the *referencing key* in some literature.

fragmentation—Fragmentation often occurs in databases when frequent or large data modifications are made. SQL Server 2000 provides methods for reducing fragmentation and improving read-ahead performance by dropping and re-creating a clustered index.

full outer join—A full outer join is a type of outer join in which all rows in all joined tables are included in a result. This literally means all rows are returned, whether or not there is matching criteria.

full-text catalog—The full-text catalog stores all of the full-text indexes for tables within a database.

full-text index—The portion of a full-text catalog that stores all of the full-text words and their locations for a given table.

full-text query—A query that searches for words, phrases, or multiple forms of a word or phrase in character-based columns. SQL Server 2000 provides rich full-text query capabilities.

full-text service—This SQL Server 2000 component provides full-text querying capabilities.

function—A section of code that operates as a single logical unit. Transact-SQL supports both built-in functions and user-defined functions. The built-in functions cannot be modified by SQL Server 2000 users, whereas users can create and modify user-defined functions.

global default—A global default applies to a specific database. This default is shared by columns of different tables.

global properties—General properties of an English Query application, such as the default year setting or the start date of the fiscal year.

global rule—A global rule applies to a specific database and this rule is shared by columns of different tables.

global subscriptions—A subscription to a merge publication with an assigned priority value used for conflict detection and resolution.

global variable—A global variable can be referenced by multiple Data Transformation Services (DTS) tasks.

grant—Applies permissions to a user account, which allows the account to perform an activity or work with data.

guest—A special user account that is present in all SQL Server 2000 databases. This account cannot be removed from any database. If a connection is made using a login that has not been assigned a user account in a database and the connection references objects in that database, it has the permissions assigned only to the guest account in that database.

heterogeneous data—Data stored in multiple formats. For example, data stored in a SQL Server database, a text file, and an Excel spreadsheet.

homogeneous data—Data that comes from multiple data sources that are all managed by the same software.

horizontal partitioning—To segment a single table into multiple tables based on selected rows.

Hypertext Markup Language (HTML)—A system of marking up, or tagging, a document so that it can be published on the World Wide Web.

identifier—The name of an object in a database. An identifier can be from 1 to 128 characters.

identity column—A column in your database that has been assigned the identity property.

identity property—The identity property generates values that uniquely identify each row in a table. When inserting rows into a table that has an identity column, SQL Server generates the next identity value automatically based on the last used identity value and the increment value specified during column creation.

idle time—A SQL Server 2000 Agent condition that defines the level of CPU usage by the SQL Server 2000 database engine that constitutes an idle state. SQL Server 2000 Agent jobs can then be created to run whenever the database engine CPU usage falls below the level defined in the idle time definition.

image data type—A SQL Server variable-length binary data type with a maximum length of 2^{31} - 1 (2,147,483,647) bytes.

immediate updating—An option available with snapshot replication and transactional replication that allows data modifications to be made to replicated data at the Subscriber.

immediate updating subscriptions—A subscription to a snapshot or transactional publication for which the user is able to make data modifications at the Subscriber.

implicit transaction—A connection option that specifies that each SQL statement executed by the connection is considered a separate transaction.

implied permission—Permission to perform an activity specific to a role.

X

index—A database object that provides fast access to data in the rows of a table, based on key values. Indexes can also enforce uniqueness on the rows in a table. SQL Server supports clustered and nonclustered indexes.

index page—A database page containing index rows.

indirect object—Word or words naming the one or ones indirectly affected by the action of the verb. For example, "Tom paid me some money." In this example *me* is the indirect object.

initial media—The first medium in each media family.

initial snapshot—Files necessary for replication. The initial snapshot is transferred to Subscribers when implementing replication.

inner join—An operation that retrieves rows from multiple source tables by comparing the values from columns shared between the source tables. An inner join excludes rows from source tables that have no matching rows in the other source tables.

Insert query—A query that copies specific columns and rows from one table to another, or to the same table.

Insert Values query—A query that creates a new row and inserts values into specified columns.

instance—An instance refers to a copy of SQL Server running on a computer. SQL Server 2000 can now run multiple instances on a single system.

int (integer) data type—A SQL Server system data type that holds whole numbers from -2^{31} (-2,147,483,648) through $2^{31} - 1$ (2,147,483,647).

integer—A data type category that includes the **bigint**, **int**, **smallint**, and **tinyint** data types.

integrity constraint—A property defined on a table that prevents data modifications that would create non-valid data.

intent lock—A lock placed on one level of a resource hierarchy to protect shared or exclusive locks on lower-level resources.

interactive structured query language (ISQL)—An interactive command-prompt utility provided with SQL Server that allows users to execute Transact-SQL statements or batches from a server or workstation and view the results returned. This utility is provided in SQL Server 2000 mainly for backward compatibility. Its functionality has been replaced by OSQL.

International Organization for Standardization (ISO)—One of two international standards bodies responsible for developing international data communications standards. International Organization for Standardization (ISO) works closely with the International Electrotechnical Commission (IEC) to define standards of computing. They jointly published the ISO/IEC SQL-92 standard for SQL.

Internet-enabled—A publication setting that enables replication to Internet Subscribers.

interprocess communication (IPC)—A mechanism through which operating system processes and threads exchange data and messages. IPCs include local mechanisms, such as Windows shared memory, or network mechanisms, such as Windows Sockets.

irregular form—A form of an English word that is an exception to the standard rules of inflection. For example, the past tense of *sit* is *sat*, not *satted*. Likewise, the plural of *alumnus* is *alumni*, not *alumnuses*.

irregular form type—The type of inflection (plural, past tense, or unknown) for which a word uses an irregular form. For example, the word *woman* has an irregular plural form—*women*—because you do not form the plural of woman in the standard way (by adding -*s* or -*es*.)

irregular noun—A noun plural that is not formed by adding -*s* or -*es*, such as *men* or *women*.

irregular verb—A verb that is not inflected in the usual ways. One example of an irregular verb is one that does not add -*ed* to the root form to create the past tense and past participle. For example, *lend* becomes *lent* not *lended*.

isolation level—The property of a transaction that controls the degree to which data is isolated for use by one process and guarded against interference from other processes. Setting the isolation level defines the default locking behavior for all **SELECT** statements in your SQL Server session.

job—A specified series of operations, called *steps*, performed sequentially by SQL Server Agent.

join—As a verb, to combine the contents of two or more tables and produce a result set that incorporates rows and columns from each table. Tables are typically joined using data that they have in common.

As a noun, the process or result of joining tables, as in the term *inner join* to indicate a particular method of joining tables.

join column—A column referenced in a join condition.

join condition—A comparison clause that specifies how tables are related by their join columns.

join filter—A row filter used in merge replication that defines a relationship between two tables that will be enforced during synchronization, which is similar to specifying a join between two tables.

join operator—A comparison operator in a join condition that determines how the two sides of the condition are evaluated and which rows are returned.

X

join path—A series of joins indicating how two tables are related. For example, **Sales.SalesRepIDSalesReps.ID**, **SalesReps.BranchIDBranches.ID**.

junction table—A table that establishes a relationship between other tables. The junction table contains foreign keys referencing the tables that form the relationship. For example, an **OrderParts** junction table can show what parts shipped with each order by having foreign keys to an **Orders** table and a **Parts** table.

kernel—In SQL Server 2000, a subset of the storage engine that is referenced in some error messages. In Windows 2000, the core of the operating system that performs basic operations.

key—A column or group of columns that uniquely identifies a row (**PRIMARY KEY**), defines the relationship between two tables (**FOREIGN KEY**), or is used to build an index.

key column—A column referenced by a primary, foreign, or index key.

key range lock—A lock used to lock ranges between records in a table to prevent phantom insertions or deletions into a set of records. Ensures serializable transactions.

keyword—A reserved word in SQL Server that performs a specific function, such as to define, manipulate, or access database objects.

latency—The amount of time that elapses between when a data change is completed at one server and when that change appears at another. (For example, the time between when a change is made at a Publisher and when it appears at the Subscriber.)

leaf level—The bottom level of a clustered or nonclustered index. In a clustered index, the leaf level contains the actual data pages of the table. In a nonclustered index, the leaf level either points to data pages or points to the clustered index (if one exists), rather than containing the data itself.

left outer join—A type of outer join in which all rows from the leftmost table in the **JOIN** clause are included. When rows in the left table are not matched by rows in the right table, all result set columns that come from the right table are assigned a value of **NULL**.

linked server—A definition of an OLE DB data source used by SQL Server 2000 distributed queries. The linked server definition specifies the OLE DB provider required to access the data, and includes enough addressing information for the OLE DB provider to connect to the data. Any rowsets exposed by the OLE DB data source can then be referenced as tables, called linked tables, in SQL Server 2000 distributed queries.

linked table—An OLE DB rowset exposed by an OLE DB data source that has been defined as a linked server for use in SQL Server 2000 distributed queries. The rowsets exposed by the linked server can be referenced as tables in distributed queries.

livelock—A request for an exclusive lock that is repeatedly denied because a series of overlapping shared locks keeps interfering. SQL Server detects the situation after four denials and refuses further shared locks. A livelock also occurs when read transactions monopolize a table or page, forcing a write transaction to wait indefinitely.

local Distributor—A server that is configured as both a Publisher and a Distributor for SQL Server Replication.

local group—A group in Windows NT 4 or Windows 2000 containing user accounts and global groups from the domain group in which they were created and any trusted domain. Local groups cannot contain other local groups.

local login identification—The identification (ID) a user must use to log in to a local server. A login ID can have up to 128 characters. The characters can be alphanumeric; however, the first character must be a letter.

local server—In SQL Server 2000 connections, an instance of SQL Server 2000 running on the same computer as the application.

When resolving references to database objects in a Transact-SQL statement, the instance of SQL Server 2000 executing the statement.

In SQL Server 2000 distributed queries, the instance of SQL Server 2000 executing the distributed query. The local server then accesses any linked servers referenced in the query.

In SQL Server 2000 remote stored procedures, the instance of SQL Server executing an **EXEC** statement that references a remote stored procedure. The local server then passes the execution request to the remote server on which the remote stored procedure resides.

local subscription—A subscription to a merge publication using the priority value of the Publisher for conflict detection and resolution.

local variable—A user-defined variable that has an assigned value. A local variable is defined with a **DECLARE** statement, assigned an initial value with a **SELECT** or **SET** statement, and used within the statement batch or procedure in which it was declared.

locale—The Windows operating-system attribute that defines certain behaviors related to language. The locale defines the code page, or bit patterns, used to store character data and the order in which characters are sorted. It also defines language-specific items such as the format used for dates and time and the character used to separate decimals in numbers. Each locale is identified by a unique number, called a *locale identifier* or *LCID*. SQL Server 2000 collations are similar to locales in that the collations define language-specific types of behaviors for instances of SQL Server 2000.

locale identifier (LCID)—A number that identifies a Windows-based locale.

lock—A restriction on access to a resource in a multiuser environment. SQL Server locks users out of a specific row, column, or file automatically to maintain security or prevent concurrent data modification problems.

X

lock escalation—The process of converting many fine-grain locks into fewer coarse-grain locks, thereby reducing system overhead.

log file—A file or set of files containing a record of the modifications made in a database.

logical name—A name used by SQL Server to identify a file. A logical name for a file must correspond to the rules for identifiers and can have as many as 30 characters (for example, **ACCOUNTING** or **LIBRARY**).

logical operators—The operators **AND**, **OR**, and **NOT**. Used to connect search conditions in **WHERE** clauses.

login (account)—An identifier that gives a user permission to connect to SQL Server 2000 using SQL Server Authentication. Users connecting to SQL Server 2000 using Windows NT Authentication are identified by their Windows 2000 login, and do not need a separate SQL Server 2000 login.

login security mode—A security mode that determines the manner in which a SQL Server 2000 instance validates a login request. There are two types of login security: Windows Authentication and SQL Server authentication.

lookup table—A table, either in a database or hard-coded in the English Query application, that contains codes and the English word or phrase they represent.

machine DSN—A machine DSN stores connection information for a database in the system registry. The connection information consists of parameters and corresponding values that the ODBC Driver Manager uses to establish a connection.

Make Table query—A query (SQL statement) that creates a new table and then creates rows in it by copying rows from an existing table.

master database—The database that controls the operation of each instance of SQL Server. It is installed automatically with each instance of SQL Server and keeps track of user accounts, remote user accounts, and remote servers that each instance can interact with. It also tracks ongoing processes, configurable environment variables, system error messages, tapes and disks available on the system, and active locks.

master file—The file installed with earlier versions of SQL Server used to store the master, model, and tempdb system databases and transaction logs, and the pubs sample database and transaction log.

measurement—In English Query, an option in the Adjective Phrasing dialog box. Using it, you can specify some measurement that is represented in an entity. For example, the relationship expressed as "the product is some category" may be represented by a product entity and a category entity.

media description—The text describing the media set.

media family—All media in a set written by a single device (for example, an initial medium and all continuation media, if any).

media header—Provides information about the backup media.

media name—The descriptive name for the entire backup media set.

media set—All media involved in a backup operation.

memo—A type of column containing long strings of text, typically more than 255 characters. This is the Access equivalent of a SQL Server **text** data type.

merge—The operation that combines two partitions into a single partition.

merge replication—A type of replication that allows sites to make autonomous changes to replicated data, and at a later time, merge changes and resolve conflicts when necessary.

message number—A number that identifies a SQL Server 2000 error message.

Messaging Application Programming Interface (MAPI)—An email application programming interface (API).

meta data—Information about the properties of data, such as the type of data in a column (numeric, text, and so on) or the length of a column.

mirroring—The process for protecting against the loss of data due to disk failure by maintaining a fully redundant copy of data on a separate disk. Mirroring can be implemented at several levels—in SQL Server 2000, in the operating system, and in the disk controller hardware.

Mixed Mode—This authentication mode combines Windows Authentication and SQL Server Authentication. Mixed Mode allows users to connect to an instance of SQL Server, through either a Windows NT 4 or Windows 2000 user account or a SQL Server login.

model—In English Query, the collection of all information that is known about the objects in the English Query application. This information includes: the specified database objects (such as tables, fields, and joins); semantic objects (such as entities, the relationships between them, and additional dictionary entries); and global domain default options.

model database—A database installed with SQL Server that provides the template for new user databases. SQL Server 2000 creates a new database by copying in the contents of the model database and then expanding it to the size requested.

money data type—A SQL Server system data type that stores monetary values from -2^{63} (-922,337,203,685,477.5808) through $2^{63} - 1$ (+922,337,203,685,477.5807), with accuracy to a ten-thousandth of a monetary unit.

multiple instances—Multiple copies of SQL Server running on the same computer. There can be one default instance, which can be any version of SQL Server. There can be multiple named instances of SQL Server 2000.

multithreaded server application—An application that creates multiple threads within a single process to service multiple user requests at the same time.

multiuser—The ability of a computer to support many users operating at the same time, while providing the computer system's full range of capabilities to each user.

.NET—A new and exciting strategy from Microsoft for their servers and applications to support Web technologies. This strategy consists of new developer tools, servers, building block services, devices, and user experiences.

name phrasing—An English description of a relationship in which one entity is the name of another entity. For example, in the sentence "Custnames are the names of Customers," *Custnames* and *Customers* are both entities.

named instance—An installation of SQL Server 2000 that is given a name to differentiate it from other named instances and from the default instance on the same computer. A named instance is identified by the computer name and instance name.

named pipe—An interprocess communication (IPC) mechanism that SQL Server uses to provide communication between clients and servers. Named pipes permit access to shared network resources.

native format—Bulk copy data files in which the data is stored using the same internal data structures SQL Server uses to store data in SQL Server databases. Bulk copy can quickly process native format files because it does not have to convert data when transferring it between SQL Server and the bulk copy data file.

nchar data type—A fixed-length Unicode data type with a maximum of 4,000 characters. Unicode characters use 2 bytes per character and support all international characters.

nested query—A **SELECT** statement that contains one or more subqueries, or another term for *subquery*.

Net-Library—A SQL Server communications component that isolates the SQL Server client software and database engine from the network APIs. The SQL Server client software and database engine send generic network requests to a Net-Library, which translates the request to the specific network commands of the protocol chosen by the user.

nickname—When used with merge replication system tables, a name for another Subscriber who is known to already have a specified generation of updated data. Used to avoid sending an update to a Subscriber who has already received those changes.

noise word—A word that does not participate in a full-text query search. For example, *a*, *and*, *the*, and *so on*.

nonclustered index—An index in which the logical order of the index is different than the physical, stored order of the rows on disk.

nonrepeatable read—When a transaction reads the same row more than once, and between the two (or more) reads, a separate transaction modifies that row. Because the row was modified between reads within the same transaction, each read produces different values, which introduces inconsistency.

normalization rules—A set of database design rules that minimizes data redundancy and results in a database in which the database engine and application software can easily enforce integrity.

noun—A part of speech that names a person, place, thing, idea, animal, quality, or action. A noun usually changes form to indicate the plural or the possessive case.

ntext data type—A variable-length Unicode data type that can hold a maximum of 2^{30} - 1 (1,073,741,823) characters. **ntext** columns store a 16-byte pointer in the data row, and the data is stored separately.

NULL—An entry that has no explicitly assigned value. **NULL** is not equivalent to zero or blank. A value of **NULL** is not considered to be greater than, less than, or equivalent to any other value, including another value of **NULL**.

nullability—The attribute of a column, parameter, or variable that specifies whether it allows null data values.

numeric expression—Any expression that evaluates to a number. The expression can be any combination of variables, constants, functions, and operators.

nvarchar data type—A variable-length Unicode data type with a maximum of 4,000 characters. Unicode characters use 2 bytes per character and support all international characters.

object—In databases, one of the components of a database: a table, index, trigger, view, key, constraint, default, rule, user-defined data type, or stored procedure.

object dependencies—References to other objects when the behavior of the first object can be affected by changes in the object it references. For example, if a stored procedure references a table, changes to the table can affect the behavior of the stored procedure.

object identifier—A unique name given to an object.

In Meta Data Services, a unique identifier constructed from a globally unique identifier (GUID) and an internal identifier. All objects must have an object identifier.

object owner—The security account that controls the permissions for an object, usually the creator of the object.

object permission—An attribute that controls the ability to perform operations on an object. For example, table or view permissions control which users can execute **SELECT**, **INSERT**, **UPDATE**, and **DELETE** statements against the table or view.

object variable—A variable that contains a reference to an object.

ODBC data source—The location of a set of data that can be accessed using an ODBC driver. Also, a stored definition that contains all of the connection information an ODBC application requires to connect to the data source.

ODBC driver—A dynamic-link library (DLL) that an ODBC-enabled application—such as Excel—can use to access an ODBC data source. Each ODBC driver is specific to a database management system (DBMS), such as SQL Server, Access, and so on.

OLE DB—A COM-based application programming interface (API) for accessing data. OLE DB supports accessing data stored in any format (database, spreadsheet, text file, and so on) for which an OLE DB provider is available.

OLE DB provider—A software component that exposes OLE DB interfaces. Each OLE DB provider exposes data from a particular type of data source (for example SQL Server database, Access database, and Excel spreadsheet).

online analytical processing (OLAP)—A technology that uses multidimensional structures to provide rapid access to data for analysis. The source data for OLAP is commonly stored in data warehouses in a relational database.

online transaction processing (OLTP)—A data processing system designed to record all of the business transactions of an organization as they occur. An OLTP system is characterized by many concurrent users actively adding and modifying data.

Open Data Services (ODS)—The layer of the SQL Server database engine that transfers client requests to the appropriate functions in the database engine. Open Data Services exposes the extended stored procedure API used to write DLL functions that can be called from Transact-SQL statements.

Open Database Connectivity (ODBC)—A data access application programming interface (API) that supports access to any data source for which an ODBC driver is available. ODBC is aligned with the American National Standards Institute (ANSI) and International Organization for Standardization (ISO) standards for a database Call Level Interface (CLI).

optimize synchronization—An option in merge replication that allows you to minimize network traffic when determining whether recent changes have caused a row to move into or out of a partition that is published to a Subscriber.

outer join—A join that includes all the rows from the joined tables that have met the search conditions, even rows from one table for which there is no matching row in the other join table. For result-set rows returned when a row in one table is not matched by a row from the other table, a value of **NULL** is supplied for all result-set columns that are resolved to the table that had the missing row.

page—In a virtual storage system, a fixed-length block of contiguous virtual addresses copied as a unit from memory to disk and back during paging operations. SQL Server allocates database space in pages. In SQL Server, a page is 8 kilobytes (KB) in size.

page split—The process of moving half the rows or entries in a full data or index page to two new pages to make room for a new row or index entry.

partitioning—The process of replacing a table with multiple smaller tables. Each smaller table has the same format as the original table, but with a subset of the data. Each partitioned table has rows allocated to it based on some characteristic of the data, such as specific key ranges. The rules that define into which table the rows go must be unambiguous. For example, a table is partitioned into two tables. All rows with primary key values lower than a specified value are allocated to one table, and all keys equal to or greater than the value are allocated to the other. Partitioning can improve application processing speeds and reduce the potential for conflicts in multisite update replication. You can improve the usability of partitioned tables by creating a view. The view, created by a union of select operations on all the partitioned tables, presents the data as if it all resided in a single table.

parts of speech—The classes into which words may be grouped according to their form changes and their grammatical relationships. The traditional parts of speech are verbs, nouns, pronouns, adjectives, adverbs, prepositions, conjunctions, and interjections.

pass-through query—A query passed uninterpreted to an external server for evaluation. The result set returned by a pass-through query can be used in the **FROM** clause of a query as an ordinary base table.

pass-through statement—A **SELECT** statement that is passed directly to the source database without modification or delay. In PivotTable Service, the **PASSTHROUGH** option is part of the **INSERT INTO** statement.

passive voice—Indicates that the subject of the verb receives the action of the verb. For example, in the sentence "The customers are sold products", the subject *customers* receives the action of the verb *are sold*.

persistence—The saving of an object definition so it will be available after the current session ends.

phrase—A sequence of grammatically related words lacking a subject or a predicate, or both.

phrasing—A way to express a relationship in English. Types of phrasings include name, adjective, subset, preposition, verb, and trait phrasings.

physical name—The path where a file or mirrored file is located. The default is the path of the Master.dat file followed by the first eight characters of the file's logical name. For example, if Accounting is the logical name, and the Master.dat file is located in Sql\Data, the default physical name is Sql\Data\Accounti.dat. For a mirrored file, the default is the path of the Master.mir file followed by the first eight characters of the mirror file's logical name. For example, if Maccount is the name of the mirrored file, and the Master.mir file is located in Sql\Data, the default physical name is Sql\Data\Maccount.mir.

physical reads—A request for a database page in which SQL Server must transfer the requested page from disk to the SQL Server buffer pool. All attempts to read pages are called *logical reads*. If the page is already in the buffer, there is no associated physical read generated by the logical read. The number of physical reads never exceeds the number of logical reads. In a well-tuned instance of SQL Server, the number of logical reads is typically much higher than the number of physical reads.

possessive case—A grammatical case that denotes ownership; for example, "the customer's order" or "the inventory's reorder point".

precision—The maximum total number of decimal digits that can be stored, both to the left and right of the decimal point.

predicate—A basic grammatical division of a sentence that consists of what is said about the subject.

prefix characters—A set of 1 to 4 bytes that prefix each data field in a native-format bulk-copy data file. The prefix characters record the length of the data value in the field, or contain -1 when the value is **NULL**.

prefix length—The number of prefix characters preceding each noncharacter field in a bcp native format data file.

preposition—A part of speech that links and relates a noun or noun substitute to another word in the sentence.

preposition phrasing—A way of expressing a relationship in English in which one entity serves as a subject and one entity serves as an object and they are linked by a preposition.

primary key (PK)—A column or set of columns that uniquely identifies all the rows in a table.

procedure cache—The part of the SQL Server memory pool that is used to store execution plans for Transact-SQL batches, stored procedures, and triggers.

pronoun—A part of speech that takes the position of a noun and functions as one, for example *she*.

proper noun—A noun that is capitalized; a specific name, such as John Sequeira.

proximity search—Full-text query searching for those occurrences where the specified words are close to one another.

publication—A collection of one or more articles from one database. This grouping of multiple articles makes it easier to specify a logically related set of data and database objects that you want to replicate at the same time.

publication database—A database on the Publisher from which data and database objects are marked for replication as part of a publication that is propagated to Subscribers.

publication retention period—A predetermined length of time that regulates how long subscriptions will receive updates during synchronizations and remain activated in databases.

published data—Data at the Publisher that has been replicated.

Publisher—A server that makes data available for replication to other servers, detects changed data, and maintains information about all publications at the site.

publishing table—The table at the Publisher in which data has been marked for replication and is part of a publication.

pubs database—A sample database provided with SQL Server.

pull subscription—A subscription created and administered at the Subscriber. Information about the publication and the Subscriber is stored.

push subscription—A subscription created and administered at the Publisher. Information about the publication and Subscriber is stored.

query optimizer—The SQL Server database engine component responsible for generating efficient execution plans for SQL statements.

question—An English form of a query, for example, "How many customers bought products last year?"

Question Builder—A tool that supports users' needs to know more about the domain objects so that they can construct questions.

question file (.eqq)—An ASCII text file containing questions that are ready for testing with the English Query engine.

question template—A structure that describes a set of questions that can be asked using a particular relationship or set of relationships.

queue—A SQL Server Profiler queue provides a temporary holding place for server events to be captured.

range query—A query that specifies a range of values as part of the search criteria, such as all rows from 10 through 100.

real data type—A SQL Server system data type that has 7-digit precision. Floating precision number data from -3.40E + 38 through 3.40E + 38. Storage size is 4 bytes.

record—A group of related fields (columns) of information treated as a unit. A record is more commonly called a *row* in a SQL database.

recordset—The ActiveX Database Objects (ADO) object used to contain a result set. It also exhibits cursor behavior depending on the recordset properties set by an application. ADO recordsets are mapped to OLE DB rowsets.

recovery interval—The maximum amount of time that the database engine should require to recover a database. The database engine ensures that the active portion of the database log is small enough to recover the database in the amount of time specified for the recovery interval.

recursive partitioning—The iterative process—used by data mining algorithm providers—of dividing data into groups until no more useful groups can be found.

referenced key—A primary key or unique key referenced by a foreign key.

referential integrity (RI)—A state in which all foreign key values in a database are valid.

relational database—A collection of information organized in tables. Each table models a class of objects of interest to the organization.

relational database management system (RDBMS)—A system that organizes data into related rows and columns. SQL Server is a relational database management system.

relationship—A link between tables that references the primary key in one table to a foreign key in another table. In English Query, a relationship is an association between entities that describes what those entities have to do with one another.

remote data—Data stored in an OLE DB data source that is separate from the current instance of SQL Server. The data is accessed by establishing a linked server definition or using an ad-hoc connector name.

remote Distributor—A server configured as a Distributor that is separate from the server configured as the Publisher.

remote login identification—The login identification (login ID) assigned to a user for accessing remote procedures on a remote server.

remote server—A definition of an instance of SQL Server used by remote stored procedure calls. Remote servers are still supported in SQL Server 2000, but linked servers offer greater functionality.

remote stored procedure—A stored procedure located on one instance of SQL Server that is executed by a statement on another instance of SQL Server. In SQL Server 2000, remote stored procedures are supported, but distributed queries offer greater functionality.

remote table—A table stored in an OLE DB data source that is separate from the current instance of SQL Server. The table is accessed by either establishing a linked server definition or using an ad-hoc connector name.

replicated data—Data at the Subscriber that has been received from a Publisher.

replication—A process that copies and distributes data and database objects from one database to another and then synchronizes information between databases for consistency.

Replication Conflict Viewer—Allows users to view and resolve conflicts that occurred during the merge replication process, and to review the manner in which conflicts have been resolved.

Replication Monitor—Allows users to view and manage replication agents responsible for various replication tasks and to troubleshoot potential problems at the Distributor.

replication scripting—The generation of SQL scripts that can be used to configure and disable replication.

replication topology—Defines the relationship between servers and the copies of data and clarifies the logic that determines how data flows between servers.

repository—A database containing information models that, in conjunction with the executable software, manage the database.

repository engine—Object-oriented software that provides management support for and customer access to a repository database.

repository object—A COM object that represents a data construct stored in a repository type library.

Repository SQL schema—A set of standard tables used by the repository engine to manage all repository objects, relationships, and collections. Repository SQL schema maps information model elements to SQL schema elements.

republish—When a Subscriber publishes data received from a Publisher to another Subscriber.

republisher—A Subscriber who publishes data that it has received from a Publisher.

result—An English answer to a question that has been posed to an English Query application.

result set—The set of rows returned from a **SELECT** statement. The format of the rows in the result set is defined by the column-list of the **SELECT** statement.

X

revoke—Remove a previously granted or denied permission from a user account, role, or group in the current database.

right outer join—A type of outer join in which all rows in the right-most table in the **JOIN** clause are included. When rows in the right table are not matched in the left table, all result-set columns that come from the left table are assigned a value of **NULL**.

role—A security account that is a collection of other security accounts that can be treated as a single unit when managing permissions. A role can contain SQL Server logins, other roles, and Windows logins or groups.

rollback—To remove the updates performed by one or more partially completed transactions. Rollbacks are required to restore the integrity of a database after an application, database, or system failure.

roll forward—To apply all the completed transactions from a database or log backup in order to recover a database to a point in time or the point of failure.

root form—The simplest form of a word. For example, the root form of *generating* is *generate*.

row—The collection of elements that form a horizontal line in the table. Each row in the table represents a single occurrence of the object modeled by the table and stores the values for all the attributes of that object.

row aggregate function—A function that generates summary values that appear as additional rows in the query results.

row filter—A filter that specifies a subset of rows from a table to be published and when specific rows need to be propagated to Subscribers.

row lock—A lock on a single row in a table.

rule—A database object that is bound to columns or user-defined data types, and specifies which data values are acceptable in a column. **CHECK** constraints provide the same functionality and are preferred because they are in the SQL-92 standard.

savepoint—A marker that allows an application to roll back part of a transaction if a minor error is encountered. The application must still commit or roll back the full transaction when it is complete.

scalar aggregate—An aggregate function, such as **MIN()**, **MAX()**, or **AVG()**, that is specified in a **SELECT** statement column list that contains only aggregate functions.

scheduled backup—An automatic backup accomplished by SQL Server Agent when defined and scheduled as a job.

script—A collection of Transact-SQL statements used to perform an operation. Transact-SQL scripts are stored as files, usually with the .sql extension.

search condition—In a **WHERE** or **HAVING** clause, predicates that specify the conditions that the source rows must meet to be included in the SQL statement.

Security Identifier (SID)—A unique value that identifies a user who is logged on to the security system. SIDs can identify either one user or a group of users.

SELECT—The Transact-SQL statement used to return data to an application or another Transact-SQL statement, or to populate a cursor.

SELECT list—The **SELECT** statement clause that defines the columns of the result set returned by the statement.

SELECT query—A query that returns rows into a result set from one or more tables.

self-join—A join in which records from a table are combined with other records from the same table when there are matching values in the joined fields.

semantic object—An object that can be represented by a database object or other real-world object. For example, an entity and a relationship are semantic objects.

serializable—The highest transaction isolation level. Serializable transactions lock all rows they read or modify to ensure the transaction is completely isolated from other tasks. This guarantees that a series of serializable transactions will always produce the same results if run in the same sequence.

server name—A name that uniquely identifies a server computer on a network. SQL Server applications can connect to a default instance of SQL Server by specifying only the server name. SQL Server applications must specify both the server name and instance name when connecting to a named instance on a server.

session—In English Query, a sequence of operations performed by the English Query engine. A session begins when a user logs on and ends when the user logs off. All operations during a session form one *transaction scope* and are subject to permissions determined by the logon username and password.

Setup initialization file—A text file, using the Windows .ini file format, that stores configuration information allowing SQL Server to be installed without a user having to be present to respond to prompts from the Setup program.

severity level—A number indicating the relative significance of an error generated by the SQL Server database engine. Values range from informational (1) to severe (25).

shared lock—A lock created by nonupdate (read) operations. Other users can read the data concurrently, but no transaction can acquire an exclusive lock on the data until all the shared locks have been released.

Showplan—A report showing the execution plan for a SQL statement. **SET SHOWPLAN_ TEXT** and **SET SHOWPLAN_ALL** produce textual showplan output. SQL Query Analyzer and SQL Server Enterprise Manager can display showplan information as a graphical tree.

X

single-user mode—A state in which only one user can access a resource. Both SQL Server instances and individual databases can be put into single-user mode.

smalldatetime data type—Date and time data from January 1, 1900, through June 6, 2079, with an accuracy of one minute.

smallint data type—A SQL Server system integer data from -2^{15} (-32,768) through 2^{15} - 1 (32,767).

smallmoney data type—A system data type that stores monetary values from -214,748.3648 through +214,748.3647, with accuracy to a ten-thousandth of a monetary unit. Storage size is 4 bytes. When **smallmoney** values are displayed, they are rounded up two places.

Snapshot Agent—Prepares snapshot files containing schema and data of published tables, stores the files in the snapshot folder, and inserts synchronization jobs in the publication database.

Snapshot Agent utility—A utility that configures and triggers the Snapshot Agent, which prepares snapshot files containing schema and data of published tables and database objects.

snapshot replication—A type of replication that distributes data exactly as it appears at a specific moment in time and does not monitor for modifications made to the data.

sort order—The set of rules in a collation that define how characters are evaluated in comparison operations and the sequence in which they are sorted.

SQL collation—A set of SQL Server 2000 collations whose characteristics match those of commonly used code page and sort order combinations from earlier versions of SQL Server.

SQL database—A database based on Structured Query Language (SQL).

SQL expression—Any combination of operators, constants, literal values, functions, and names of tables and fields that evaluates to a single value.

SQL Mail—A component of SQL Server that allows SQL Server to send and receive mail messages through the built-in Windows NT or Windows 2000 Messaging Application Programming Interface (MAPI). A mail message can consist of short text strings, the output from a query, or an attached file.

SQL query—A SQL statement, such as **SELECT**, **INSERT**, **UPDATE**, **DELETE**, or **CREATE TABLE**.

SQL Server Authentication—One of two mechanisms for validating attempts to connect to instances of SQL Server. Users must specify a SQL Server login ID and password when they connect.

SQL Server Event Forwarding Server—A central instance of SQL Server that manages SQL Server Agent events forwarded to it by other instances.

SQL Server login—An account stored in SQL Server that allows users to connect to SQL Server.

SQL statement—A SQL or Transact-SQL command, such as **SELECT** or **DELETE**, that performs some action on data.

SQL-92—The version of the SQL standard published in 1992. The international standard is ISO/IEC 9075:1992 Database Language SQL. The American National Standards Institute (ANSI) also published a corresponding standard (Data Language SQL X3.135-1192), so SQL-92 is sometimes referred to as ANSI SQL in the United States.

sql_variant data type—Data type that stores values of various SQL Server-supported data types except **text**, **ntext**, **timestamp**, and **sql_variant**.

statement permission—An attribute that controls whether a user can execute **CREATE** or **BACKUP** statements.

step object—A Data Transformation Services (DTS) object that coordinates the flow of control and execution of tasks in a DTS package. A task that does not have an associated step object is never executed.

stored procedure—A precompiled collection of Transact-SQL statements stored under a name and processed as a unit. SQL Server supplies stored procedures for managing SQL Server and displaying information about databases and users. SQL Server-supplied stored procedures are called *system stored procedures*.

string—A set of contiguous bytes that contain a single character-based or binary data value. In character strings, each byte, or pair of bytes, represents a single alphabetic letter, special character, or number.

string functions—Functions that perform operations on character or binary strings. Built-in string functions return values commonly needed for operations on character data.

Structured Query Language (SQL)—A language used to insert, retrieve, modify, and delete data in a relational database. SQL also contains statements for defining and administering the objects in a database.

subject—A basic grammatical division of a sentence. The subject is a noun or noun clause about which something is asserted or asked in the predicate, which it usually precedes. For example, in the sentence "The customer placed the order," the word *customer* is the subject of the sentence.

X

subquery—A **SELECT** statement nested inside another **SELECT**, **INSERT**, **UPDATE**, or **DELETE** statement, or inside another subquery.

subscribe—To request data from a Publisher.

Subscriber—A server who receives copies of published data.

subscription—An order used in replication that defines what data to publish, when the data should be published, and to which Subscriber.

subscription database—A database at the Subscriber that receives data and database objects published by a Publisher.

subset phrasing—A way of expressing a relationship in English in which one entity or word is a subset of another entity. For example, in the sentence "Some employees are managers," *managers* is a subset of *employees*.

superlative form—A form of an adverb or adjective that refers to a comparison or denotes the greatest degree. Shorter adjectives and some adverbs typically form their superlative degree by adding *-est*, as in *youngest* or *strongest*.

synchronization—Synchronization is the process in replication of maintaining the same schema and data at a Publisher and at a Subscriber.

synonym—A word that means the same thing as another word. For example, *workers* can be a synonym for *employees*.

system administrator—The person or group of people responsible for managing an instance of SQL Server. System administrators have full permissions to perform all actions in an instance of SQL Server. System administrators are either members of the sysadmin fixed server role, or log in using the sa login ID.

system catalog—A set of system tables that describe all the features of an instance of SQL Server. The system catalog records metadata such as the definitions of all users, all databases, all objects in each database, and system configuration information, such as server and database option settings.

system databases—A set of four databases present in all instances of SQL Server that are used to store system information. These system databases are master, tempdb, model, and msdb.

system functions—A set of built-in functions that perform operations on and return the information about values, objects, and settings in SQL Server.

system stored procedures—A set of SQL Server-supplied stored procedures that can be used for actions such as retrieving information from the system catalog or performing administration tasks.

system tables—Built-in tables that form the system catalog for SQL Server. System tables store all the metadata for an instance of SQL Server, including configuration information and definitions of all the databases and database objects in the instance.

table—A table is a two-dimensional object, consisting of rows and columns, used to store data in a relational database. SQL Server 2000 databases are typically made up of many tables with these tables related to each other through keys.

table data type—A special data type used to store a result set for later processing.

table lock—A lock on a table, including all data and indexes.

table scan—A data retrieval operation where the database engine must read all the pages in a table to find the rows that qualify for a query.

table-level constraint—Constraints that allow various forms of data integrity to be defined on one column (column-level constraint) or several columns (table-level constraints) when the table is defined or altered.

tabular data stream (TDS)—The SQL Server internal client/server data transfer protocol. TDS allows client and server products to communicate regardless of operating-system platform, server release, or network transport.

tape backup—A backup operation to any tape device supported by Windows NT 4 and Windows 2000.

task object—A Data Transformation Services (DTS) object that defines pieces of work to be performed as part of the data transformation process.

tempdb database—The database that provides a storage area for temporary tables, temporary stored procedures, and other temporary working storage needs.

temporary stored procedure—A stored procedure placed in the temporary database (tempdb) and erased at the end of the session.

temporary table—A table placed in the temporary database (tempdb) and erased at the end of the session.

text data type—A SQL Server system data type that specifies variable-length non-Unicode data with a maximum length of $2^{31} -1$ (2,147,483,647) characters. The **text** data type cannot be used for variables or parameters in stored procedures.

thread—An operating system component that allows the logic of multiuser applications to be performed as several separate, asynchronous execution paths.

timestamp data type—A SQL Server system data type that is a monotomically increasing counter whose values are always unique within a database.

tinyint data type—A SQL Server system data type that holds whole numbers from 0 through 255. Its storage size is 1 byte.

trace file—A file used by SQL Profiler to record monitored events.

X

trait—An attribute that describes an entity. For example, "blood type" is a trait of "patients."

trait phrasing—A way of expressing a relationship in English description in which a minor entity describes a major entity. For example, in the phrase, "ages of customers," *ages* is the trait (or minor entity), and *customers* is the major entity.

Transact-SQL—The language containing the commands used to administer instances of SQL Server, create and manage all objects in an instance of SQL Server, and to insert, retrieve, modify and delete all data in SQL Server tables. Transact-SQL is an extension of the language defined in the SQL standards published by the International Organization for Standardization (ISO) and the American National Standards Institute (ANSI).

Transact-SQL cursor—A server cursor defined by using the Transact-SQL **DECLARE CURSOR** syntax. Transact-SQL cursors are intended for use in Transact-SQL batches, stored procedures, and triggers.

transaction—A group of database operations combined into a logical unit of work that is either wholly committed or rolled back. A transaction is atomic, consistent, isolated, and durable.

transaction log—A database file in which all changes to the database are recorded. It is used by SQL Server during automatic recovery.

transaction processing—Data processing used to efficiently record business activities, called *transactions*, that are of interest to an organization (for example, sales, orders for supplies, or money transfers). Typically, online transaction processing (OLTP) systems perform large numbers of relatively small transactions.

transaction rollback—Rollback of a user-specified transaction to the last savepoint inside a transaction or to the beginning of a transaction.

transactional replication—A type of replication where an initial snapshot of data is applied at Subscribers, and then when data modifications are made at the Publisher, the individual transactions are captured and propagated to Subscribers.

transformable subscription—A subscription that allows data movement, transformation mapping, and filtering capabilities of Data Transformation Services (DTS) during replication.

trigger—A stored procedure that executes when data in a specified table is modified. Triggers are often created to enforce referential integrity or consistency among logically related data in different tables.

trusted connection—A Windows network connection that can be opened only by users who have been authenticated by the network. The users are identified by their Windows login ID and do not have to enter a separate SQL Server login ID.

two-phase commit—A process that ensures transactions that apply to more than one server are completed on all servers or on none.

Unicode—Unicode defines a set of letters, numbers, and symbols that SQL Server recognizes in the **nchar**, **nvarchar**, and **ntext** data types. Unicode includes characters for most languages.

Unicode collation—Unicode collation acts as a sort order for Unicode data. It is a set of rules that determines how SQL Server compares, collates, and presents Unicode data in response to database queries.

Unicode format—Data stored in a bulk copy data file using Unicode characters.

Union query—A query that combines two tables by performing the equivalent of appending one table onto the other.

UNIQUE constraints—Constraints that enforce entity integrity on a nonprimary key. These constraints ensure that no duplicate values are entered and that an index is created to enhance performance.

unique index—An index in which no two rows are permitted to have the same index value, thus prohibiting duplicate index or key values. The system checks for duplicate key values when the index is created and checks each time data is added with an **INSERT** or **UPDATE** statement.

uniqueidentifier data type—A data type containing a unique identification number stored as a 16-byte binary string used for storing a globally unique identifier (GUID).

update—The act of modifying one or more data values in an existing row or rows, typically by using the **UPDATE** statement.

update lock—A lock placed on resources (such as row, page, table) that can be updated. Updated locks are used to prevent a common form of deadlock that occurs when multiple sessions are locking resources and are potentially updating them later.

Update query—A query that changes the values in columns of one or more rows in a table.

update statistics—A process that recalculates information about the distribution of key values in specified indexes. These statistics are used by the query optimizer to determine the most efficient way to execute a query.

user (account)—A SQL Server security account or identifier that represents a specific user in a database. Each user's Windows account or SQL Server login is mapped to a user account in a database. Then, the appropriate permissions are granted to the user account. Each user account can only access data for which it has been granted permission to work.

user database—A database created by a SQL Server user and used to store application data. Most users connecting to instances of SQL Server reference user databases only, not system databases.

user-defined data type—A data type that is based on a SQL Server data type and created by the user for custom data storage. Rules and defaults can be bound to user-defined data types, but not to system data types.

user-defined event—A type of message, defined by a user, that can be traced by SQL Profiler or used to fire a custom alert. Typically, the user is the system administrator.

user-defined function—A user-defined function is a Transact-SQL function defined by a user. Functions encapsulate frequently performed logic in a named entity that can be called by Transact-SQL statements instead of recoding the logic in each statement.

varbinary data type—A SQL Server system data type that holds up to 8,000 bytes of variable-length binary data.

varchar data type—A SQL Server system data type that holds variable-length non-Unicode data with a maximum of 8,000 characters.

variables—Defined entities that are assigned values. A local variable is defined with a **DECLARE@localvariable** statement and assigned an initial value within the statement batch where it is declared with either a **SELECT** or **SET@localvariable** statement.

verb—A part of speech denoting action, occurrence, or existence. A verb can consist of one or more words.

verb phrasing—A way of expressing a relationship in English in which one entity is the subject in an action, which is expressed with a verb. For example, suppliers provide products. Here *suppliers* is the entity, *provide* is the verb, and *products* is the direct object.

vertical filtering—Vertical filtering is used with replication and allows you to create a table article that contains only selected columns from the publishing table.

vertical partitioning—Vertical partitioning segments a single table into multiple tables based on selected columns. Each of the multiple tables has the same number of rows but fewer columns.

view—A database object that can be referenced the same way as a table in SQL statements. Views are defined using a **SELECT** statement and are analogous to an object that contains the result set of this statement.

WHERE clause—The portion of a SQL statement that specifies which records to retrieve.

wildcard characters—Use wildcard characters, including underscore (_), percent (%), and brackets ([ ]), with the **LIKE** keyword for pattern matching in queries.

wildcard search—A wildcard search refers to your ability to use placeholders (such as * or ?) to perform a search for data in a table or field.

Windows Authentication—Windows Authentication is one of two mechanisms for validating attempts to connect to instances of SQL Server. Users are identified by their Windows user or group when they connect. Windows Authentication is the most secure mechanism for connecting to SQL Server.

Windows collation—A set of rules that determines how SQL Server sorts character data. Windows collation is specified by name in the Windows Control Panel and in SQL Server 2000 during Setup.

word generation—The process of determining other forms of the word(s) specified. The Microsoft Search Service currently implements inflectional word generation. For example, if the word *swim* is specified, SQL Server also searches for *swim*, *swam*, and *swimming*.

write-ahead log—A transaction logging method in which the log is always written prior to the data.

Index

B

D

T